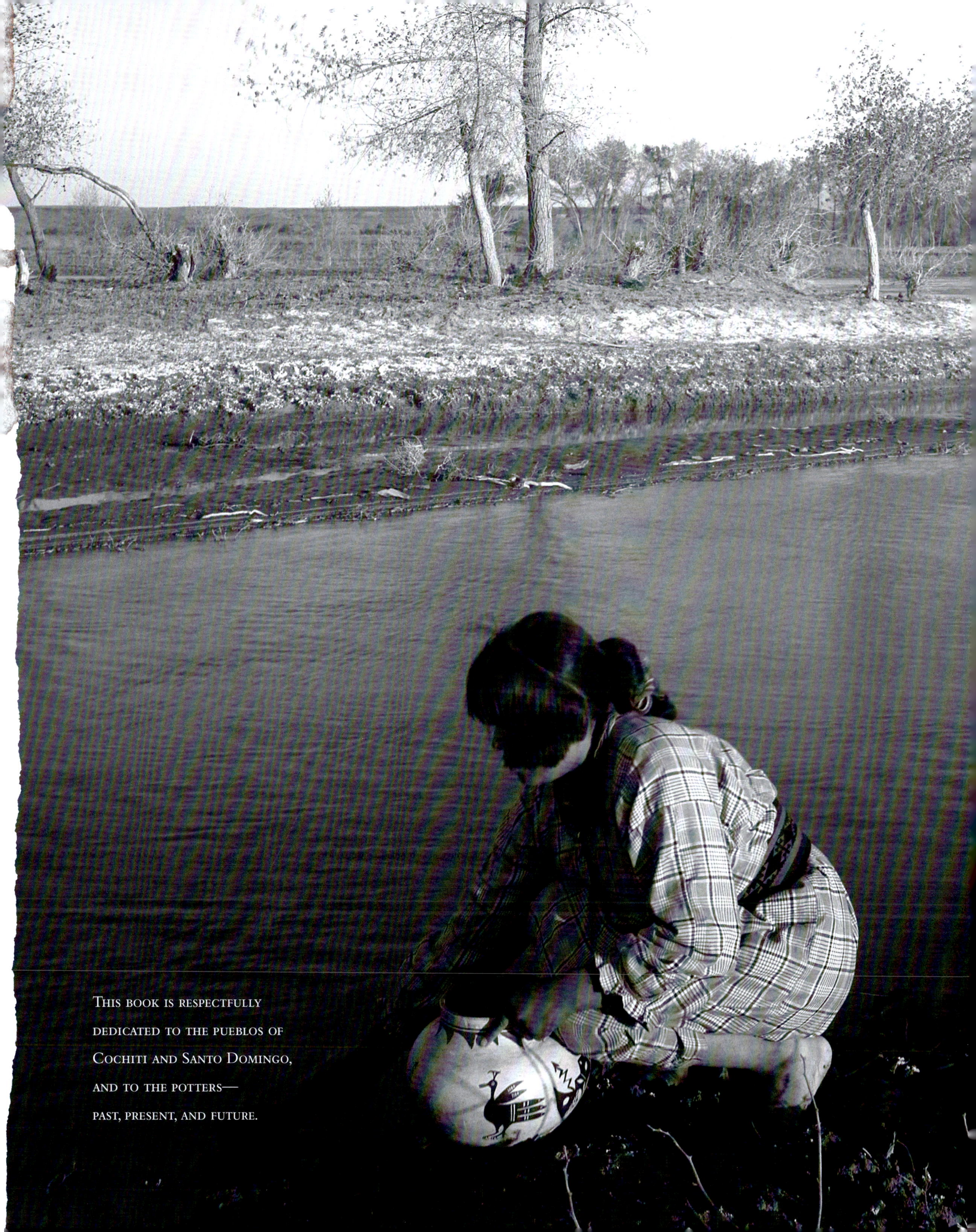

This book is respectfully dedicated to the pueblos of Cochiti and Santo Domingo, and to the potters—past, present, and future.

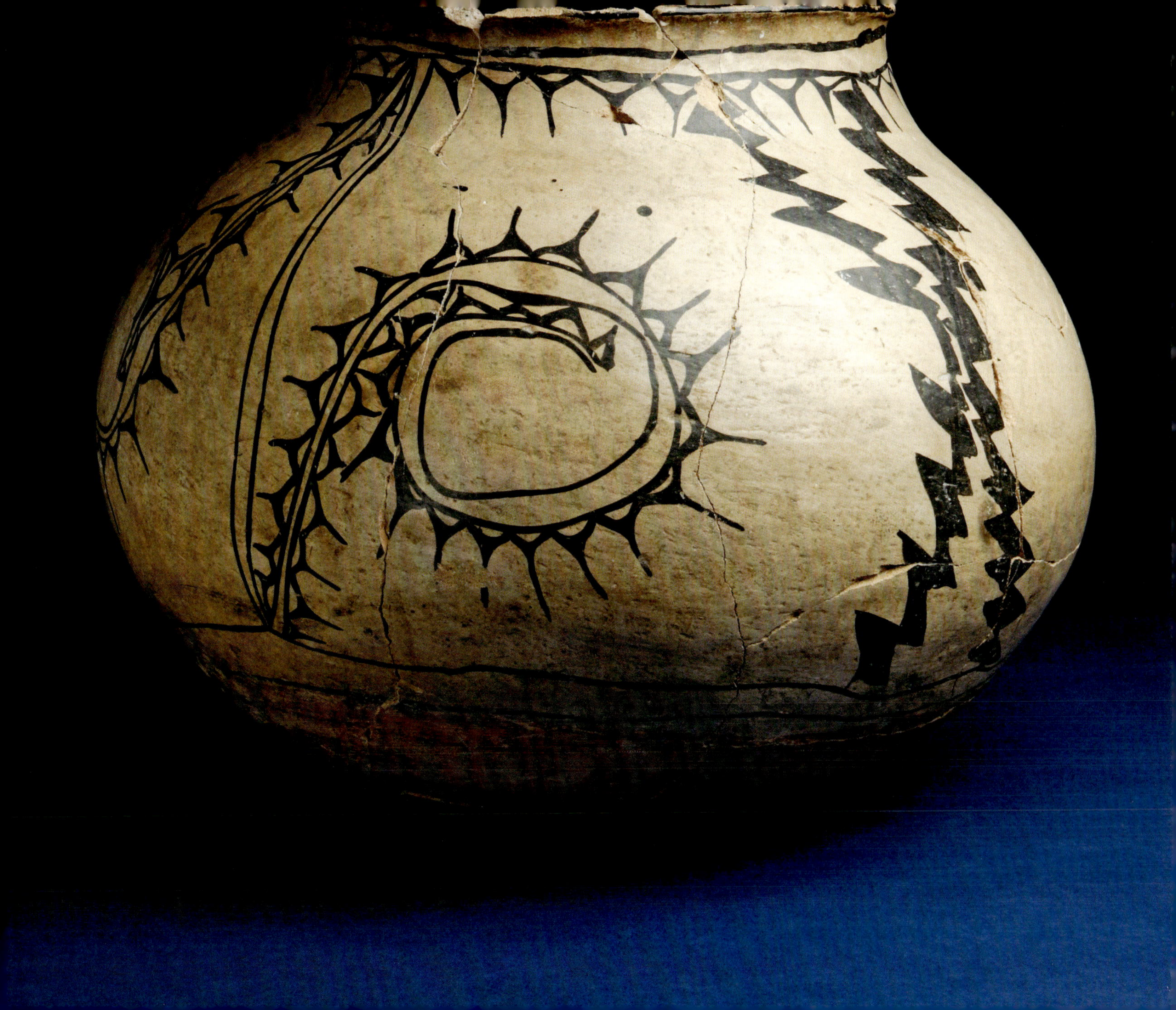

A River Apart

The Pottery of Cochiti & Santo Domingo Pueblos

EDITED BY VALERIE K. VERZUH

PRINCIPAL PHOTOGRAPHY
BY ADDISON DOTY

MUSEUM OF NEW MEXICO PRESS   SANTA FE

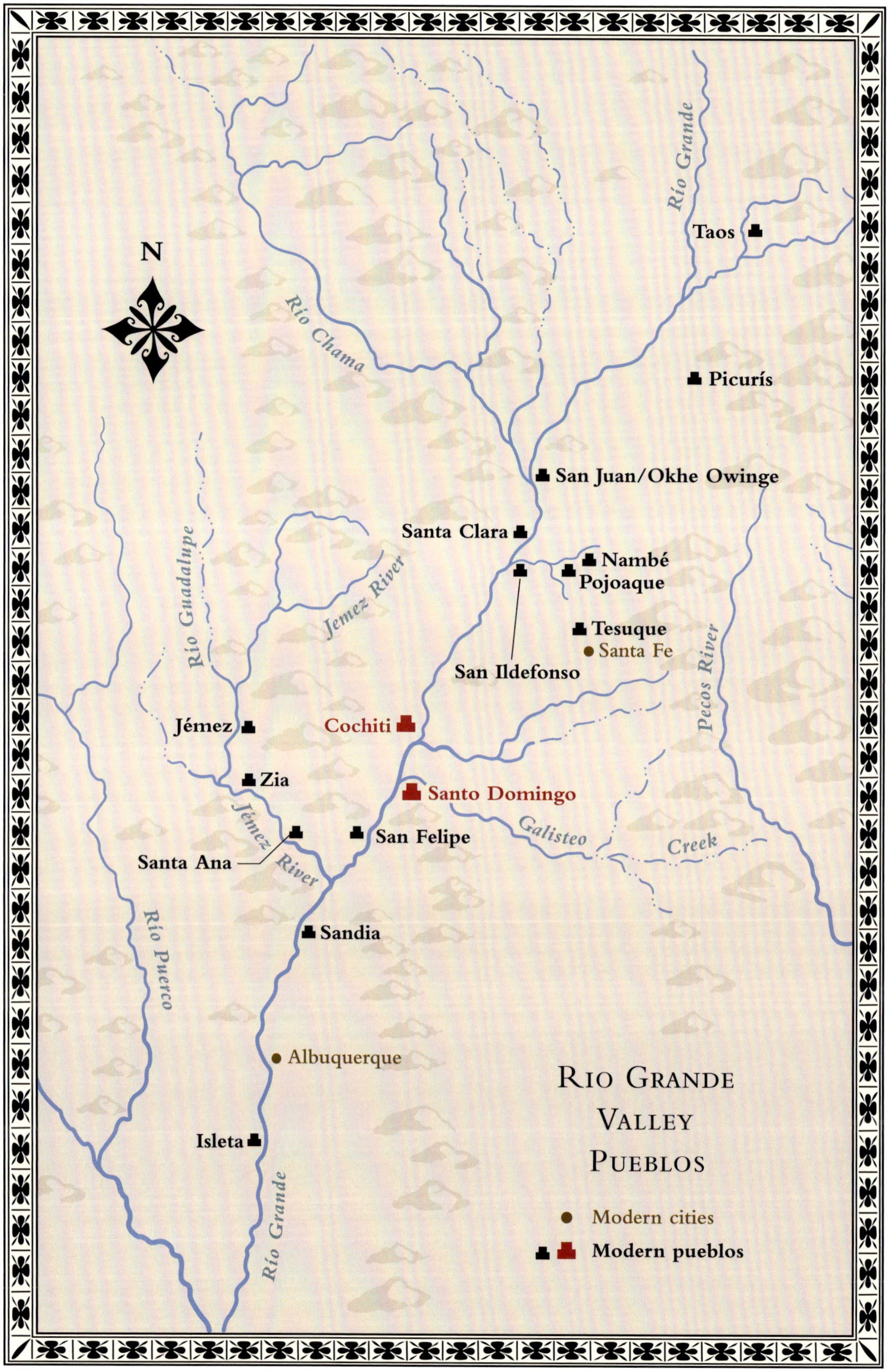

N
Rio Grande
Taos
Rio Chama
Picurís
San Juan/Okhe Owinge
Santa Clara
Nambé
Pojoaque
Jemez River
Rio Guadalupe
Tesuque
Santa Fe
San Ildefonso
Pecos River
Jémez
Cochiti
Zia
Santo Domingo
Jémez
River
Santa Ana
San Felipe
Galisteo
Creek
Río Puerco
Sandia
Albuquerque
Isleta
Rio Grande
Rio Grande Valley Pueblos
Modern cities
Modern pueblos

Contents

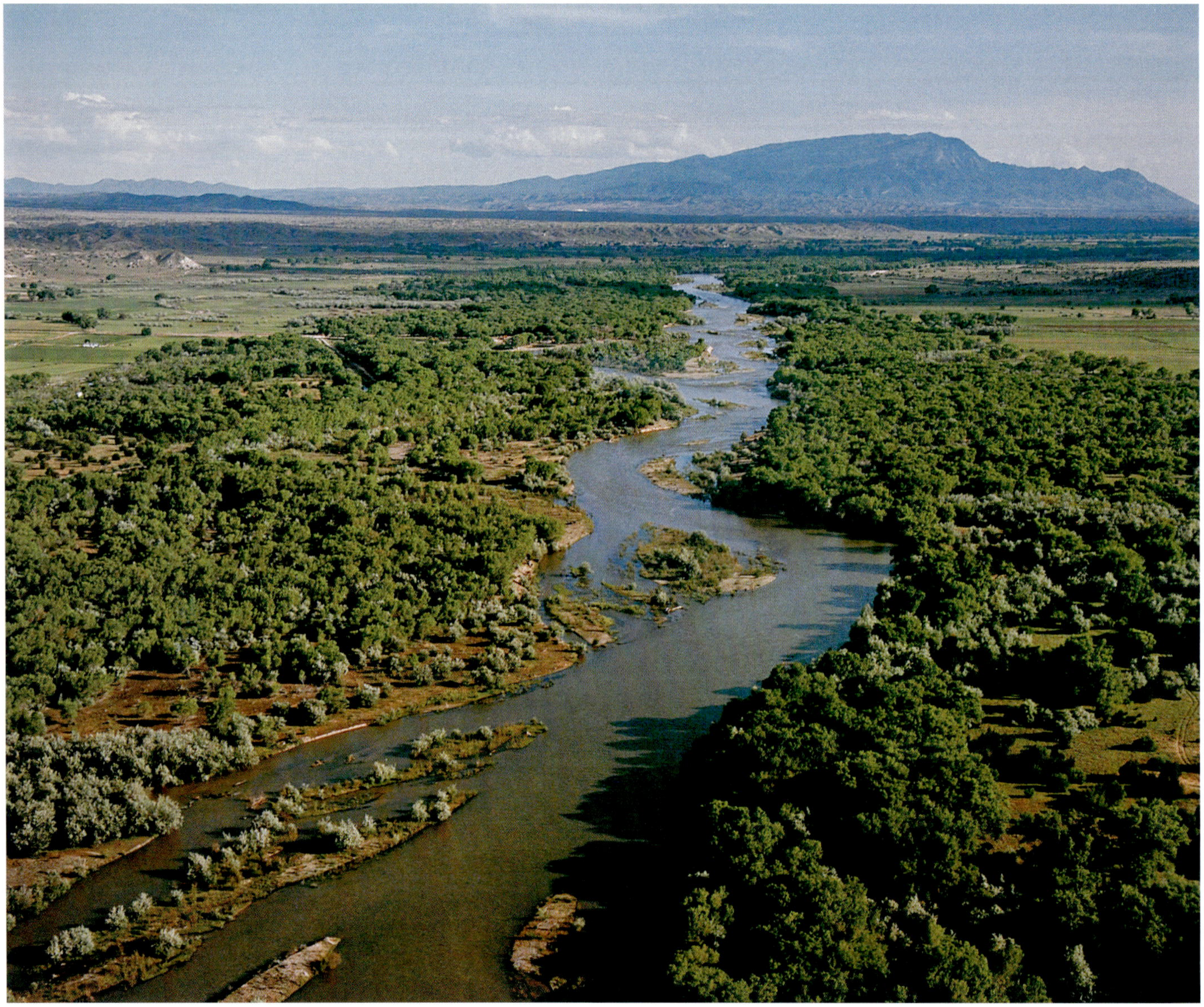

Aerial photograph of the Rio Grande, looking south from Cochiti to Santo Domingo, ca. 1980. Paul Logsdon, photographer. Courtesy of the Estate of Paul Logsdon. Collection of the Museum of Indian Arts & Culture/Laboratory of Anthropology (MNM/DCA) 51561.

Foreword

The Museum of Indian Arts & Culture/Laboratory of Anthropology (MIAC/LAB) collections have a long and significant history in American and international scholarship. Its collections are divided into two curatorial units: Archaeological Research Collections (ARC) and Individually Catalogued Collections (ICC). Research based on them, in whole or in part, has led to seminal discussions of archaeological systematics and Southwest prehistory as well as classic descriptions of historic and contemporary arts, including ceramics, textiles, jewelry, basketry, and fine art. If the material culture in museums can be seen as a statement of the personal, political, and cultural motives of its collectors, then the MIAC/LAB holds a unique place in both its focus on the material culture of the Rio Grande pueblos and the intention behind the formation of its collections.

In the early 1920s, a group of professional anthropologists at major northeastern universities interested in establishing an anthropological field station envisioned a new institution in Santa Fe that would combine research, collecting, education, and professional training. In 1927, as the Committee on the Organization of the Anthropological Laboratory, they incorporated as the Museum and Laboratory of Anthropology, or Lab, Inc. The anthropological community saw the Laboratory as a home base in the midst of traditional Native communities. The local Santa Fe community saw the facility as a place dedicated to the preservation and promotion of Indian arts. Eventually, the Lab merged the two interests—investigating indigenous communities through research and encouraging Native arts through collecting and exhibiting.

Beginning in the early 1900s, projects were developed to recapture the traditional quality of Pueblo ceramics. Masterminding these efforts were individuals and organizations intimately connected with the Laboratory of Anthropology, most significantly the Lab's first curator, Kenneth Chapman. Chapman's firsthand involvement with pottery—and the people who made it—became the guiding narrative for the formation of the Lab's collections. The nearly 3,500 vessels in the historic period pottery collections do not constitute an encyclopedic reference work of material culture; rather, they attest to an active engagement with community. Today, the museum's donor and catalog records are reflective of the many communities, institutions, and individuals involved with Pueblo pottery over the past eighty years.

The State of New Mexico mandates that all its departments—one of which is the Department of Cultural Affairs, the museum's parent organization—actively consult with Native American tribal governments and community members on matters affecting their cultural heritage. For its part, the MIAC/LAB has an active consultative relationship with Native communities of the Southwest through its Indian Advisory Panel, and Native American staff members who are involved in the development of major programs and exhibits. The MIAC/LAB also has established innovative partnerships with Indian leadership to implement the Native American Graves Protection and Repatriation Act (NAGPRA).

The museum's core exhibition *Here, Now and Always,* a precedent-setting collaboration between the museum and the indigenous communities of the Southwest, represents the first step in the museum's long-range plan to fully incorporate Native voices in the telling of the story of the Southwest. *A River Apart* provides the museum with an opportunity to expand on this first step toward the presentation of a variety of themes and stories based on the intercultural exchange of ideas expressed by multiple voices through a variety of media. Toward this end, the museum's Individually Catalogued Collections (ICC) staff—which oversees the historic-period collections from Cochiti and Santo Domingo—has initiated two projects to document the collections with the ultimate goal of making the information fully accessible to indigenous communities, scholars, and the general public. Funding from the National Endowment for the Humanities in 2003 supported the comprehensive documentation and cataloging of the historic-period ceramics, textiles, and fine arts collections. This was accomplished with the assistance of Native artists, cultural specialists, and scholars. ICC staff is currently completing a major project to digitize those collections with funding provided by the Institute for Museum and Library Services in 2006. The combined product of the two projects will provide access to the collections through the museum's website, onsite computer terminals, and exhibitions. In addition, tribal communities and individual artists can obtain CDs with catalog information and images of the material culture of their communities represented in the collections. Through initiatives like these, the museum staff continues to learn respect for and appropriate ways to care for and interpret Native American cultural patrimony. Collections are no longer viewed as objects on a shelf—instead, each pot, each textile, each basket or piece of jewelry has a story and a life of its own.

This volume brings together the multiple stories relating to Cochiti and Santo Domingo pottery. Listen carefully and you will hear the story of each maker and learn where each artifact was made, how it was made, what it was made for, and what it meant to the community it served. It is these stories that are carried as messages on the wind—we only need to stop long enough to listen.

Shelby Tisdale, Ph.D., Director
Museum of Indian Arts & Culture/
Laboratory of Anthropology

Acknowledgments

My proposal for an exhibition of Cochiti and Santo Domingo pottery would never have come to fruition without the enthusiastic acceptance of the notion by my cocurator Antonio Chavarria, and his subsequent involvement in all aspects of the creative process. The concept for this catalog and the exhibition was developed during lively discussions held by catalog and exhibition team cocurators, along with advisers Bruce Bernstein, J. J. Brody, Diego Romero, Mateo Romero, and William Wanker. Their wonderfully odd and exciting ideas—too numerous for this project—are already finding their way into others.

During 2007 Indian Market, we invited Cochiti and Santo Domingo potters and their families to collections storage to visit, talk about, photograph, and sketch the pottery of their pueblos and families. Those who accepted our invitation assisted with identifications and enriched our understanding of Pueblo pottery. Our profound gratitude is extended to Martha Arquero, Clyde Arquero, April Arquero, Ambrose Atencio, Cippy Crazyhorse, Crucita Melchor, Marlene Melchor, Dominic Melchor, Elizabeth Trujillo, and Erma Trujillo.

Of special note are the potters who participated in three pottery firings at Santo Domingo Pueblo between 2006 and 2008: Robert Tenorio, Ione Coriz, Warren Coriz, Paulita Pacheco, and Gilbert Pacheco. They were unbelievably gracious when we peered over their shoulders as they worked, asked tedious questions, and got in their way snapping endless pictures. Their work and unique talents are represented here by photographs captured by the cameras of Antonio Chavarria and Elysia Poon.

Special recognition is due to the Luce Foundation for providing funding for conservation of the Cochiti and Santo Domingo collections in preparation for the *A River Apart* exhibition. The foundation also provided support for a symposium that brought potters from the pueblos together with consulting conservator Landis Smith and Museum of New Mexico conservation staff members Mark MacKenzie, Maureen Russell, Mina Thompson, Larry Humetewa, Conor McMahon, and Anya McDavis.

At the MIAC/LAB I would like to thank director Shelby Tisdale for her early and continuing support of this project. Also of assistance were librarians Michelle Garcia and Minnie Murray, educator Dawn Kaufmann, archivist Diane Bird, and project intern Kami O'Brien. Volunteers at the Individually Catalogued Collections Division also deserve recognition. They include Joanne Bol, Tukey Cleveland, Robert Kasal, and Carol Warren.

The impetus for this volume was the research and documentation for the Cochiti and Santo Domingo ceramic collections completed during a 2003–2006 grant from the National Endowment for the Humanities, Division of Preservation and Access. Special thanks for the success of that project go to grant research assistants Renee Cannon, Emily O'Brien, and Cheryl Paddock.

The photographs in the catalog section of this volume were made possible by an Institute of Museum and Library Services, Museums for America–Sustaining Cultural Heritage grant, "Imaging the Southwest: Digitization of the Ethnographic Collections." The initiative's goal was to create quality digital images of objects in the MIAC/LAB's Individually Catalogued Collections Division, including historic-period ceramics, and to make them available for a wide range of projects. Special thanks for the success of this grant go to project photographers John Torres-Nez, John Frank, Claire Lighton, Diana Sherman, and Ricardo Martinez.

Research and photo assistance were provided by a number of individuals and institutions, including Daniel Kosharek at the Palace of the Governors Photo Archives; Laura Holt and Jennifer Day at the School for Advanced Research; Vernon Lujan, Phillip Karshis, and Nadine Ulibarri at the Poeh Center; and Lou Stancari at the National Museum of the American Indian.

This exhibition is only the third to be installed in the MIAC/LAB's newly renovated Masterpieces Gallery. Funding for the gallery and its exhibitions was generously provided by Masterpieces Gallery campaign donors: the Thaw Charitable Trust, the McCune Charitable Foundation, Adobe Gallery, Charmay Allred, John Berl and Bob Bauernschmitt, Blue Rain Gallery, Lynn and Norman Brown, Jane and Bill Buchsbaum, Joan and Richard Chodosh, Linda and John Comstock, Darla and George Cox, Sarah and Benjamin Crane, Susan and Ronald Dubin, the family of Colleen Cloney Duncan, Gail and Jim Goodwin, Doris Rosen and Ron Klein, Gloria and Marvin Lieberman, Rosalind Wells Lustig and Harry Lustig, Janice and David Matthews, Helene Singer Merrin and Seymour Merrin, Edwina and Charles Milner, Kathryn O'Keeffe, Doris and Arnold Roland, Mary Frances Schottstaedt, Edith and Ernest Schwartz, Georgia and Jim Snead, Warren von Preissig, Nancy and Gil Waldman, and Carol and Bob Warren.

Photographer Addison Doty spent over a week in a dark room peering through a camera lens to capture portraits of the pots. His feeling for each pot's "best side" and his connection with each one's unique personality are evident in every photograph.

Additional thanks to JoAnn and Bob Balzer, Lynda and Don Shoemaker, Kerry Green, and Glen Green for their individual assitance on this project.

Finally, this book is the product of the patience and perseverance of the staff at the Museum of New Mexico Press. The book would not exist without the initial support of director Anna Gallegos and the ministrations of editorial director Mary Wachs and art director David Skolkin.

Introduction

A River Apart

Valerie K. Verzuh

Multivocality, Communities, and Museums in a Postmodern World

Water is a rare and essential element in the arid Southwest. Two major rivers and their tributaries—the Colorado River and the Rio Grande—have shaped both the landscape and the distribution of indigenous villages. Neighboring New Mexico pueblos on the banks of the northern Rio Grande—just a river apart—the communities of Cochiti and Santo Domingo join a ceramic tradition extending back almost 1,500 years. For centuries, the women—and more recently the men—of both pueblos have made pottery for use in their homes and ceremonial spaces, for sale as tourist curios at roadside stands, and for placement as objects of longing in high-end galleries. The materials, construction techniques, painted designs, and intended functions of each piece of pottery made in these two villages intimately reflect each community's social, religious, and institutional values as well as the land that supports and nourishes them. Over the past two centuries, countless of these carefully constructed pieces, isolated from their original contexts, have become aesthetic and sociocultural specimens of beauty and utility in art and anthropology museums throughout the Western world. Historically, these institutions have preserved the pieces as iconic representatives of dying cultures whose histories they reconstructed in exhibitions and publications.

The Pueblos themselves have preserved their histories by the telling and retelling of myths and legends, and through the ceremonial performance of songs and dances. They have recorded their histories upon the landscape with the settlements and artifacts they constructed and abandoned during generations of migration and change. These indigenous "museums" of the Southwest were and are part of a living landscape (Colwell-Chanthaphonh and Ferguson 2006) subject to time and environment, as well as to the movements and interpretations of contemporary Puebloans.

The authoritative voice of Western museums resides in the classification and definition of people through representations of material culture. Usually, these are indigenous people, or cultural "others," meaning that presentation and interpretation of cultural diversity in museums has always been problematic. Over the past two decades, and notably since the passage of the Native American Graves Protection and Repatriation Act (NAGPRA), third- and fourth-world communities, attempting to establish and maintain a sense of self and to assert their social, religious, political, and economic rights from within the dominant Western culture, have challenged the right of established institutions to control the presentation of their cultural artifacts and community identities.

In traditional museum exhibitions, Western cultural points of view have assumed a universal significance—historically, European and American museums have presented the authoritative view of the "expert" outsider looking in and "explaining" indigenous cultures. Typically, this approach portrays Pueblos and other indigenous peoples as something out of the past and fixed in time. Many contemporary museums have begun to explore the challenge to their authority through an interpretive theory known as multivocality.

Multivocality, which entered anthropological discourse in the 1980s adjunct to the postmodern movement of the 1970s, is an approach to interpreting material culture in a manner that seeks to represent and reconcile contested meanings (Foucault 1970; Lyotard 1984, 1992; Crapanzano 1992). Within the context of multivocality, anthropologists and their subjects, and museums and the cultures they represent, participate in an exchange of perspectives and beliefs. Multivocality, as applied to museum anthropology, advocates a plurality of voices in the production of knowledge and emphasizes that there is no single "correct" viewpoint within this theoretical framework. The postmodern museum curator questions accepted concepts and engages with other points of view.

Postmodern theorists advocate bridging the gap between anthropologists and their subjects by giving credence to the views of the observed. They have posited that it is impossible for anyone to have objective and neutral knowledge of another culture. This view comes from the notion that each of us interprets the world in a unique way, concordant with our cultural background, the language we speak, and our personal experiences. Opposition to this approach contends that postmodernists eschew empirical data and scientific method in favor of a humanist political model based on empathy with third- and fourth-world peoples. Opposing viewpoints also reject the overly relativistic stance they predict as the outcome of this position. In anthropological discourse, postmodernism is an ongoing debate, especially in regard to the definition of anthropology as a scientific or humanistic discipline (Spiro 1996; D'Andrade 1995).

The postmodern anthropologist replaces the metanarrative—an abstract theory or idea which orders and explains all knowledge and experience—with multiple theoretical perspectives or narratives. In much the same way, the intent of this collection of essays is to examine and interpret, from several different perspectives, the pottery traditions of Cochiti and Santo Domingo pueblos. As a critical analysis of various aspects of Pueblo pottery, the collected essays are meant to present perspectives while giving the reader enough room to develop his/her own viewpoint. The essayists provide information related to reading and interpreting material culture in general, and Pueblo pottery specifically. Each author's singular way of thinking about Pueblo pottery comes from a range of disciplines—anthropology, art history, practice of art, and museum studies.

The river that marks the physical division between Cochiti and Santo Domingo also can be seen as a metaphorical demarcation between the dissimilar responses of the two pueblos to outside influences, between insiders and outsiders, and between the varying perspectives explored by the six essays in this volume. The honesty and passion in Antonio Chavarria's essay belies what I often hear from Santa Fe residents and museum visitors: their feelings that behind Pueblo secrecy is a hollowness harboring only political aspirations. Chavarria's characterization of Pueblo pottery as "shifting and changing" is the tie that binds the multiple perspectives of the essays in this volume—although all the essays are directed at the same target, they reach their goal by following different paths. Even the painted designs on pottery have "multiple levels of meaning," Chavarria informs us, and choosing one interpretation over another "gives short shrift to the complexity of the art and cultures." A museum curator from the pottery-producing Pueblo of Santa Clara, Antonio Chavarria emphasizes the artist's point of view in his study of southwestern pottery. The artistic tradition he writes about recognizes those potters who understand their work as creating and continuing life, rather than making inanimate objects. Chavarria notes that archaeologist, ethnologist, collector, and dealer must all work within an understanding that pottery is made from Mother Earth—it is from the earth that Pueblo people form and sustain their lives; thus, when artists gather and use a material which literally and metaphorically makes life, they are involved in the creation of people, family, relations, and the continuity and vitality of life itself.

Chip Colwell-Chanthaphonh investigates a part of ceramic vessels rarely seen in exhibitions and catalogs—the underside. There he finds written a hidden story about the production and consumption of Pueblo pottery over the last century. In his essay Colwell-Chanthaphonh considers the origin and significance of artists' signatures on Pueblo ceramics to illuminate what signed (and unsigned) pieces can tell us about the relationships between individual and community, fine art and folk art, and matter and spirit. He explicates the recontextualization of Pueblo pottery by exploring the history of signatures in Western art and the ramifications of transferring this European fine art tradition to previously unsigned Pueblo pottery. "No longer were objects honored for their contribution to the community or the degree to which they venerated the ancestors, but rather for their achievement of individual creativity and mastery of the craft," he writes.

Bruce Bernstein's personal and professional relationship to Puebloans and Pueblo pottery is at the thematic center of his two-part essay. While storytelling is not the usual modus operandi of anthropologists, Bernstein in Part I relates personal experiences to shed light on the ways Anglo-Americans, or outsiders, perceive the Pueblos, as well as how the Pueblos perceive outsiders. After more than two decades of living and working in the Southwest, he recognizes the central importance of pottery to Pueblo life—Native societies use the ceramic arts to teach others about themselves, as well as to strengthen their families, their communities, and their resolve for survival. In Part II, Bernstein reflects on anthropology's contributions to the understanding of this artistic tradition, while questioning the efficacy of the academic approach in isolation from Pueblo perspectives. Keeping this in mind, Bernstein proposes new ways to simultaneously interpret scholarship and engage indigenous artistic communities.

Painter and Cochiti community member Mateo Romero expresses his opinions about museums, and the scholars associated with them, in graphic and poignant terms. He recognizes that museums are one way to educate people about cultural heritage, but questions the extent to which Western museums present their collections as ethnographic truth and the means they have employed to amass them. As a Native artist from Cochiti, he addresses issues of cultural rights and the role of art in ownership and management of cultural knowledge. Today Romero and other indigenous artists are redefining stereotypical imagery as a means of reasserting self-identity: reclaiming the past to build the future.

J. J. Brody writes from a personal perspective shaped by sixty years of academic training and professional work as, successively, a visual artist, archaeologist, art historian, museum professional, and university professor. His interest in the closely linked pottery traditions of Cochiti and Santo Domingo is filtered by an immersion, since about 1954, in the 1,500-year history of Pueblo art, especially the medium of painted pottery. His perception as an art historian is that the visual arts, including painted pottery, are nonverbal communications constrained within a medium, expressive of history, and structured by local social contexts. While Bruce Bernstein introduces the difficulty of painting on a curved surface in Part I of his essay, Brody hypothesizes on exactly how it is done and constructs an overarching aesthetic philosophy that explains its application.

figure 1
Wedding Vase
Santo Domingo and Santa Clara
Monica Silva
1960
31.0 x 38.0 cm

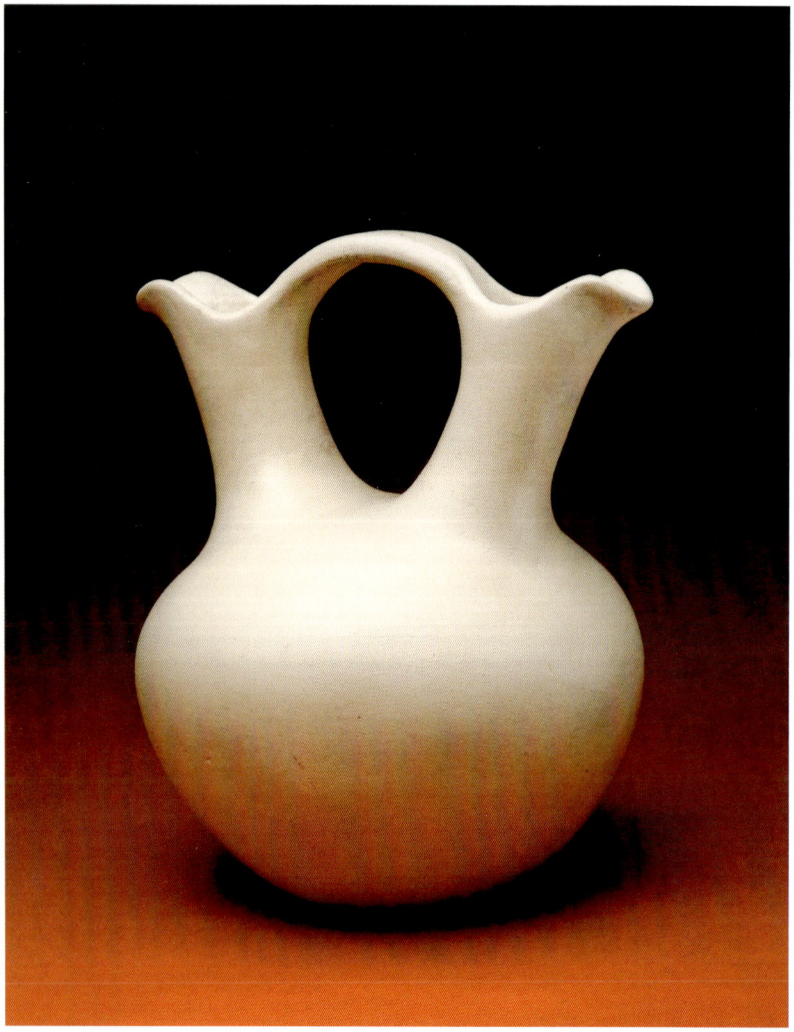

The Pueblos of Cochiti and Santo Domingo—A Historical Perspective

Living in the Southwest's harsh environment, a marginal area for agriculture, meant that Ancestral Puebloans migrated constantly in search of sustainable farming conditions. The Keresan-speakers of the present-day Rio Grande Pueblos are descendants of the Ancestral Pueblos of the Four Corners area. They trace their origin to the underworld, from which they emerged from an opening called a *sipapu*. According to tradition, over a very long period of time they migrated from the *sipapu* to an area north of their present location, where they constructed cliff dwellings at Rito de los Frijoles, or Tyuonyi. Long before their first contact with Coronado in 1540—the start of the historic period—the Keresan people had moved to a number of autonomous villages along the Rio Grande. In 1540 when the Spanish arrived in the region, they encountered over 40,000 indigenous people living in nearly 100 villages. In reference to their village lifestyle, the Spanish named the people "pueblo" or "town-dwellers." Cochiti and Santo Domingo are two of the twenty pueblos now extant in the Southwest. Although Puebloan peoples never constituted a single tribe—each Pueblo village is an autonomous political entity—they have engaged each other continually—trading, visiting, and intermarrying (figs. 1–3). While the people of some Pueblo villages spoke the same or similar languages, others spoke entirely unrelated languages. Amongst today's twenty pueblos there are five unique language groups—

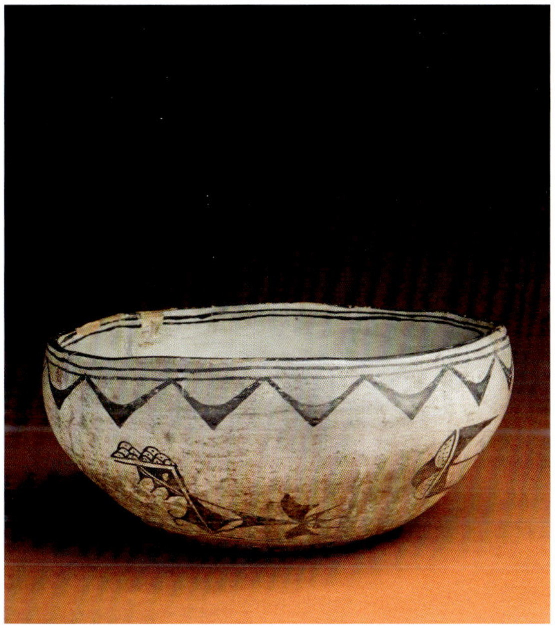

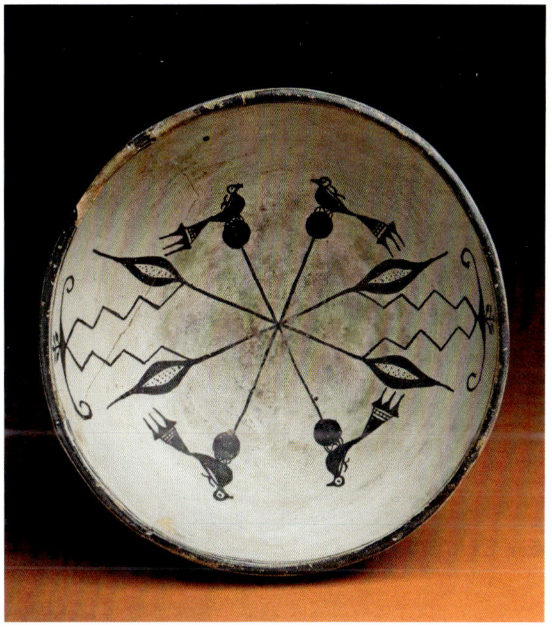

figure 2
Bowl (two views)
Cochiti and
San Ildefonso
Tonita Peña
ca. 1920
12.6 x 29.1 cm

bottom left:
figure 3
Mermaid Figurine
Cochiti and Acoma
Rita and Ivan Lewis
1987
16.3 x 9.0 x 26.2 cm

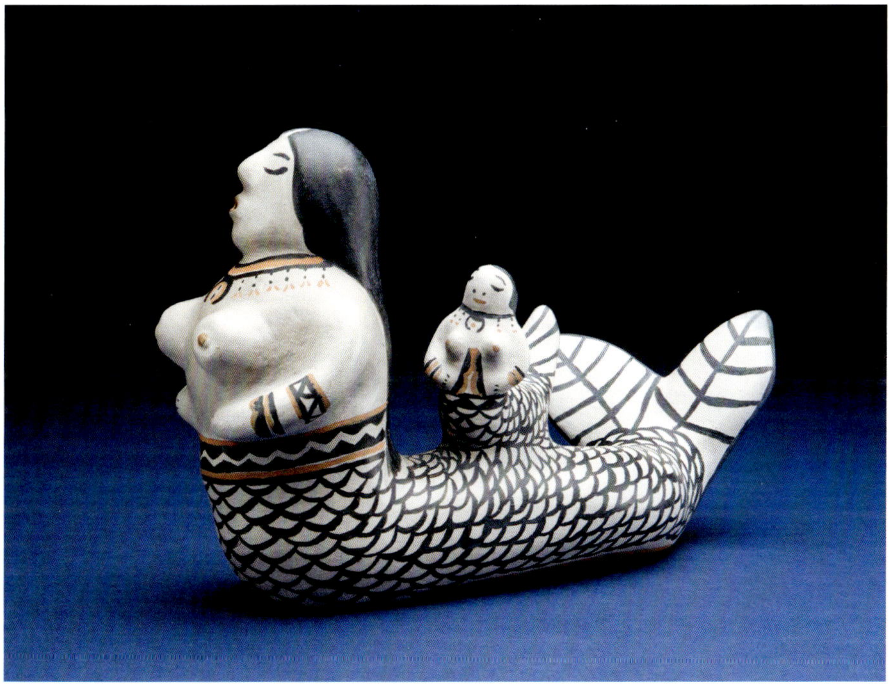

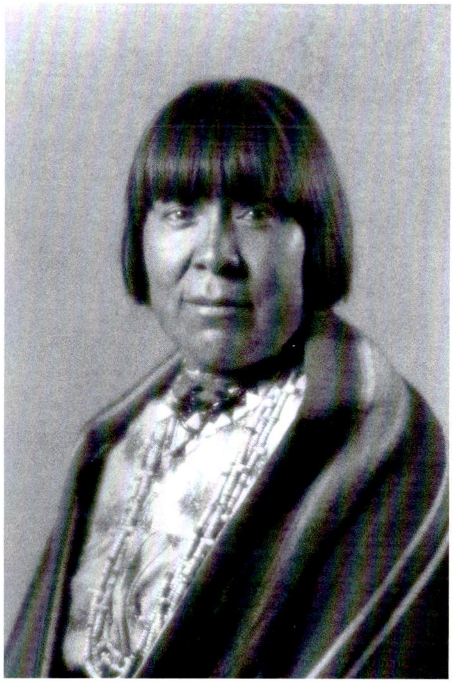

Tonita Peña, ca. 1930. T. Harmon Parkhurst, photographer. Courtesy Palace of the Govenors (MNM/DCA), 46988.

Cochiti and Santo Domingo people are Keresan speakers, along with the Pueblos of Acoma, Laguna, San Felipe, Santa Ana, and Zia.

The traditional homeland of the Puebloans is the high arid plateau country of northern Arizona and northwestern and central New Mexico. Their village lifestyle is made possible in this harsh environment by irrigation-based farming. (Before Spanish contact, their cultivars included maize [corn], beans, squash, cotton, and tobacco.) The strong societal bonds that ensure the cooperation of the large numbers of people needed to support village life are evident in the social, political, and especially religious organizations that persist today. In this world where the success or failure of crops is critical yet uncertain, a central element of the yearly religious

top:
View of Cochiti Pueblo, ca. 1880. John K. Hillers, photographer. Courtesy Palace of the Governors (MNM/DCA), 3964.

bottom:
View of Santo Domingo Pueblo, ca. 1920. T. Harmon Parkhurst, photographer. Courtesy Palace of the Governors (MNM/DCA), 2812.

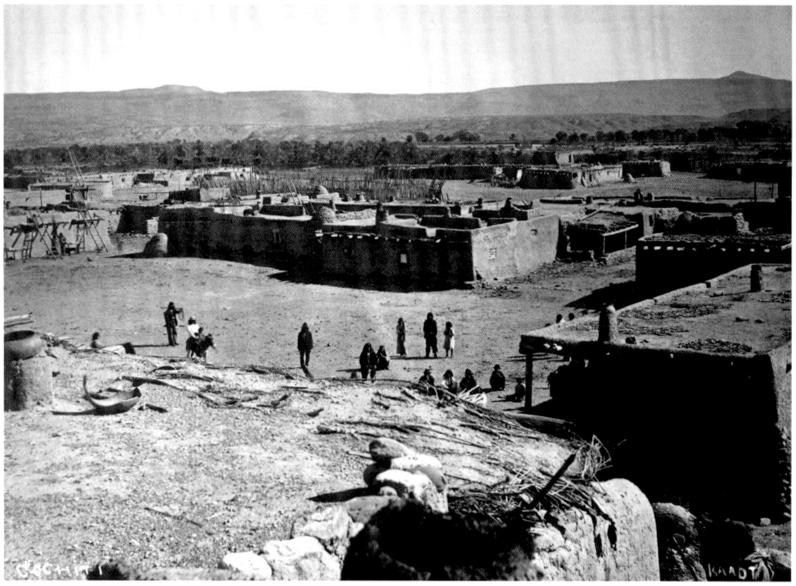

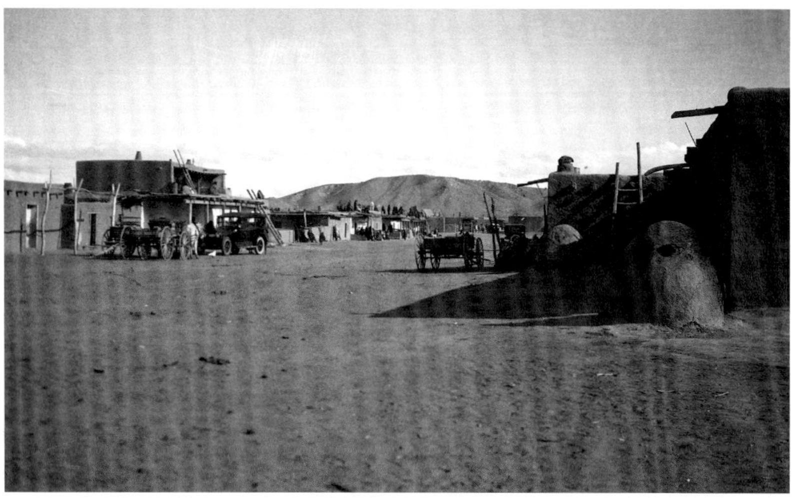

cycle emphasizes rain in both its physical and spiritual manifestations. Strict adherence to religious life is believed to result in a bountiful harvest.

Both Cochiti and Santo Domingo are theocracies with secular governments appointed by religious leaders. Religious life, the center of Pueblo existence, revolves around the Catholic Church as well as the *kivas* and society houses that are the focal points of traditional religious practices. Roman Catholicism has maintained a strong presence at both pueblos since its introduction during the first Spanish expeditions in the mid-1500s, so that each pueblo's annual calendar of religious activities represents a blending of Catholicism and Native religious beliefs. Today, at Santo Domingo (and to a lesser extent at Cochiti) there is a general and persistent reticence to discuss or reveal internal Pueblo life, the legacy of centuries of religious and social oppression by colonizing peoples.

On the west bank of the Rio Grande, Cochiti is northernmost of the eastern Keresan groups. The Cochiti people have occupied their present village, about 25 miles southwest of Santa Fe, since at least 1700. Currently, they administer 53,779 acres of land and have jurisdiction over the adjoining Kasha-Katuwe Tent Rocks National Monument. The total population at the 2000 census was 1,502. Cochiti's annual feast day, San Buenaventura's Day, is celebrated on July 14 with a performance of the Corn Dance. The Cochiti people traditionally are agriculturists, and today some of their land is under cultivation in the form of family plots. A portion of the water from the Rio Grande, which flows through pueblo lands, is stored behind Cochiti Dam, making it possible for the pueblo to develop a Farm Enterprise Plan, which includes the restoration of large acreages of traditional farmland. Although historically Cochiti has had no private economic enterprises, in 1995 the pueblo acquired the Town of Cochiti Lake and created the Cochiti Community Development Corporation. This initiative has been a primary revenue source for the community.

On the east bank of the Rio Grande, about 35 miles southwest of Santa Fe, Santo Domingo is the largest of the Rio Grande pueblos. As with the Cochitis, the Santo Domingo people have occupied their present village since at least 1700. Currently they administer approximately 75,000 acres of land. The total population at the 2000 census was 3,166. Santo Domingo's annual feast day, Saint Dominic's Day, is celebrated on August 4 with a performance of the Corn Dance, artisan booths, and a festive carnival. Ironically, although Santo Domingo is probably the most conservative and insular of the pueblos, it is also among the best known. Santo

Domingo's location—directly on or near established roads from the Camino Real of early Spanish times, to the railway and the state and federal highways of today—has contributed to its high profile and, reflexively, to its conservative stance toward innovation and change. Except on feast day, the presence of outsiders at the pueblo is generally discouraged.

For more than four hundred years now, pressures from Euro/Anglo-American communities have had a profound effect on the evolution of Pueblo pottery. We know that outside influence on Pueblo material culture from 1540 to American rule in 1848 was considerable. However, a definitive picture of Pueblo pottery during this period has never

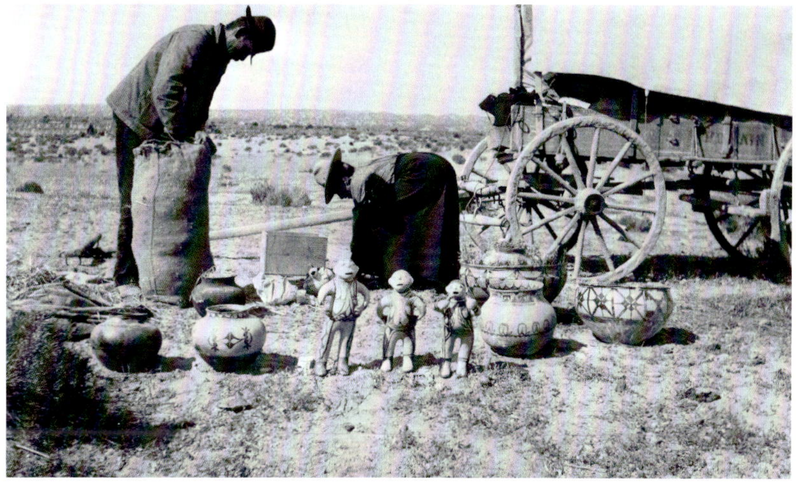

American Museum of Natural History curator George Pepper packing Cochiti pottery for shipment east to the museum, 1903. Courtesy National Museum of the American Indian, Smithsonian Institution, N32657.

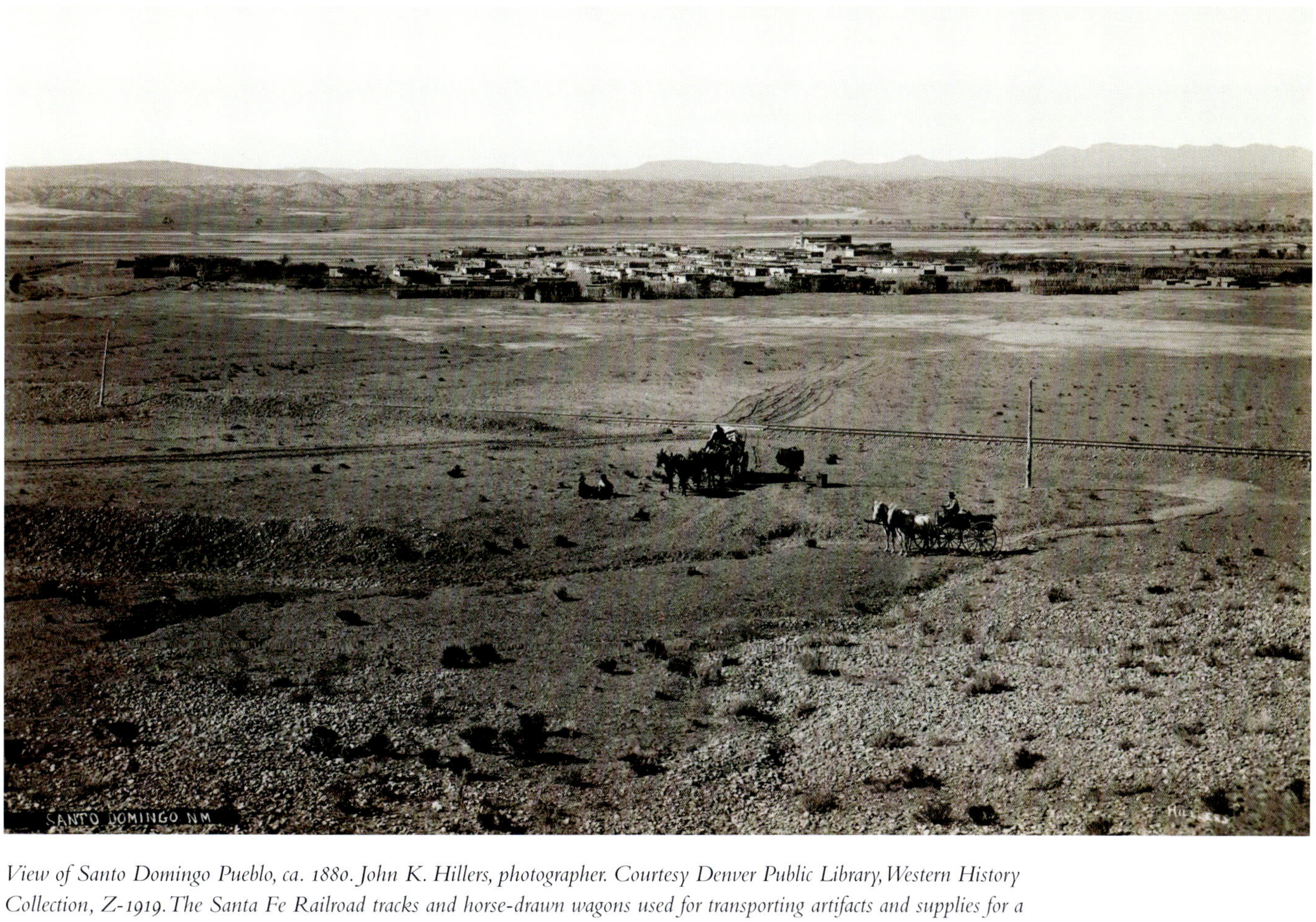

View of Santo Domingo Pueblo, ca. 1880. John K. Hillers, photographer. Courtesy Denver Public Library, Western History Collection, Z-1919. The Santa Fe Railroad tracks and horse-drawn wagons used for transporting artifacts and supplies for a James Stevenson collecting expedition are shown in the foreground. Between 1880 and 1925, eastern museums mounted major collecting expeditions to the Southwest pueblos with the mission of creating systematic and encyclopedic ethnographic and archaeological material culture study collections. The expedition recorded here may be the one organized by the Bureau of American Ethnology, which included James Stevenson, Matilda Coxe Stevenson, Frank Hamilton Cushing, and photographer John K. Hillers.

been developed as whole vessels from that period are rare for a number of reasons. One is that pottery was used at the pueblos as long as it was serviceable and then discarded in the village trash heap. A second significant reason is that because almost all the pueblos occupied since the Spanish reconquest of the 1690s are alive and vibrant villages today, archaeological excavations have been limited. Consequently, even fragmentary vessels made between the conquest and 1879, when museums began to collect and preserve them, are scarce.

By the mid-nineteenth century, the pace of social, political, and economic change had accelerated. Competition for land between the Pueblos, Hispanic communities, and new Euro/Anglo-American immigrants put increasing pressure on indigenous populations. With the arrival of American rule in 1848, the Puebloan land base and water rights were further impinged, and disastrous disease epidemics that began with first contact with outsiders continued to cause population decline. With the Spanish and early Euro/Anglo-American settlers, the Pueblos had continued a traditional economic system of subsistence, barter, and exchange. In exchange for the new consumer goods, Pueblo potters had developed pottery types specifically for settler households, including pitchers, cups and saucers, and candlesticks. With American rule, Pueblo people became consumers instead of producers for the first time in their long history. People accustomed to a gifting, bartering, and a subsistence economy were forced to become dependent on the new cash economy and manufactured goods. American rule also brought the railroad, then automobile travel, and with them a booming tourist industry. Potters rethought the forms of their utilitarian wares and developed new styles, such as figurines and miniatures, for the burgeoning tourist market. Beginning in the 1920s, Santa Fe museum personnel—most significantly Edgar L. Hewett and Kenneth Chapman—began developing initiatives to "improve" the craft they saw as degraded by the introduction of tourist wares. Today we see their influence in the judging of pottery at annual summer events including the Southwest Association for Indian Art's Indian Market, the Eight Northern Pueblos Arts and Crafts Show, and the MIAC/LAB's Native Treasures Indian Arts Festival. While these events promote "high-quality" pieces, contemporary potters throughout the Southwest continue to produce a wide variety of wares, from pieces for use in Pueblo homes and for community ceremonial events to wares which fall on a continuum from inexpensive tourist pieces to fine art.

Curators, Collectors, and Catalogs

Contemporary Pueblo ceramic wares are the result of centuries of a fluid and adaptive tradition. These wares reflect diverse influences: continual migrations necessitated variation in materials; dietary and household changes required functional shifts in shape and size; and multiple markets—such as other pueblos, other Native communities, Hispanic and Euro/Anglo-American villagers, and, more recently, tourists and high-end collectors—resulted in adaptations that would appeal to these varied buyers. Over the last two centuries, the Pueblo pottery market has been an important contributer to the continued vitality of village life by bringing needed income to communities, and by giving potters a way to support their families while living and working at home. Throughout the historic period in the Southwest, outsiders have appropriated Pueblo cultural and natural resources for personal, political, and monetary gain.

Curators, collectors, and the exigencies of imposed cataloging systems recontextualize Pueblo pottery as museum artifacts, often losing sight of their indigenous identities in the process. Because of this, it is important to cast an ever critical eye on the circumstances of collecting, the assumptions and

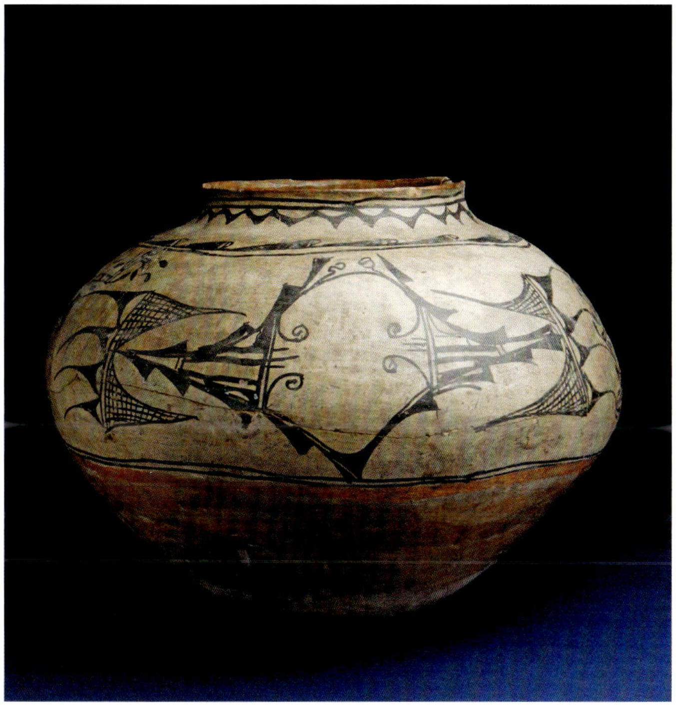

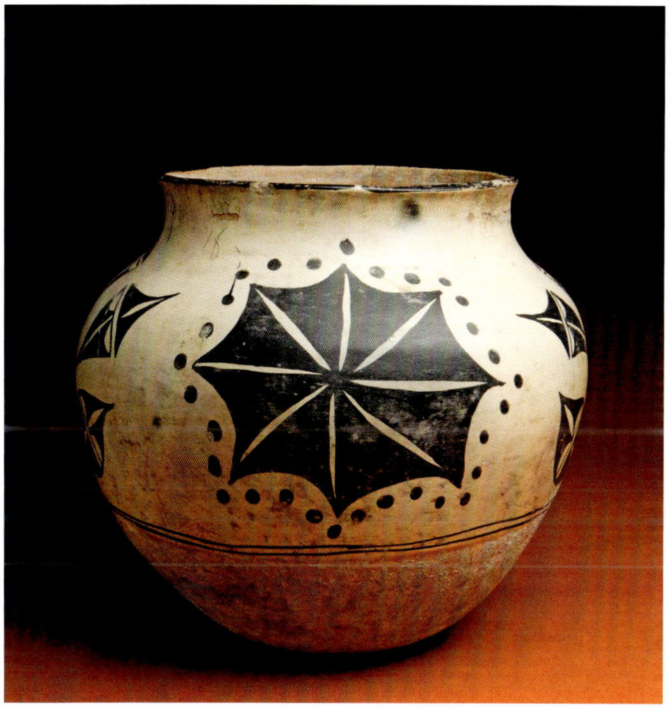

motivations of curators and collectors, and the changing meanings and values attached to Pueblo pottery in museum collections over time and space. Today those of us who work in Southwest regional museums—and who are in the unique position of living, working, and socializing on a daily basis with the very alive and very real people represented by our collections—have to recognize their legal and ethical right to determine how their traditional knowledge and products are to be interpreted and represented, as well as their right to demand some kind of recognition and compensation for their appropriation by others. An often-repeated story told by former curator of ethnology Edmund Ladd, which he swore was true, illustrates the tight control museums have exercised over representation of America's indigenous populations. Tourists, returning from a visit to the several northern New Mexico pueblos, were convinced that the museum peopled the villages as a living exhibit. "They don't really live there, do they?" the tourists asked. To combat a widely accepted and romanticized view of Indian people as the mysterious past occupants of abandoned ruins, the essays in this volume seek to present Cochiti and Santo Domingo as the dynamic and living cultures that they are today.

figure 4
Jar
Cochiti
Artist Unknown
ca. 1880
40.0 x 55.5 cm

figure 5
Jar
Cochiti
Artist Unknown
ca. 1900
29.4 x 32.8 cm

SECTION I

Artistic Community

My metaphor for the Pueblo world, both past and present, is a stream. Composed of many diverse and varied currents, connected together at all points simultaneously, yet with a degree of distinction in the currents. Some people, villages, artwork, dances might seem at first glance to be more central, essential, or forceful within the flow of the stream. In the end, it is enough for me to say that when I had the chance in my life, I chose to be part of the flow.

Mateo Romero, Cochiti Pueblo
from *Painting the Underworld Sky*

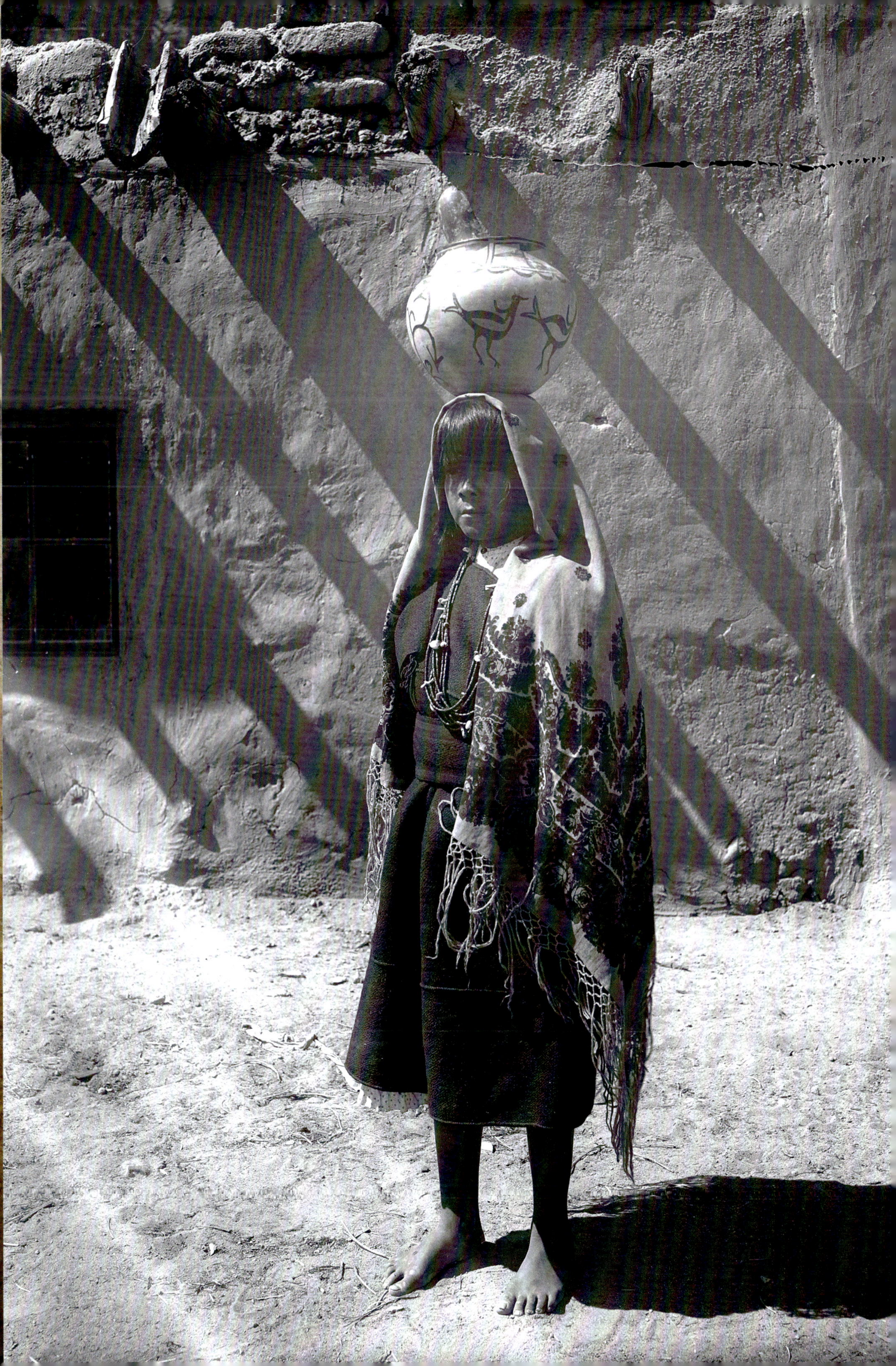

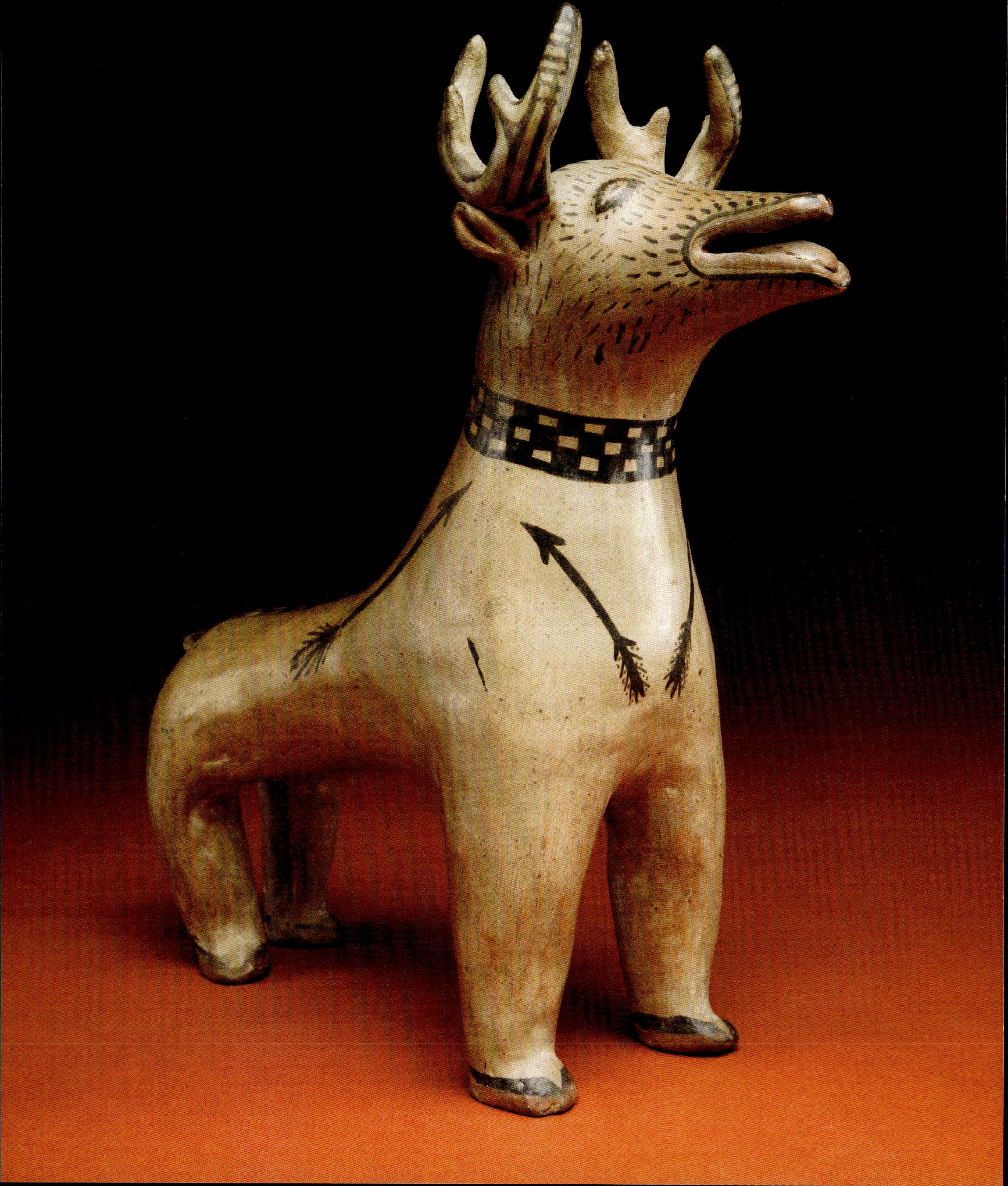

Making Pottery, Seeking Life

Antonio Chavarria

In this essay about how the artists of Cochiti and Santo Domingo work and the worldview behind their work, I write from my perspective as an anthropology museum professional—Curator of Ethnology at the Museum of Indian Arts & Culture/Laboratory of Anthropology (MIAC/LAB)—and as a Pueblo person—Tewa from the Pueblo of Santa Clara. I concentrate on pottery production, the shifting relationship between tribes and museums, and the role of a museum in preservation. As a Tewa, I respect the private nature of Keresan religious practices and discuss spiritual aspects of pottery making only in the broadest of terms. Readers should note that mine is only one among any number of shifting and changing interpretations.

Indians as Anthropologists—and Potters, Too

I have always thought of American Indian people raised in traditional households as de facto anthropologists. Raised in one "culture" with definite rules and behavioral norms, we must also participate in a dominant society whose conventions and expectations are very different. We learn through participant/observation how that society works and how to negotiate through it. Like anthropologists, Native people seek to understand the perceived "other," and ultimately learn more about themselves in return. Indian artists experience this dichotomy on a number of levels—they must balance traditionalist community practices, art market economics, aesthetic contradictions, and the competing definitions of Pueblo pottery constructed by collectors, dealers, curators, and art competition judges. My viewpoint is that while these community outsiders give intermittent standing to the indigenous perspective, the game—selling and buying—is played by their rules and on their turf, outside of the pueblos.

This is not to deny the increasing influence of Native voices in the art market. Many artists have formed committees that promote their interests in classification and judging. Yet the dominant aesthetic remains that of the Western eye and the product, pottery, still is developed to fill that niche. Well-crafted, pleasing pots always have been part of the Pueblo aesthetic: a jar that will hold water is a

figure 6
Deer Figurine
Cochiti
Artist Unknown
ca. 1910
29.5 x 9.8 x 30.5 cm

previous spread:
Cochiti girl, 1894–1910
See page 43.

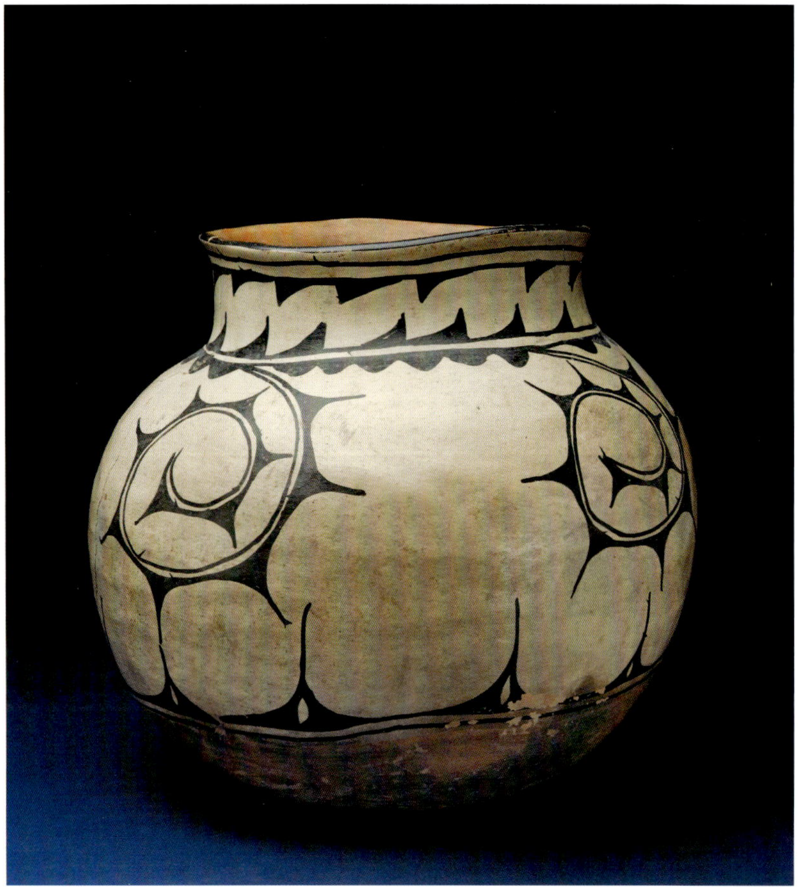

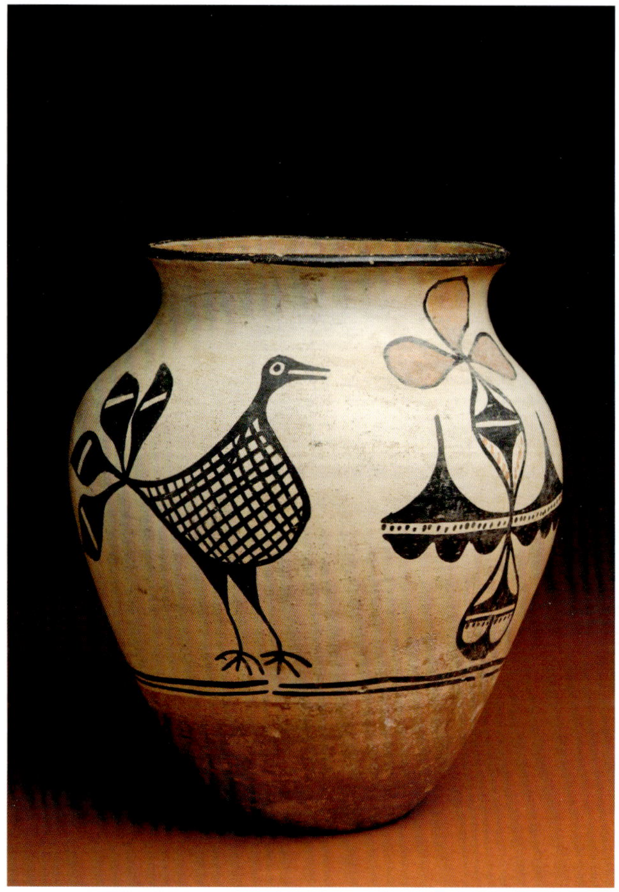

figure 7
Storage Jar
Cochiti
Artist Unknown
ca. 1900–1920
37.0 x 37.5 cm

figure 8
Storage Jar
Santo Domingo
Artist Unknown
ca. 1910
26.3 x 23.0 x 25.1 cm

necessity, but so is one that carries the mark of humanity in all its flawed beauty—a shaky line, a scratch, a crack in the slip, a divot, or off-hue firing are all products of aging eyes, weathered hands, and imperfect humans. Looking over museum collections, especially those of MIAC/LAB, I am captivated by the element of human touch visible in pottery. In museum collections, ancient Pueblo pots with asymmetrical bulges and crackled surfaces are declared masterpieces (figs. 7–8); however, if they were entered in Indian art competitions today, they wouldn't make it past the intake table. This focus on finely crafted product has replaced revealing expressions of traditional communities with an art that reveals more about the community for which it is produced. Such is Art.

In the potter's mind, a fired piece ready for sale or household use is not an end product. The process is a journey on which every completed piece marks a step on the path. For many potters it is the path their ancestors forged; it is how the clay is gathered, how the clay slips are mixed, how the wood is gathered, how the form is shaped, and how the pot is fired. This process—steeped in tradition, cyclical repetition, and cumulative action—is a journey that doesn't end with a prize or a sale. The process and practice is passed on through generations, and even when teachers' lives are interrupted by outside circumstances, we have seen the journey re-created by singular or communal acts. One person may choose to learn pottery making and, after they have grown in skill, will teach others, or a village may fund a pottery-making class to revitalize a traditional practice. Nevertheless, contemporary potters may work with clays and other materials that they did not gather from the earth but from commercial sources. Cochiti potter Diego Romero learned the traditional meth ods and then branched out on a journey that didn't

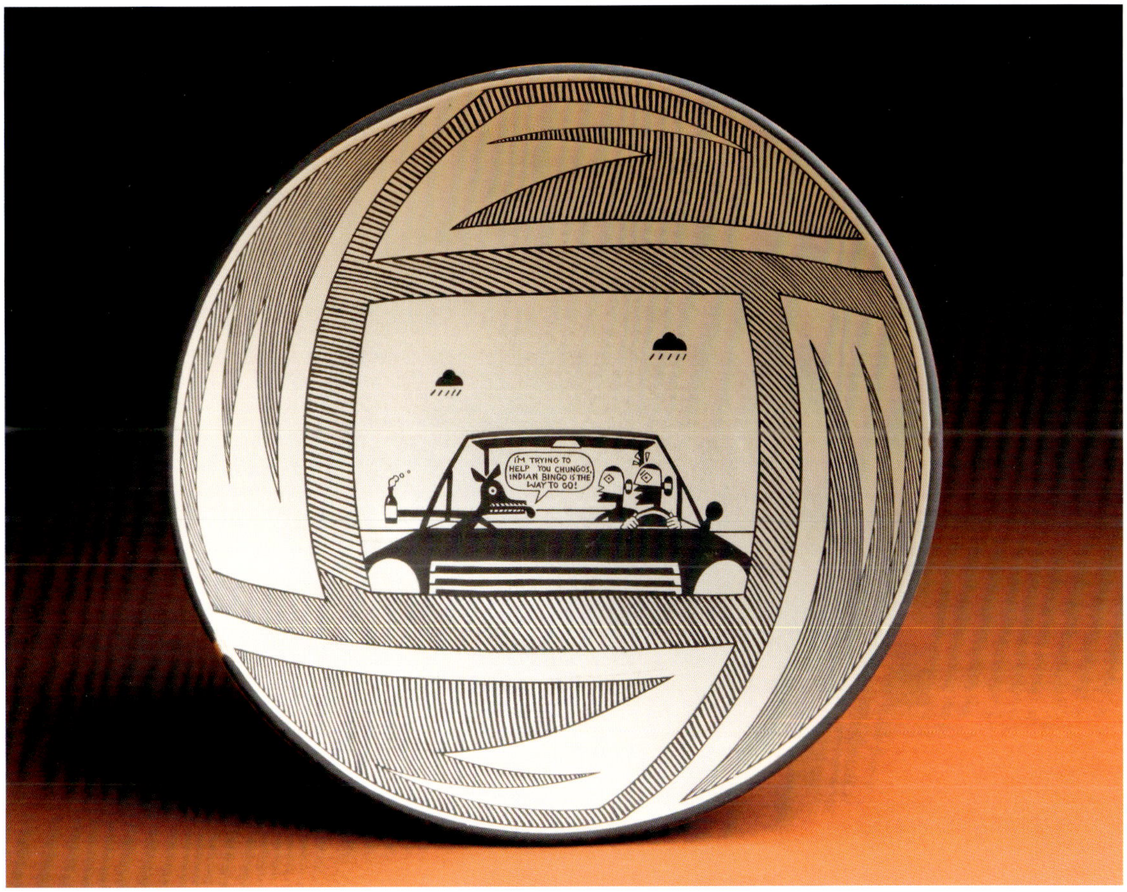

figure 9
Chongo Brothers Bowl
Cochiti
Diego Romero
1994
13.2 x 7.8 cm

repeat the past but instead explored new materials and artistic expression that would continue to evolve and challenge (fig. 9). In the footsteps of their ancestors, Romero and other contemporary potters are adapting to influences that come from over the horizon. Whether we on the outside call them contemporary, traditional, or innovative, the potters of Cochiti and Santo Domingo are informed by an ancient practice that links their origin, life, and spirit (figs. 10–11).

Making Pottery, Seeking Life

Pottery is family. In the Puebloan view, pots, like people, are creations from the earth. Clay is referred to and thought of as a mother. The literal Mother Earth or, more accurately, Old Clay Earth Mother, is a nurturer of life, and from her gifts people sustain life in all its forms, including pottery. Since their emergence from within this earth, Indian people, after many trials and migrations, came to create from the earth vessels as aides to both material and spiritual existence. Clay, in its manifesting of life and creation, plays a vital role in Pueblo lifeways. Represented in origin stories, cosmology, songs, and stages of life, pottery is intricately connected to Pueblo existence. The importance of the communal aspect of pottery making cannot be stressed too strongly. Even members of a community who do not shape vessels or paint their surfaces with meaningful designs play a part in this tradition.

Nuclear and extended families gather clay and the associated materials at carefully selected areas close to their communities. Some potters believe the materials interact with each other as people do, based on a common area of origin or familiarity—clays work with slips or paints more readily if they "know" each other. One Cochiti potter is hesitant

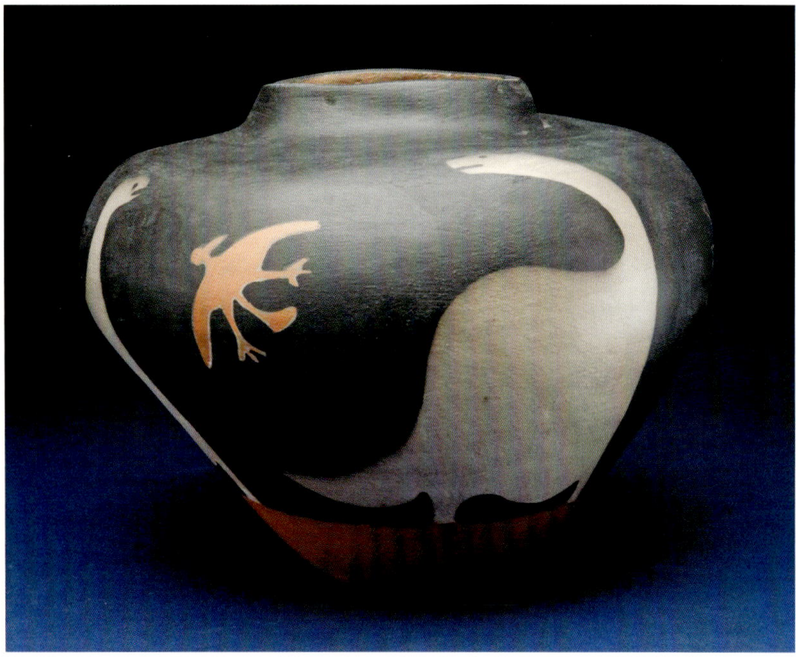

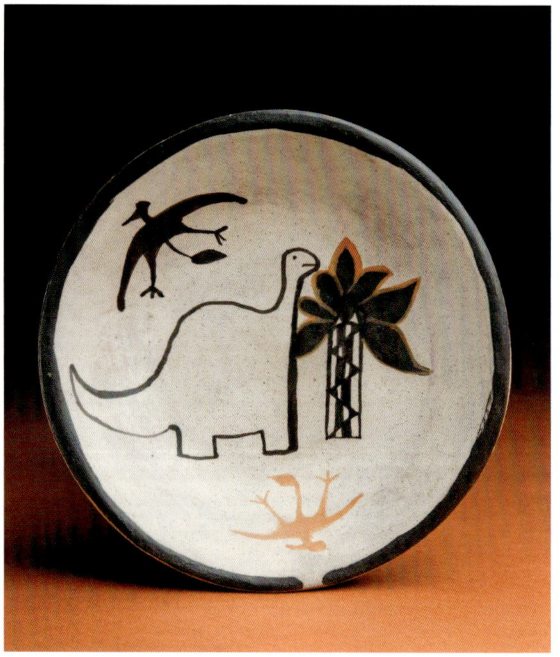

figure 10
Jar
Santo Domingo
Andrew Pacheco
1991
26.7 x 31.2 cm

figure 11
Plate
Santo Domingo
Andrew Pacheco
1991
4.2 x 20.1 cm

to use a North Dakota clay slip with her local clay as she does not know if they will "get along." (I have personally experienced this lack of compatibility when I tried to use a La Bajada red earth as a plaster for a Santa Clara mud oven.)

Clay is needed to make pottery but, as a group effort, gathering clay carries an aspect beyond that of utility. Gathering clay, slip, stones, and plants for paint and brushes requires an exchange or offering. A family will gather what they need, keeping an active dialog with the earth throughout the process and asking that they may do well with what they are given. After clay is carried home the family, working together, breaks it into smaller clods for drying on a prepared surface—a large slat of wood, a large screen, or even the top of a camper shell. The dried clods are pulverized into a rough screen to remove any impurities. After multiple screenings through finer and finer mesh, the earth is soaked in buckets to become an early stage of clay.

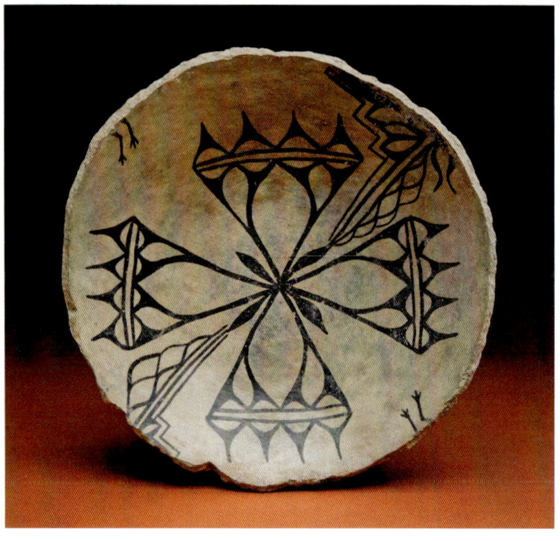

figure 12
Bowl Fragment or Puki
Artist Unknown
ca. 1910
6.1 x 30.0 cm

The family then adds a temper, usually a volcanic ash gathered locally, to the wet clay, handful by handful. The balance of temper and clay is not a fixed measurement, so each clay preparation is unique—the potter knows by feel when the proper balance is achieved. Too much temper can make the clay dry and lacking in the adhesion between coils, too little will allow the clay to shrink too much as it dries and cause the surface to crack. I have witnessed and participated in "over salting," or adding too much temper. The quick fix is to add more clay if it is on hand and, if not, to steep the current batch in a bucket of water until more clay is available. I must add that before this, the temper is also screened over and over until it is a very fine powder, another

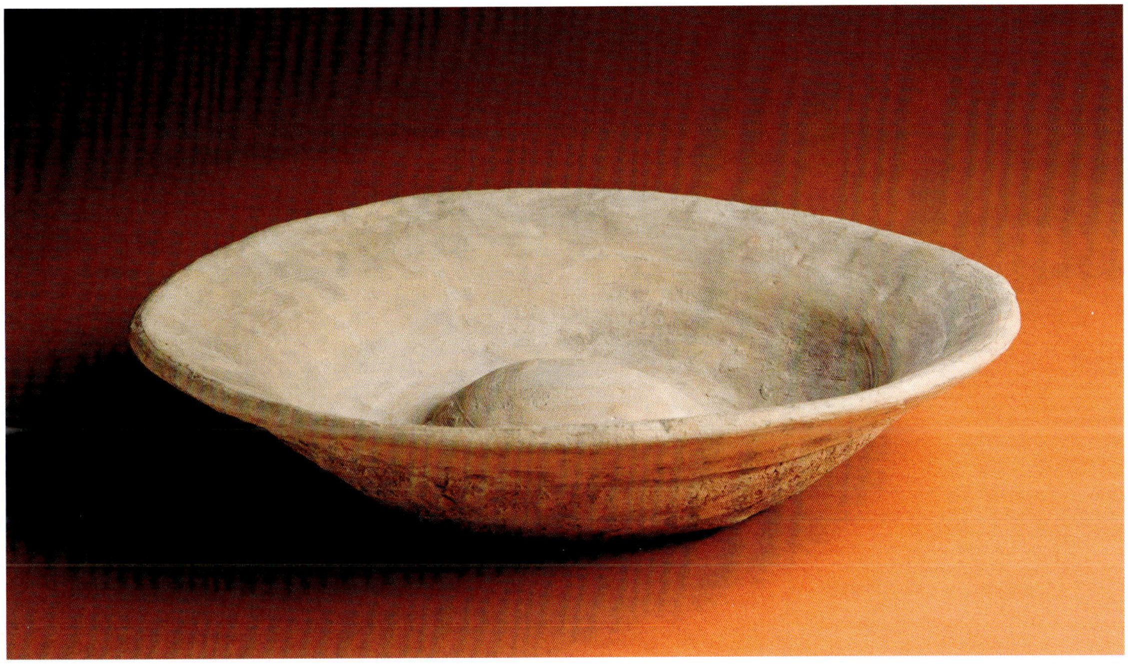

figure 13
Puki
Santo Domingo
Artist Unknown
ca. 1925
6.9 x 29.8 cm

labor-intensive process that requires help from others. Seeking balance involves multiple hands.

After a proper batch is made, all under the watchful eye of the potter or potters, the damp clay is ready to be used. For larger vessels, the potter uses a mold in the form of a basket or dried clay structure as a foundation. Called a *puki* in the Tewa language, it can be one of a Pueblo potter's prized heirlooms (fig. 13). A good *puki* helps midwife many a jar. From this foundation, the potter creates the vessel by adding coils of clay on top of each other to the desired height. In Keresan pueblos, coils are generally applied above and inside of each other, while in the Tewa region, coils are generally applied above and outside of each other. The coils are then scraped smooth, often with a smoothed section of gourd, the tool of choice as it has a little "give" but is sturdy enough to give form to the clay. Even the figurines for which Cochiti potters are famous are built using this coil and scrape method.

The potter's fingers are the tools used for the vessel's finishing touches. In the MIAC/LAB collections, pots can be found with fingerprint whorls where potters pressed the still damp clay. Robert Tenorio of Santo Domingo Pueblo can recognize "conversation rims" on jars and bowls of the older pots. Potters in conversation, shaping the rim between thumb and forefinger while they talk, create these rims which bring to mind the communal aspect of pottery, not only in gathering and preparing clay, but also in shaping the forms. Today, many potters work in solitude with the occasional assistant. Lucky are the Pueblo potters who work among others and can exchange ideas, techniques, or gossip as they give life to earth.

After shaping, the vessel is allowed to dry and is inspected for any cracks appearing among the coils. If the flaws are too severe and it is not feasible to continue making the pot, it can be returned to a clay bucket with water and later take on a new shape. Potters speak of clay finding its own shape or becoming what it wants to be. The artist's hand only guides what is already there waiting to take shape on a physical plane. The dry pot is sanded with a fine grit sandpaper to create a surface ready for application of slip. Red or white slips are added to create the painting surface. Slips are added in multiple coats, creating a creamy background to allow the

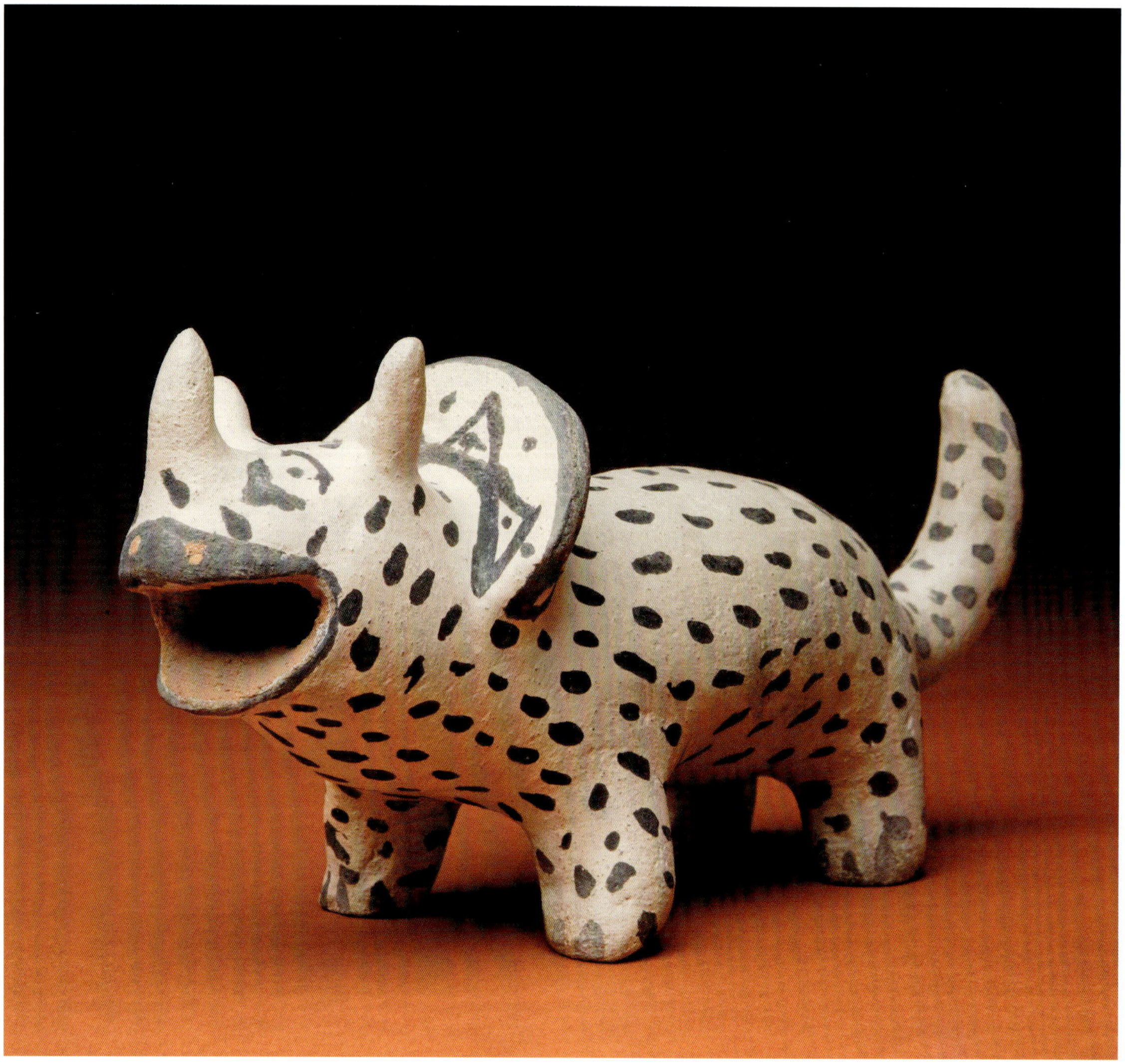

figure 14
Dinosaur Figurine
Cochiti
Damacia Cordero
ca. 1985
10.2 x 22.1 x 7.8 cm

below:
Cochiti potter Martha Arquero, her husband Clyde Arquero, and her daughter potter April Arquero with figurines made by her mother and teacher, Damacia Cordero, in MIAC/LAB collections storage, 2007. Antonio Chavarria, photographer. Arquero's humorous and mischievous figurines are a family tradition that began with her mother and includes the work of her three sisters: Josephine Arquero, Gloria Herrera, and Marie Laweka.

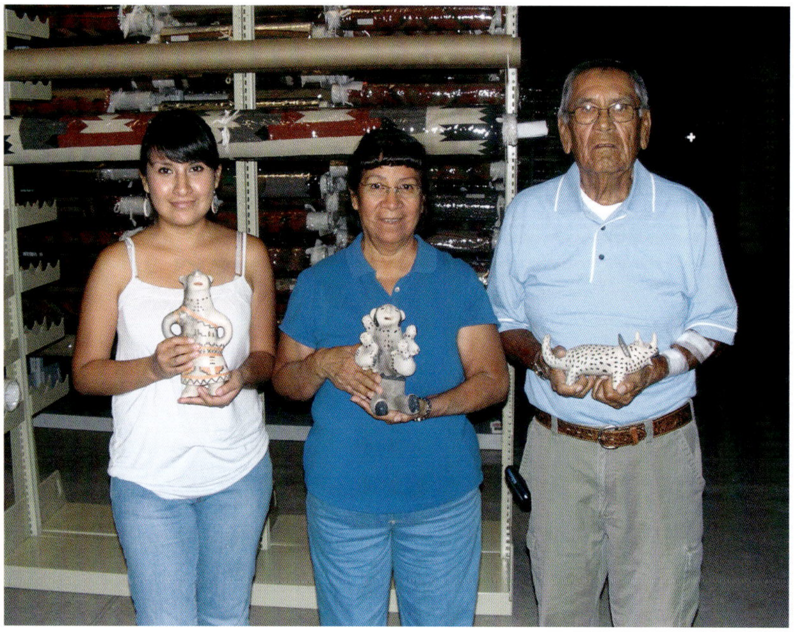

painted design to stand out. The white slip used at Cochiti and Santo Domingo is now in short supply. The land where it was once gathered is under private ownership, and the clay source for the slip has been lost to development and earth moving. "It's like gold now," says Ambrose Atencio of Santo Domingo. Cochiti potter Martha Arquero remembers being offered a flour sack of white slip for the unheard of price of twenty-five dollars back in the 1980s. Just a few years later, she and her mother Damacia Cordero "went halfers" on a similar sized sack for one hundred dollars. Potters are now using the existing supply and looking for another source. Some have begun using a mixture of slips from other sources, using the local source as the base coat; others occasionally use a mixture of commercial slips and locally gathered clay. The use of "nontraditional" materials, such as commercial slips and paints, brings up the debate on authenticity, which, while not the focus of this essay, is an ongoing issue among everyone interested in Pueblo pottery, most of all among the artists. Some potters I have spoken to feel that using commercial materials makes the product something other than Pueblo pottery. Cochiti potter Elizabeth Trujillo used outside ceramic paints for a short period but was never comfortable with the material. Other artists differentiate between using commercial and traditional materials, and price their pieces accordingly.

Pueblo people meet challenges by adapting. Experimental archaeologists, Native students at New Mexico Tech, and amateur rock hounds are working together in the search for new slip sources or suitable replacements. Elizabeth Trujillo has experimented with slips from Acoma, "it wipes off after the first coat," and from Hopi and San Felipe with similar results. In the meantime, the dwindling supply is causing a surge of creativity. Inspired by earlier "Aguilar" style designs (fig. 15)—a reverse-painted style of Santo Domingo pottery where large geometric forms of black and red cover most of the white-slipped background—contemporary potters are creating new organic, graphic designs. Lisa Holt

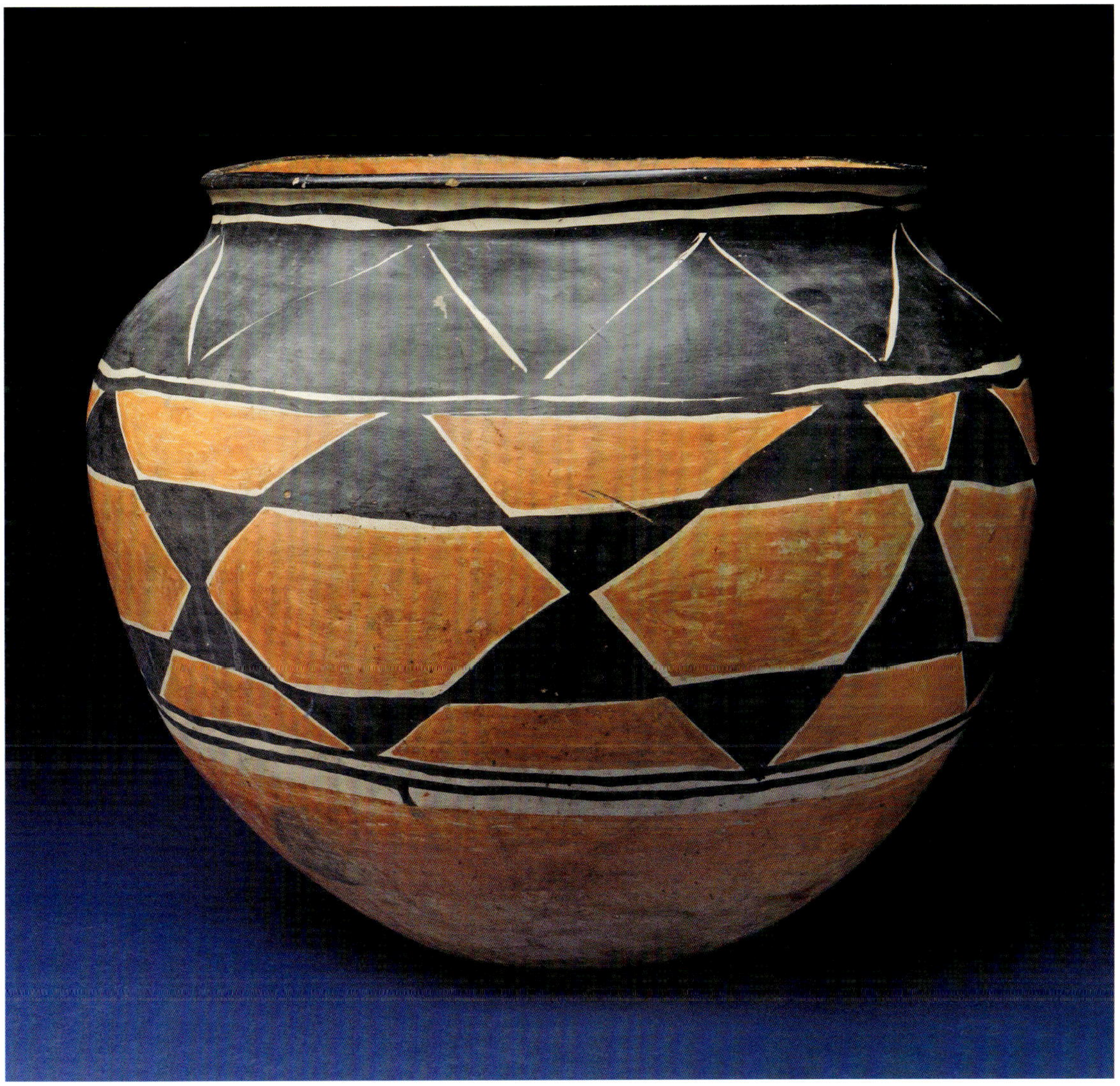

figure 15
Jar
Santo Domingo
Attributed to the Aguilar Family
ca. 1910
34.5 x 44.0 cm

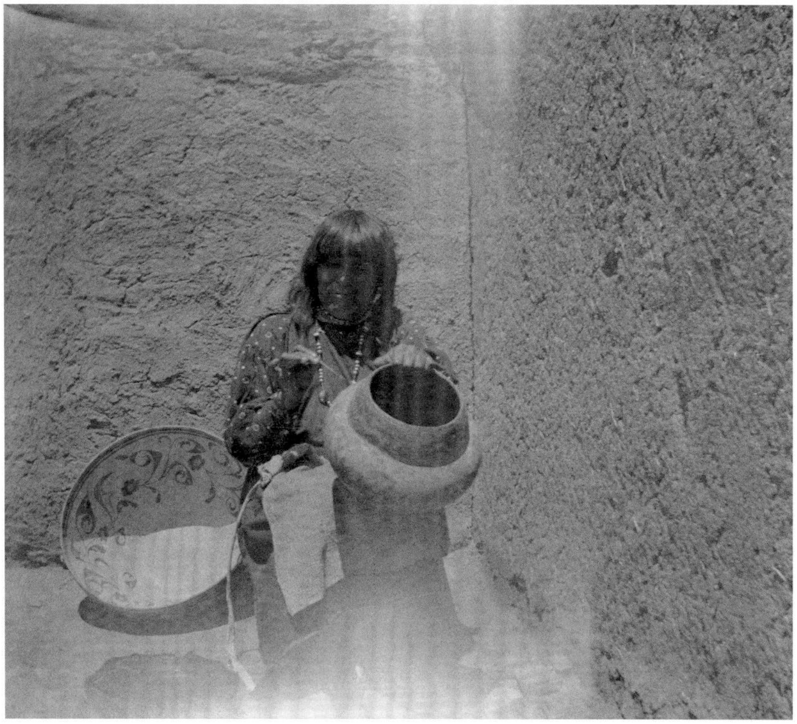

A Cochiti potter (identified only as Ben Trujillo's mother) painting a pot with a yucca paintbrush, ca. 1900. Mary E. Dissette, photographer. Courtesy Palace of the Governors (MNM/DCA), 45452.

(Cochiti) and Harlan Reano (Santo Domingo) are an artistic team working in this emerging style.

The paints that make up the Keresan Polychrome Pottery tradition are both mineral and organic based. The reds, whites, and creams are all clay slips, each color having a different source in the land. Occasionally, red and white slips are mixed to make a tan-color slip. The black paint, which makes for most of the line work in the designs, is carbon based, meaning it is an organic paint that is made from plant material. By far the most common plant used is the Rocky Mountain Beeplant (*Cleome serrulata*). When collected, the plant is thanked for giving of itself and harvested whole. The plants are boiled down into a black paste and allowed to dry into dark, porous cakes. This processing is done outside for the most part as the smell of the boiling sludge can be overpowering. The dried cakes are distributed and stored for future use. Potters also experiment with wild teas, spinach, and other plants to make carbon paint. Robert Tenorio even had success using a tea purchased at Starbucks, but when he tried again with another batch, it was not as successful.

Many Pueblo potters today, not only at Cochiti and Santo Domingo, continue to use a paintbrush made from the narrowleaf yucca (*Yucca angustissima*), the spiny flowering desert plant. They cut the narrow leaves into medium-length strips and chew one end to create the bristles. Using a yucca paintbrush is not like using a similarly sized camel hair brush. The yucca leaf bends to the contour of the surface being painted, enabling long, deliberate strokes. During my own attempts at painting pottery using yucca brushes, I experienced it not as applying paint with brush strokes but carefully laying and dragging a thin line of nearly invisible ink. The paint in its watery form is visible only as a faint gray or blue, the "black" manifesting after firing. Given the challenges of the materials, the brushes, and the only faintly visible carbon paint, I am in awe of the potter's ability to successfully employ ancient techniques. Keresan artists fire their pots within a few days after painting the designs; after a week or so, the blacks will not be as vibrant and will take on gradient hues of gray. Today some potters will use commercial paint or mix it with the beeplant to create a denser black. When this is the case, it must be applied after firing, as the commercial paint will not "fire on."

A Few Words on Designs

A common question asked of the Pueblo potter is, "What do the designs mean?" Other books and guides will offer up multitudes of interpretations; this essay is not one of them. If there is anything I have learned by observing Pueblo artists it is that symbols incorporated into pottery designs have multiple levels of meaning. Choosing one interpretation gives short shrift to the complexity of the art *and* culture. When asked about meaning, the artist will often give the most literal interpretation—a loose, basic meaning most palatable to the outsider. This is not disingenuous, but is the artist's way of giving information on a mutually acceptable level. Symbols can be layered with meaning in terms of placement and sequence. In another instance, sometimes on the same vessel, symbols are combined to give multivocal meanings to a society, to a family, or to an individual painter. There are instances where a potter has a very specific meaning in mind when a design is painted and is happy to share with anyone interested. Robert Tenorio has painted designs that tell vivid stories, and designs that are amalgams of symbols from other communities where the message is his appreciation of the talents of his ancestors (fig. 16).

Certain designs are identified with particular pueblos. Though this sense of possession can be a response to market forces, it also comes from the artist's teachers. Design styles or elements are learned and repeated until a novice becomes a teacher and the cycle repeats itself. Some designs are shared or borrowed. There are a significant number of pots in the museum's collections where a specific pueblo or origin is still being debated due to the similarity or oddness of a design that doesn't speak to our notion of a certain village style. Polychromes of the middle Rio Grande can be quite tricky to the museum cataloger and elude easy classification. Designs also can be handed down through generations of one family, or can cross family lines. Intermarriage is an important catalyst for bringing new forms, designs, and techniques from one pueblo to another. Monica Silva, originally from Santa Clara Pueblo, brought along many Tewa influenced aspects of pottery making when she married into Santo Domingo. Designs can be inspired by older pots seen in museums or stores, can come to mind in the middle of the night, or are momentary thoughts quickly drafted on a piece of paper. Others may result from playing with mundane daily visual prompts—Elizabeth Trujillo bases some designs on stylized versions of her initials.

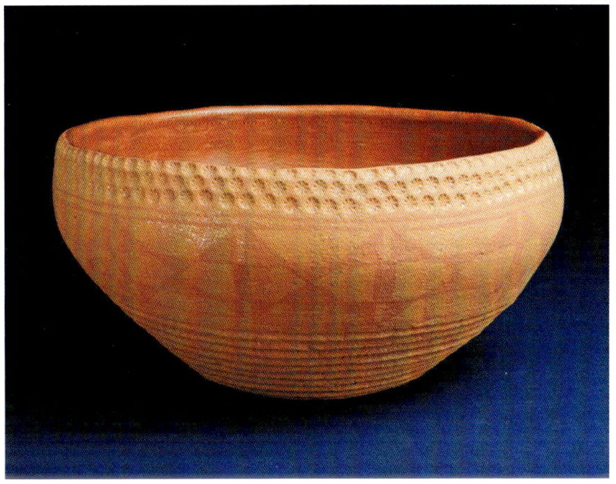

figure 16
Bowl
Santo Domingo
Robert Tenorio
1975
15.5 x 33.1 cm

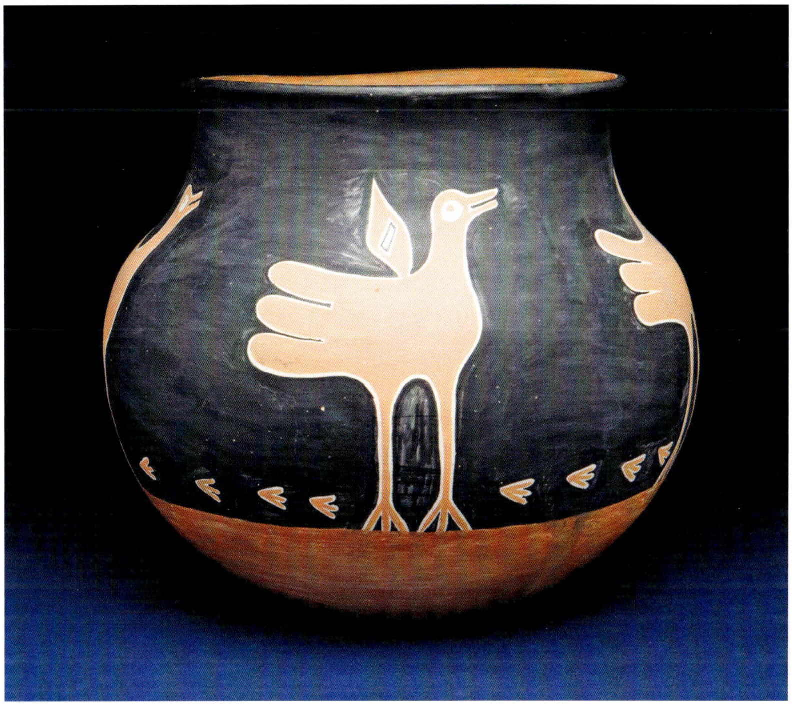

figure 17
Jar
Santo Domingo
Santana and
Crucita Melchor
ca. 1976
31.0 x 25.5 cm

Other designs are a result of a village's *gestalt*, and here we come to the striking difference between Cochiti and Santo Domingo pottery. Santo Domingo Pueblo is famous for its perceived conservative nature. Enforced by secular and religious authorities, this conservatism is exemplified both by the cloistered nature of their village and the abstract nature of their pottery designs. Rarely are plants or animals—and never humans—depicted on Santo Domingo pottery (fig. 17). Cochiti, on the other hand, goes all out—plants, animals, humans, clouds, rain, and

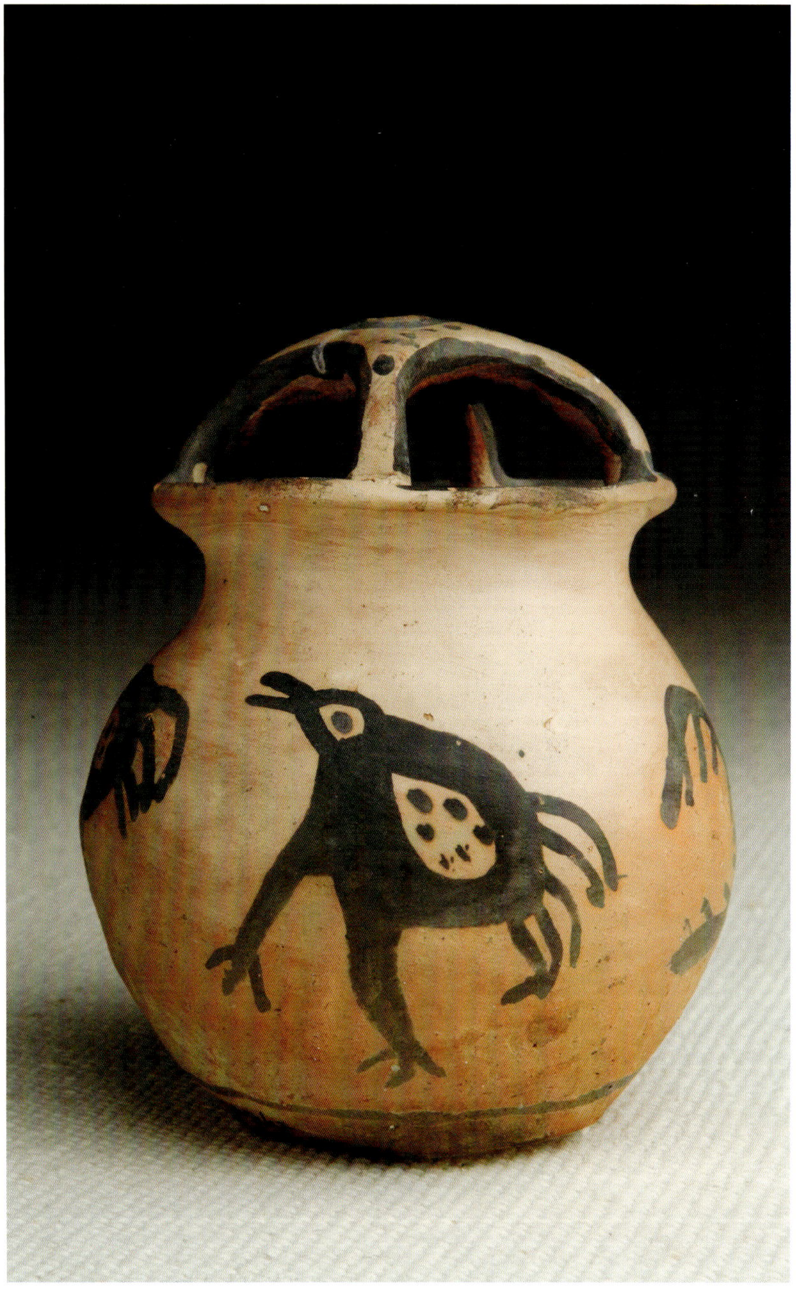

figure 18
Jar
Cochiti
Artist Unknown
ca. 1910
12.5 x 10.0 cm

just about everything else found in heaven or on earth has appeared on Cochiti pottery (fig. 18). Surely this openness of subject and line speaks of a village of modern, freewheeling folks. Taking a closer look, we can see that each statement contains elements of truth, but, in the larger picture, things are much more complicated (compare figs. 19–20).

Santo Domingo is a conservative pueblo but, then again, so is Cochiti. Cochiti Pueblo is a hospitable village brimming with artistic expressions, and so is Santo Domingo. Santo Domingo welcomes thousands of people to take part, via observation, in very important religious celebrations such as the harvest dances of August 4 performed every year. Every Labor Day weekend, Santo Domingo opens its village to visitors and other Native artists to participate in its arts and crafts fair. Santo Domingo artists and craftsmen are extremely active in the art tourism market of Albuquerque and Santa Fe. Hardly isolated or reclusive, they are major players in the tourist economy of New Mexico. Cochiti has produced some of the most renowned contemporary Indian artists: Virgil Ortiz, his sisters Janice and Inez, the Romero brothers Diego and Mateo, and Cippy Crazyhorse. At Santo Domingo, Robert Tenorio, William Andrew Pacheco, Ambrose Atencio, Ione Coriz, and Warren Coriz create work that shifts preconceived notions of what Santo Domingo pottery is. These artists and others are recognized for creating art outside set notions of "Indian art." Yet each in their own way works within community values and traditions. Each ascribes sacredness to a medium, such as clay, or to symbols that the artist will treat differently and hold in a unique regard (fig. 21).

Puebloan adaptation to Spanish oppression by keeping religious matters private and internal manifests in different ways in each village and each individual artist. Openness and seclusion are matters of perception or degree, just as designs are. It is perfectly all right if an outsider cannot comprehend Pueblo religion or Pueblo design—sometimes that is the point. Sometimes the lack of specificity in an explanation is not meant to obfuscate or to frustrate, but is the result of the combining and layering of symbols and meaning, each with multiple interpretations, depending on time, place, and person. Ultimately, designs and the pots they are painted on can be accepted and appreciated for what they truly are, expressions of art originating from an ancient American culture.

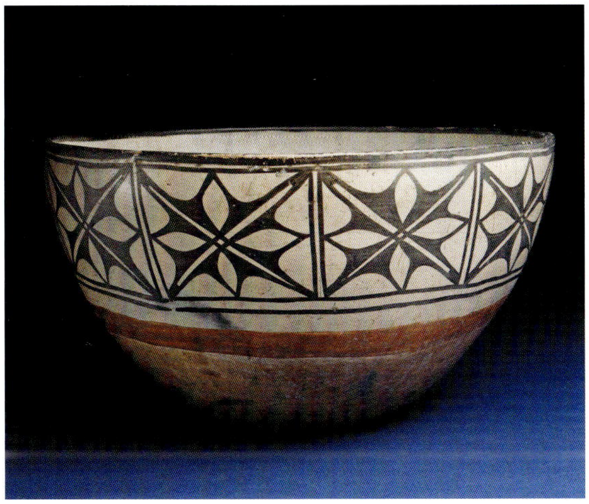

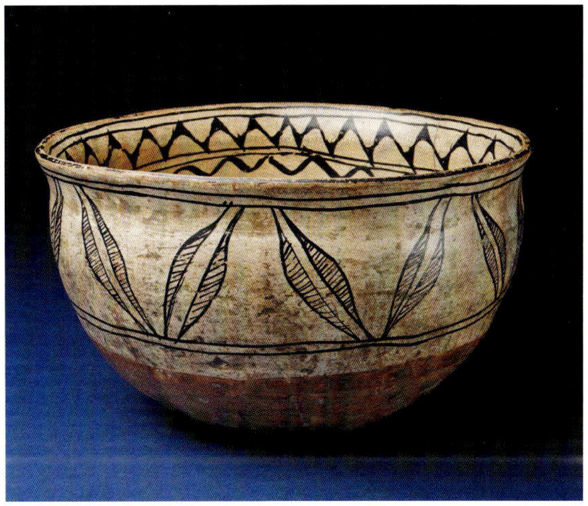

figure 19
Dough Bowl
Santo Domingo
Artist Unknown
ca. 1915
26.5 x 49.0 cm

figure 20
Dough Bowl
Cochiti
Artist Unknown
ca. 1860
19.2 x 35.7 cm

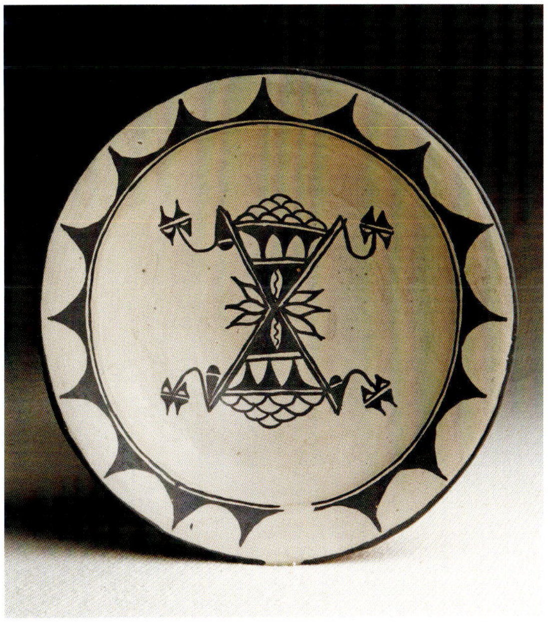

figure 21
Bowl
Cochiti
Magdalena Melchor
prior to 1948
6.3 x 23.6 cm

To the Fire

In pre-European times, pottery firing included large family or community groups. Pots of every type were fired in pits by the dozens. For many Keresan potters, firing pottery remains a family activity. As with gathering clay, many hands are needed to make a firing happen—wood has to be gathered, tins and other materials for supporting, covering and housing pots have to be found, and enough painted pots have to be ready to go. As with all aspects of the pottery-making tradition, there is a personal and a sacred element to firing. During the firing is when a pot is fully transformed. Taking on color and strength, it reaches a new level of being. A firing is a serious but lighthearted affair—while working with the fire to bring the gifts of earth to life, talk about the work is exchanged, last-minute painting is completed, and food shared.

A small fire is lit to heat the earth, and then the ash and coals are brushed aside to make space for setting up the tins that cradle the pots. Metal milk crates, balanced upon tin cans, are ideal. My grandma used a child's wagon as the cradle for her firing. The pots are placed within and covered with flat tins or heavy screens. Some potters will use slabs of rock or large pottery sherds as well, a method used often in older times. Slats and small broken branches or wood are placed above and below the pottery. Many potters prefer pine or cottonwood; however, at one firing in Santo Domingo potters used a supply of warped 2×2 boards. Cottonwood bark is excellent for use as the top cover around the tin and wood.

The popping and crackling of the wood, a joyful part of the song of the transformation, is occasionally punctuated by a "pop," usually meaning one thing: a pot has returned to Mother Earth. The loss of a pot in the firing is part of the cyclical process and part of the lessons learned as one becomes a proficient artist. Potters will not compliment or openly admire a pre-fired piece of pottery so as not to make it too irresistible to Clay Mother. This cautionary practice also means that potters will not sell a piece before it is fired. When I was a very young

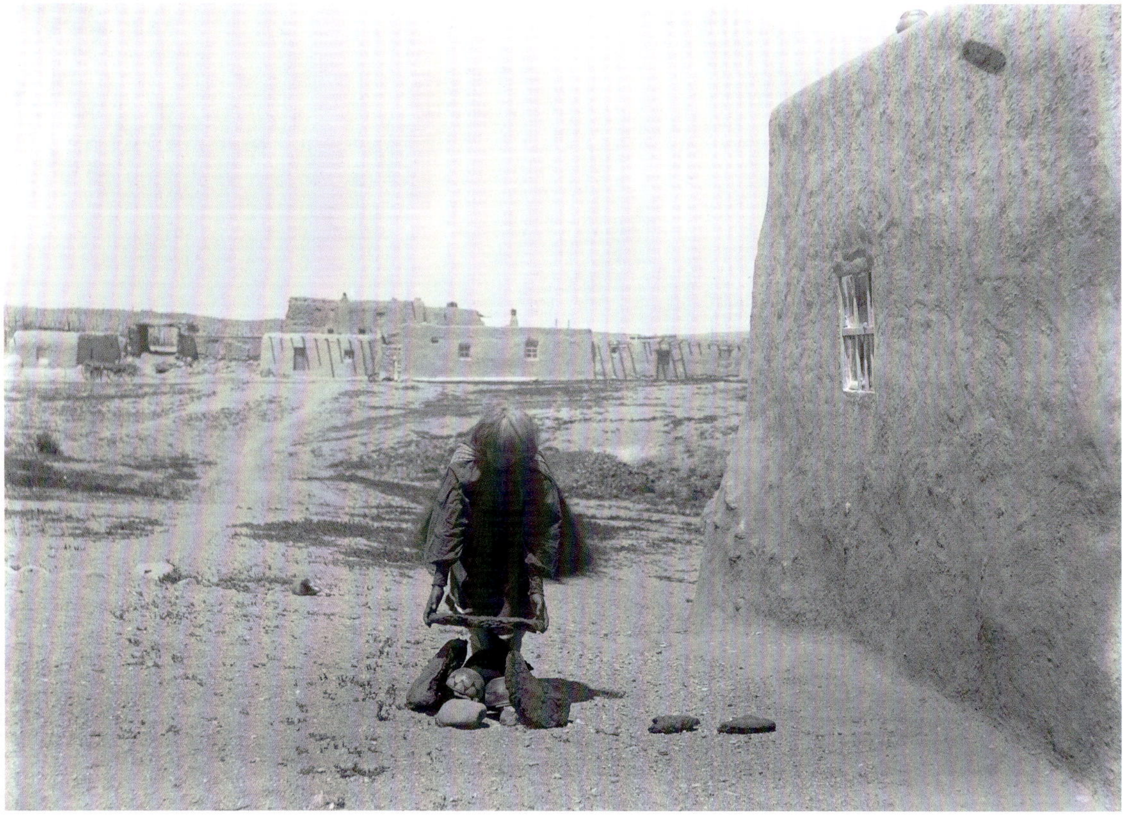

In this image, probably staged for the photographer, a lone Cochiti potter prepares to fire a pot outdoors with cow dung fuel, 1894–1910. Courtesy National Museum of the American Indian, Smithsonian Institution. N15622.

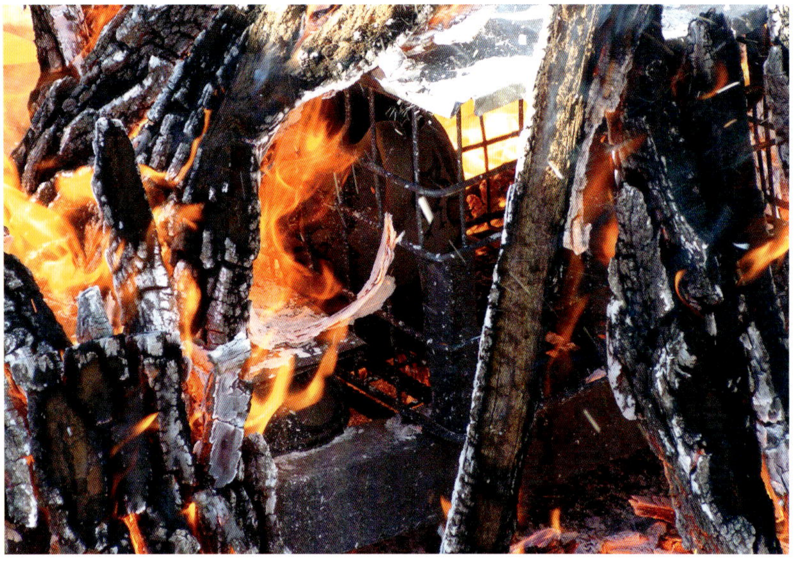

In the fire, Santo Domingo, 2007. Antonio Chavarria, photographer.

potter, one of my dinosaur figurines lost a leg during the firing. Only ten years old, I was upset and whined openly. My grandma admonished and at the same time comforted me by saying the dinosaur was liked by Clay Mother so much that she decided to take it, and it was not proper to be upset as our Mother already gives us so much. That I was a novice potter also had something to do with it, but that too was part of the lesson.

When a pot breaks during a firing, it can damage pottery next to it; because of this possibility some contemporary potters fire their pieces individually. The Santo Domingo and Cochiti potters my colleagues and I have spoken with continue to fire pots in groups in whatever number is on hand. This can be from a relative few to more than a dozen. When asked, they perceive the risk of breaking as part of the practice and believe that in the right heart and state of mind, it is nothing to be overly concerned about. Outsiders lucky enough to observe a firing are amazed at the short firing time: from beginning to end, less than an hour passes. Potters casually remove the pieces from the faint embers with sticks and tongs and, brushing away the ashes, carefully examine them while still warm from the flames. After cooling, some potters coat their pots with a mixture of boiling water and egg whites, swirling it on the interior of a bowl or applying it

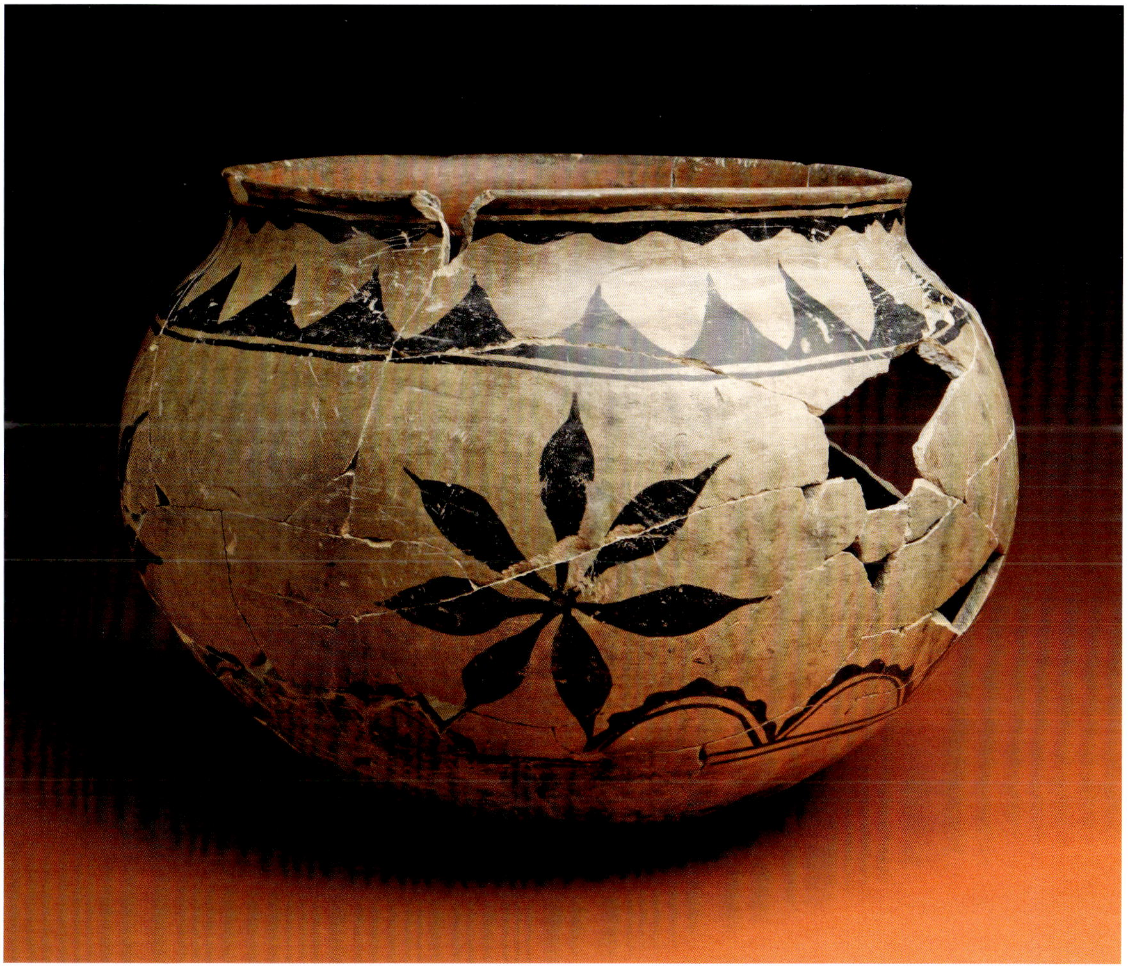

figure 22
Jar
Cochiti
Artist Unknown
ca. 1850–1900
40.2 x 6.0 cm

figure 23
Bowl
Santo Domingo and Santa Clara
Attributed to Monica Silva
ca. 1960
8.7 x 26.3 cm

like a varnish to the exterior. Additional luster is the product of oil or lard in very small amounts. Now the pottery is ready for its new life. Many pieces are sold to admirers; some are used in the household or within the community. When a visitor buys a Pueblo pot, it is imbued with an individual's talent, a family's labor, and a community's tradition (figs. 22–23).

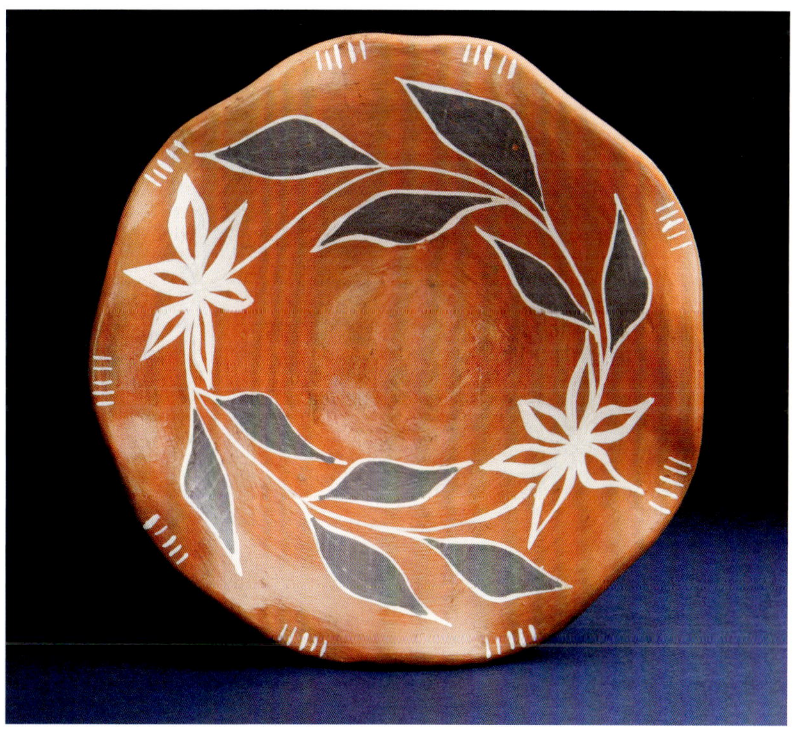

A Century in the Museum

Pots are the same as people—both come from the earth, become part of families, then age and return to the earth. Some are repaired to last just a little longer, others live and work in a household until they are physically unable. This was the life cycle before museums and anthropologists. With the interest in the ancient Southwest by the new discipline

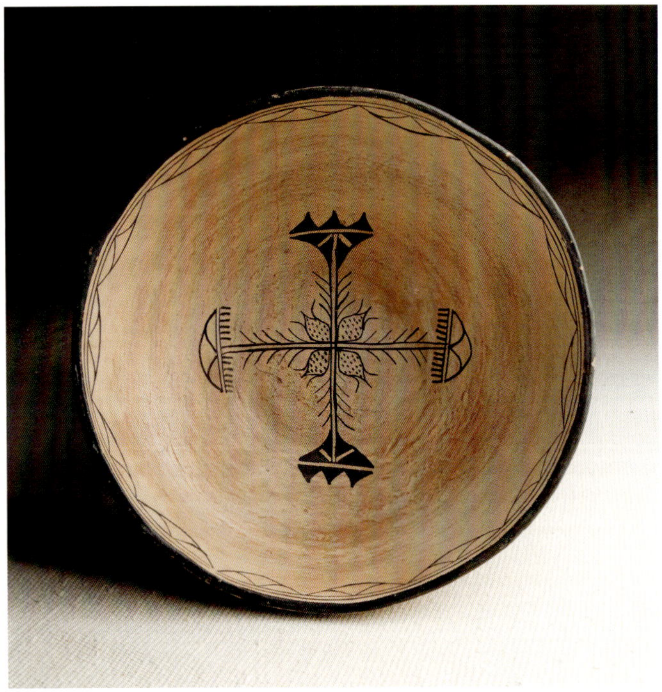

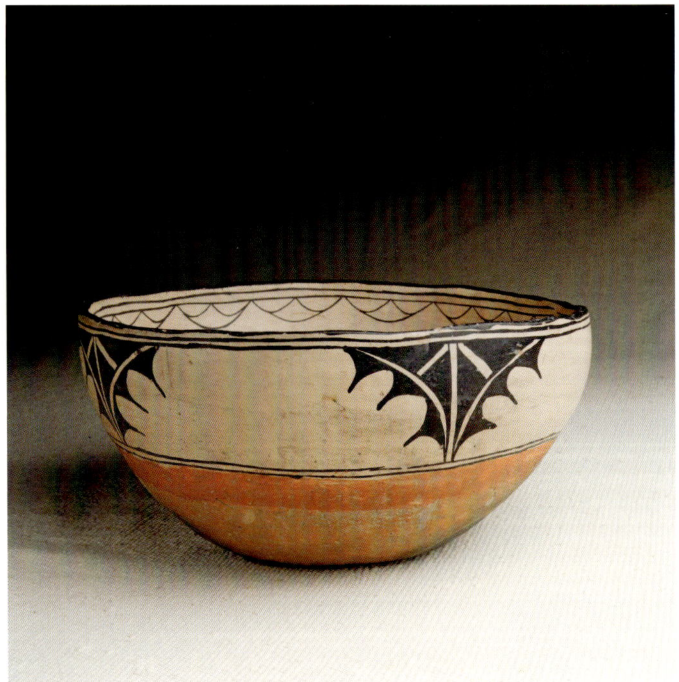

figure 24
Bowl (two views)
Cochiti
Attributed to
Frances Suina
ca. 1920
12.2 x 26.0 cm

of archaeology/anthropology, the lives of pots changed. Older museum collections, like those of the Museum of Indian Arts & Culture/Laboratory of Anthropology, contain pottery once part of families and communities now transformed into scholarly specimens (fig. 24).

Museums and Native people have a long and contentious history. Museums collect artifacts from indigenous communities as a form of cultural preservation, but from *their* perspective without thinking about the consequences to the communities. Yes, the communities participated, but during a time when financial pressures from the newly introduced cash economy, along with population decline in the villages due to several epidemics, led to the marketing of objects of community significance, once used in personal homes or in society houses. They now sit on shelves in isolated storage areas or in exhibit cases, examples of America's cultural patrimony.

From a museum's perspective, collecting older and contemporary works enables scholars to extrapolate the "true nature" of Native peoples. Most important is constructing a portrait of Pueblo people before European influence, locked in time and culturally pure—a people who never really existed. The Southwest has always been a place of trade, travel, exchange, and influence. Adapting to whatever comes their way is a preeminent Pueblo trait, if I can be so bold as to assign one trait to an entire people. Adapting to a changing environment, other tribal groups, other cultures, other economic and religious systems, while seeking balance within their cosmology, is what Pueblo people do. Today there are the additional challenges—loss of language and land—that are recognized and addressed by each pueblo individually. Most importantly, Pueblo people are not frozen in the past, nor have they abandoned their culture for the shopping mall and the Internet. We all navigate these treacherous waters using tradition to guide our way and to help us move forward. We strive for political clout, self-determination, preservation of traditional beliefs and practices, and economic development that creates jobs in or near the villages so community members can participate in the yearly cycle of religious and social activities.

Today, the MIAC/LAB seeks to present a broad picture of Pueblo art outside of a framework built out of past biases that defined "real" Indian art. As the twenty-first century presents new challenges to survival of the pueblos, the museum seeks to be a partner rather than a predator. Recent documentation projects in the museum's collections have brought together artists, academics, and museum staff to reexamine the pottery collection and develop more concise and accurate information. This new documentation can then be shared with the communities of origin. By returning information to the Native communities whose material culture makes up the collections, museums can serve as a place of preservation for the pueblos, preservation based on their needs. Today, when tribes are actively engaged in programs for health, art, and language retention, the museum can be a helpful tool by opening up its doors and sharing its resources. By doing this, it can build a stronger foundation for both museum and community. During her recent visit to the MIAC/LAB collections, I asked Cochiti potter Martha Arquero her thoughts on seeing so many of her mother's pieces in museum storage. She said knowing that these works of her mother were there made her "feel proud knowing the gifts my mother made are here, and a few things I made are here with her." When potters visit the museum's storage areas initial reactions are quiet awe, respect, and admiration of the lasting power of the pottery. There is also a humble pride in the outside recognition of the work of their community or family. Santo Domingo potter Ambrose Atencio quietly walks the aisles, occasionally touching a certain curve or tracing a particular design. Soft comments of, "I like that one…that shape is hard to do…that's my mother's" intersperse the stillness while museum staff stand aside impatiently holding our pads, pencils, and questions. Pueblo pottery speaks, especially to Pueblo potters. Today's potters listen intently to their teachers, from elder to youth, from ancestor to descendant. They know personally the knowledge, skill, patience, and hard work the pottery in the collections represents. Potters bring a deep and academic appreciation to the museum's holdings. These last words are those spoken by Elizabeth Trujillo during her visit to the collections in 2007: "It touches my heart to see all these older pots. I think of the old people gone away who put their hands and their hearts on the clay because I *know* how hard it is to do….I ask their guidance to keep on the tradition with my work."

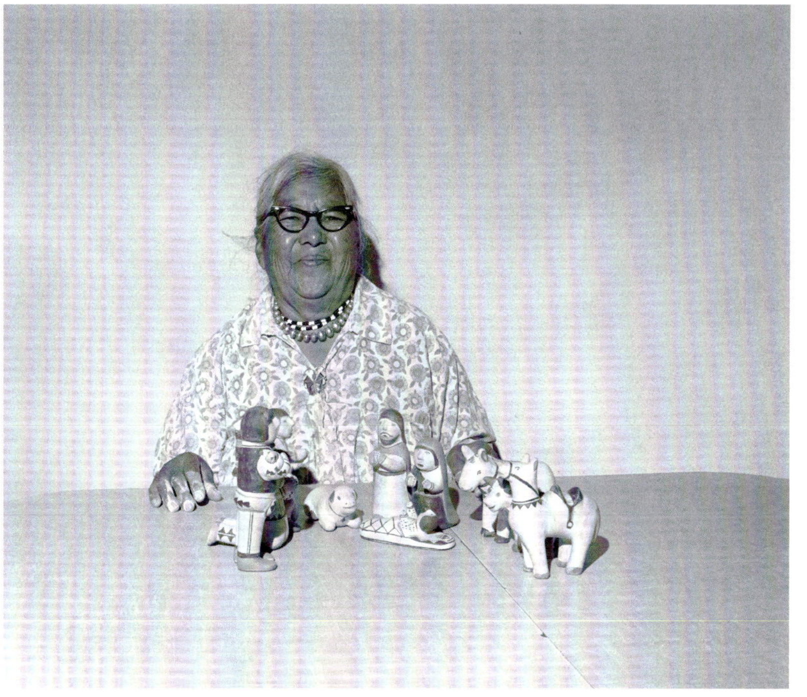

Cochiti Potter Francis Suina, 1974. David Donocho, photographer. Courtesy Palace of the Governors (MNM/DCA), 157155

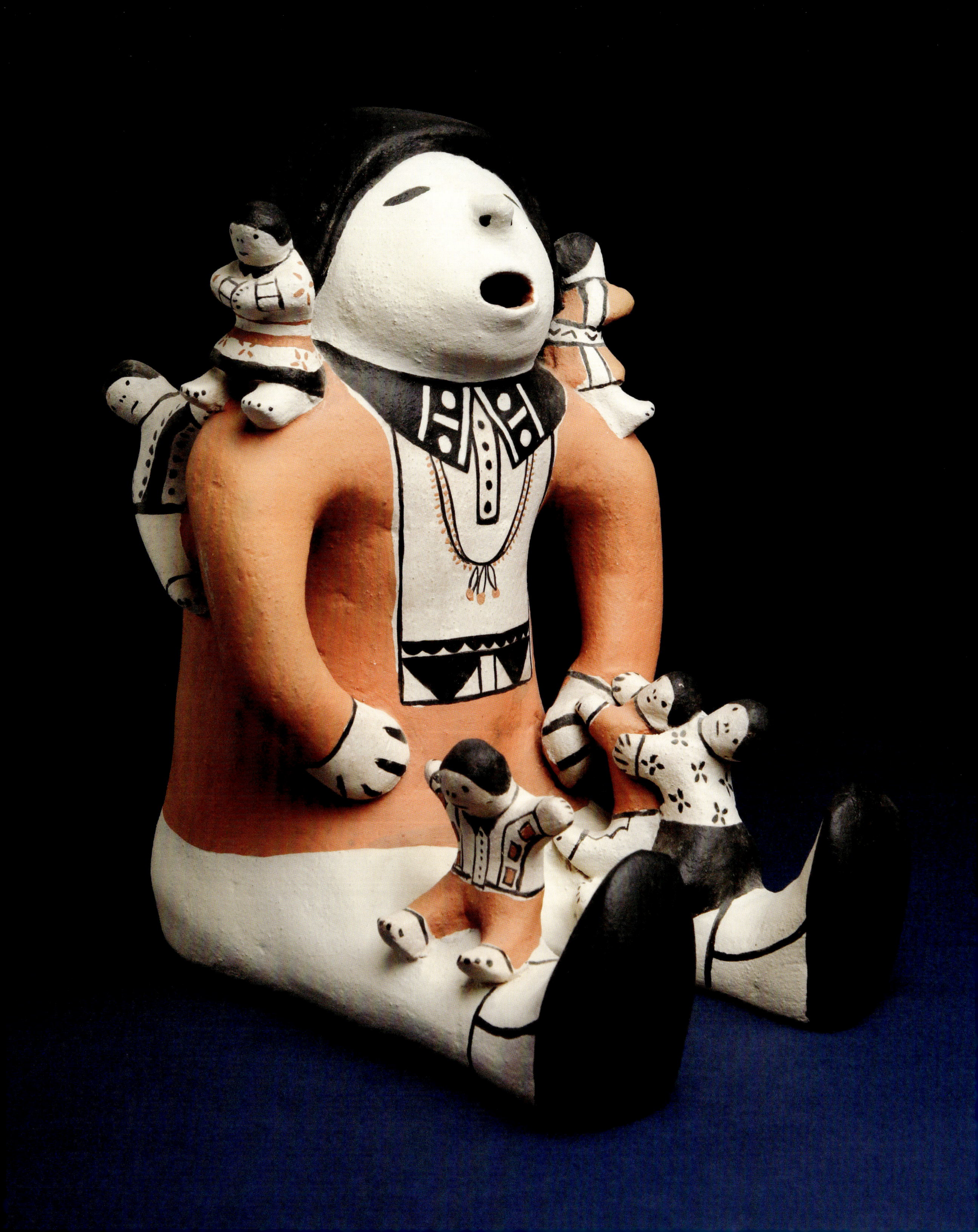

Artist Unknown

The Significance of Signatures on Pueblo Pottery

Chip Colwell-Chanthaphonh

Name : Vessel

The ideal view of a Pueblo pot is from its side and slightly above, the perspective at which the unity of the vessel comes through—a symphony of form, shadow, color, and texture. In turn, many bowls and not a few jars are best seen from a bird's-eye view, an aerial perspective that allows the viewer to take in the whole of the design field and the vessel's balance and symmetry. If one of these beautiful vessels were to be placed in your hands, the last place you would probably look, if you looked at all, would be the vessel's bottom. It is not a mystery why the bottom is rarely seen: it is the remnant of a vessel's beginning that is easily forgotten by the vessel's end. For a ceramic vessel to stand upright, for it to be viewed in its stationary mode, it must have a bottom to rest on the ground. Thus a necessary facet of pots and figurines must remain unseen. As a result, a vessel's bottom is often plain and unfinished, without polish or paint, scratched and fragmented, or worn thin from use. The underside of ceramics often belies the vessel's beauty in every other dimension, save the maker's signature.

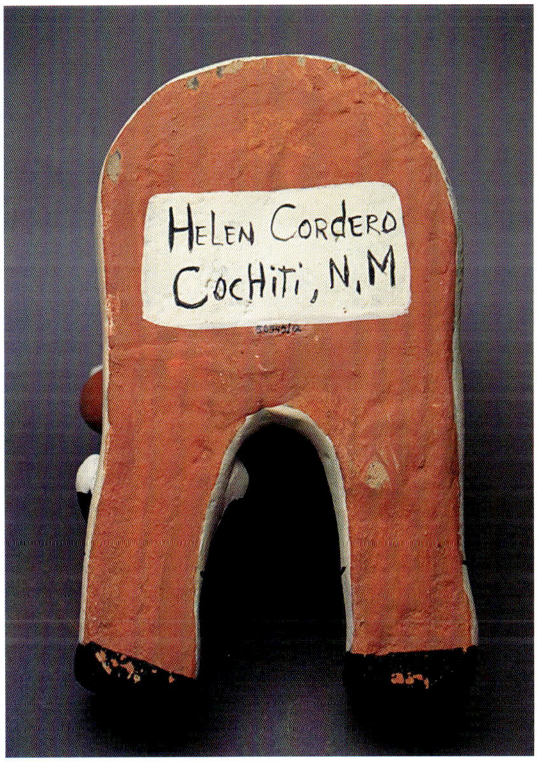

figure 25
Storyteller Figurine (two views)
Cochiti
Helen Cordero
ca. 1980
27.5 x 18.3 x 25.5 cm

The equivalent of an exhibit of Pueblo pottery that doesn't show the undersides would be an exhibit of Pablo Picasso paintings with a black square pasted on every canvas corner. You would only see his name on a placard adjacent to each image rather than his distinctive mark, a brand now in itself, sold on posters and stamped on perfume bottles. To see Picasso's signature you would have to furtively and gingerly pry the black squares from the corners and find for yourself Picasso's signed name.

In part, by signing his work, Picasso was merely following a long tradition in European fine art in which the artist left a signature when done. As far back as the Attic vase tradition of ancient Athens, nearly three thousand years ago, ceramics were signed, both by those who made the pots and those who painted them (Cohen 1991). However, centuries would pass before signing works became the norm. It was not until the 1400s that Europeans began regularly signing their paintings, although religious works were signed as a means of prayer more than a mark of authorship (Rubin 2006:567; see also Wilmerding 2003:1–38). Artwork was signed for different reasons at different times in the subsequent generations, but included signing as a stamp of authenticity, as advertising, and by the late 1800s, for artists such as Edgar Degas, as an aesthetic device. Into the twentieth century, signatures most clearly meant, "It is mine, it is genuine, it is finished" (Haus 2004). One modern artist, Thomas Moran, in 1919 even went so far as to impress a fingerprint into the wet paint, as John Wilmerding has written, "to authenticate his canvas in the most modern of ways" (Wilmerding 2003:75).

Still, it is worth mentioning that many celebrated works of art were left unsigned. Leonardo Da Vinci's *Mona Lisa* bears no signature. Michelangelo signed only a single work of art, the marble statue *Pietà* in Saint Peter's Basilica (Wang 2004). Some contemporary artists have refused to sign their pieces in the belief that "a great artist was like a religious disciple, not someone to deal with the issue of his own ego or talk about himself" (Haus 2004). For others, the artist's signature became a kind of mad game. The Spanish surrealist Salvador Dalí is known to have signed his name 678 different ways (Zavrel 2006).

Of course, Picasso did not have to sign his paintings: his aesthetic style was so visually distinctive that a signature was in essence superfluous. But Picasso understood there were other values to a signature than merely the ability to ascribe a painting to its creator. A story, perhaps apocryphal, goes that Picasso once paid for dinner by creating an impromptu drawing on the bill (Haus 2004). The restaurateur, more than pleased, asked him to sign it. "I'm buying the meal," Picasso replied, "not the restaurant."

Picasso undoubtedly also signed his art because he understood his signed name held more than an economic value: to sign his artwork was to claim possession, authority, and right. "The placing of a signature on a painting is a conscious act by the painter that establishes his or her presence," art historian Louisa C. Matthew has observed. "That presence communicates outward to the viewer, but it also communicates information about the painter's relationship inward, to the painting itself: its form, subject, and even the process of its creation" (Matthew 1998:616). Picasso's signature did not merely state that he made the piece but that, with his name interwoven into the fabric of the design, he claimed the piece as his own. It was this realization that the signature could make the art (and not the other way around) that underpinned Marcel Duchamp's ironic "ready-made" sculpture *Fountain*, a urinal placed in a gallery and signed "R. Mutt." It was the signature that in large part transformed the utilitarian object into a piece of fine art (Basalla 1982:194).

This brief walk through art history illustrates that the artist's signature is neither innocuous nor made for obvious reasons. Rather, historically, marking artwork creates economic value and has complex social repercussions. With this premise, the essay here will explore the underside of ceramics, aiming to encourage readers to consider a side of pottery rarely seen and even less discussed.

Individual : Community

The Hopi-Tewa potter Nampeyo was already an accomplished artisan, making ceramics in the "old Hopi" pattern, when she first saw the fifteenth- and sixteenth-century designs on the pottery being excavated from the site of Sikyatki in the late 1800s (Brody 1971:67; Frisbie 1973; McChesney 1994:6; Nequatewa 1943). She emulated the bold polychrome designs and soon helped launch the "Sikyatki revival," which was an instant success in Arizona's flowering tourist market. Although other Hopi potters incorporated Sikyatki designs, Nampeyo's work stood out like a jazz song, a beautiful improvisation on an ancient style. In 1905, Nampeyo demonstrated her techniques at the Grand Canyon's Hopi House, and soon her popular pottery made there bore stickers declaring "Made by Nampeyo, Hopi" (McChesney 1994:7). As Lea S. McChesney has detailed, over the next decade Nampeyo herself "became a tourist commodity" as "Nampeyo's name was known through the United States and Europe, and every visitor to the Southwest brought home a souvenir of her work" (McChesney 1994:7). With Nampeyo's celebrity and success, by the 1920s it was clear to traders that pottery identified with specific potters made plain economic sense.

Similarly, though more self-consciously, in 1908 Edgar Lee Hewett and Kenneth Chapman began excavating archaeological sites on the Pajarito Plateau and encouraged a San Ildefonso potter named Maria Martinez to revive the ceramic traditions they were unearthing (Bernstein 1994a:74). By 1915, Maria's skill had surpassed many potters along the Rio Grande. "She could make three pots while other women made one," it was said, "each pot perfect in execution" (Peterson 1977:98). As her work gained popularity, collectors and curators began encouraging her to sign completed vessels. Fascinatingly, several of her earliest signed pieces bore her Tewa name "Poh've'ka" not signed on the bottom of the ceramics but rather more visibly along the side, as if the vessel itself were a painter's canvas (Fox 1976:262–263). Although she signed these pieces in the 1910s, it was not until the mid-1920s that she was regularly signing her name—now on the bottom of the vessel—at first "Marie" because she was told this name would appeal more to her Anglo buyers (Fox 1976:259; Peterson 1977:98). Later, after 1934, her pottery bore the signature "Marie & Julian" to recognize the efforts of her husband, who painted the vessels. Then after Julian's death in 1943, the name of her other collaborators appeared on her pots—"Marie & Santana," "Maria & Popovi," and finally her own name "Maria Povéka" (Peterson 1977:98-99; Spivey 2003:161–166).

Like Nampeyo, for Maria a main motivation was economic considerations. "On a work of art [a signature] confirms originality to a dealer or purchaser, even when an unsigned work has all the stylistic and technical characteristics of that artist's hand," Wilmerding has explained. "A buyer instinctively feels more confident if a signature is present, and its absence can often affect the market value considerably" (Wilmerding 2003:ix). However, the presence of a signature by no means guarantees authenticity. A name can be forged, as has been done with Maria's signature, and for many years Maria herself would sign pots brought to her with a felt tip pen (Spivey 2003:161). The only problem was some of the pots weren't hers; out of kindness, Maria didn't want to disappoint her hopeful visitors.

Although by the early 1930s many Pueblo potters were signing their pots, the practice of uniquely identifying one's work is in fact a longer tradition. As anthropologist Bruce Bernstein has recounted, San Ildefonso potters at the 1927 Southwest Indian Fair in Santa Fe resisted signing their work, expressing that "our own people knew who made the pots" (Bernstein 1993:18). About the time of the Indian Fair, ethnologist Ruth L. Bunzel recorded that Pueblo potters knew which vessels they made, and in turn which their family members made and those by other women in their community. "If I painted my bowls like every one else, I might lose my bowl when I took dinner to the dances in the plaza," one Zuni potter explained to Bunzel. "I am the only person who makes a checkerboard design around the rim, so I can always tell my bowl by looking at the edge. I don't have to use any mark on my bowl because I recognize my design" (Bunzel 1929:65). Looking over photographs of ceramics during an interview with a Laguna woman, Bunzel was told, "My aunt always made designs like that" (Bunzel 1929:65). Signatures, it might be said, can be inscribed without signing a name.

For centuries, pottery was a communal activity in Pueblo societies. Ceramic technology and design were taught by elders to the young—the location of clays and tempers, how to form coils and smoothly scrape them, the right decorations for beauty and prayer, and the means of transforming clay through fire. This knowledge was collective, not owned by any one individual. Women would sit together for hours sharing their lives and their knowledge of the ancient craft. Change would come slowly, perhaps when the community migrated to a new village or established new rituals. The containers would have been used and seen by all—blackened jars with stews on an open hearth, and then finer bowls used to serve the steaming food to family and guests. Special vessels were used in rituals, in both public ceremonies at which all would see the containers and at more private rites held in *kivas*. Although individuals left their own marks of creativity and personal identity on pottery they produced, ceramics in Pueblo society long embodied the traditions and practices of the community as a whole over generations.

A signature on Pueblo pottery is thus more than economic: it signals a deep change in the relationship between individual and community. One dough bowl has the name "KAY" written on it with a bright white enamel paint, presumably scrawled not by the maker but so that on feast days when the vessel was brought to the plaza, it could easily be found by its owner (fig. 26). This bowl suggests the beginning of a change in the community in which pottery is not used or widely made enough so that all the community members easily know the owner based only on the vessel's design. It signals a deeper change of selling pottery to outsiders. The signatures indicate a wholly new context for pottery: the circulation of objects beyond the shared knowledge of the community. A century ago, no name was needed to identify a potter because everyone knew that Aunt Maria used this design on her pots; but when Aunt Maria's pot goes up on the trader's shelf for purchase, the pot's creator is not definitely known by the tourist from Wisconsin. The signature on the bottom of that pot is evidence of this radical recontextualization of Pueblo pottery.

The equation seems clear: name is to vessel as individual is to community. So as names were increasingly placed on Pueblo vessels, increased focus was placed on the artistic achievement and promise of the individual. It is not coincidental that as names became habitually inscribed on pottery, prizes came to be an important part of Indian arts fairs (Bernstein 1994a:70). No longer were objects honored for their contributions to the community or the degree they venerated the ancestors, but rather for their achievement of individual creativity and mastery of the craft. In today's litigious atmosphere, a few artists have taken this to the next logical step: copyrighting their pottery (Brown 2003; Nicholas and Bannister 2004). On the one hand, it is an understandable desire to control where and how an object is to be represented and used. On the other hand, it might seem that Pueblo pottery is the collective effort of countless Pueblo people over thousands of years.

Nampeyo, although a dazzling success in many people's eyes, also suffered reproaches of her own community. "Whether conscious or not, in allowing this name to be commoditized and promoted she

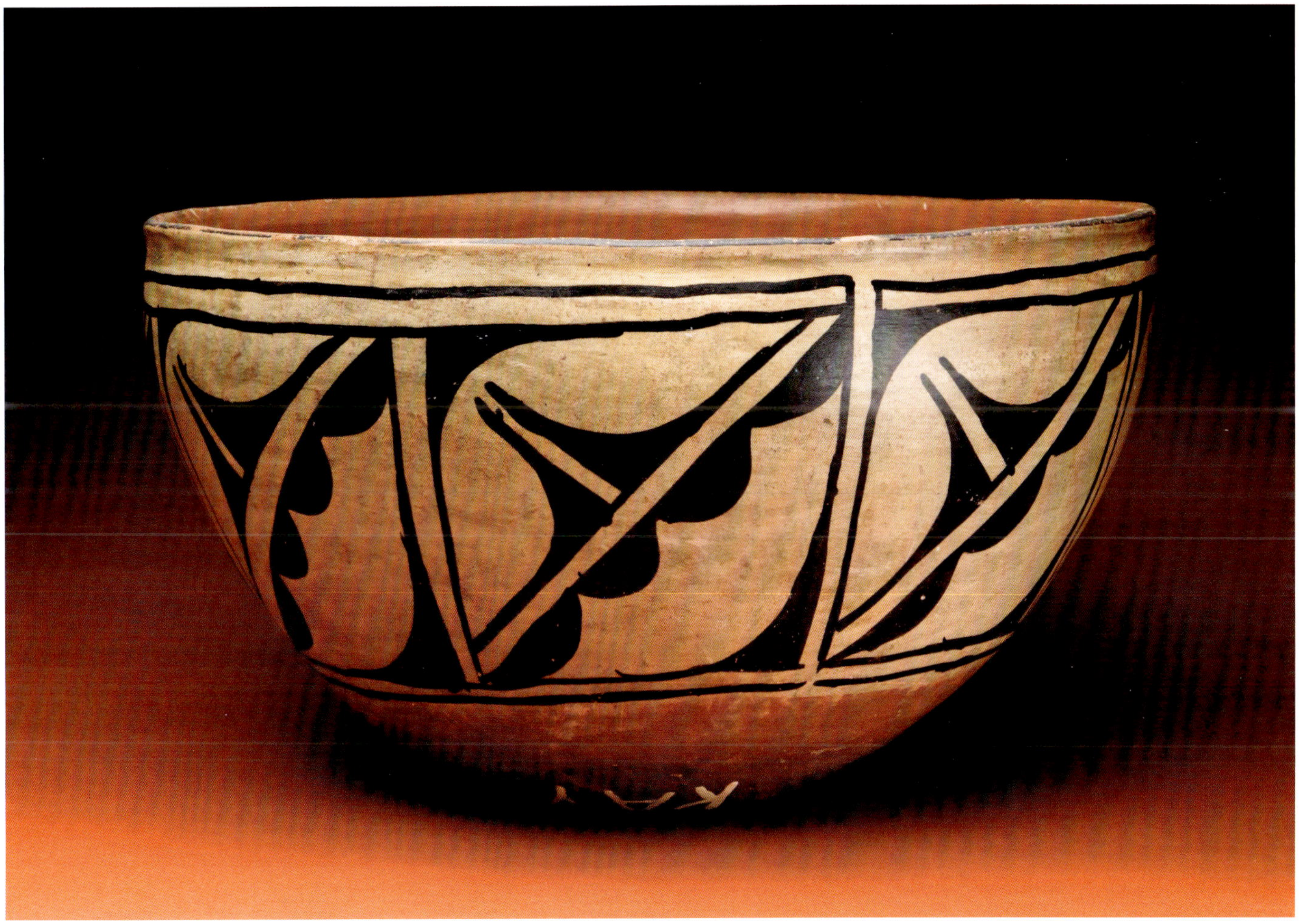

precluded recognition of the larger work of pottery production that was recognized at First Mesa, especially among the Hopi women of her father's matrilineage," McChesney has written of Nampeyo, following interviews on the Hopi Mesas. "Individuals have commented to me that pottery making did not belong to Nampeyo" (McChesney 1994:13). Many Hopis were not pleased that Nampeyo claimed for herself—implicit in her signed pieces—what they believed to belong to no one person.

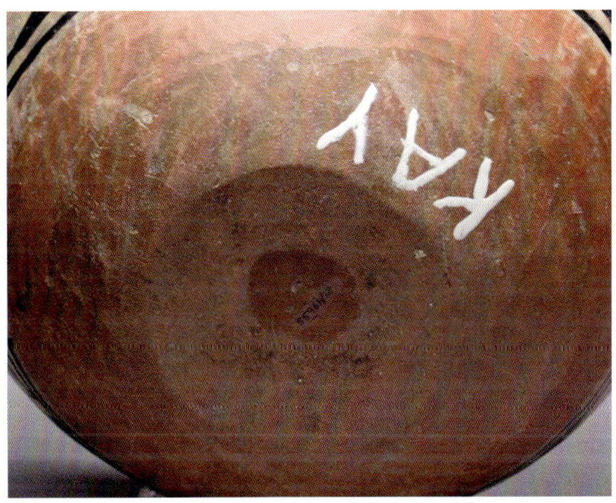

figure 26
Dough Bowl
(two views)
Santo Domingo
Artist Unknown
ca. 1930
25.8 x 46.4 cm

Fine Art : Folk Art

At the same time names began appearing on Pueblo pottery, collectors and curators were working hard to ensure that these objects were seen by mainstream Americans as objects of fine art rather than folk art. As anthropologist Karl A. Hoerig has written, the early Indian fairs in the 1920s and 1930s had the explicit intention to promote "good" Indian art, a response of Anglo organizers "appalled by what they saw as abysmal work being produced for the curio trade" (Hoerig 2003:185). The so-called curio-dealers had a brisk business in New Mexico during the late 1800s, selling just about everything under the sun and, as an 1881 handbill advertised, pottery in a "variety of grotesque designs, Idols, Dogs, Horses, Birds, Bowls, Cups, Pitchers, Saucers, Urns, Baskets, Pipes, Ash-Receivers, Flower-Pots, Tea-Pots, etc." (Batkin 1998:72).

By the 1920s, a handful of promoters sought to create stable markets for Indian arts and to encourage the persistence of traditional crafts. In 1922, the first Southwestern Indian Fair was held in Santa Fe, an event that eventually turned into the city's celebrated annual Indian Market (Bernstein 1994b). At first, the Indian Fair only allowed "traditional" ceramic forms, but in 1930 the organizers allowed "modifications from traditional shapes and designs…if by the changes the articles become more suitable for the white man's uses and are thus more saleable" (Bernstein 1993:47).

Part of the goal of the Southwestern Indian Fair, then, was to improve the quality of objects sold to tourists and collectors, but also to ensure that buyers understood every object was uniquely made, a true piece of art. A signature on the bottom of each vessel could thus play an important role: to prove that the object was not mass-produced (Hoerig 2003:189). Perhaps just as importantly, the signature indicated to the buyer that the object was not the result of an anonymous artisan but rather the creative expression of a specific Indian artist. This shift helped move Pueblo pottery from the category of "folk art" to that of "fine art," significantly, a move that had a clear economic advantage for both artists and their dealers (Hoerig 2003:177).

And so the equation can be expanded further: name is to vessel as fine art is to folk art. A name on an object marks the creative product of an individual, which for European and American elites has long been requisite for the production of "fine art." In turn, an unsigned object indicates that a master did not make it but rather an anonymous artisan working from timeless ancestral traditions. With the rise to prominence of "primitive art" in the 1920s, these anonymous objects were not without merit, elite collectors told themselves (Blocker 1994; Errington 1998; Price 1989). However, the objects were not equal in worth to those created by the artistic genius laboring in self-inspired isolation: folk art is collective, fine art is individualist.

Native peoples themselves have rejected such a dichotomy, emphasizing that individual masters can fully express themselves within folk traditions. One example was the exhibit of Pomo basketry titled "Remember Your Relations" (Brovarney et al. 1996). In this exhibit, it was made clear that each weaver of Pomo baskets has her own agency and biography. For Elsie Allen, who built the collection, to not collect information about who made what basket indicated a lack of care about the individual. Ignoring a weaver's name is akin to ignoring the weaver's humanity.

Pueblo life, past and present, tends towards emphasizing community over individual and thus would likely not similarly insist on the identification of individuals. For instance, initially the Museum of Indian Arts & Culture planned to call a new exhibition space the "Masterpieces Gallery." However, the museum's Indian Advisory Panel members, mainly from Pueblo communities, were greatly discomforted by this label. They felt that the objects to be shown in the gallery were not individual masterworks so much as community traditions. A masterpiece is an object taken out of context, to show us the brilliance of a thing in itself.

Perhaps signing pottery on the unseen bottom of each vessel is ideal for the Pueblo artist. The vessel stands by itself, an object of art but without any overt sign of the individual, no name scrawled in the vessel's corner. Only underneath, almost always out of sight, is the claim the individual makes for the work. In this way, signed pots and figurines offer a unique balance between individual and community, fine art and folk art.

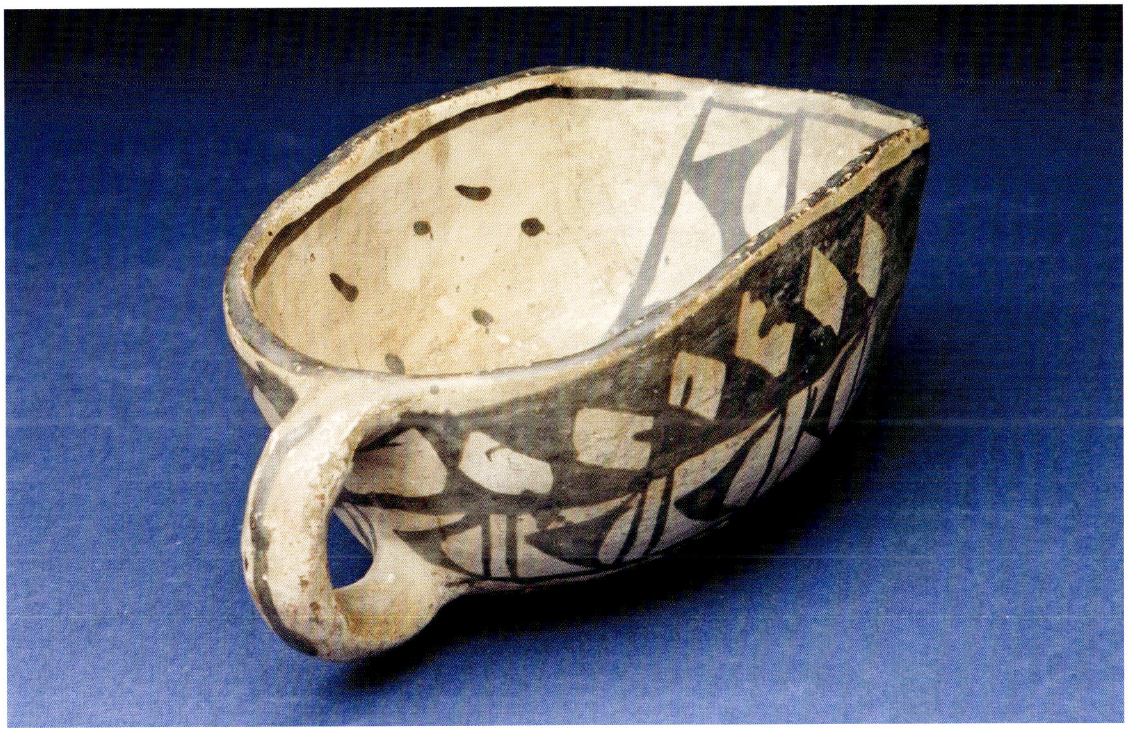

figure 27
Pitcher or Scoop
(two views)
Santo Domingo
Artist Unknown
ca. 1900–1915
7.1 x 10.2 x 19.2 cm

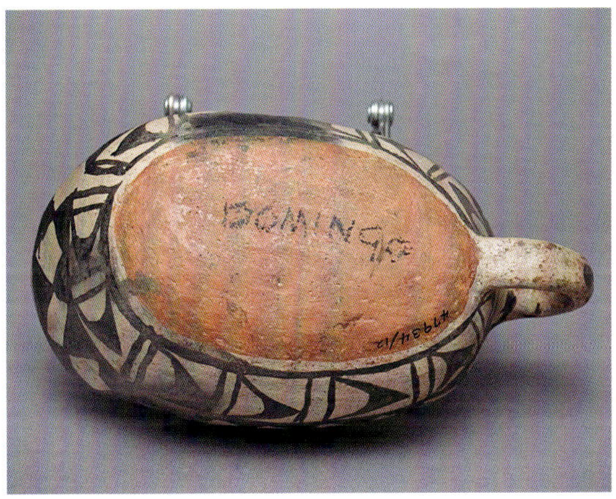

Cochiti and Santo Domingo Pueblos

When querying the catalog records for Santo Domingo and Cochiti vessels, the most common response to the artist's name is "artist unknown." Today, there is something unsettling for curators and museum visitors alike to have hundreds of objects made by anonymous hands. We feel compelled to know who these people were and about their lives as artists. So great is the desire to identify individuals that even when museum curators don't have detailed information about who made what in the collections, they study and group vessels so as to discover the "hand" of an individual artist.

In collections, when we do know the artist it is largely because the artist elected to sign her or his work, or because the dealer or collector wrote down the name on behalf of the artist. Closely examining signatures and other markings on the hidden bottoms of vessels tells us about the transformation of Santo Domingo and Cochiti pottery from folk art to fine art, and provides clues about the changing relationship between the individual artists and their respective communities. Signatures also tell us about the culture of collecting and the nature of the collections as a whole. In the Museum of Indian Arts & Culture collection, only about 75 out of more than 400 Cochiti and Santo Domingo pots and figurines were signed at all.

The earliest signed vessels, in the early 1900s, ascribe authorship not to individuals but to entire communities, demarcating in pencil either "Cochiti" or "Domingo" (fig. 27). The first "signed" vessels—likely marked by dealers—thus implicitly

figure 28
Jar
Santo Domingo
Artist Unknown
ca. 1880
43.4 x 48.0 cm

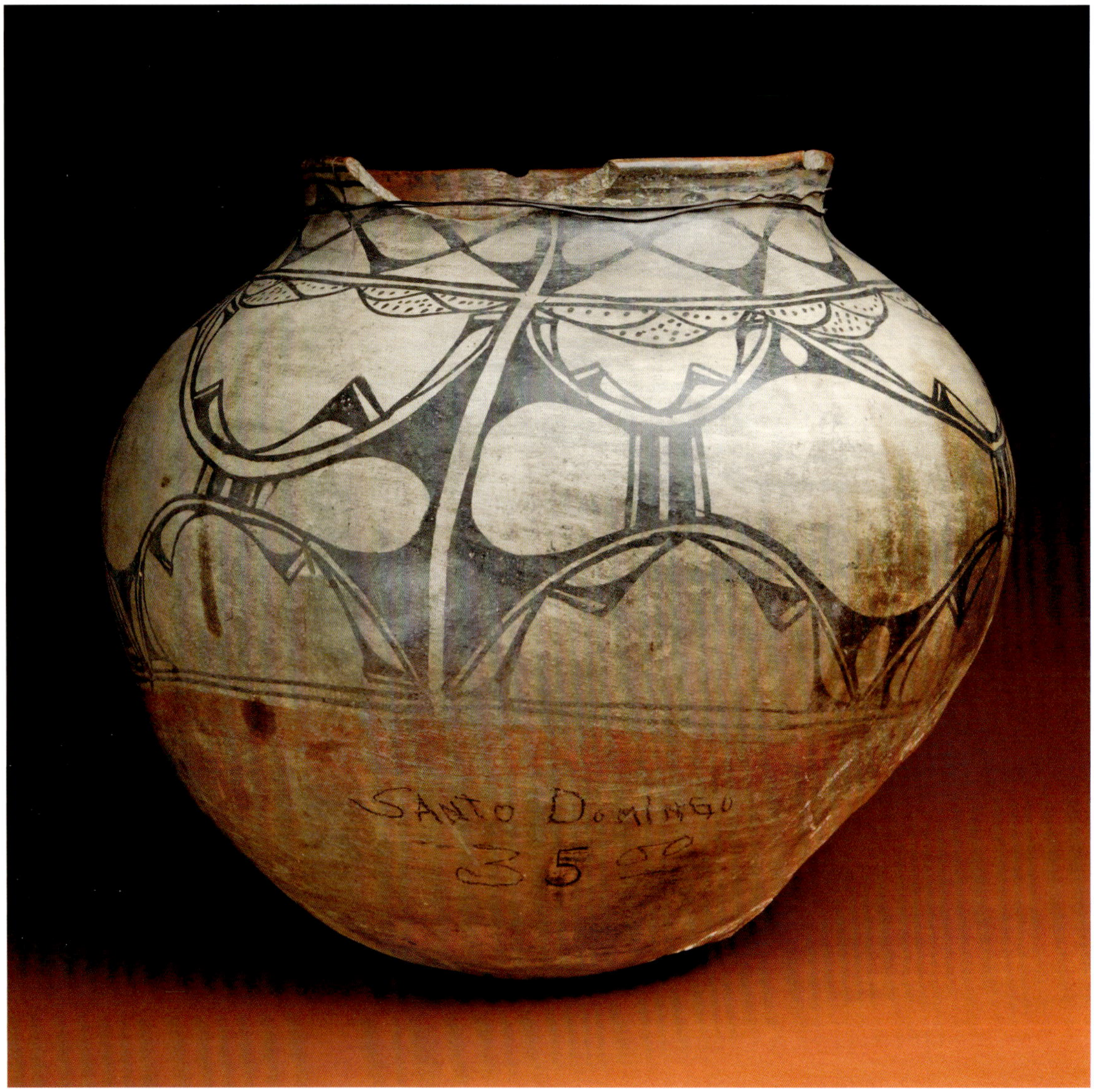

emphasized the relationship between pot and community. However, it is significant that decades later when ceramic artists started signing their names, they consistently continued the tradition of also including the village they are from. Even today, Cochiti and Santo Domingo ceramicists continue to link their work to home (fig. 28).

Noticeably, one of the first vessels with a named individual in the Museum of Indian Arts & Culture collection points to collector and curator rather than the artist. A Santo Domingo jar, made sometime around 1850, bears the label "San Diego Museum / W. Bradfield – 1914" (fig. 29); it is the earliest vessel that unambiguously bears an individual's name. For decades, while vessels did not display the name of their creators, those who owned the pottery were sure to place their mark (fig. 30). These labels are a means for collectors and museum professionals to express ownership and control. They are also visual signs of the recontextualization of pottery, announcing that the objects now belong behind glass in a museum instead of on a table holding food for a Pueblo family.

One signature of ownership and valuation is the curatorial "X" mark left by Kenneth Chapman. A Cochiti bowl made around 1930 has Chapman's

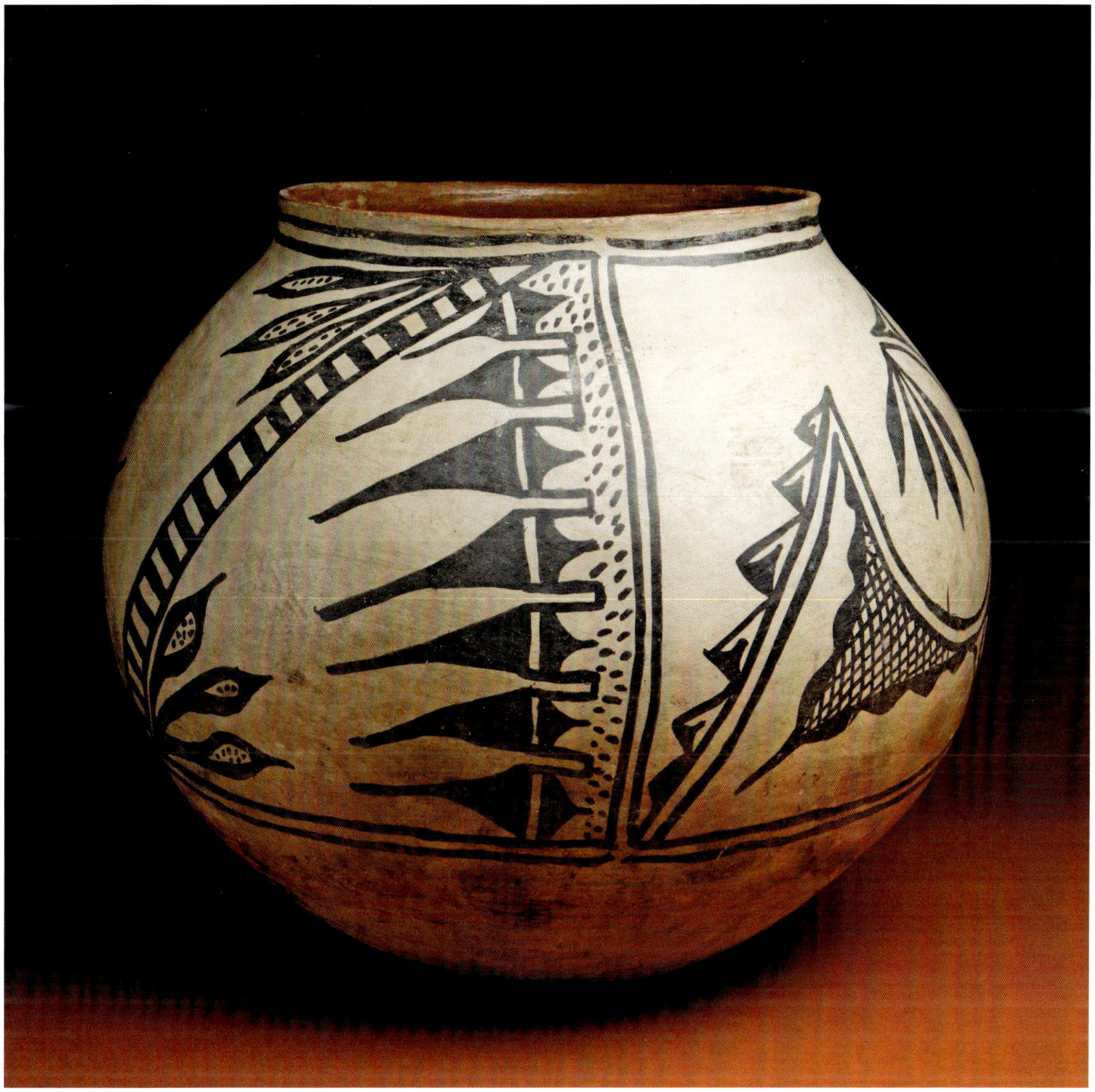

figure 29
Jar (two views)
Keresan Polychrome
Artist Unknown
ca. 1850
40.5 x 46.0 cm

distinct "X" on the bottom (fig. 31). Chapman regularly evaluated vessels entering the collections as museum quality or not; those he felt were not received the "X" indicating suitability for sale or exchange for more appropriate examples.

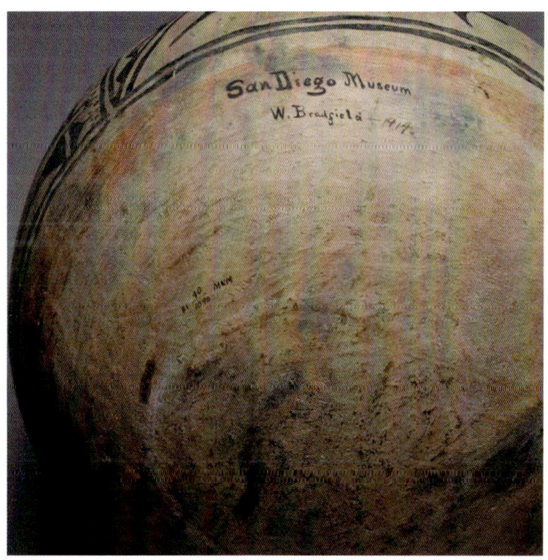

An early definite signature appears on the underside of an elegant bowl dating to 1933. The signature is itself a kind of decorative element, given its beautiful looping curls, etched to express "Maria Calabaza." An earlier vessel, made in 1923, declares in a faint hand, "Santo Domingo Made by Juan Cate," but the signature written in pencil likely was not Cate's, but rather inscribed by the seller or

figure 30
Jar (two views)
Santo Domingo
Artist Unknown
ca. 1915
35.5 x 37.5 cm

This vessel bottom is marked with M.N.M., for Museum of New Mexico.

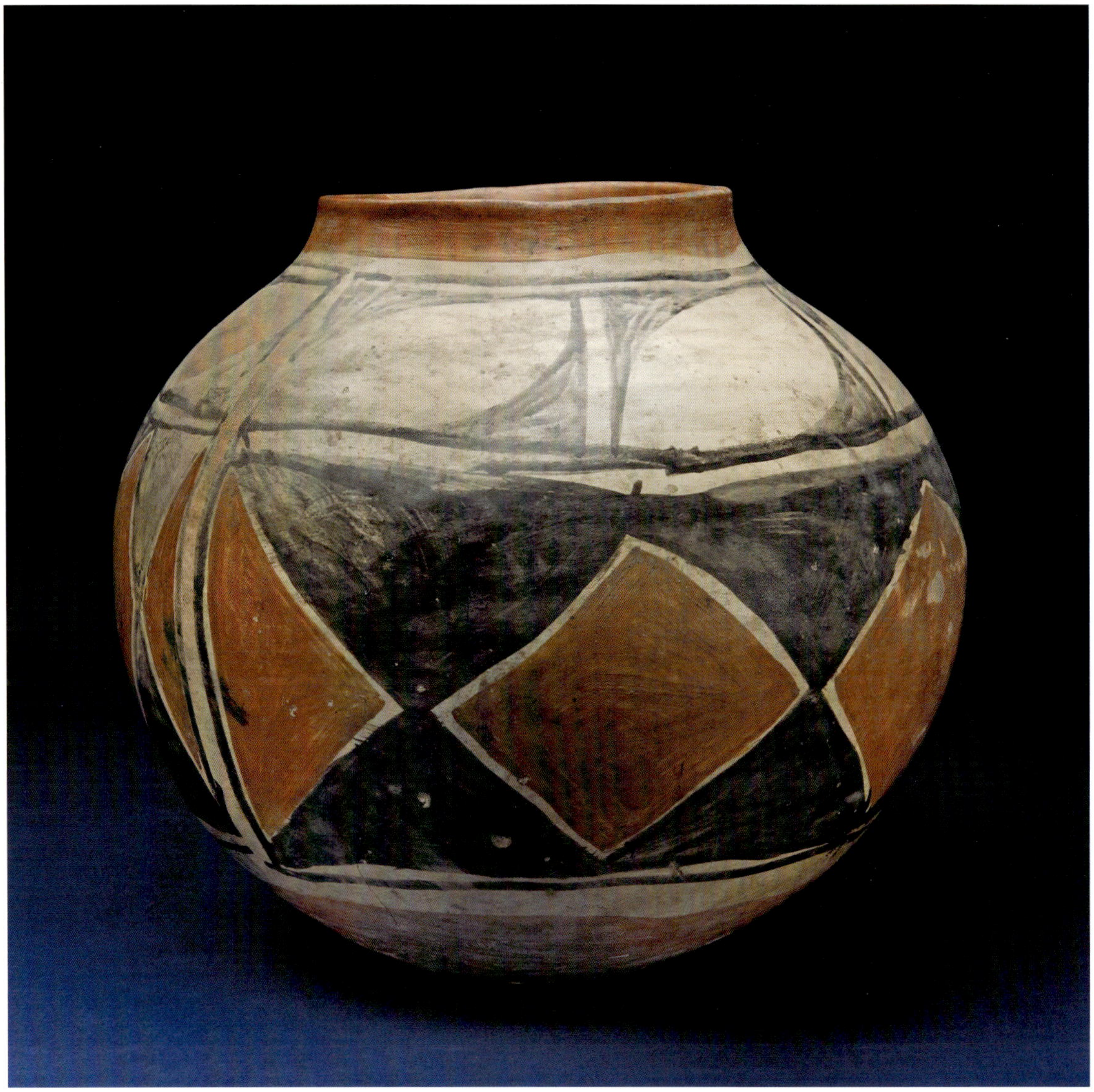

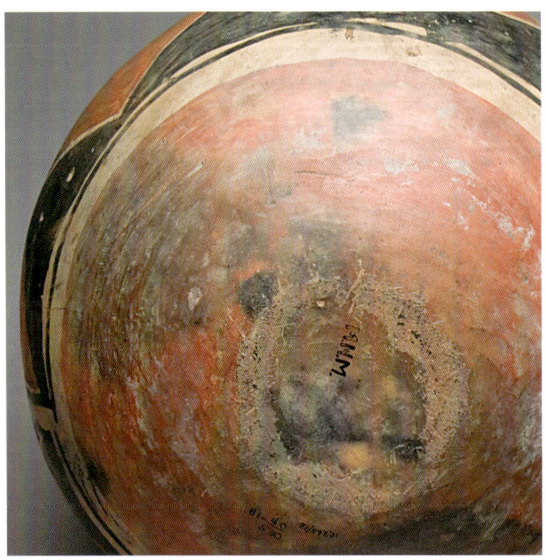

buyer. The statement "made by" emphasizes that the signature is meant to authenticate the piece, reminiscent of the early labels put on Nampeyo's pottery sold in the Grand Canyon. Indeed, labels still attached to the vessels from this time period emphasize that the purchase of authentic pieces was central in the growing market in the 1920s and 1930s. "Guaranteed Hand-made Santo Domingo," reads one label, "Indian Pueblo, New Mexico/ Southwest Arts and Crafts / Santa Fe, New Mexico /Price. 3.60."

The emphasis on place—Santo Domingo and Cochiti pueblos—between the 1910s and 1930s

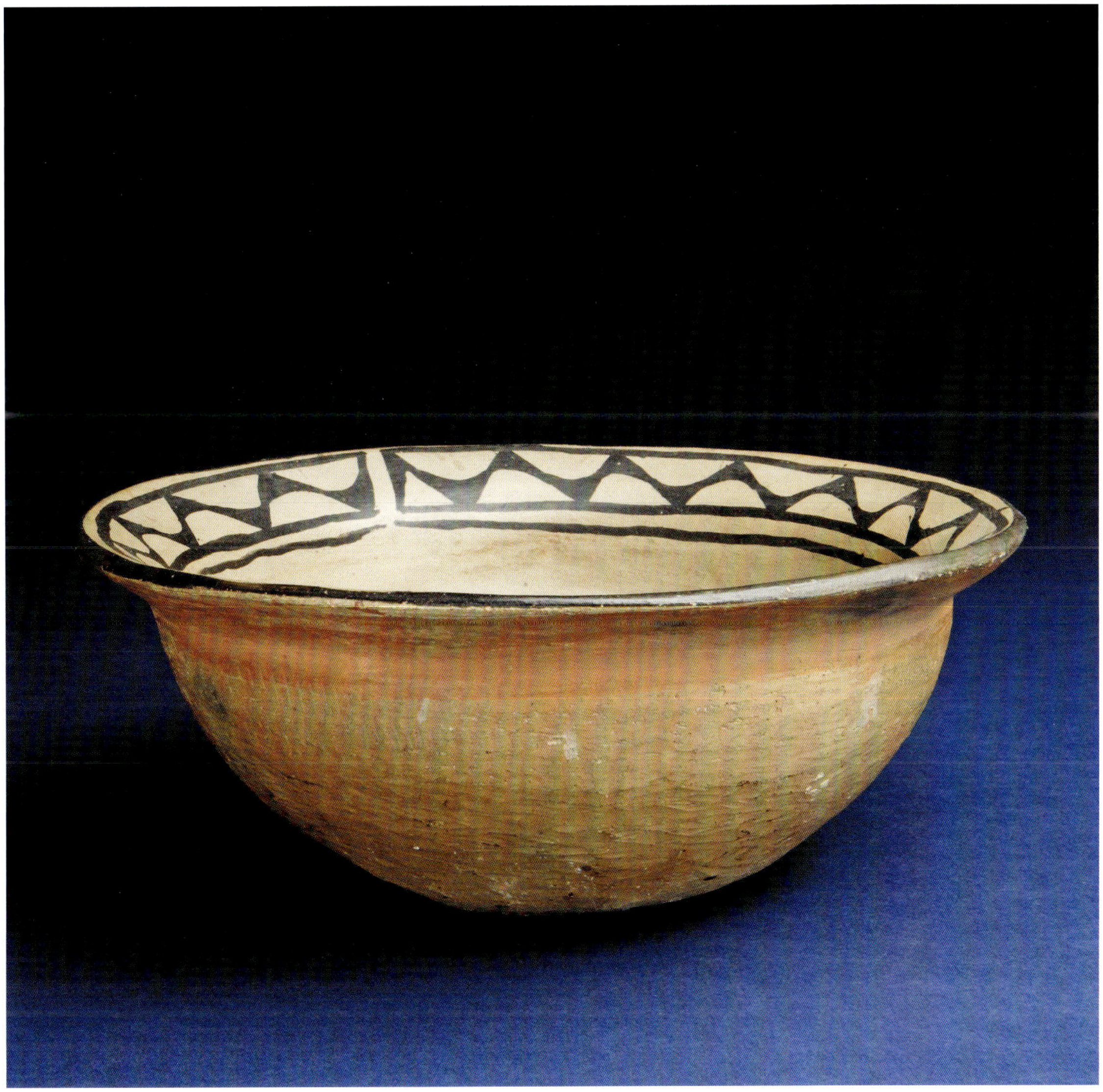

figure 31
Bowl (two views)
Cochiti
Artist Unknown
ca. 1930
10.1 x 26.4 cm

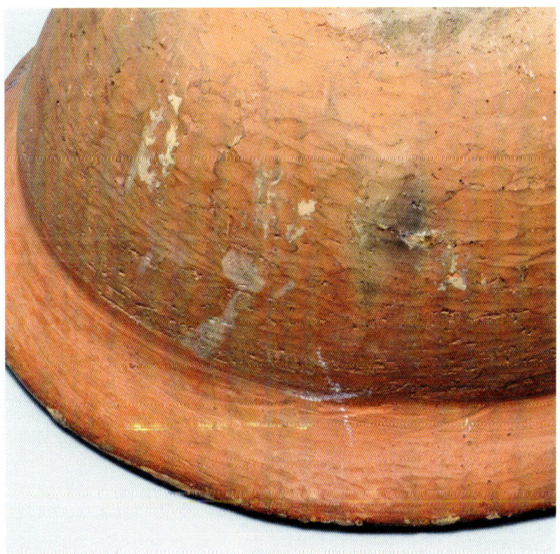

would soon give way to an emphasis on the individual artists and the time when the individual piece was made. No longer were Pueblo vessels timeless generic objects made by a collective knowledge, but they became singular objects, the creative expression of individuals at a particular time. In the 1950s, the penciled signature of Cochiti artist Teresita Romero, probably written by a dealer, appears on several figurines, as is the case for Laurencita Herrera in the next decade. Into the 1970s, the signatures become clearer, with rising prices. Herrera's signed figurine was selling for $8 in 1965, compared to $300 for Aurelia Suina's 1975 artist-signed figurine

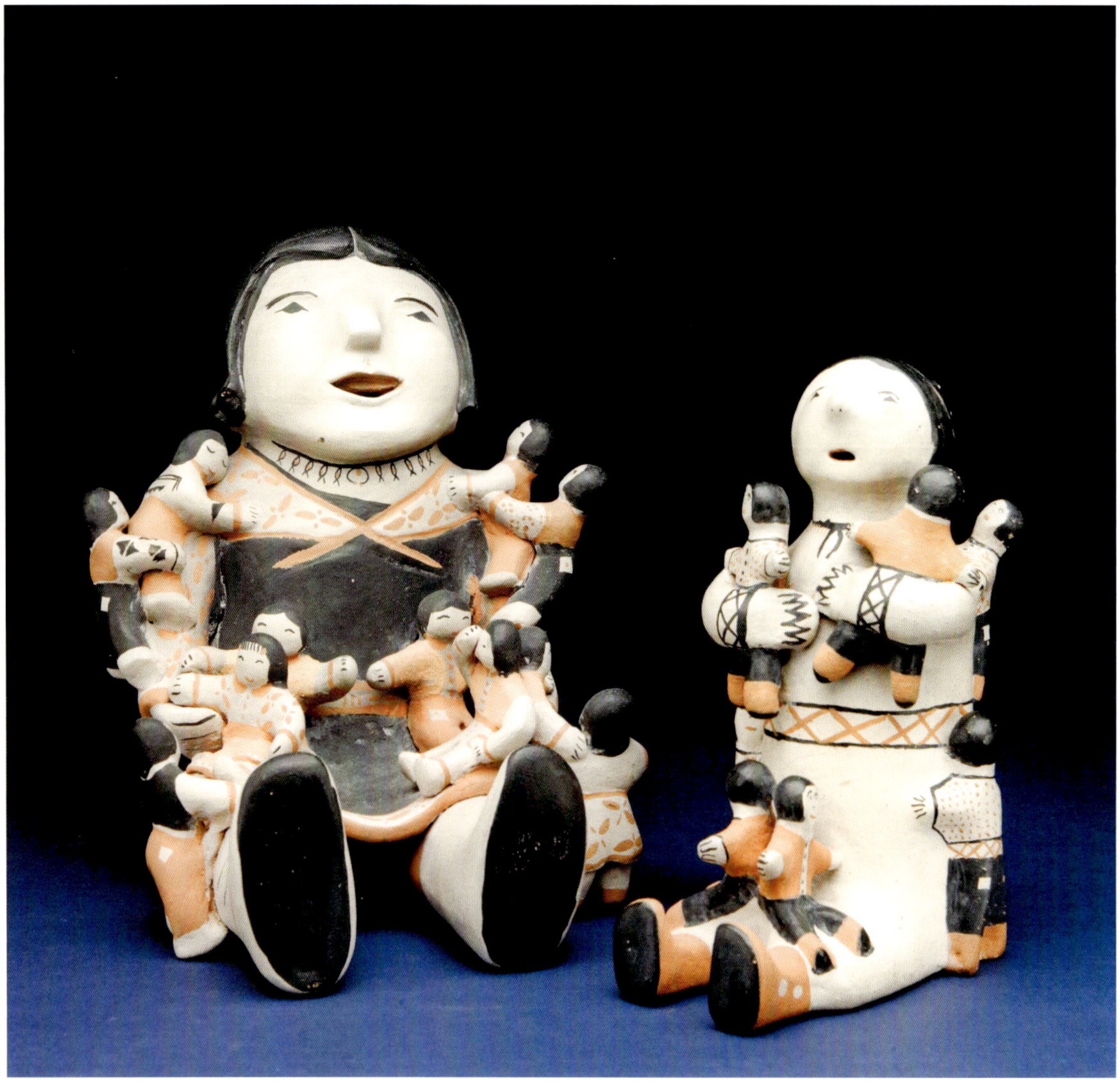

figure 32
Storyteller Figurines
(two views)
Cochiti
Aurelia Suina and
Ada Suina
1975; 1982
20.8 cm; 24.0 x 20.0 x 25.0 cm

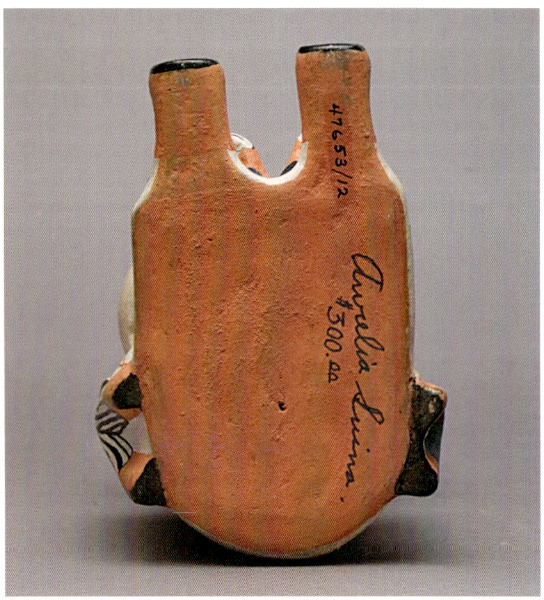

(fig. 32). The signatures at this time are no longer in pencil or dubiously penned by the artisans. Rather, they are bold as can be seen with Crucita Melchor's painted signature—and they are proud as Helen Cordero's large and very conspicuous signature (fig. 25). By the 1980s and 1990s, signatures are commonplace. Signing pieces becomes so standard that artists find increasingly creative ways to sign their work, as does Robert Tenorio (fig. 33). And some, such as Virgil Ortiz, even begin to use the maker's mark as a symbol of creativity (fig. 34); adjacent to his signed name is an elaborate insignia reminiscent of the tangled signatures used by Spanish conquistadores.

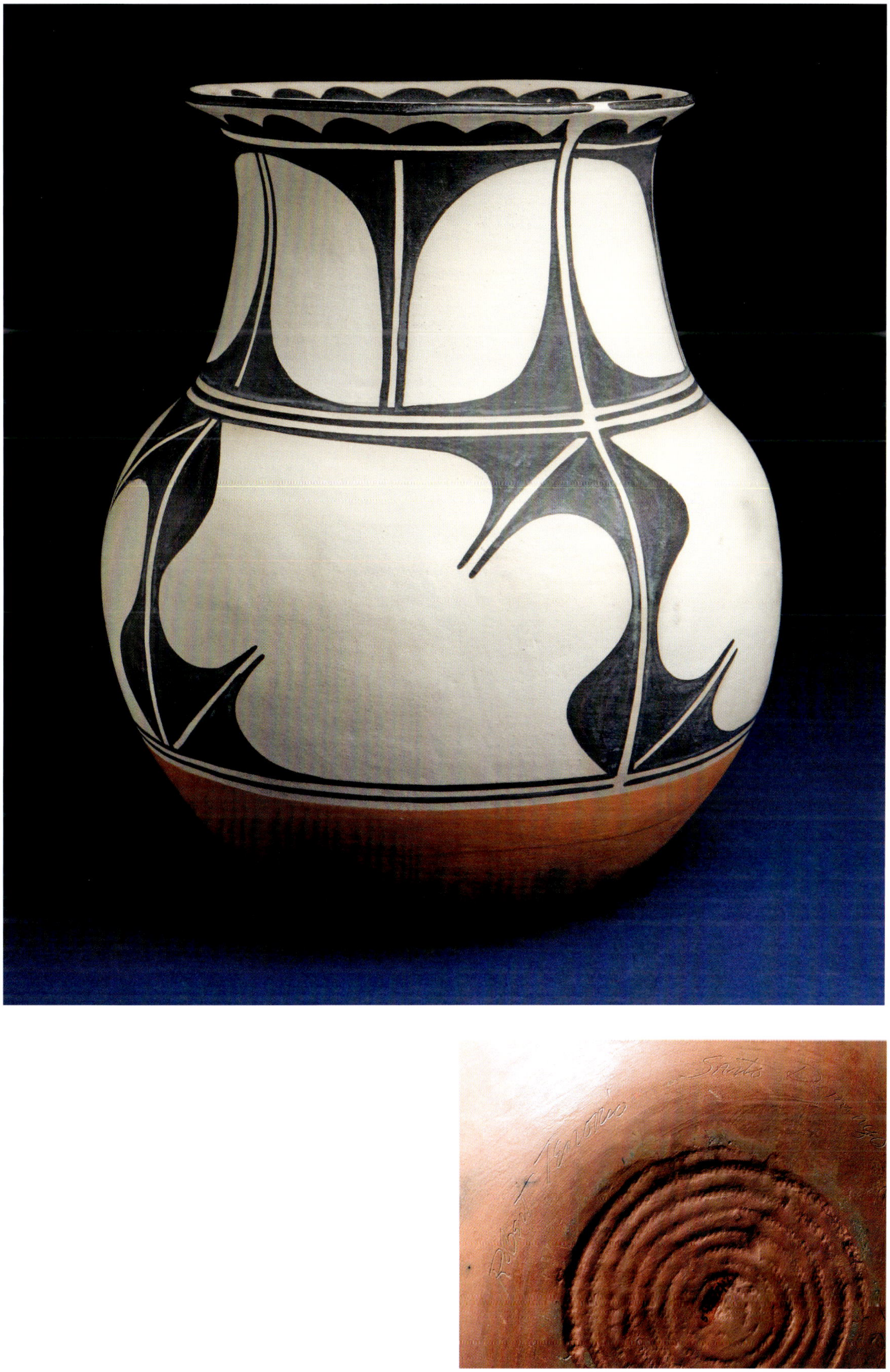

figure 33
Jar (two views)
Santo Domingo
Robert Tenorio
ca. 1985
35.5 x 30.8 cm

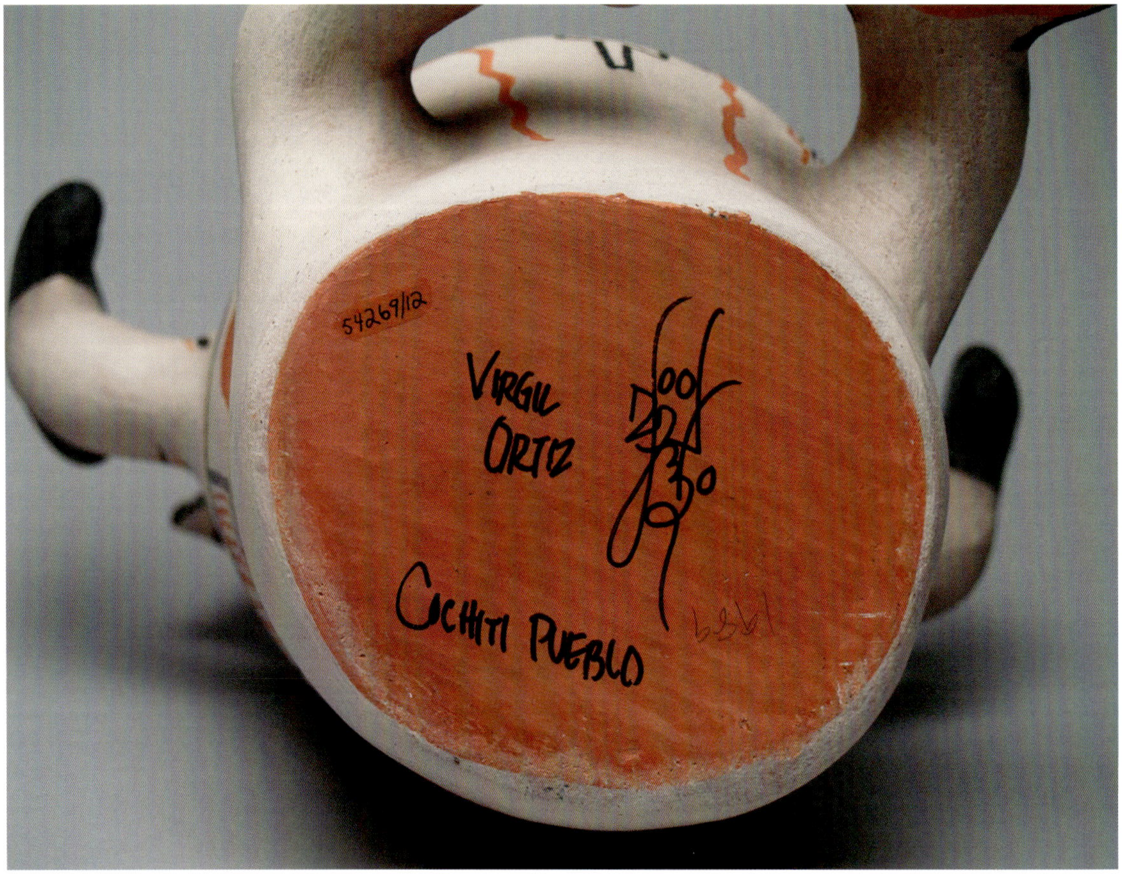

figure 34
Male Figurine
Cochiti
Virgil Ortiz
1989
28.4 x 27.5 x 21.1 cm

MATTER : SPIRIT

A study of signatures is a study in the ambiguity of modern Pueblo pottery. Born of tradition, reinvigorated in recent generations, and expanded to creative heights, Pueblo pottery today is a statement of the past and present in a single breath. The visible dimensions of pottery—form, color, texture—are traditions built by millennia of unnamed artists, but today, on the bottom, rarely seen, is clear evidence of the individual who took those ancestral ideas and traditions and made them her or his own.

Signatures on Pueblo pottery perhaps best reflect what Tessie Naranjo describes as living between two worlds, Western and Pueblo (Naranjo 1994). Much has been gained from the exchange between Pueblo artisans and outside anthropologists, dealers, and connoisseurs over the last century plus. As Bruce Bernstein observes, pottery sales to non-Indians have provided vital income for Pueblo artists while at the same time preserving aspects of Pueblo culture. "For example, at Santa Clara [Pueblo] over 300 people living in the village identify themselves as potters. Since they can work in the pueblo they are able to participate in community events as the need arises and to be near family," he has written. "Potters say that pottery making allows them to express their 'Santa Claraness' both to 'Mother Earth for the clay' and to the non-Pueblo buyer. It also permits them to maintain the reciprocal relationship central to the communal life of the pueblo, a reciprocity they extend to their work" (Bernstein 1994b:16–17). The art market has provided the means for the flourishing of Pueblo pottery production and the celebration and worldwide recognition of Pueblo artistry.

Tessie Naranjo writes that these benefits have not come without costs. The rise of the market—so perfectly embodied in those names tucked under pots—has also resulted in a vain pursuit of individualism, competition, and perfection. These, she suggests, are anathema to the origin and purpose of pottery in Pueblo society. "The role of pottery in our life is to bring the human into oneness with the earth through clay," Naranjo states, after describing the interdependence among land, water, prayer, ancestors, amity, and ceremony in the making and using of ceramics. "Pottery production is a symbolic expression of the creative potential of the human spirit in collaborative and cooperative interaction with the earth" (Naranjo 1994:47).

Following from Naranjo, the equation can perhaps be expanded further still: name is to vessel as matter is to spirit. The names on ceramics suggest a profound change in the numinous aspect of pottery production and consumption—an embodiment of the clash between market forces and the spiritual experiences of transforming clay. It is these interlinked connections that artist Nora Naranjo-Morse also brings to mind. In her poem "Mud Woman's First Encounter with the World of Money and Business," Naranjo-Morse relates a potter's sorrowful initiation into the art world (Naranjo-Morse 1992:35–37). While the artist is proud of each object's "idiosyncrasies, that made each piece her own," the gallery owner cares only about the artist's family name and whether the things will sell. The gallery owner reluctantly buys several pieces, and the creator reluctantly lets them go. Mud Woman, the maker of the pieces, walks away from the gallery crestfallen, "leaving behind her / shaped pieces of earth."

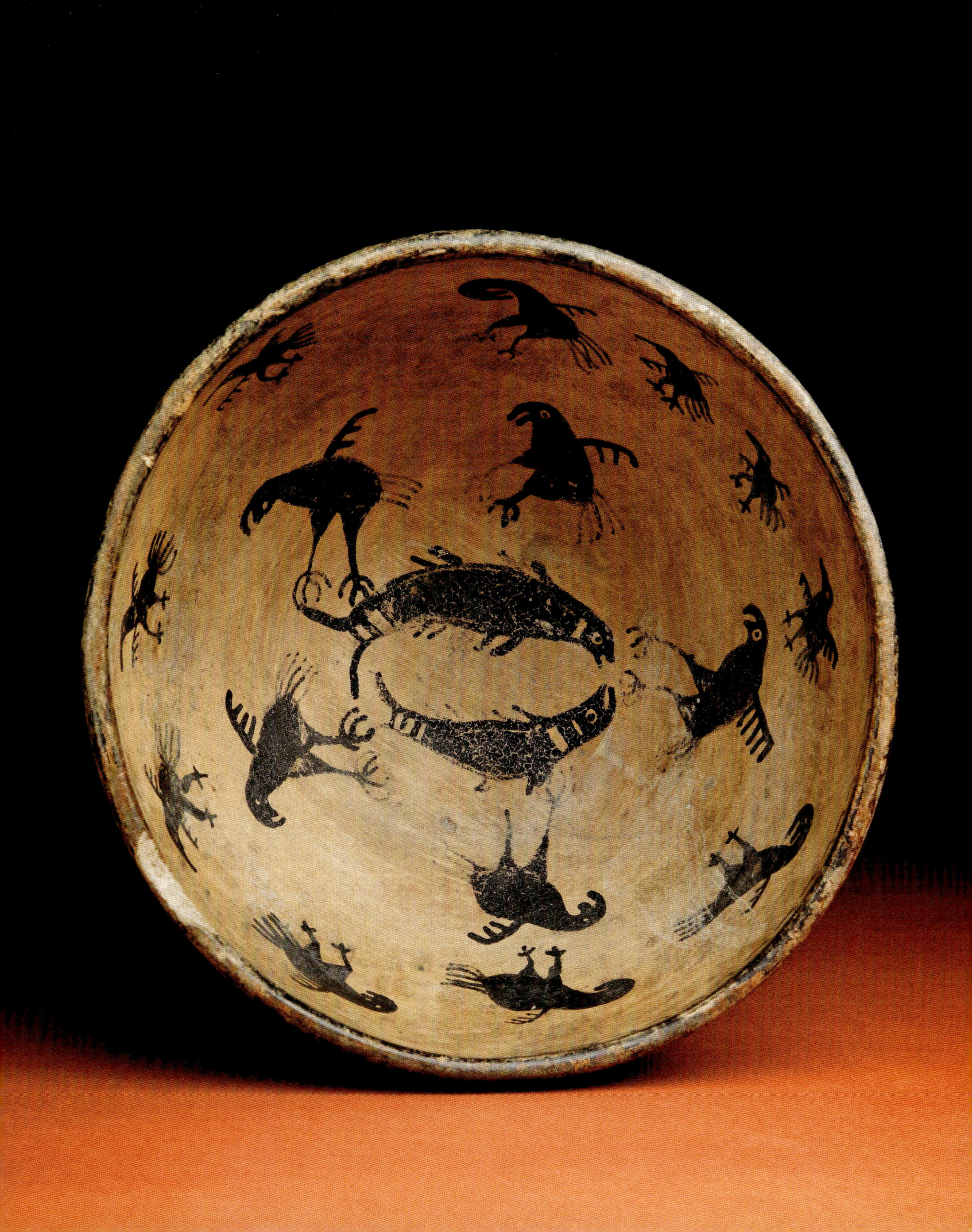

Looking into the Bowl

Part I: Artists and Outsiders

Bruce Bernstein

Introduction

Cosmologically, the Pueblo world can be visualized as two bowls put together to form a sphere—the upper the Father or Sky and the lower the Mother or Earth. This perspective expands when you equate the bottom of the bowl with the bare yet fertile ground that constitutes a central pueblo plaza. On the Earth bowl interior are painted designs describing a fecund world from which can be seen the vast New Mexico sky that marks the horizon of the outside world just above and beyond the rim. Pueblo potters use their work to express themselves and teach outsiders about their communities—each pot they make contains Pueblo values and beliefs, including sacred concepts about fertility and life. Seen from this perspective, making pottery is a courageous act; selling or giving it away is even more courageous, especially when this intrinsically pious and exceedingly Pueblo-centric entity ends up in a non-Pueblo home or museum. I have learned that no matter how much those of us in the outside world embrace and immerse ourselves in Pueblo pottery, we always remain outsiders looking into the bowl.

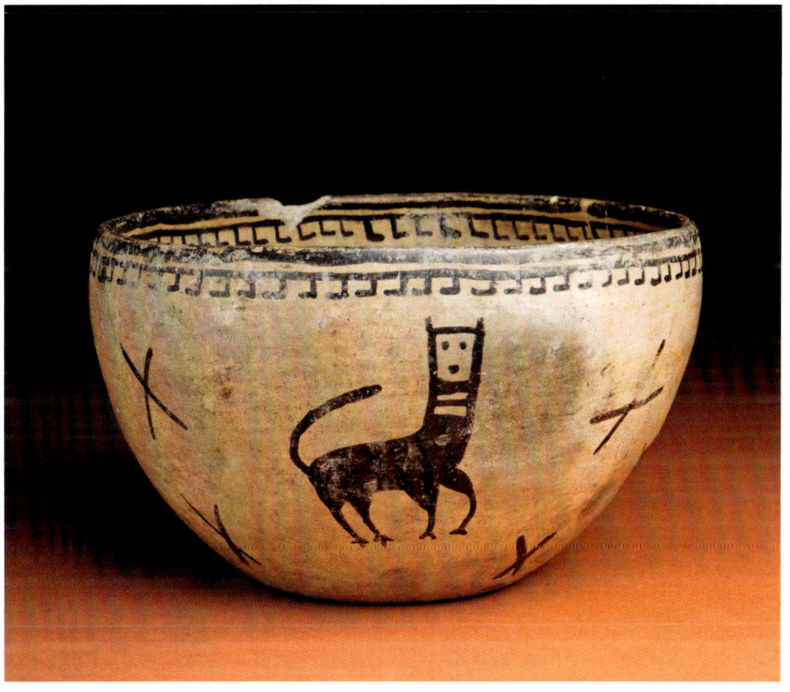

figure 35
Bowl (two views)
Cochiti
Artist Unknown
ca. 1880
13.6 x 23.3 cm

For some outsiders, a momentary encounter with a pot in a museum or store is enough to gain an appreciation of the survival and vibrancy of Pueblo culture. To those of us who wish to understand more, many potters regularly give of themselves through talks and demonstrations, sometimes sharing profound insights into their work: inspirations for designs, difficulties securing traditional materials, experiments with firing, and attention to detail. Other potters might offer participants the opportunity to paint a pot. The novices quickly discover how difficult it is to paint on curved surfaces—the concave and convex—and their awkward designs look like doodles on a page. At one of these demonstrations I began to think about the difficulties inherent in translating life onto a surface, a metaphor that epitomizes my plight here as well: describing multi-dimensional life with words on flat pages.

The Artists: Creating and Selling Pottery

In today's Southwest, Native societies use the arts to strengthen themselves and to affirm their resolve for survival. We know that Pueblo pottery is constantly changing, creating a moving picture recounting a culture that remains strong by adapting and absorbing new influences, as well as by shielding its members from intrusions and rapid, unwanted changes. The world outside the pueblo sometimes entices members away, but the arts generally, and pottery in particular, provide a way for people to live and work at home, to be near family, to participate in community events, and to live a traditional life. By providing a means to enter the American cash economy without leaving home for employment, pottery making is one example of how artists can profitably fit an old pattern to contemporary needs.

Potters tell us that making pots is giving birth—a truism of pottery when you consider the bringing together of the fertile elements of earth and water—earth the substance from which First Person is formed, and water the single most important life force of the Southwest and a focus of religious life. While the Pueblos are known for their protective secrecy, seeing and holding a pot made from the same substance that comprises First Person is revealing. Today, we understand that heirloom pottery contains village history and family genealogy—holding pottery is holding Pueblo life. In the late 1800s a travel writer noted that "When an Indian will not sell his blankets, pottery, beadwork or dance costumes it shows that he has plenty to eat and is thoroughly prosperous" (Eickemeyer 1895:101). So, what does it mean to sell and to buy Pueblo pottery?

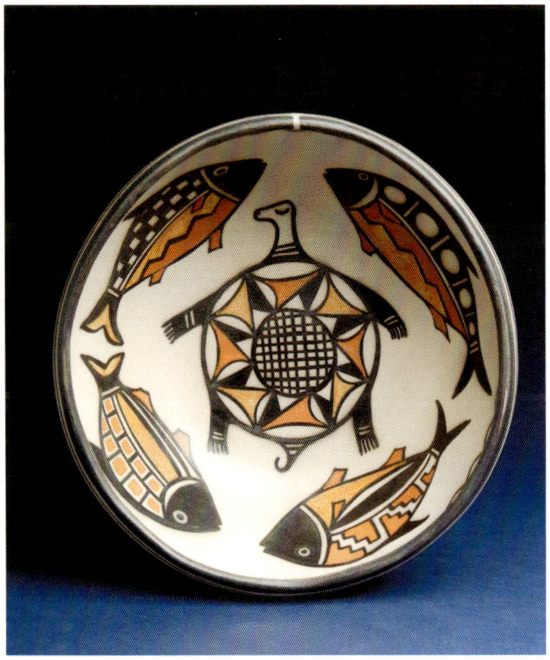
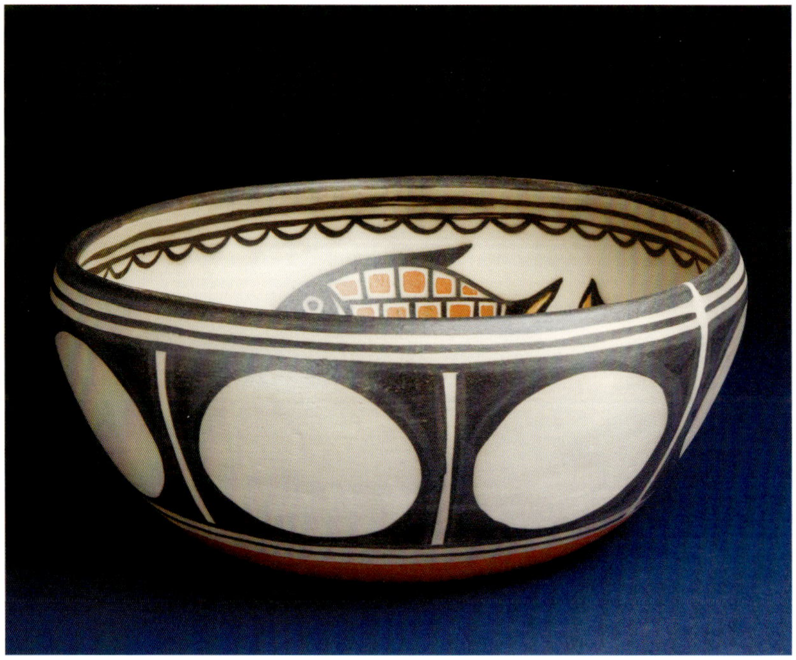

figure 36
Bowl (two views)
Santo Domingo
Robert Tenorio
13.6 x 33.4 cm

Santo Domingo communities discourage figurative depictions on pottery, preferring that artists confine their imagery to more abstract, and less revealing, geometric designs. Figurative representations like these are usually designed with collectors in mind, and only marginally relate to ancestral designs.

In 1968, Santo Domingo potter Robert Tenorio enrolled in the Institute of American Indian Arts, Santa Fe, to study jewelry, but he soon discovered that his heart was in the ceramics studio. At the institute, he began by working in stoneware, a commercial clay that he kiln fired; however, today Tenorio primarily uses traditional clays and paints, and fires outdoors in a cottonwood fire. Over the years, Tenorio and I have spent a considerable amount of time discussing pottery. While he assiduously avoids revealing anything too private about Santo Domingo, as I watch him construct, paint, and fire pots, and listen as he speaks about his work, I perceive in his lively discourse the joy with which he engages with life and with his culture. Sometimes what he tells outsiders is well rehearsed as he answers familiar questions about materials, techniques, and designs and dispels preconceived notions. From Tenorio I have learned that to understand Pueblo pottery, we outsiders must experience it as intended, and not as objects of our own cultural longing (fig. 36).

The work of contemporary Cochiti potter Diego Romero illustrates and articulates this and the past, present, and future of Pueblo pottery. Romero grew up in the San Francisco Bay Area and was heavily influenced by comic books and by the Art Department at the University of California, Los Angeles, where he earned an MFA in ceramics. He sees himself as a Pueblo potter steeped in the very Pueblo tradition of experimentation and innovation, and thus independent of the labels imposed by the contemporary Indian art market. Even though his materials, technique, painting style, and subject matter are contemporary, to talk to Romero is to be immersed in Cochiti clay. "I make pots and don't care to theorize, because one hundred years from now, my pots stacked up will be part of a long conservative tradition," he says. Seen in the short view, Romero's pottery is unique; however, in the long view it nestles comfortably within the long tradition from which he draws inspiration (fig. 37, see fig. 9).

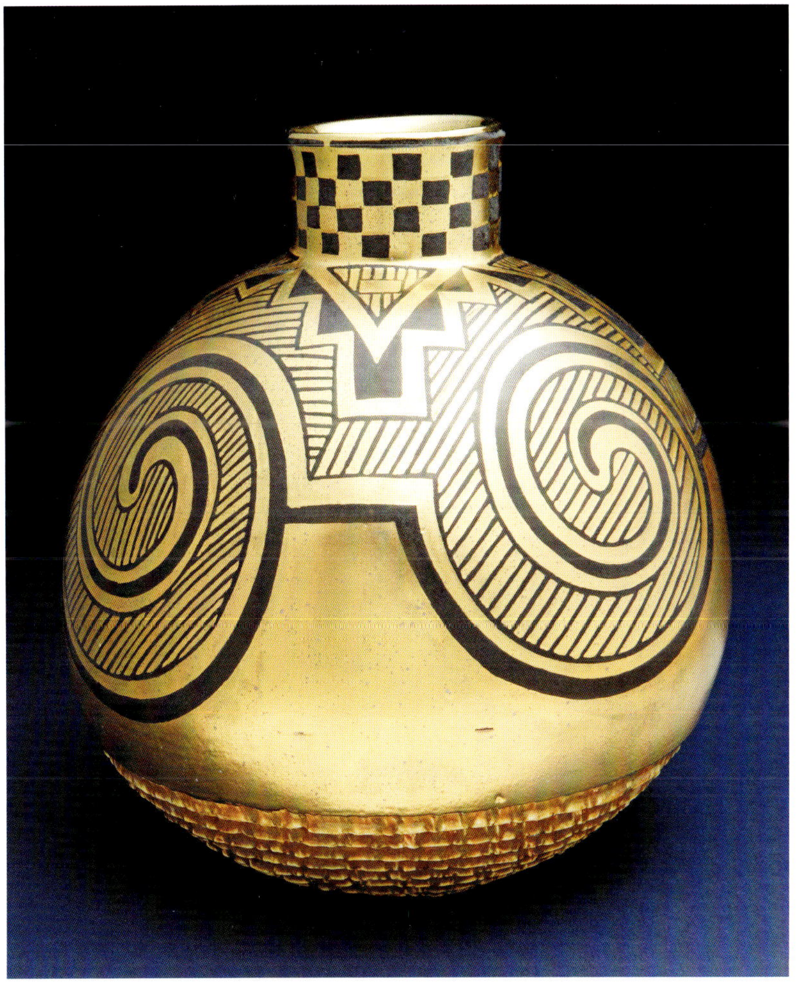

figure 37
Jar
Cochiti
Diego Romero
ca. 1994
24.8 x 23.6 cm

The Outsiders: Buying and Selling Pueblo Pottery

The Southwest Indian curio business originated with the completion of the transcontinental railroad in 1880. Excursion trains brought tourists who besieged the curio shops of Albuquerque, Santa Fe, and smaller towns for souvenirs of their travels. They also purchased directly from Pueblo vendors at railroad stations and stops. In the Puebloan world, people from Santo Domingo are renowned for their trading prowess, and in the late nineteenth and early twentieth centuries, Santo Domingo men boarded the trains to sell their wares, including pottery, riding from the Santa Fe area as far as Gallup. The 1905 photograph of a Santo Domingo peddler provides an idea of one apparently well-traveled man's inven-

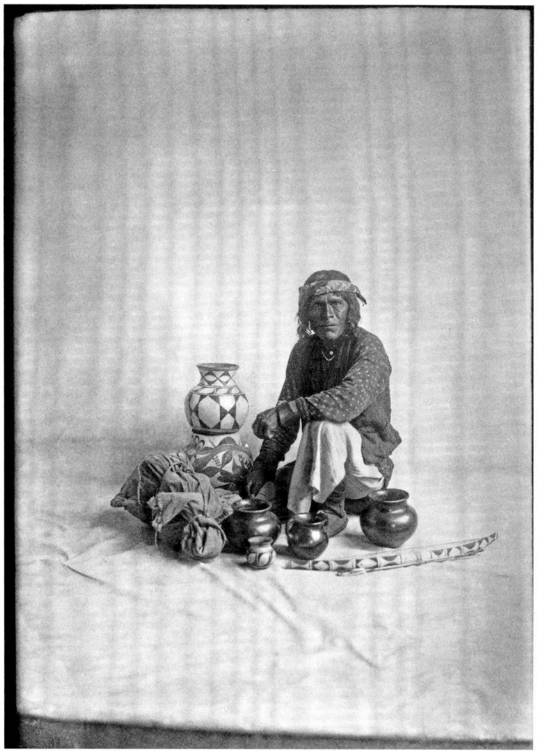

Santo Domingo peddler, ca. 1905. Karl E. Moon, photographer. Courtesy Palace of the Governors (MNM/DCA), 200110. Here a Santo Domingo trader sits among his presumed wares, some unwrapped, some still in cloth carrying squares. There is one Santo Domingo jar, others from Ohkay Owingeh, and a Mohave bow. Santo Domingo traders still ply their trade, traveling between pueblos exchanging feathers, clay slips, jewelry, and agricultural products.

below:
Pueblo women selling pottery in front of the Indian Building, Fred Harvey's Hotel Alvarado, Albuquerque, ca. 1900–1910. Harry H. Lake, photographer. Courtesy Denver Public Library, Western History Collection, L-484. When early travelers alighted from the trains at Albuquerque, they walked the gauntlet of potters and jewelers to the Harvey Company's Indian arts and crafts store, where they might meet artists demonstrating and see historic Indian art. The undignified concept of sitting on the ground selling outside was artificially constructed to provide travelers with an exotic experience.

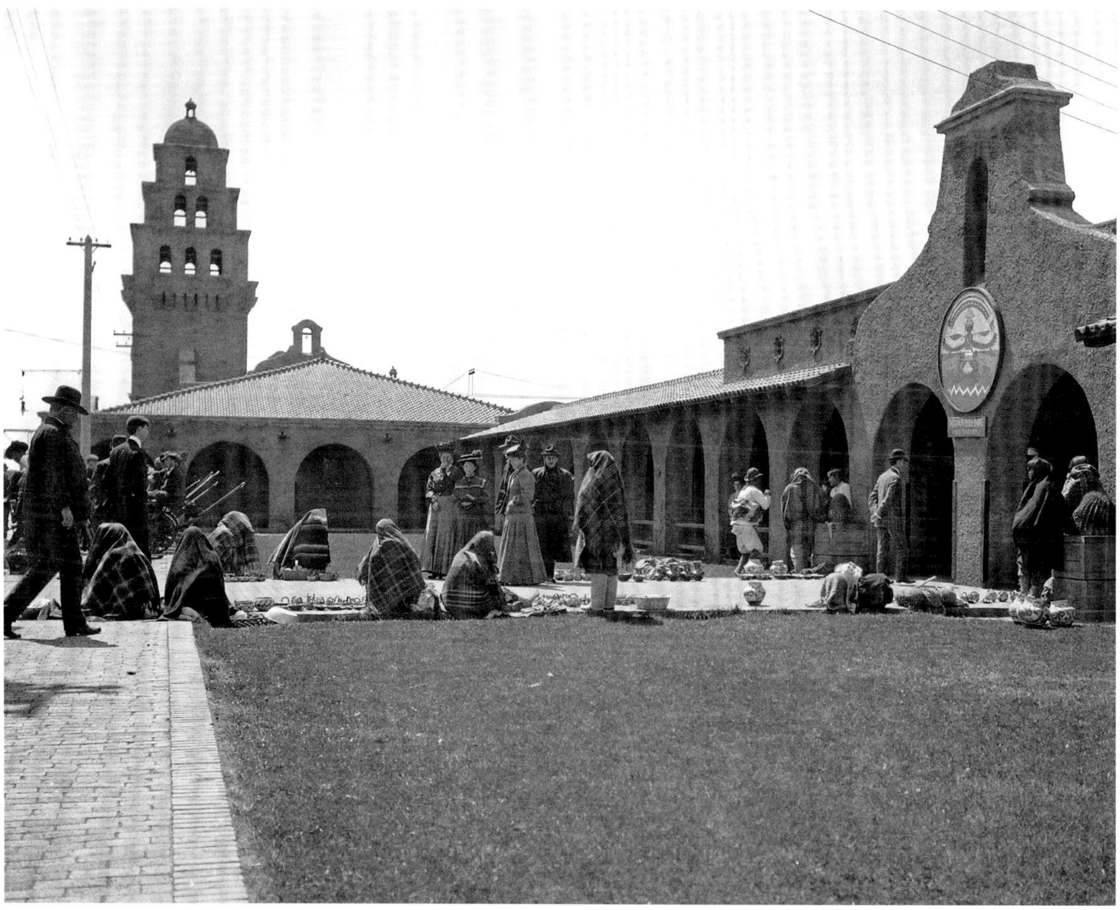

tory. To serve this trade, curio dealers often purchased pottery by the wagonload or by the barrel, with the potter receiving a few cents, or at most a dollar, for a full-sized vessel. Dealers encouraged potters to produce "marketable" wares (Batkin 1998; Bernstein 1993), or "Indian pots," without further elaboration needed as to village of origin or maker, and without recognition of quality or aesthetics. An 1881 handbill describes the type of nontraditional pieces traders preferred: "a variety of grotesque designs, idols, dogs, horses, birds, bowls, cups, pitchers, saucers, urns, baskets, pipes, ash-receivers, flower pots, tea-pots &c." (Batkin 1998). Other marketing strategies associated Pueblo pottery with regional myths about Montezuma and a northward Aztec and Toltec migration, going so far as to have Tesuque potters imitate pre-Columbian ceramics (Batkin and Lange 1999:52–54).

Pottery sales, of course, meant more money in the pueblos and thus increased acquisition of and reliance on non-Puebloan products. Store-bought goods undermined the theocracy—if villagers could purchase flour or have their wheat threshed and ground outside the pueblo, carefully orchestrated labor and communal work systems would no longer have complete efficacy. At Santo Domingo Pueblo the introduction and use of American goods and agricultural products and, importantly, the acquisition of money to buy them, was doubtless frowned upon. Money could only be earned by working for outsiders or by selling to outsiders; moreover, while men's success in the cash economy was tolerated, women—the potters—were actively discouraged from having contact with the outside world. One well-documented incident supports the commonly held viewpoint that Santo Domingo's leaders did not want their village's wares sold in stores: on discovering a pair of armbands for sale in Santa Fe, community leaders punished the villager who had sold them and confiscated the armbands from the store owner.

By 1900, all the pottery-producing pueblos had formulated wares for the non-Indian market. The pieces generally were smaller, simpler in design and surface finish; to add value, some pieces were sold as being of religious use or, short of that, the painted design was reputed to be of deep religious significance. Cochiti's potters incorporated the outsiders' tastes, creating small items for tourists (fig. 38) as well as figurative pottery mimicking the non-Cochiti world (fig. 39), while Santo Domingo kept the outside world at arm's length.

In the first two decades of the twentieth century, Santo Domingo is almost certainly the singular exception to what pottery scholars refer to as the low point in traditional Pueblo potting history. As noted above, while by 1900 Cochiti potters were producing for the curio and tourist market, at Santo Domingo domestic pottery production and use remained preeminent. The market for small tourist pieces seems to have puzzled the potters of Santo Domingo, who made few curios. As noted by Kenneth Chapman, Santo Domingo discouraged visitors and other outside intrusions in the pueblo:

> In 1881, the building of a railroad within a quarter mile of the pueblo aroused the resentment of the elders who have since objected strenuously and consistently to the location of a Government school, the digging of wells, and every successive innovation of the Indian Service. While this policy of aloofness is relaxed during their principal feast days, only the purchase of pottery or other products now gives visitors freedom of the village for more than the briefest of visits and with the relocation of the new transcontinental highway five miles to the eastward, the potters are urged to sell their wares there as a further means of discouraging visits of tourists to the pueblo (Chapman 1936).

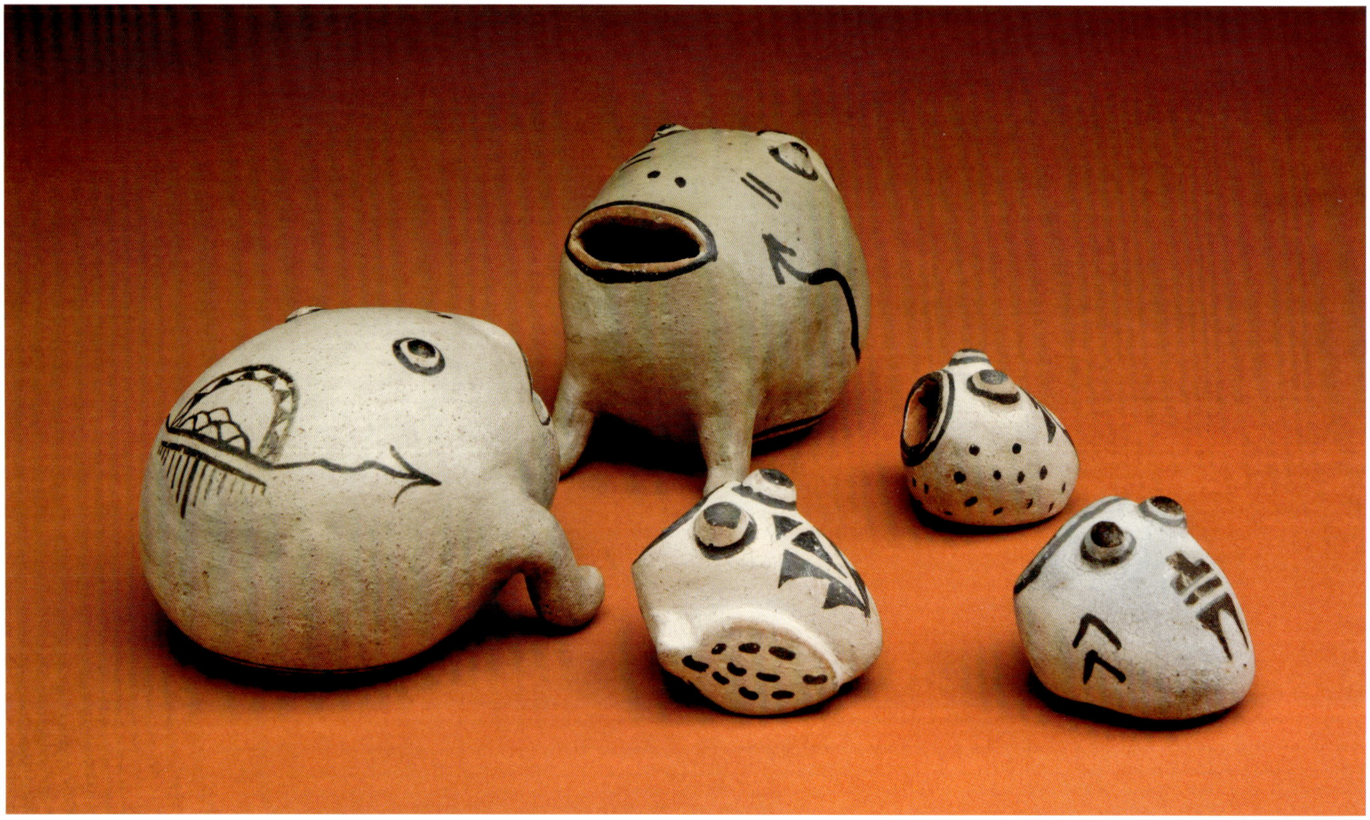

figure 38
Frog Figurines
(two large)
Cochiti
Artist Unknown
ca. 1960
6.2 x 8.1 x 8.9 cm
ca. 1925–1945
7.2 x 7.0 x 9.6 cm

Frog Figurines
(three small)
Trini Herrera
ca. 1930–1940
3.7 x 3.8 x 4.0 cm;
3.9 x 3.8 x 4.3 cm;
4.0 x 5.0 x 5.0 cm

figure 39
Male Figurine
Cochiti
Artist Unknown
ca. 1910
47.5 x 24.0 x 13.0 cm

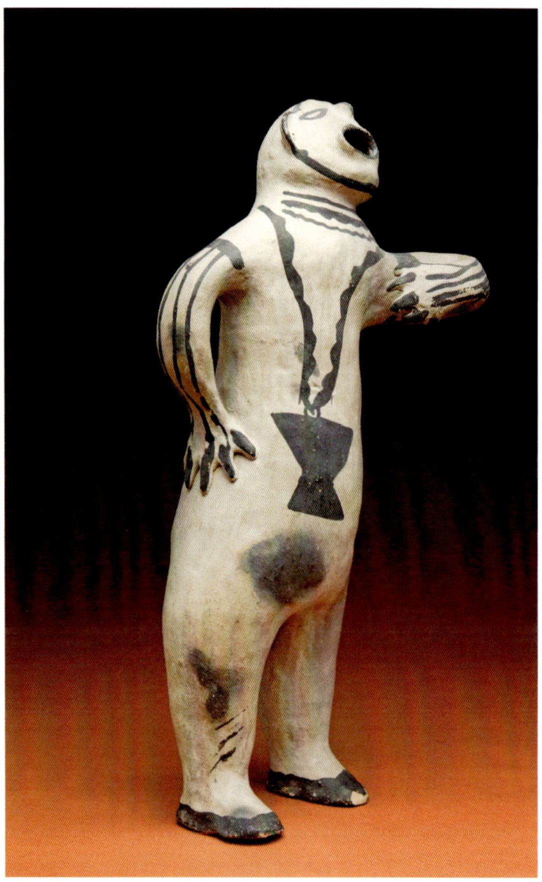

Today, it is easy to get to Santo Domingo or Cochiti—broad paved highways take you right to the villages, many of the houses are now numbered, and people have telephones, cell phones, and the Internet. Before the 1980s I-25 Interstate Highway Improvement projects, Santo Domingo was accessible by a left turn off the highway rather than today's overpass, and villagers stood along the highway waiting to catch the bus or to hitch a ride. Many visitors who traveled through New Mexico previous to the 1970s remember encountering Pueblo vendors at roadside stands:

> At the sound of an approaching motor they emerge from their brush or stone shelters, their bright costumes fluttering, their arms waving that you might stop and see the pottery of their villages located miles off the highway. Reticent sales agents these, yet appreciative of your interest, and

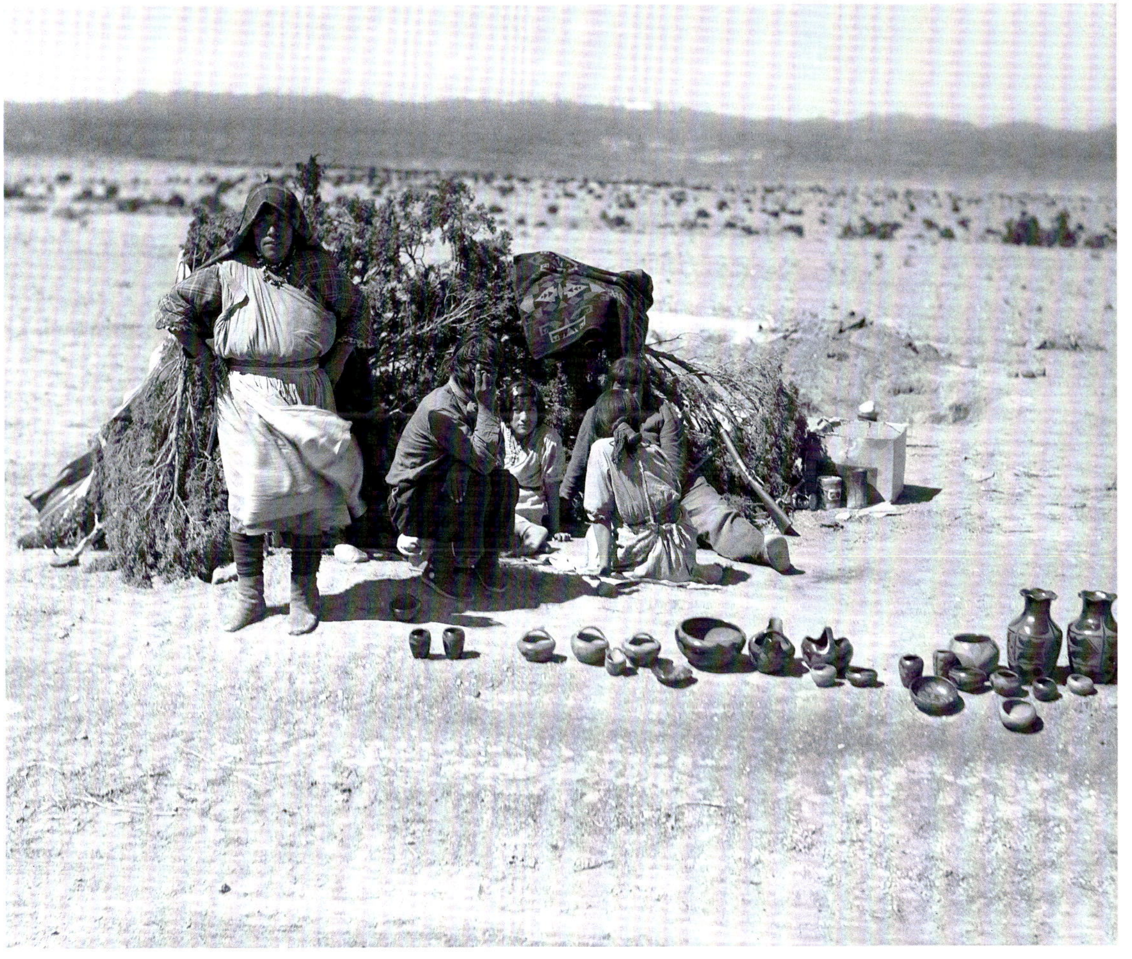

Santo Domingo pottery vendors, ca. 1935. T. Harmon Parkhurst, photographer. Courtesy Palace of the Governors (MNM/DCA), 4368. While few pots were made for sale at Santo Domingo prior to 1920, tourist wares comprised almost all of the pottery made after that date. These Santo Domingo potters have set up roadside stands to sell their wares, as well as that of family members. The insular nature of Santo Domingo's people did not change when they began interacting with outsiders—none of these vendors looks pleased about being photographed; some have turned away from the camera.

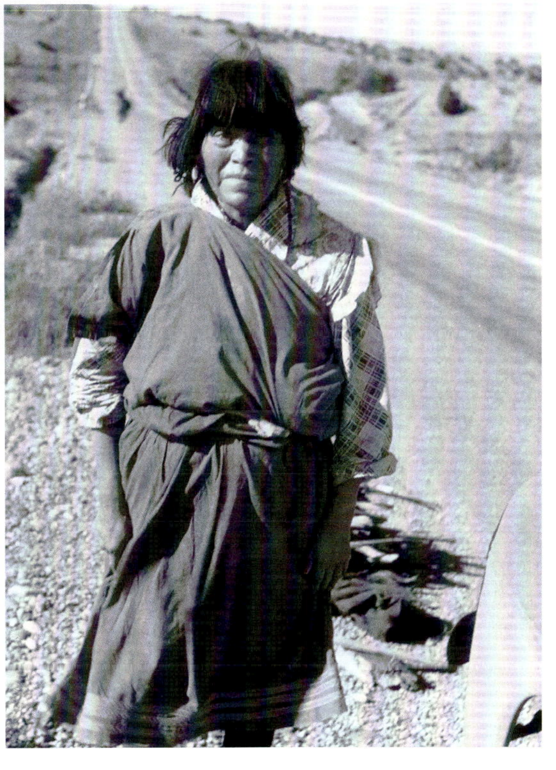

Santo Domingo pottery vendor Crucita Tenorio, February 1941. Courtesy Denver Public Library, Western History Collection, X-33507. Photographs like this one capture some of the disparities between the Native and non-Native worlds. Although we just recently learned her name, Tenorio's likeness probably resides in museum and library photo archives, as well as in individual memories and scrapbooks.

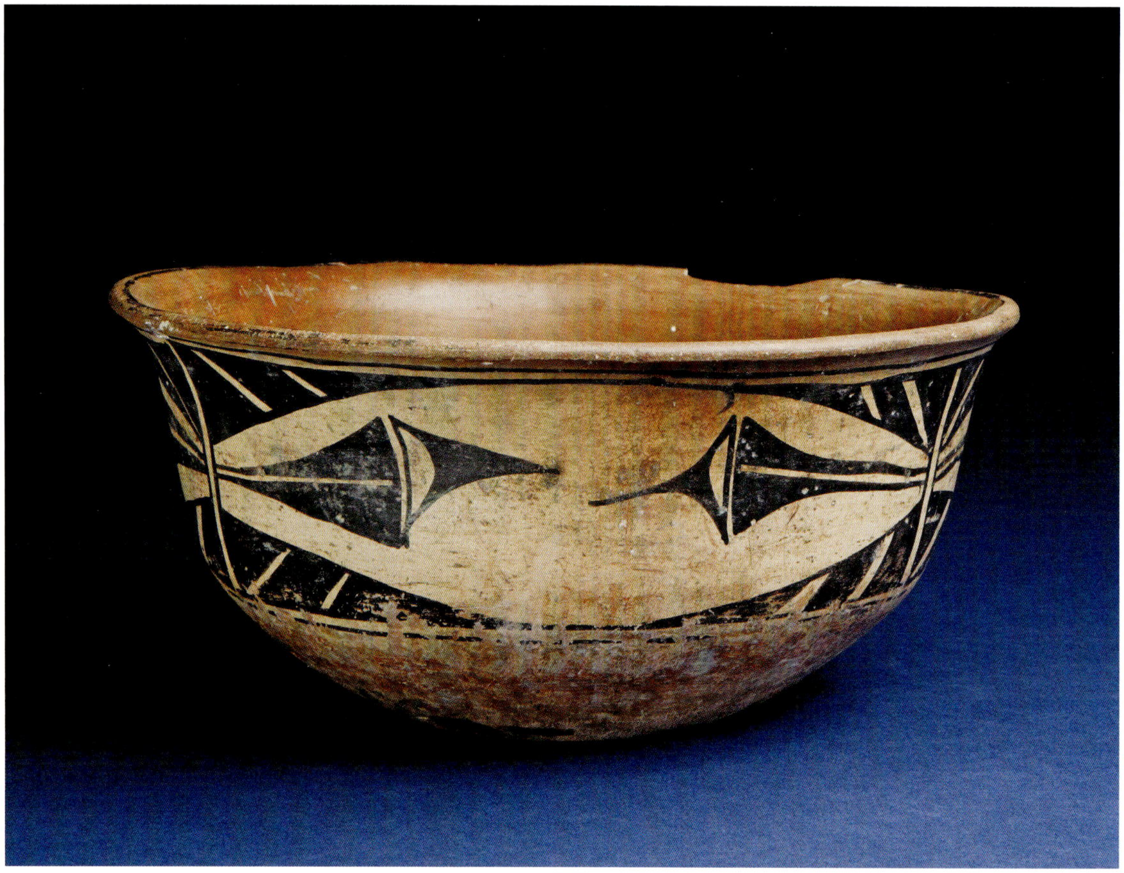

figure 40
Bowl
Santo Domingo
Artist Unknown
14.8 x 33.0 cm
ca. 1880–1900

In 1906, Julius Seligman and his brothers, Sigfried, Carl, and Ernest, opened the Bernalillo Mercantile Company in Sandoval County, New Mexico. Because religious leaders at Santo Domingo discouraged direct pottery sales at the pueblo, potters commonly marketed their wares through traders and dealers, such as the Seligmans. This bowl was a gift from the Seligmans.

> if you recognize shapely forms, good firing and neat brush-strokes they feel, perhaps, that their great labor has been worth the smallness of their wage (Chapman 1936:1).

> ...potters...mostly offer their imitations of the latest and most popular wares of other pueblos, usually crudely molded and decorated, and poorly fired, although a fine black on creamy buff can sometimes be found in the village proper (Chapman 1936:3).

Children were the primary mediators between the Santo Domingo and tourist worlds, no doubt because of their knowledge of English and the American customs that they learned at school. For a short period of time, selling by the roadside was de rigueur for most young Santo Domingo girls; during tourist season they sat along the roadside and waited for passing cars to stop. They must be the subject of hundreds of tourist photographs now stuffed in scrapbooks and shoeboxes. One 1923 tourist sent a postcard back home, writing her correspondent, "Bought pottery directly from Indians on La Bajada Mt. outside of Santa Fe." Unfortunately, primary source documents for this period are rare, with only a few photographs publicly available to provide evidence of a once thriving industry.

Today, a tribally owned gas station and travel center with an arts and crafts store have displaced the individual vendors who once lined the roads; a ragtag assortment of wooden booths and torn cloth covers the only remnants of a bygone era. Today, neat cinderblock stalls are permanent year-round reminders of Santo Domingo people's continued dependence on arts production. After the 2007 Indian Market, I asked Santo Domingo potter Crucita

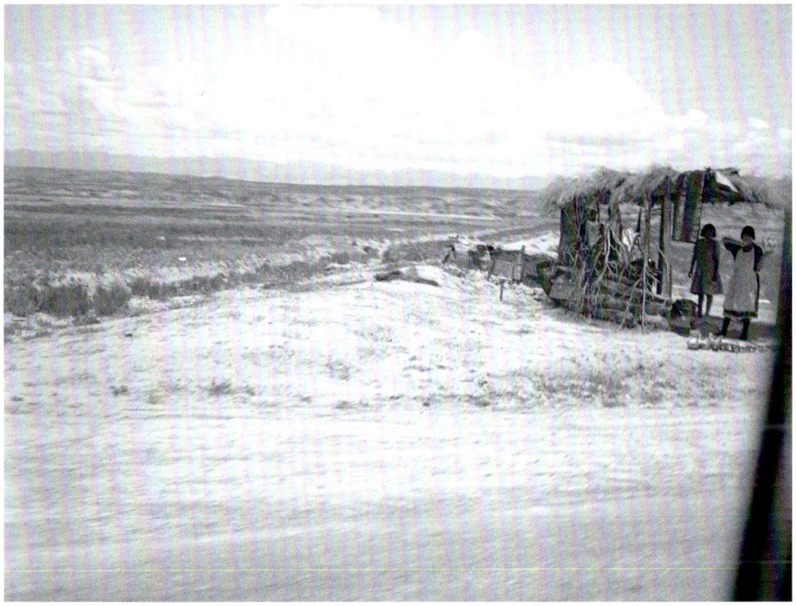

Santo Domingo girls selling pottery at a roadside stand, as taken from a passing car window, ca. 1920s. Courtesy National Museum of the American Indian, Smithsonian Institution, N47791. These two young girls are selling pottery from a brush shelter along the highway east of Santo Domingo. One traveler noted, "Bought pottery directly from Indians on La Bajada Mt. outside of Santa Fe."

Melchor whether she had sold pottery along the roadside. She answered yes and recounted walking or riding in a wagon the few miles to her family's shelter along the roadside, remembering that they made and ate fresh tortillas there. Because friends from other villages had told me of the shame they felt when cars visited their northern villages, I asked if she felt badly about selling pottery along the roadside. "Oh, no," she explained, "I was happy to be of use to my family." While highways make it easier to visit the villages, my exchange with this distinguished elder suggests that highways alone cannot

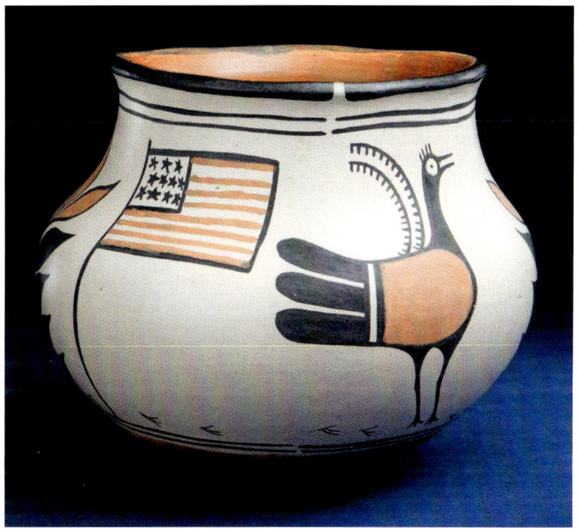

figure 41
Jar
Santo Domingo
Santana and Crucita Melchor
1976
19.0 x 17.0 x 23.5 cm

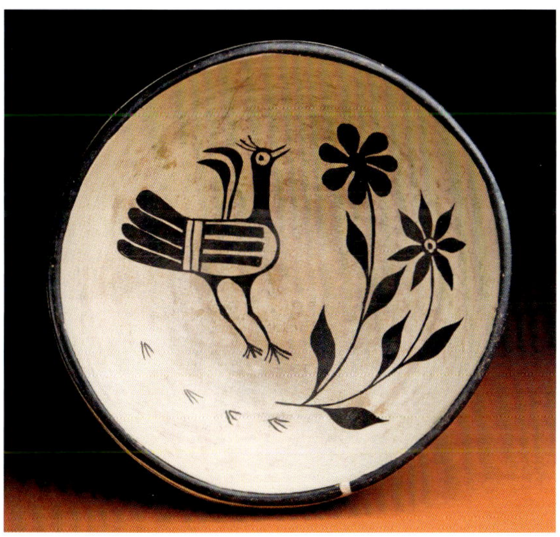

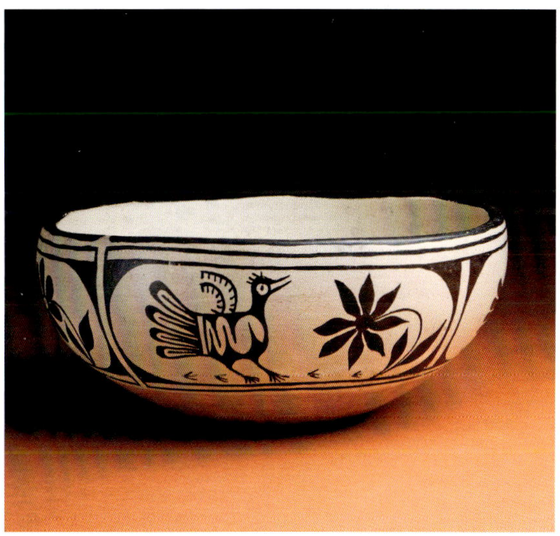

figure 42
Bowl (two views)
Santo Domingo
Crucita Melchor
ca. 1976
14.1 x 32.5 cm

figure 43
Dough Bowl
Santo Domingo
Artist Unknown
ca. 1880–1900
12.0 x 22.0 cm

The oily patina on this dough bowl suggests that it saw significant domestic use.

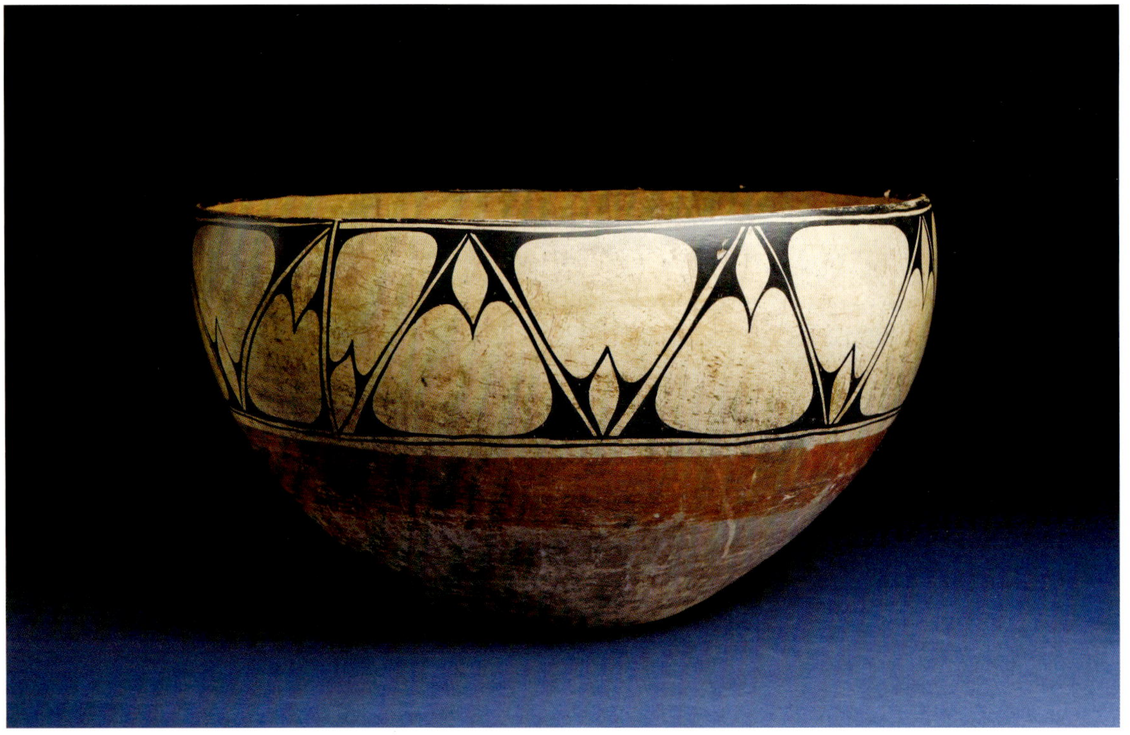

figure 44
Storage Jar
Cochiti
Artist Unknown
ca. 1870–1880
39.5 x 50.5 cm

Use wear patterns on the interior rim and interior bottom of this jar indicate that it was used in a Pueblo home.

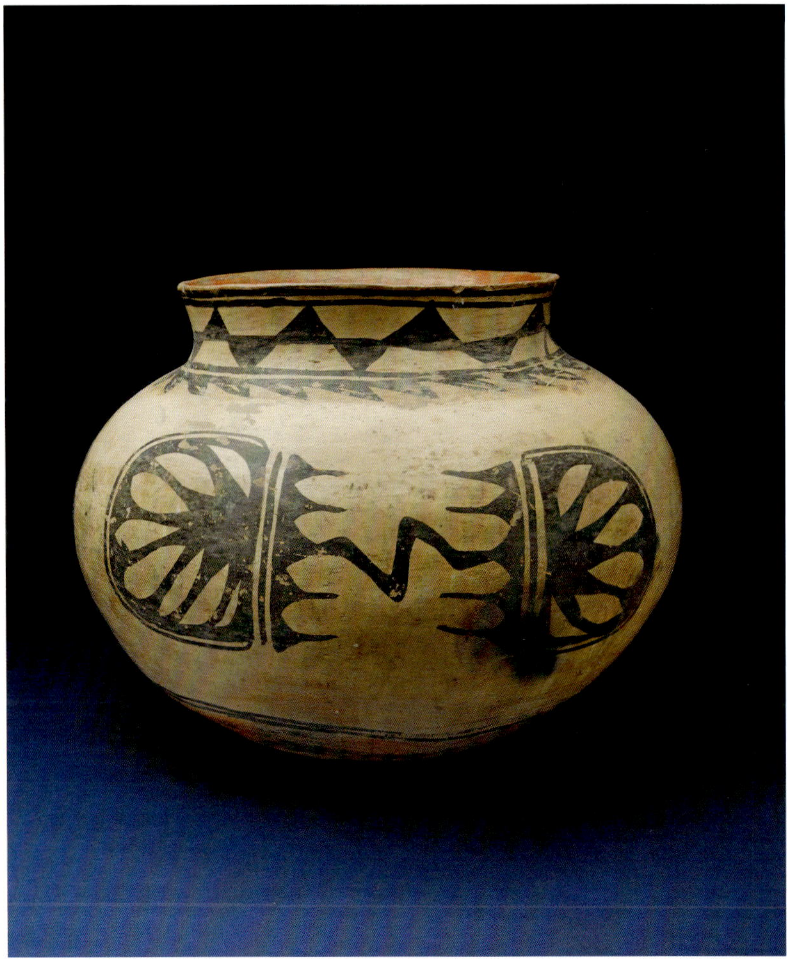

always bridge worlds. Driving from Santa Fe to Albuquerque, as I pass by the exit to Cochiti, I always admire the exposed red clay escarpment favored by many potters. Continuing down the highway, passing Budaghers, the rich clay beds of the area again come to mind, here because they are now made inaccessible by the restrictions of private land ownership. At this point I become aware that I am sharing the highway with Santo Domingo cars pulling onto or off the highway. They remind me that although our highways crisscross the land, we remain but ephemeral visitors in the Pueblo world.

The Outsiders: Museum Expeditions to the Southwest

When museum-collecting expeditions first arrived at the Southwest pueblos in the late 1880s, they acquired relatively few wares at Cochiti and Santo Domingo. Usually, the reasons are assumed to be that in shopping for "traditional" wares, curators avoided Cochiti's curios, while Santo Domingo's reticence toward outsiders precluded collecting opportunities there. The resistance to outsiders, often referred to as Pueblo secrecy, may be less a cultural artifact born of ancient Pueblo traditions and more a historical artifact born of unpleasant experiences with Spanish and American outsiders. Along with the acquisition of cultural knowledge by outsiders, the acquisition of pottery by anthropologists, curators, collectors, dealers, and tourists may be interpreted as further inroads by the infrastructure supporting colonial domination and control, and just as intrusive and destructive as any rules or laws imposed from the outside.

On the other hand, consider an alternate way of thinking: that it is the strength of pottery production and its continued domestic use at both pueblos that prevented museums from amassing significant collections at Cochiti and to a greater degree at Santo Domingo. In 1879–1880, 125 pieces were collected from Cochiti and only 38 from Santo Domingo. Museum curators clearly met obstacles at Santo Domingo: early Smithsonian collections from the pueblo lack domestic use bowls and storage jars, a glaring omission given the numbers of these containers collected in later years by the American Museum of Natural History (1910–1916) and the Laboratory of Anthropology and Indian Arts Fund (1922–1935) (figs. 43–44). The strength of pottery in the two villages manifests itself as continued domestic use, whereas other pueblos primarily produced curios for sale. Also, limited acquisition excursions to the Southwest meant that eastern museum collections were typically built over a period of just a few years; furthermore, many museums collected conveniently, meaning they purchased from dealers in Albuquerque or Santa Fe, acquiring only the limited range of styles and ages of wares readily available. In contrast, curators at Santa Fe museums remained in continuous contact with the villages and the potters. As a result, over a period of more than a century, Santa Fe museums were a ready market as circumstances at the villages or in families allowed or necessitated the sale of pottery.

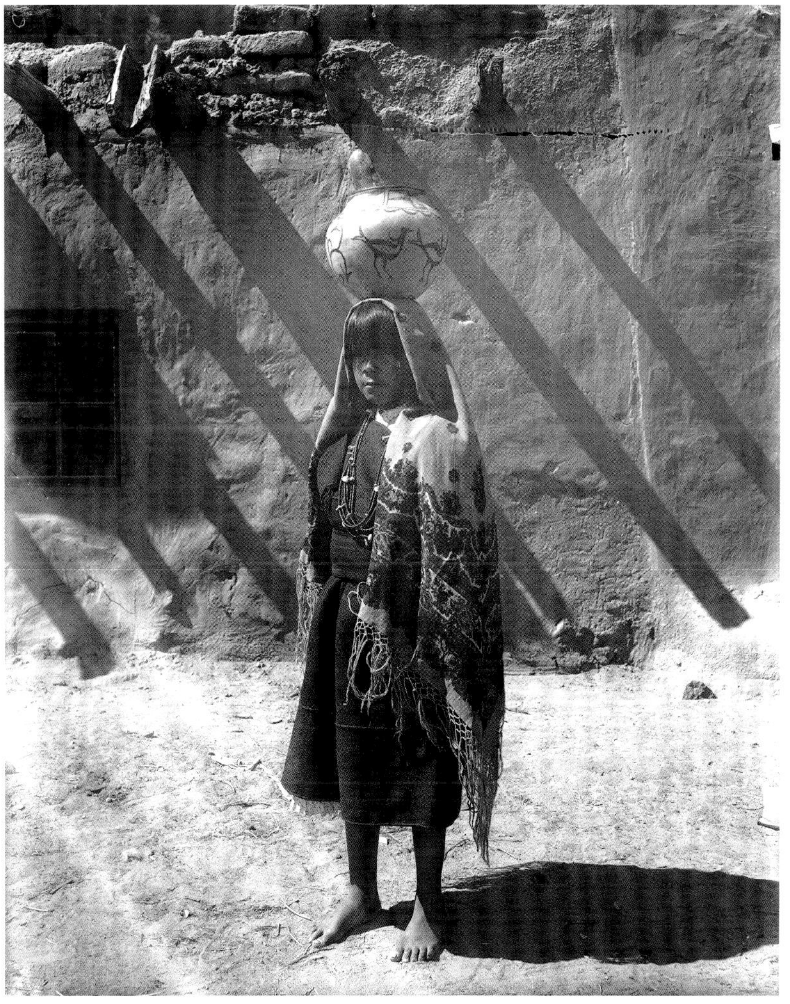

This Cochiti girl is still using a traditional Cochiti water jar, 1894–1910, suggesting continued traditional use of domestic pottery at the pueblo. George Pepper, photographer. Courtesy National Museum of the American Indian, Smithsonian Institution, N15746. Pottery jars were used to transport water from wells, cisterns, and large storage jars. Balancing a pot on top of the head was traditional for women.

The Outsiders: Indian Fair/Indian Market

Between 1900 and 1920, almost all Pueblo potters reformulated their wares for the marketplace. This adaptation resulted from the combination of incen-

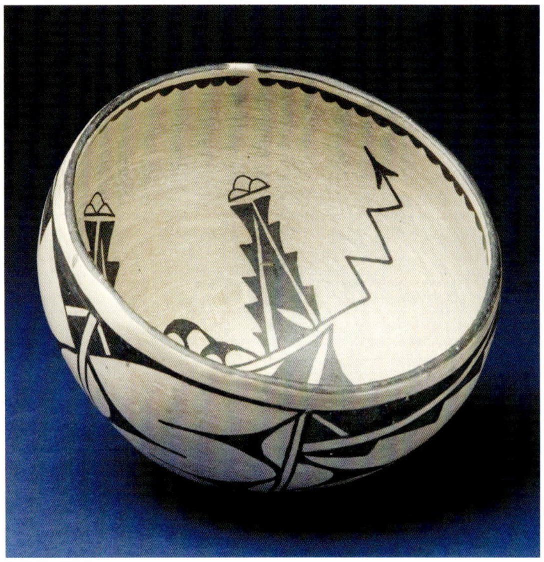

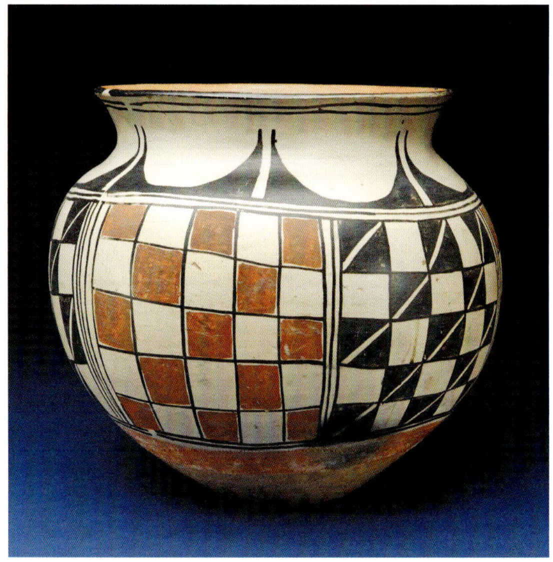

figure 45
Bowl
Cochiti
Ascension Chavez Benada
1933
13.8 x 22.2 cm

figure 46
Jar
Santo Domingo
Artist Unknown
ca. 1910–1920
30.3 x 34.2 cm

tives given to individual artists to end curio mass production and an increasing need for cash. Consequently, the first Indian Fairs (the antecedent of today's Indian Market) of the 1920s in Santa Fe showcased new styles, instead of the intended goal of building a market for traditional pottery (figs. 45–46). Few Santo Domingo potters participated in the markets until the 1970s, and Indian Fair organizers banned Cochiti's hallmark figurative pottery as a trader-introduced invention. It was not until the 1940s that awards were given to figurative pottery: Damacia Cordero won in the late 1940s, and in 1964 Cordero took first prize in sculpture and Seferina Ortiz second; in 1976 Ada Suina won second place for a drummer figurine; and in 1979 Ortiz took first place with a set of three drummers (figs.47–49). Contemporary Cochiti artist Virgil Ortiz, son of Seferina Ortiz, continues to push the boundaries and transform the non-Pueblo into Pueblo in his ceramic works as well as his fashion designs. One of Virgil Ortiz's first figurative pieces is in the museum's collections: At the suggestion of American ceramic artist and Pueblo pottery collector and dealer Rick Dillingham, Virgil Ortiz made a one-headed and four-armed figure based on a circa 1880 image (fig. 50).

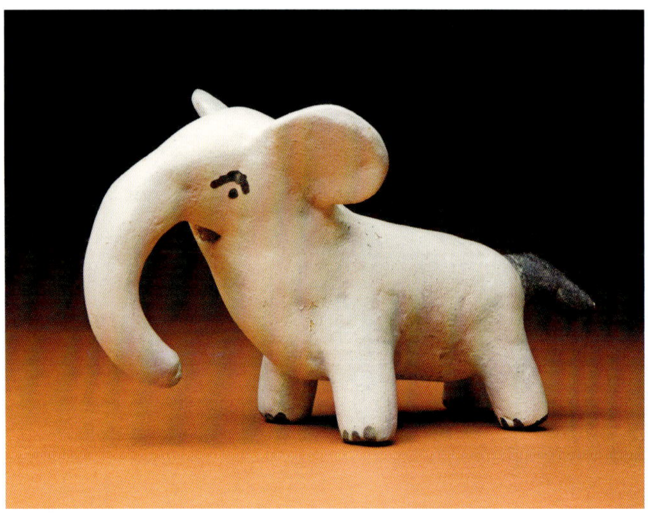

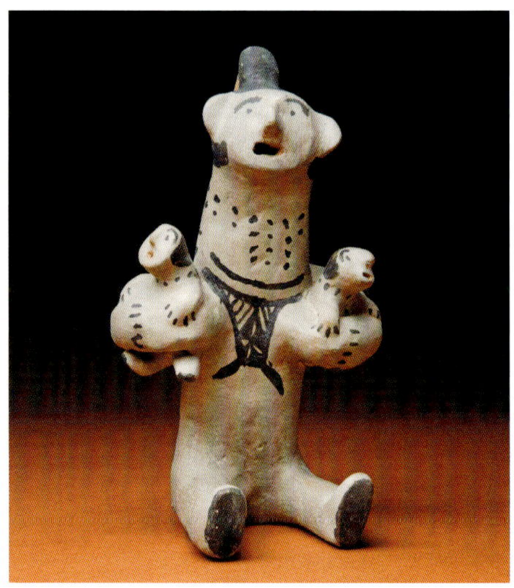

figure 47
Elephant Figurine
Cochiti
Damacia Cordero
ca. 1980
14.8 x 10.8 x 23.7 cm

figure 48
Singing Mother Figurine
Cochiti
Damacia Cordero
ca. 1985
24.1 x 13.6 x 11.5 cm

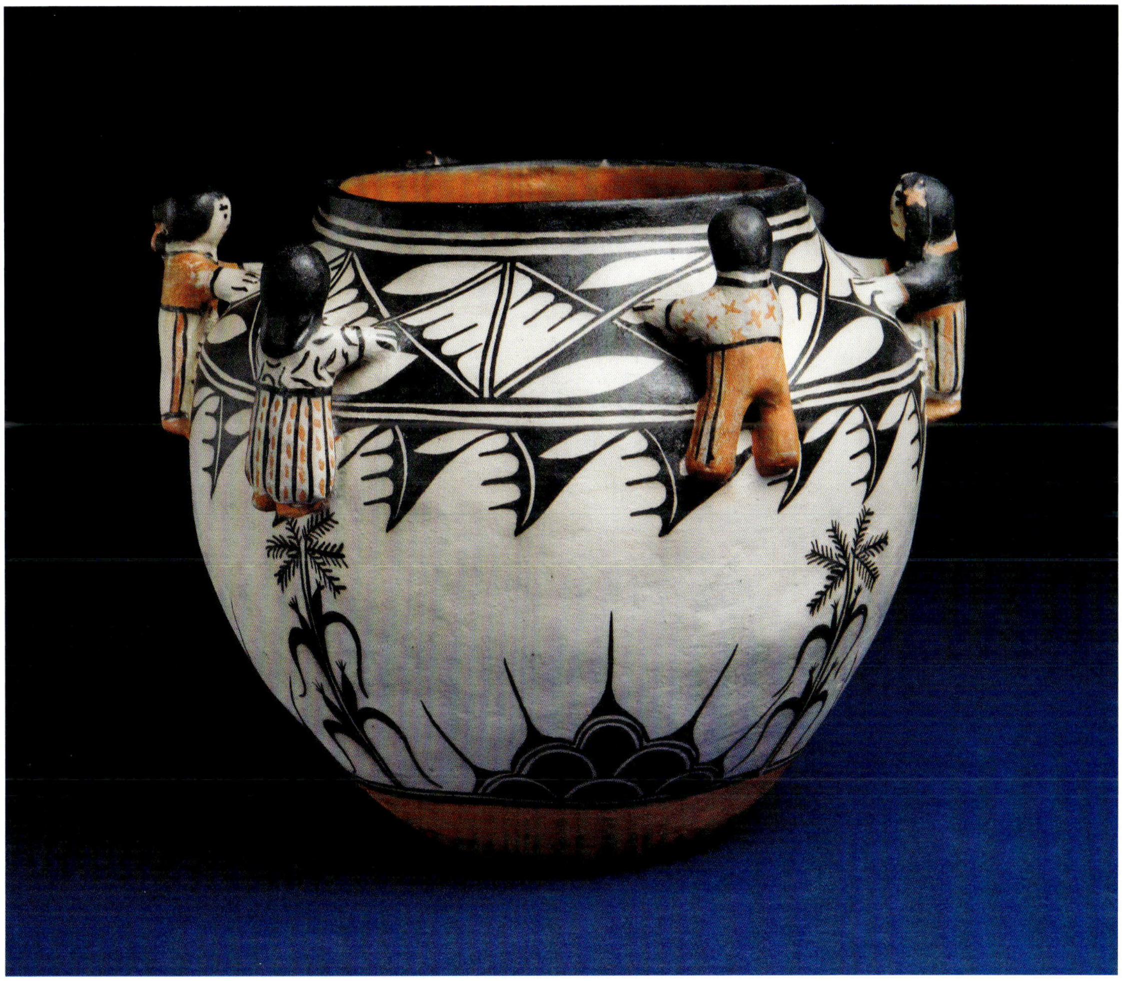

figure 49
Jar
Cochiti
Seferina Ortiz
ca. 1992–1997
20.0 x 25.3 cm

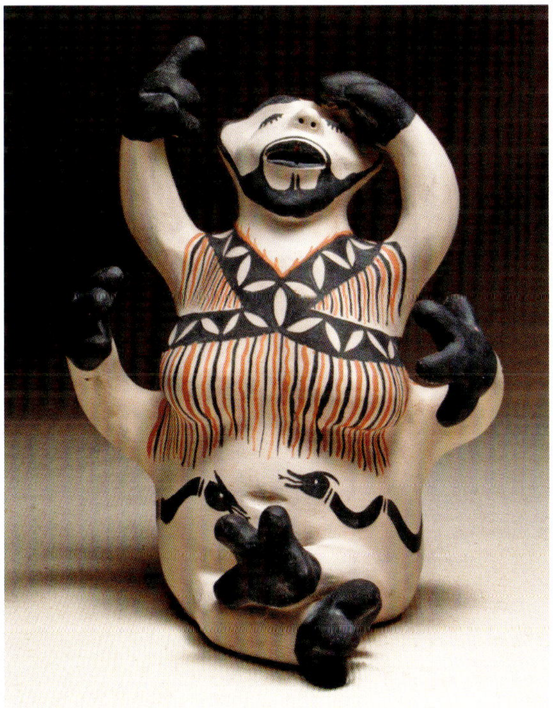

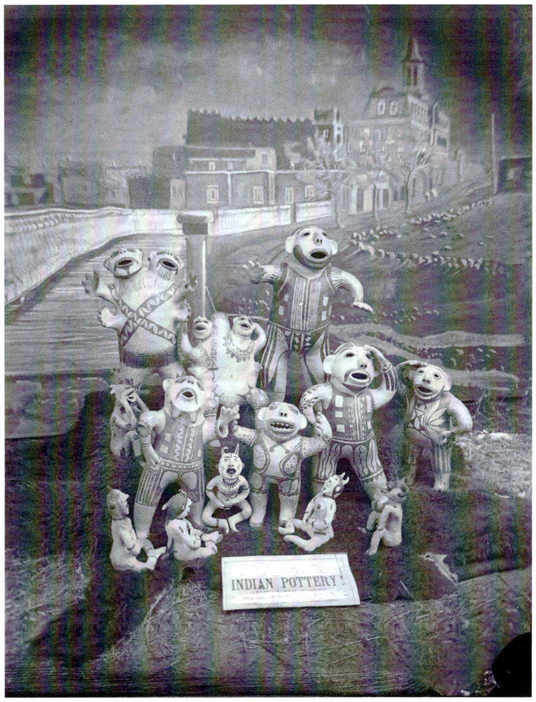

figure 50
Male Figurine
Cochiti
Virgil Ortiz
1989
28.4 x 27.5 x 21.1 cm

Cochiti figurines at Parker's Indian Trading Post, Albuquerque, 1885. Ben Wittick, photographer. Courtesy Palace of the Governors (MNM/DCA), 16293.

figure 51
Jar
Santo Domingo and Santa Clara
Monica Silva
1959
33.0 x 40.3 cm

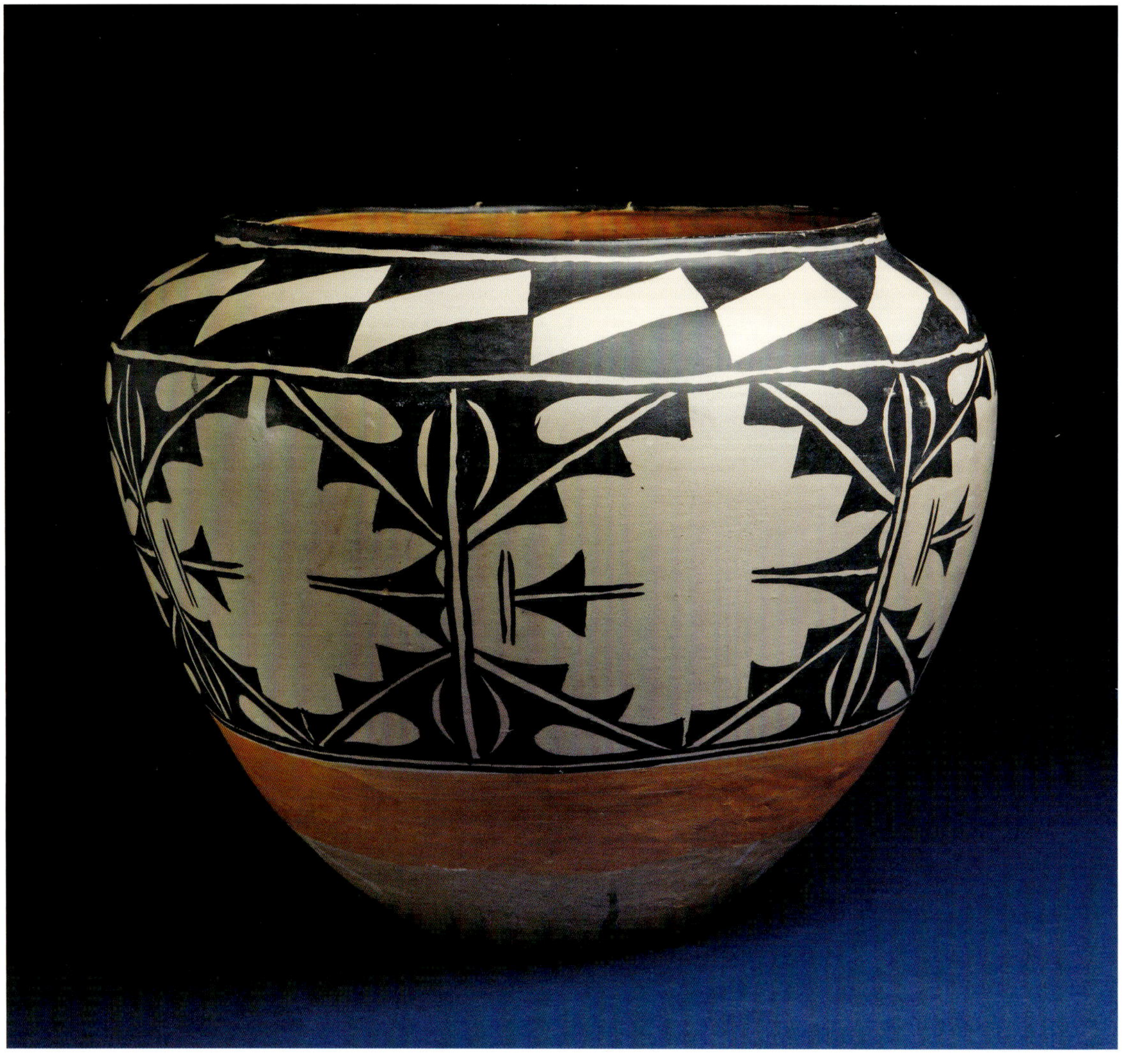

figure 52
Jar
Santo Domingo and Santa Clara
Monica Silva
ca. 1930
16.4 x 24.4 cm

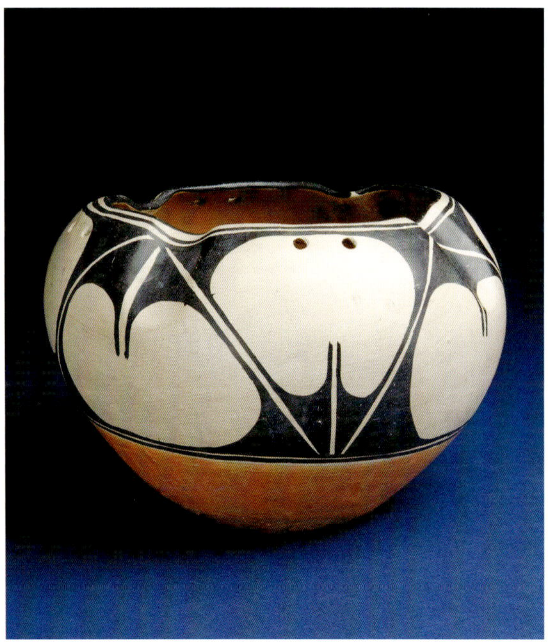

figure 53
Jar
Santo Domingo and Santa Clara
Monica Silva
ca. 1930
17.0 x 26.0 cm

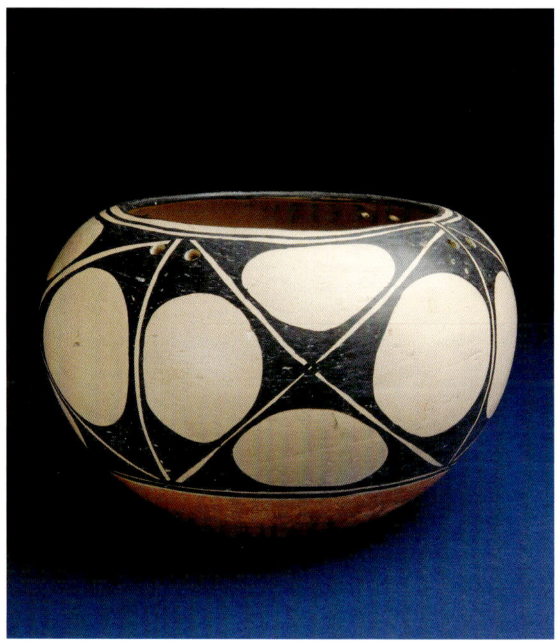

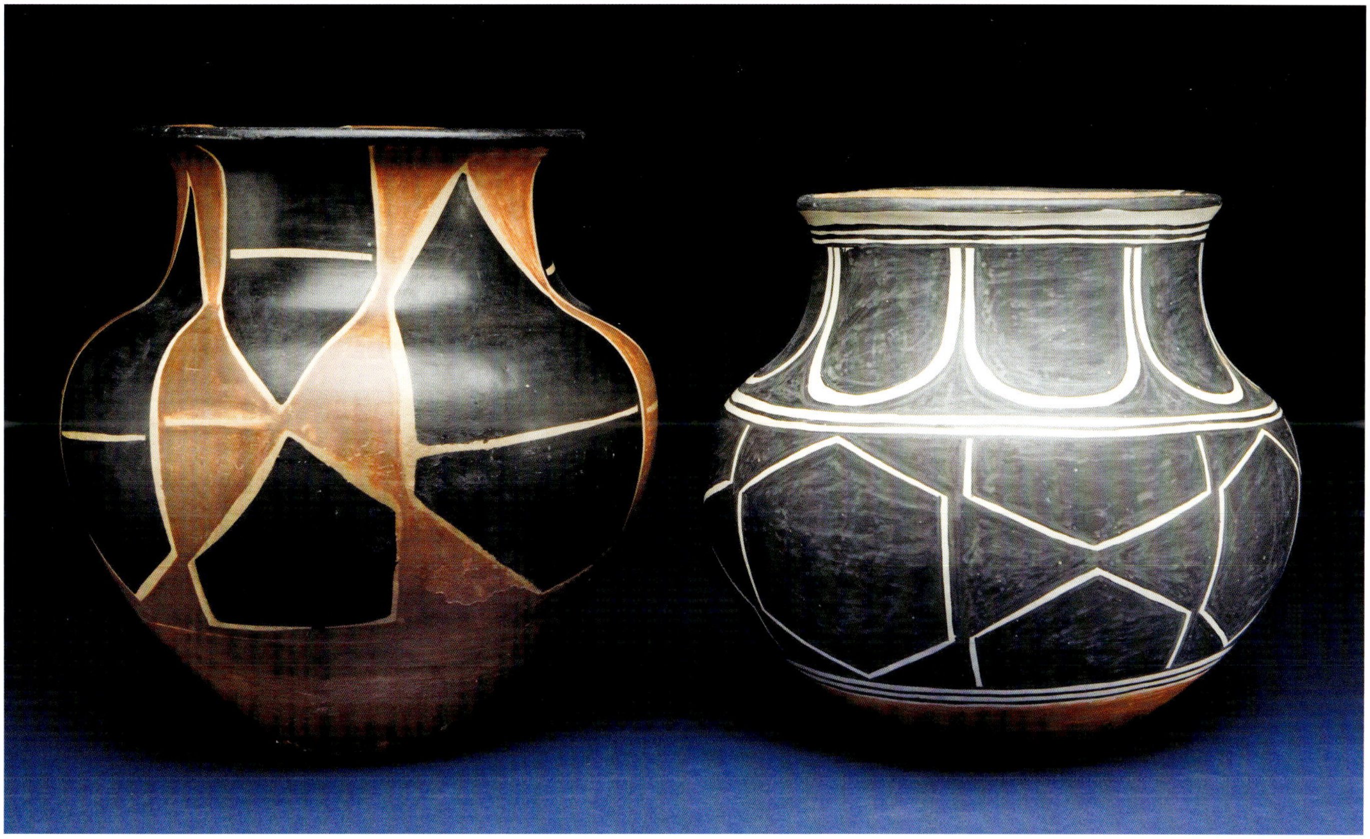

Given their reticence towards the outside world, it is not surprising that Santo Domingo was not well represented in the first Indian Fairs of the 1920s. Santo Domingo residents were discouraged from participating in the Santa Fe Fiesta and fairs: "It was against the wishes of the pueblo officials that these women came to the Fair, but last year a third potter risked the wrath of the elders, and after returning from the Fair with money from sales and prizes, and ribbons to prove her success, it may be possible that she scorned their wrath and will come back again next year with several of her sisters" (Halseth 1926:152). Monica Silva is the only Santo Domingo potter's name recorded through the first four years of Indian Fairs (1922–1925), when she is consistently listed as both the first and second prizewinner. In 1929, Chapman noted that there was "no worthy entry" for first prize; nonetheless, Silva, a Santa Clara woman who married into the village, won the second prize of three dollars (figs. 51–53). In 1926, Silva won first prize and Felipita Aguilar second. Aguilar was a member of the extended family that originated the "Reverse" or "Aguilar" style. By reversing traditional design colors, Aguilar and her sisters invented a dynamic and distinctive, but unmistakably Santo Domingo, pottery style. When the Cleveland Art Museum contacted the Museum of New Mexico to acquire examples of pottery in 1923–24, it was the work of Felipita Aguilar, her sister Asuncion Aguilar Cate, and their sister-in-law Mrs. Ramon Cate Aguilar that went to Cleveland. Their pottery also was purchased for the American Museum of Natural History, the Denver Art Museum, and the Laboratory of Anthropology. Upon the death of one of the sisters in 1925, production of this pottery style came to an end (Batkin 1987:99) (fig. 54).

figure 54
Reverse Ware Jars
Santo Domingo
Mrs. Ramon Cate Aguilar, ca. 1910–1915;
Santana Melchor, October 26, 1977
29.8 x 27.9 cm;
27.0 x 20.0 cm

Cochiti potters also were few in number at the early fairs, undoubtedly due to a misconception on the part of the fair's organizers that their spe-

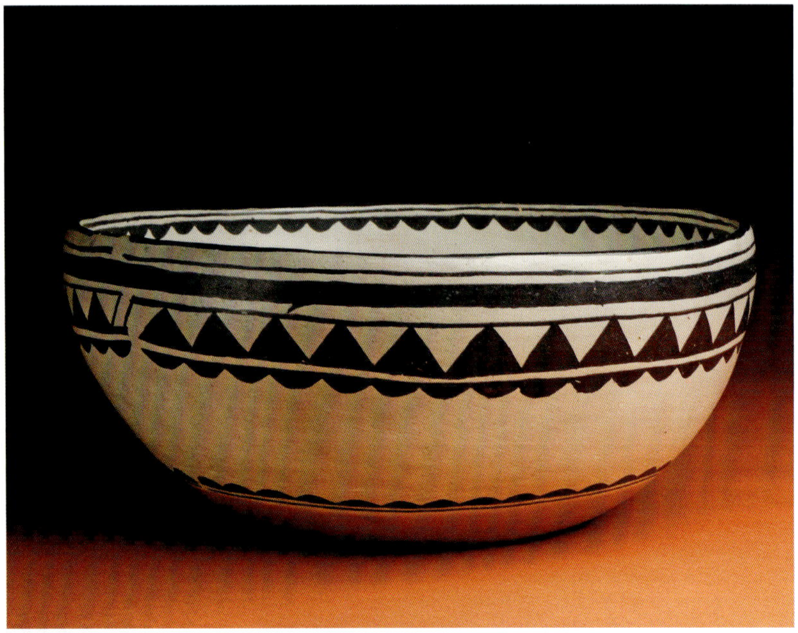

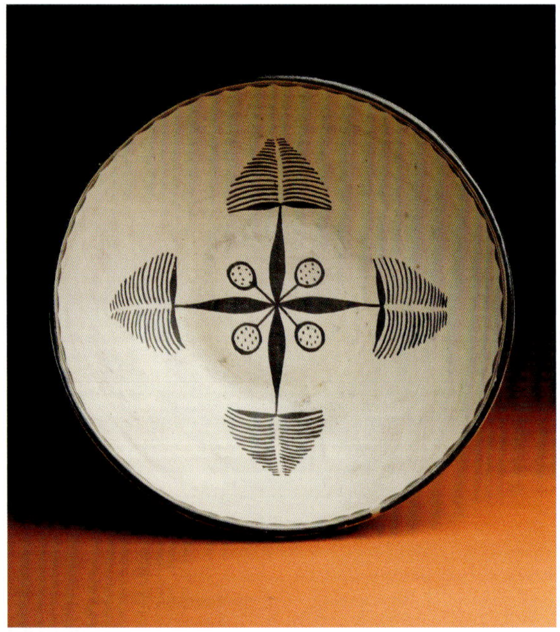

figure 55
Bowl (two views)
Cochiti
Ignacita Suina Arquero
ca. 1935
14.6 x 34.8 cm

figure 56
Jar
Cochiti
Estefanita Herrera
ca. 1950–1954
19.0 x 22.8 cm

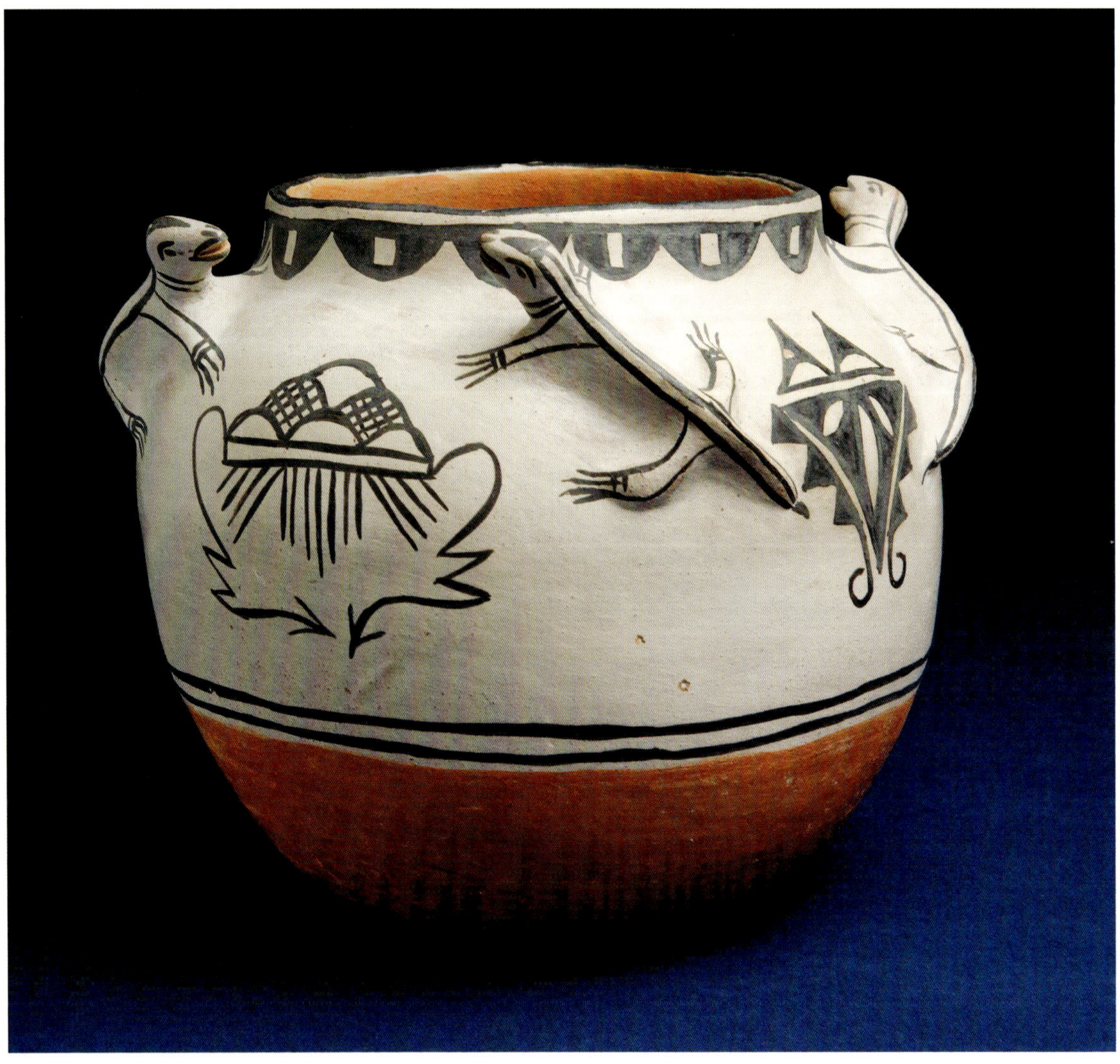

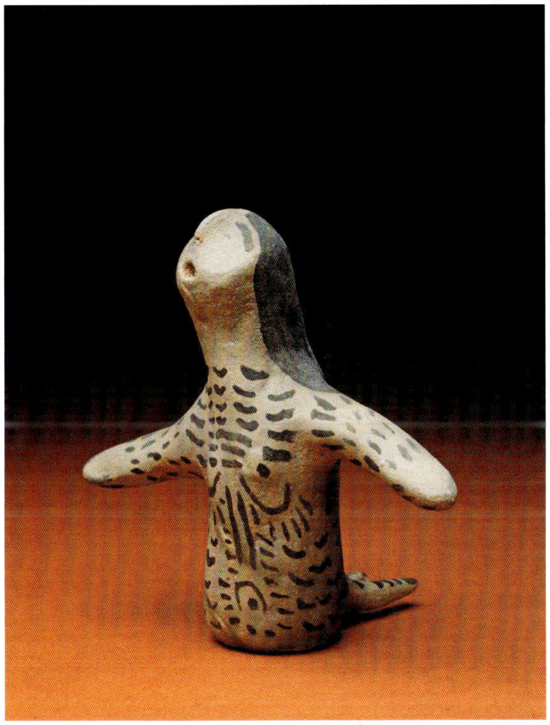

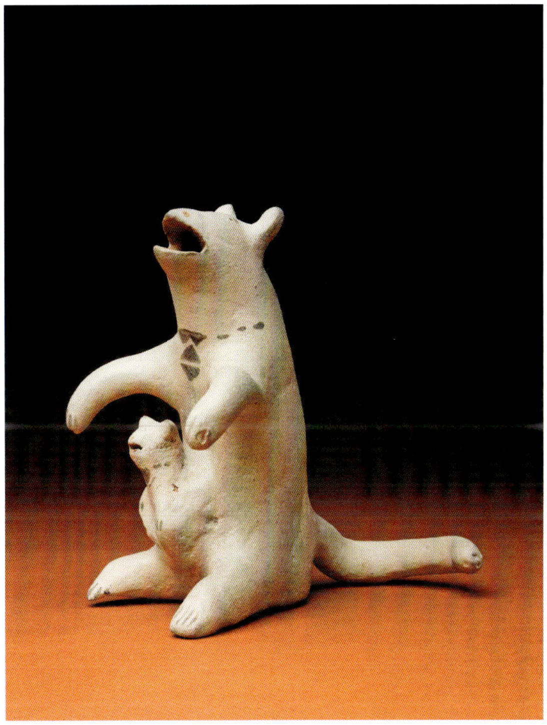

figure 57
Mermaid Figurine
Cochiti
Damacia Cordero
ca. 1985
17.3 x 17.9 x 10.3 cm

figure 58
Kangaroo Storyteller Figurine
Cochiti
Damacia Cordero
1987
18.4 x 15.5 x 9.5 cm

cialty, figurative pottery, was not traditional, but a curio market introduction. Nevertheless, early winners included Laurencita Herrera and Ignacita Suina Arquero (1922) (fig. 55), Merced Montoya (1923), Victoria Quintana (1926), and Lupita Chavez and Reyes Romero (1928). Estefanita Herrera would win her first prizes in the 1930s and would continue winning awards through the early 1950s (fig. 56). Later in the century, Helen Cordero would be credited with reviving Cochiti's figurative pottery traditions with her storyteller figurines (see figs. 25, 112); however, records indicate that Damacia Cordero entered figurines and won awards in the late 1940s (figs. 57–58), and Seferina Ortiz in 1964. While Cordero's own vision and artistic ability remain unquestioned, further research suggests her work is part of an already distinguished tradition. Appropriately, it was Seferina Ortiz's son Virgil who defied the overly precious jury and judging systems of Indian Market with his dynamic autobiographic creations of bisexuality and metrosexual fashion. In 2002, Virgil Ortiz mysteriously disappeared from Market to the hallow halls of the New York fashion industry, replaced by a series of posted handbills claiming him as MIA and daring readers to find him.

By the first outdoor modern Indian Market in 1936, a newspaper article reported that "Cochiti makes good drums, and will have all sizes. Indian drums are gay, and make a noise—also the large ones make handsome tea tables. A fine large one shown some weeks back will be exhibited again. Ignacia [Suina]—well famed for her model fireplaces—will be among the potters, and Tonita [Pena] (Quah-Ah), one of the best known Indian artists will be there with her pictures" (*New Mexican* August 1936). These are significant platitudes given that just the previous year, 1935, Amelia White and Kenneth Chapman reported that at Cochiti they "found the Arts and Crafts exhibition so disgracefully poor that we gave reprimands instead of prizes" (Chapman 1935). These critiques are about authenticity and the calcification of what constituted traditional pottery. At the same time, reports were that Santo Domingo pottery made for tourists was unfired and decorated with commercial paint and shoe polish. Collections do suggest that within one or two generations domestic Santo Domingo pottery shifted from principally for home use to made-for-sale. Perhaps the change was inevitable, but it is stunning in its swiftness and finality. Other than the obvious increasing reliance on cash to supplement agricultural products, there is not a good explanation for this sudden and seemingly complete change.

Conclusion: Artists and Outsiders

My personal experience with Pueblo pottery is both that of a museum professional and a consumer. In the larger museum world, my interaction is with pottery as objects of scholarly discourse sitting on shelves; as a consumer my interaction has been more personal. A number of years ago, I met a Santo Domingo man and his Acoma wife selling their pottery under the Palace of the Governors portal. We struck up an easy conversation talking about kids, pottery, and selling under the portal. They made classic Santo Domingo bowls to which they sometimes added Acoma concepts, and later a few things I showed them in the MIAC/LAB collections. My family home quickly filled with their sturdy and beautiful bowls, as did the homes of relatives who were the recipients of some of our bounty. What my family and I enjoy most is using the bowls for serving. Owning and using the bowls, I have come to

figure 59
Bowl
Santo Domingo
Santana and Dolorita Melchor
ca. 1975
7.1 x 18.7 cm

This bowl comes from the personal collection of Rick Dillingham. The oily residue on the interior indicates its use as a salad bowl.

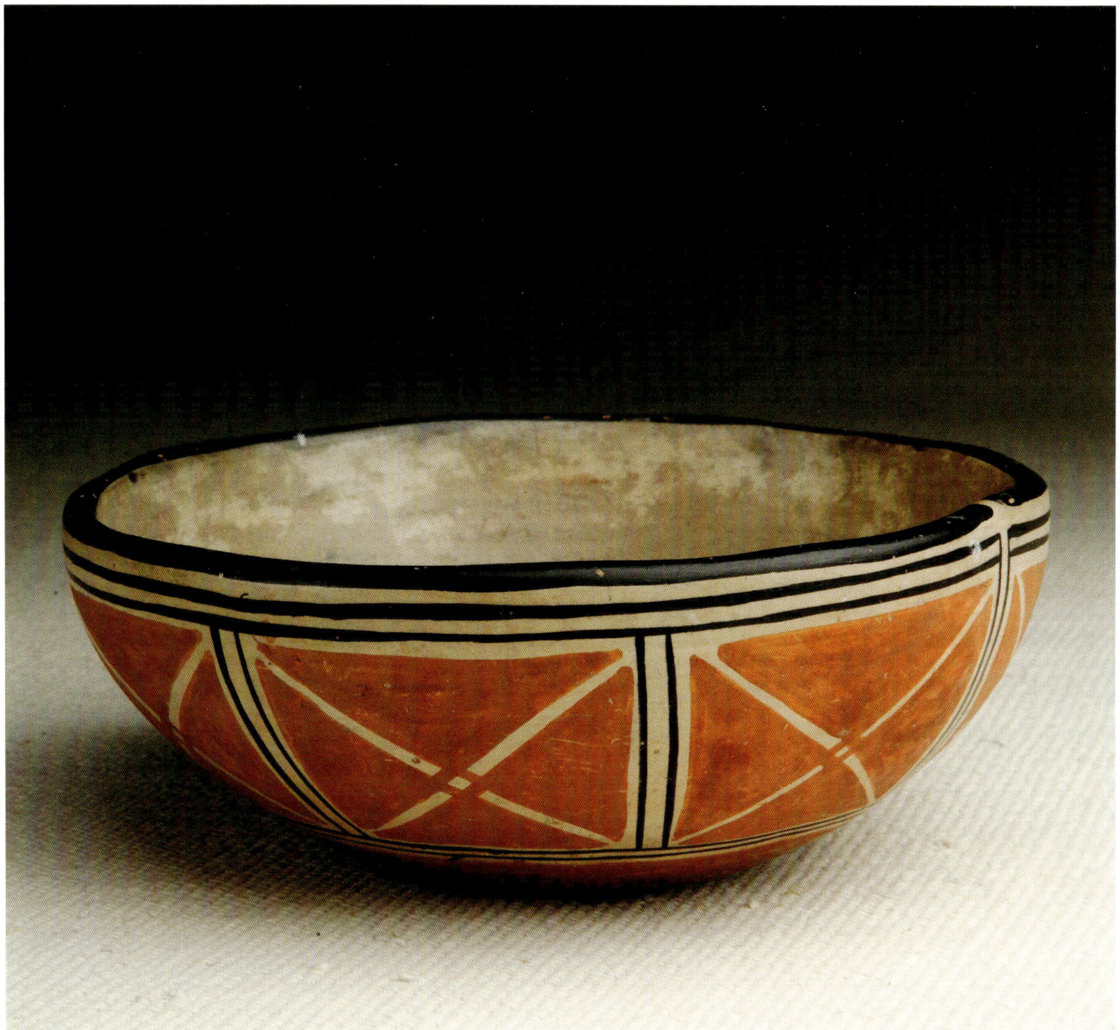

understand Pueblo pottery in different ways. Each use creates a memory and subtly alters the look, smell, and feel of the bowls (fig. 59).

More recently, my wife and I asked a young museum intern from New York City to join us on August 4 for Santo Domingo's feast day. He was studying pottery in the rarified atmosphere of a New York City museum, pondering its origins and researching ways to better preserve it. He gaped at the tables of pottery for sale that lined the pueblo's streets, but he was truly flummoxed by potter Robert Tenorio's home, both because of the bowls full of chile on the table, as well as the hundreds of pots that fill every surface of his home. The young man returned to his studies transformed by the experience. Tenorio and the thousands of people in the village that day obliterated his preconceived idea that pottery was something of the past. Now, when this intern is at work in his museum lab, he will remember the images of that day and the aliveness of Pueblo pottery. Now he knows that Pueblo pottery is always contemporary. Now he understands that buying and selling Pueblo pottery is dealing in a commodity of consciousness.

SECTION II

Perspectives

In the beginning Itc'tinaku considered how the people should live. She said to herself, "My old father and my old mother must go down to the people and be Clay (mitsi) Old Woman and Clay Old Man." In Shipap she made the old man and woman into Clay Old Woman and Clay Old Man. The old woman began to mix the clay with sand and soften it with water. When she had finished she made it into a ball and wrapped it in a white manta. She began to coil and pot with her clay, and Clay Old Man danced beside her singing while she worked. All the people gathered in the village and watched her all day long. When she had made her pots so high (about eighteen inches) and the old man was singing and dancing beside her, he kicked it with his foot and it broke in many pieces. The old woman picked up his stick and chased him all around the plaza. She overtook him in the middle of the kiva. They made friends again and she took the broken pot and rolled it into a ball again. The old man took the pot and gave a piece of it to everybody in the village. They each took it and made pottery as Clay Old Woman had made it. This was the time they learned to make pottery. Clay Old Man told them never to forget to make pottery. In those days they only indented it with the marks of their fingers. Ever since when we do not make pottery these two masked dancers come with the dance to remind us of the clay they gave to the people. They tell us not to forget our grinding stones and always to grind our own corn flour.

Collected at Cochiti Pueblo by Ruth Benedict, 1924.

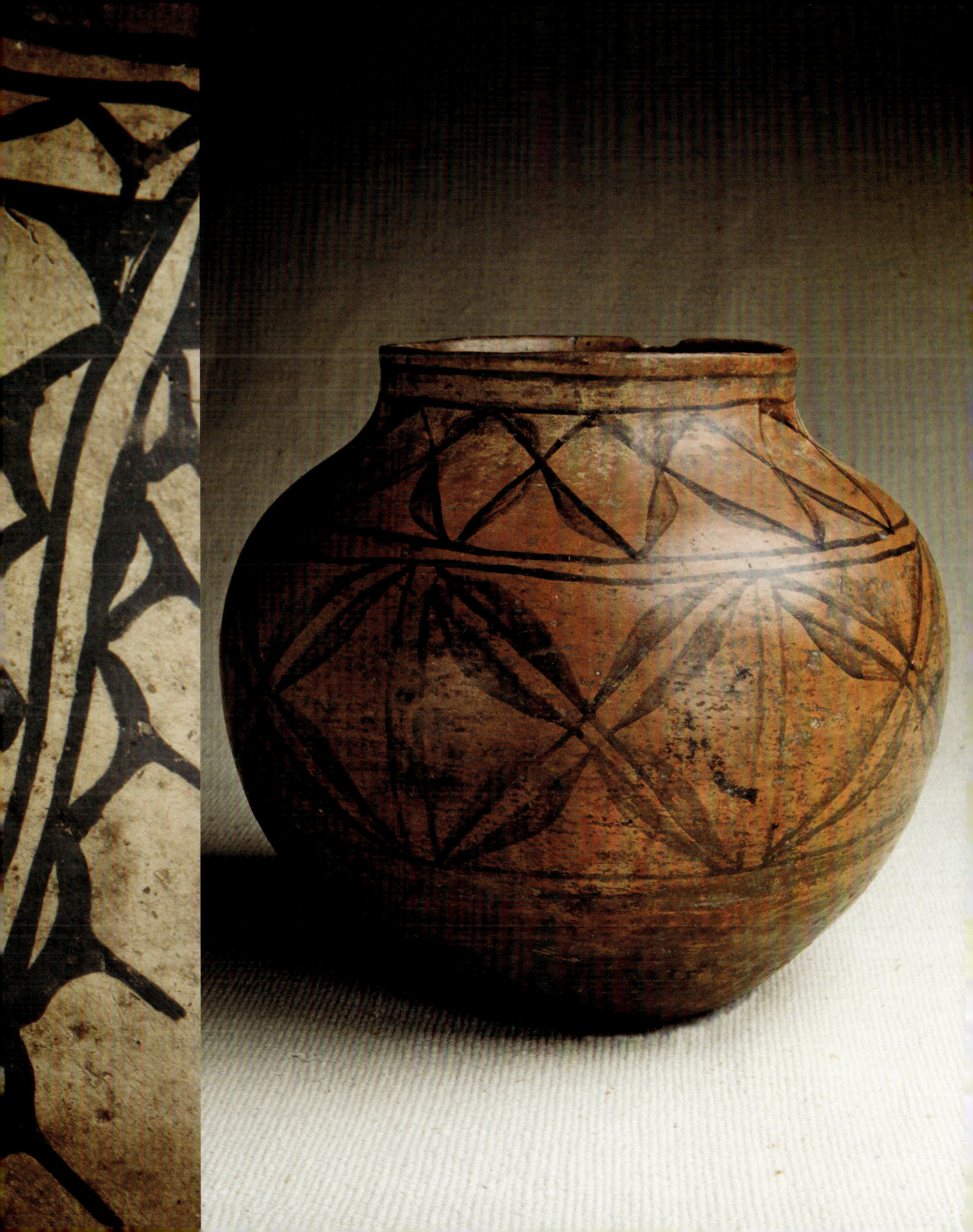

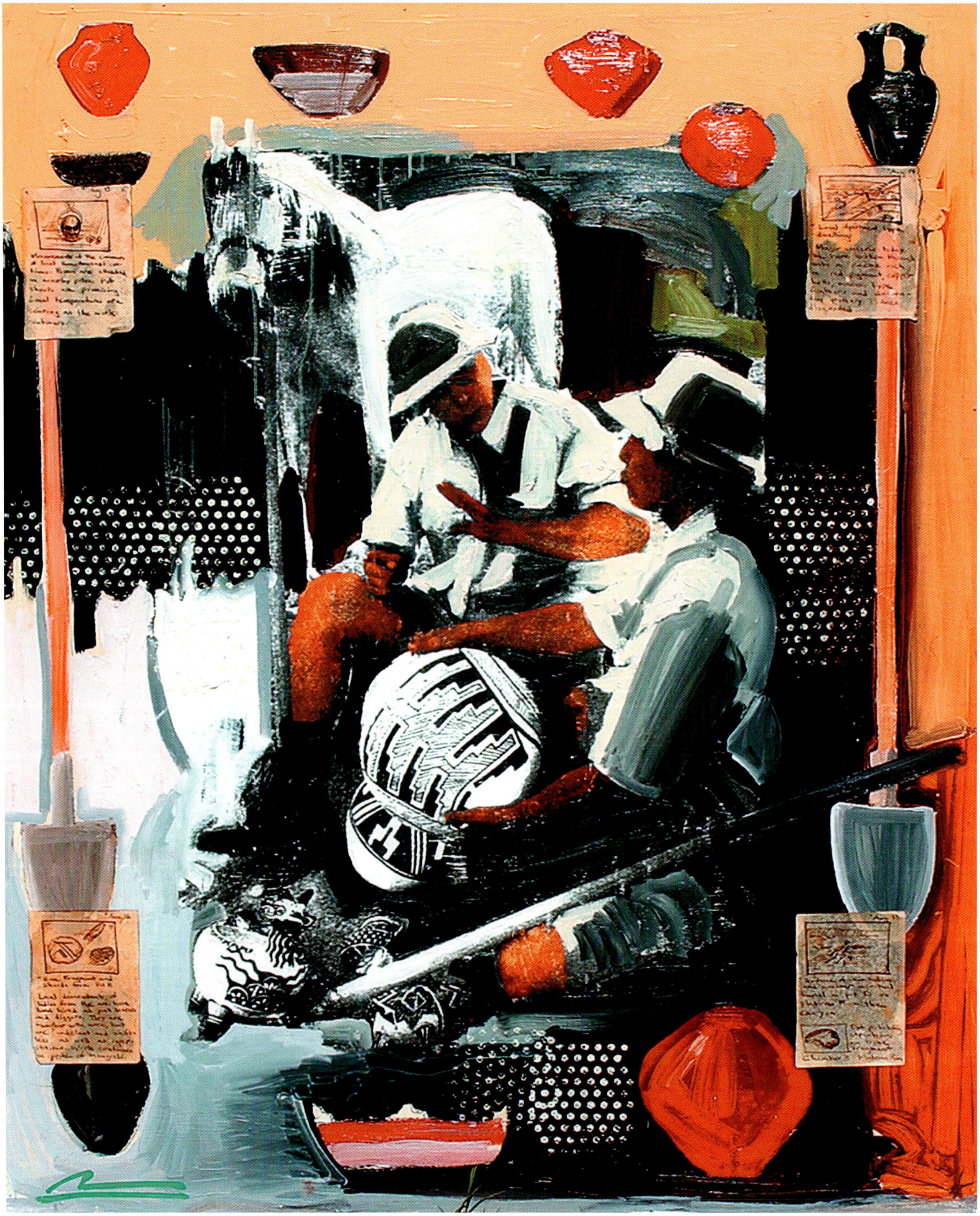

Pot Hunters/ Pray for Rain

Mateo Romero

"Pot Hunters" is the title of a series of paintings I began in 2002. The central theme of these paintings is the greed and avarice of people who defile ruins and graves in pursuit of the holy grail of southwestern archaeology: Mimbres and Ancestral Pueblo pottery. While Native belief systems hold that ancestral ruins, the dead, and the materials associated with their internment are sacred, the modern-day pot hunter's creed holds nothing too personal or important to halt desecration by bulldozer for quick, enormous cash profits. This state of affairs is not unique to the Southwest but occurs everywhere Western colonizers encounter indigenous peoples. How do we honor the spirit of our dead grandfathers and grandmothers between their sacred burial ground and the blade of the bulldozer?

Pot Hunters #2 represents the culmination of the "Pot Hunters" series to date. The central figures are my brother Diego Romero and me dressed as faux circa 1900 archaeologists. Surrounding us is a series of Mexican pots painted to mimic Ancestral Pueblo historic pottery. In the background, Tewa sculptor Roxanne Swentzell's horse Toucha poses as a pack animal. The pot hunters are feverishly discussing the latest priceless artifacts they have pillaged from ancestral ruins. Around the edges of the picture plane are pre-orgasmic depictions of the pots they so desperately desire to uncover. Faux archaeological journal-entry pages, collaged at the four cardinal points, communicate disparaging racist commentaries about the Native laborers working at the dig, and the objects of Native culture uncovered.

My uncle from Cochiti, a fetish carver and distinguished artist in his own right, once told me a story of how he made faux Rosetta stones and gave them to archaeologists on a dig at the village, along with a tall tale about their discovery. It is this sense of humor about the whole state of affairs that keeps us going; however, some incidents are just too disturbing. One such incident involved the Cochiti lion shrines at the site of Potrero de Los Idolos in Bandelier National Monument, a sacred site just beyond Cochiti. Archaeologists from the University of New Mexico removed one of the lion shrines (carved from several tons of rock) from the site and put it on display at their museum. The Cochitis lob-

Mateo Romero (Cochiti)
Pot Hunters #2, 2002.
Oil and collage on panel,
122 x 30.5 cm.
Photo-transfer image, Jennifer Esperanza; Phillip Karshis, photographer.
School for Advanced Research, 2006–7.1, gift of Ronald N. and Susan Dubin.

previous spread:
figure 60
Jar
Keresan Polychrome
Artist Unknown
ca. 1850
23.6 x 26.9 x 22.8 cm

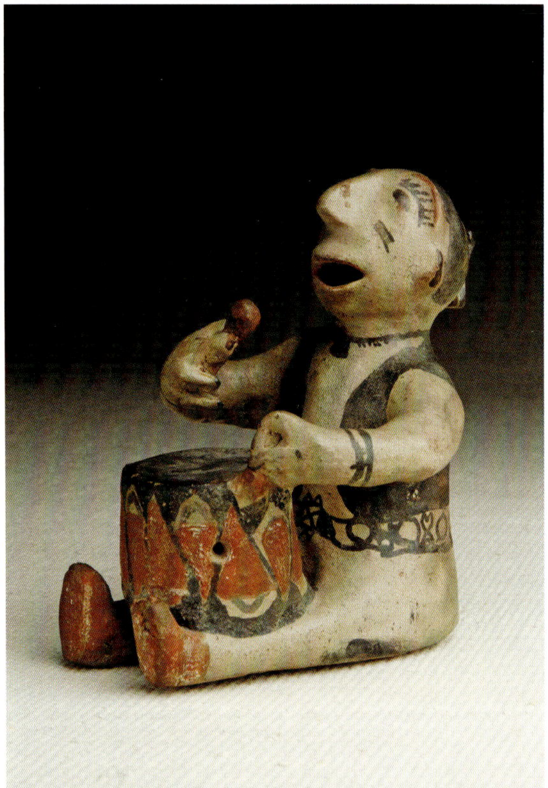

figure 61
Singing Drummer Figurine
Cochiti
Teresita Romero
ca. 1945
13.9 x 9.8 x 12.6 cm

bied for its return, succeeded, and watched the lion be transported back by helicopter *in situ*, one foot breaking as it was lowered to its earth-navel of origin. Another incident concerns a stone petroglyph of a Medusa-like head, which I saw as a young boy in Witch's Cave above Cochiti Dam, being cut out of the rock and probably sold into a private collection. Also gone missing are the Giant's pots, two large vessels carved out of the face of a stone outcropping. Has a collector appropriated these pieces of indigenous heritage, or did they just take a look around and head out on their own for a better time, a better place? This is part of the conundrum of my time, the rapacity of consumption and the speed at which we destroy the past to create a lackluster, frame-housed, linoleum-tiled future. One of my professors at the University of New Mexico, Dr. J. J. Brody, would say that we are complicit in destroying our father's songs to make our own.

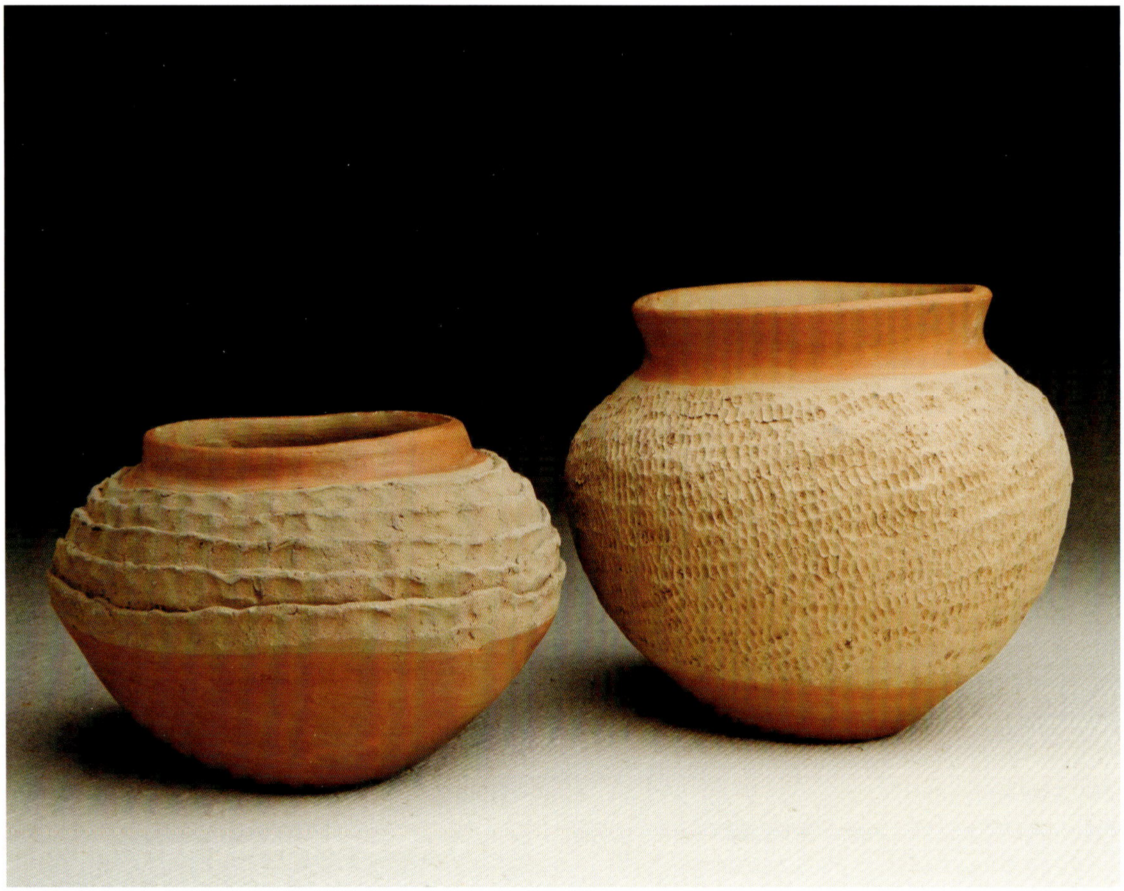

figure 62
Corrugated Jars
Cochiti
Teresita Romero
ca. 1950–1957
12.0 x 17.0 cm; 15.7 x 18.0 cm

Family

Most indigenous people I know are engaged in a process of cultural diaspora and return; we search for experience and meaning beyond our birth culture, while maintaining the core ideologies that are quintessentially Puebloan. My father, Santiago Romero, was born at Cochiti Pueblo to Keres-speaking parents who were active participants in the ceremonial life of the village. He grew up in a time when Pueblo kids in the village still hunted deer, made pilgrimages with their fathers to the shrines, fished and swam in the Rio Grande, honed their field craft, and developed patience. Dad, though, was an iconoclast. A product of the Bureau of Indian Affairs boarding school experience at the Santa Fe Indian School and later the Marine Corps, my father's view of himself was ethnically and culturally challenged. His search for self ultimately led him to Berkeley, California, in the 1960s, and to my mother.

My grandmother and brother chose the path of potters (figs. 61–62). Teresita Romero was a noted Cochiti Pueblo pottery revivalist. I believe that her amazingly gestural beeplant lines, eccentric vessel shapes, appliquéd lizards, painted turkeys, human life forms, and voluptuous plants are the most direct source of the art that flows through me. My brother, Diego Romero, is also an extraordinary potter and the author of monthly neo-Mimbres-inspired comic strips that have emerged on the inside of his pots for more than two decades (see fig. 37).

My father Santiago and I chose to be painters. Dad was an accomplished three-dimensional watercolorist at a time when Dorothy Dunn was teaching a flat, two-dimensional ethnographic style of painting at the Santa Fe Indian School. The Dunn School style—usually executed in opaque watercolor paint on illustration board—featured high-craft aestheticism and the depiction of scenes of "untouched" Native life, dance, and ceremonialism. When I was a child, my grandmother Cornelia saw a public television program on Dartmouth College's Native American Studies Program. I matriculated to Dartmouth in 1985. There I studied with noted painter Ben Frank Moss and construct master Varujan Boghosian. I received my Master of Fine Arts degree from the University of New Mexico, where I was privileged to study with José Rodriguez, Lydia Madrid, Alfonso Ortiz, J. J. Brody, and the artists at the Tamarind Institute.

The quintessentially Puebloan act of concealment has existed for centuries as a survival mechanism, but I believe we shouldn't hide anymore, that it is too late to hide. I believe in an honest, open, and cathartic attitude toward problems in Indian country. In the spring of 1992, my MFA thesis exhibit was a series of paintings about the dysfunctional elements of Native communities—domestic violence, gambling, addiction, and fetal alcohol syndrome. The paintings are about breaking the collective taboo, of breaking the silence maintained for the last five hundred years of bare existence and talking about healing and growth in the present.

Although I am from Cochiti Pueblo, I live with my wife Melissa Talachy, an accomplished contemporary Pueblo potter, in her village of Pojoaque Pueblo. In more conservative Pueblo social conventions, the wife usually follows the husband to his village, assuming his clan affiliations and status. But Pojoaque is where I feel most at ease, with my wife and children. On a good day, the kids are at school, my wife is working on her pottery, and I am painting the landscape just outside my door.

Survival

If you are a Native person in this time and place, you are the survivor of five hundred years of cold, hunger, lethal disease, and bullets. You live in a country that has dreamed about and hungered after your death in many stark and violent ways. Now there is a brief break in this pattern as the country turns to-

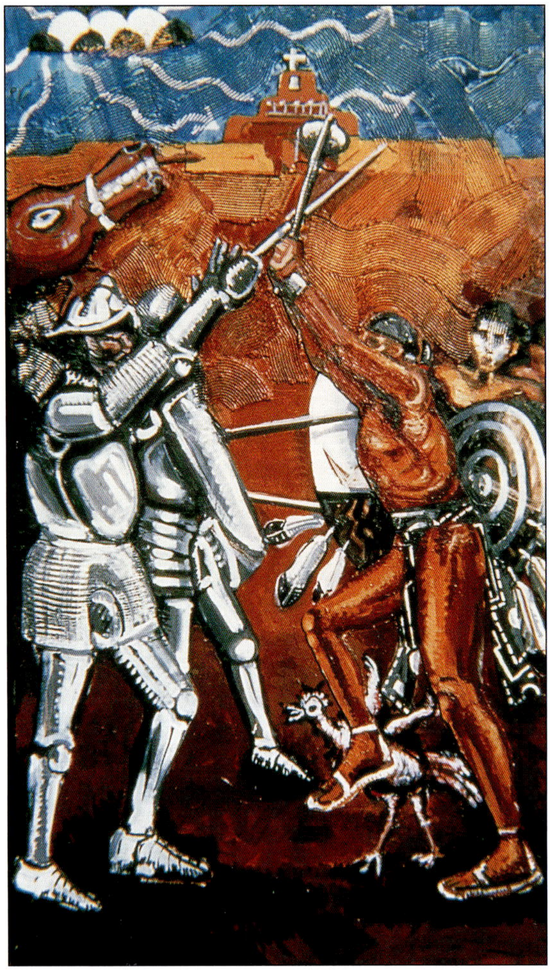

Mateo Romero (Cochiti) Pueblo Revolt Series #1, 1992. *Acrylic on gator board, 122 x 182.9 cm*

ward newly perceived threats and terrors, towards other dark-skinned people to hate.

This pattern of oppression began to take form in 1540 with the Spanish *conquistadores*. The picture of Pueblo life under the Spanish is one of the persecution and mutilation of Pueblo medicine people, physical and sexual bondage of Pueblo women, *encomienda/repartimiento* peonage of Pueblo farmers, and senseless brutality. Dominating this picture is religious persecution, compulsory conversions to Catholicism, and the imposition of European ideology. In the wake of this enforced change—our names, our religions, our very souls—the Pueblo world erupted in armed conflict.

The year is 1680. Popé, a religious leader from Ohkay Owengeh (San Juan Pueblo)—along with forty-six other respected medicine men—has been captured by the Spanish, imprisoned in Santa Fe, tortured, and finally released. To the horror of the Pueblo world, four of the imprisoned men are taken to the plaza, where they are hung by the neck until dead. Sequestered at Taos Pueblo, Popé begins planning one of the only successful indigenous revolutions mounted against a European colonial power.

Two knot-keepers run from village to village along the Rio Grande, leaving a yucca cord tied in knots at each. They also carry a message: At the end of each day, untie one knot. When all the knots are untied, the revolution begins. For safety, a secret message is embedded in the first—three days *before* the last knot is untied, the revolution begins. At Dry Spot (present-day Tesuque) the knot-keepers are captured. At this point in the run they are Tesuque youths, Catua and Omtua. They are strong, fast, beautiful, favorites of the young girls in the village. They are taken to Governor Antonio de Otermin in Bead Water (present-day Santa Fe); they are interrogated. Catua and Omtua are taken to the plaza, where they are hung by the neck until dead. They are only about seventeen years old, and they die in the power of their youth.

On August 10, 1680, the outlying districts of Bead Water are sacked by Keres and Tewa war captains and their troops. On August 13, Northern and Southern Pueblo armies link up at Bead Water. Twenty-five hundred Pueblo warriors descend on the one hundred fifty soldiers and one thousand civilians. The Pueblo war cry is "God and Santa Maria are dead!" The Spanish defenses are broken, and they retreat to Mexico. Santa Fe becomes Bead Water, *tierra india*, once again and remains so for twelve years, until the Spanish reconquest. The Palace of the Governors is occupied by Pueblo Indians. Four sacred kiva spaces are built on the four corners of the plaza, and sacred dances and ceremonies, once forbidden by the Spanish, are performed again.

Commodification

Some experiences are culturally unique and do not translate into other cultural perspectives or experiences. A common perception about and among contemporary Native people is that the historic, frozen-in-time, archaeological/ethnographic experience of their ancestors, grandparents, mothers, and fathers is more authentic, inherently real, and culturally relevant than their own current experience. This skewed perspective is emphasized by the mainstream world at many points, particularly in the value they assign to the past, to "museum-quality" Indian artifacts, and to staged and calcified imagery. As Bruce Bernstein points out, a more complex approach to the contemporary indigenous experience acknowledges that Native communities have been interacting throughout time with other communities—both Native and non-Native—in a state of cultural synergy, idea exchange, technology exchange, and flux.

Route 66 is a painting about the commodification of traditional Native culture, about the consumption of traditional Native systems of thought, value, and culture by modernity, technology, and the culture of tourism. On the left side of the painting, a Tewa woman butterfly dancer is performing the intricate motions of her dance. On the right side, an oncoming steam train rushes forward, threatening to overwhelm the dancer and the viewer. In the upper left quadrant, a neo-kitsch sign from the Chief's Inn in Española, New Mexico, fires an arrow. In the bottom right quadrant, the Route 66 logo is placed over a sketch of a Route 66 map.

This all brings us to the question of the indigenous artist's role in the vibrancy of culture. As an artist I am able to capture moments in time and place—sunrises and sunsets, war and love, hot and cold, Summer and Winter clans, and Pueblo dances that signify life, fertility, rain, abundant harvest, rebirth.

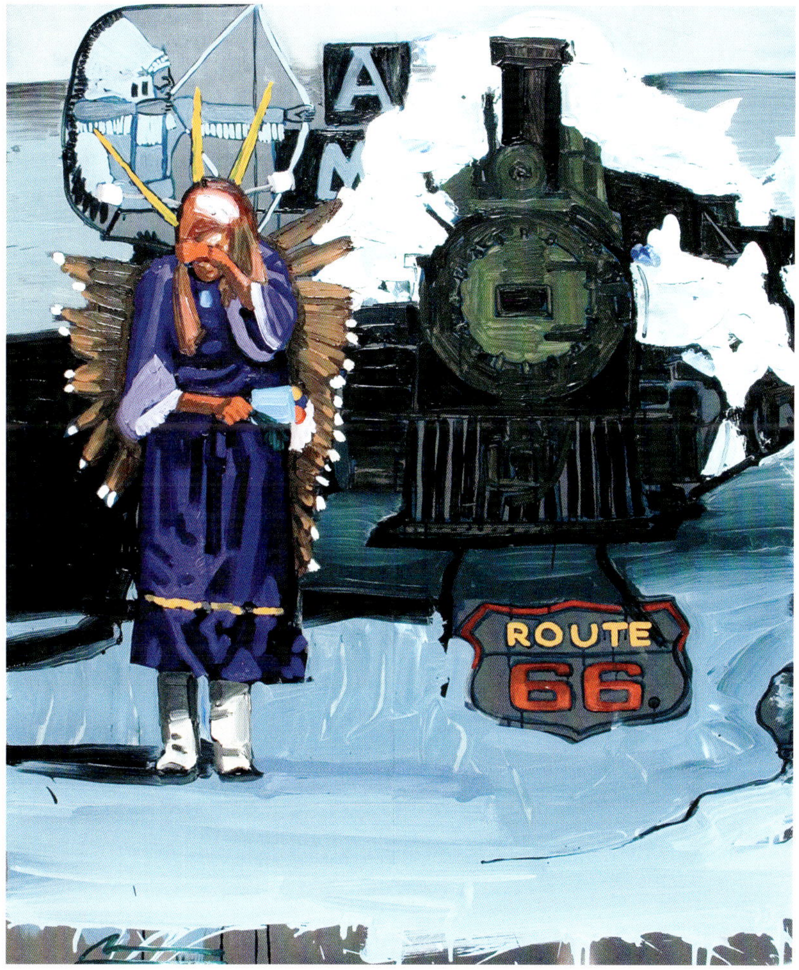

Mateo Romero (Cochiti) Route 66, 2002. *Oil and acrylic on aluminum flashing on panel, 122 x 152.4 cm. Courtesy Poeh Museum, Pojoaque, NM. Phillip Karshis, photographer.*

In my opinion, political and social activists engage in acts of civil disobedience to change some of the world's problems. Artists tend to make artwork about political activists for purposes of self-promotion and access, apparently without any tangible positive change in the world. Finally, the purpose of a painting is not to tell the viewer what to think or to do but to prompt the viewer to think and to form their own opinions about the artwork, about the actions depicted, about what it means to them. Some things just have to be experienced on your own. A basic structural precept in Puebloan ideology is that as long as rain falls, crops continue to grow, fertility is encouraged, and life harbors the possibility of balance. Pray for rain.

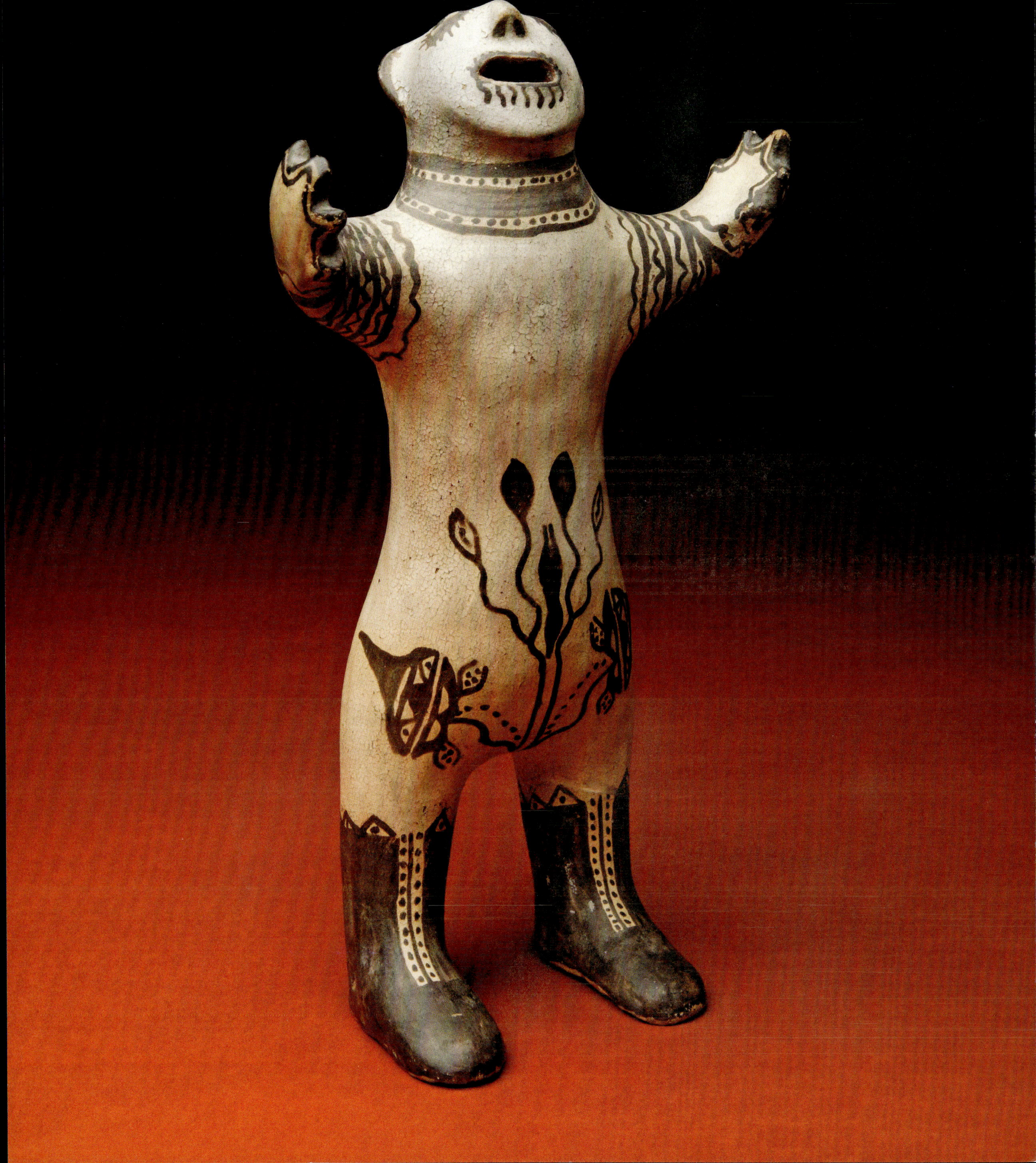

The Anomalous Painted Pottery of Santo Domingo and Cochiti Pueblos

A Brief History

J. J. Brody

The Painted Pottery of Cochiti and Santo Domingo Pueblos

Keresan is one of six distinct native languages spoken by the Pueblo Indian people of New Mexico and Arizona. Cochiti and Santo Domingo are among the seven Keresan-speaking pueblos, all but one of which, San Felipe, still have active pottery-painting traditions. Those are the most northerly of the Keresan communities, and their relative isolation may partially explain why their painted pottery is notably different from that of the other Keresan towns: Santa Ana, Zia, Laguna, and Acoma. Each of the others is noted for a different variant of a white-slipped red and black painted ware that is often graced by fanciful curvilinear bird, flower, and feather motifs interacting within well-defined picture spaces. By contrast, the paintings on Cochiti and Santo Domingo pottery tend to use static, black-on-cream pictorial units that favor visually ambiguous angular, geometric positive-negative abstractions.

In many respects, this anomalous Keresan tradition more closely resembles the painted pottery of eighteenth- and nineteenth-century northern Rio Grande Tewa-speaking pueblos than it does that of any other Keresan tradition, past or present. Still, all three of those pictorial modes fit neatly within a generic Puebloan pottery-painting esthetic and demonstrate how that esthetic works as a self-renewing mechanism. I examine that esthetic as well as some historical and geographical factors that may explain when, why, and how the anomalous northern variation of it developed. In passing, I also speculate about when, why, and how its Tewa prototypes were so modified in later times as to become virtually invisible.

Painted Pottery in the Pueblo World: An Overview

Prototypes for traditional painted pottery made in recent centuries at all pueblos are deeply buried in the collective pottery-painting traditions of the southwestern Pueblo Indian past. Everywhere, uniquely recognizable pottery paintings were, and are, created that are expressive of ancient Puebloan

figure 63
Male Figurine
Cochiti
Artist Unknown
ca. 1890–1900
28.6 x 16.3 x 7.0 cm

aesthetic philosophies modified over time by local histories and conditions. Puebloan people began painting their pottery about 1,500 years ago on the Colorado Plateau of the northern Southwest and, from the beginning, were guided by the aesthetic principles of more ancient arts. Over time, countless regional pottery-painting stylistic variations developed, each with its own temporal, historical, cultural, technical, and idiosyncratic dimensions. But, as at Santo Domingo and Cochiti, those variations almost always expressed and were structured by the over-arching pan-Pueblo aesthetic philosophy. That philosophy as it applies to pottery paintings is described below, and its principles still provide the intellectual foundation for many modern Pueblo Indian pottery painters.

Those principles are based upon the knowledge that one or both visible sides of a portable hemispherical or globular container will be the primary surface on which paintings are made. Consequently, a pottery painting is conceived of as a kind of two-dimensional skin applied snugly over the surface of a three-dimensional container. Rather than being thought of as illusions of three-dimensional reality on two-dimensional plane surfaces, pottery paintings are understood to be true three-dimensional pictorial structures. For that reason, artists must be comfortable with the knowledge that all of their painted lines will be arcs and that the forms and motifs they create will occupy real-world space. In those respects pictorial illusions created on pottery are fundamentally different from those made when artists paint pictures on two-dimensional plane surfaces.

Further, Pueblo aesthetic principles rarely, if ever, distinguish in any significant way between one kind of pictorial subject matter, for example figurative motifs, and any other, for example, nonfigurative motifs. A fundamental precept of the Pueblo pictorial system seems to be that all subjects painted on pottery have equal value as intellectualized abstractions that are simultaneously decorative and meaningful. Finally, in the Pueblo system each pottery painting is expected to be an individual expression, constrained by local visual expectations to illustrate some aspect of the collective shared knowledge and experience of Pueblo people about the way the world is and how it works.

No other pottery tradition anywhere else in pre-Columbian North America relied so heavily or for so long a time on the use of portable pottery containers as the primary surface for painting pictures that would regularly be seen and used in daily life. Therefore all Pueblo pottery paintings are, or were, fundamentally utilitarian. Except when self-consciously made for an entrepreneurial art market, all Pueblo pottery today is, as it always has been, based upon the assumption that clay pots are tools made to function as containers. But even though paintings on pottery may seem to serve no particular functions and have little or no obvious bearing on the fundamental utility of their containers, they are not without utility. A "pot is not complete unless there is a painted design" says Santo Domingo potter Robert Tenorio (Bernstein and Brody 2001:68), underlining the fact that a three-dimensional pictorial composition is as much a part of the fabric of a pottery container as is the clay itself.

Technology, Aesthetic Choice, and Shared Basics through Time and Across Space

Pottery is made of clay, a potentially plastic material that becomes permanently hardened when fired above certain temperatures. Until firing occurs clay can be manipulated in an almost infinite number of ways: it can be pushed, pulled, pinched, braided, shaped, scraped, burnished, combed, and covered by shiny glazes to name just a few. Pueblo potters have always known about the potential plasticity of clay and, at the most fundamental level, manipulate it in order to make appropriately shaped containers for all sorts of useful purposes, simultaneously modulating those shapes to fit aesthetic as well as utilitarian ideals. And, from the time they first made pottery, Pueblo potters often textured unpainted vessels decoratively by using one or more of the procedures noted above. So even if we cannot explain why Pueblo potters choose to paint pots, we can be sure that they are aware of alternative ways to make aesthetically desirable utilitarian pottery and that their painted wares are the products of an informed, corporate decision-making process.

A variety of vessel forms and proportions have always characterized sub-traditions of Pueblo pottery. As a rule, most vessels are either made as bowls shaped into relatively simple, open hemispheres generally wider than high, or as jars that are generally globular, somewhat higher than wide, and often with a flared-rim, tubular, or conical neck. Relatively minor variations of those basic forms define regional and temporal sub-traditions. For example, jars made before about 1300 in the Mesa Verde region of the northeastern quadrant of the Colorado Plateau tend to be squat with low centers of gravity and have short necks or none at all, while those made somewhat earlier in the Chaco-Cibola area of the southeastern quadrant of the Colorado Plateau may also lack necks but are taller and have higher centers of gravity.

Almost all Pueblo pottery containers are made of clays that fire at relatively low temperatures, and those that are to be painted are usually covered with a smoothed, light-colored clay slip that serves as a ground for the painting. For traditional wares, slips and paints are applied before firing, and vessels are only fired once (but see Crown and Wills 2003 for archaeological exceptions). During the first 700 years of the Pueblo painted-pottery tradition, most painted vessels were bichromatic and usually painted on white grounds with black pigments. Depending upon local and regional paint manufacturing preferences, "black" pigments vary in color: today, as in the past, they range from soft, ebony-black carbon-based paints that soak into the slip to mineral-enhanced dark red-brown paints that sit on top of it. Background slips also vary in color, texture, and other qualities. For example, they are relatively thick, white, burnished, and have reflective surfaces if from the ancient Kayenta and Mesa Verde regions of the Colorado Plateau, but those from the Chaco-Cibola area are often nonreflective washes of thin, streaky, dull gray-white clay.

Starting in about the late 1100s when Pueblo people began migrating toward the south, away from the Colorado Plateau, and especially after interactions began with agriculturalists from the Mogollon highlands of the southern Southwest, an increasingly large proportion of Pueblo pottery was painted with three or more colors. And, since the 1300s, such polychromatic wares using combinations of yellow, red, and white slips as background color have dominated at most pueblos where painted pottery was made.

From about 1250 to 1700, wherever colored background slips were in common use, slip paints supplemented and enhanced linear patterns and motifs. At many places those patterns and motifs were painted with translucent or transparent brown, green, or purple lead glaze paints that, unless applied on light-colored slips, generally appear to be black or dark brown. Among the pueblos, glazes were used exclusively to paint linear designs and never, as in most other parts of the world, to cover a vessel with a decorative, waterproofing material.

Increasingly, in the decades just before the 1680 Pueblo Revolt against the excesses of Hispanic rule, linear glazes were applied so thickly that they spread and ran, thereby obscuring painted motifs and patterns. That seemingly deliberate effort to defeat pictorial clarity was linked somehow to the hardships of that stressful period (fig. 64). In some regions neither glaze paints nor polychrome slips were ever used; instead, pottery paintings continued to be made on

figure 64
Jar
Kotyiti Glaze Polychrome
Artist Unknown
ca. 1670
24.3 x 22.5 cm

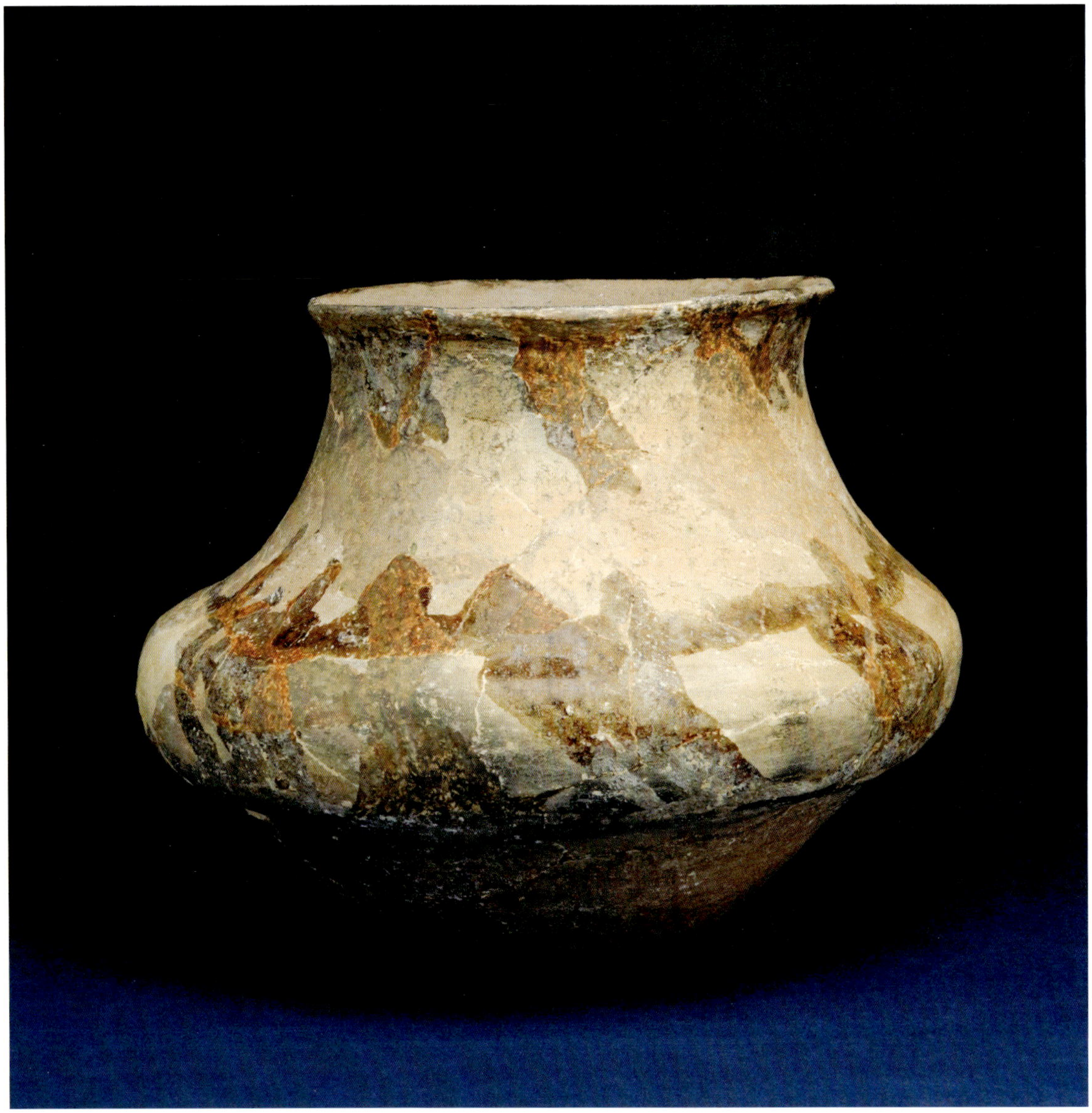

bichromatic wares using white, cream, or gray background slips and either of the two primary variants of matte black paint. For the most part, glaze paints were no longer used in the Pueblo world after 1700, and since then matte-paint polychrome wares have been dominant at most pottery-painting pueblos.

Vessel Form and Design Structure: Deep Are the Roots

Comparison between Pueblo painted-pottery traditions and much older local visual traditions on woven basketry and textiles shows that at its inception Pueblo pottery painting was a by-product of those earlier pictorial modes. For technological reasons pictures woven into baskets and textiles are often thoroughly integrated with the containers of which they are a part. That integration contrasts strongly with pottery paintings that are always applied by processes that are entirely independent of ceramic technology. Yet even though pottery paintings have no necessary association with vessel form, in the Pueblo system they are generally composed as though they are integral to the containers on which they are placed. The conclusion seems inescapable that familiarity with woven pictorial media not only provided many of the visual elements that came to be used by pottery painters, but more fundamentally also provided the structural logic for organizing painted images on potentially mobile, portable containers that are made using other media.

Almost from the first, despite occasionally radical visual innovations, Pueblo pottery painters generally composed their pictures as southwestern basketry and textile artists had done for millennia. A vessel was divided into framed picture spaces that were logically structured by the architectonic qualities and potential mobility of that vessel. For example, bowl paintings were composed as though bowls would remain empty so that pictures painted in their interiors were always visible mobile compositions best seen from above or from just below eye level. Pictorial spaces, therefore, were generally framed and organized to control all available interior spaces including the upper walls.

In all periods and most places when the interior space of a pottery vessel was to be painted, it was usually divided into framed areas subdivided into a complex of arithmetically rational repeat motifs whose logic was determined by one of several locally preferred symmetrical systems (Washburn 1977:11–22; Zaslow and Dittert 1977:4–15). Motifs were usually composed of geometric units such as triangles, diamonds, rhomboids, or rectangles that were combined into more complex design units or motifs. The central space of a bowl interior was either an unpainted void, the visual equivalent of the central orifice of a jar, or was used as the field for a dominant motif. Until the fourteenth century, bowl exteriors were usually left unpainted, but in all periods, when they were painted, their designs were considerably different from those placed on the interiors of the same vessel.

For obvious reasons, jar paintings were placed on exterior surfaces and either organized as unified overall compositions or in sequences of framed horizontal registers. In either case, they can be seen in their entirety only by rotating the vessel. Jar paintings were ordinarily composed as though best viewed from above, and they are often visually unintelligible unless seen from that vantage point. At times an entire jar exterior was treated as a single picture space and covered by a network of interlocking elements that shrank or expanded in response to the swelling or shrinking of the vessel contours.

When jar paintings were organized into horizontal bands, the shape of the container ordinarily determined the size and placement of those bands. As in bowl paintings, each band was often treated as an isolated picture space and divided into a series of three, four, or more panels. Panel motifs were usually repeated within a register in AAAA or ABAB sequences so that the pictorial logic was arithmetical. Pictorial unity was maintained by using predictable repeat rhythms of related motifs in all bands painted on a vessel. From the top down, design area placement on jars usually depended on vessel architecture. Distinct and separate design zones were defined by the central orifice, neck, handle (or handles), upper shoulder, waist, lower body, and base of a jar. Orifices and bases were almost always isolated by simple lines, and necks might be left unpainted or emphasized by a framed band of repeat motifs. Handles were often treated idiosyncratically with patterns unrelated to any others on a vessel or were manipulated into braids or other tactile forms.

Depending upon vessel shape, upper shoulders generally provided the largest and most dominant picture spaces on jars. When a jar was globular with little or no geometric or visual definition of neck and shoulder, upper picture spaces were often defined by the artist arbitrarily painting a band or register to suggest those forms. The waist of a jar was often marked by a narrow paneled band, but lower bodies were usually left unpainted except for a single broad line that defined the base.

As noted, each register usually carried a different set of designs that were visually related to all others by use of similar elements and motifs. As a rule, regardless of vessel shape or regional or temporal variants, most Pueblo pottery paintings through most of time relied upon a limited number of small-scale geometric elements. Depending upon local traditions, these might be painted solid black as in the Mesa Verde and Kayenta areas or, as in the roughly contemporaneous Chaco-Cibola area, might be outlined and filled with thin parallel lines to create a gray color that could be contrasted with solid black motifs. In either case, elemental design units could be combined and recombined into an infinite variety of geometric motifs suggestive of black, white, or gray geometric shapes trapped inside a kaleidoscope.

Patterns could be dynamic or static, painted with precision or otherwise, and often made to circulate around an implicit central point in a bowl bottom or the mouth of a jar. When solid black motifs were paired with solid white ones as in the Mesa Verde and Kayenta traditions they could form dazzlingly ambiguous positive-negative visual illusions. Alternatively, as in the Chacoan tradition, play of three subtle values—gray, gray-white, and solid black—created pseudo-polychromatic patterns that can be imagined as anticipating the truly polychrome paintings of later times.

Such details and others are the variations that describe both ancient and more modern local Pueblo pictorial traditions and temporal periods. With rare exceptions, the basic Puebloan aesthetic philosophy combined with local pictorial and visual habits provided the underlying structure for all variations. That philosophy and those habits of thought still define pan-Pueblo pottery-painting traditions that are practiced at the pueblos of Cochiti and Santo Domingo today.

The Pottery Traditions of Cochiti and Santo Domingo Pueblos: 1650–1850

The northern Keresan pueblos of Cochiti, Santo Domingo, and San Felipe have all been at or near their present locations since the seventeenth century or earlier. However, since few painted pottery vessels are known to have been made at San Felipe, that community does not figure in this discussion. And, since almost no information is available about pottery making at Santo Domingo until after 1800, any account of the earlier pottery of those pueblos has mostly to be about Cochiti.

Traditional Cochiti history and the archaeological record both place ancestral Cochiti people north of their present location between the thirteenth and the early seventeenth centuries. During those years they established several large pueblos in the southern part of the Pajarito Plateau not far from ancestral Tewa communities in what is now Bandelier National Monument (Rohn 1989:17, 19). The boundary between the two language groups was Frijoles Canyon, where the ruins of Tyuonyi, the most northerly Pajaritan Cochiti town, are located. That canyon seems also to have served as a ceramic boundary between the two populations with glaze-paint wares found toward the south, presumably made by ancestral Cochiti potters, and matte-paint wares to the north, presumably the work of Tewa potters (Powers and Orcutt 1999:389). Thus, for several centuries, interactions between the Cochiti and Tewa people seem to have been more regular and intense than interactions were between Cochiti and any other Keresan group.

Tewa matte-paint wares of the Pajarito Plateau are considered to be "the first clear antecedents of historic Tewa ceramics, as indicated by vessel form, ceramic paste, firing technology and decorative treatment" (Powers and Orcutt 1999:399). Variations in detail suggest that they were made at many different places on the Pajarito but all used gritty and relatively friable local clays, and were painted with black carbon paint similar to that used centuries earlier by the Mesa Verde pottery painters of the Colorado Plateau. In form, however, these vessels were generally more similar to contemporaneous Rio Grande area glaze-ware vessels. Bowls were relatively large and by the sixteenth century often had elaborately shaped rims. Jars, like those of the ancestral Mesa Verde people, tended to be squat, with low centers of gravity, well-defined sloping shoulders, wide-mouthed orifices, and short necks (fig. 65). The design structures of those early Tewa vessels, many of their motifs, other stylistic qualities, and most especially their use of dark-light, positive-negative designs also suggest Mesa Verde prototypes. Those visual qualities contrast sharply with the polychrome glaze paintings that were made during those centuries by most other Rio Grande Pueblo potters.

Clays suitable for making and slipping glaze-ware vessels and some of the raw materials for making glaze paints have been identified on the Pajarito Plateau (Powers and Orcutt 1999:407). Those resources as well as the tangible evidence of late seventeenth-century Cochiti glaze pottery all support the probability that most glaze-ware pottery found on the Pajarito was locally made by ancestral Cochiti people. Regular interactions between the two groups are demonstrated by archaeological evidence that Pajaritan glaze-ware vessels were used by Tewa people north of Frijoles Canyon, and contemporaneous Tewa matte-paint wares were used at the Cochiti towns of the Pajarito Plateau (Powers and Orcutt 1999:407). Both wares are especially com-

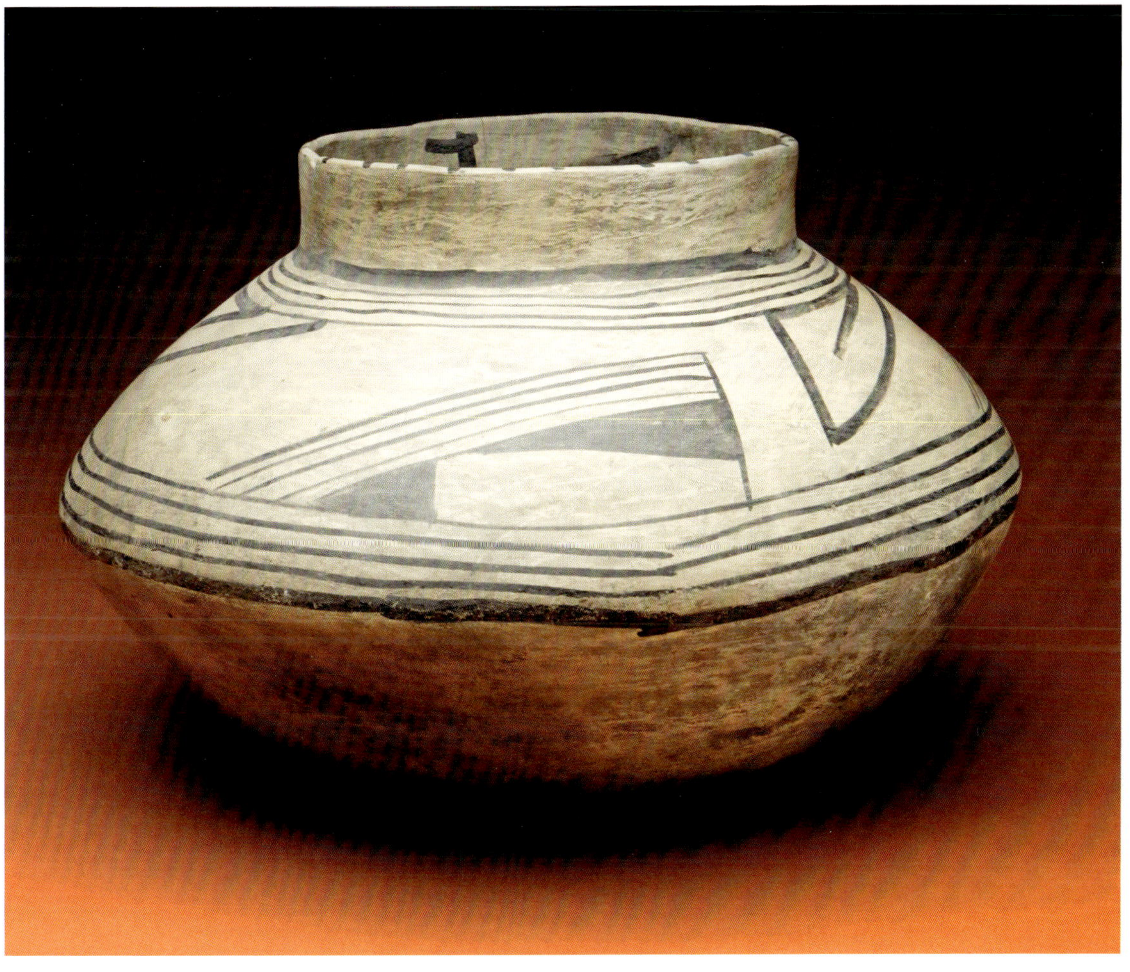

figure 65
Jar
Bandelier
Black-on-cream
ca. 1300–1600
Artist Unknown
25.3 x 39.1 cm

figure 66
Jar
Sakona Polychrome
Artist Unknown
ca. 1680
26.5 x 32.3 cm

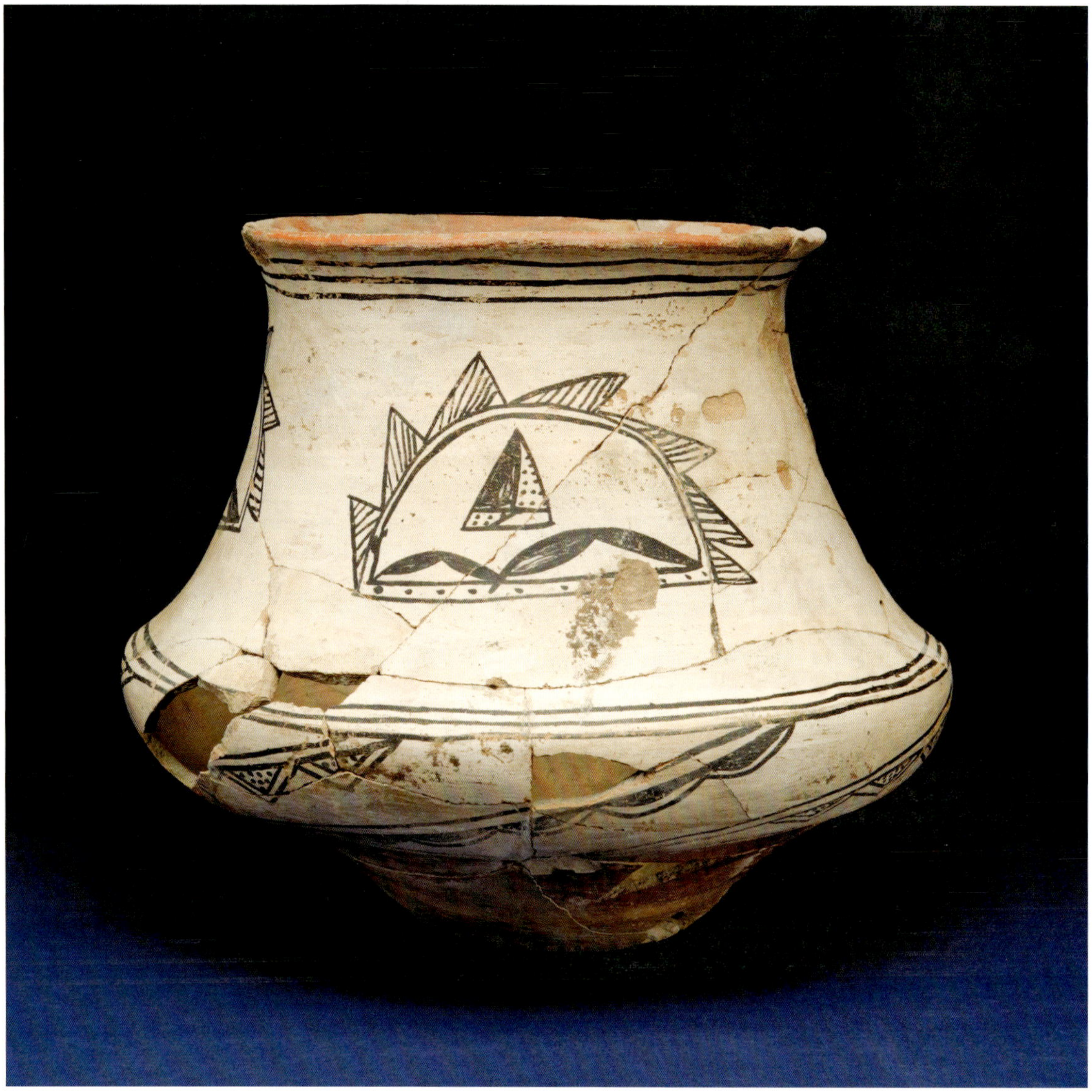

monplace in the Tewa-Keresan borderland areas, and it is obvious that potters from each group were thoroughly familiar with the quite different wares made by the other.

Spanish colonization of the region seems to have impacted Rio Grande Pueblo pottery making by the early seventeenth century, by which time both Tewa and Keresan people were moving off the Pajarito Plateau and toward the Rio Grande valley. The Tewa went eastward and the northern Keresans toward the south, and each established new communities not far from where their present towns are located. Tewa jar forms had already changed significantly by the 1550s and by the 1700s featured elegant, high, sloping shoulders, rims that were almost invisible, low, bulging, narrow waists, and indented bases. That form of jar came also to be used by Keresan potters, including those from Cochiti, who made a glaze-painted variant (compare figs. 64 and 66).

Initially, in the Tewa system, paintings on those jars were limited to a narrow band around the waist and an even narrower one just below the orifice. The vessel shoulder, its largest potential picture space, was left blank. That pictorial austerity reached a logical conclusion in the eighteenth century when Tewa artists simply stopped painting those jars and instead finished them as highly burnished black- or red-ware vessels. There are no known Pueblo prototypes either for that jar form, especially its indented base, or for the use of burnished red or black finishes, and it is reasonable to conclude that Hispanic or Mexican Indian sources introduced those novelties. Related forms continued to be made by Tewa potters until well into the twentieth century.

Potters from other pueblos meanwhile painted those same-shaped vessels in a variety of much more elaborate ways as did Tewa potters in the late nineteenth and early twentieth centuries. The Kotyiti glaze paint variant is distinctively austere and named for the defensively located late seventeenth-century Cochiti village of Kotyiti. It was made from about 1650 to 1700, and, typically for that time, the glaze paints on it melted so thoroughly during firing that the painted designs became illegible as though symbolizing the chaotic times during which they were made. Those fifty years were among the most difficult in Pueblo history, characterized at first by intense religious, economic, and political repression by Spanish religious and secular authorities, followed by the successful Pueblo Revolt of 1680, and finally ending with the bloody reconquest of the 1690s.

During and after the 1680 Revolt and the defensive struggles that followed, many Pueblo people, transcending linguistic and other differences, created new inter-pueblo ties or renewed old ones by collectively taking refuge from Spanish military force. Long-lasting relationships were established in that time of stress, creating the potential for a sharing of traditions, including visual ones. For example, some time after 1680, Cochiti allied with northern Keresan neighbors and with people from several other places, including Tewa- and Tiwa-speakers from northern Rio Grande pueblos. Together, they fortified the defensively sited village of Kotyiti, where they held out against the Spanish until 1694. Similar refugee sites in Tewa areas attracted Keresan people among others and also resulted in the formation of new or the strengthening of older inter-pueblo relationships.

Kotyiti glaze-wares had been traded both to Tewa pueblos of the north and Keresan ones southwest of Cochiti, and may have been the only late seventeenth-century painted pottery made in the area. But almost nothing is known of any later eighteenth-century Cochiti wares, and on the basis of slim evidence whatever there was is thought to be a variant of Kotyiti glaze-ware painted with a matte black, Tewa-like carbon-based paint (Harlow 1973:45–46). In any case, it seems likely that most painted pottery used in the eighteenth century by the northern Keresan pueblos was either imported from Tewa towns to the north or from the Keresan ones of Santa Ana and Zia to the southwest (Batkin 1987:93). In both areas pottery paintings were dominated in that time by stylized feather and bird motifs derived in part from earlier adaptations of western Pueblo iconography. But avian motifs were rarely used in pottery paintings at Cochiti or Santo Domingo until late in the nineteenth century, and our knowledge of eighteenth-century northern Keresan wares is so limited that no detailed discussion of them is currently possible.

Between about 1800 and 1850 the painted wares of Cochiti and Santo Domingo were virtually indistinguishable from one another (Harlow 1973: 46). And, throughout the nineteenth century, pottery from those two pueblos more closely resembled that of Tewa-speaking neighbors to the north than of any of the other Keresan pueblos. Even today points of similarity with Tewa prototypes are numerous and range from such technical matters as the use of distinctive pottery-making and pottery-painting materials to the form, shape, and proportion of pottery vessels, and to many details of design structure and pictorial motif. Perhaps the most obvious of similarities show the systematic use in both areas of geometrically interactive and intentionally

figure 67
Jar
Tewa Polychrome
Artist Unknown
ca. 1770–1820
26.0 x 26.2 cm

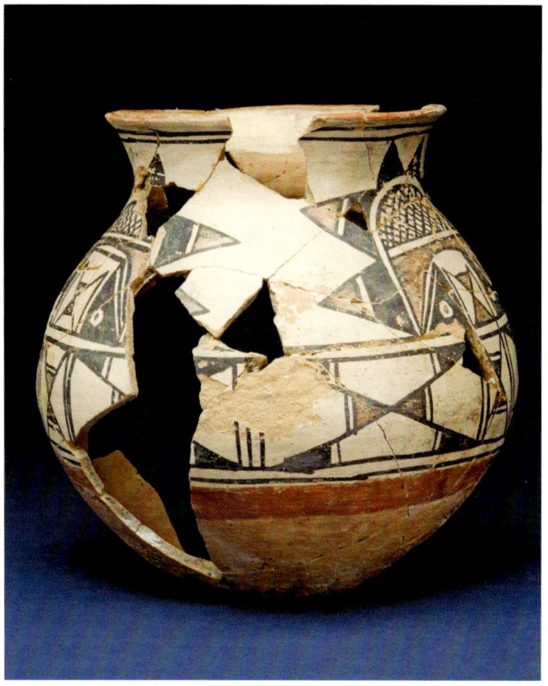

figure 68
Storage Jar
Santo Domingo
Artist Unknown
ca. 1910
37.5 x 42.0 cm

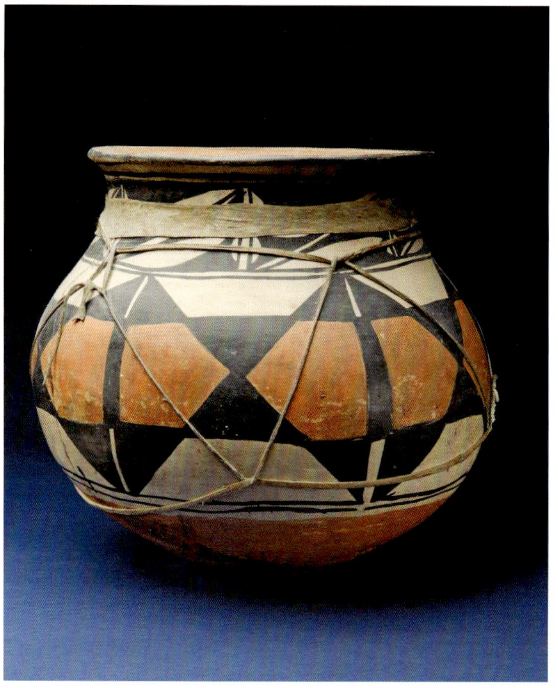

figure 69
Dough Bowl
Santo Domingo
Artist Unknown
ca. 1900–1910
22.8 x 37.6 cm

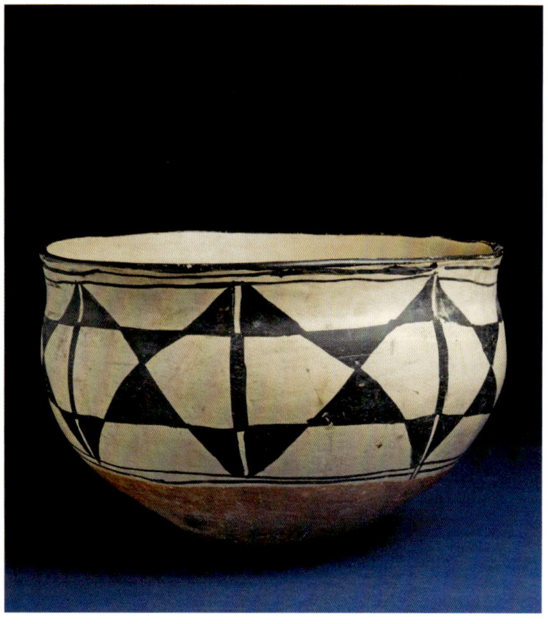

figure 70
Pitcher
Cochiti
Artist Unknown
ca. 1920
11.7 x 13.4 x 15.7 cm

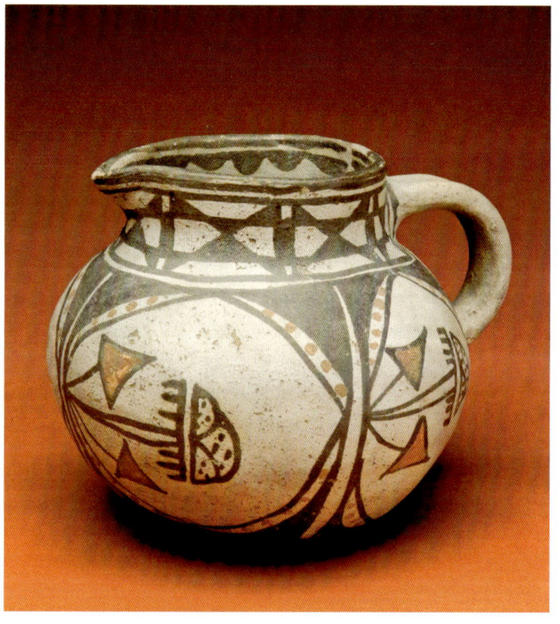

ambiguous positive-negative patterns and motifs (compare fig. 67 to figs. 68–70).

History, geology, and propinquity had laid the groundwork for close similarities between Tewa and northern Keresan pottery paintings of the late eighteenth and nineteenth centuries. Pottery paintings in the two areas have differed significantly since the early twentieth century, but similar clays are still used by potters of both areas to form vessels that are then slipped with almost identical red, creamy-white, or gray-white bentonite slip clay. And, wherever Tewa and northern Keresan painted wares are made they are painted with black carbon-based paint that soaks into the slip in contrast to the non-penetrating, iron-bearing red-black paint used by all other Keresan pottery painters. It may be that carbon-based

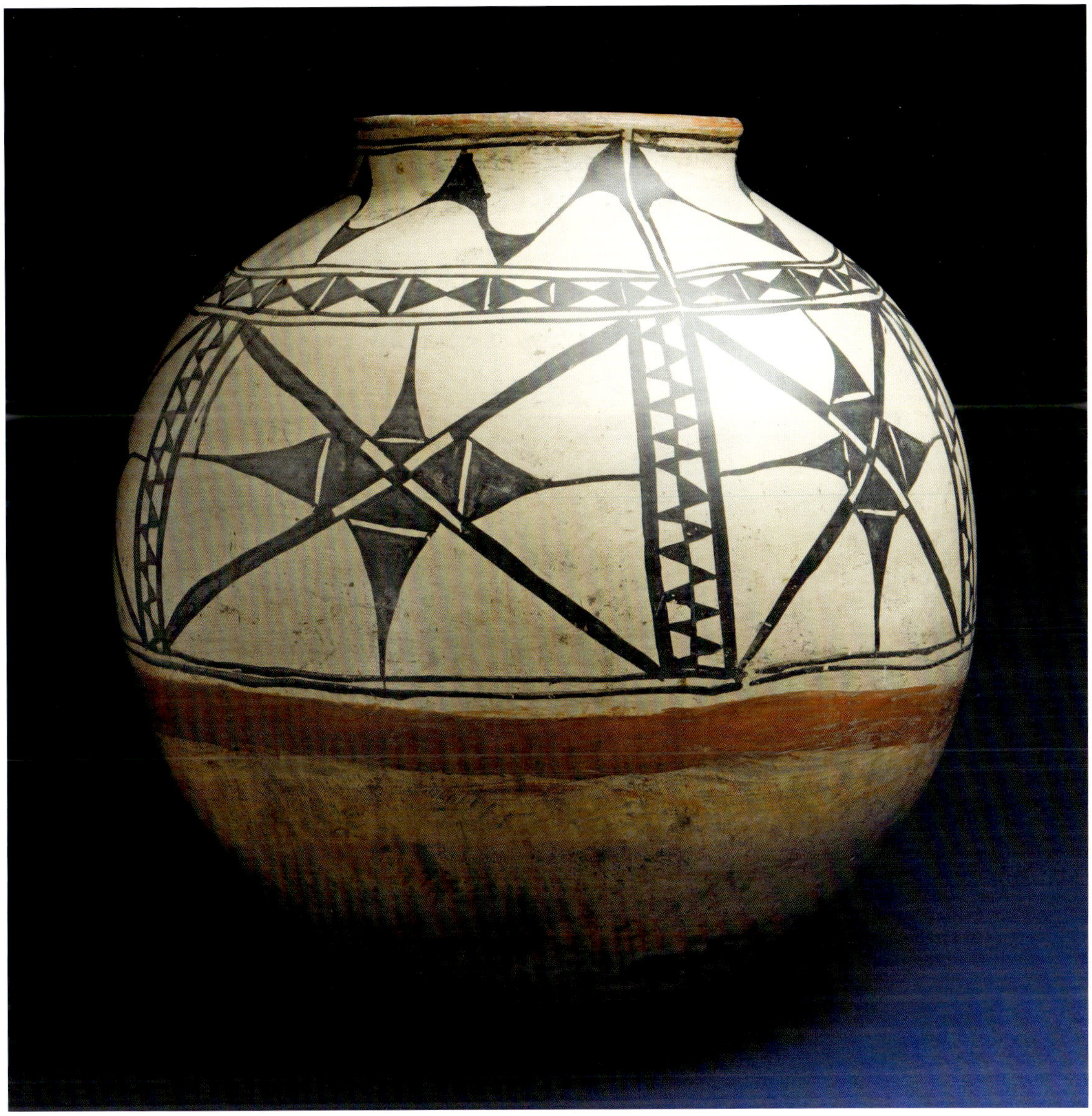

figure 71
Jar
Tewa or
Keresan Polychrome
Artist Unknown
1760–1850
59.0 x 58.0 cm

paints work better on bentonite slips than on other surfaces, but in any case paint choice is clearly a function of local histories and collective decision making.

Similar historical factors as well as unpredictable idiosyncratic ones may also explain similarities in vessel forms and the paintings on them that characterized Tewa, Cochiti, and Santo Domingo wares of the late eighteenth century. In an important deviation from Puebloan esthetic principles, large globular jars made at those pueblos were painted in novel ways. Instead of using framed bands with repeat motifs on the large, upper body pictorial fields of those jars, those spaces were left open and unframed to be painted with one or more large, isolated motifs. Similarly, the central interior spaces of bowls were also used as fields for isolated motifs. In contrast, however, bowl exteriors and the lower portions of globular jars were used for bands of interlocking black (positive) and creamy white (negative) triangular or rectangular repeat motifs.

Finally, new forms, including large, lidded storage jars, were made at many Rio Grande pueblos in response to the introduction of wheat by the Spanish during the seventeenth century (fig. 71). Wheat had important economic consequences and also impacted the Pueblo diet by introducing leavened bread, which required such new tools as large, round-bottomed, bread-kneading, dough-rising bowls. Those novel forms were integrated into most pueblos by structuring the paintings made on them in traditional ways. For example, the designs and motifs painted on northern Keresan dough bowls differ only in scale from those used on much smaller contemporaneous food-serving bowls.

Variation, Modernity, and Idiosyncrasy

The more recent pottery traditions of Cochiti and Santo Domingo pueblos are discussed elsewhere in this volume so I will close with a brief look at the transition to modernity that took place at those two pueblos during the late nineteenth and early twentieth centuries. Pictorial patterns and vessel forms that had been in use for more than a century at Tewa and northern Keresan pueblos were largely abandoned by the Tewa in the latter years of the nineteenth century and have since become identified almost exclusively with Santo Domingo and Cochiti. The Tewa, because of their proximity to Santa Fe, had been more seriously challenged than most other pueblos by nineteenth-century Euro/Anglo-American pressure to replace Native manufactures with industrially made goods while replacing their barter-based economy with a monetary one. Those pressures began with the opening of the Santa Fe Trail in 1823, accelerated after New Mexico was brought into the United States about thirty years later, and culminated after 1880 when Santa Fe was linked to the rest of the country by the transcontinental railroad.

Yet even as imported goods stimulated radical changes, the transportation links that had made it all possible, especially railroads, simultaneously brought potential new consumers and created new functions for formerly utilitarian hand-made Pueblo goods. Curio-hunting tourists, art collectors, immigrants, and newly created wholesale and retail institutions revolutionized the production and distribution of Pueblo pottery. Traditional forms of painted pottery were modified to function in novel ways for novel markets, and new forms were invented to accommodate the new audiences.

Unpredictably, the new products came to be perceived by their consumers as encapsulating and symbolizing the ethos of individual pueblos, and so they somehow mediated relationships between the pueblos and influential segments of the soon-to-be-dominant Euro/Anglo-American audience. Before long also, some in the new audience applied a new value—"art"—to characterize older, "antique" painted-pottery vessels and thereby stimulated revivals of older traditions. By the 1920s, the category "art" was also applied to newly invented forms of Pueblo pottery, for example vessels made by Tewa artists who modified newly made utilitarian forms by burnishing them to an extraordinary degree before painting or carving designs on them and then firing them as black- or red-ware vessels. Other than beautifully conceived and executed utilitarian forms, "art pottery" as such was almost unknown at either Cochiti or Santo Domingo until recent years (fig. 72).

Throughout that transitional period and continuing to the present, traditional forms of painted pottery survived, continued in use as intended, and even thrived at more isolated pueblos, including Cochiti and Santo Domingo. At such places, paintings on pottery, whether on traditional vessels or on novelties made for the curio market, were still conceptualized as a kind of skin applied over the surfaces of three-dimensional utilitarian containers. They still conformed to and helped articulate the physical qualities of those containers, and all pictorial content, no matter how novel, could still be treated as equally meaningful.

Even before the arrival of the railroad, some Cochiti potters had made fantastic effigy canteens, jars, and other forms of human and animal figurines

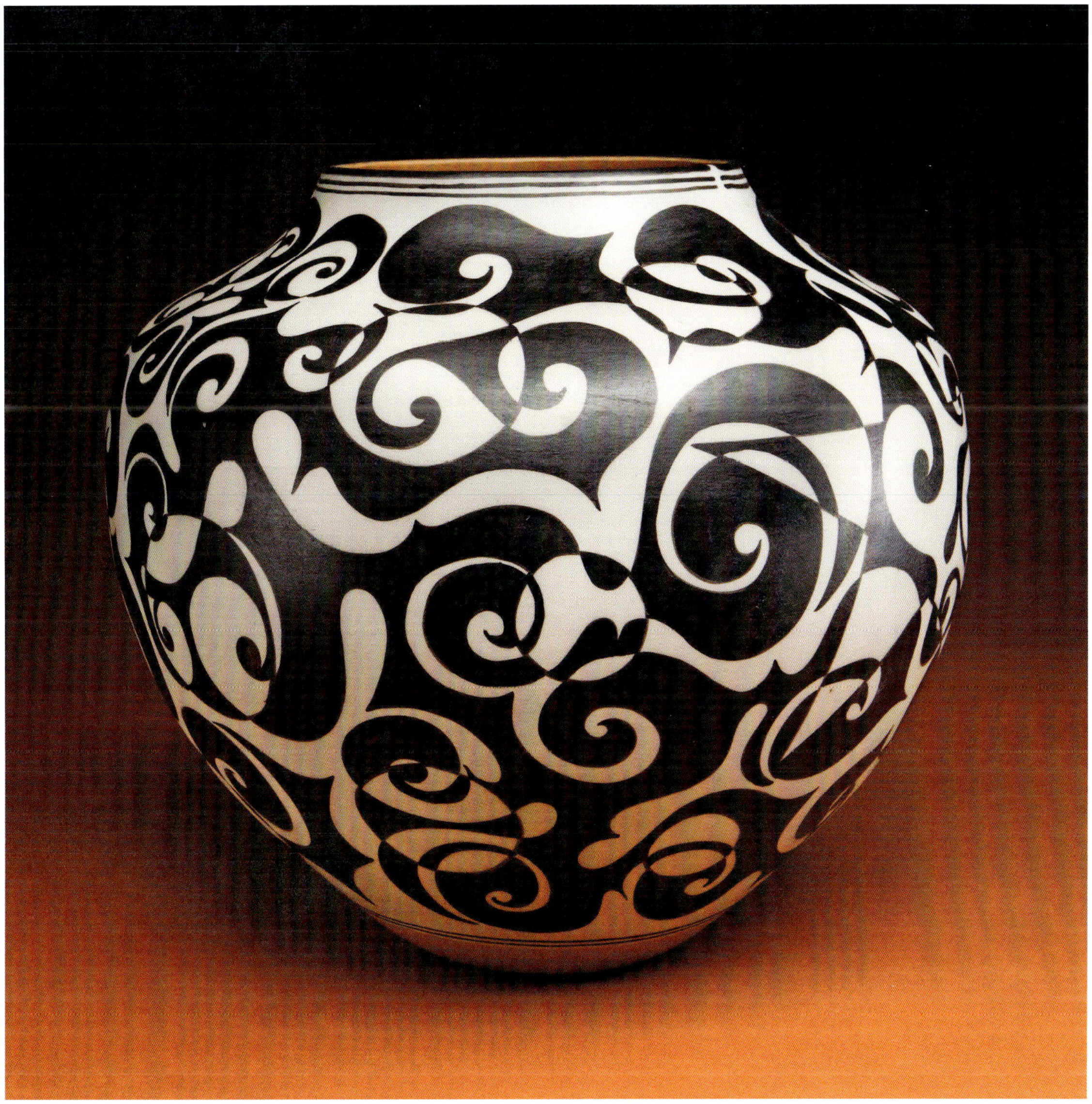

figure 72
Jar
Cochiti and Santo Domingo
Lisa Holt and Harlan Reano
2006
30.5 x 33.9 cm

for sale to the incipient curio market (Stevenson 1883:405–409). Dealers in Santa Fe vigorously (and falsely) marketed such figurines, made also at other pueblos, as Indian "idols" (Batkin 1987:110–111). Within a decade Cochiti figurines, other kinds of human and animal effigies, and other pottery trinkets, all slipped and painted in typical Cochiti fashion, were sold in barrel-loads to Santa Fe curio dealers and wholesalers, the latter shipping them to retail outlets across the country.

At Cochiti, no matter how bizarre the forms the paintings applied to them were organized as though the figurine or other novelty was a bowl or jar. Thus they were organized in terms of vessel architecture with body parts such as neck and base framed off to make separate pictorial spaces (figs. 63, 73–74, 78). By the 1890s, the Cochiti figurine tradition was well established, and by then stylized floral motifs, star-like forms, and fanciful animals were often painted within framed spaces on such effigies. By 1900 similar motifs were also used on the interior and exterior spaces of utilitarian bowls and jars, and they remain a vital and constantly evolving aspect of the Cochiti painted-pottery tradition.

Beginning in about the middle of the nineteenth century, novel stylized bird and floral patterns

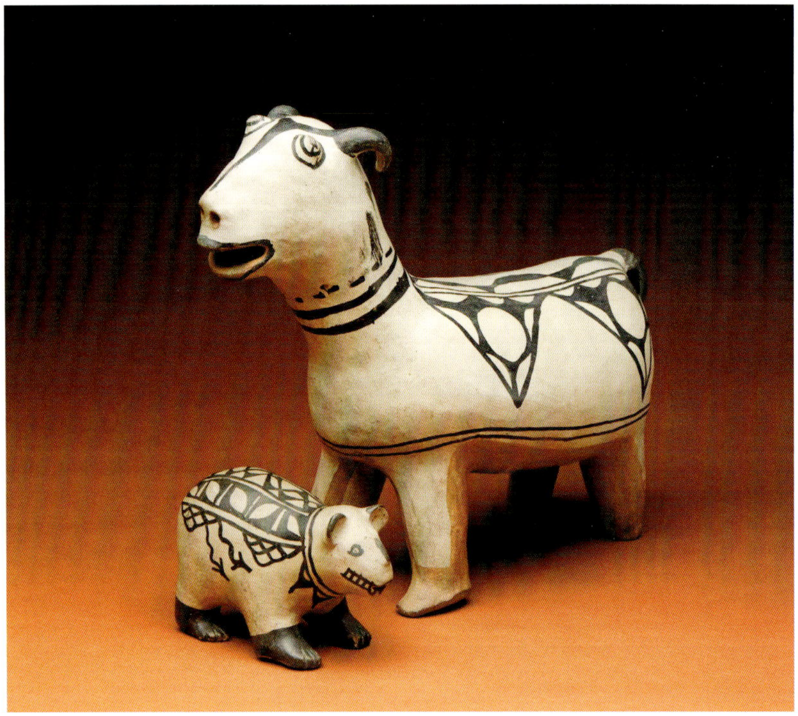

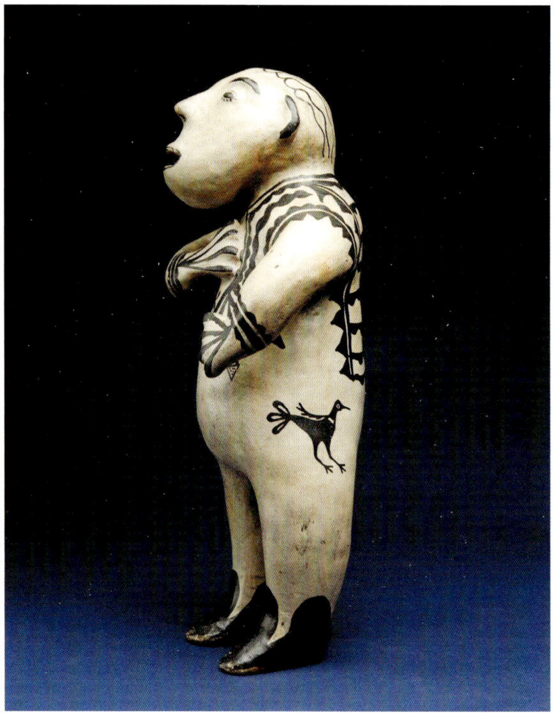

figure 73
Goat and Bear Figurines
Cochiti
Artists Unknown
ca. 1890–1920
29.8; 9.4 x 17.1 cm

figure 74
Male Figurine
Cochiti
Artist Unknown
ca. 1890
46.9 x 22.5 cm

figure 75
Bowl (two views)
Cochiti
Artist Unknown
ca. 1900
23.0 x 43.4 cm

of unknown European "folk" antecedents, with their floral patterns often modified by Pueblo artists to resemble stylized feathers, were integrated into the pottery paintings of Tewa and Keresan pueblos everywhere—except at first at Cochiti and Santo Domingo. But by the 1880s, large and small bird motifs, stylized yet clearly representational, had made their appearance at both northern Keresan pueblos (Batkin 1987:96; Frank and Harlow 1990: figs. 84–86). At Cochiti these were often drawn with a thin, almost scraggly line that soon became an identifying Cochiti characteristic (fig. 75) (Batkin 1987:104, 106). Meanwhile some Santo Domingo pottery painters using bolder linear applications oc-

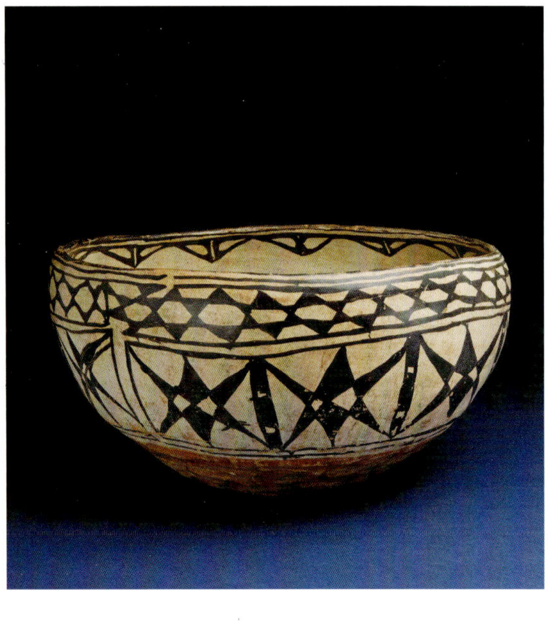

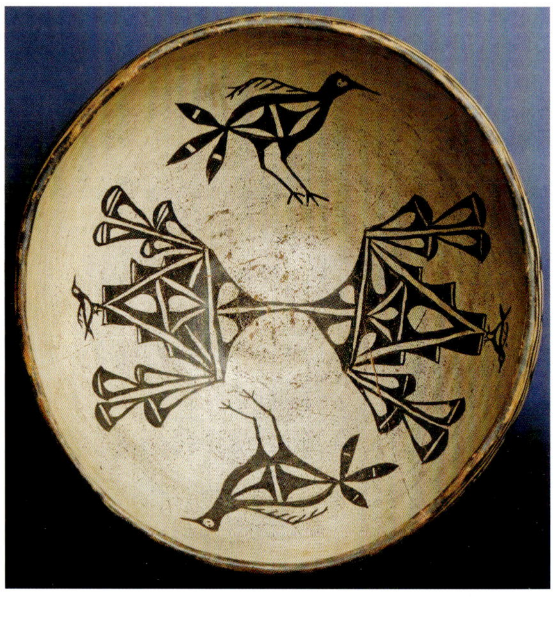

casionally painted fanciful birds, sometimes framed within rainbow bands, that were clearly derived from prototypical western Keresan rainbow-framed parrot-like birds (fig. 76) (Frank and Harlow 1990: fig. 80).

Also at Santo Domingo, use of large isolated motifs similar to those used on the large, globular eighteenth-century Tewa and eastern Keresan jars, continued in use to the present, though now often applied on smaller vessels. But by far the most characteristic Santo Domingo paintings are more highly structured and often create networks of interlocking dark-light geometric blocks. They use dark black carbon paint on creamy white slips to create constantly changing geometric forms that can simultaneously and ambiguously be read as stars, leaves, feathers, or almost any other imaginable image.

There are endless variations on those themes that may have originated in the Mesa Verde area in the 1200s and then been carried south by people who seem to have been ancestral Tewa. In the eighteenth century, the Tewa used those themes as the basis for a characteristic new tradition, and they were soon adopted, adapted, and transformed by northern Keresan artists. A century later no longer used by Tewa pottery painters, those themes were transformed once again to become the northern Keresan hallmark most especially identified today with Santo Domingo Pueblo. That story very neatly summarizes the lengthy history of the visual traditions of the Pueblo world. Over and again, at different times and places, those traditions have undergone such transformations and renewals, each time revitalizing and carrying forward the fundamental aesthetic philosophy of the Pueblo people.

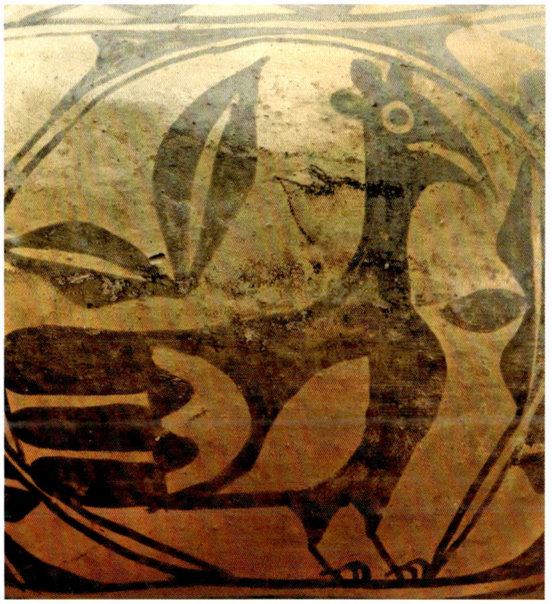

figure 76
Jar
Santo Domingo
Artist Unknown
ca. 1910–1920
25.8 x 25.4 cm

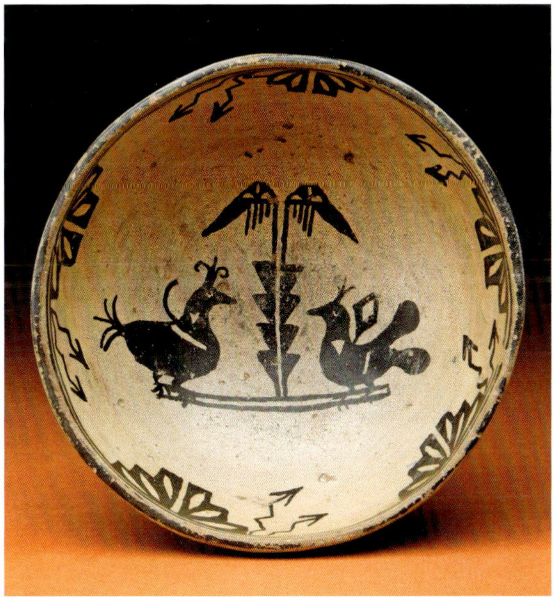

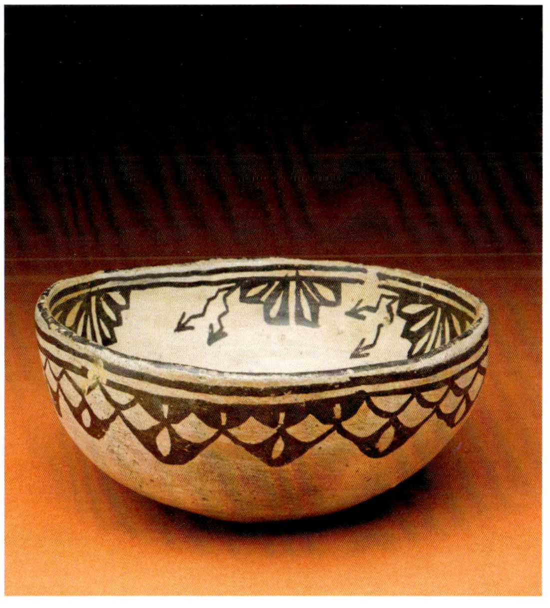

figure 77
Bowl (two views)
Cochiti
Artist Unknown
ca. 1920
9.0 x 20.0 cm

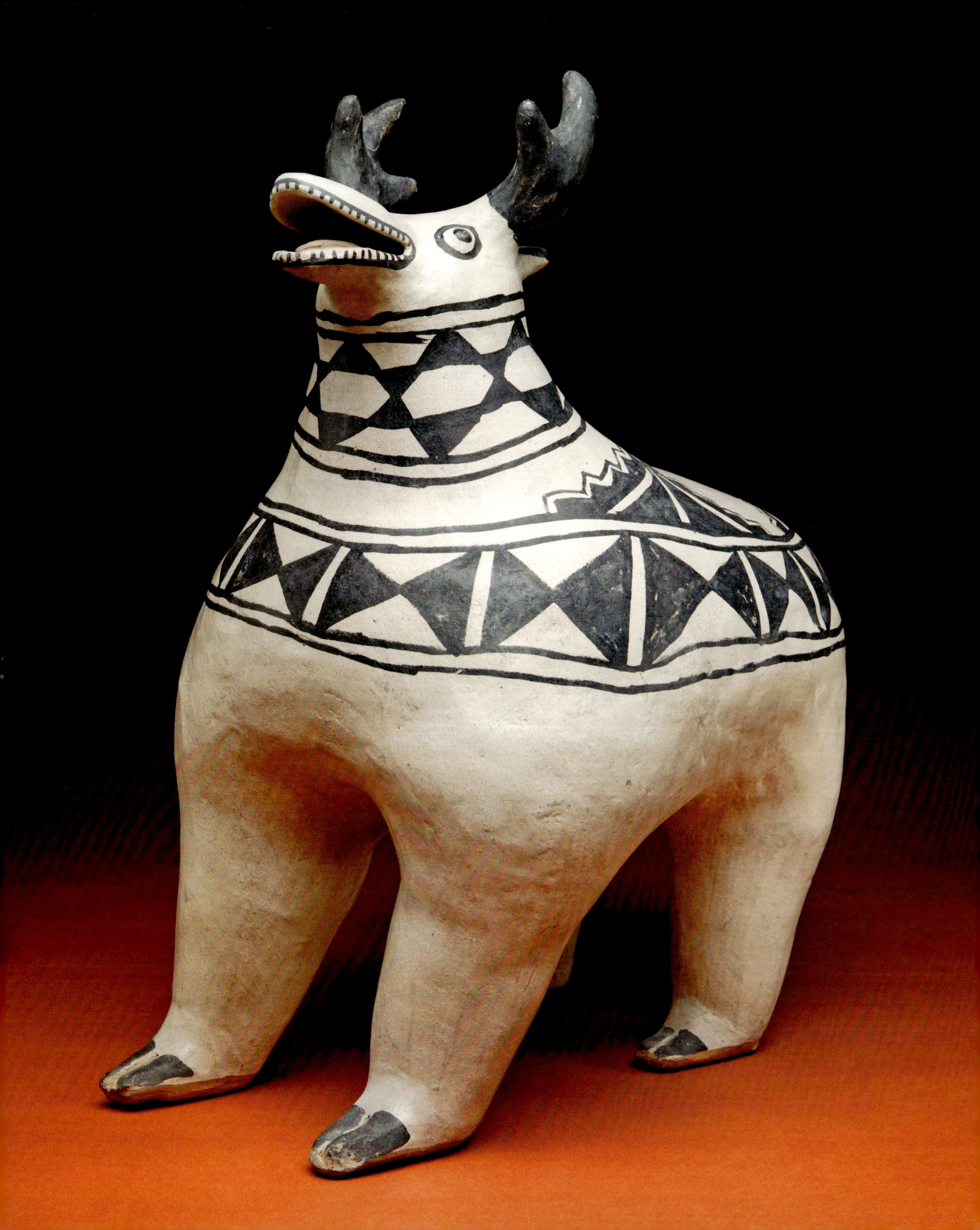

Looking into the Bowl

Part II: An Anthropologist's View of Cochiti and Santo Domingo Pottery

Bruce Bernstein

I [Kenneth Chapman] was impressed with the relative integrity and simplicity of the decorative art in the abundant supply of pottery then in general domestic use; and . . . in 1920 . . . determined to undertake a survey of the conditions then existing in the nearby pueblos, ... I chose the ceramic decorations of Santo Domingo because . . . of the relative abundance of material still available at that pueblo (1936:xii).

Anthropologists and other scholars have written scores of volumes on archaeological pottery but relatively little on pottery dating from the historic period through the present. The aversion to such studies might be anthropology's own self-interest in the past and the constructed authenticity it continues to represent to the discipline. The lack of scholarship in contemporary pottery also may be attributable to Museum of New Mexico founding director Edgar L. Hewett's advancement of a cultural nationalism that looked to the past for models of identity, or his promotion of southwestern tourism. Pottery scholar Kenneth Chapman recognized and assessed the situation in 1936:

> Doubtless it was the lure of the unknown that has prompted so much digging, but if the archaeologists had only realized that the rarest of all Pueblo pottery is that of the two centuries following the Conquest, they might have diverted at least a part of their energy to ferreting out the remnants of the antique ceramics of each pueblo. A mistaken belief that pottery making was influenced by contact with the invaders was long current among those who based their conviction on nothing more tangible than the wide variance between the pre-Spanish and the later wares of each pueblo. The fallacy is now fully exposed, for Pueblo pottery of the past three centuries proves to be a normal development, in which scarcely a trace of European contact can be traced (1936:xi).

figure 78
Antelope Figurine
Cochiti
Artist Unknown
ca. 1890–1900
43.2 x 26.3 x 39.4 cm

What has been written about historic-period pottery is largely based upon archaeological models; these typologies or classification systems are based on observable traits rather than the ideology of living people. When assessing Pueblo pottery, I believe that using extant Pueblo explanatory systems is as valuable as using imposed ones. But rather than entering this debate here, what follows is a view from the outside looking in—how non-Puebloans might understand pottery. While it is true that we will never comprehend Pueblo pottery as insiders do, we still can learn a good deal about and from pottery. So how and what can we know?

A History of Change

In perspective, Pueblo pottery history changes every few hundred years in response to social change. While the changes in visual patterns and styles are obvious, their meanings are more difficult to comprehend. For example, Kenneth Chapman in his study of Santo Domingo pottery included 79 plates of disarticulated pottery design elements to illustrate only twelve pages of text. He doesn't document if meaning was located in the discrete element or in combinations of elements. We have records of only one inconclusive conversation between Chapman and San Ildefonso potter Maria Martinez that provides insight into Native thinking and belief on the matter—it is clear from Maria's recorded comments that she viewed both the discrete design elements and their combinations as stories possessing meaning (Chapman n.d.). As today, Chapman was able to access pottery visually and physically, but the mental object proved to be less obtainable.

Puebloan societal change is reflected in the choices potters make. Following the collapse of the Chacoan world in the twelfth century and Mesa Verde in the thirteenth century, Puebloan pottery production focused on polychrome glazewares, with new design iconographies and vessel shapes, which replaced centuries of black-and-white pottery traditions. Polychrome glazewares continued to evolve until the late sixteenth and early seventeenth centuries when Pueblo response to Spanish settlement resulted in new pottery styles, designs, shapes, and functions. "Material culture can be actively or intentionally manipulated to signal identity…choices are often intentionally manipulated to convey social information. Intentional manipulation of ceramic variability was related to the complimentary processes of resistance and identity formation following the Pueblo Revolt, and that this was one means by which women participated in the resistance process" (Mills 2002:86).

The Historic Period: 1540–1880

I define the historic period as beginning with Puebloan first contact with Europeans in 1540 to the railroad's arrival in the Southwest in 1880. Spanish explorers were impressed by Pueblo pottery; in 1581 they praised Piro and Tiwa pottery as "better quality than the pottery of New Spain…and Portugal" (Hammond and Rey 1966:82, 85 quoted in Snow 1973:61). That Spanish settlers became dependent on Pueblo wares for household and other needs is amply demonstrated in the archaeological record (Snow 1973:61). During the first period of Spanish settlement (1598–1680), some pueblos made ceramic pieces for Spanish consumption, particularly pieces such as censers, chalices, bowls for holy water, candlesticks, and other items made for religious function at the behest of the Franciscan missionaries. For the most part, however, Pueblo people did not adopt these shapes permanently into their ceramic repertoire.

The Pueblo Revolt of 1680 (see Romero this volume) and the ensuing twelve years of freedom from Spanish domination was a turning point in pottery development. Following the 1692 reconquest, potters abandoned their traditional glaze-

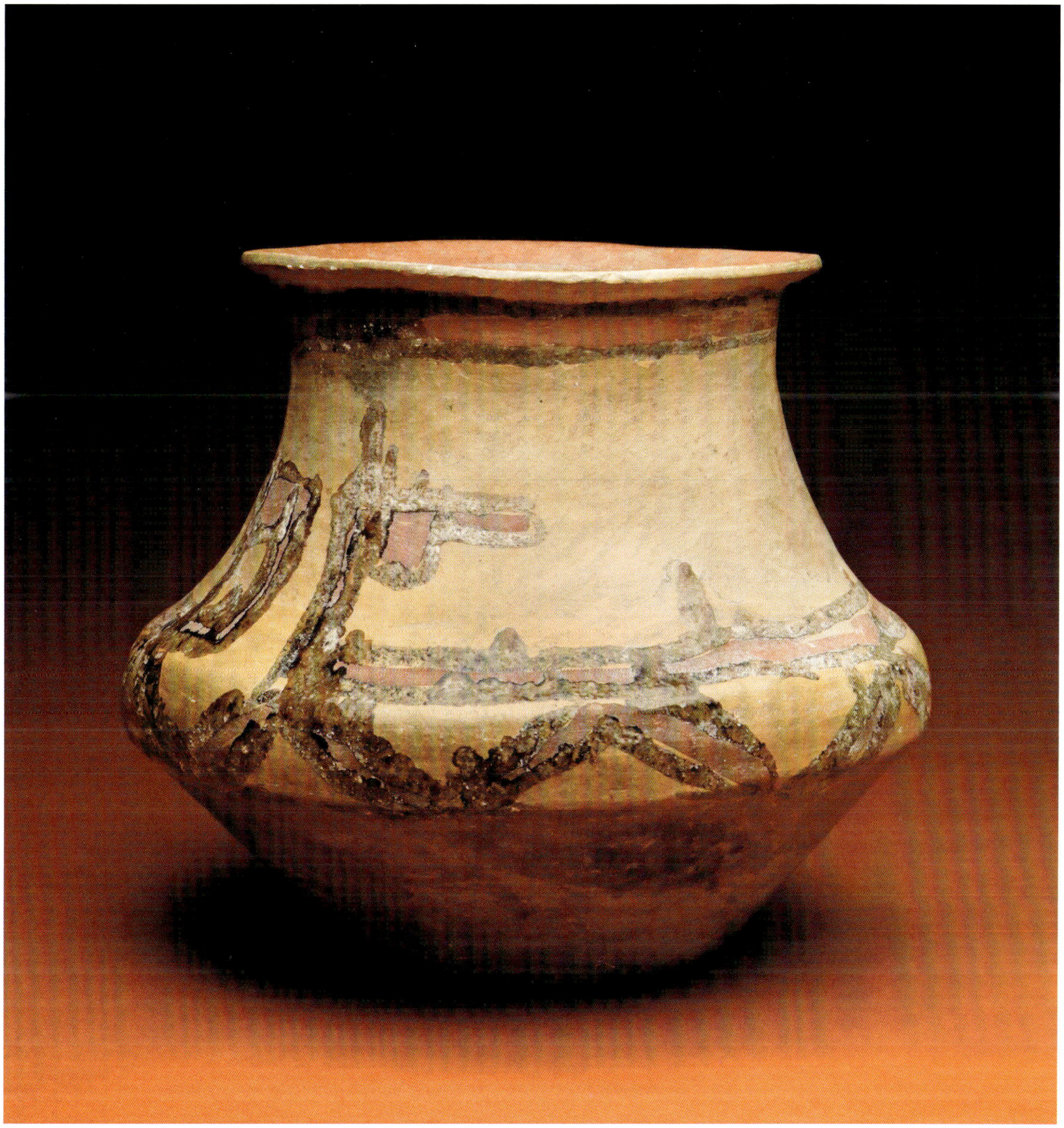

figure 79
Jar
Kotyiti Glaze Polychrome
ca. 1680
22.5 x 25.0 cm

paint pottery for matte-paint pottery, and began using red paint to create polychrome vessels; and they replaced their round-bottomed, bulbous disk-shaped jars with ones that featured tall necks and indented bottoms (fig. 79). It appears that potters changed from imprecise glaze paint to vegetal and mineral paints in order to control the clarity and complexity of their designs (Frank 1991:283). (The concept also may have been brought to mind by the ceramic wares the Spanish imported from Mexico and Europe.) Habicht-Mauche (2006) suggests that the dwindling source of lead was the reason glaze-paint design elements were abandoned; it is more likely that glazewares were associated with Spanish rule and discontinued as a component of the Pueblo Revolt. Following the revolt, new matte-paint pottery styles were introduced. In comparison, the dramatic transformation of the period 1760–1820 reflects the vast social changes brought on by declining Pueblo populations resulting from a smallpox epidemic (Simmons 1966 in Carrillo 1997:55) and from unrelenting raids by Apachean, Ute,

figure 80
Storage Jar
Cochiti
Artist Unknown
ca. 1850
50.0 x 18.0 x 42.0 cm

figure 81
Storage Jar
Keresan Polychrome
Artist Unknown
ca. 1820
48.0 x 51.5 cm

figure 82
Dough Bowl
Santo Domingo
Artist Unknown
ca. 1880
22.5 x 54.3 cm

figure 83
Dough Bowl
Santo Domingo
Artist Unknown
ca. 1880–1900
21.8 x 37.9 cm

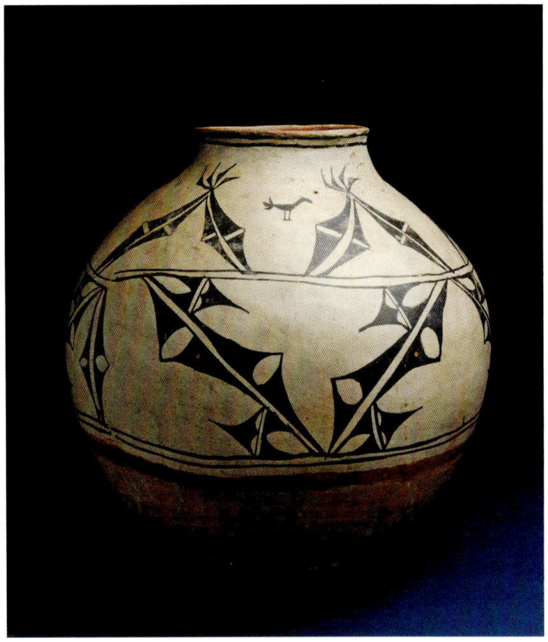

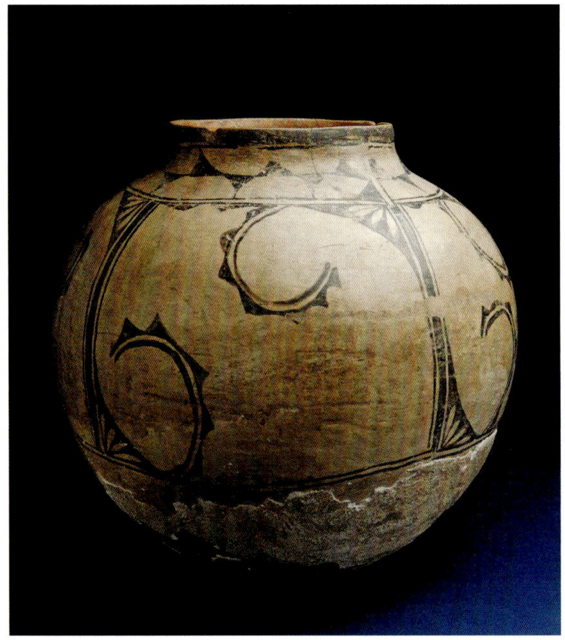

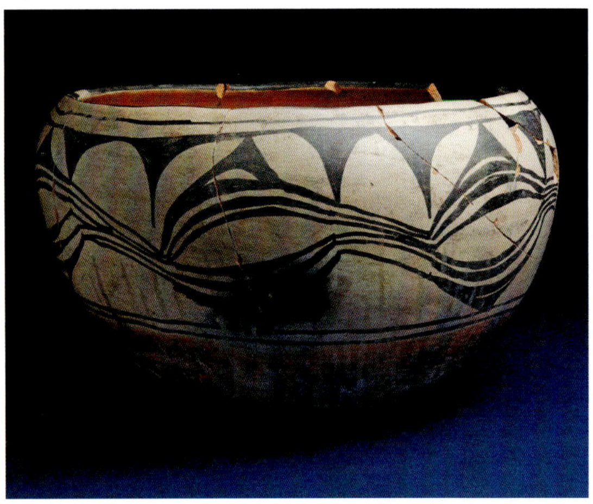

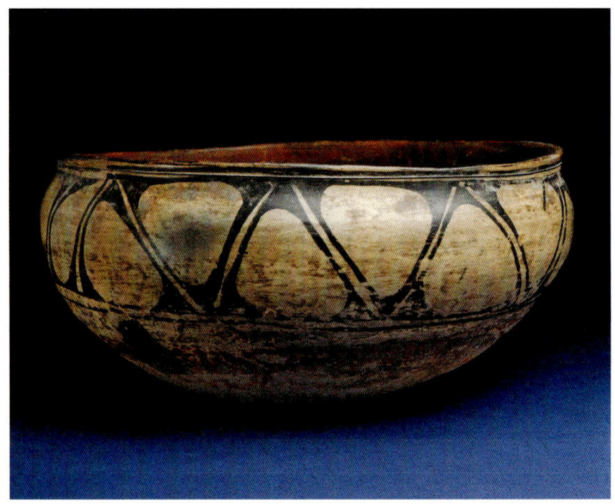

Navajo, and Comanche Indians (Carrillo 1997; Frank 1991; and Spicer 1962). Other significant social changes included the full integration of wheat agriculture into the Pueblo economy, and a *vecino* (native born) takeover and alteration of what had been a lively aboriginal trade system. Throughout the period, the Pueblos adapted to the increasing political and social control of the ascendant Spanish. Nowhere is this more obvious than in pottery production (Frank 1991:315).

At the close of the eighteenth century, wheat agriculture and new trading patterns resulted in new pottery forms, most notably round-bottomed storage jars—whose consistent size and capacity suggest they doubled as measurement devices—and large, thick-walled bowls for mixing and rising bread dough (figs. 80–83). At both Cochiti and Santo Domingo large storage jars and bowls for domestic use were made well into the twentieth century (Lange 1959) (fig. 84). At the same time, Cochiti and Santo Domingo potters began using a bentonite slip that could be wiped on rather than applied through the tedious process of stone polishing (Hedges and Dittert 1984). And, further, in 1803 the first documented use of animal dung to fire pottery occurred (Carrillo 1997:170), reducing the firing temperature

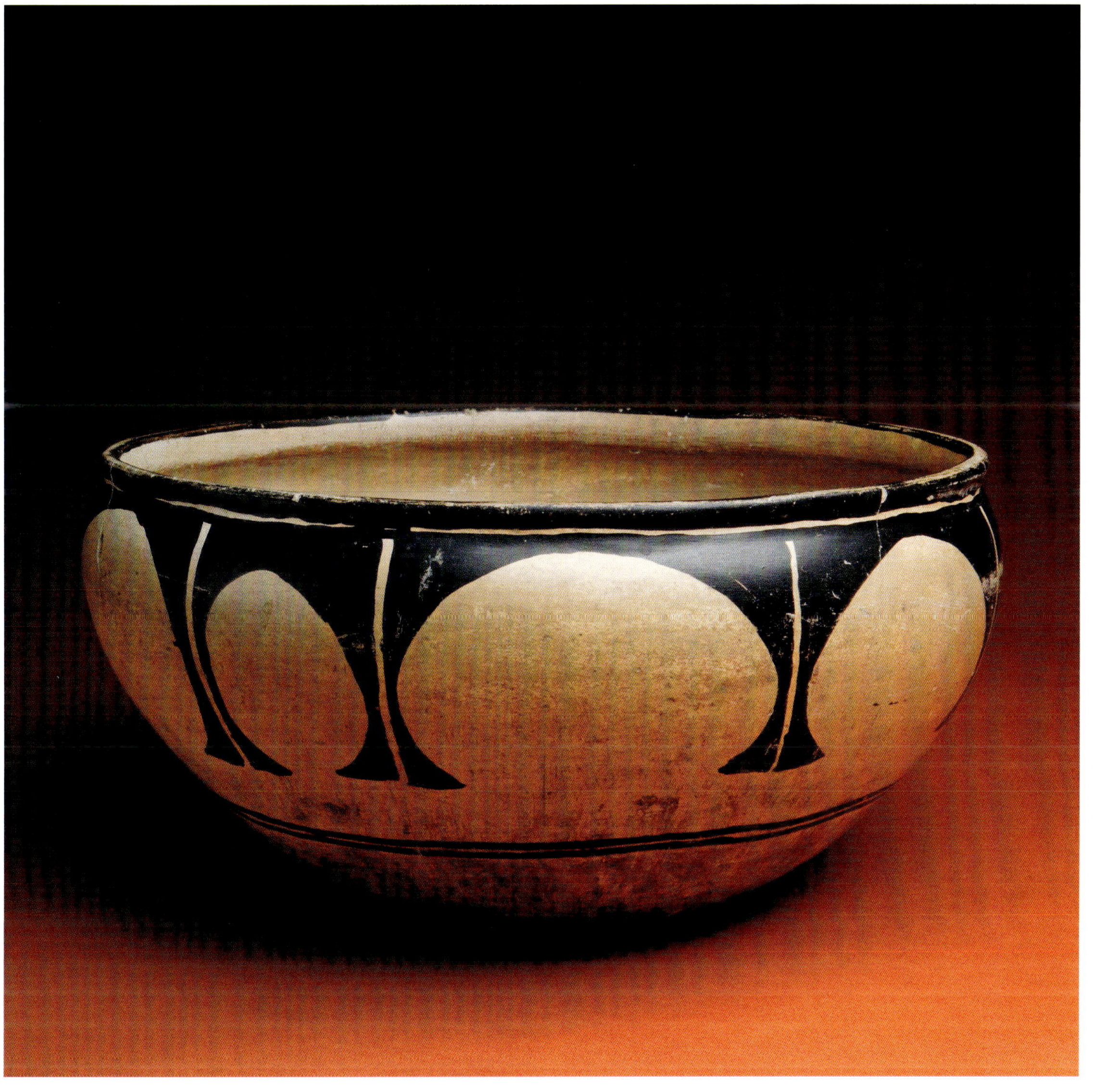

figure 84
Dough Bowl
Santo Domingo
Artist Unknown
ca. 1920
19.0 x 28.9 cm

and, ultimately, the domestic serviceability of the wares. (The change in firing fuel might be a result of mid-eighteenth-century Spanish consolidation of authority and attendant changes in land use and ownership—under Spanish rule, once large open tracts of land became highly regulated and community owned and controlled, reducing access for wood collection.) Low firing and slipshod finishes seem to indicate a carelessness of manufacture that is usually interpreted to mean that the vessels were not being made for people's own use but for trade or sale to others. Certainly, the ascendant power of the *vecino* population might be the direct cause. Also occurring in the historic period is an increase in the presence of micaceous wares and polished black pottery (Kapo Blackware). Both have been suggested as the introductions of Mexican indigenous populations who came to New Mexico with the Spanish; however, the Jicarilla Apache's change of settlement pattern from nomadic to sedentary agricultural in the mid-nineteenth century may have been responsible for the revitalization of micaceous wares in the upper Rio Grande area. At the end of the historic period, as at its beginning, New Mexico's nonindigenous population relied on Pueblo-made pottery for daily household use. Davis

left to right:
figure 85
Pitcher
Santo Domingo
Artist Unknown
ca. 1930
13.5 x 13.0 x 18.8 cm

figure 86
Pitcher
Cochiti
Artist Unknown
ca. 1940
18.0 x 18.6 x 22.0 cm

figure 87
Stew Bowl
Santo Domingo
Artist Unknown
ca. 1920
9.0 x 20.3 cm

figure 88
Stew Bowl
Santo Domingo
Artist Unknown
ca. 1910
8.1 x 20.3 cm

figure 89
Stew Bowl
Santo Domingo
Artist Unknown
ca. 1900–1910
10.8 x 24.9 cm

figure 90
Stew Bowl
Santo Domingo
Artist Unknown
ca. 1910–1920
9.9 x 21.9 cm

figure 91
Stew Bowl
Santo Domingo
Artist Unknown
ca. 1925
8.7 x 20.9 cm

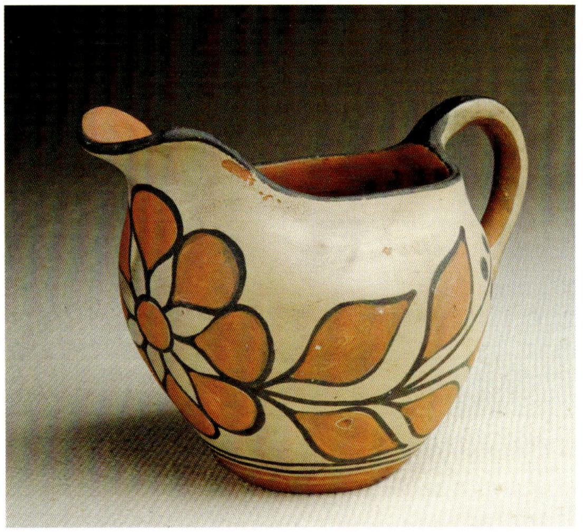

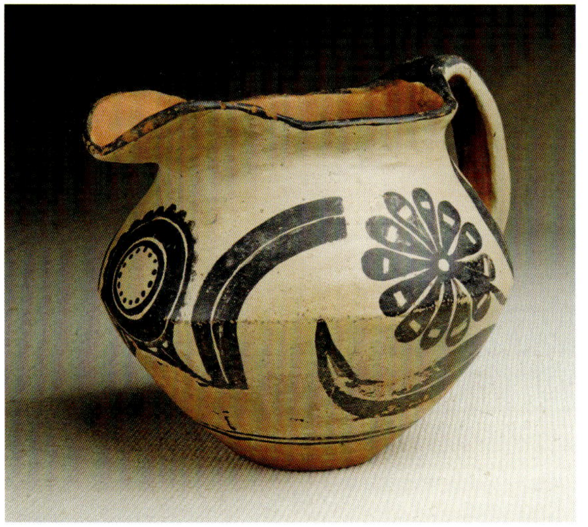

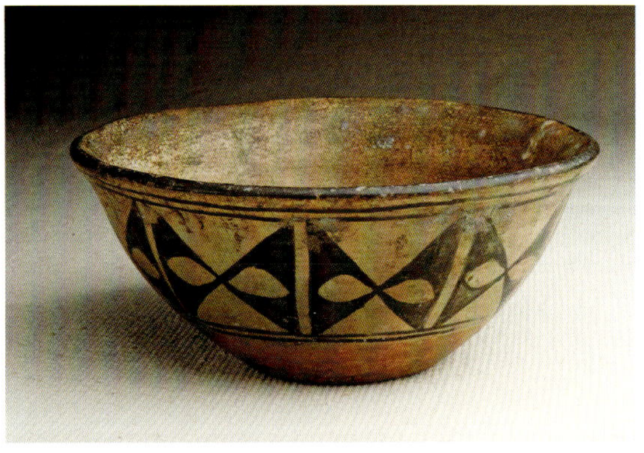

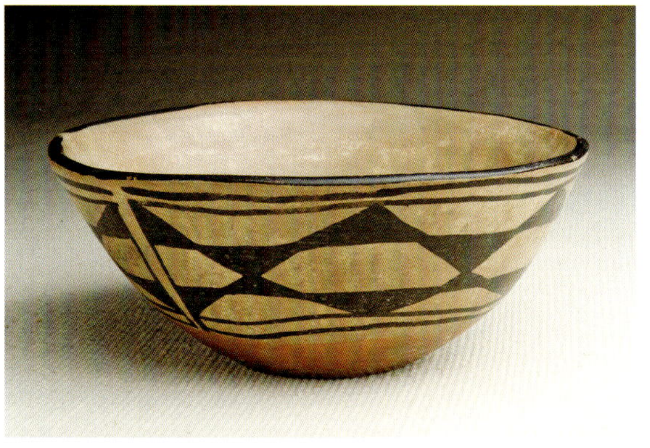

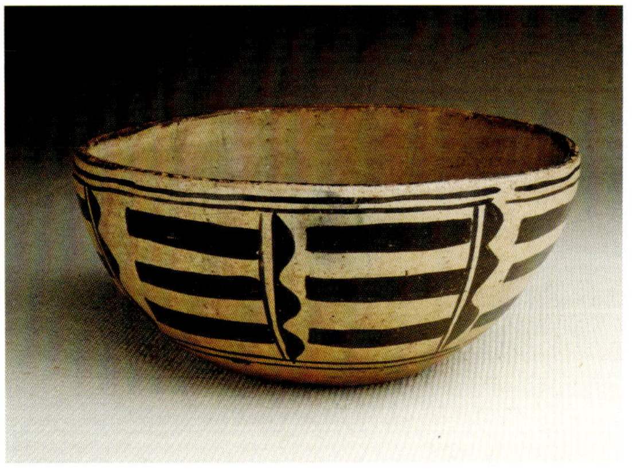

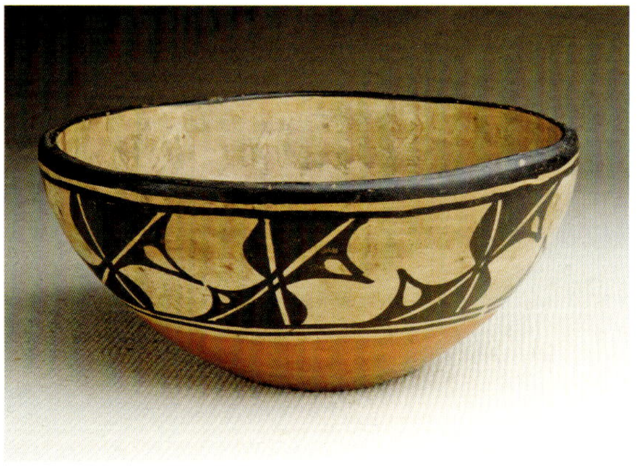

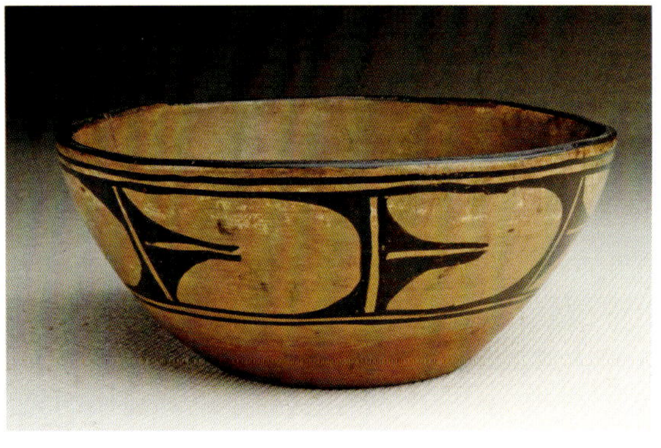

(1938:327 in Snow 1973:62) noted in 1857 that Pueblo pottery "is in universal use in the territory." Museum collections attest to the various serving and eating bowls, cooking and water jars, and the relish bowls and vinegar jars in use in Puebloan, Spanish, and American homes (figs. 85–91).

Keresan Pottery and Historic-Period Scholarship

Kidder (1931) and Kidder and Shepard (1936) were the first to attempt a ceramic chronology of the period, relying on changes in bowl rims to date wares. However, this method was inadequate for demonstrating all of the changes in pottery since Spanish contact. Harry Mera (1939 cf. 1932, 1933) chose the olla, or water jar, as his index of chronology, and his work continues to serve as a foundation for understanding the developmental sequence of historic-period Pueblo pottery. Mera based his chronology on the upper Rio Grande region (Batkin 1991:2). Francis Harlow (1971, 1973; Frank and Harlow 1974; Harlow, Anderson, and Lanmon 2005:33–119) has substantially contributed to our understanding of historic-period pottery, building and expanding on Mera's publication, refining chronologies and suggesting new ceramic types. Jonathan Batkin has provided a convincing critique of the serviceability of chronologies in general and, in particular, of the viability of the specific proposed chronologies of Chapman, Mera, and Harlow.

Two factors hinder the development of a definitive chronology of historic-period pottery: the natural attrition of pottery vessels, which were deposited in the village trash heap when no longer serviceable; and the fact that most pueblo villages of this period continue to be occupied, so archaeological evidence is limited (but see Ellis and Brody 1964). Historic archaeology of abandoned villages has contributed to historic-period chronologies. Of particular importance are excavations done in collaboration with Cochiti Pueblo at Kotyiti, a village occupied by Cochiti people from 1683–1694 (Preucel 1998, 2000, 2002; Capone and Preucel 2002), and Las Huertas (Ferg 1984); see also Barnett (1969); Lambert (1981); Smith, Woodbury, and Woodbury (1966); Toulouse (1949); and Wade and McChesney (1981)). Of seminal importance are documented vessels from the Gobernador Canyon of northwestern New Mexico (Carlson 1965, 1977), where many people of the Rio Grande pueblos fled after the Pueblo Revolt (1680) or in response to the Spanish reconquest. In cogent arguments, Frank (1991) and Snow (1983, 1984) demonstrate the utility of historical information to provide contexts and explanation for Pueblo pottery changes in the 1760–1820 period, rather than relying solely upon stylistic analysis.

A Chronology of Historic-Period Pottery

Kenneth Chapman and Laboratory of Anthropology curator Harry Mera developed their historic-period pottery chronology by building the Indian Arts Fund (IAF) pottery collection (Dauber 1993), now housed at the School for Advanced Research in Santa Fe. The temporality of the collection is suggested through Chapman's idea of "non-reducibility," an evolutionary model of stylistic change representing increasing complexity of shape and design. Data continues to support Chapman's and Mera's hypothesized chronology, which has been further refined by the work of Harlow and Batkin. Others, such as Snow and Frank, provide cultural contexts for artistic change, growth, and retrograde.

While the IAF collection is filled with historically and artistically significant pots, there is little historical evidence that attests to the veracity of the sequence it was assembled to illustrate (Batkin 1987, 1991). Ethnographic documentation of the collection is virtually nonexistent and associated historic information sketchy; indeed, most of the collection was purchased from dealers and collectors. A few

figure 92
Jar
Cochiti
Artist Unknown
ca. 1890
44.8 x 45.0 cm

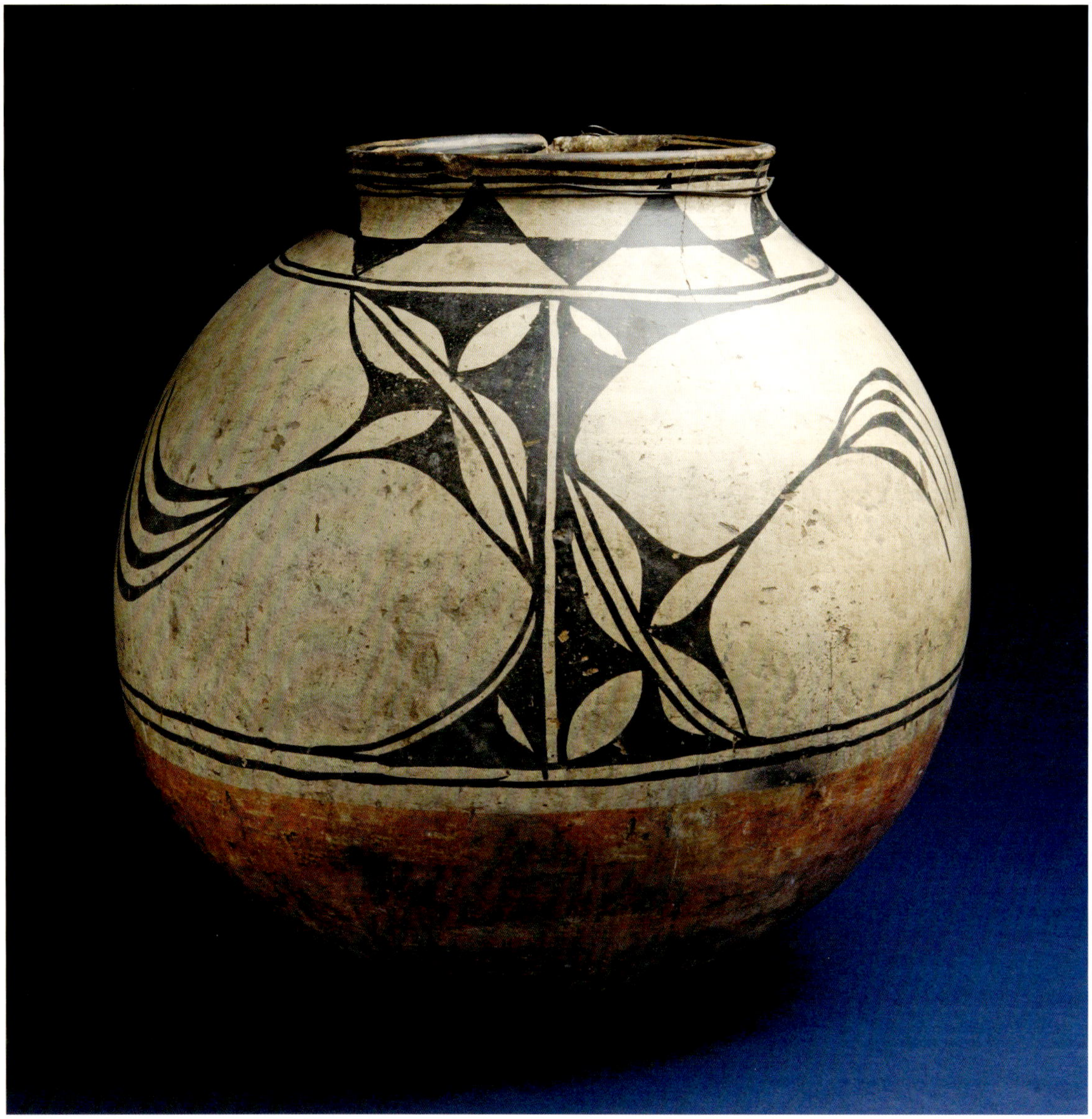

pots in the IAF collection (see Dauber 1993; Chapman n.d.) were purchased in the villages; however, they lack the manufacture dates necessary to verify the sequence. Although the IAF is a collection of historic-period pottery (1600–1880), Chapman nonetheless included new pieces that he clearly believed to be authentic facsimiles of pre-1880 styles. Importantly, other private and public collections also include significant examples of historic-period pottery (cf. Frank and Harlow 1974; Harlow 1990; and Harlow and Silverman 2001). Historical pottery has many potential meanings, but first we must relearn to read and interpret the pottery without imposed structures.

Chapman's (1936, 1970) primary work with the IAF collection was an attempt to dissect historic-period pottery, creating a series of discrete and interchangeable components which could be directed toward providing models for use in improving Pueblo pottery, as described below (Bernstein 1994). Chapman's definitions of authenticity abound in the IAF collection. The IAF was intended to inspire, to be used as pattern and example for living potters. In contrast, the MIAC/LAB collection—

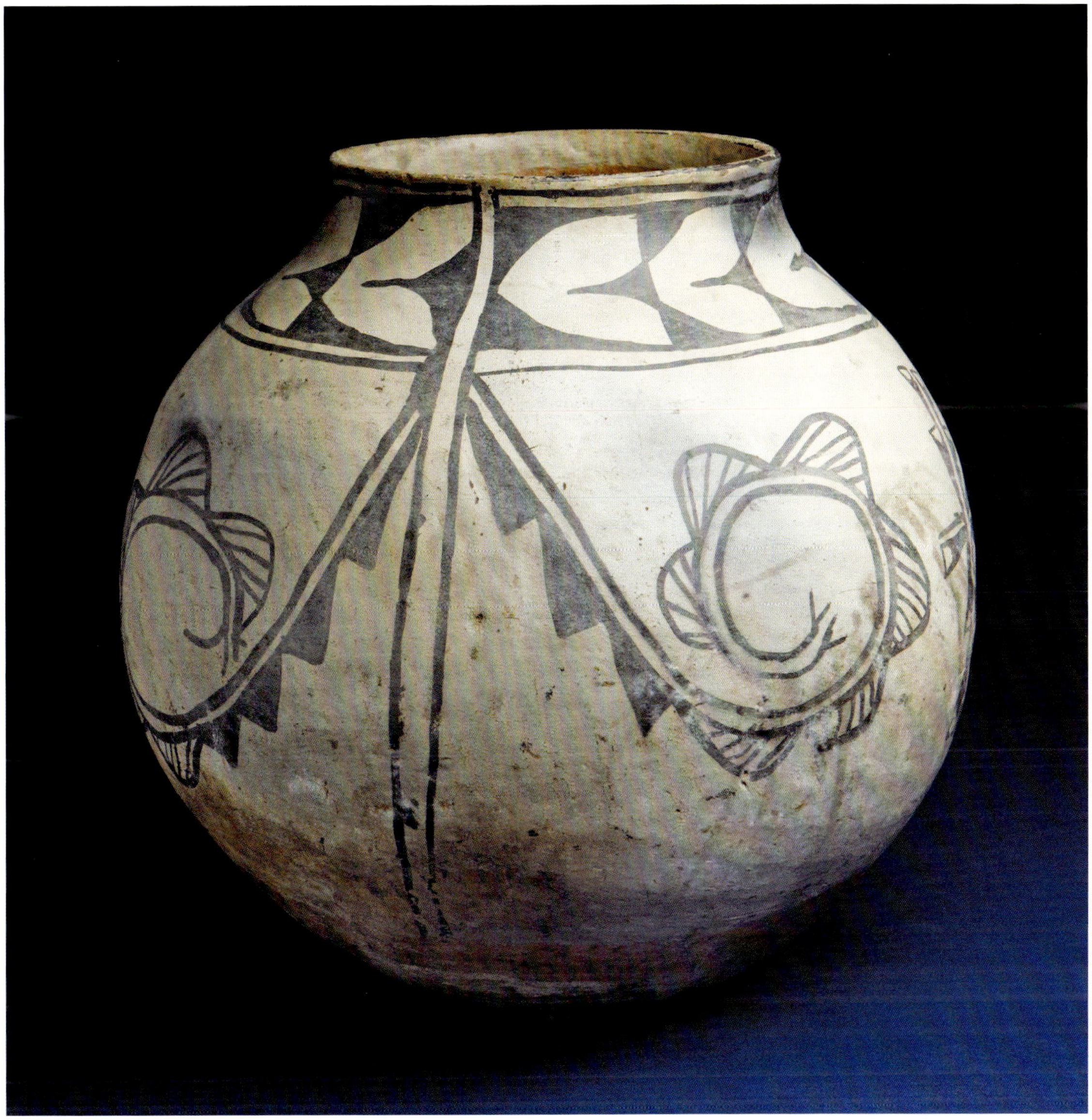

figure 93
Jar
Keresan Polychrome
Artist Unknown
ca. 1860–1880
35.3 x 36.4 cm

also curated by Chapman—includes many pieces that did not fit into Chapman's schema of historic pottery. Moreover, it includes pottery from a variety of acquisition sources and donations rather than within the limited scope of Chapman collecting pots to illustrate a single sequence (figs. 92–93).

The use of style trends in the dating of historic-period pottery is difficult because of the considerable overlap. One style may take generations to morph into the next because of the vicissitudes of individual and family pottery-making aesthetics. Keresan pottery holds promise for unlocking an accurate Rio Grande pottery history. In particular, the dates and documentation from Kotyiti provide critical evidence of when, how, and by whom pottery adapted to Spanish rule, the Pueblo Revolt, and the factionalism that the Spanish exploited to resettle New Mexico in the 1690s. The conservatism of Santo Domingo also is instructive in understanding the concepts of tradition and innovation. The Keresan style, for example, persisted for about five generations of potters, with change evident only after the aggressive introduction of American farming methods and manufactured goods in the 1920s (figs.

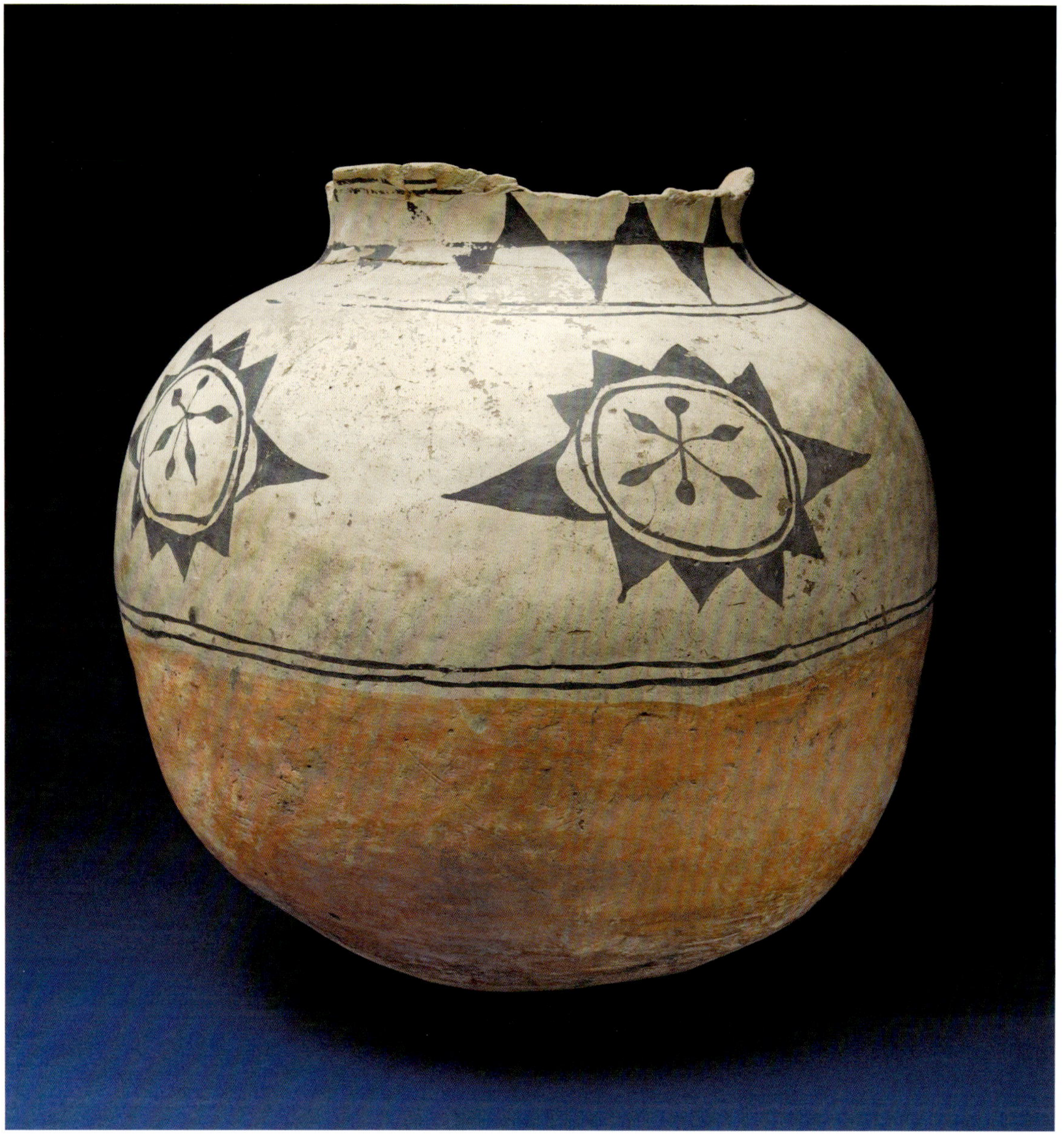

figure 94
Jar
Keresan Polychrome
Artist Unknown
ca. 1850–1880
50.0 x 48.5 cm

94, 118). This suggests the perils of developing chronologies on the basis of stylistic analysis alone, because within a period of two centuries individual innovation and cultural change were occurring simultaneously.

Relatively speaking, Cochiti potters turned their backs on domestic-use ware to produce pottery for economic commodity (figs. 106, 110). In contrast, Chapman observed that many pots were in use at Santo Domingo in 1909, but when he returned twenty years later to purchase historic-period pottery he found willing sellers. As late as the 1980s Santo Domingo families were selling their large heirloom pots; however, I still see large vessels in the homes of friends living at the pueblos. Today, instead of practical containers in daily use, they are objects of cultural heritage and pride.

The Modern Period, 1880–1950

Anthropologists and museum curators voraciously collected the Southwest, and in particular, pottery

(Parezo 1985; see also Fane, Jacknis, and Breen 1990; Wade and McChesney 1981). The Smithsonian Institution collected some 34,000 Puebloan objects in just twenty-five years, two-thirds of these between 1879–1885. Collecting could not have happened at a worse time. With American rule in 1846 came the incessant replacement of domestic pottery with manufactured goods, as well as the establishment of a cash economy (fig. 95). Museum collecting removed many models for future pottery making from the villages, as is particularly evident at Zuni, where pottery in 1880 is substantially different from that of 1900. Nevertheless, Pueblo peoples' own desire for change and modernity guided the era, and it is sentimental to suggest that if collecting had not happened indigenous use-oriented pottery production would have persisted longer.

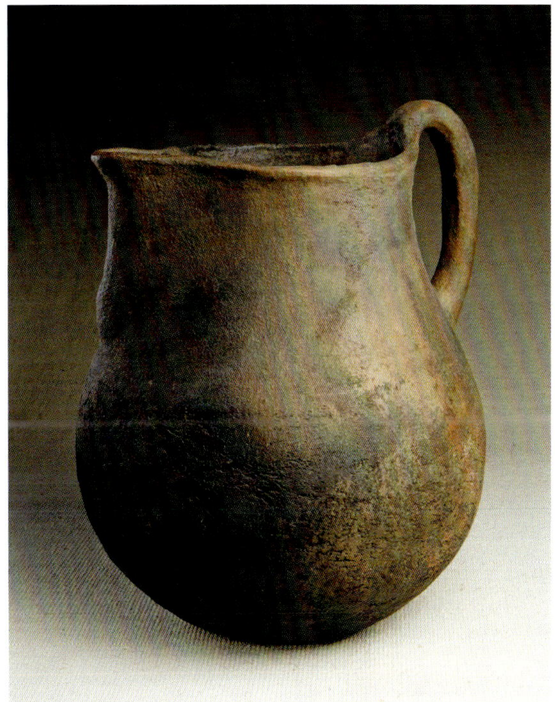

figure 95
Coffee Pot
Santo Domingo
Artist Unknown
ca. 1880
32.8 x 27.1 cm

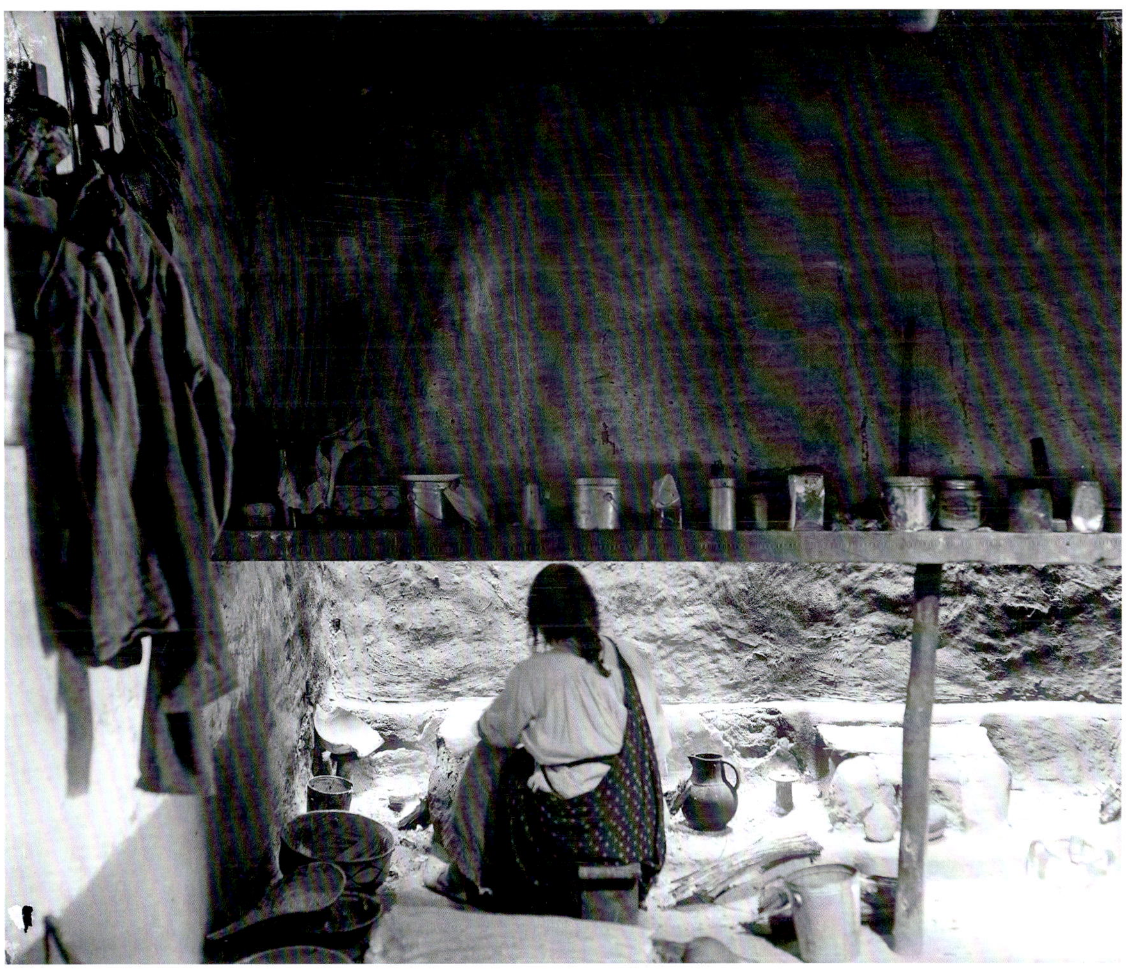

Pueblo woman in her kitchen, ca. 1894–1910. Courtesy National Museum of the American Indian, Smithsonian Institution, N15742. A typical Cochiti kitchen of a hundred years ago mixed the Spanish-style fireplace with traditional pottery and Anglo-American manufactured metal and ceramic containers. Potters often replicated American goods in clay for village household use.

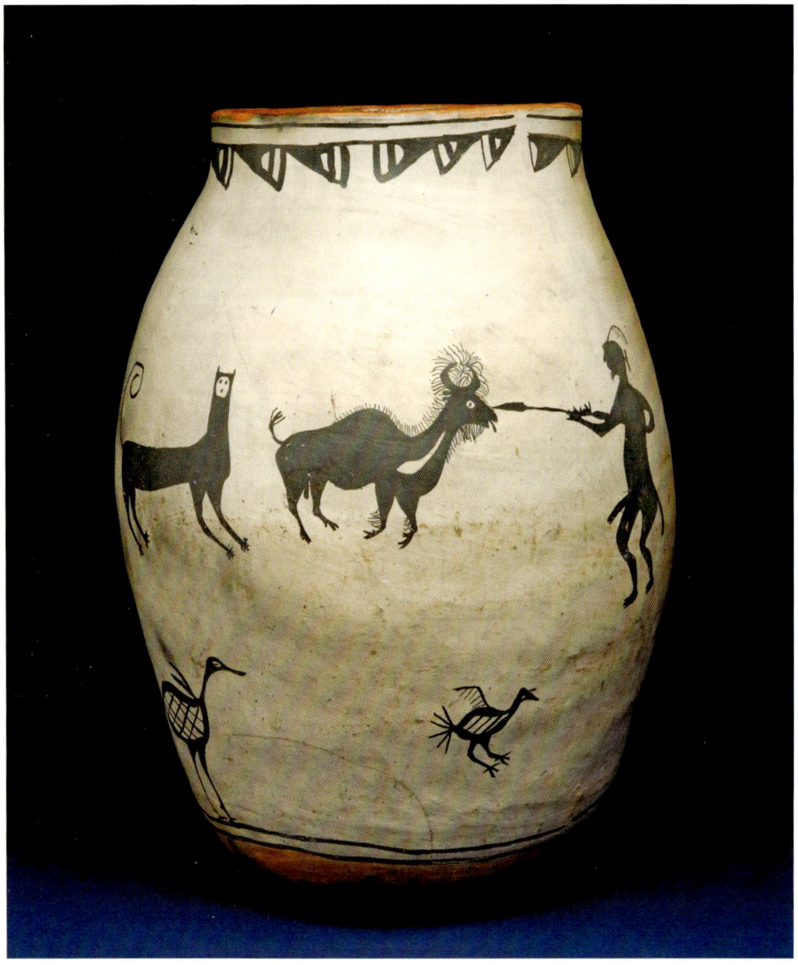

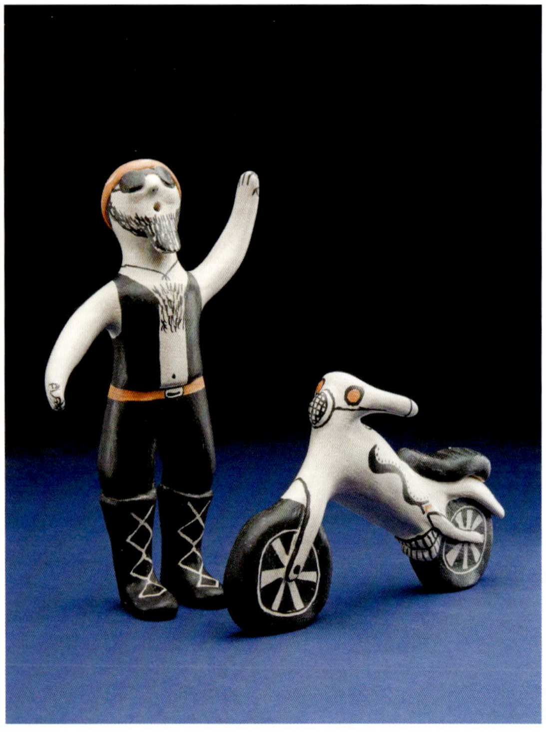

figure 96
Storage Jar
Cochiti
Trinidad Montoya
ca. 1910
54.6 x 40.9 cm

figure 97
Motorcycle Man
Figurine
Cochiti
Joyce Ortiz
1997
21.0 x 14.0 x 4.2 cm

There was a burgeoning production of story pots in the late nineteenth and early twentieth centuries. They depict idiosyncratic scenes of hunting or other daily events, as well as encounters with the supernatural (fig. 96). Because male activities such as hunting and public dance are depicted, I deduce that men painted these pots. Although their origins might be in water and meal bowls for religious use, story pots are invariably secular wares. The telling of hunting stories and other exploits may have been encouraged when Pueblo men made contact with outsiders; the direct style and subject of the paintings suggest that we are to take the hunting scenes literally, to understand that man's foibles and exploits are part of the continuity of life. (A few similarly "autobiographical" bowls were produced by Ancestral potters from the Mimbres and Four Corners region.) Also at this time, Cochiti potters used figurines to engage in social criticism, conducting a discourse—often through parody—on the changing occupants of the Southwest. The figurines expressed the multiple ways potters viewed those who differed from themselves (figs. 39, 63, 97). While it is impossible to understand individual potters' intentions, we can infer that the making of figurines was a means of coping with foreigners as well as a form of social empowerment (Batkin and Lange 1999:43). Story pots include this same discourse and, apparently, parody. Story pots have a directness lacking in other vessels—making a water jar in the shape of a waterfowl or filling its surface with swimming creatures is a deliberate artistic decision (figs. 98–101). In this manner, ceramic wares were used to integrate and tell stories of daily life, from the mundane to the extraordinary (Batkin 1999; Lange 2002).

Cochiti story pots and figurines may have been an element of the nativistic movement that swept through the Rio Grande pueblos in the mid-nineteenth century. During Spanish rule and following the Pueblo Revolt, Native religious imagery

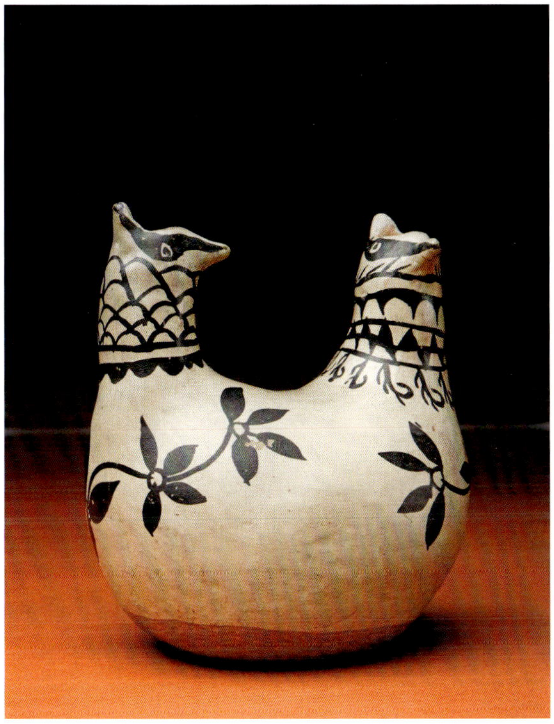

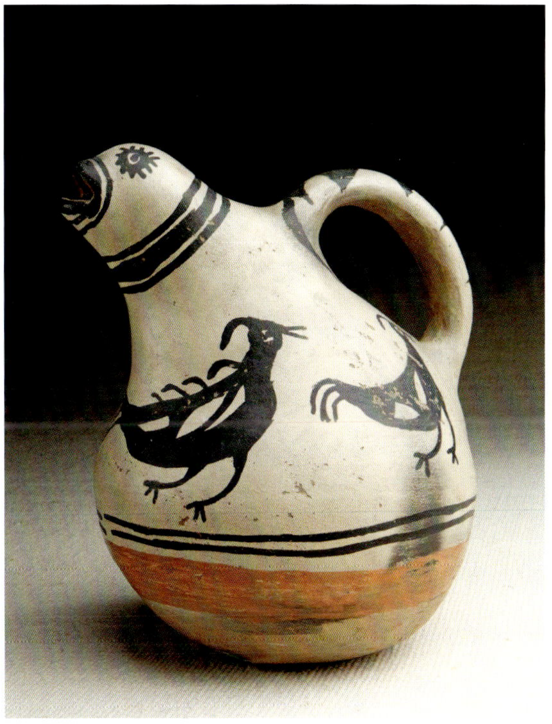

figure 98
Double Bird Jar
Cochiti
Artist Unknown
ca. 1890
17.9 x 12.7 x 16.2 cm

figure 99
Bird Pitcher
Cochiti
Artist Unknown
ca. 1890–1910
23.2 x 16.5 x 20.5 cm

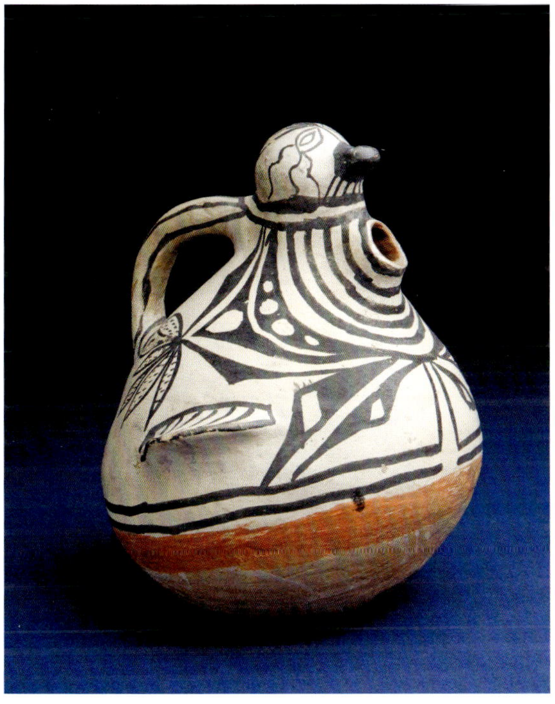

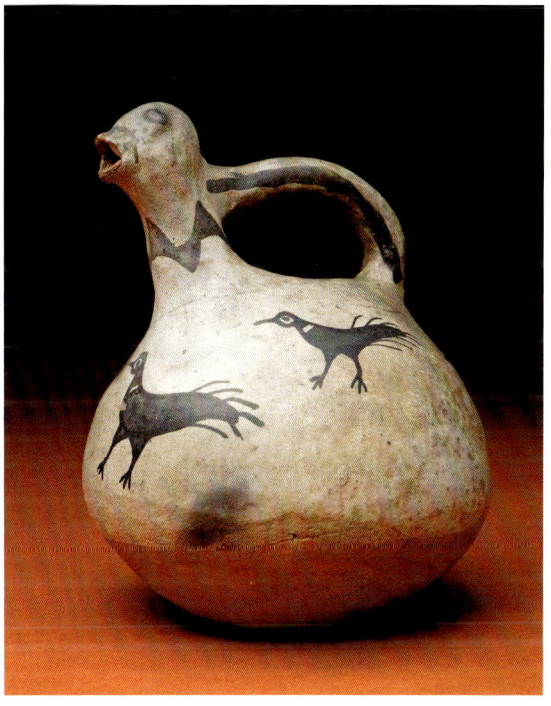

figure 100
Bird Pitcher
Cochiti
Artist Unknown
ca. 1910
22.0 x 20.0 x 19.0 cm

figure 101
Bird Pitcher
Cochiti
Artist Unknown
ca. 1870
20.3 x 6.4 cm

—Katsina figures, altars, and prayer sticks—was replaced with more generalized symbolism (Mills 2002). But after two centuries of rapid change and aggressive colonization, and although Catholicism and new agricultural crops were fully integrated into Puebloan cultural practices, potters once again began expressing deep cultural values on pottery. By the mid-nineteenth century, isolated sacred motifs and iconography began surfacing on large and small vessels, both for home use and for sale. This in-

figure 102
Jar
Cochiti
Artist Unknown
ca. 1910
17.9 x 26.8 cm

figure 103
Jar (two views)
Cochiti
Artist Unknown
ca. 1910
26.5 x 32.4 cm

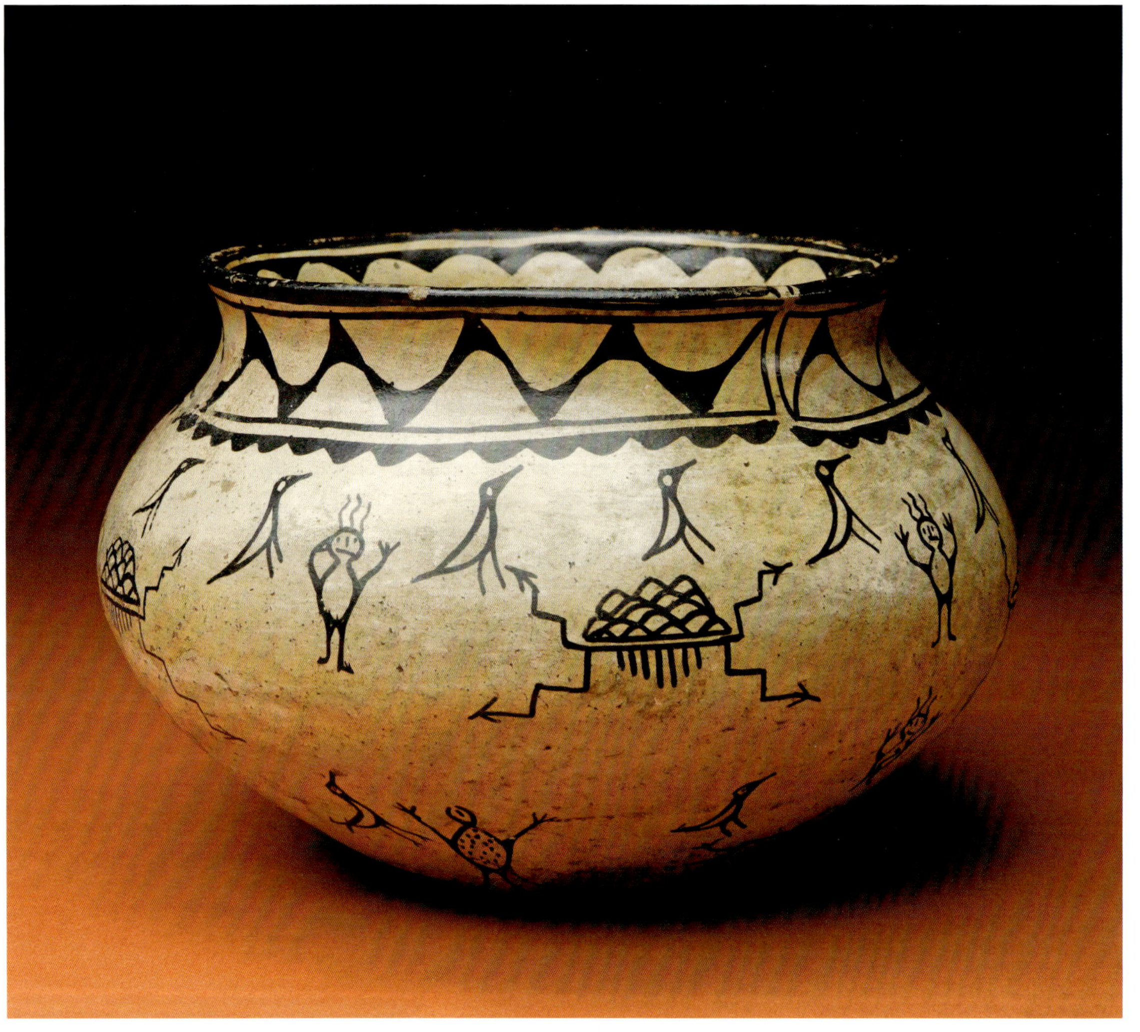

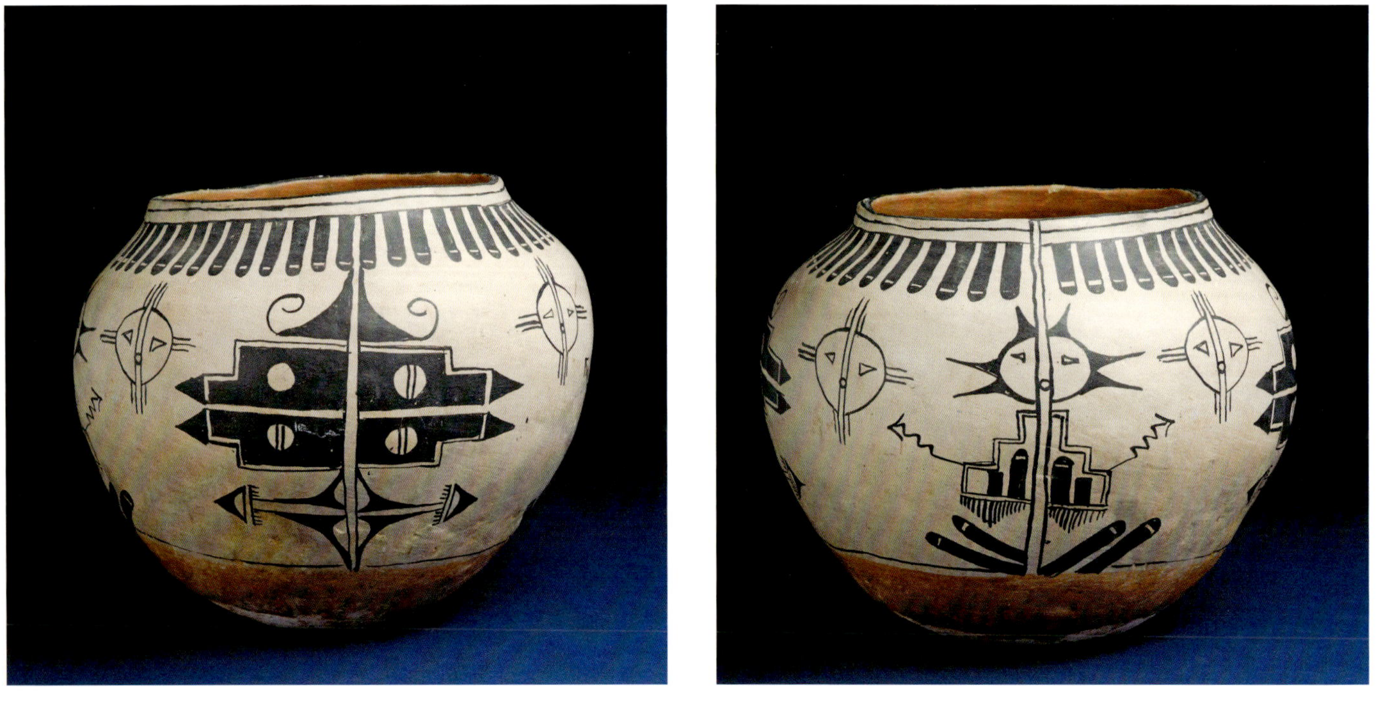

creased use of ancient Puebloan ceremonial motifs may be seen as representing a nativistic assertion of "we are still here" (figs. 102–104).

Creating a clear picture of pottery production after 1880 is filled with paradoxes. While Stevenson's (NAA Stevenson to Powell, October 27, 1880) assessment of Santa Clara is upbeat—"great quantities of black-glazed pottery are made..."—others recorded that Santa Clara pottery was on the decline and was not used in households after 1870 (Jeancon 1904–30 in Hill 1982:83). Of San Ildefonso Stevenson (1883b:432–433) wrote, "The people of this pueblo devote their time chiefly to agricultural and pastoral pursuits, and have almost abandoned the manufacture of pottery. That in use by them at the present time being mostly obtained from neighboring pueblos." In 1881, Bourke (1936:278, 1937:47) noted that pottery in use at both Taos and Picuris came from San Juan Pueblo. Bunzel (1929:82–83) wrote that Santo Domingo pottery production had reached a "lamentable state of decay." Conceivably, this was because pottery was no longer vital for survival. Lange (1959:159) observed that in the late 1940s pottery made at Cochiti and other pueblos was still extensively used but noted (Lange 1959:154) the Cochiti preference for Zia, Acoma, and Zuni water jars obtained through trade, as much of their own pottery production was directed toward the tourist market. White (1962:56) observed that instead of making their own pottery, Santa Ana and Jemez obtained their wares from Zia. Others wrote about the effects the curio and tourist markets had on pottery: "The country is flooded with cheap and, scientifically speaking, worthless earthenware made by the Pueblo Indians to supply the tourist trade" (Holmes 1889:320). Stevenson (1883a:330) observed that potters made "large quantities for sale in addition to what they make for their own use" (figs. 105–110).

While there are several publications about Cochiti figurative pottery (Babcock 1986; Batkin

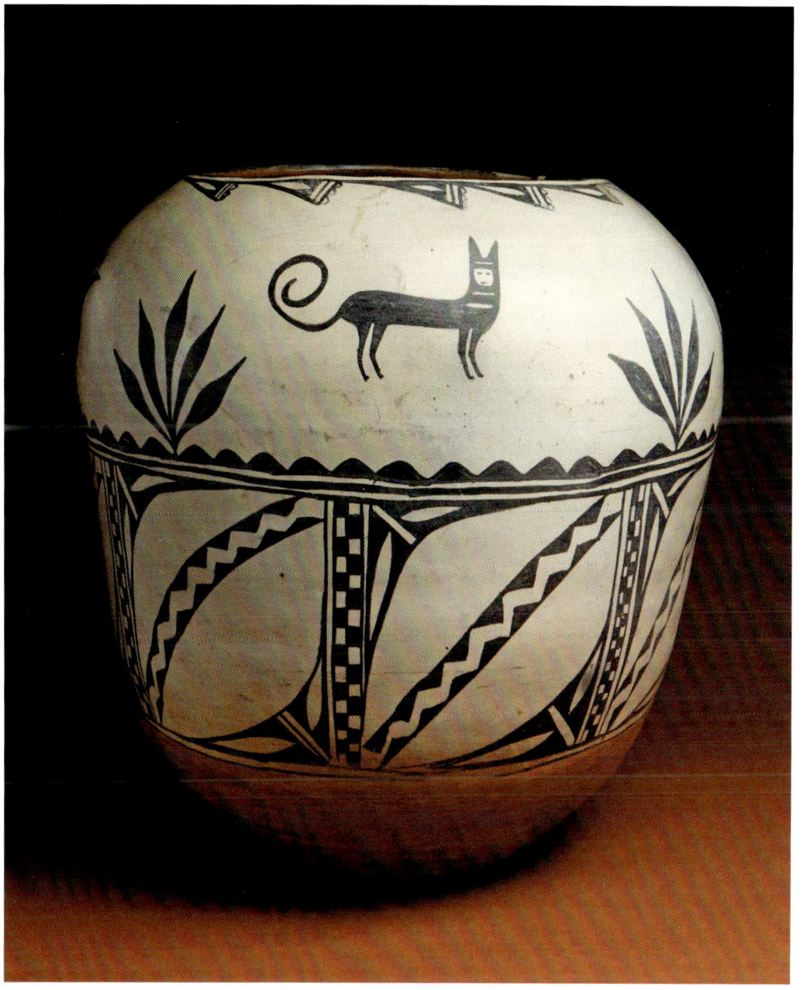

figure 104
Jar
Cochiti
Artist Unknown
ca. 1935
55.0 x 52.0 cm

1999; Lange 1993; 1998; 2002), there is only one book about the fuller repertoire of Santo Domingo pottery (Chapman 1936), although Lange (1959) and White (1935) discuss pottery in their general ethnographic studies. Even though he had a good rapport with potters, Chapman's Santo Domingo book has limitations. His pottery studies emphasize the stylistic analysis of painted design systems and the reconstruction of a chronological sequence. In a manner of speaking, Chapman's Santo Domingo publication is a sanitized view of the village's pottery. Nowhere, for example, do we learn what was stored in storage jars, or if particular designs were used only for particular types of wares or foods. Moreover, the illustrations in the book, executed by Chapman, remove all of the individuality, all of the expressiveness of unsteady lines and variability from the pottery

figure 105
Bird Jar
Cochiti
Artist Unknown
ca. 1890–1910
17.0 x 15.5 cm

figure 106
Owl Jar
Cochiti
Artist Unknown
ca. 1910
17.2 x 9.8 cm

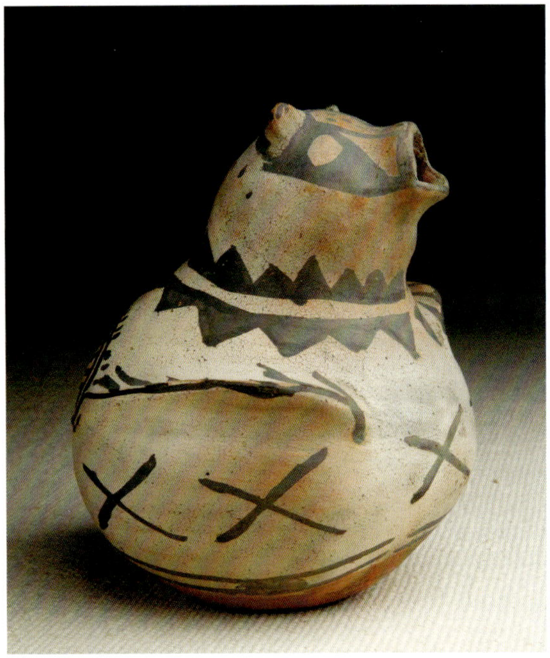

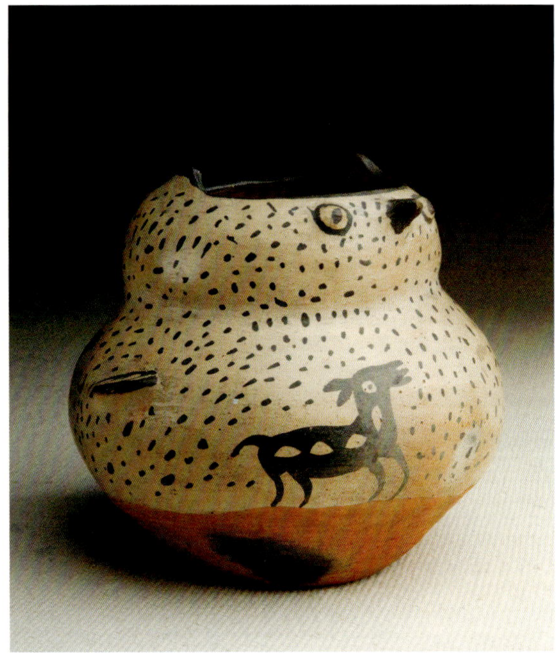

figure 107
Jar
Santo Domingo
Artist Unknown
ca. 1920
37.3 x 42.5 cm

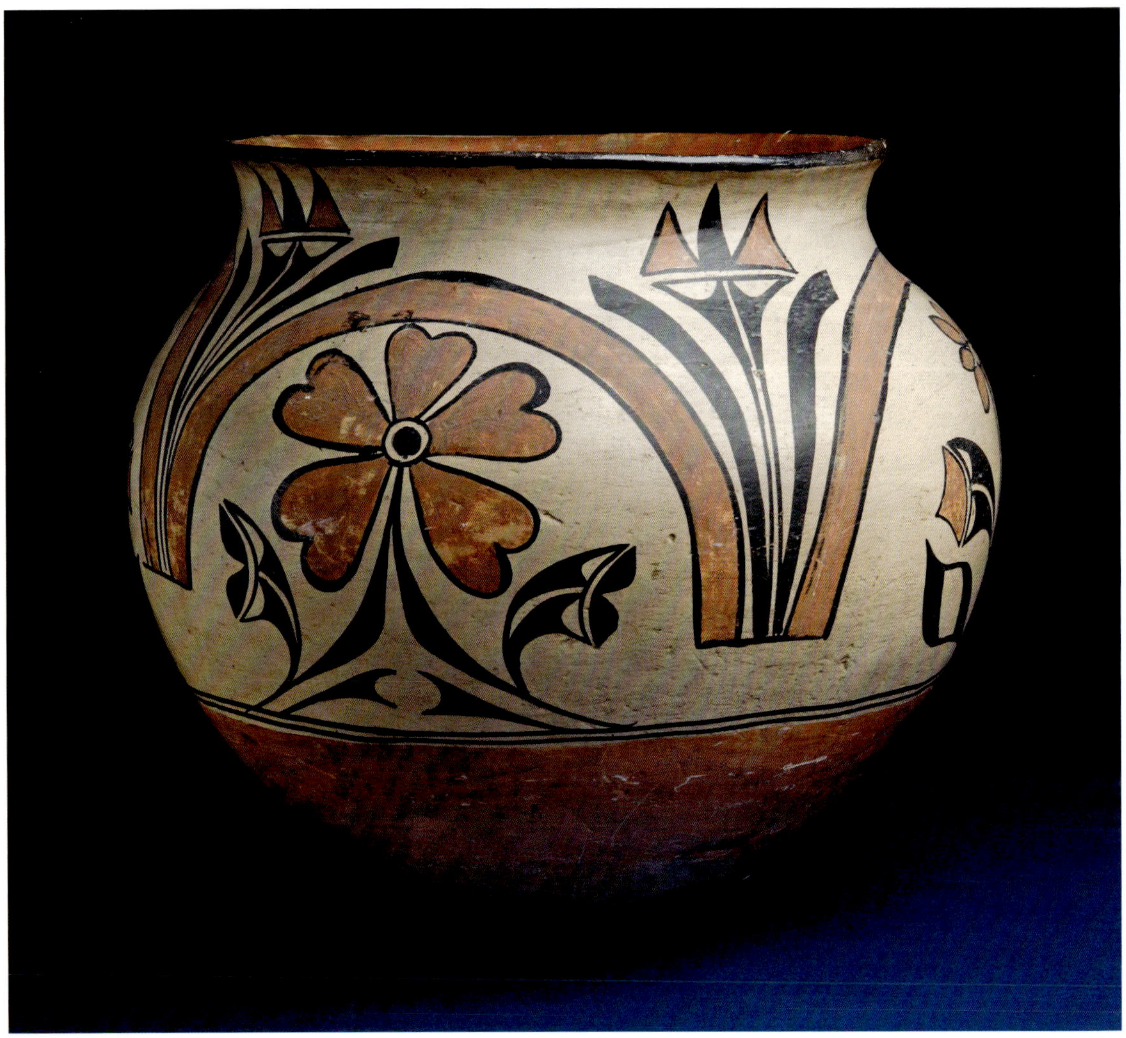

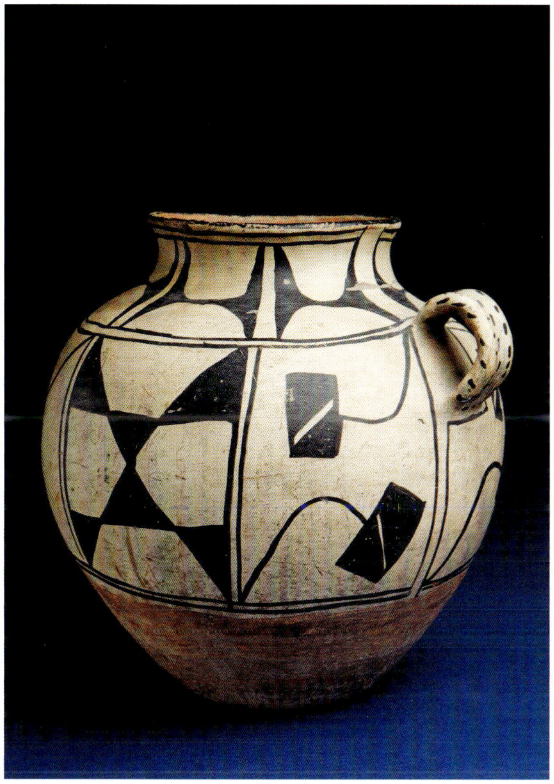

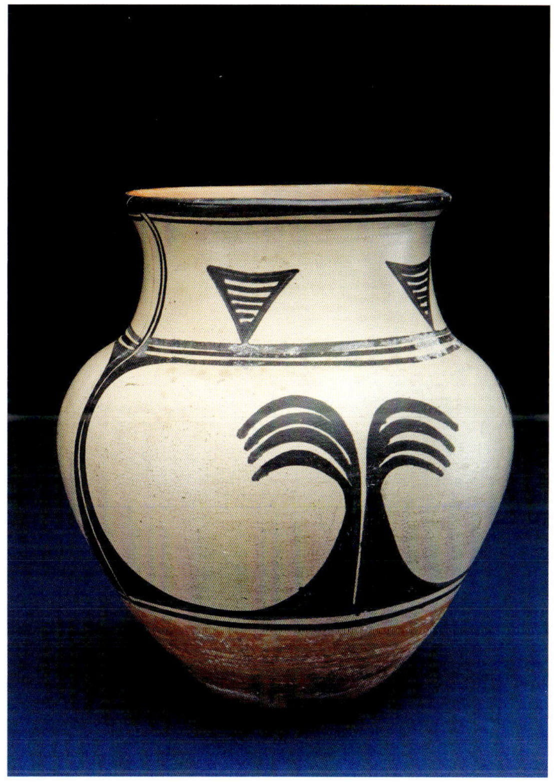

figure 108
Jar
Santo Domingo
Artist Unknown
ca. 1915–1920
27.3 x 28.1 cm

figure 109
Jar
Santo Domingo
Artist Unknown
ca. 1920
19.6 x 18.0 cm

figure 110
Jar
Cochiti
Artist Unknown
ca. 1900–1920
36.5 x 38.0 cm

motifs. He created a perfected world of art, which to this day is held out to Pueblo potters as an archetype. Santo Domingo was a pueblo continuing to use pottery in daily life and making relatively few curios for sale, yet throughout his book Chapman seeks to return what he called a "dignity" to pottery through a return to "ancient symbolic ornamentation and decorative motifs that give the old . . . ware distinction and distinctiveness" (Anonymous 1917:101).

Other early observers gave some of the first descriptions of Pueblo pottery making based on what they saw at Cochiti (Bandelier April 3, 1882; and Eickemeyer 1895:101–102). Lange (1959:159) reported that although the great majority of household utensils are of modern manufacture and are obtained from outside sources, pottery made at Cochiti and other pueblos is still extensively used. This is particularly true of large storage jars, which are handed down from mother to daughter and highly prized. "Smaller bowls are used for chili [*sic*]. . . .

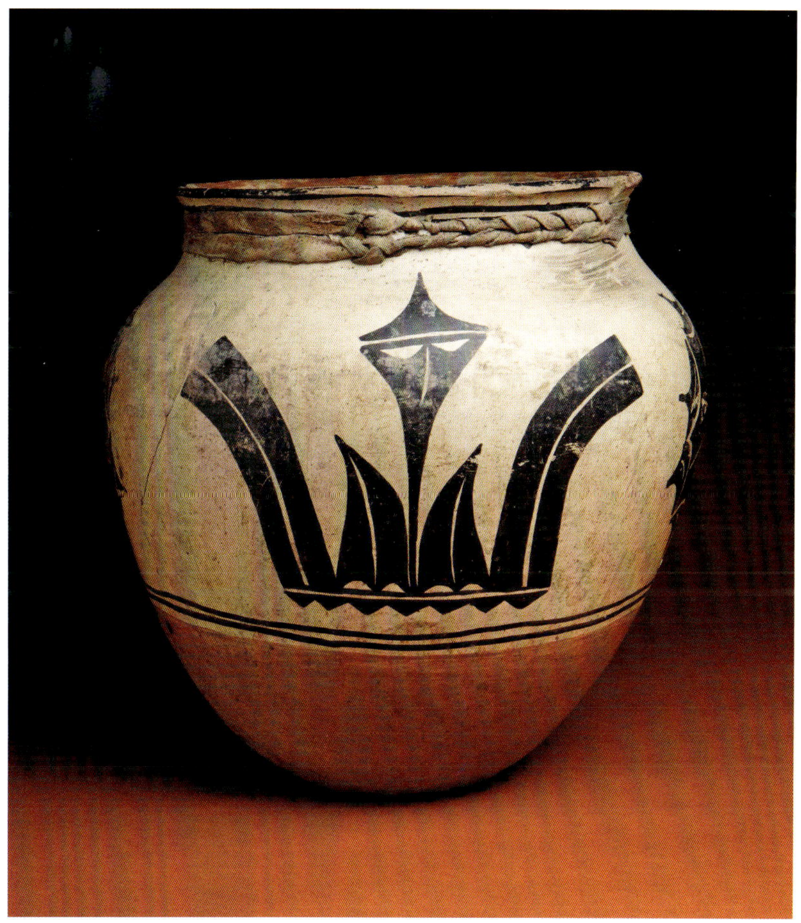

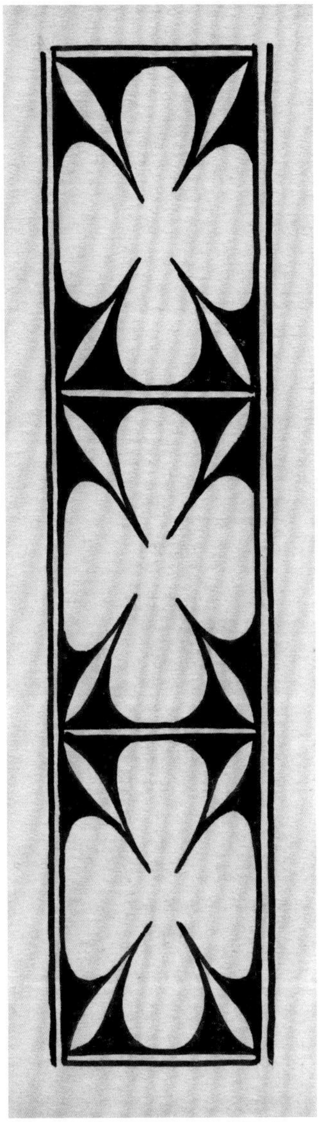

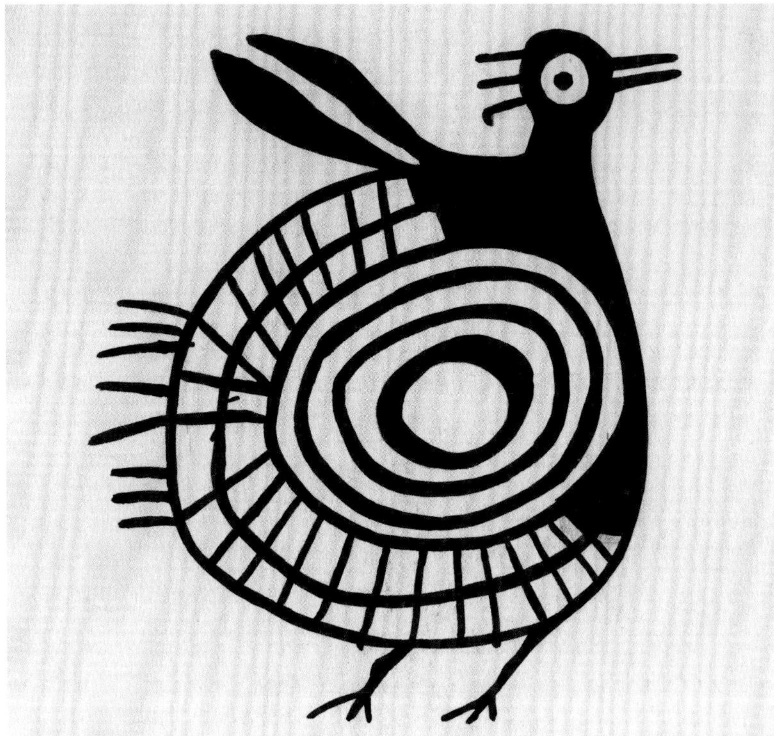

Santo Domingo pottery neck design element, Kenneth Chapman, ca. 1930–1936. Courtesy School for Advanced Research, Transfile AC02:570. Chapman drew hundreds of discrete design elements from Santo Domingo pottery as part of his pottery studies.

Santo Domingo water jar bird design element, Kenneth Chapman, ca. 1930–1936. Courtesy School for Advanced Research, Transfile AC02:570. Chapman made these drawings to show potters the proper designs to use when painting the high-quality Santo Domingo pottery he believed should be their legacy.

Local pottery, though fairly well-made and often water tight, is considered by the Cochiti to be inferior to many Zia water jars." Lange (1959:161) noted pottery was preheated before firing in wood stoves, while an early undated photograph indicates that *horno*, or outdoor bread ovens, were used for the same purpose. Men began decorating pottery in the twentieth century: "Some men make designs on paper first, a few patterns being copied from sherds of prehistoric wares found in the vicinity. These designs are borrowed and copied by others, invariably by relatives. Favorite designs are kept in notebooks so that they may be used again" (Lange 1959:161). Lange notes that most pottery made in the 1940s was intended for the tourist market, the vast majority small eccentric curio pieces such as miniature ovens, ashtrays, or animal banks. Maria Seferina Arquero is noted as one of the first to make large dolls or human forms for sale (Lange 1959:161). Larger vessels were rarely made at the time because the financial return was small for the amount of work—"other things, like beadwork and drums, are a lot easier, and you get more money for them" (Lange 1959:162). Nevertheless, potters Estefanita Herrera,

Lupita Chavez, Teresita Romero, and Ascension Chavez Benada were making larger vessels.

Regardless, MIAC/LAB and the Indian Arts Fund collections have few curios or plain-ware household vessels because Chapman and others intended the collections to be examples of the best of Pueblo ceramic heritage, and not documents of what they considered degenerative traditions (Bernstein 1994). Both collections are notable for their exclusive representation of Pueblo pottery history by what Chapman and others considered to be the truest and noblest examples of the tradition—painted pottery. Within this schema, plain or utilitarian wares were not part of a great art tradition, and pottery made for sale was inauthentic. Chapman's books on Santo Domingo and San Ildefonso pottery (1936 and 1970) carried this schema to an extreme (Bernstein 1994) and has resulted in generations of ahistorical pottery studies focused on creating an "advanced art beyond the stage of simple utilitarian wares" (Frank and Harlow 1974:8) rather than more inclusive studies of the continuities and innovations that have defined pottery for millennia. Beauty and significance were attributed to observable traits—the surface painting and the end product—rather than to the traditions of learning, function, and family. In their place is a stylistic analysis of painted design systems and reconstruction of a chronology based upon the very basic art history diachronic of simple to complex. The end creation of this schema is pottery of an idealized Pueblo past as defined by outsiders, instead of by the Pueblos themselves. In Chapman's hands, ancient emblems of the continuity and solidarity of modern Pueblo people with the past become only design systems. No doubt he perceived these motifs as precontact and thus purer, as sound canons of Native art devoid of the polluting influences of Spanish or American design, or of tourism and other economic forces. Consequently, Chapman's book has served as a ready Pueblo design reference and was republished in 1995 under the title *Pueblo Pottery Designs.*

The broader and indigenous cultural contexts in which these design systems were created and maintained remain in Cochiti and Santo Domingo as part of their worldviews, as part of their aesthetic or materialization of the world. Reuniting their worldviews with their visualizations can only provide additional insight and understanding.

SECTION III

Collections

Imagine a world without things, your things: The things that make your life comfortable; the things necessary to your survival; the things that bring beauty to the spaces you occupy; the things that express your identity to others. Then, imagine that a wild fire swept through and destroyed your community, the livelihood of your family, your personal home and possessions. What would be left to express and validate your identity? Imagine that the wildfire was not a literal fire but a fire of outside colonizers, of land and natural resource loss, of disease, of social and religious persecution, of political domination. What would remain of your community, family, and your personal life? How would you survive? Would you give up everything you believe, the way you lived, and become part of the colonizing culture? Or would you become private, go underground, disguise and secret away the things important to you that others coveted or disapproved of and sought to destroy? If you are a member of a Pueblo community you don't have to imagine this, it is what happened.

V.K.V.

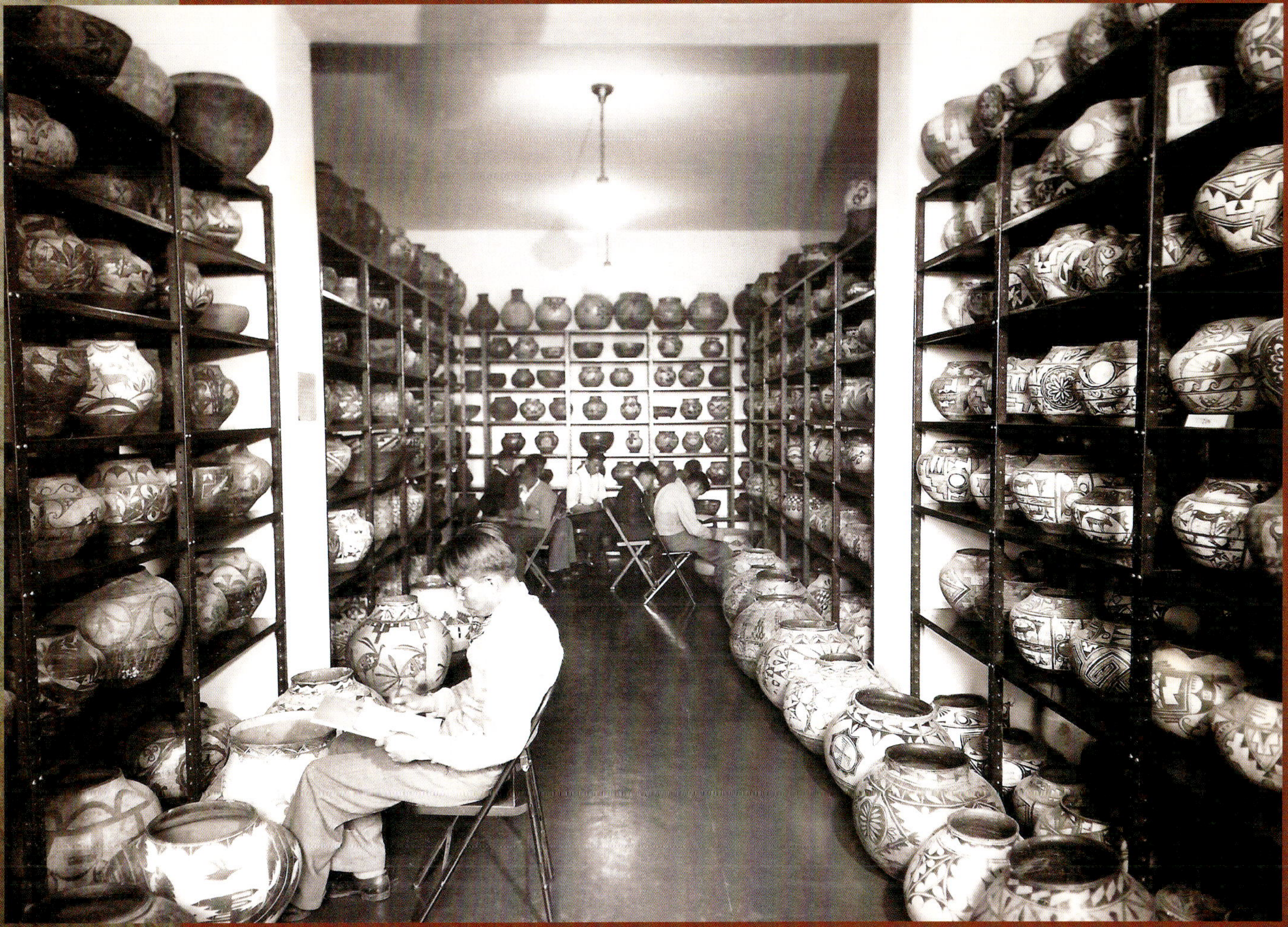

Dorothy Dunn Studio students, Santa Fe Indian School, copying pottery designs in ceramic storage, Laboratory of Anthropology, ca. 1940. Courtesy Laboratory of Anthropology Archives (MNM/DCA), 70.1/2276. The founders of both the School of American Research and Laboratory of Anthropology Southwest Collections intended that they be used for research and study by both scholars and Native American artists. In the early days of both institutions, Native artists and students had access to the collections; as the collections grew in scholarly importance and monetary value, and the institutions became nationally accredited museums, terms of access became more stringent and visitors fewer.

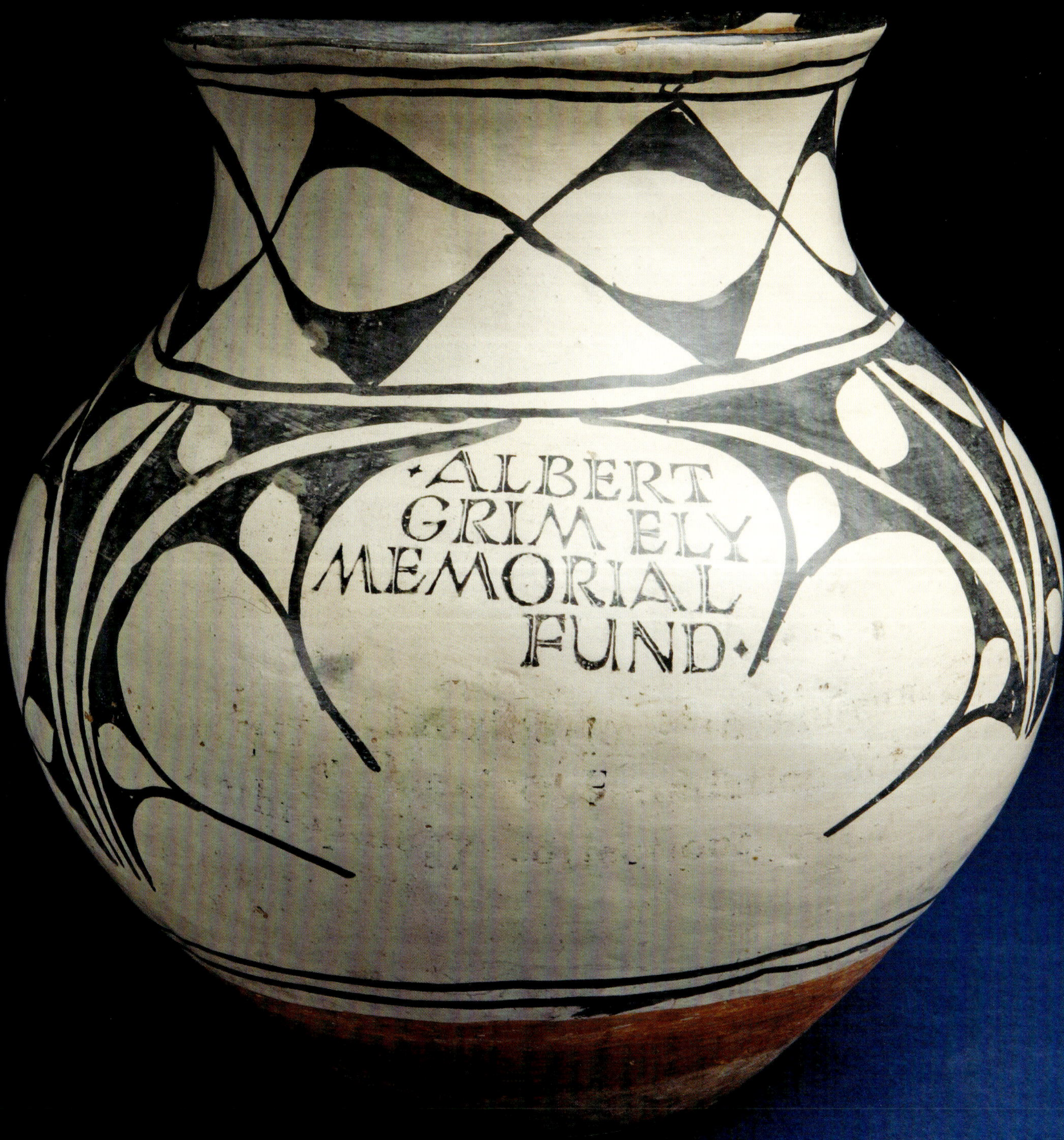
ALBERT
GRIM ELY
MEMORIAL
FUND

Collecting, Preserving, and Giving Back

A Catalog of the Collections

Valerie K. Verzuh

As is true with most publications about Pueblo pottery, the potters themselves did not write the essays in this volume. Their focus resides in the actual creation of pots, and less in constructing discourse about cultural and scholarly significance, artistic quality, circumstances of use, monetary value, or the possible past and future trajectories of the oeuvre. This catalog of the Cochiti and Santo Domingo pottery collections is included in part because this is where the artists' voices reside. Examining the museum's extensive pottery collection in all its diversity—locating the individual pots in time and space, becoming familiar with the shapes and sizes, with the use of color, with the types of painted designs and their purposeful placement on the vessels, with all their visual attributes—is an entryway to the Pueblo perspective. So, to emphasize the potters' voices and in the spirit of individual inquiry, this catalog section contains no interpretive information other than object name, name of artist if known, artist's pueblo, creation date, dimensions, and donor's name; here there is no curator to act as an intermediary between you—the viewer—and the pots.

Still, we all need tools to translate physical objects into mental objects, and I encourage you to also examine the catalog pieces from the multiple perspectives provided by the essayists: artistic, anthropological, historical, curatorial, cultural, and personal. Using some of the tools they have provided, as well as your own insights, critique the generally accepted authorities on the subject as well as your own assumptions about the meanings of pottery inside Pueblo culture and outside in the tourist and art markets. And keep in mind that although we are able to name only a very few of the artists, each piece is the work of a talented, creative, and unique individual and an eloquent, although mute, statement (fig. 112).

Another means to intellectually access the pottery in this section is in the same manner we catalog our collections. My museum colleagues and I collect and preserve Pueblo material culture to understand how the people lived when no written records exist, or at least none from the point of view of a cultural insider. We believe that all artifacts can tell us their story, if only we know the right ques-

figure 111
Jar
Santo Domingo
Artist Unknown
ca. 1920
25.5 x 25.6 cm

This jar was used as a donation pot in the early 1970s, when it was inscribed with the name of a Laboratory of Anthropology collections manager.

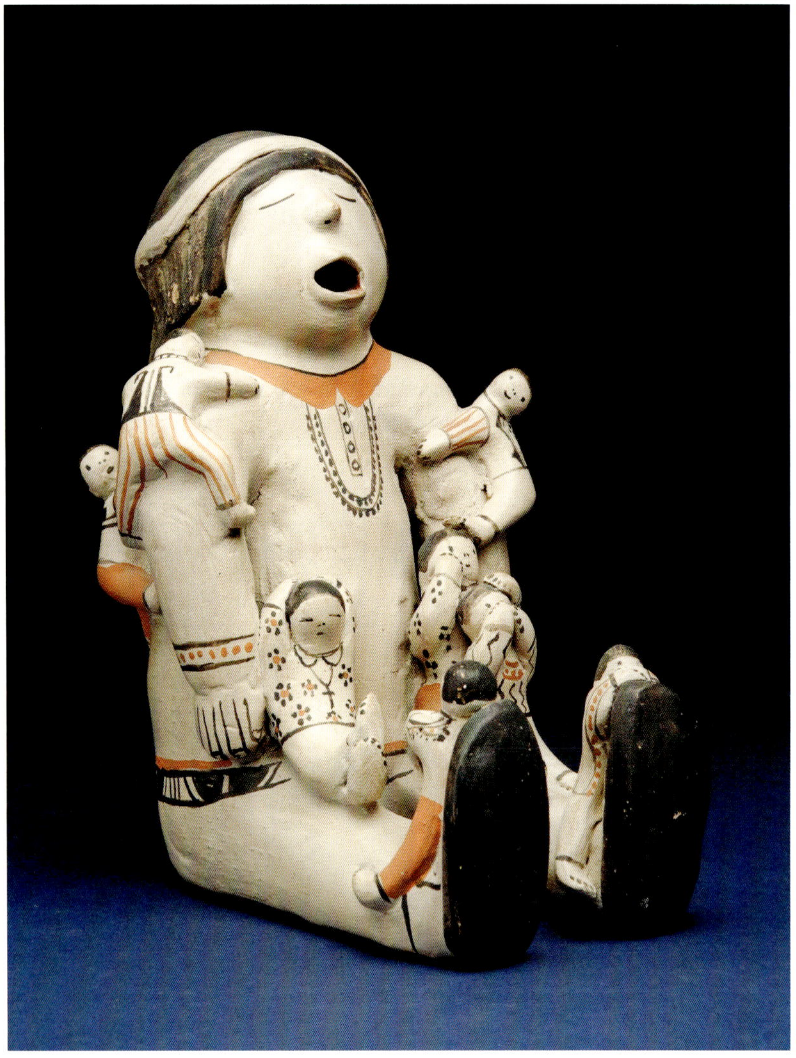

tions to ask. To give our Cochiti and Santo Domingo ceramic collections meaning within a museum context, to catalog them and to organize them in storage—to make our own kind of sense of them—we catalog each piece within the theoretical framework of typological, or chronological, classification. In part two of his essay in this volume, Bruce Bernstein discusses how typology is only one way to "read" pottery and its limitations; however, it is a very significant and principal approach for museum curators. Ceramic taxonomists construct typologies by studying combinations of traits or attributes including: form or shape, the composition of the paste, the method of manufacture, the slips and paints, the surface finish, and the elements of any painted design. For historic-period collections, typological evaluation—essentially asking questions of a pot—is crucial when historic or ethnographic documentation of an artifact is lacking. As is common with many American museum collections formed in the late nineteenth and early twentieth centuries, very little written documentation was collected with the objects. In such cases, the usefulness of typology is in determining culture, place, and date of manufacture, and sometimes even the individual maker. We can

figure 112
Storyteller Figurine
Cochiti
Helen Cordero
ca. 1970
22.8 x 19.4 x 14.9 cm

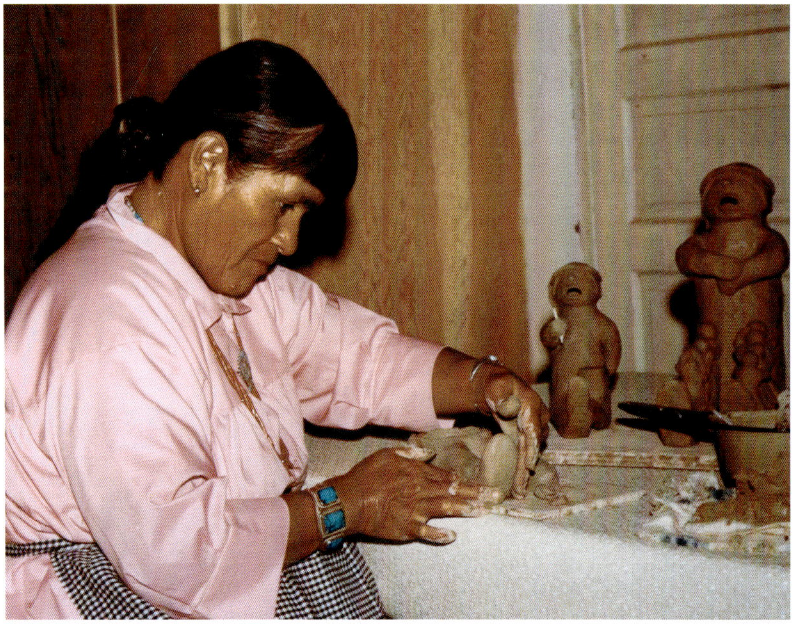

Helen Cordero, Cochiti, 1970. Leonard C. Turner, photographer. Courtesy Palace of the Governors (MNM/DCA), 50300. Cordero, the originator of the storyteller figurine, made her first one in 1964. She is often quoted as having said that her inspiration was her grandfather, Santiago Quintana, who was a notable oral historian at Cochiti. In homage to Quintana, her classic storyteller is a man with closed eyes "because he is thinking" and open mouth because he is "telling stories."

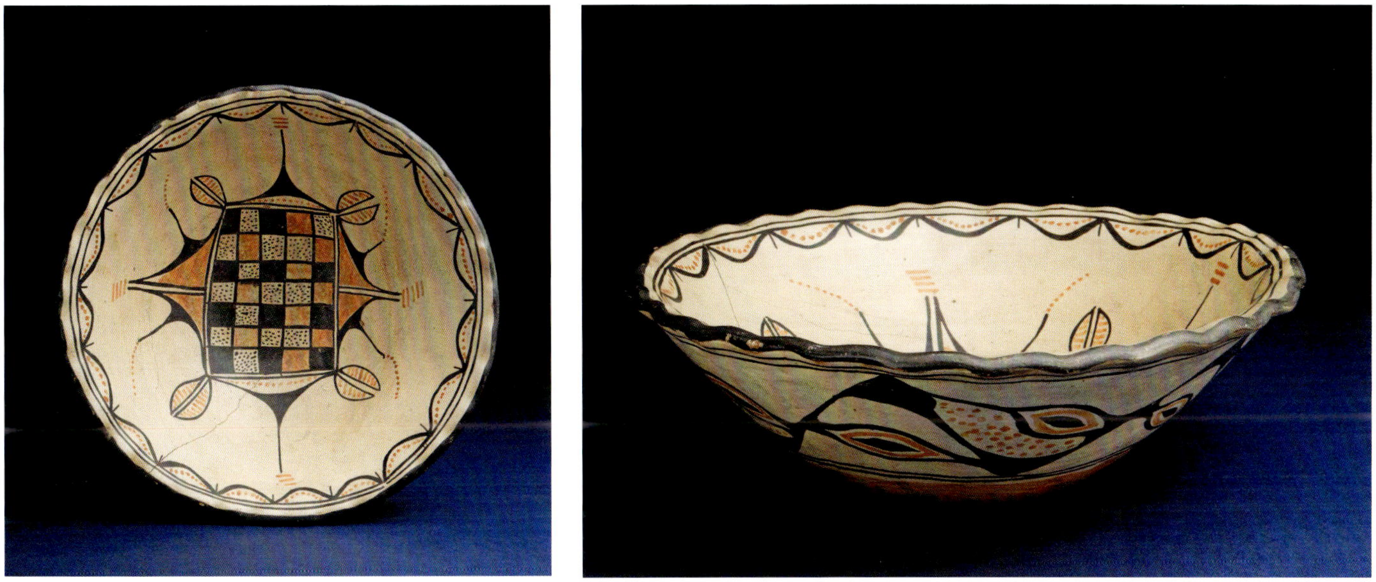

figure 113
Bowl (two views)
Cochiti or Santo Domingo
Artist Unknown
ca. 1920–1940
10.8 x 33.3 cm

deduce the identity of each vessel—where it was made, when it was made, who made it, what it was made for—by "reading" its individual traits. When reading artifacts we take into account four principal traits: material, construction technique, design, and function (often determined by the analysis of ethnographic wear patterns and any deposits acquired during use). After studying these traits, we can locate the vessel in a place, time, and tribal tradition, and further study and comparative analysis may lead to the identification of specific potting families or individual potters (figs. 114–115).

Current identifications of the individual collection objects are based upon recent research in the museum's accession and catalog records, review of publications which include specific objects, and by inviting scholars and indigenous community members to review the collections. The catalog is divided into five parts: Ancestral Puebloan wares, including antecedents, either Powhoge Polychrome or Keresan Polychrome; Cochiti; Santo Domingo; and wares inconclusively from Cochiti or Santo Domingo. Together, the Cochiti and Santo Domingo historic-period collections consist of a total of 473 objects. Two hundred and thirty-five are conclusively Cochiti Pueblo; 214 are conclusively Santo Domingo; 21 are either Cochiti or Santo Domingo; and 26 artifacts in the catalog are Ancestral Pueblo, or prior to the historic-period, and are included to give a perspective on the genesis of the ceramic wares under consideration. Three hundred and eleven of the artifacts are by "artist unknown," meaning that only 165 vessels have identified makers (these are the work of 75 named makers). The vessels date from the mid-nineteenth century to the present, with the bulk of the collections dating from 1900 through 1950. The collections consist almost exclusively of

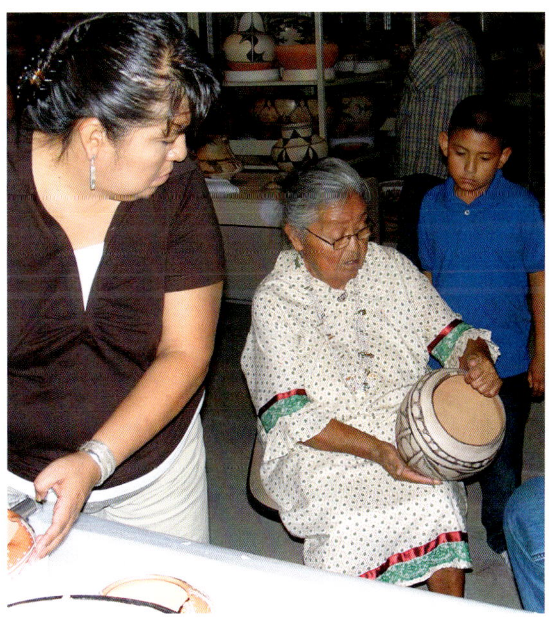

Marlene, Crucita, and Dominic Melchor in the MIAC/LAB collections, 2007. Antonio Chavarria, photographer.

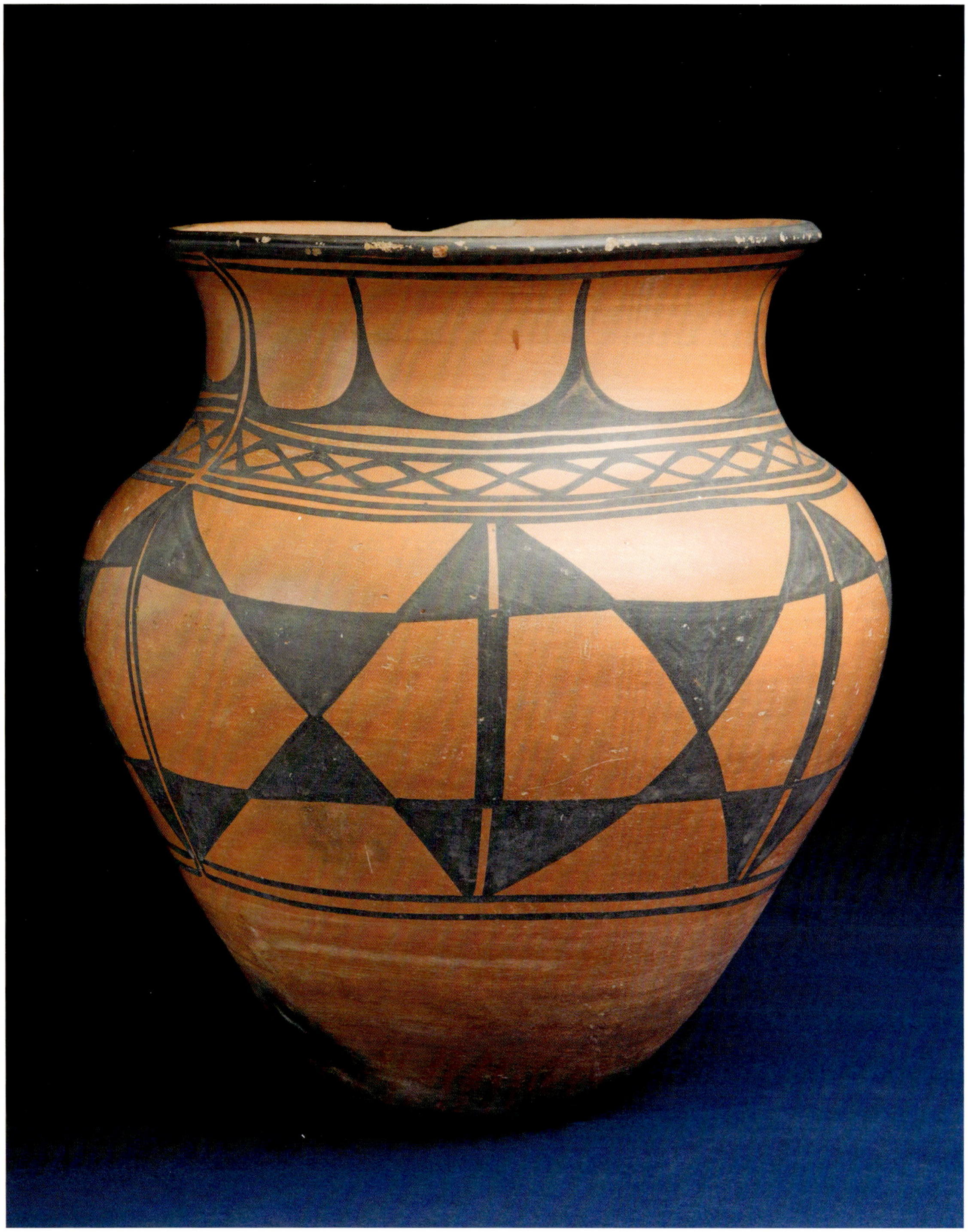

figure 114
Jar
Santo Domingo
Artist Unknown
ca. 1900–1920
31.6 x 29.0 cm

polychrome painted pottery, with few examples of utilitarian plainwares, or anomalous wares such as Blackware and Black-on-black.

The Laboratory of Anthropology, which opened its doors on September 1, 1931, was established as a field station which ethnologists and archaeologists could use as a home base when working in the Southwest, as well as a permanent facility which would house their research field notes and collections. The proposal for its founding listed its purposes as "anthropological research, public education, welfare of the native races in the Southwest,

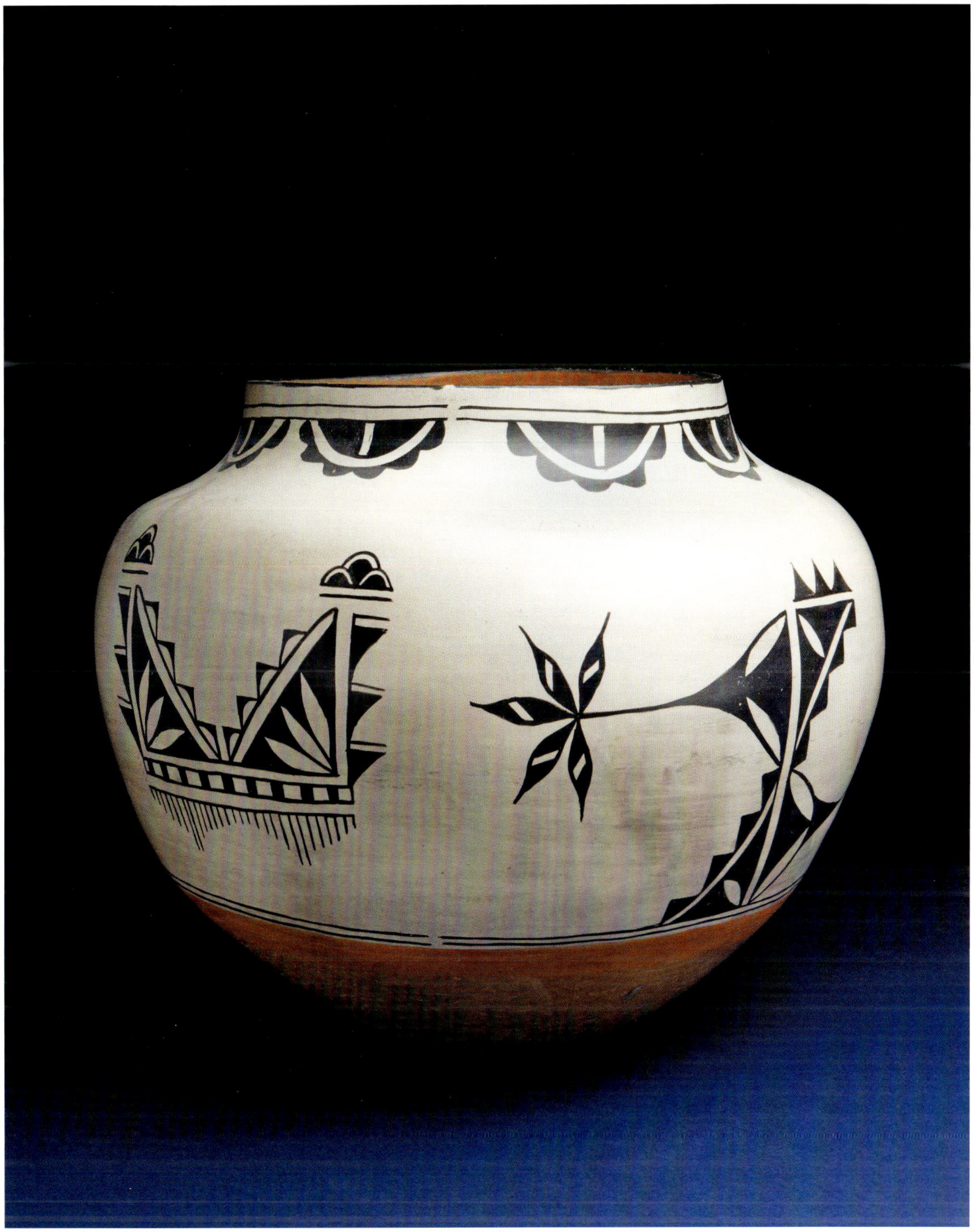

figure 115
Jar
Cochiti
Reyes Q. Romero or
Estefanita Herrera
ca. 1930–1935
40.6 x 53.4 cm

and publication." Curator of anthropology Kenneth Chapman had been on staff since 1927, when the Lab was incorporated as a private institution. It was Chapman who was primarily responsible for bringing the Indian Arts Fund (IAF) collection to the Lab. The historic-period ceramic collections, including those of Cochiti and Santo Domingo, were formed on the framework of the IAF collection. (Briefly, the IAF was a group of Santa Fe individuals who banded together to improve Pueblo pottery by creating a collection of exemplary examples.) Over time, the Lab's collections grew in depth and

figure 116
Bowl
Cochiti
Possibly Estefanita Herrera
ca. 1945–1950
23.0 x 44.5 cm

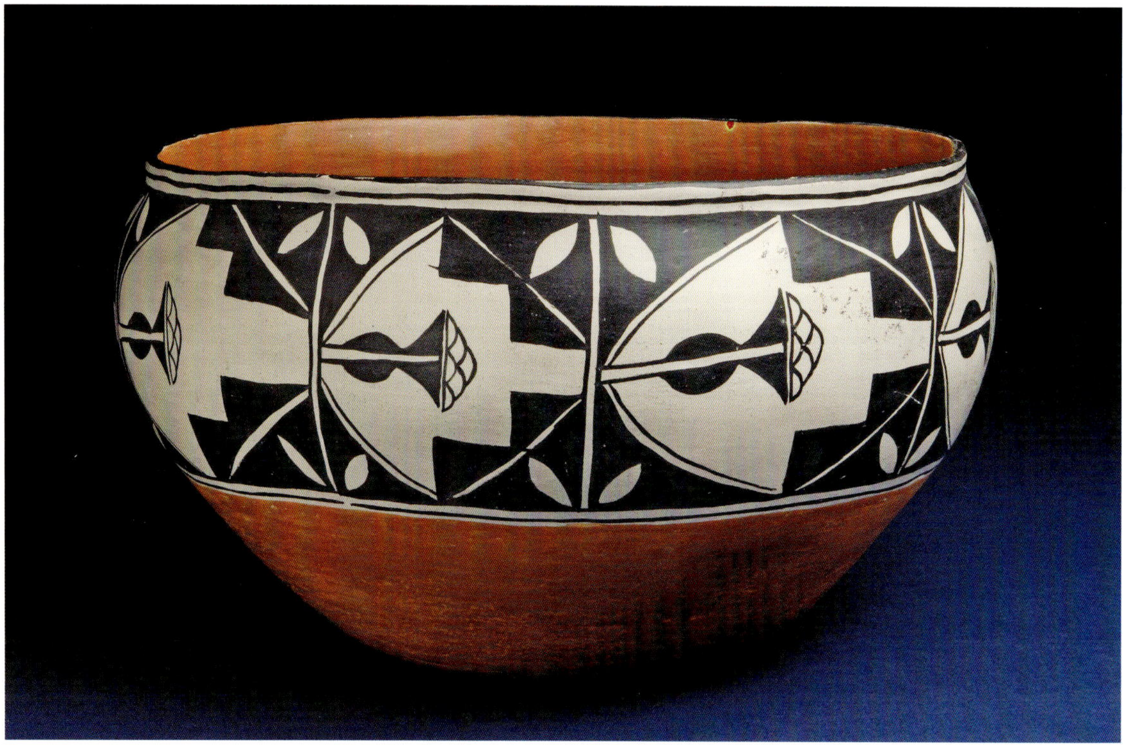

figure 117
Jar
Cochiti
Antonita Quintana
ca. 1910
43.2 x 42.0 cm

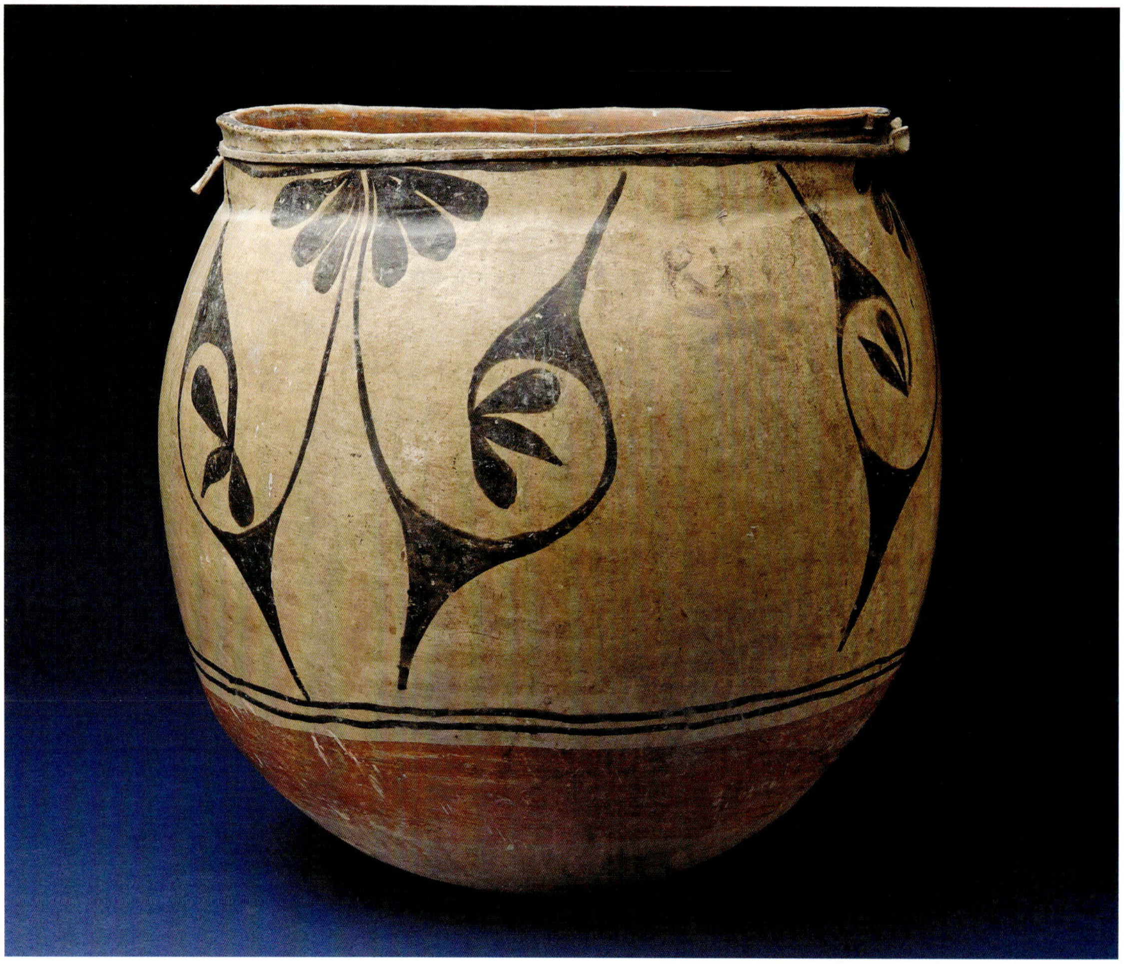

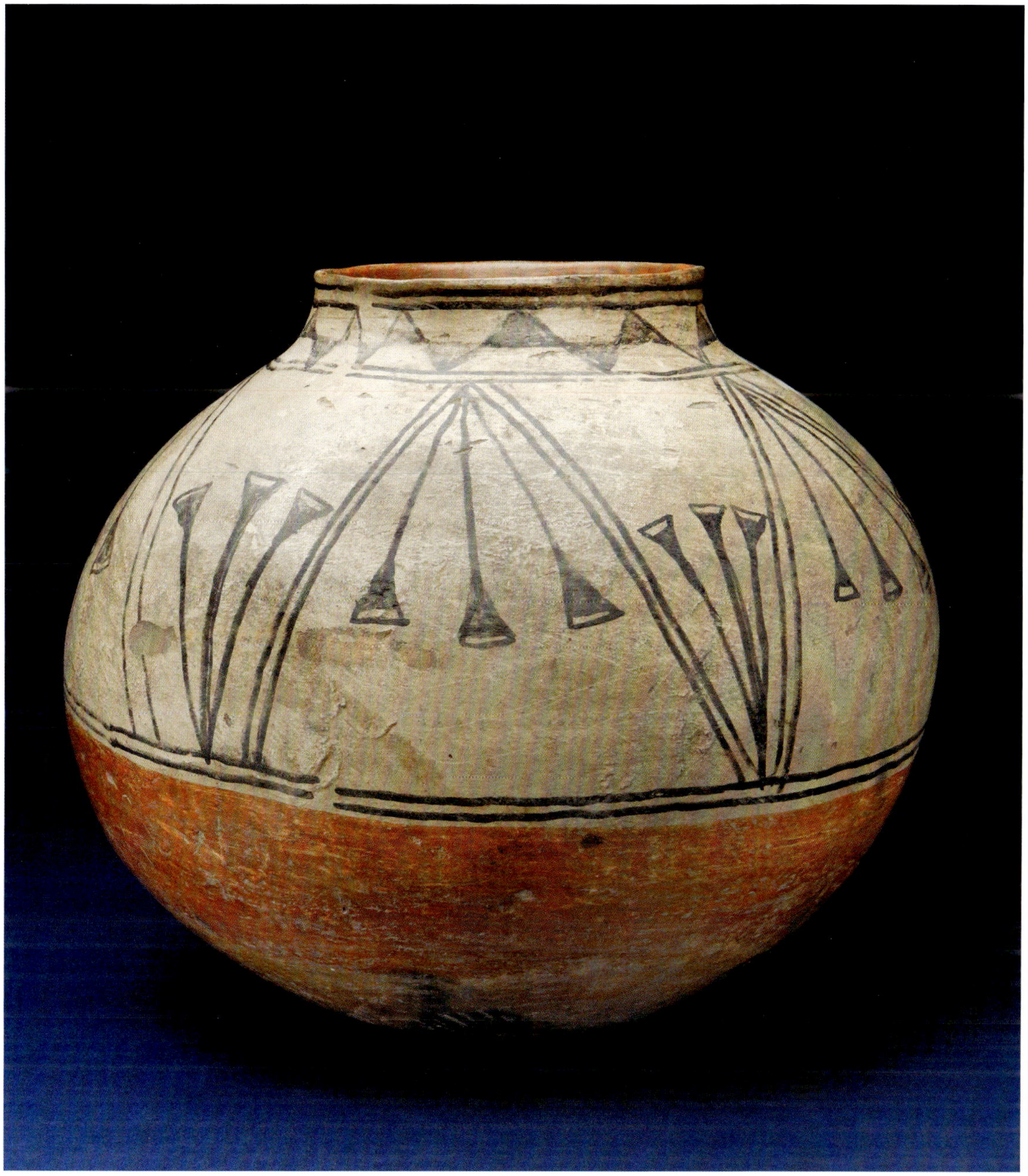

figure 118
Jar
Keresan Polychrome
Artist Unknown
ca. 1850
44.4 x 36.8 cm

breadth through archaeological excavation, directed purchases by museum curators from pueblo community members (fig. 119) and traders or dealers, and through individual donations, with the greater percentage donated by Santa Fe or New Mexico community members with a personal interest in Pueblo domestic and fine arts, or with an interest in the preservation of traditional indigenous communities (fig. 120). Eventually, the IAF collection was deeded to the School of American Research (now the School for Advanced Research). Today, our collections continue to grow through gifts as well as through purchases funded by the museum's support groups, notably the Friends of Indian Arts and the organization that produces Native Treasures market each year. We continue to add to the collection by acquiring individual specimens that paint a complete picture of Pueblo artistic production, from

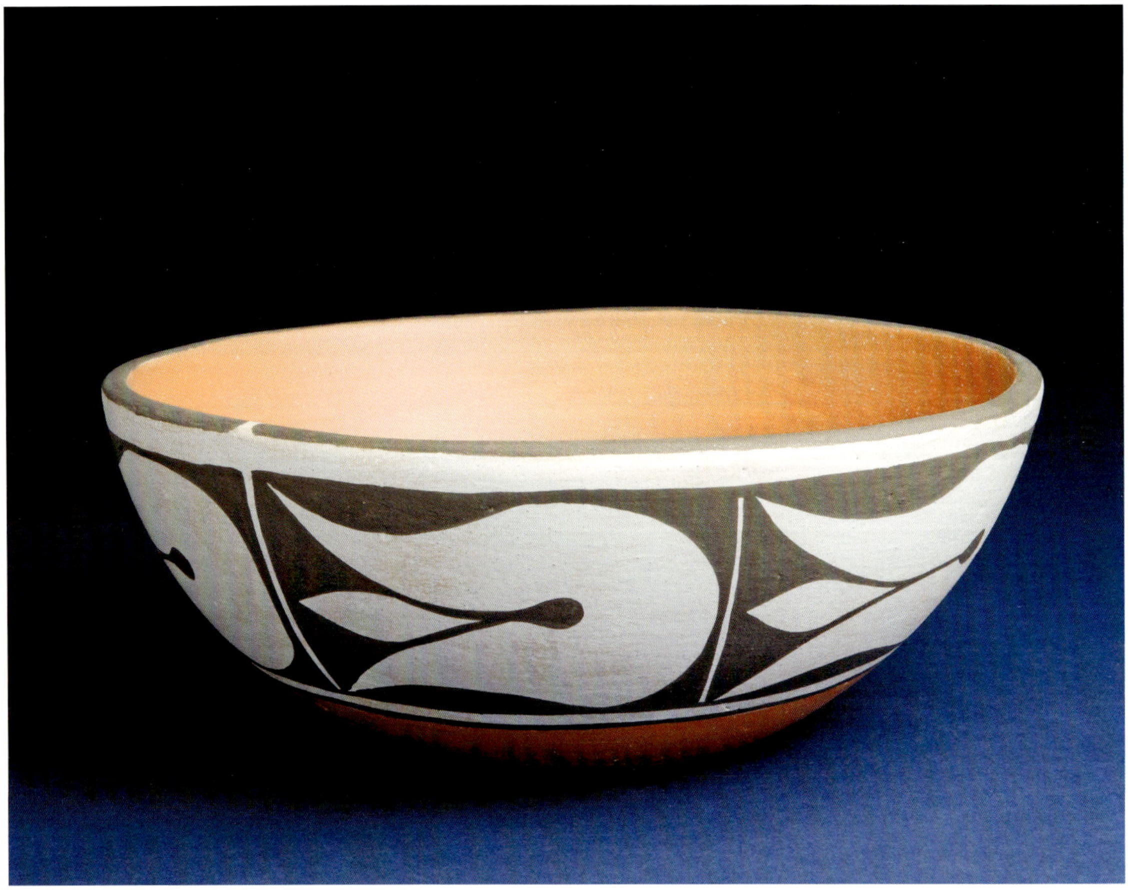

figure 119
Bowl
Santo Domingo
Petra G. Garcia
1989
10.6 x 29.3 cm

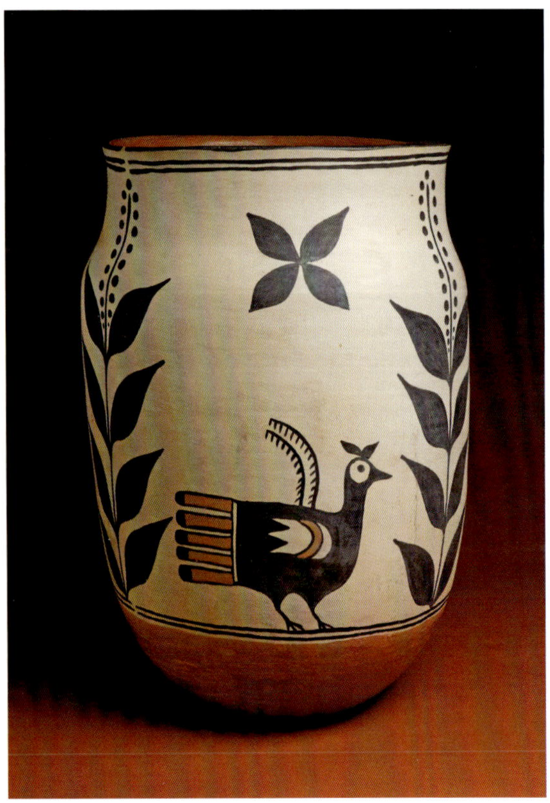

figure 120
Jar
Santo Domingo
Santana and
Crucita Melchor
1964
57.8 x 40.9 cm

"museum quality" examples of high art to "made for sale" pieces.

The Laboratory of Anthropology was conceived as a place of learning where the collections could be accessed for research both by Euro/Anglo-American and indigenous scholars and artists. Recognizing that giving, sharing, and empathy are qualities of community building that historically have been found lacking in ethnographic museums around the world, we today seek to sustain that founding philosophy. Giving back—supporting a community and its unique culture—is an integral part of Pueblo community life and increasingly a guiding principle of the Museum of Indian Arts & Culture/Laboratory of Anthropology. Giving back is at the core of this catalog section. Sharing the pottery in the Cochiti and Santo Domingo collections with the communities that made and used them, that collected or donated them, and those who now

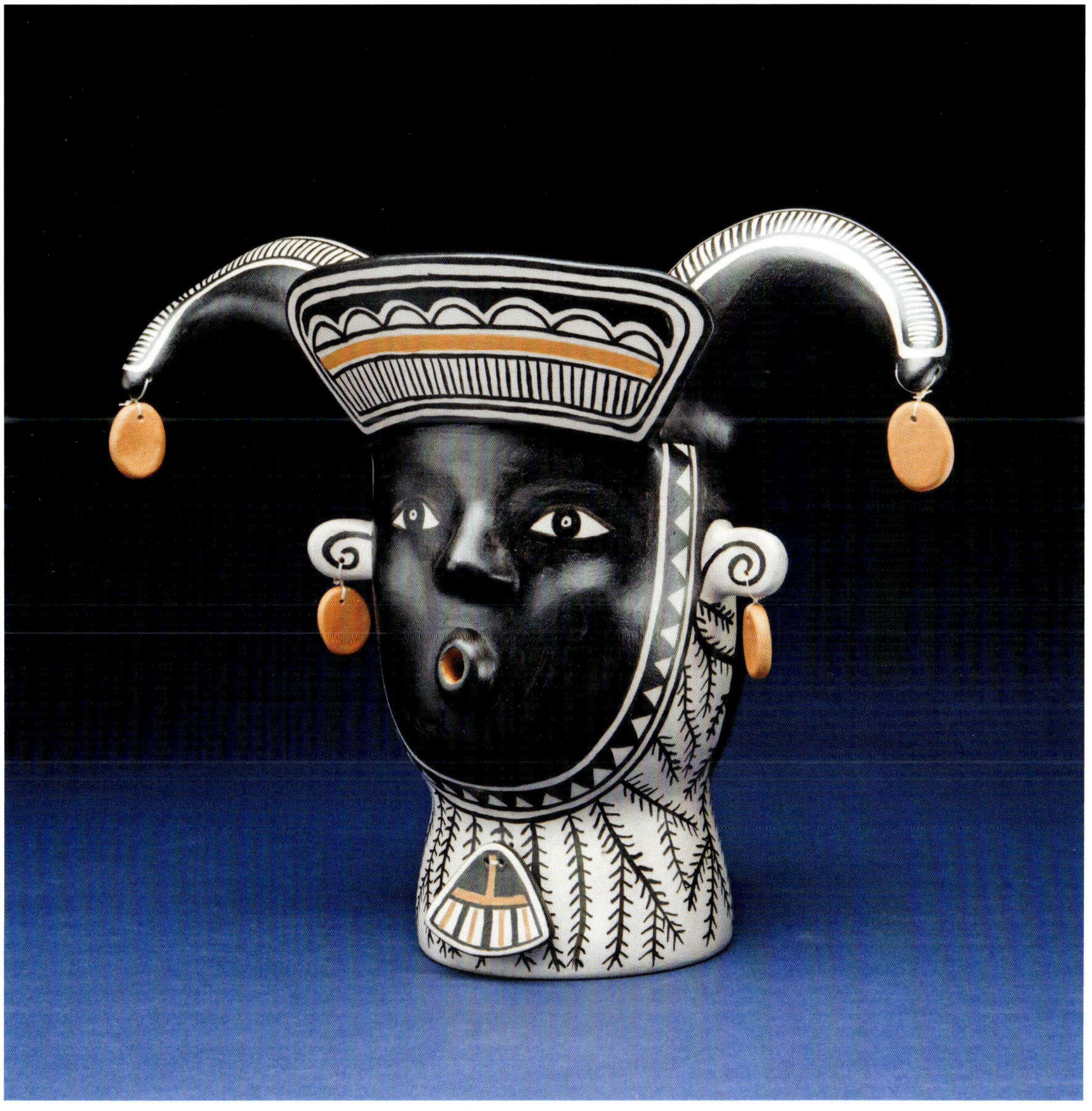

figure 121
Bighorn Sheep Dancer Figurine
Cochiti
Janice Ortiz
2007
27.5 x 35.0 x 17.5 cm

research and write about them, not only preserves and promotes Southwest indigenous traditional arts, it renders the museum contemporary, meaningful, and relevant. Finally, in creating this catalog section my colleagues and I have been guided by sensitivity to how knowledge is held, shared, and perpetuated in conservative Pueblo communities. These concerns have resulted in ongoing consultations with representatives of both Cochiti and Santo Domingo, and ultimately in the restriction of physical, visual, and documentary access to some objects in the collections.

PART I

Ancestral Puebloan

Photographs by
John Torres-Nez

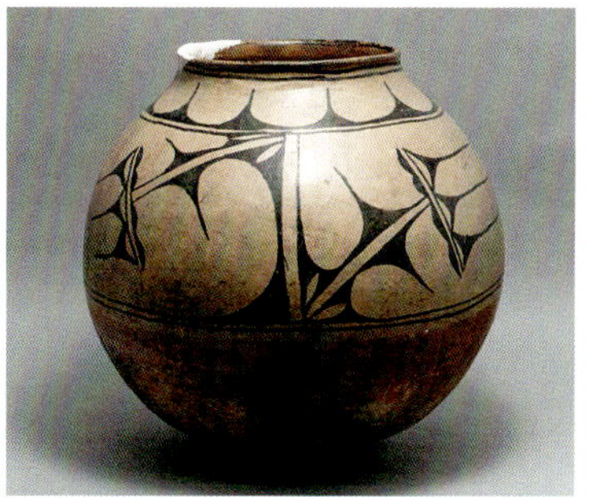

Jar
Keresan Polychrome
Artist Unknown, ca. 1880
43.0 × 45.0
Museum Purchase,
Rogers and Schafer, Albuquerque
11104

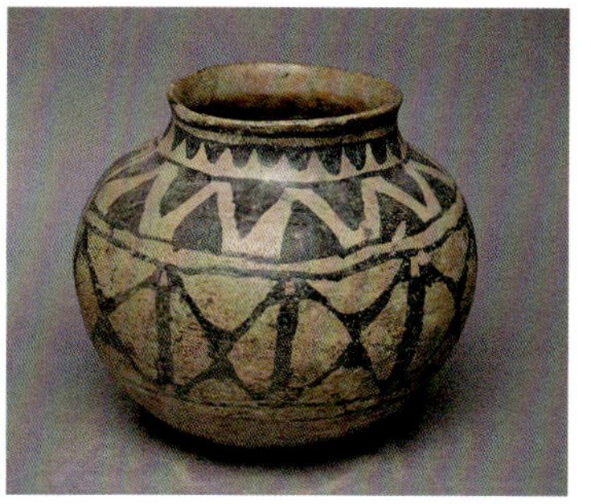

Jar
Keresan Polychrome
Artist Unknown, ca. 1850
20.2 × 23.9
Nelson Collection
12268

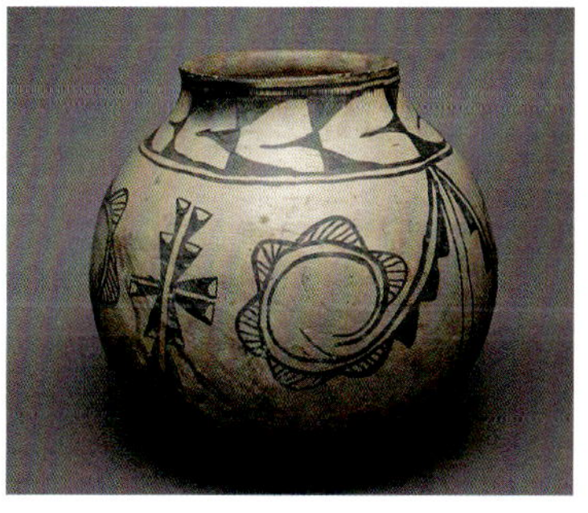

Jar
Keresan Polychrome
Artist Unknown, ca. 1880
35.3 × 36.4
Museum Purchase,
Rogers and Schafer, Albuquerque
11107

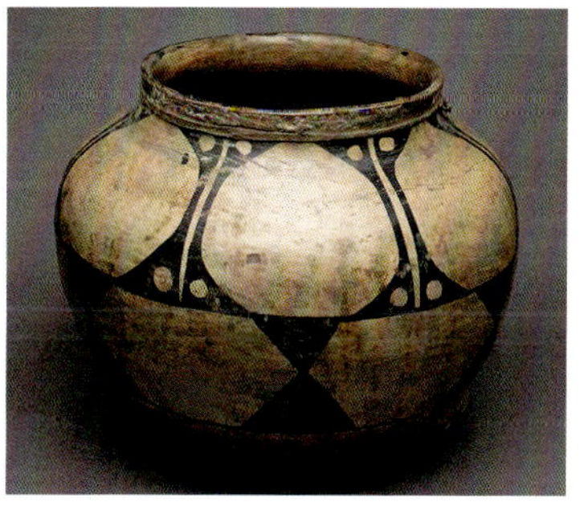

Jar
Keresan Polychrome
Artist Unknown, ca. 1860
38.0 × 44.3
Museum Purchase, Mrs. Julius Gans
35773

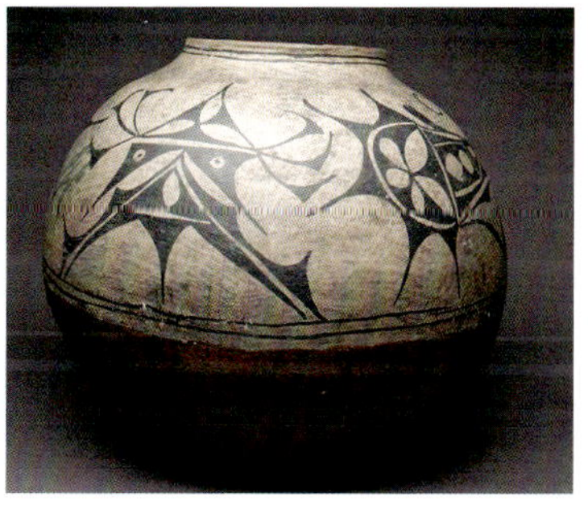

Storage Jar
Keresan Polychrome
Artist Unknown, ca. 1840
48.5 × 57.0
Museum Collection
12172

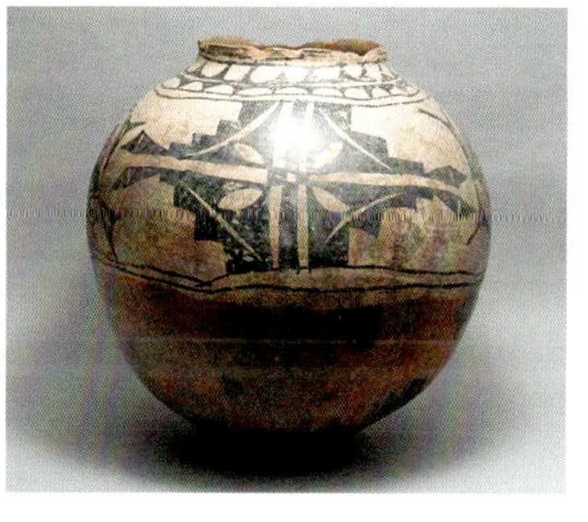

Jar
Powhoge Polychrome
Artist Unknown, ca. 1800
54.0 × 52.5
Museum Collection
41807

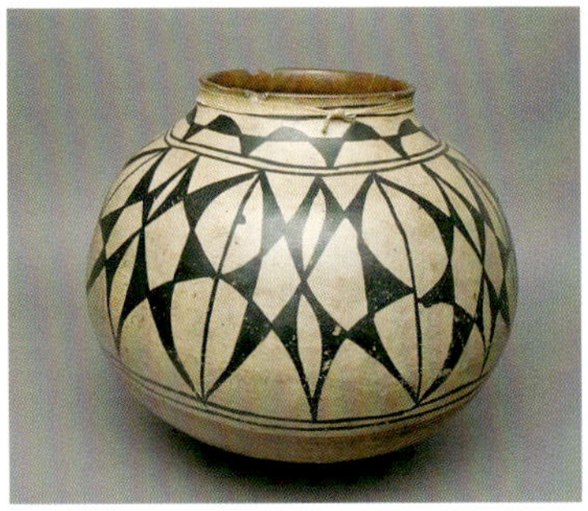

Jar
Powhoge Polychrome
Artist Unknown, ca. 1850
35.0 × 40.0
Gift of Marie Wolfe
45611

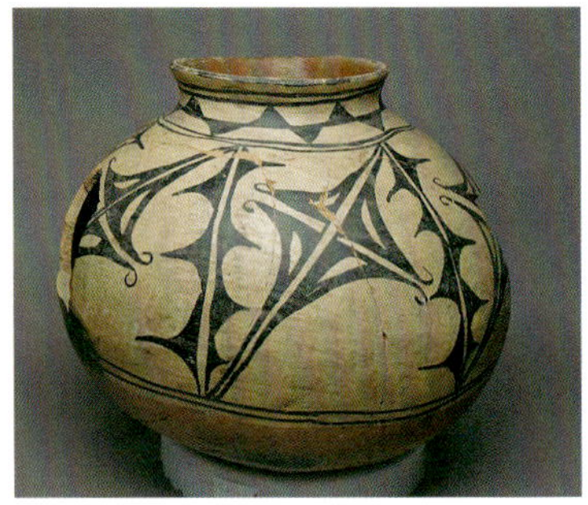

Jar
Keresan Polychrome,
Artist Unknown, ca. 1870
38.8 × 46.3
Gift of the Fred Harvey Company
53893

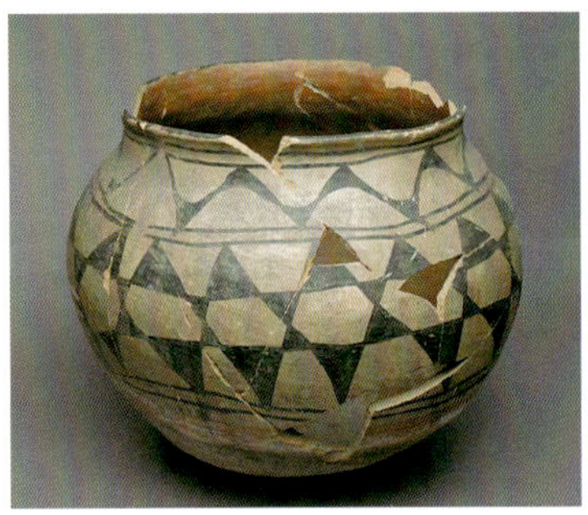

Jar
Keresan Polychrome
Artist Unknown, ca. 1840–1850
41.6 × 42.7
Gift of the Fred Harvey Company
53859

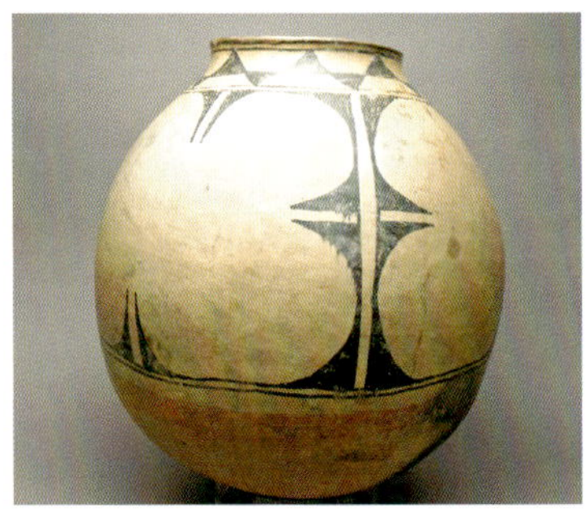

Storage Jar
Keresan Polychrome
Artist Unknown, ca. 1840
49.4 × 47.3
Gift of Francis H. and Patricia N. Harlow
55802

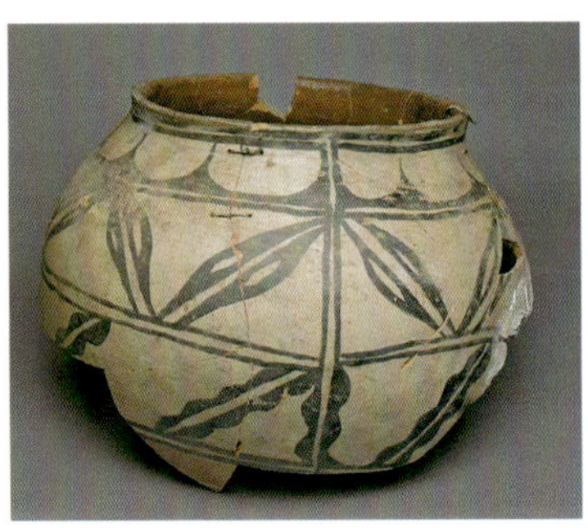

Jar Fragment
Keresan Polychrome
Artist Unknown, ca. 1860
28.5 × 44
Museum Collection
53876

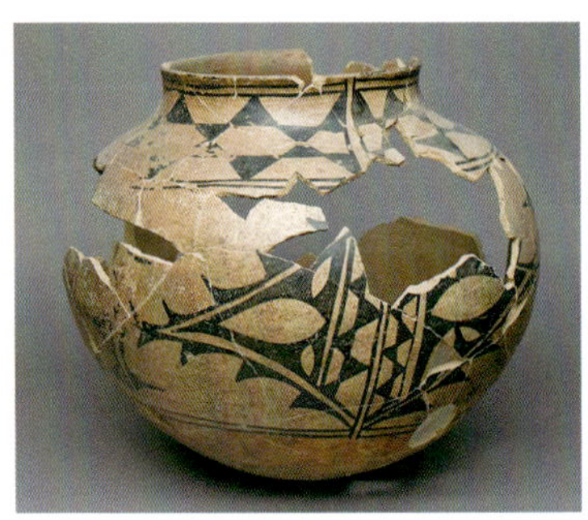

Jar
Keresan Polychrome
Artist Unknown, ca. 1850
36.0 × 39.6
Gift of the Fred Harvey Company
53880

PART II

Cochiti

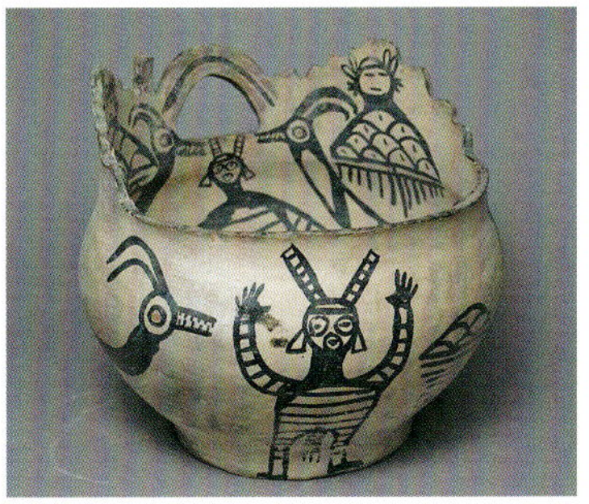

Bowl
Artist Unknown, ca. 1910
24.7 × 29.1
Museum Purchase, Jim Riley
5912

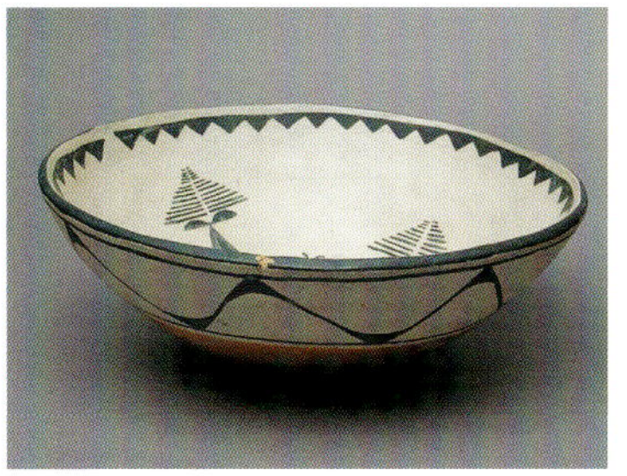

Bowl
Ascension Chavez Benada,
ca. 1925–1930
8.2 × 24.0
Kenneth M. Chapman Collection
7731

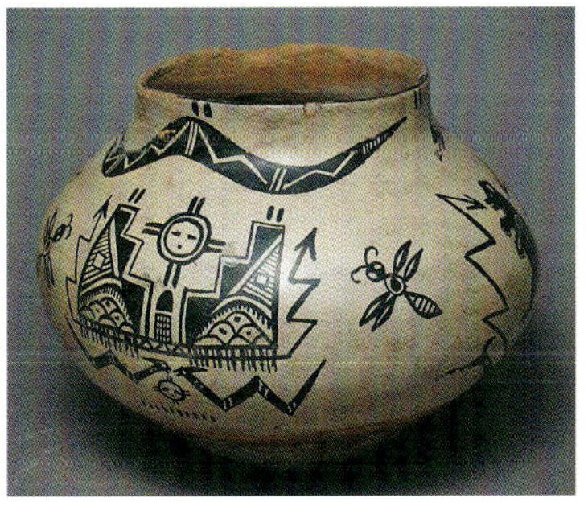

Jar
Artist Unknown, ca. 1890
22.5 × 28.6
Museum Purchase, Presciliana Roybal
7696

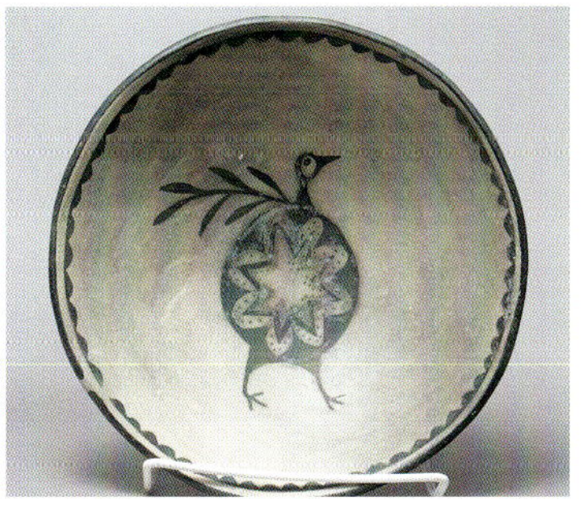

Bowl
Artist Unknown, ca. 1925
7.5 × 22.1
Kenneth M. Chapman Collection
7732

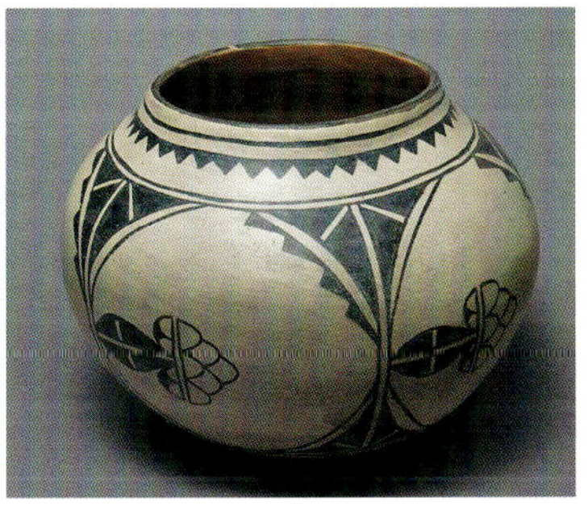

Jar
Ascension Chavez Benada,
ca. 1925–1930
21.0 × 27.2
Kenneth M. Chapman Collection
7726

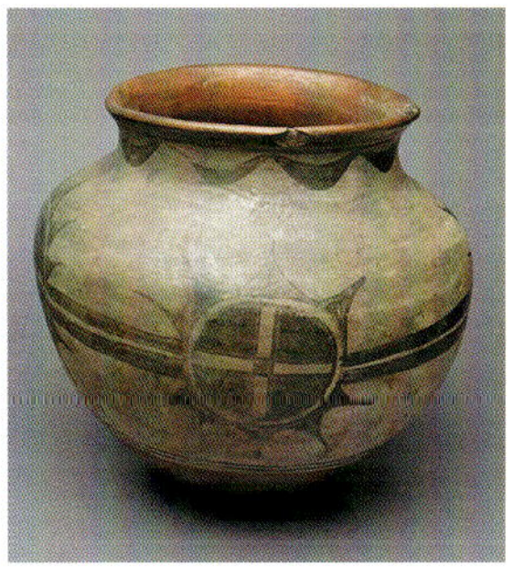

Jar
Artist Unknown, ca. 1875
25.3 × 28.3
Museum Purchase, J. F. Collins, Inc.
7737

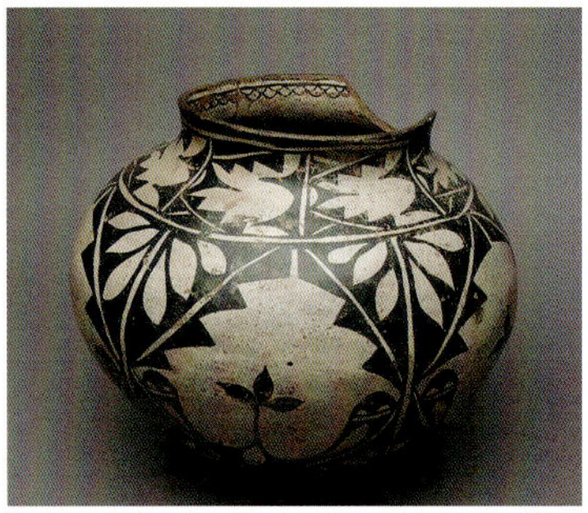

Jar
Artist Unknown, ca. 1925–1930
23.0 × 28.2
Kenneth M. Chapman Collection
7784

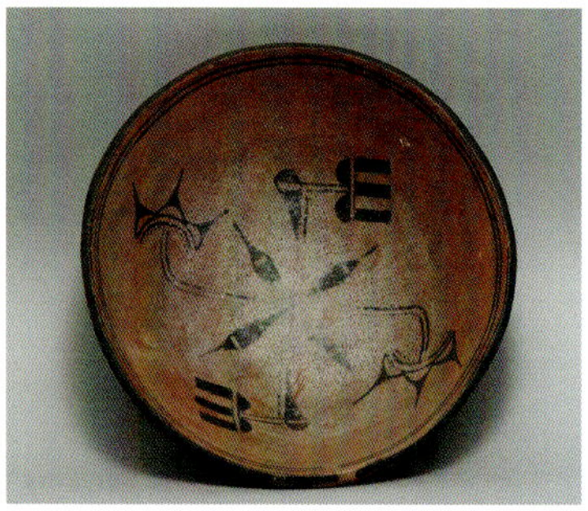

Bowl
Artist Unknown, ca. 1920
6.7 × 19.0
Kenneth M. Chapman Collection
7798

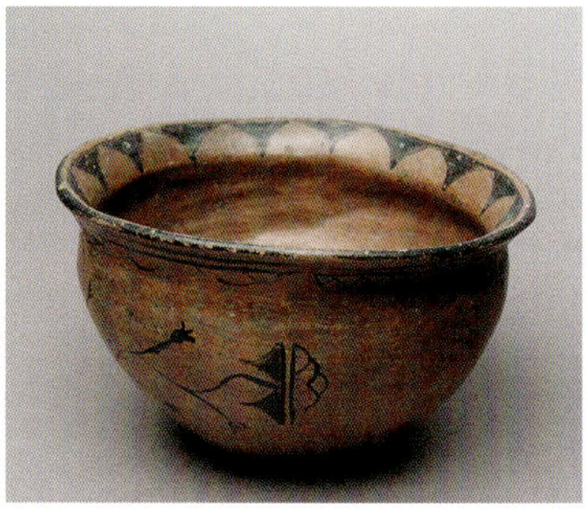

Bowl
Artist Unknown, ca. 1890
8.8 × 15.0
Museum Purchase, D. M. Bacalski
7897

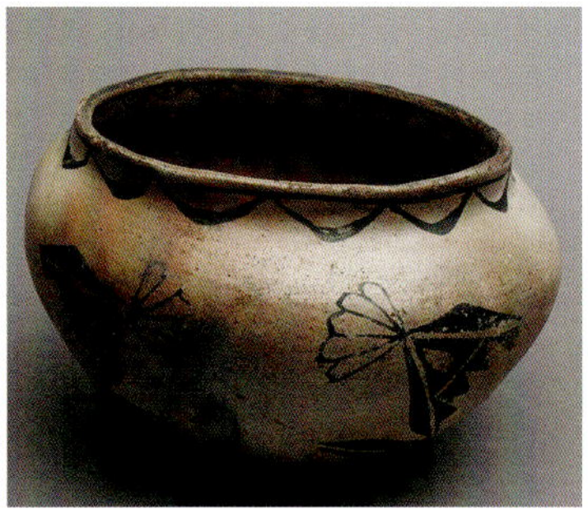

Bowl
Artist Unknown, ca. 1900
10.5 × 18.0
Kenneth M. Chapman Collection
7793

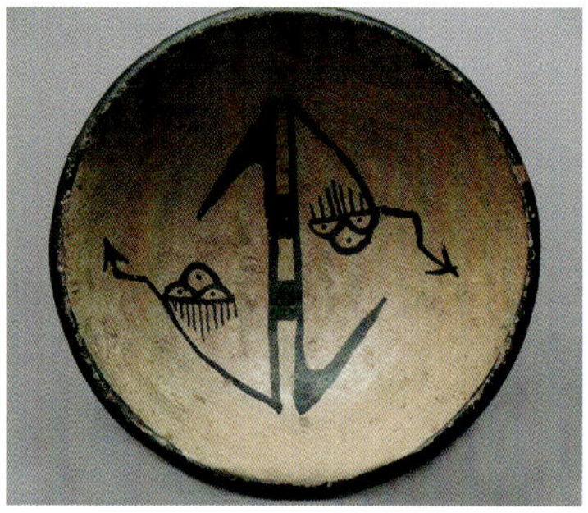

Bowl
Artist Unknown, ca. 1925–1930
5.0 × 14.9
Kenneth M. Chapman Collection
7799

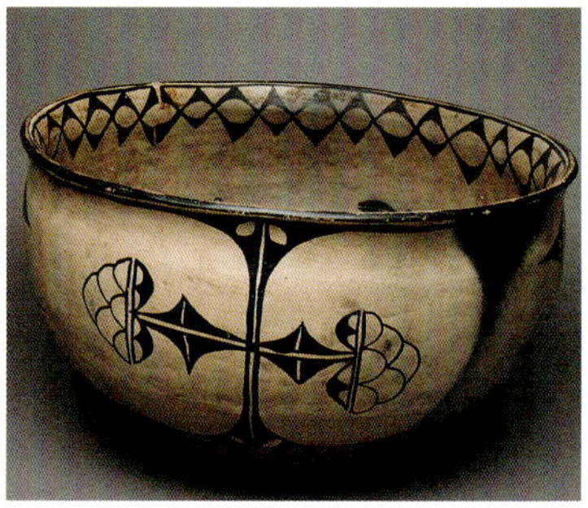

Dough Bowl
Estefanita Herrera, ca. 1910
25.2 × 45.1
Museum Purchase, Juan Poncho
7899

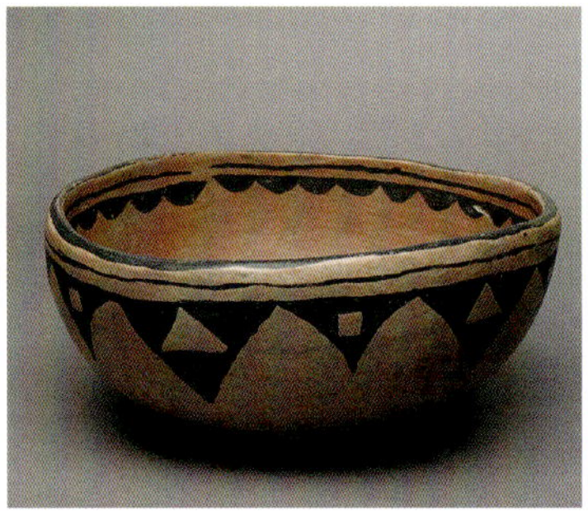

Bowl
Artist Unknown, ca. 1920
9.0 × 21.0
Kenneth M. Chapman Collection
7795

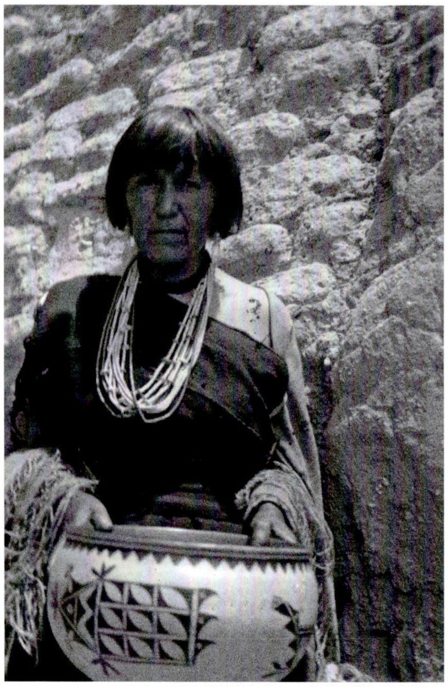

Cochiti Pueblo Fiesta prizewinner (identified as Estefanita Herrera) and her winning pot, 1932. Courtesy Denver Public Library, Western History Collection, X-30181.

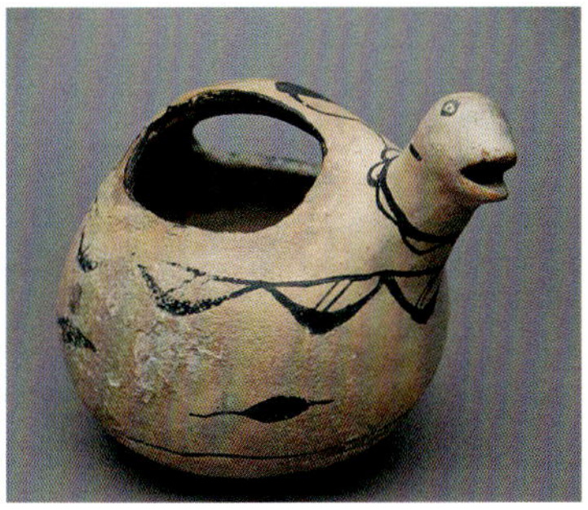

Bird Pitcher
Artist Unknown, ca. 1920
16.7 × 15.9 × 21.4
Gift of Majeed Fattah
7900

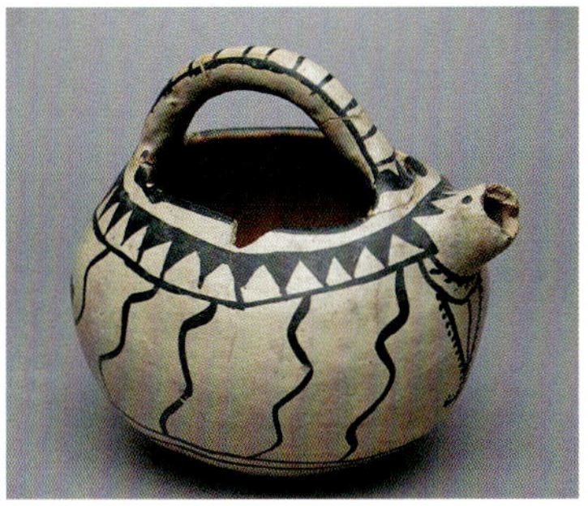

Bird Pitcher
Artist Unknown, ca. 1925
16.0 × 15.7 × 17.8
Gift of Mrs. John W. Chapman
7933

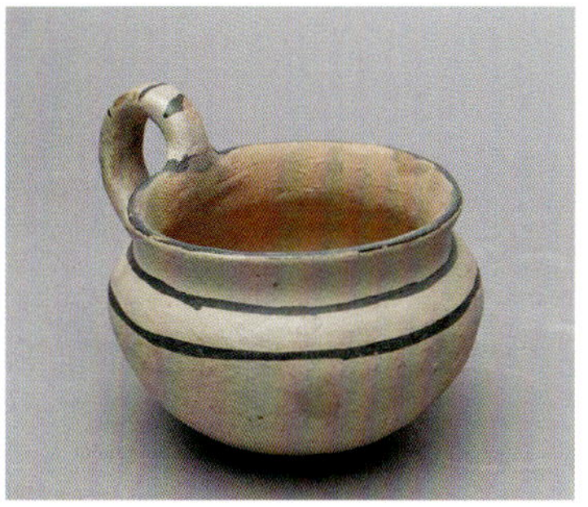

Cup
Artist Unknown, ca. 1925
7.3 × 11.5 × 9.6
Gift of Henry Dendahl
7986

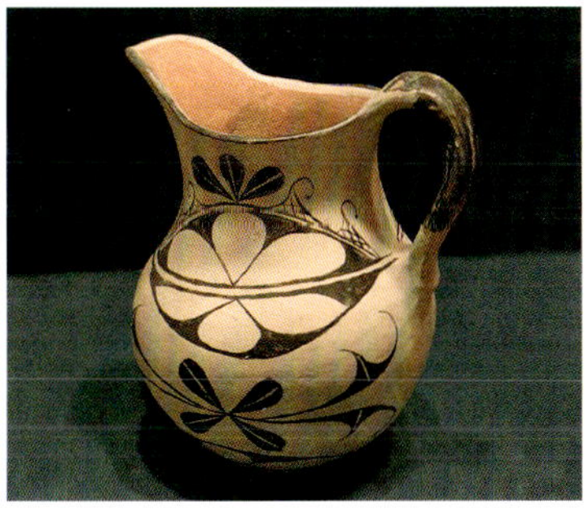

Pitcher
Artist Unknown, ca. 1920
20.0 × 18.0
Gift of Mrs. John W. Chapman
7930

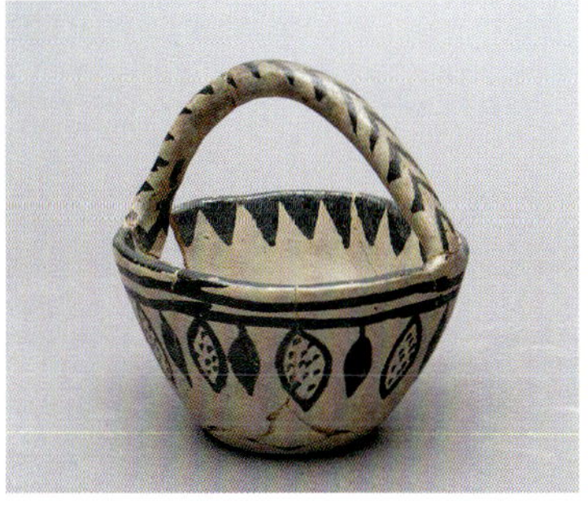

Bowl
Artist Unknown, ca. 1925
10.0 × 9.4
Gift of Mrs. John W. Chapman
7934

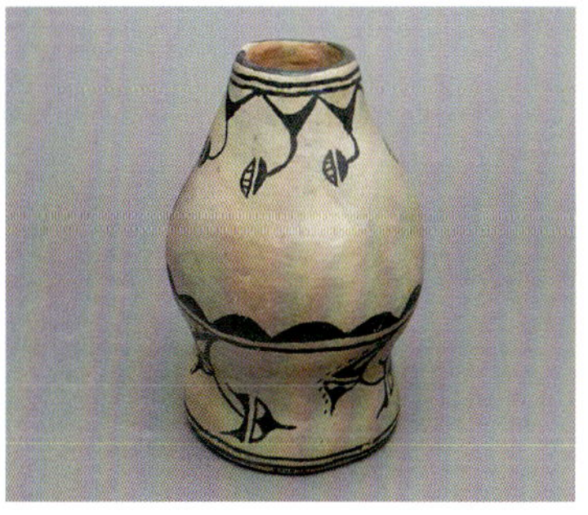

Jar or Lamp Base
Artist Unknown, ca. 1920–1930
16.0 × 10.7
Gift of Majeed Fattah
8009

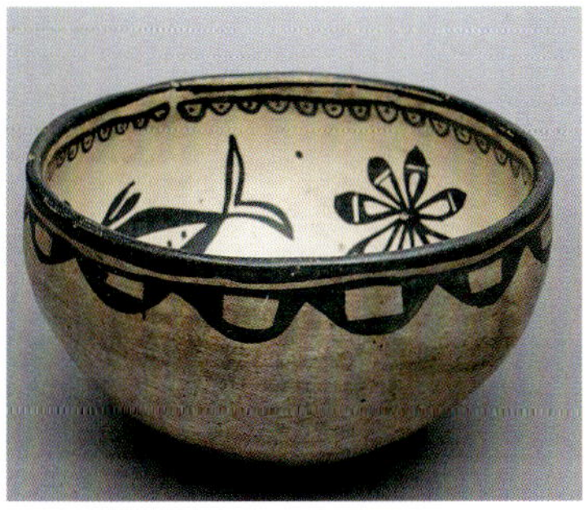

Bowl
Artist Unknown, ca. 1915
11.0 × 19.4
Gift of Mrs. John W. Chapman
7932

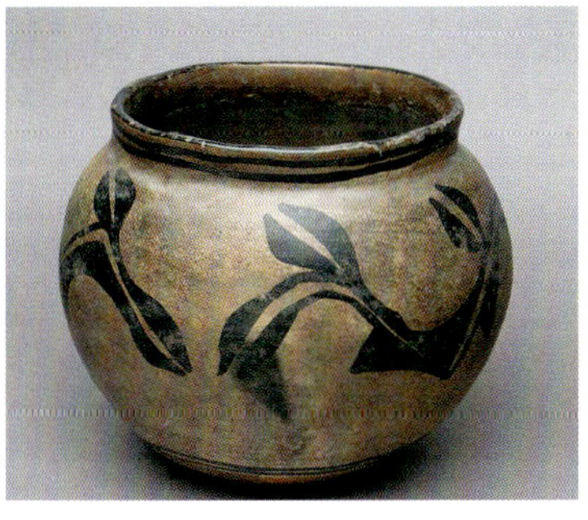

Jar
Artist Unknown, ca. 1890–1900
17.9 × 22.9
Museum Purchase,
William A. Jacobson
7942

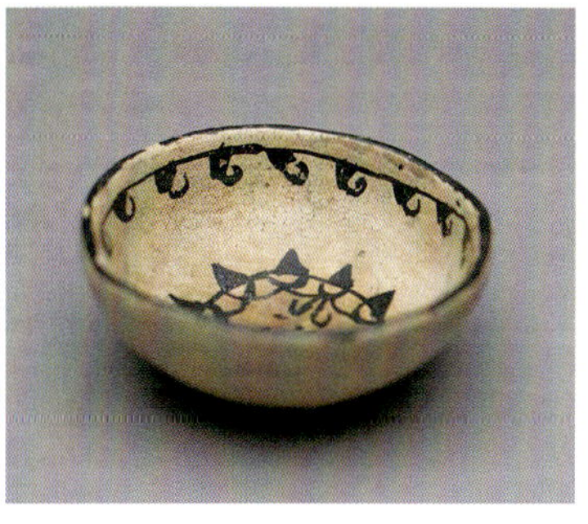

Bowl
Artist Unknown, ca. 1925
4.0 × 10.4
Ina Sizer Cassidy Collection
8016

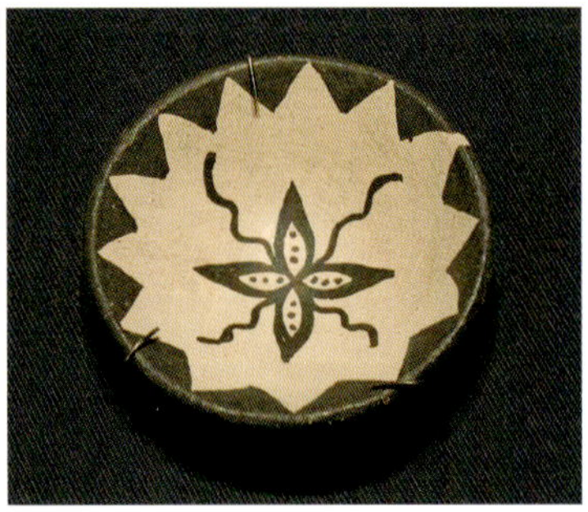

Bowl
Artist Unknown, ca. 1960
2.0 × 6.5
Gift of Marjorie F. Lambert
10044

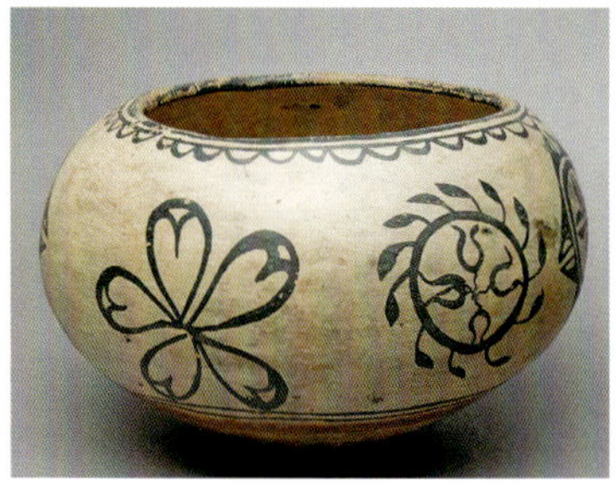

Jar
Artist Unknown, ca. 1900
15.5 × 25.5
Museum Collection
11085

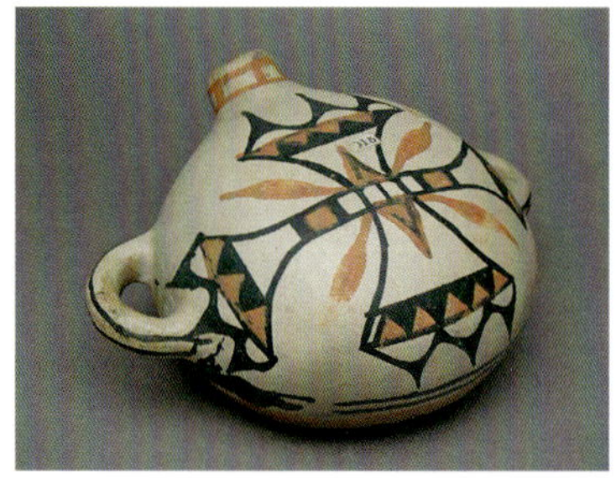

Canteen
Cochiti or San Ildefonso
Artist Unknown, 1890s
8.0 × 19.5
Museum Collection
11168

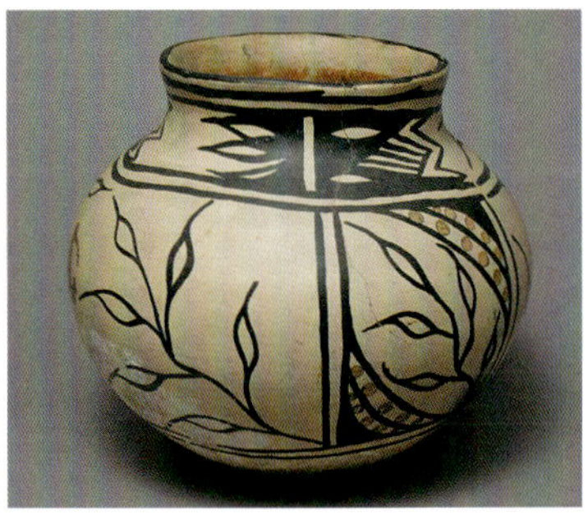

Jar
Artist Unknown, ca. 1900–1920
19.4 × 22.4
Museum Purchase,
Rogers and Schafer
11083

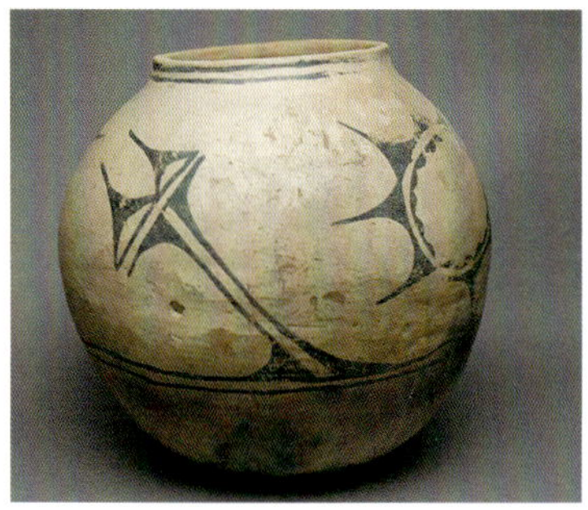

Jar
Artist Unknown, ca. 1820–1840
42.5 × 43.0
Gift of Frank Applegate
11099

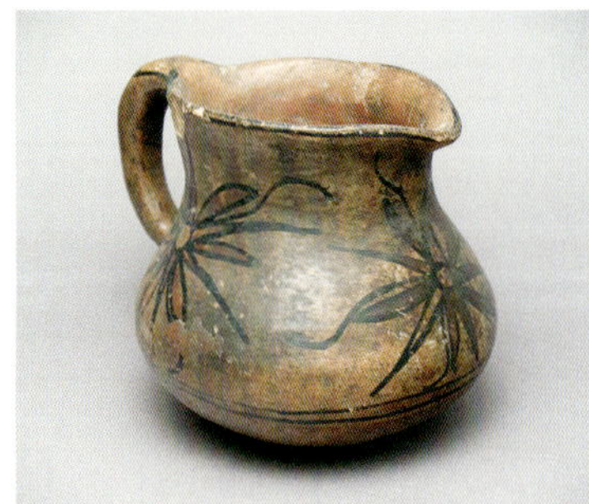

Pitcher
Artist Unknown, ca. 1915
15.6 × 16.2 × 19.5
Museum Purchase, Rogers and
Schafer, Albuquerque
11191

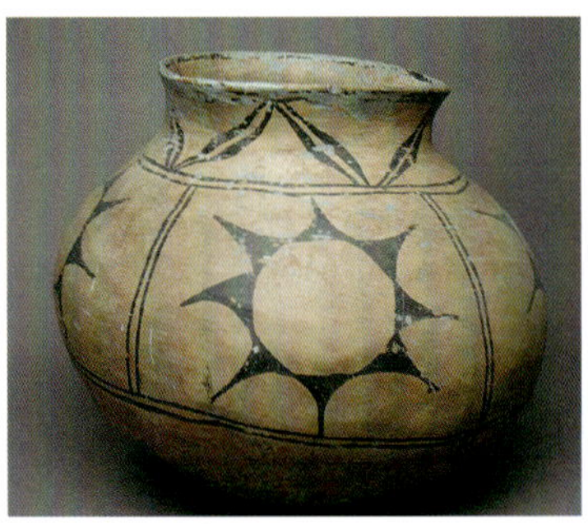

Storage Jar
Artist Unknown, ca. 1900
39.0 × 44.5
Museum Purchase, Rogers and
Schafer
11084

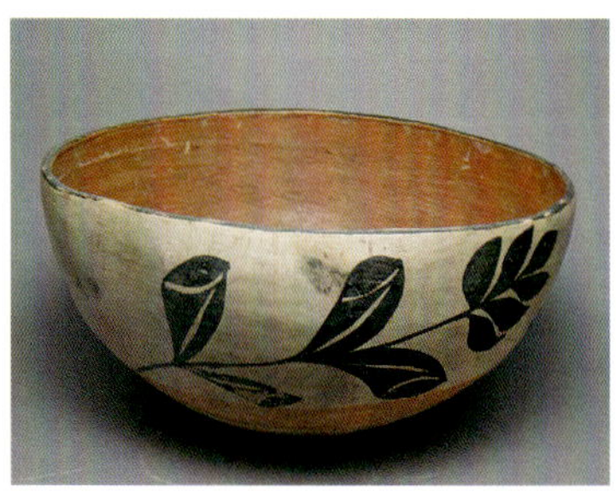

Bowl
Artist Unknown, ca. 1930
22.0 × 43.0
Museum Purchase, Rogers and
Schafer
11113

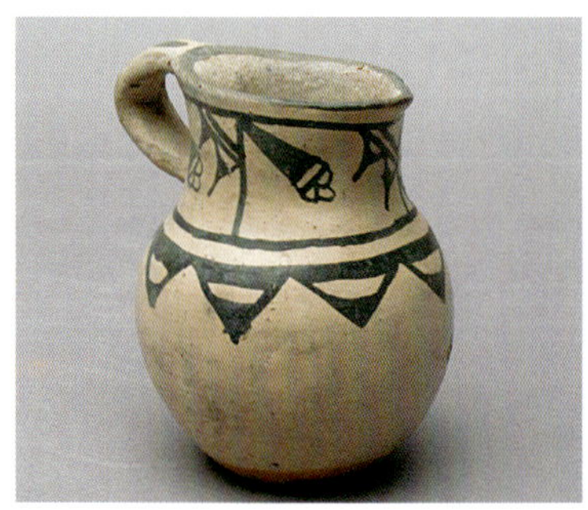

Pitcher
Artist Unknown, ca. 1925–1930
9.9 × 7.8 × 9.0
Kenneth M. Chapman Collection
11227

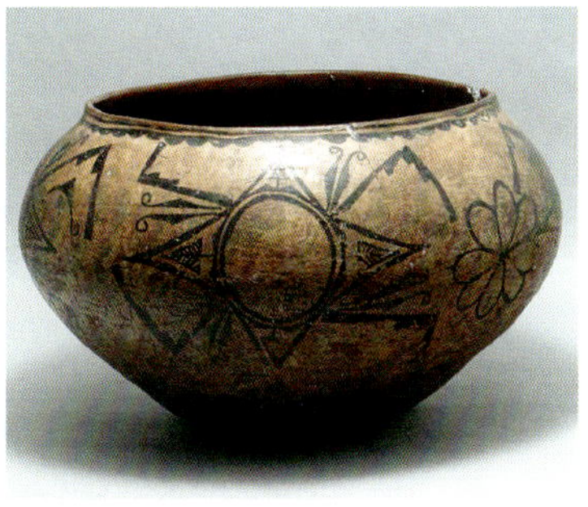

Bowl
Cochiti or Tesuque
Artist Unknown, ca. 1860–1880
32.5 × 57.0
Museum Collection
12108

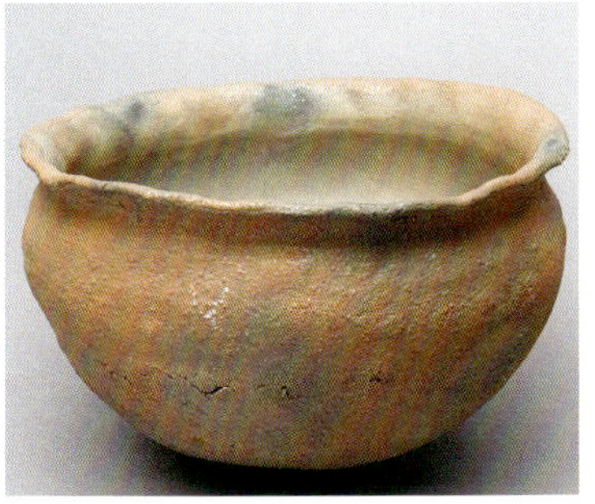

Bowl
Artist Unknown, ca. 1920
9.5 × 15.6
Gift of the Historical Society of New Mexico
12138

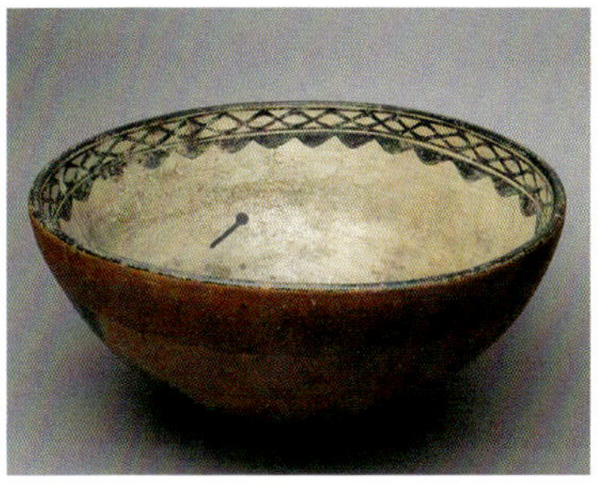

Bowl
Artist Unknown, ca. 1920
16.1 × 35.0
Gift of the Philadelphia Museum
12175

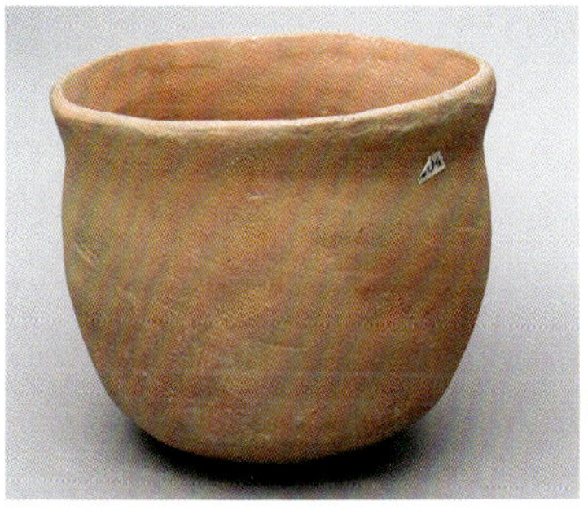

Jar
Artist Unknown, ca. 1920
14.6 × 17.0
Gift of the Historical Society of New Mexico
12132

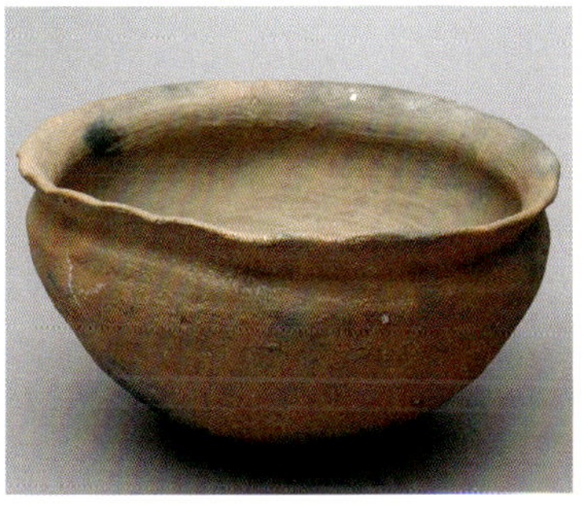

Bowl
Artist Unknown, ca. 1920
9.4 × 17.8
Museum Collection
12139

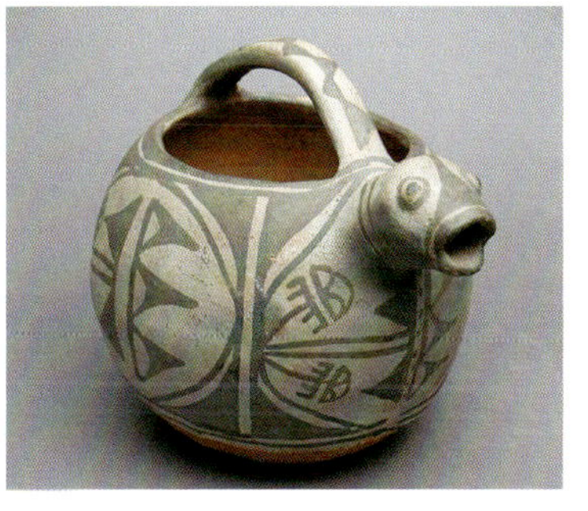

Bird Pitcher
Artist Unknown, ca. 1920
19.5 × 19.2 × 25.1
Gift of the Historical Society of New Mexico
12176

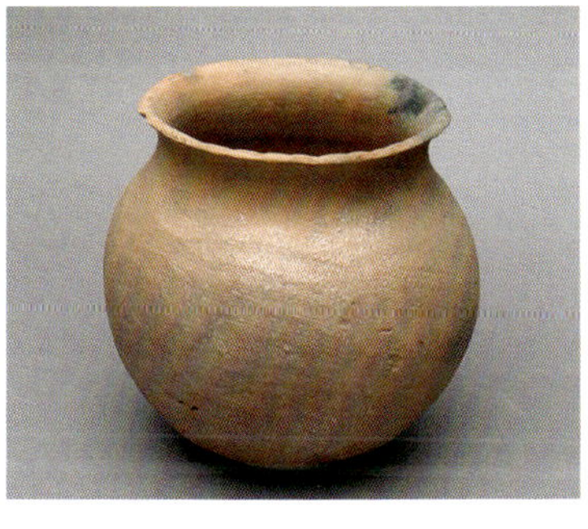

Jar
Artist Unknown, ca. 1920
15.7 × 17.3
Gift of the Historical Society of New Mexico
12133

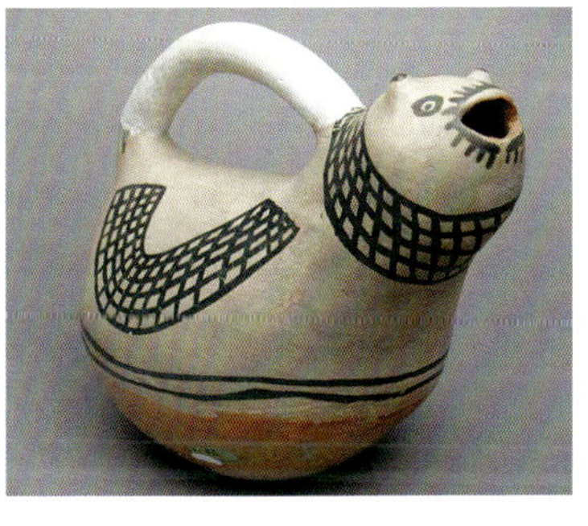

Bird Pitcher
Artist Unknown, ca. 1900
19.1 × 14.9 × 21.3
Gift of the Historical Society of New Mexico
12173

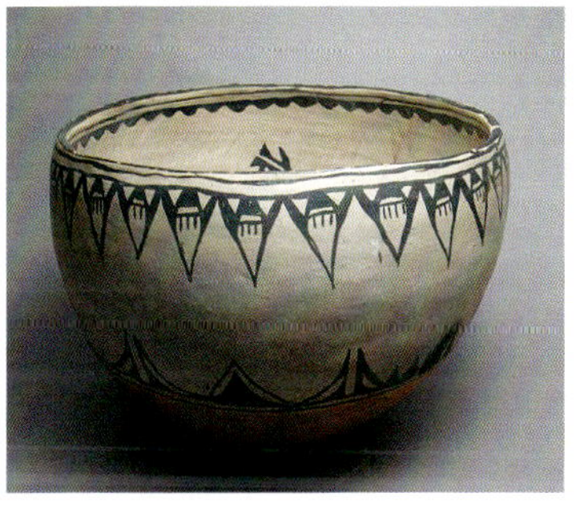

Bowl
Artist Unknown, ca. 1930
26.0 × 39.0
Gift of the Historical Society of New Mexico
12178

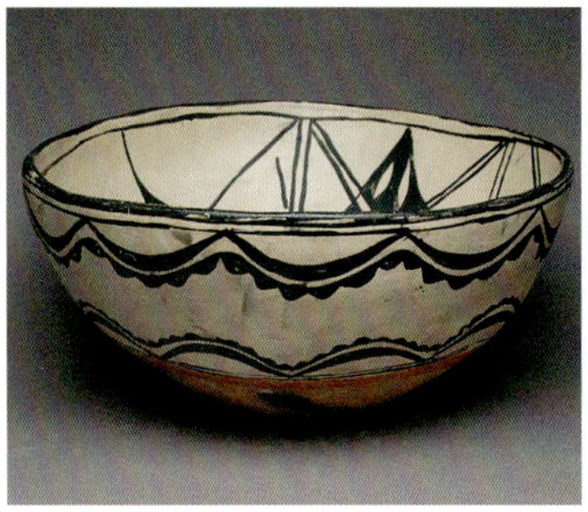

Dough Bowl
Artist Unknown, ca. 1910–1915
18.7 × 38.6
Gift of the Historical Society of New Mexico
12260

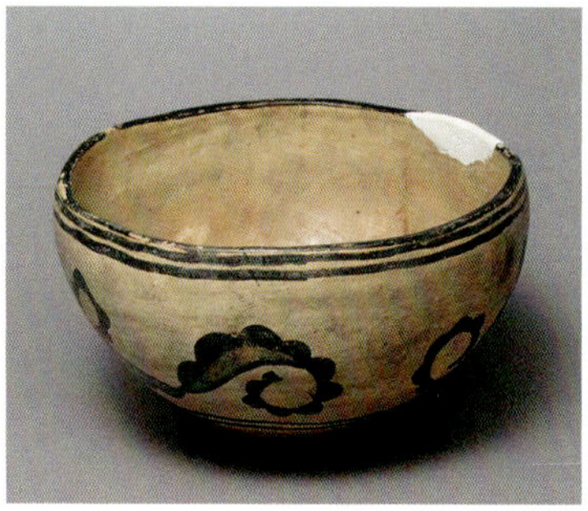

Bowl
Artist Unknown, ca. 1940
10.6 × 19.3
Nelson Collection
12441

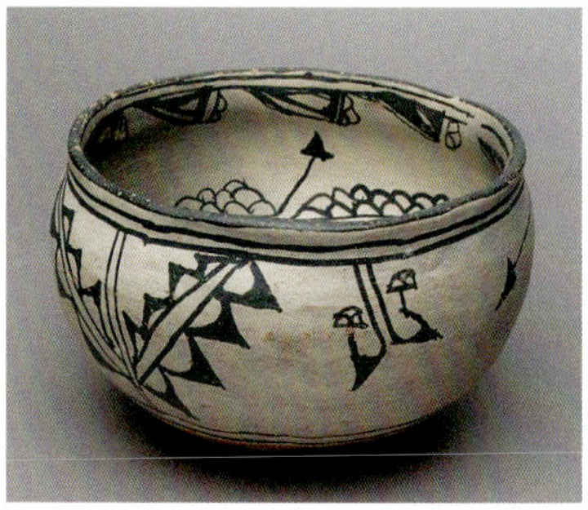

Bowl
Artist Unknown, ca. 1930
10.0 × 16.2
Nelson Collection
12444

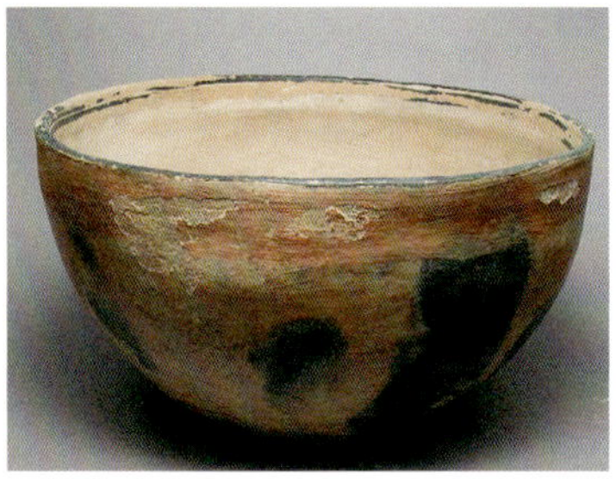

Bowl
Artist Unknown, ca. 1900
20.0 × 36.0
Gift of the Historical Society of New Mexico
12261

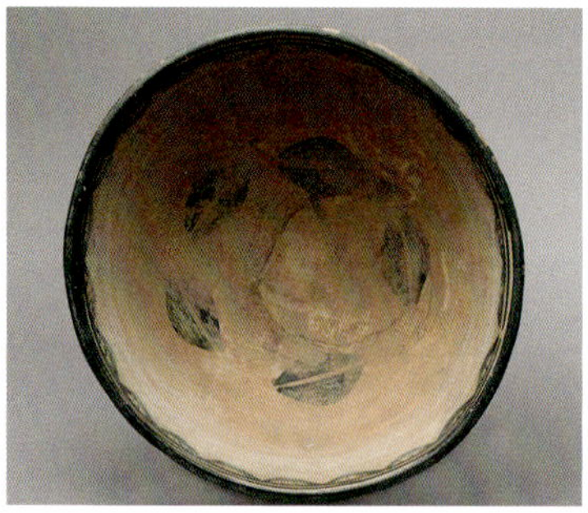

Bowl
Artist Unknown, ca. 1930
9.5 × 19.7
Nelson Collection
12442

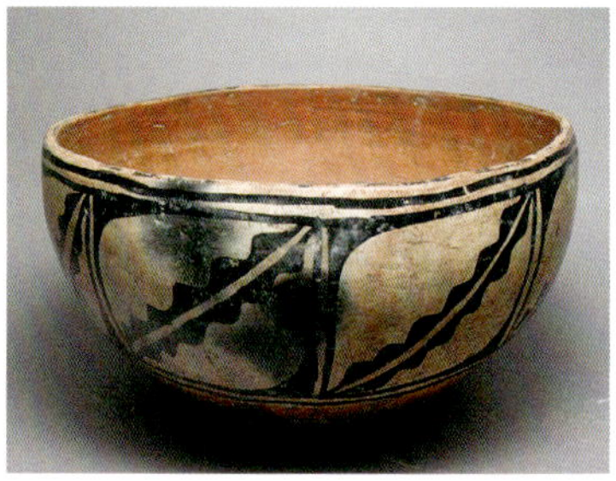

Bowl
Artist Unknown, ca. 1920
23.0 × 38.0
Kenneth M. Chapman Collection
16183

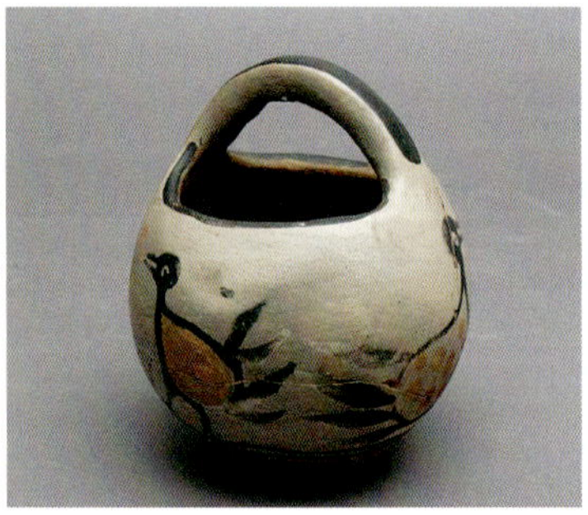

Bowl
Artist Unknown, ca. 1920
10.8 × 9.3
Gift of the Historical Society of New Mexico
12436

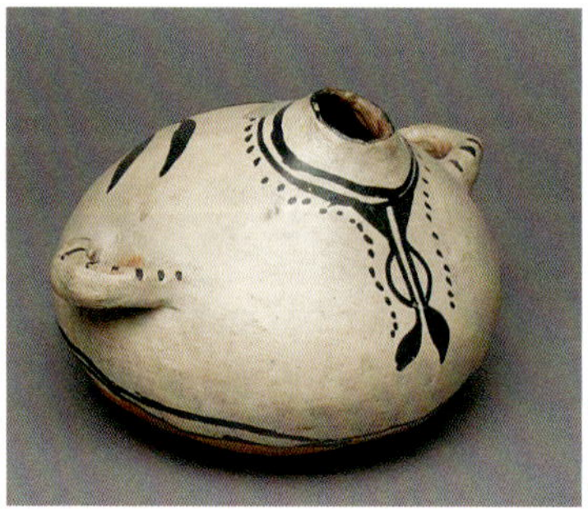

Canteen
Artist Unknown, ca. 1890
14.5 × 11.4
Museum Purchase
12443

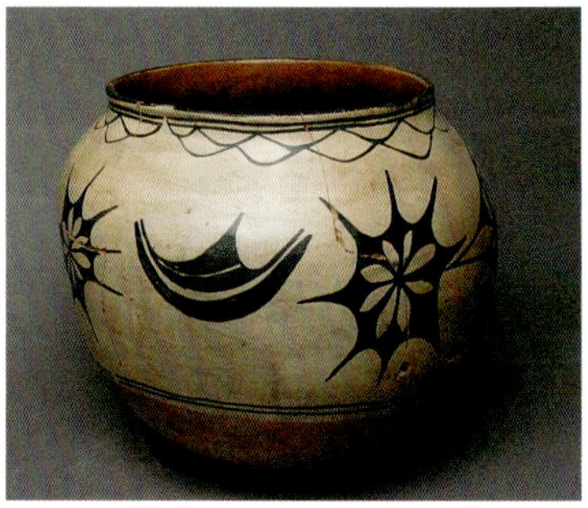

Jar
Artist Unknown, ca. 1900–1920
34.5 × 37.5
Museum Collection
16194

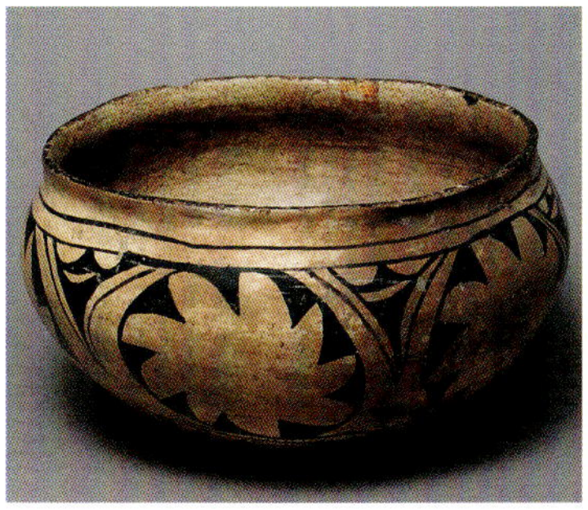

Bowl
Artist Unknown, ca. 1925–1930
14.0 × 26.4
Kenneth M. Chapman Collection
16197

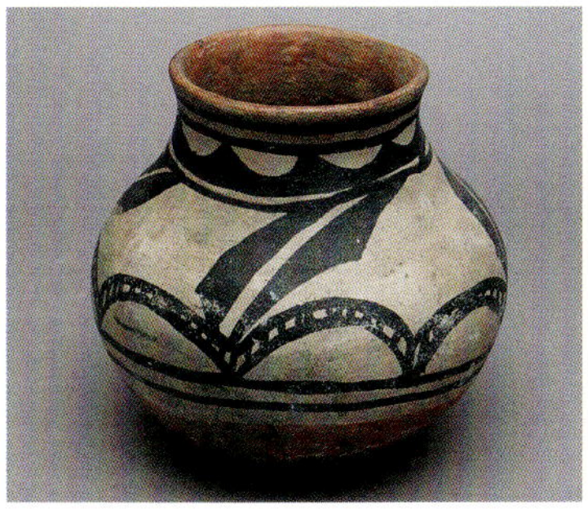

Jar
Artist Unknown, ca. 1920
13.8 × 15.0
Gift of the Historical Society of New Mexico
18728

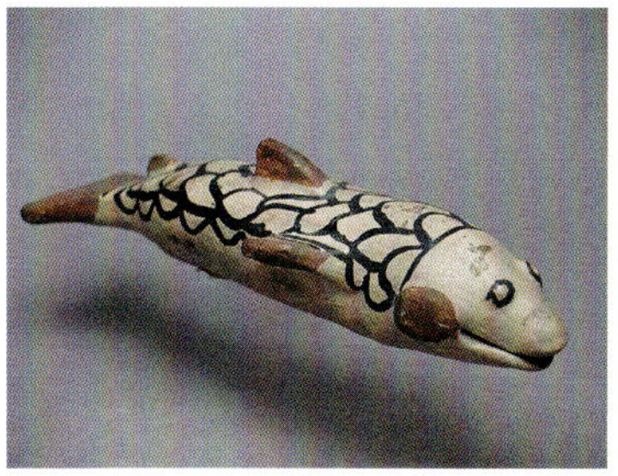

Fish Figurine
Artist Unknown, ca. 1900
6.0 × 9.5 × 27.1
Museum Collection
18803

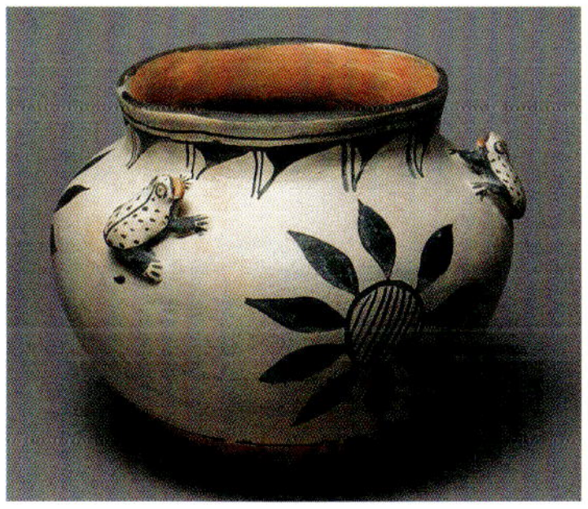

Jar
Teresita Romero, ca. 1950–1960
15.6 × 19.3
Museum Collection
18668

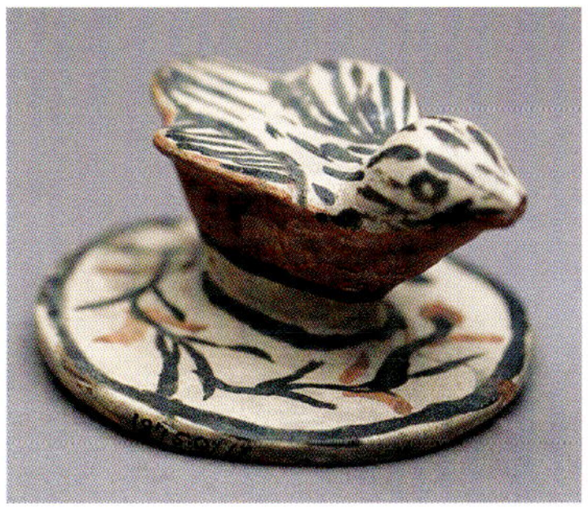

Bird Figurine or Jar Lid
Artist Unknown, ca. 1930
5.3 × 8.5 × 9.6
Gift of the Historical Society of New Mexico
18750

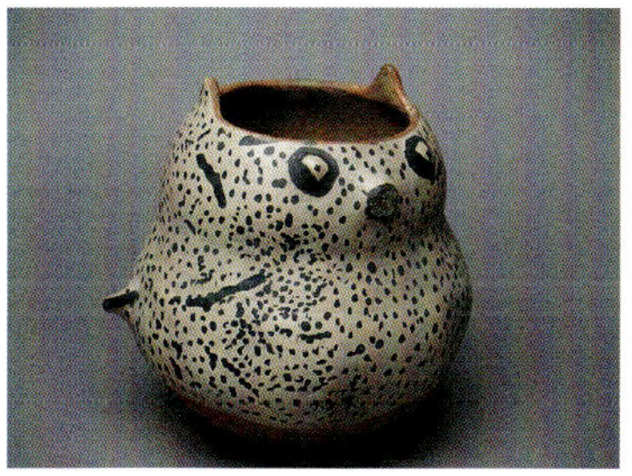

Owl Jar
Artist Unknown, ca. 1940
18.0 × 18.5
Museum Collection
18822

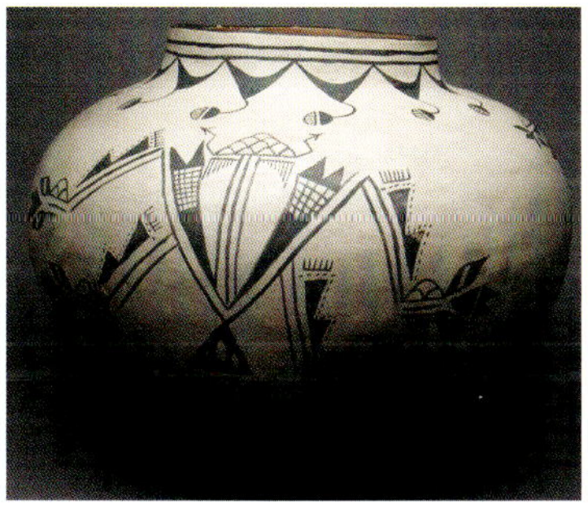

Storage Jar
Agrapina Quintana, ca. 1925
40.6 × 50.6
Gift of Lydia Trowbridge
18685

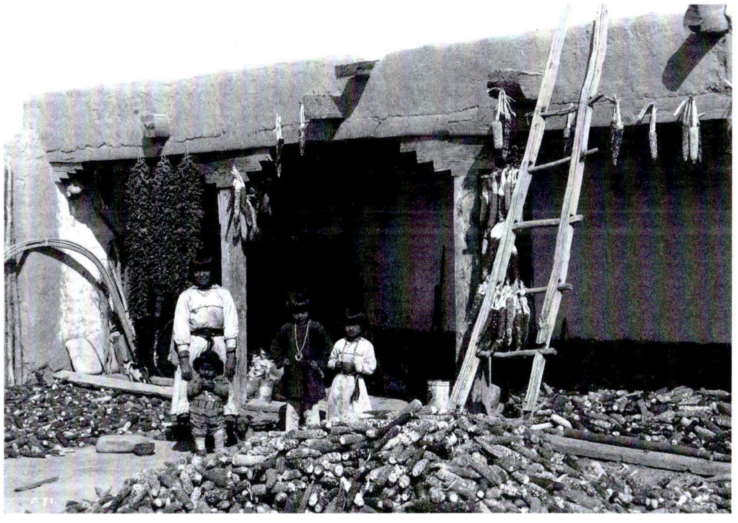

Potter Agrapina Quintana and children with drying corn and chili, Cochiti Pueblo, ca. 1920. Courtesy Palace of the Governors (MNM/DCA), 41532.

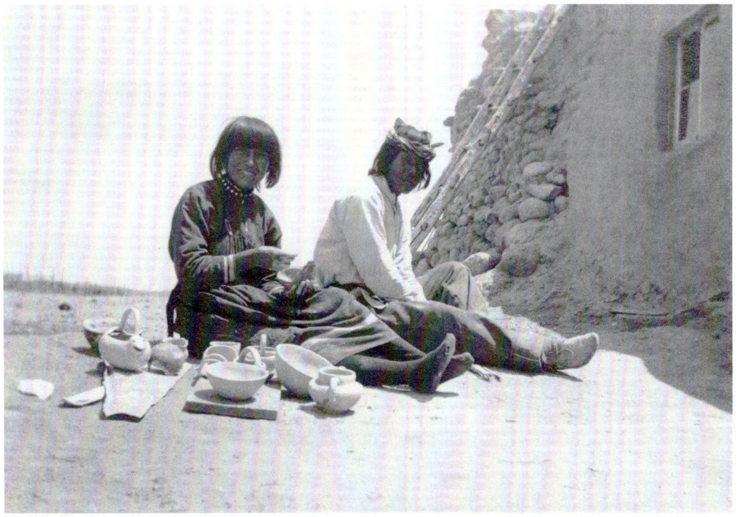

Potter Ignacita Arquero and her husband Santiago Arquero, Cochiti Pueblo, ca. 1920. Courtesy Palace of the Governors (MNM/DCA), 2322.

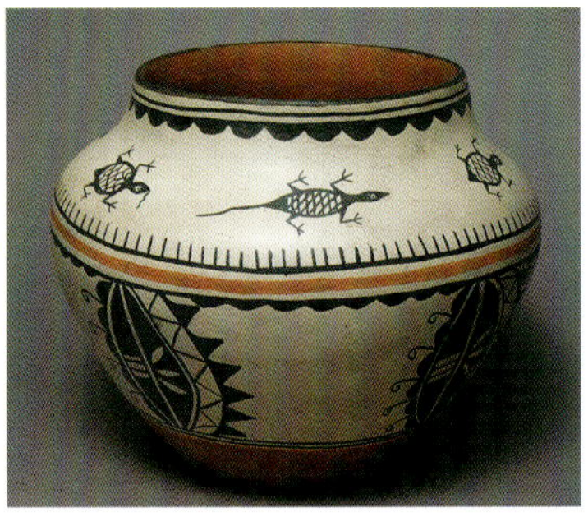

Jar
Ignacita Arquero, 1940
17.6 × 22.1
Museum Purchase, Louisa Ponicha
18879

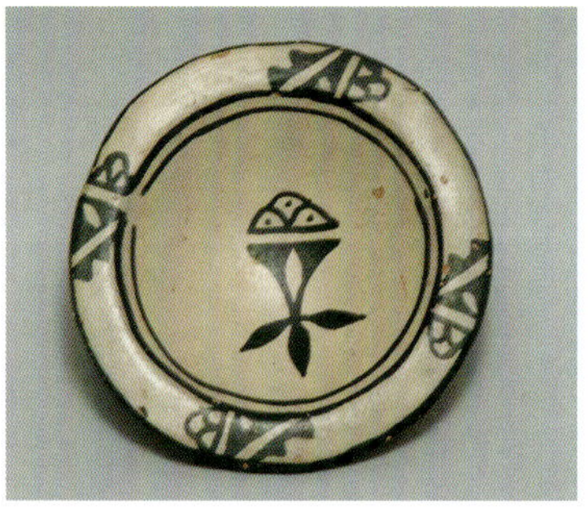

Plate
Artist Unknown, ca. 1940
Museum Purchase, Trowbridge
18927

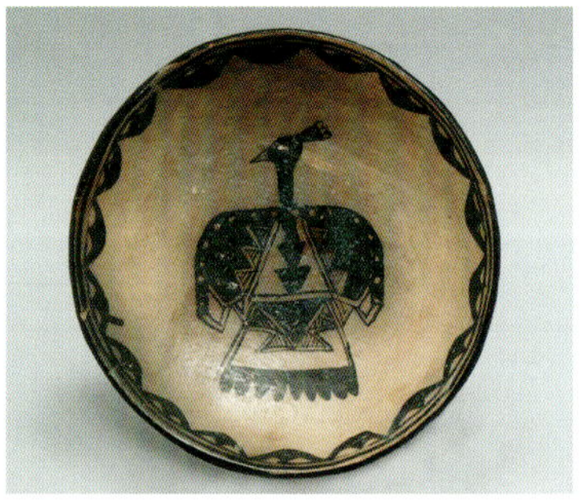

Plate
Artist Unknown, ca. 1940
4.5 × 22.7
Gift of Hugh Bryden McGill
19069

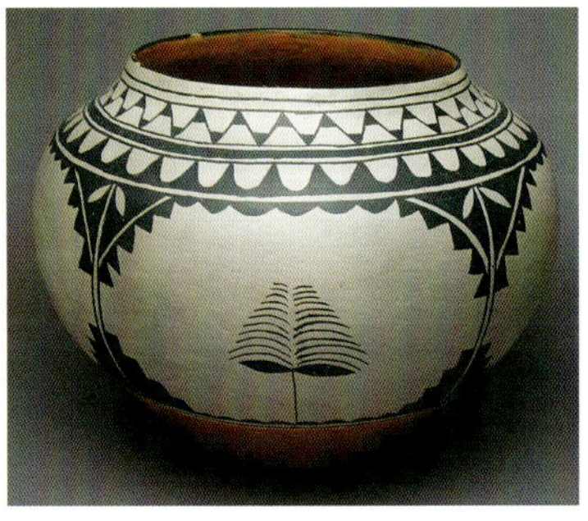

Jar
Ignacita Arquero, 1940
25.5 × 35.0
Museum Purchase, Ignacita Arquero
18882

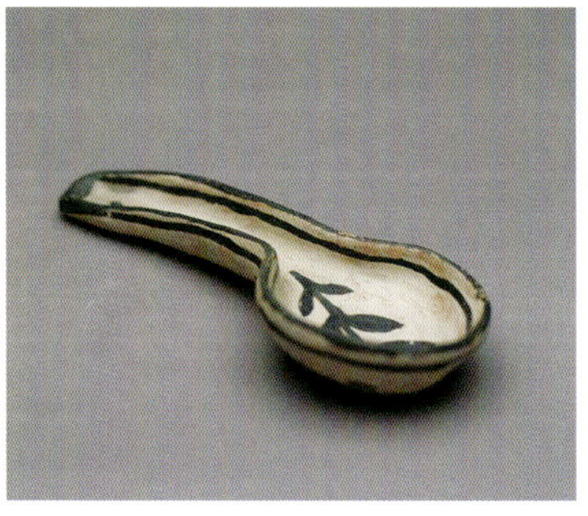

Spoon
Artist Unknown, ca. 1930
2.6 × 5.9 × 14.5
Gift of Henry Dendahl
18974

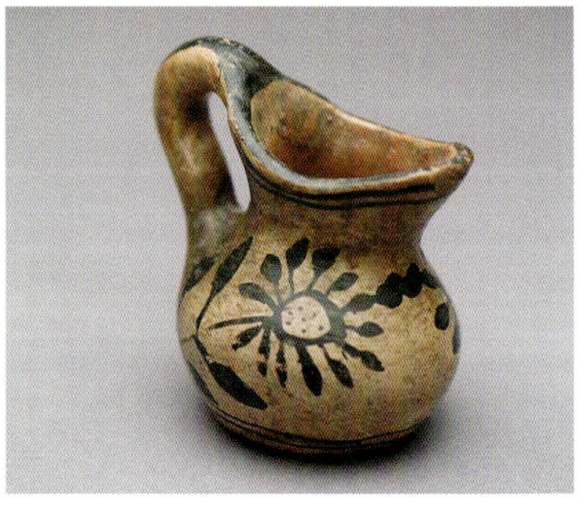

Pitcher
Artist Unknown, ca. 1940
8.0 × 7.3 × 8.5
Museum Purchase, Tony Garcia
19083

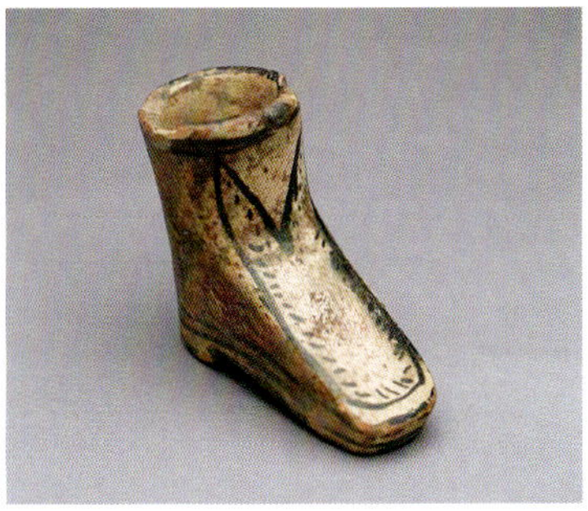

Candlestick
Artist Unknown, ca. 1930
8.0 × 4.5 × 9.3
Museum Purchase, Tony Garcia
19084

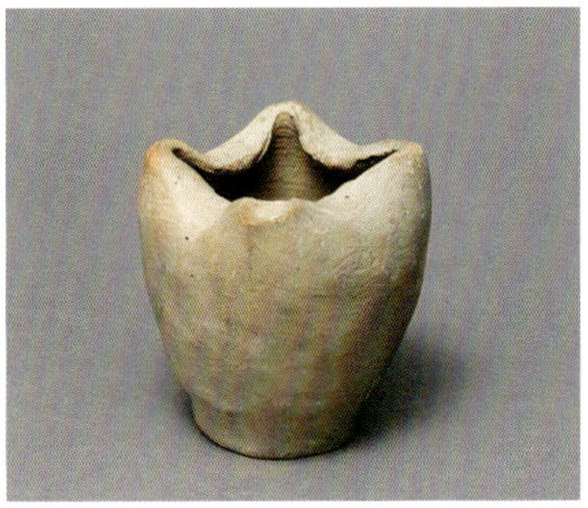

Jar
Artist Unknown, ca. 1940
6.4 × 6.2
Gift of Norma Sweringer
19127

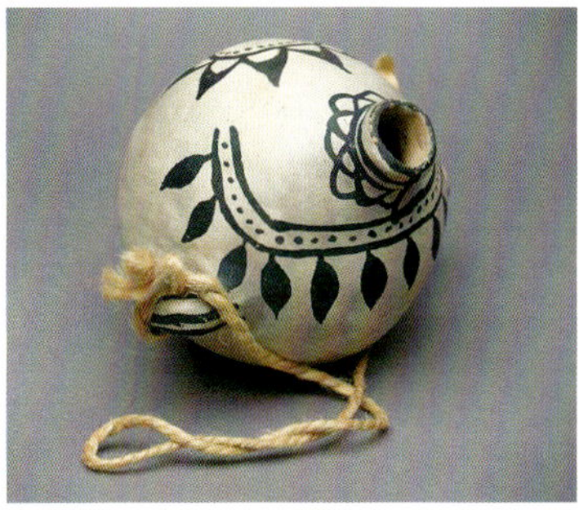

Canteen
Artist Unknown, ca. 1920
11.1 × 12.0 × 13.7
Gift of Byron Harvey III
19271

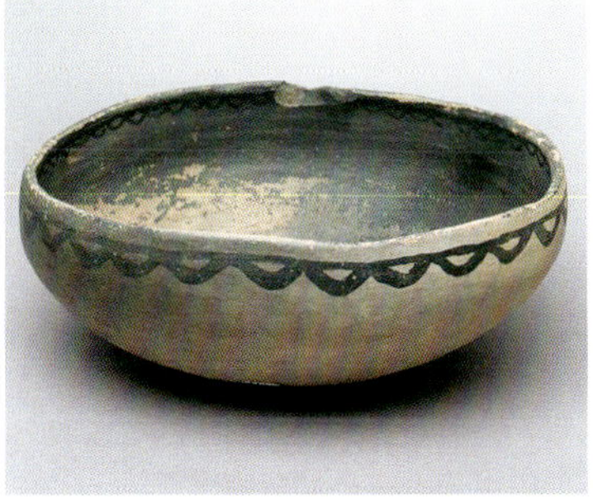

Bowl
Artist Unknown, ca. 1930
8.5 × 23.6
Gift of Norma Sweringer
19125

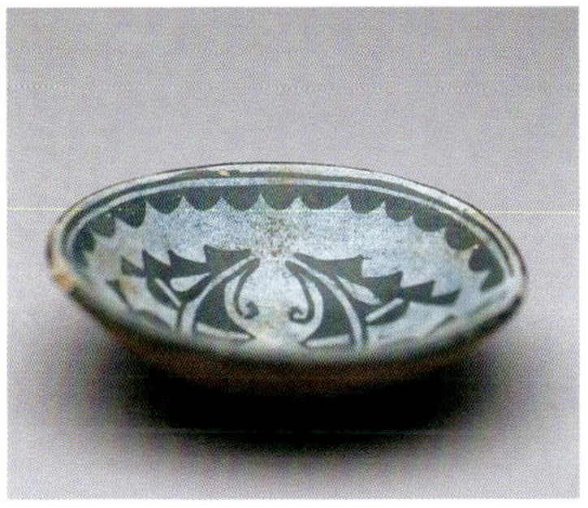

Bowl
Artist Unknown, ca. 1940
3.8 × 11.2
Museum Collection
19177

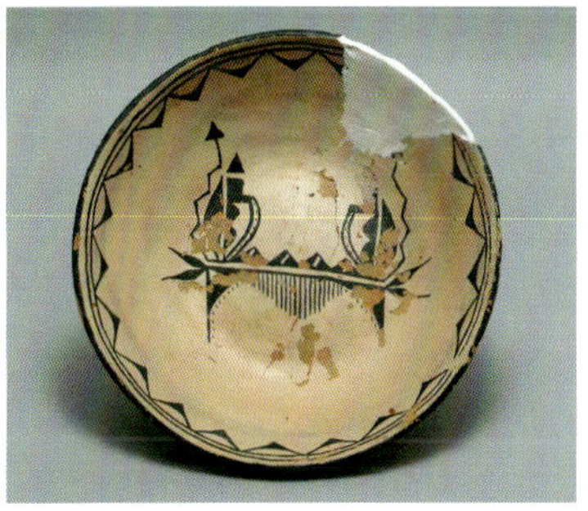

Bowl
Signed Juanita, possibly
Juanita Trujillo, ca. 1940
6.5 × 24.4
Gift of Dorothy N. Stewart
19303

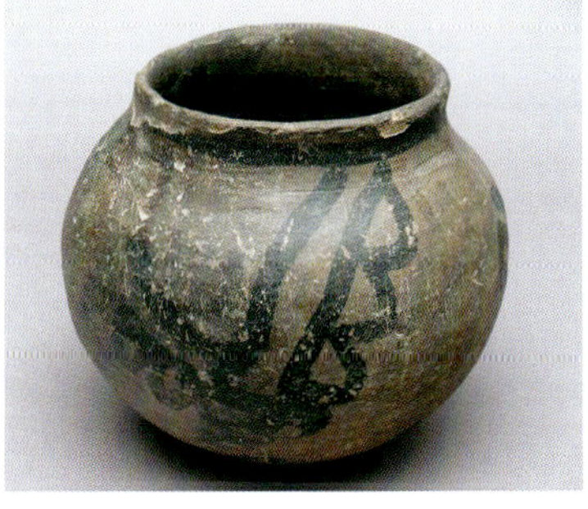

Jar
Artist Unknown, ca. 1920
12.1 × 14.9
Gift of Norma Sweringer
19126

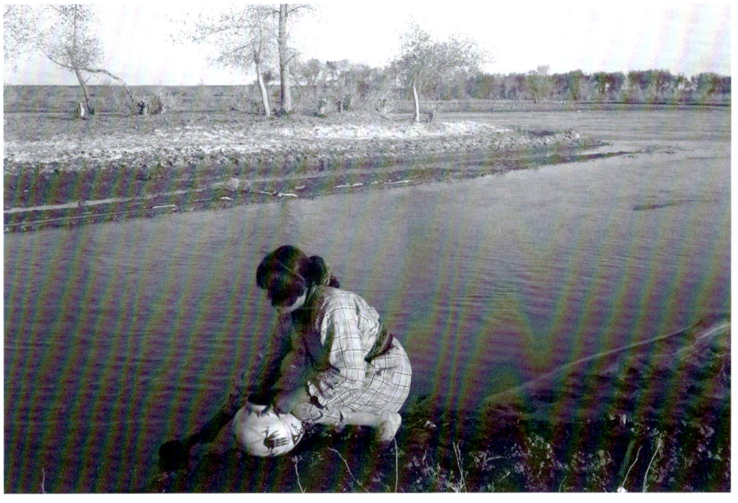

Potter Juanita Trujillo, Cochiti Pueblo, ca. 1940–1945. T. Harmon Parkhurst, photographer. Courtesy Palace of the Governors (MNM/DCA), 2322.

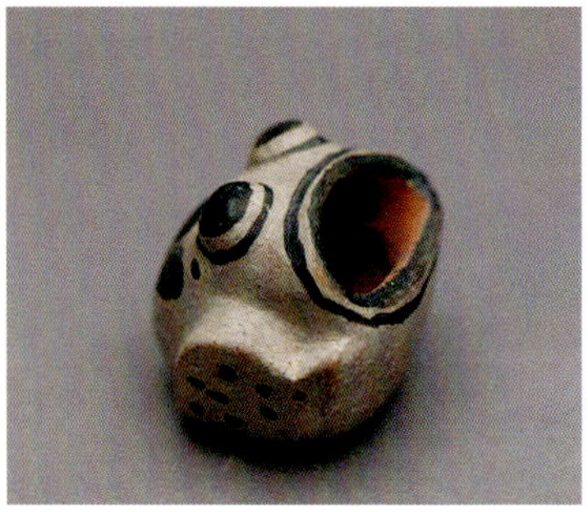

Frog Figurine
Trini Herrera, ca. 1930
3.5 × 4.0 × 3.5
Mrs. Stewart Harvey Collection
19310

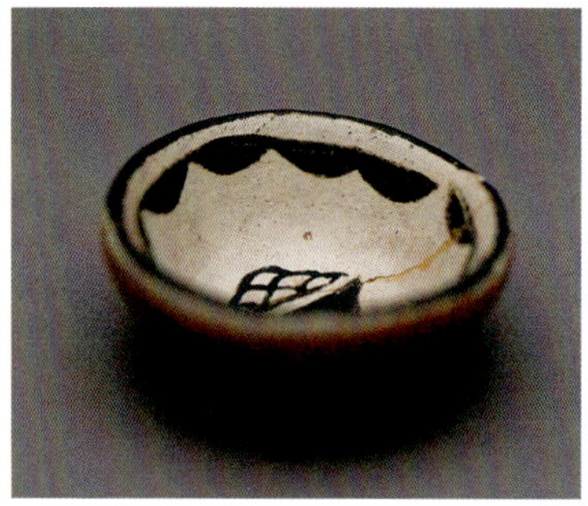

Bowl
Attributed to Estefanita Herrera, ca. 1930
2.1 × 5.0
Museum Purchase, Estefanita Herrera
19375

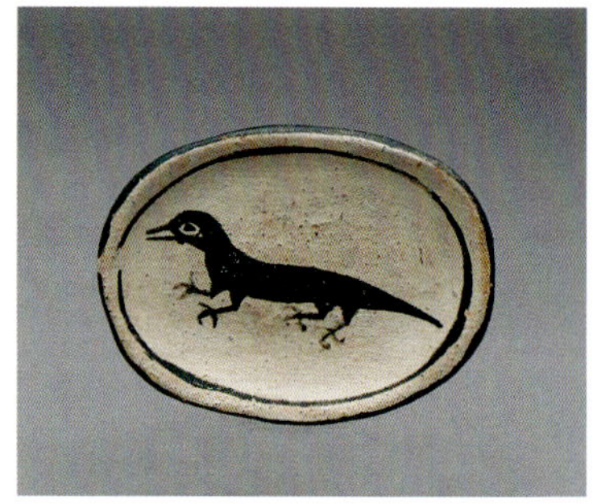

Plate
Attributed to Estefanita Herrera, ca. 1930
9.0 × 5.2 × 7.0
Museum Purchase, Estefanita Herrera
19378

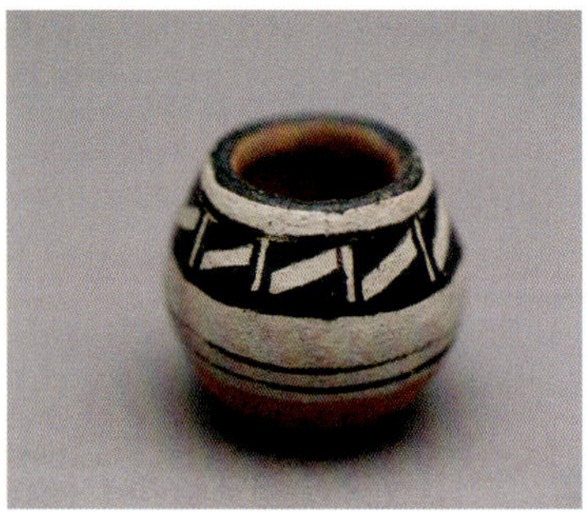

Jar
Attributed to Estefanita Herrera, ca. 1930
3.3 × 3.5
Museum Purchase, Estefanita Herrera
19372

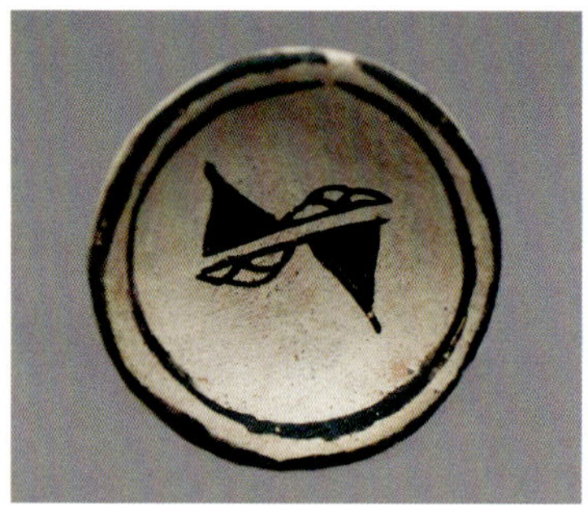

Plate
Attributed to Estefanita Herrera, ca. 1930
1.0 × 4.0
Museum Purchase, Estefanita Herrera
19376

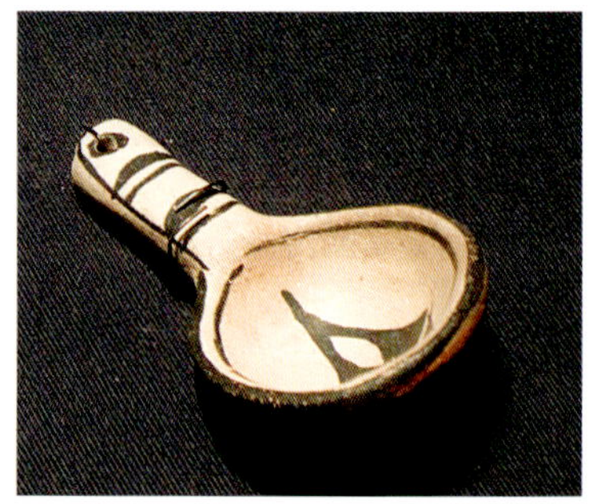

Ladle
Attributed to Estefanita Herrera, ca. 1950
3.1 × 4.5 × 8.5
Museum Purchase, Estefanita Herrera
19379

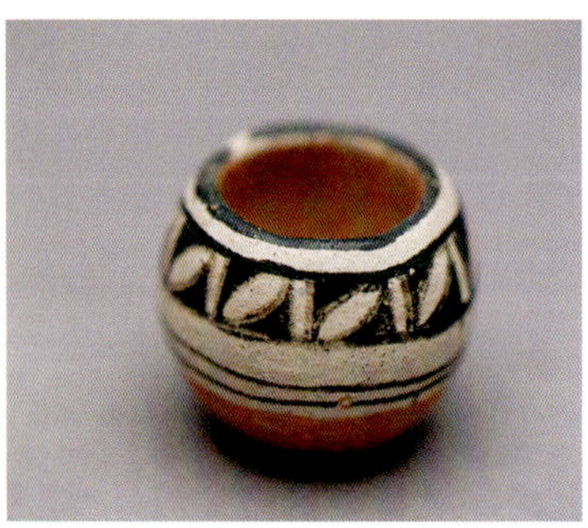

Jar
Attributed to Estefanita Herrera, ca. 1930
3.4 × 3.8
Museum Purchase, Estefanita Herrera
19373

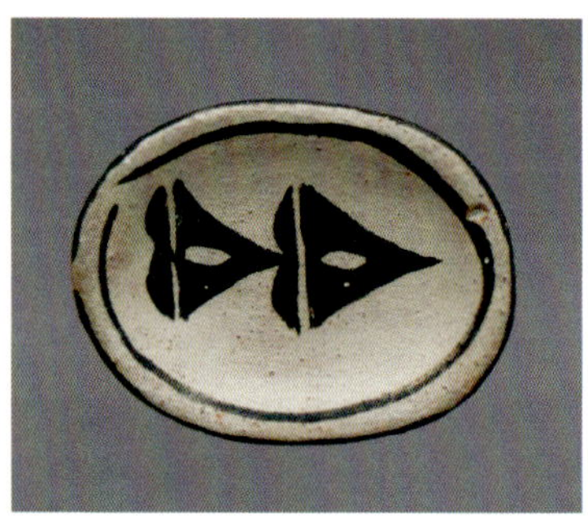

Plate
Attributed to Estefanita Herrera, ca. 1930
1.0 × 4.3 × 5.6
Museum Purchase, Estefanita Herrera
19377

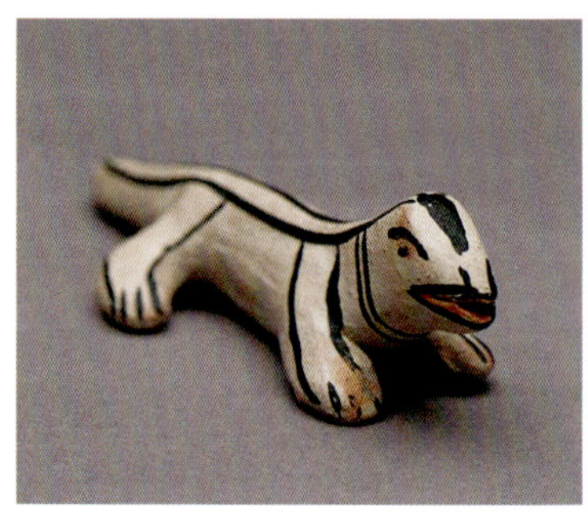

Lizard Figurine
Attributed to Estefanita Herrera, ca. 1935
3.0 × 4.4 × 10.0
Museum Purchase, Estefanita Herrera
19380

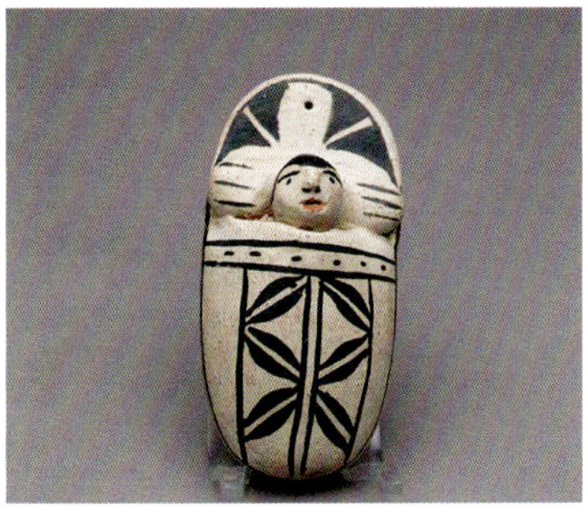

Infant Figurine
Attributed to Estefanita Herrera, ca. 1935
3.1 × 5.0 × 9.9
Museum Purchase, Estefanita Herrera
19381

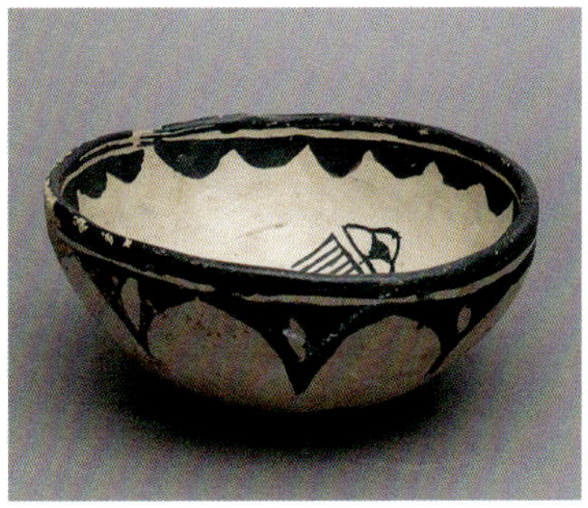

Bowl
Artist Unknown, ca. 1930
6.4 × 15.3
Nelson Collection
24822

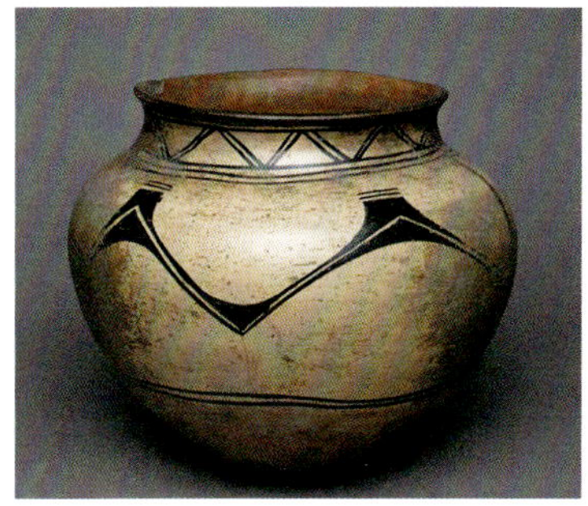

Jar
Artist Unknown, ca. 1900
23.5 × 29.2
Museum Purchase, Mrs. Julius Gans
35760

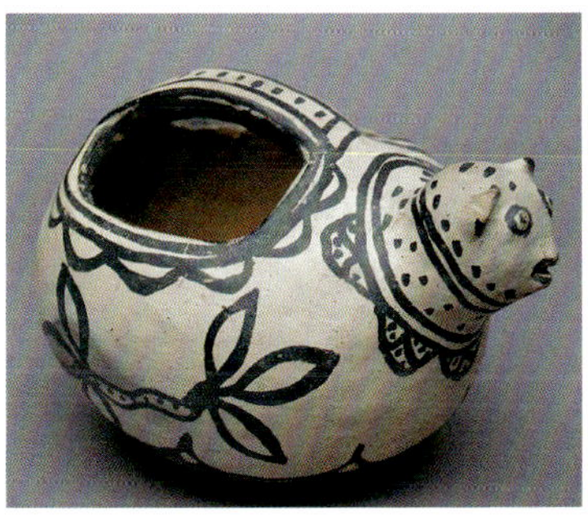

Bird Pitcher
Artist Unknown, ca. 1930
13.8 × 17.0 × 20.3
Peltz Collection
19395

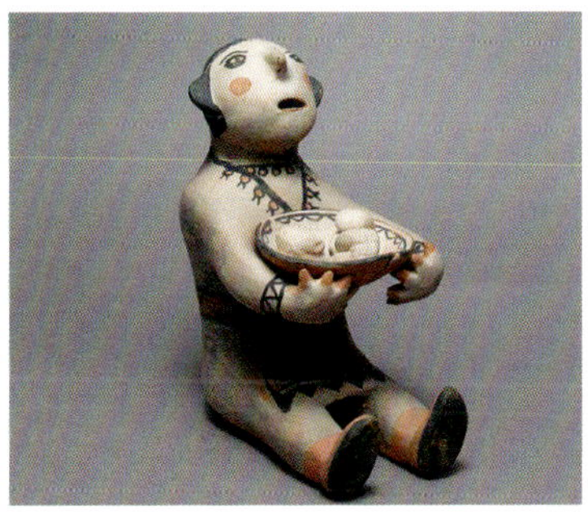

Female Figurine
Teresita Romero, 1960
18.0 × 10.0 × 14.6
Museum Purchase, Sallie Lippencott
25114

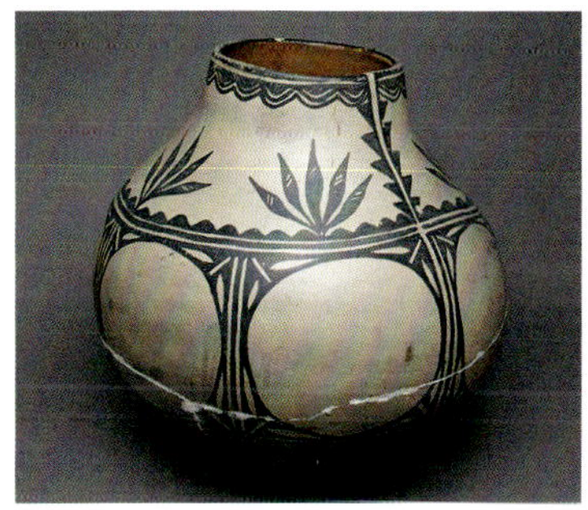

Jar
Artist Unknown, ca. 1900
47.5 × 50.0
Gift of Julius Gans
35767

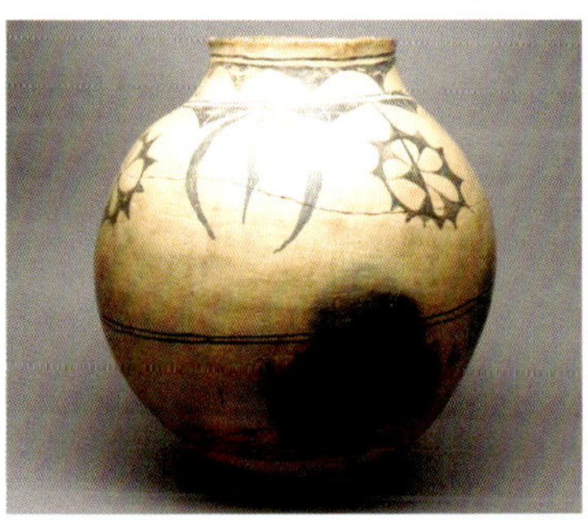

Jar
Antonita Quintana, ca. 1890–1910
54.0 × 43.0
Museum Collection
22751

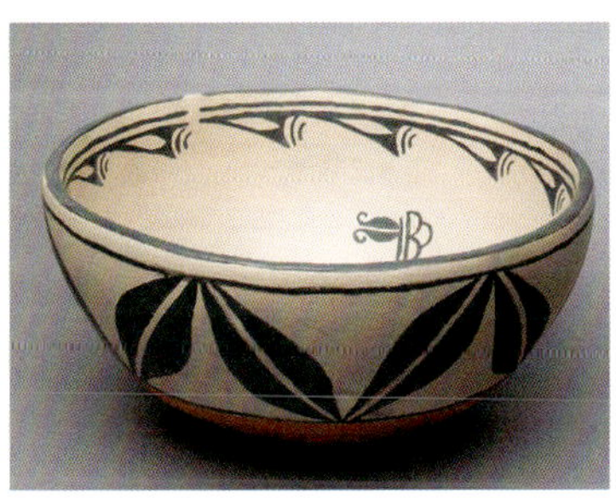

Bowl
Laurencita Herrera, 1961
11.2 × 24.0
Museum Purchase, Sallie Lippencott
25828

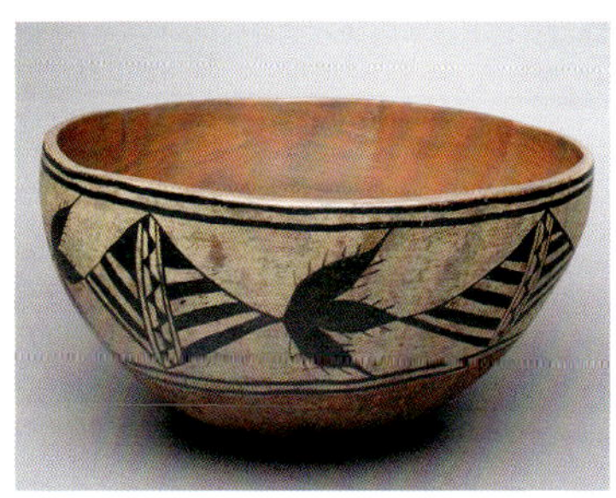

Bowl
Artist Unknown, ca. 1920
16.0 × 31.3
Museum Collection
36553

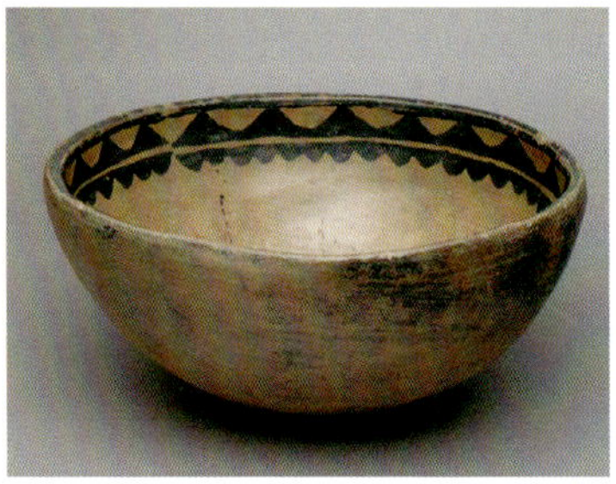

Bowl
Artist Unknown, ca. 1920
11.2 × 26.1
Kenneth M. Chapman Collection
37744

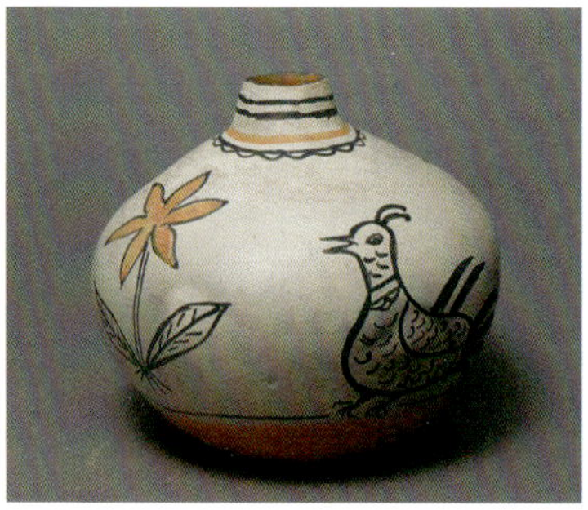

Jar
Teresita Romero, ca. 1960–1962
12.9 × 14.9
Museum Purchase, Sallie Lippencott
38141

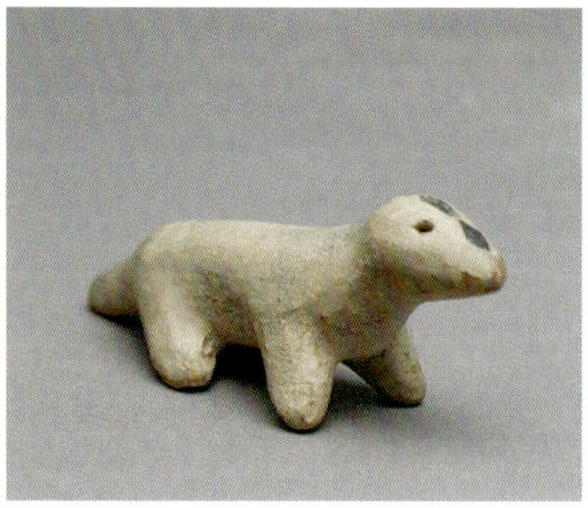

Lizard Figurine
Artist Unknown, ca. 1930
3.7 × 3.4 × 10.0
Gift of Mr. and Mrs. Bud Noltersmeyer
43733

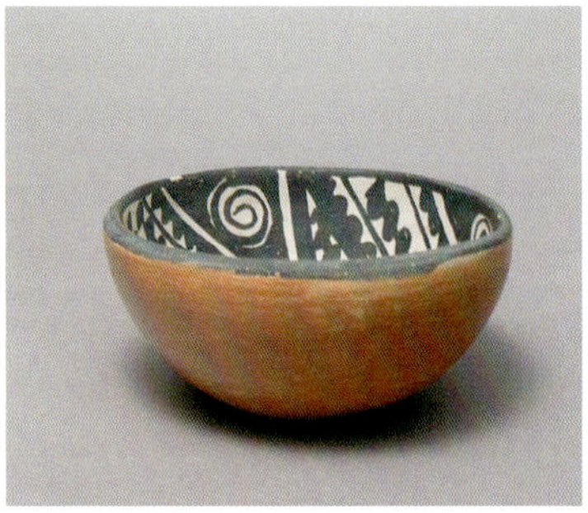

Bowl
Teresita Romero, ca. 1960–1962
5.7 × 12.2
Museum Purchase, Sallie Lippencott
38139

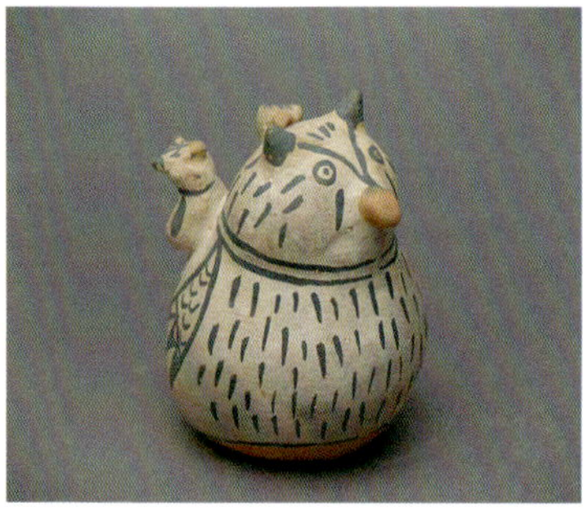

Owl Figurine
Artist Unknown, ca. 1958
11.1 × 7.4 × 7.5
Museum Purchase, Sallie Lippencott
38143

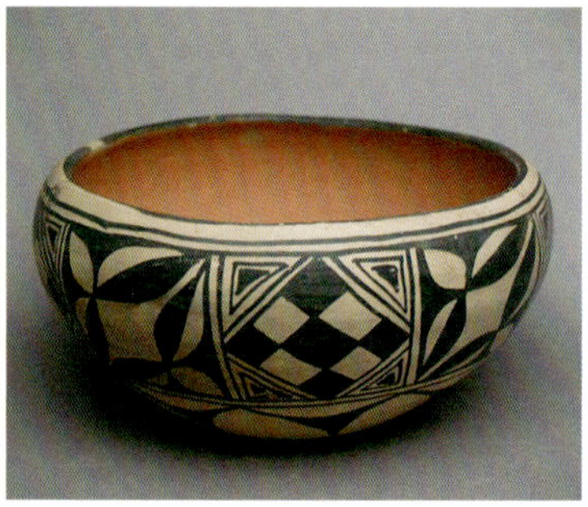

Bowl
Artist Unknown, ca. 1935
11.9 × 25.0
Gift of Erik K. Reed
45794

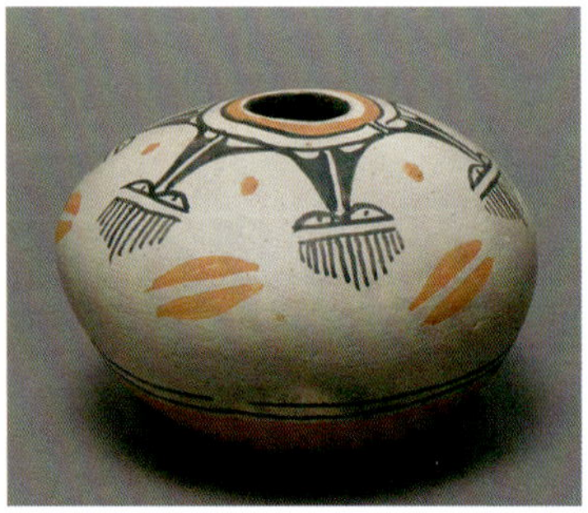

Jar
Teresita Romero, ca. 1952–1962
8.8 × 12.6
Museum Purchase, Sallie Lippencott
38140

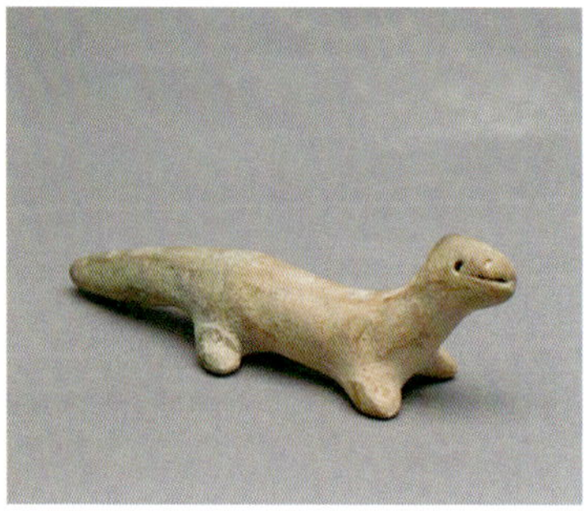

Lizard Figurine
Cochiti or Tesuque
Artist Unknown, ca. 1940
3.4 × 3.6 × 11.0
Gift of Mr. and Mrs. Bud Noltersmeyer
43732

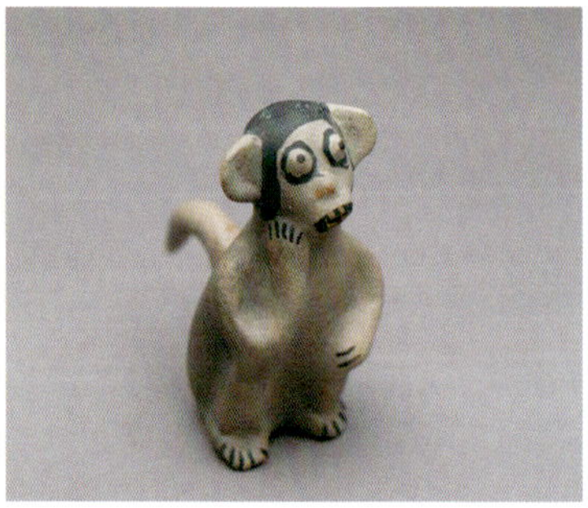

Monkey Figurine
Artist Unknown, ca. 1950
10.0 × 5.0 × 8.0
Mrs. E.V. Lambert Collection
45575

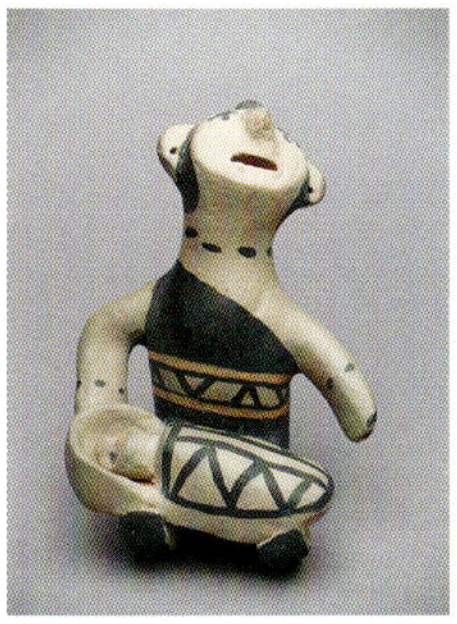

Singing Mother Figurine
Damacia Cordero, ca. 1956–1957
14.4 × 10.9 × 8.6
Mrs. E.V. Lambert Collection
45967

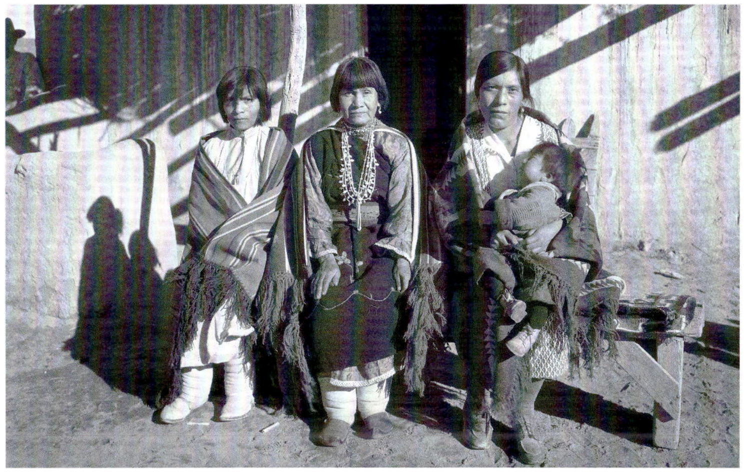

Lucinda Suina and daughters potter Damacia Cordero and Veronica Trujillo, Cochiti Pueblo, ca. 1935. Courtesy Palace of the Governors (MNM/DCA), 7474.

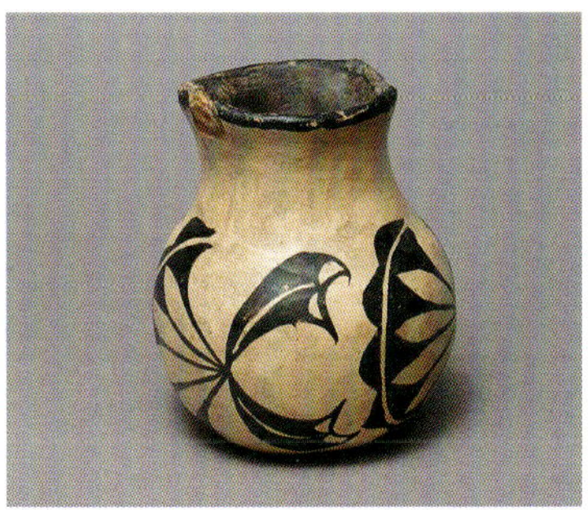

Jar
Artist Unknown, ca. 1930
10.5 × 9.4
Pansy Stockton Bequest
46187

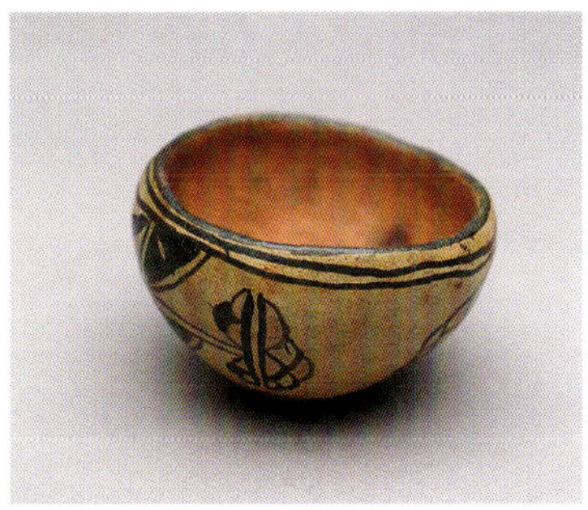

Bowl
Artist Unknown, ca. 1935
4.5 × 7.1
Gift of Jane Baumann
47937

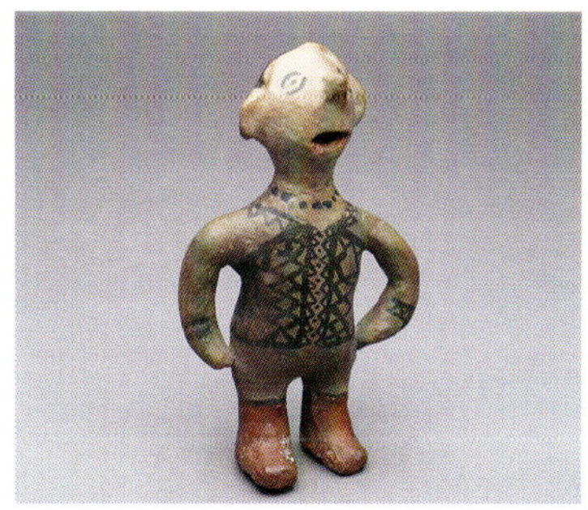

Male Figurine
Artist Unknown, ca. 1930
16.5 × 9.8 × 4.0
Gift of Jane Baumann
47940

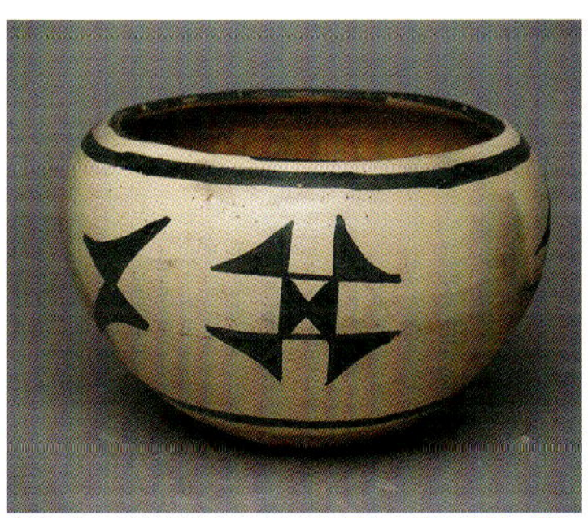

Bowl
Artist Unknown, ca. 1925
12.3 × 19.8
Pansy Stockton Collection
46216

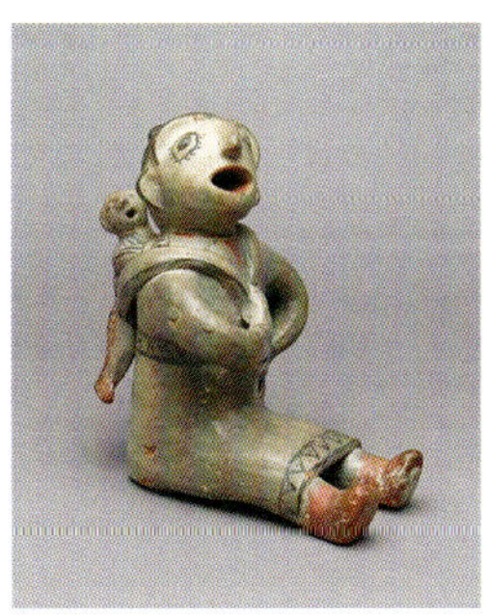

Mother and Child Figurine
Artist Unknown, ca. 1935
15.3 × 14.6
Gift of Jane Baumann
47939

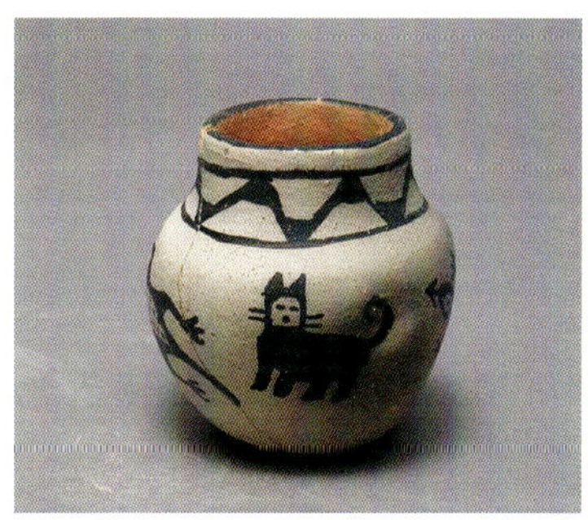

Jar
Artist Unknown, ca. 1965
6.8 × 6.5
Gift of Mrs. E.V. Lambert
48036

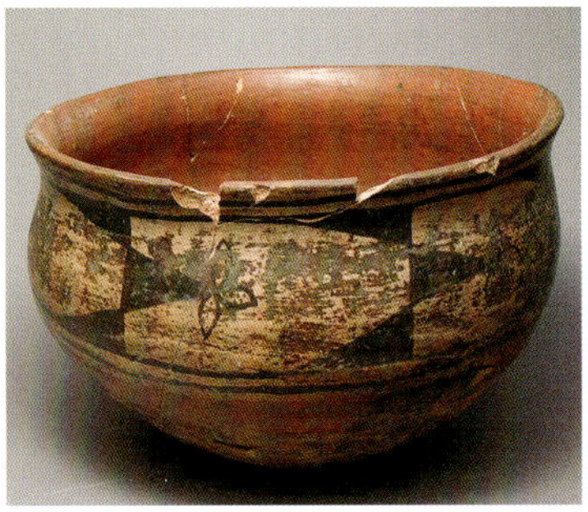

Bowl
Artist Unknown, ca. 1880–1900
27.5 × 40.0
Gift of the Fred Harvey Company
48248

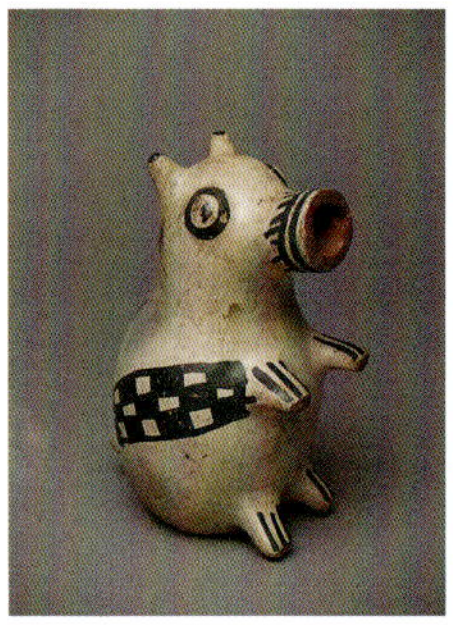

Pig or Prairie Dog Figurine
Artist Unknown, ca. 1912
13.8 × 9.4 × 9.0
Gift of Phyllis Harroun
50009

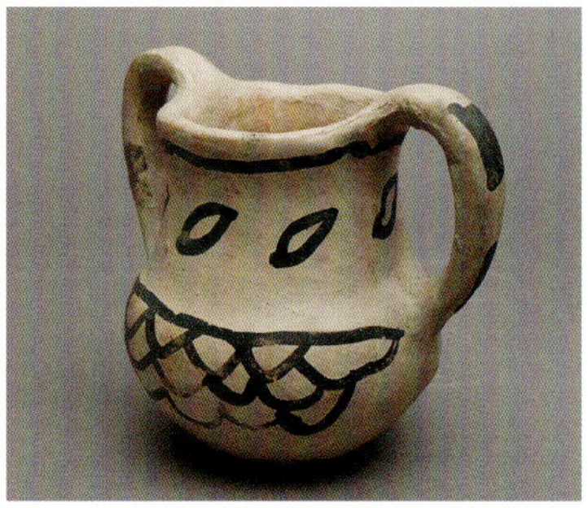

Vase
Artist Unknown, ca. 1920
10.6 × 9.0 × 12.7
Museum Collection
50056

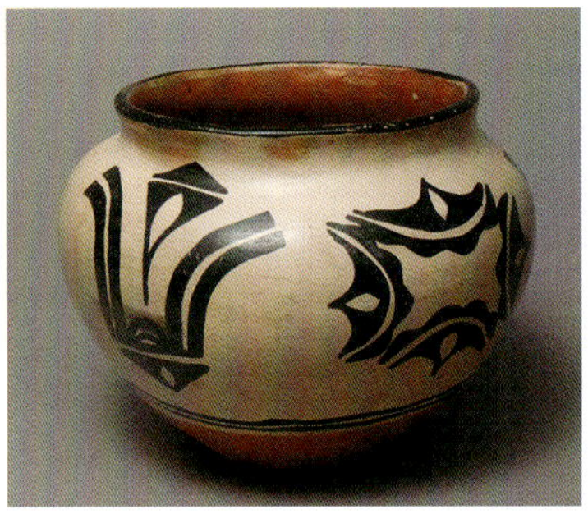

Jar
Artist Unknown, ca. 1945–1950
13.7 × 18.2
Kenneth M. Chapman Collection
48636

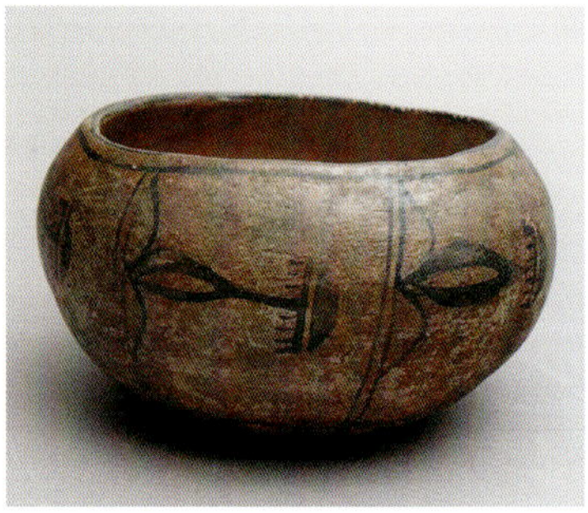

Bowl
Artist Unknown, ca. 1900–1915
8.6 × 16.0
Museum Collection
50026

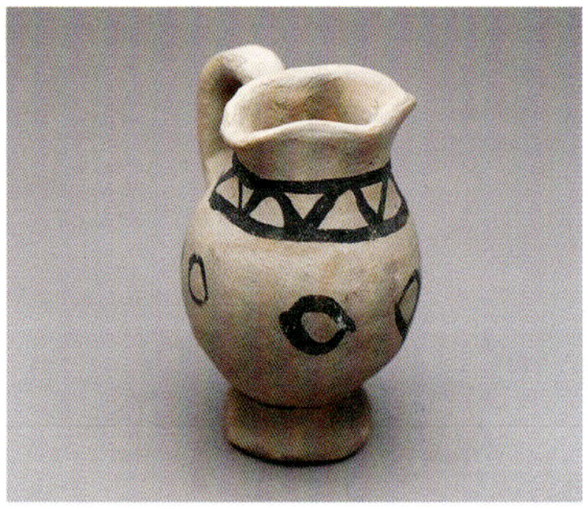

Pitcher
Artist Unknown, ca. 1960
9.1 × 7.5 × 8.5
Museum Collection
50057

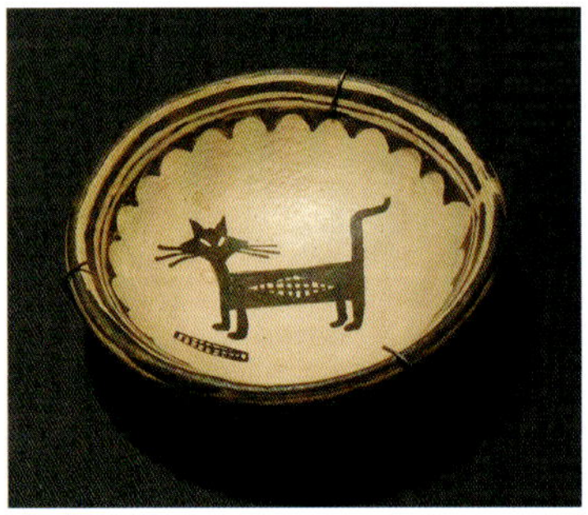

Plate
Artist Unknown, ca. 1955
3.3 × 8.4
Julia K. Shishkin Bequest
49705

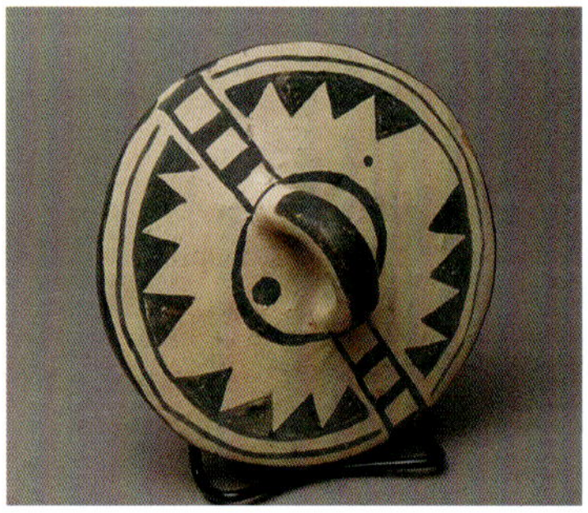

Jar Lid
Artist Unknown, ca. 1900–1940
4.8 × 13.2
Kenneth M. Chapman Collection
50055

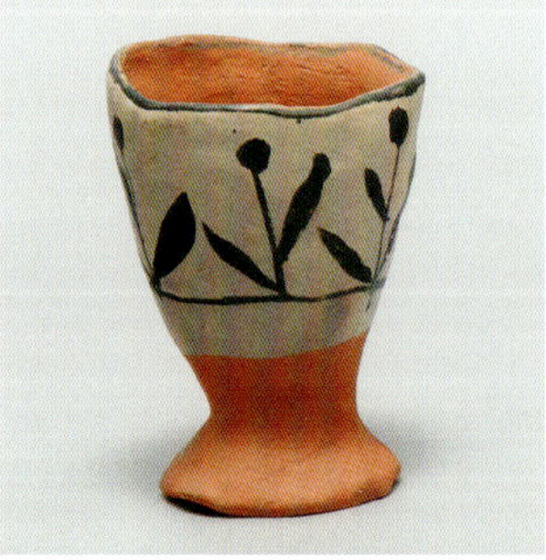

Cup
Artist Unknown, ca. 1940
8.3 × 6.3
Museum Collection
50058

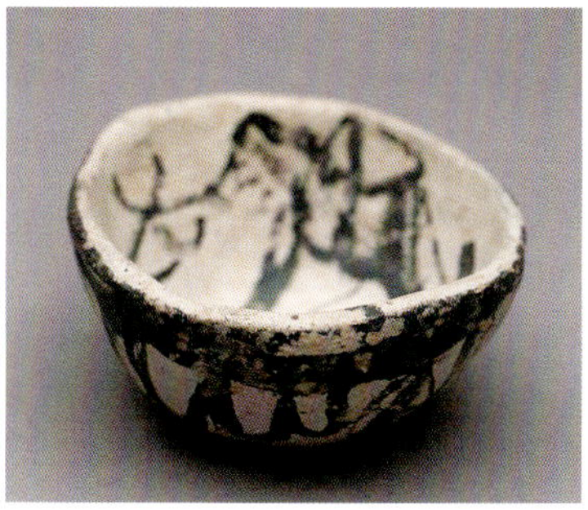

Cup
Artist Unknown, ca. 1930–1950
4.4 × 8.9
Museum Collection
50059

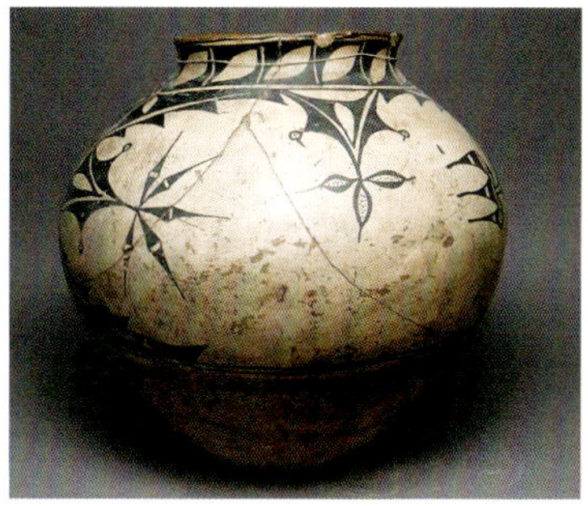

Jar
Artist Unknown, ca. 1840
44.5 × 51.0
Margaret Moses Bequest
50204

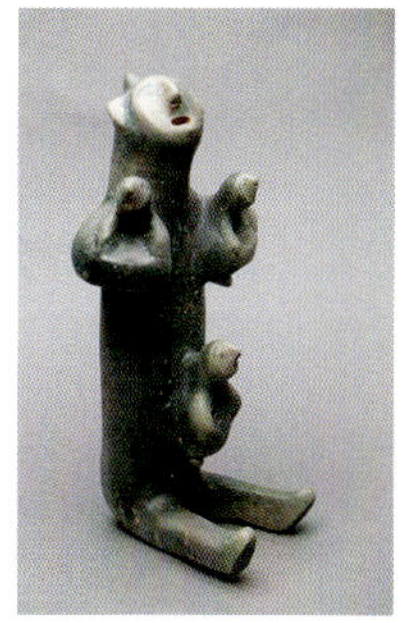

Storyteller Figurine
Damacia Cordero, ca. 1960
29.8 × 14.3 × 10.4
Gift of Gilbert R. Hitchcock
51131

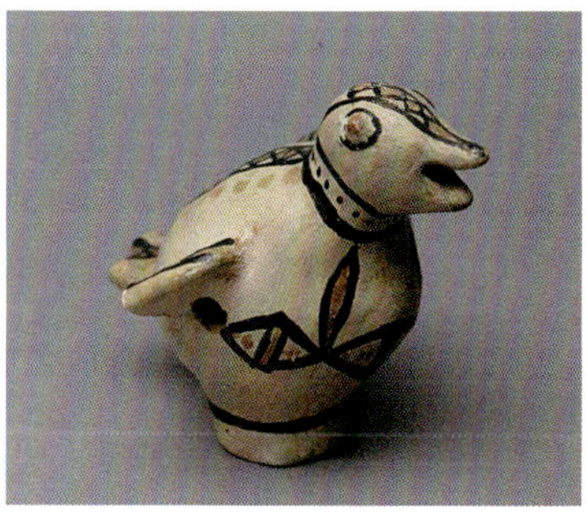

Bird Figurine
Artist Unknown, ca. 1900
10.1 × 8.7 × 12.3
Gift of Phyllis Harroun
50181

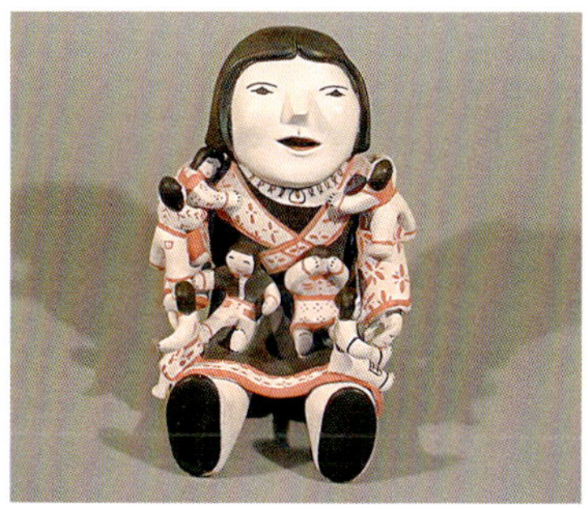

Storyteller Figurine
Ada Suina, ca. 1975
Gift of Gilbert R. Hitchcock
51129

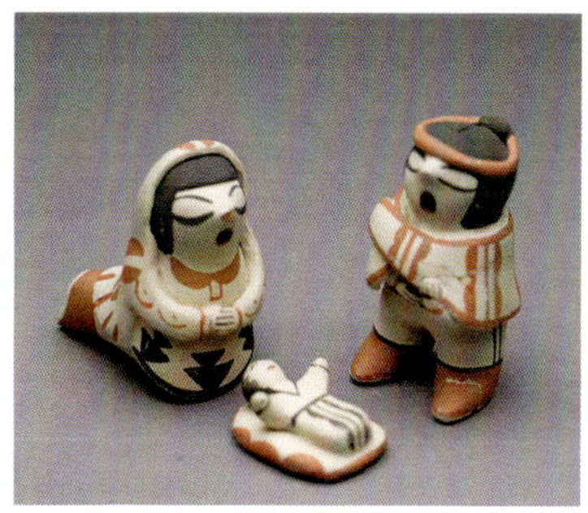

Jesus, Mary, and Joseph Figurines
Judith Suina, ca. 1980
8.5 × 4.7
Gift of the Museum of
New Mexico Shops
51327

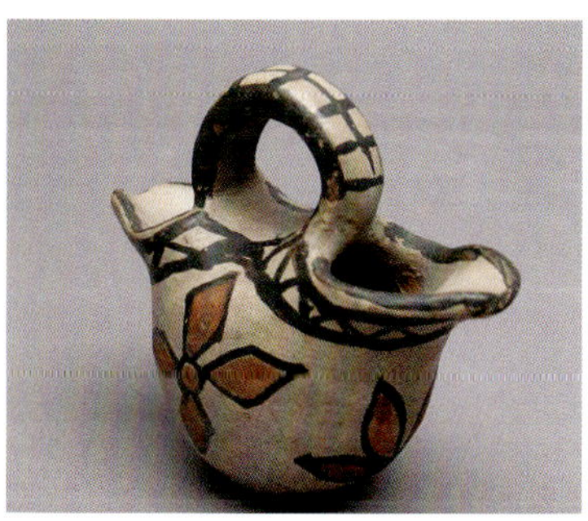

Wedding Vase
Artist Unknown, ca. 1910–1912
8.3 × 5.2 × 9.5
Gift of Phyllis Harroun
50182

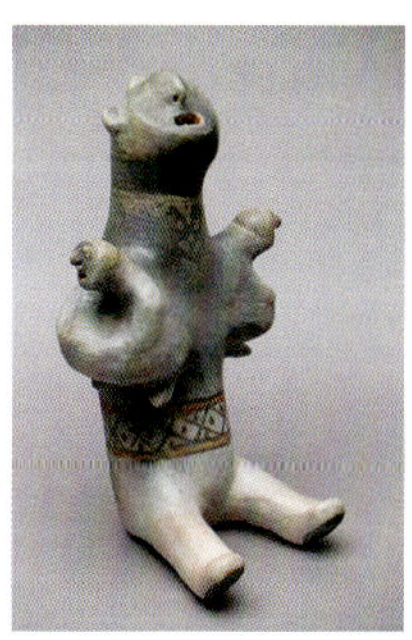

Storyteller Figurine
Damacia Cordero, ca. 1960
23.3 × 13.5 × 11.3
Gift of Gilbert R. Hitchcock
51130

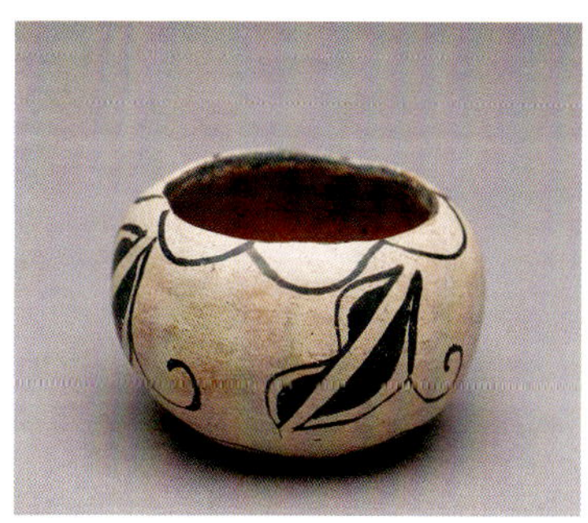

Bowl
Artist Unknown, ca. 1930
5.3 × 7.5
Gift of Warren and Lois von Preissig
and Sue Bacharach
53146

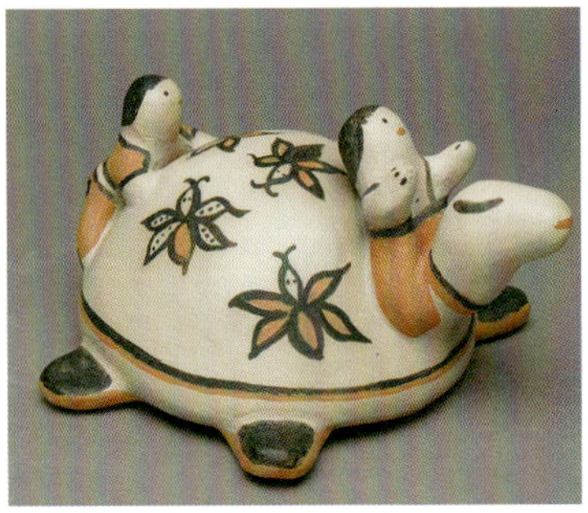

Turtle Figurine
Rita Lewis, ca. 1985
7.8 × 13.7 × 16.5
Gift of Adam and Justin Dewey
53211

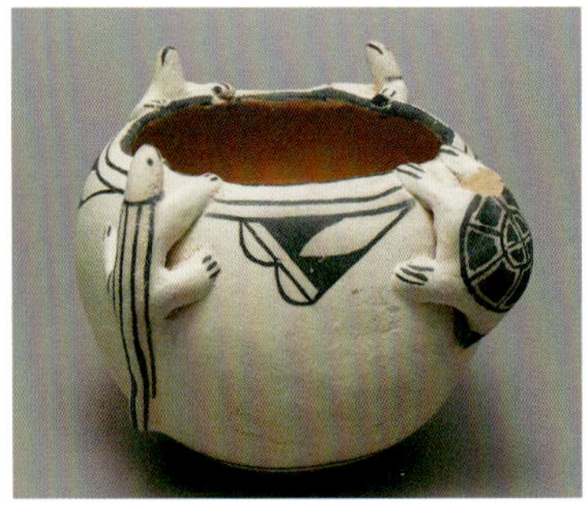

Jar
Laurencita Herrera, ca. 1975
12.6 × 16.1
Rick Dillingham Collection
53604

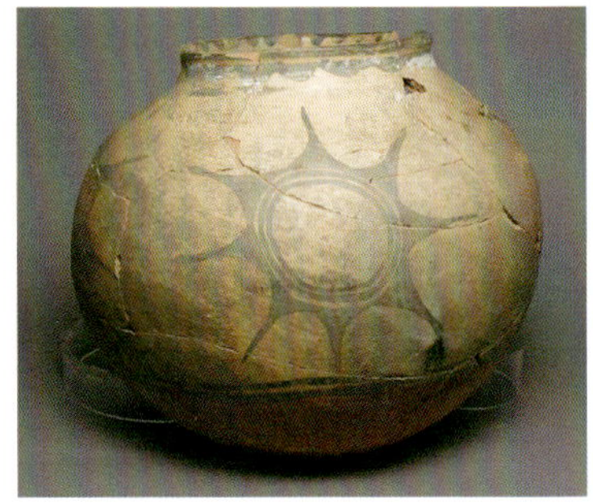

Storage Jar
Artist Unknown, ca. 1900
33.0 × 37.7
Gift of the Fred Harvey Company
53886

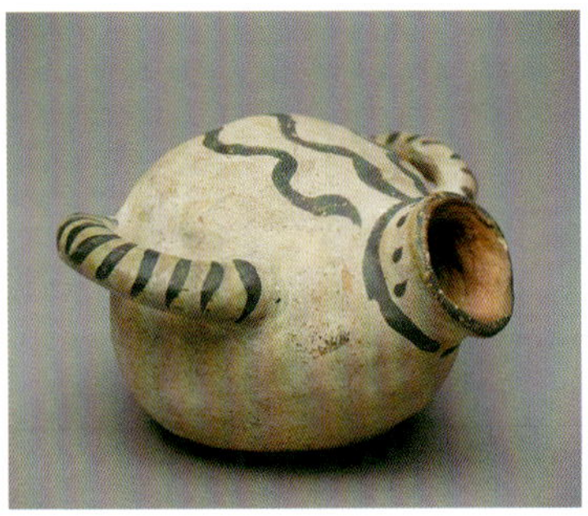

Canteen
Artist Unknown, ca. 1930
7.6 × 7.7 × 12.1
Gift of John Kania
53252

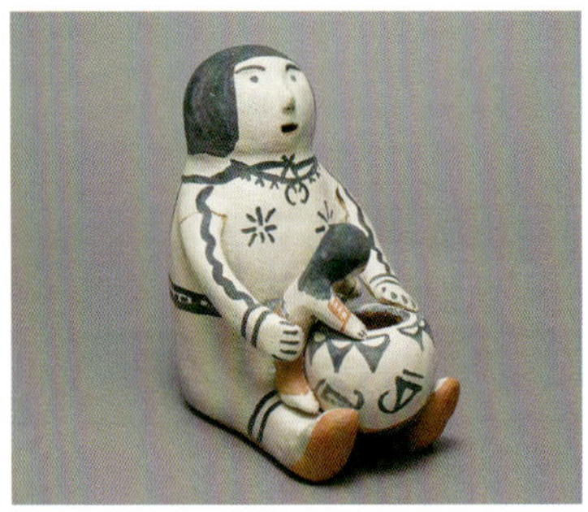

Mother and Child Figurine
Laurencita Herrera, ca. 1985
14.5 × 8.1 × 13.2
Rick Dillingham Collection
53605

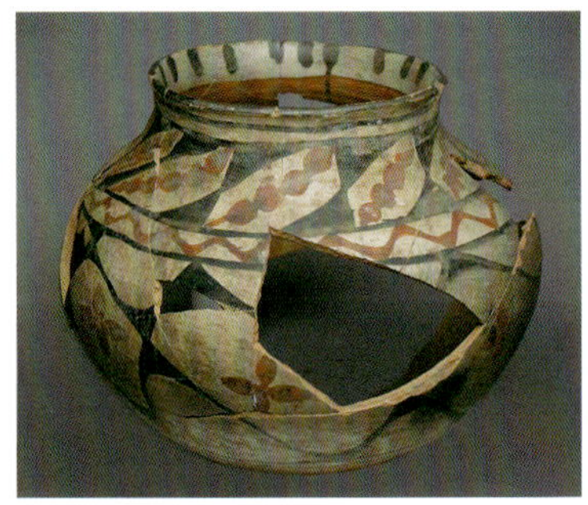

Jar
Artist Unknown, ca. 1890–1900
32.0 × 34.3
Gift of the Fred Harvey Company
53889

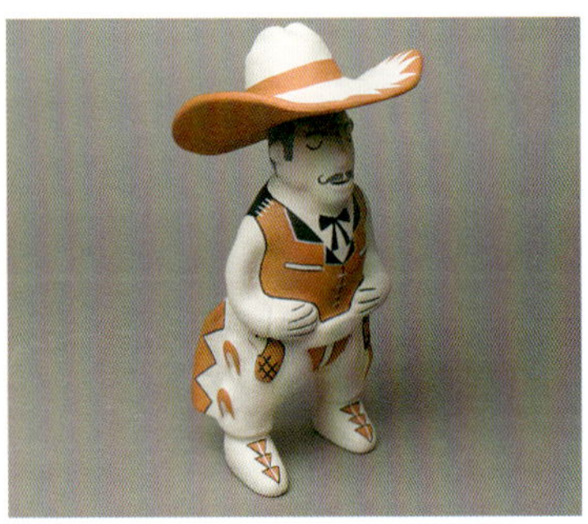

Gaucho Figurine
Ivan Lewis, 1992
19.1 × 9.9 × 5.7
Museum Purchase, Ivan Lewis
53553

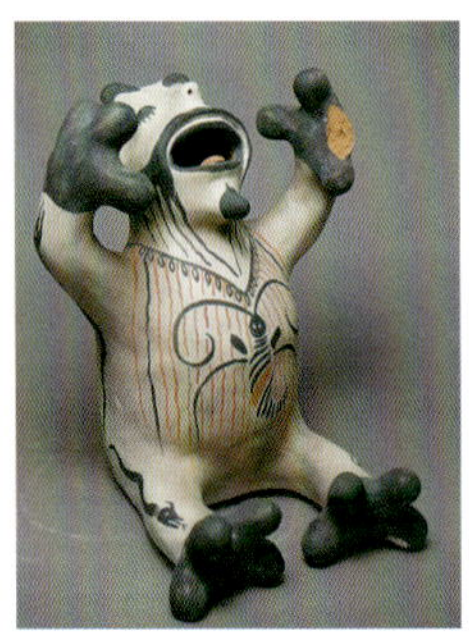

Male Figurine
Virgil Ortiz, ca. 1990
26.9 × 23.3 × 21.5
Rick Dillingham Collection
53651

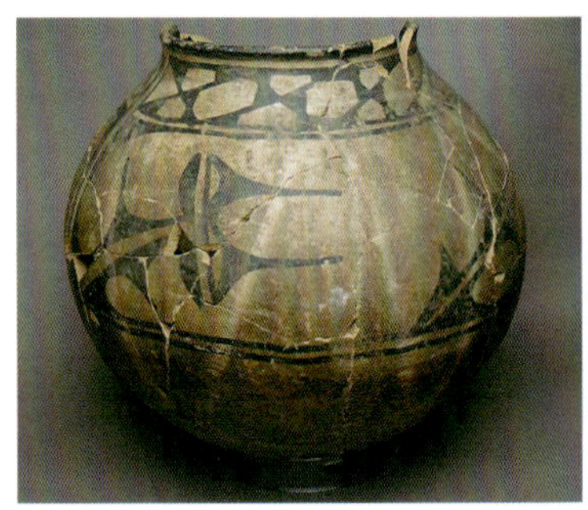

Jar
Artist Unknown, ca. 1880
43.4 × 44.9
Gift of the Fred Harvey Company
53896

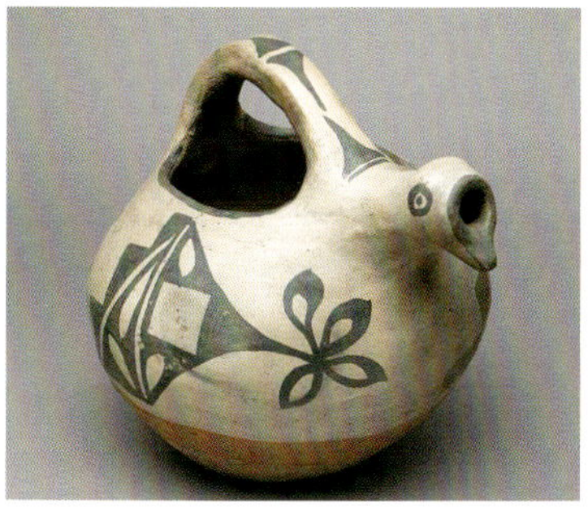

Bird Pitcher
Artist Unknown, ca. 1880
19.0 × 18.0 × 22.0
Gift of the Charleston Museum
54058

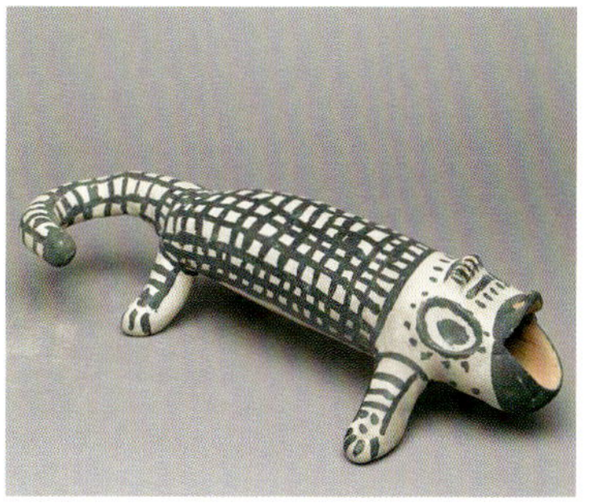

Alligator Figurine
Damacia Cordero, 1980
6.8 × 28.7 × 13.5
Rick Dillingham Collection
54246

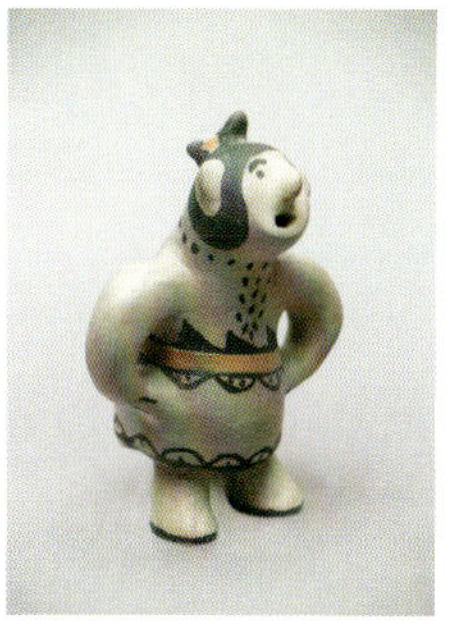

Female Figurine
Damacia Cordero, ca. 1975
17.7 × 13.7 × 7.8
Rick Dillingham Collection
54250

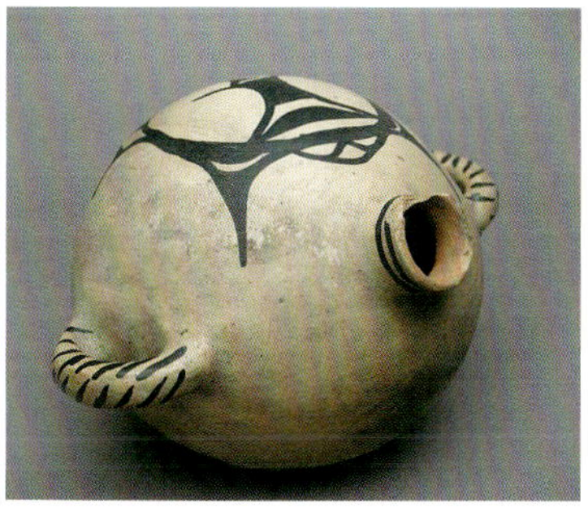

Canteen
Artist Unknown, ca. 1890
18.6 × 22.8 × 15.5
Gift of the Charleston Museum
54067

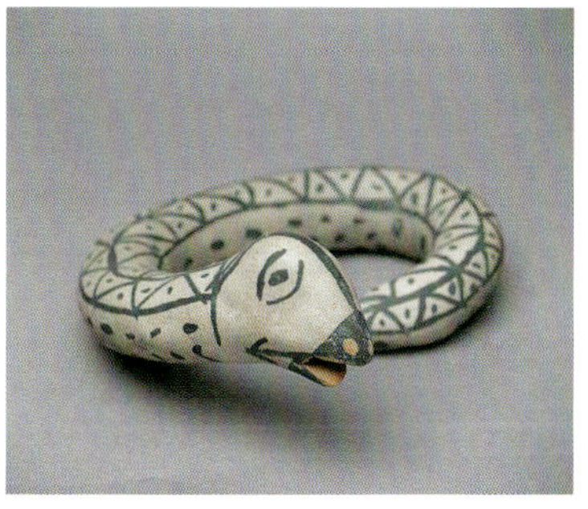

Snake Figurine
Damacia Cordero, ca. 1981
6.3 × 14.2 × 2.6
Rick Dillingham Collection
54248

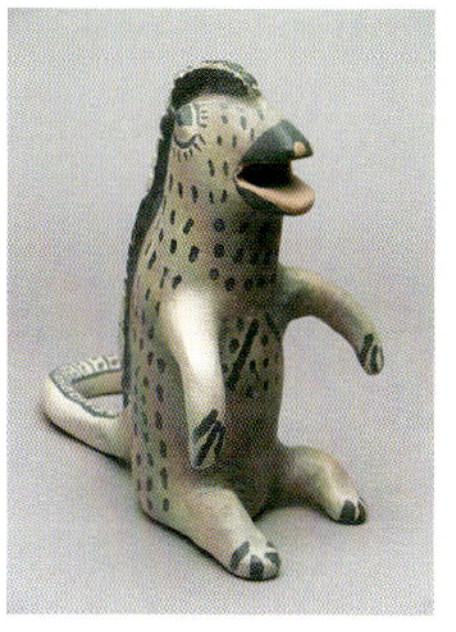

Dinosaur Figurine
Damacia Cordero, 1981
19.0 × 10.5
Rick Dillingham Collection
54251

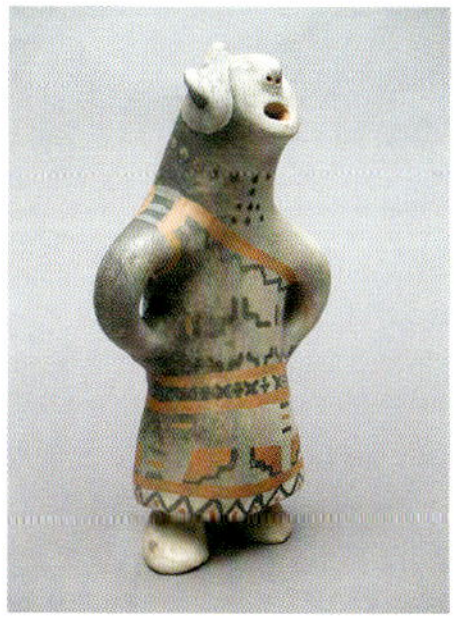

Female Figurine
Damacia Cordero, 1981
25.1 × 14.4 × 6.7
Rick Dillingham Collection
54245

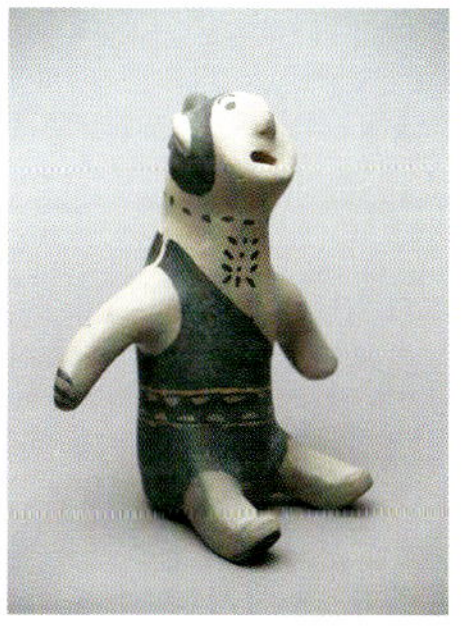

Female Figurine
Damacia Cordero, ca. 1980
19.0 × 16.1 × 10.5
Rick Dillingham Collection
54249

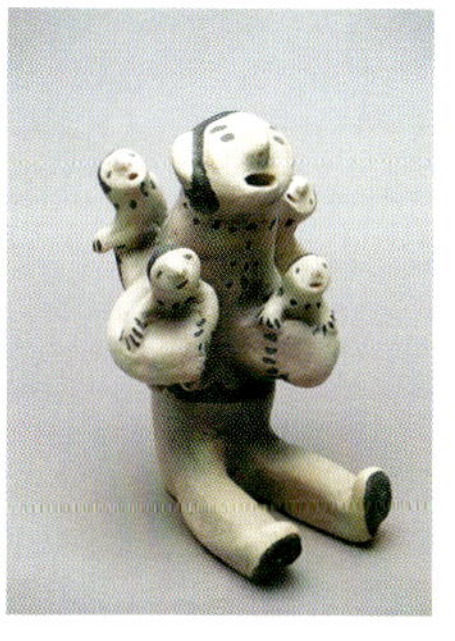

Storyteller Figurine
Damacia Cordero, ca. 1975
20.7 × 13.3 × 14.3
Rick Dillingham Collection
54252

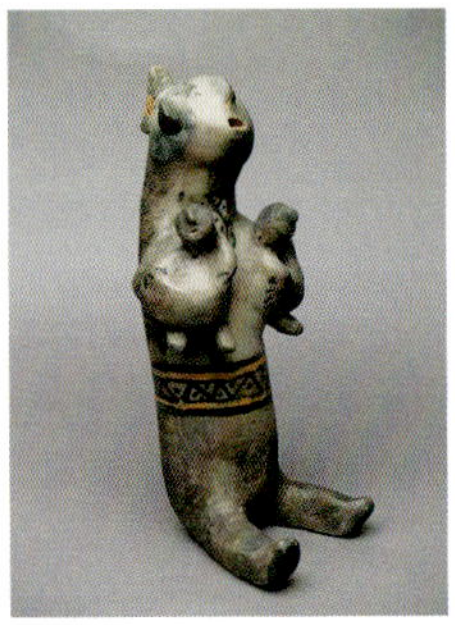

Storyteller Figurine
Damacia Cordero, ca. 1965
26.1 × 12.0 × 10.4
Rick Dillingham Collection
54253

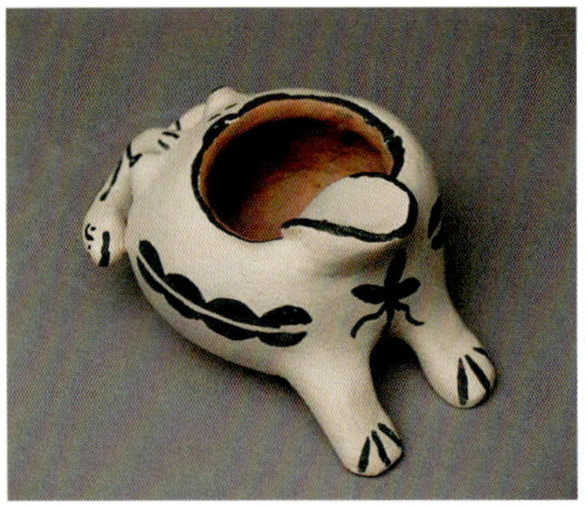

Frog Figurine or Ashtray
Maria Laweka, ca. 1985
7.2 × 10.4 × 13.2
Rick Dillingham Collection
54259

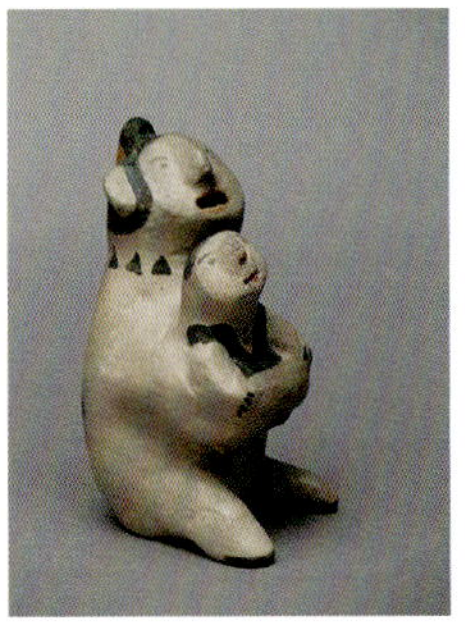

Storyteller Figurine
Damacia Cordero, ca. 1985
14.2 × 8.4 × 8.7
Rick Dillingham Collection
54263

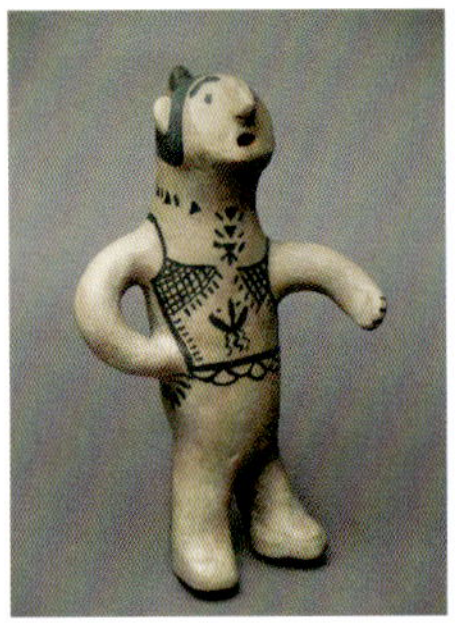

Male Figurine
Damacia Cordero, ca. 1982
25.4 × 15.6 × 8.3
Rick Dillingham Collection
54255

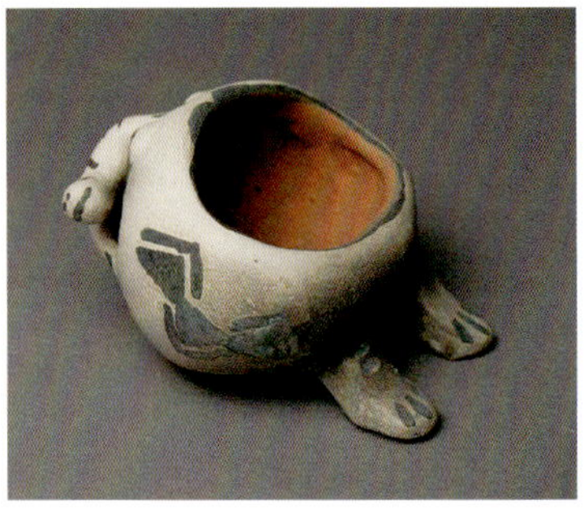

Frog Figurine or Ashtray
Maria Laweka, ca. 1980s
5.8 × 7.9 × 7.8
Rick Dillingham Collection
54260

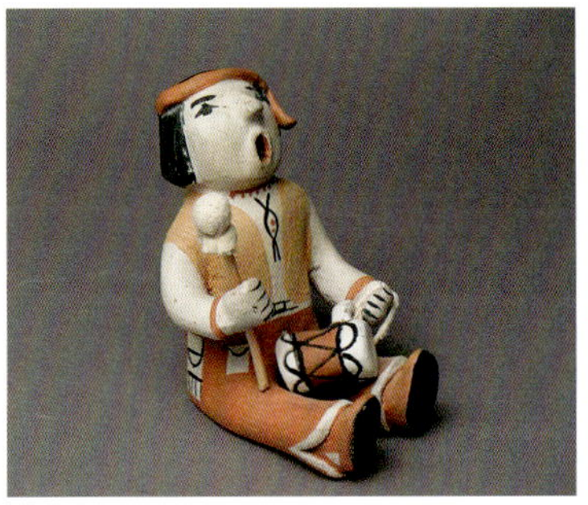

Singing Drummer Figurine
Artist Unknown, ca. 1980s
10.6 × 7.1 × 8.3
Rick Dillingham Collection
54267

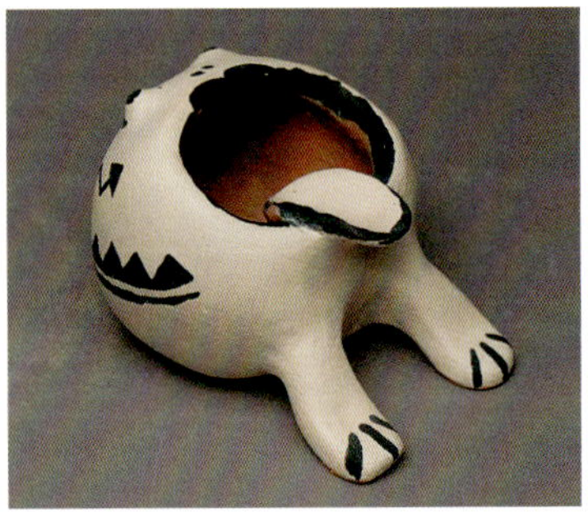

Frog Figurine or Ashtray
Maria Laweka, ca. 1985
7.8 × 12.8 × 10.0
Rick Dillingham Collection
54258

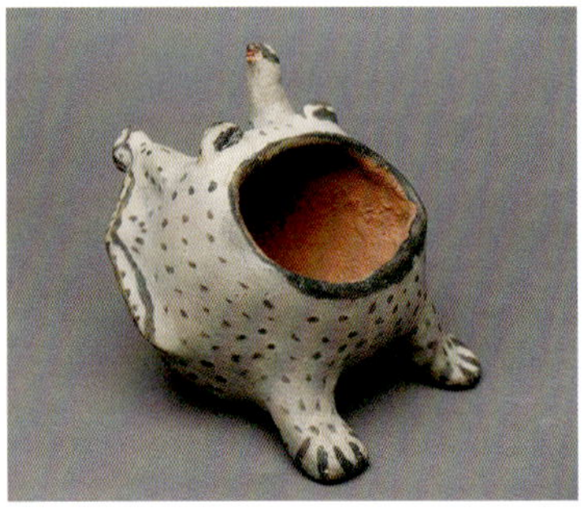

Frog Figurine or Ashtray
Damacia Cordero, ca. 1985
14.7 × 10.1 × 9.3
Rick Dillingham Collection
54262

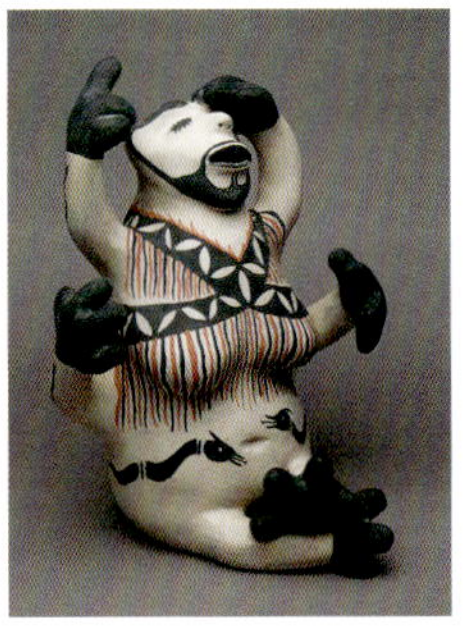

Male Figurine
Virgil Ortiz, ca. 1990
30.0 × 23.5
Rick Dillingham Collection
54268

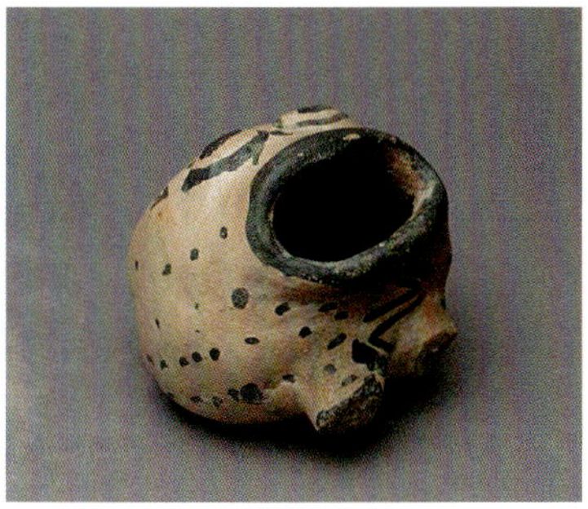

Frog Figurine
Artist Unknown, ca. 1950
7.7 × 7.9 × 8.4
Rick Dillingham Collection
54270

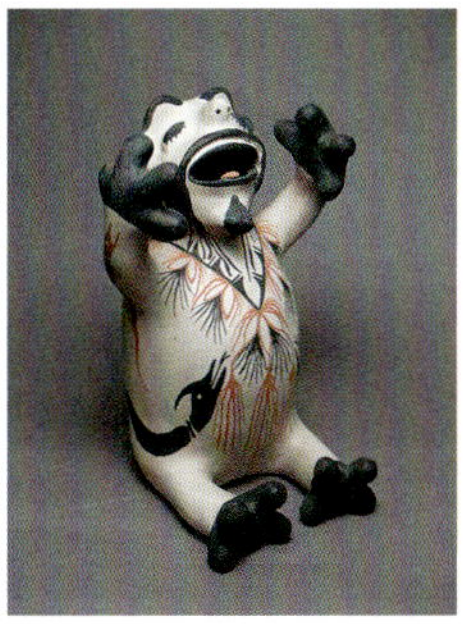

Male Figurine
Virgil Ortiz, ca. 1990
31.9 × 21.7 × 21.1
Rick Dillingham Collection
54273

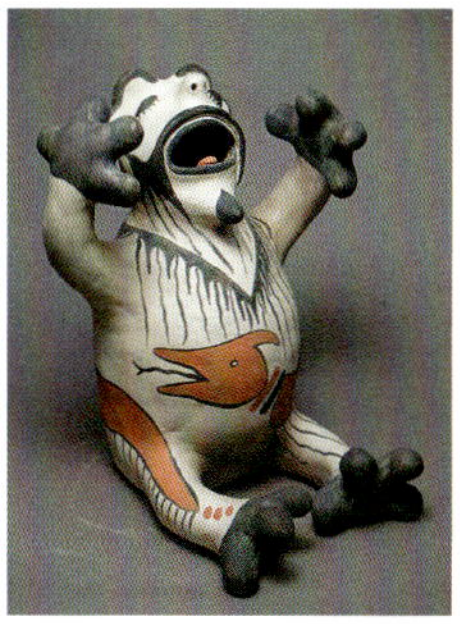

Male Figurine
Virgil Ortiz, ca. 1990
29.3 × 24.7 × 24.1
Rick Dillingham Collection
54275

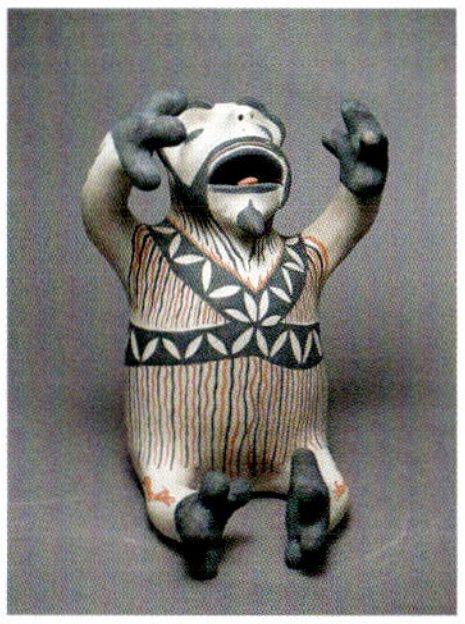

Male Figurine
Virgil Ortiz, ca. 1990
28.1 × 20.4 × 23.2
Rick Dillingham Collection
54271

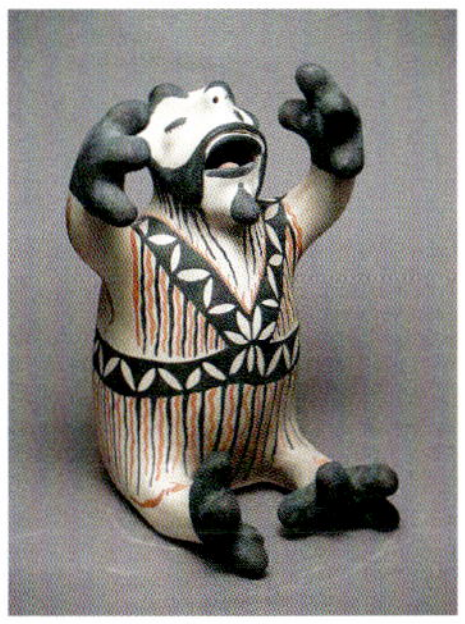

Male Figurine
Virgil Ortiz, ca. 1990
28.0 × 20.1 × 22.5
Rick Dillingham Collection
54274

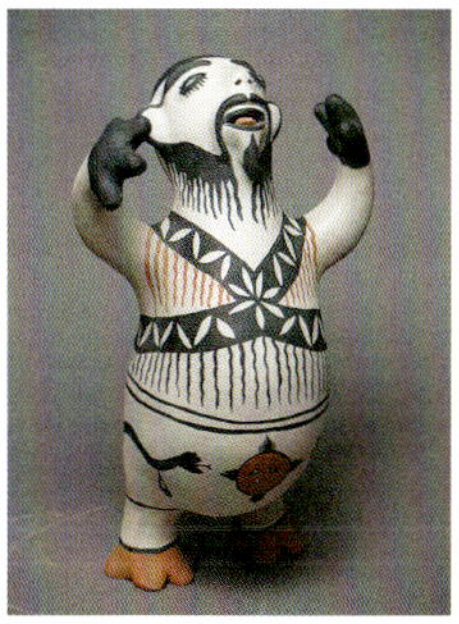

Male Figurine
Virgil Ortiz, ca. 1990
34.1 × 20.1 × 15.7
Rick Dillingham Collection
54276

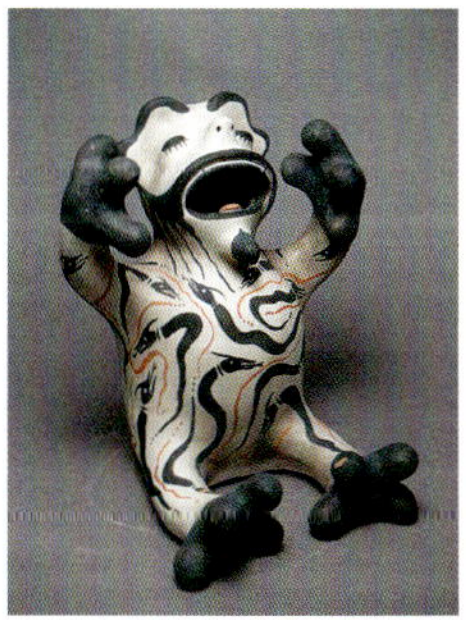

Male Figurine
Virgil Ortiz, ca. 1990
26.2 × 22.6 × 23.0
Rick Dillingham Collection
54272

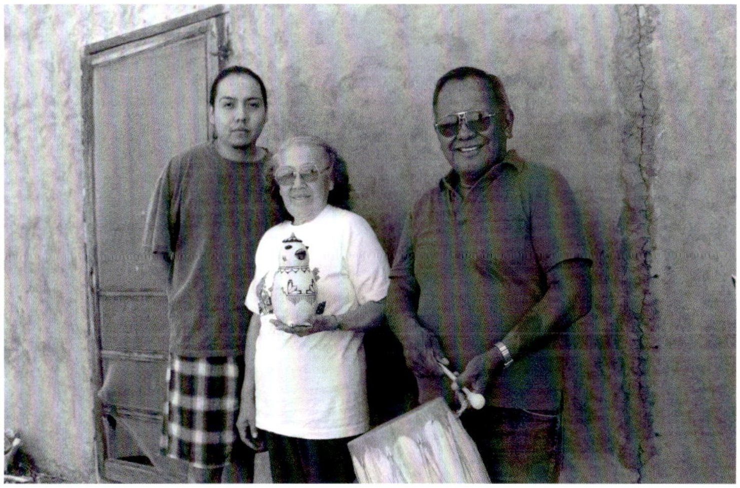

The Ortiz family of potters: Seferina Ortiz, her son Virgil, and husband Guadalupe Ortiz, 1993. (See fig. 50 for another example of Virgil's work and fig. 49 for an example of Seferina's work.) Courtesy National Museum of the American Indian, Smithsonian Institution, P23654.

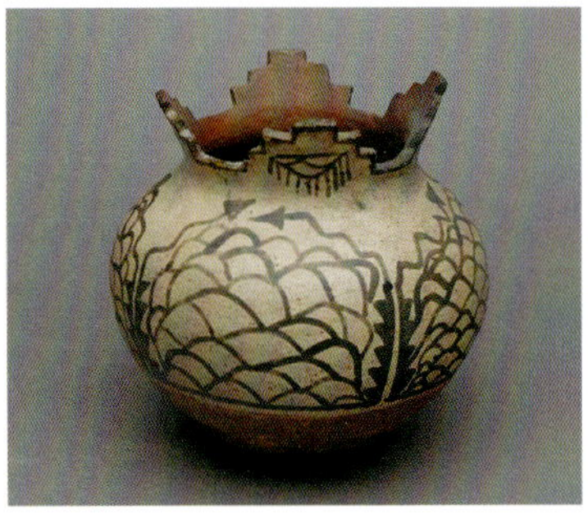

Jar
Artist Unknown, ca. 1890s
13.7 × 14.3
Rick Dillingham Collection
54277

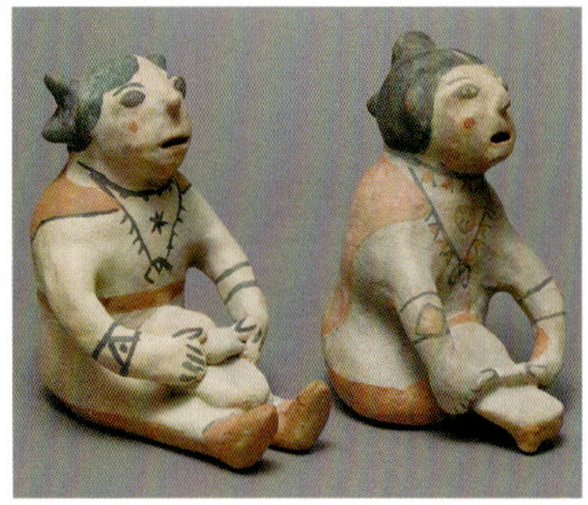

Female Figurines
Teresita Romero, 1955
14.3 × 6.1
Gift of Sanford and Diane Besser
55442

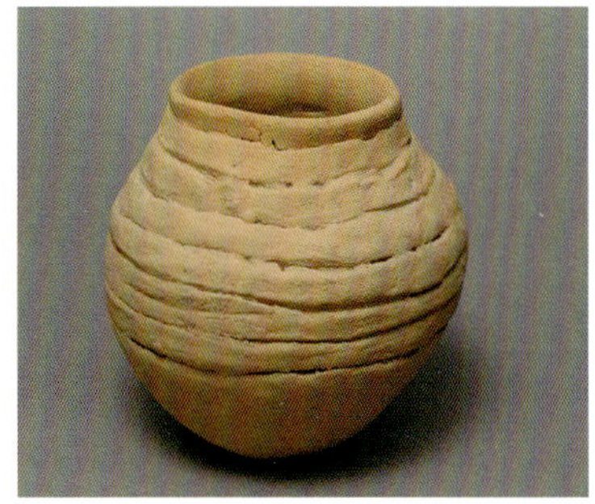

Jar
Teresita Romero, 1957
13.6 × 13.2
Gift of Pat Lange
56614

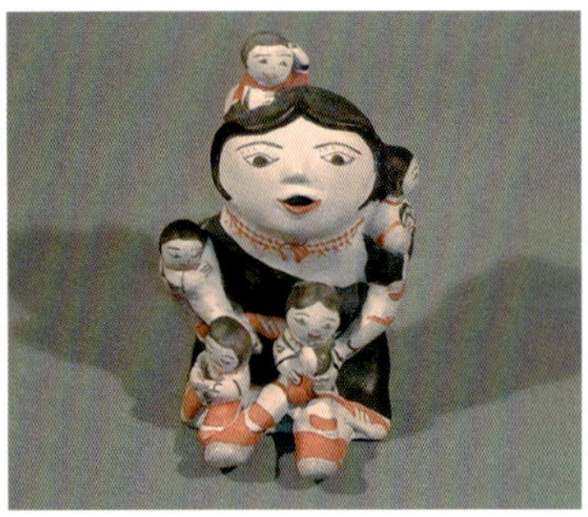

Storyteller Figurine
Felecita Eustace, 1993
15.0 × 9.5
Gift of Robert Nichols
54404

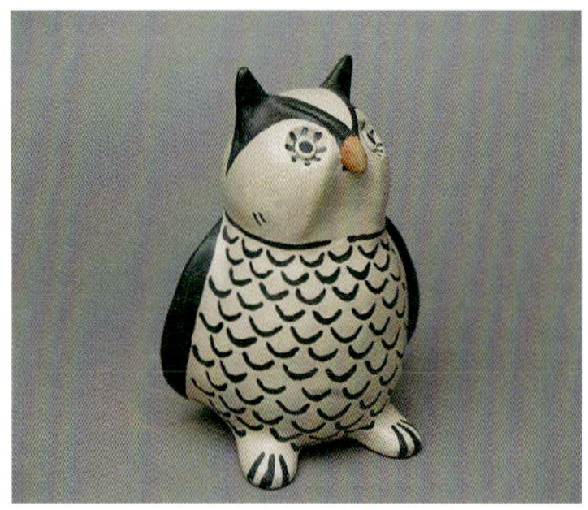

Owl Figurine
Laurencita Herrera, 1965
16.9 × 12.6 × 12.3
Gift of Thomas NK Godfrey
56143

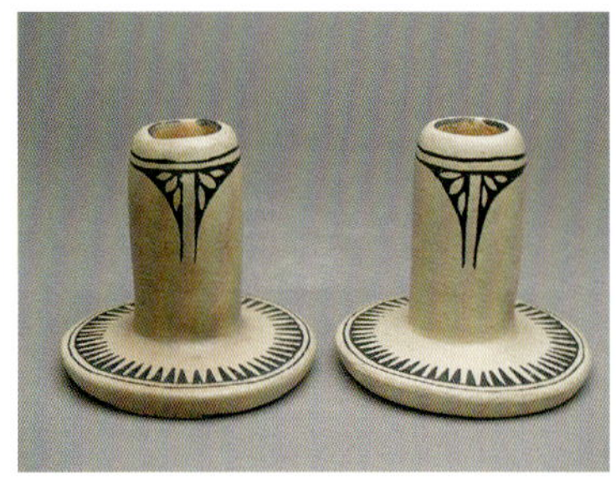

Candlesticks
Artist Unknown, ca. 1940
11.0 × 11.0
Gift of J. Mark Sublette
56823

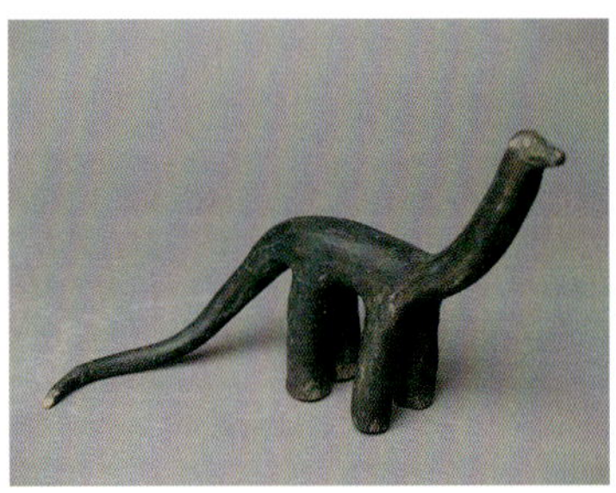

Dinosaur Figurine
Josh Lewis, ca. 1995–1996
11.7 × 6.4 × 19.5
Gift of the Robert Nichols Gallery
55277

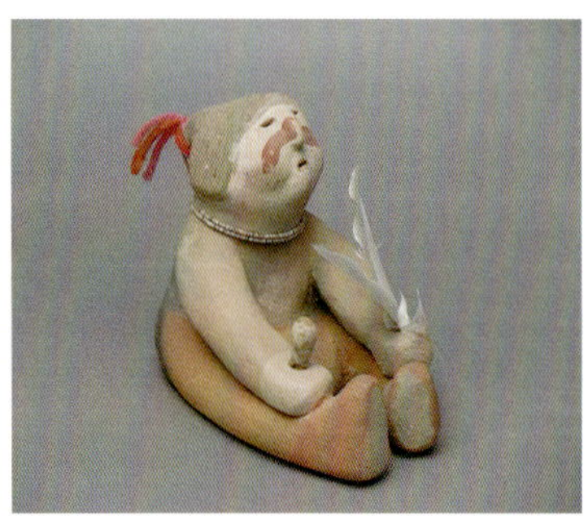

Drummer Figurine
Encarnacion Pena, 1979
11.8 × 8.5 × 15.1
Gift of Judith M. Liersch and Al Jennings
56552

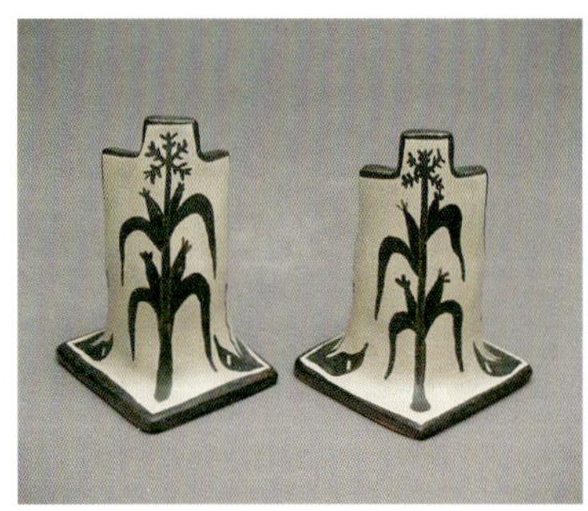

Candlesticks
Virgil Ortiz, ca. 2000
9.0 × 5.7 × 5.2
Gift of J. Mark Sublette
56847

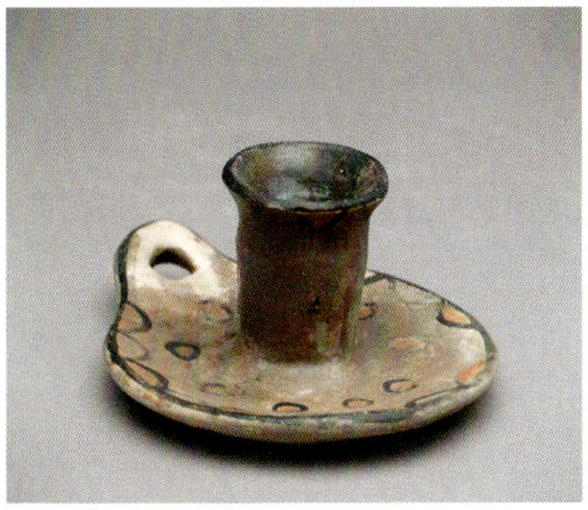

Candlestick
Artist Unknown, ca. 1920
6.5 × 14.0 × 11.5
Gift of J. Mark Sublette
56904

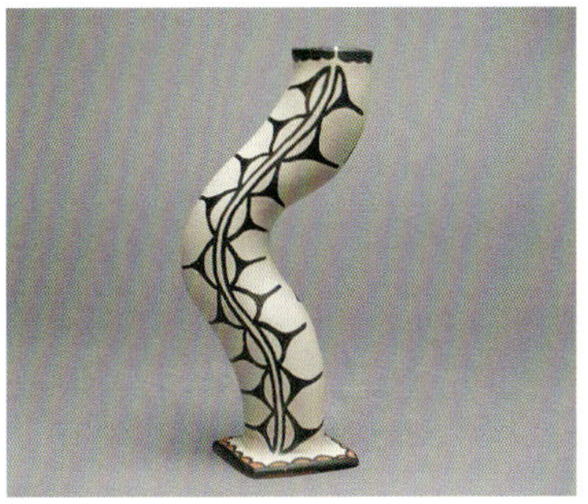

Candlestick
Virgil Ortiz, ca. 1995
19.4 × 8.7 × 7.5
Gift of J. Mark Sublette
56915

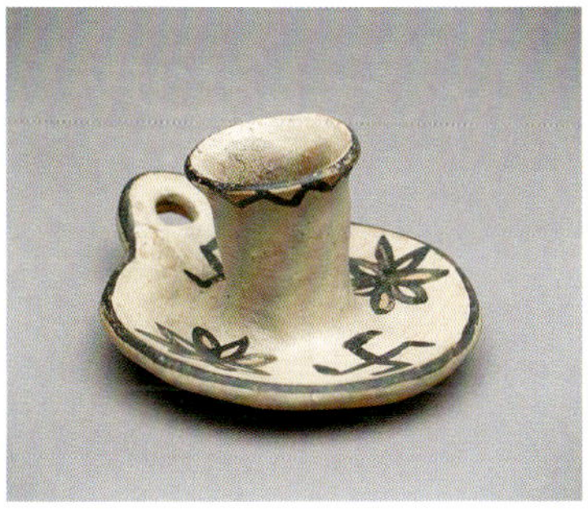

Candlestick
Artist Unknown, ca. 1920
6.7 × 15.0 × 11.8
Gift of J. Mark Sublette
56906

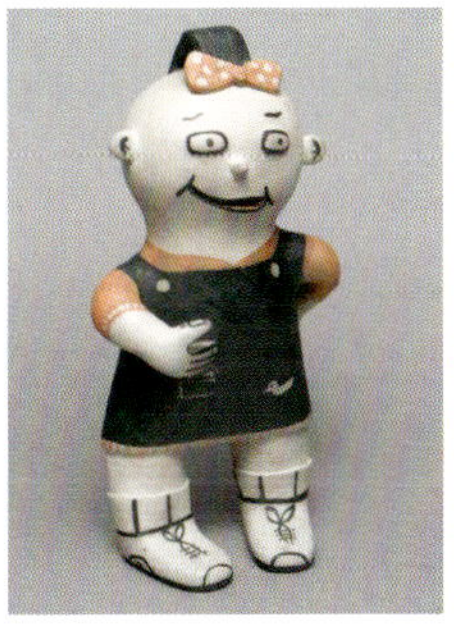

Rugrats Figurines
Juanita Ortiz, ca. 2004–2005
24.0 × 11.9 × 8.5
Gift of Native Treasures Committee
56959

PART III

Santo Domingo

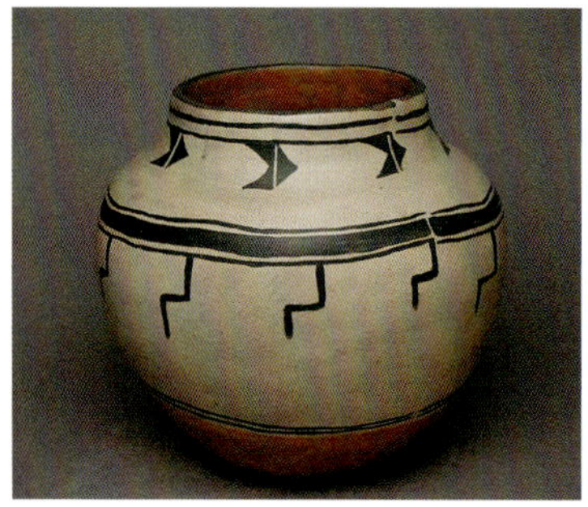

Jar
Artist Unknown, ca. 1935
22.7 × 25.3
Gift of Norma Fisk
594

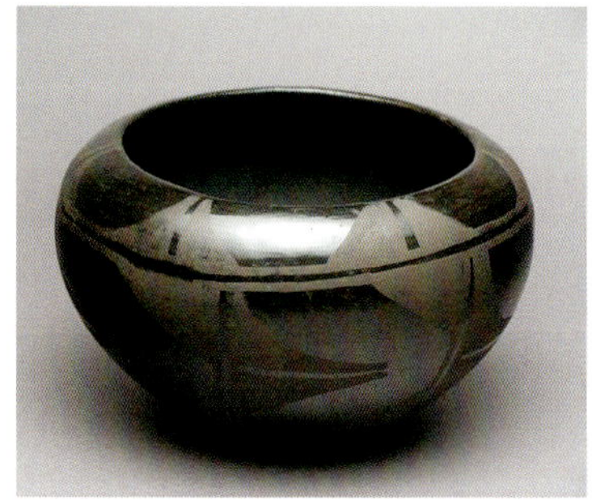

Bowl
Maria Calabaza, 1933
11.4 × 20.1
Kenneth M. Chapman Collection
7727

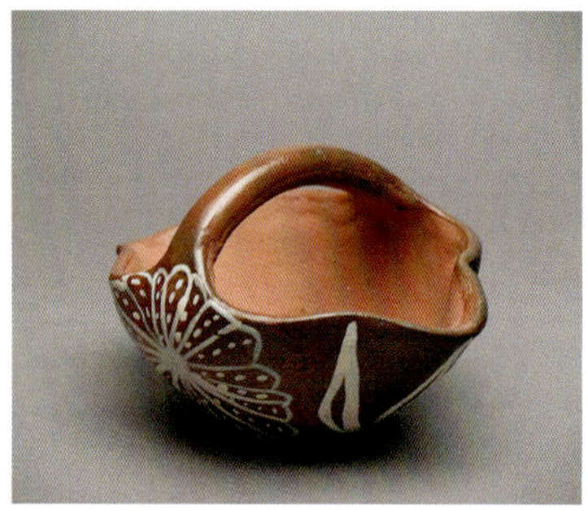

Bowl
Santo Domingo or Taos
Lena Archuleta, 1920s
9.0 × 11.3 × 4.6
Museum Purchase, Lena Archuleta
736

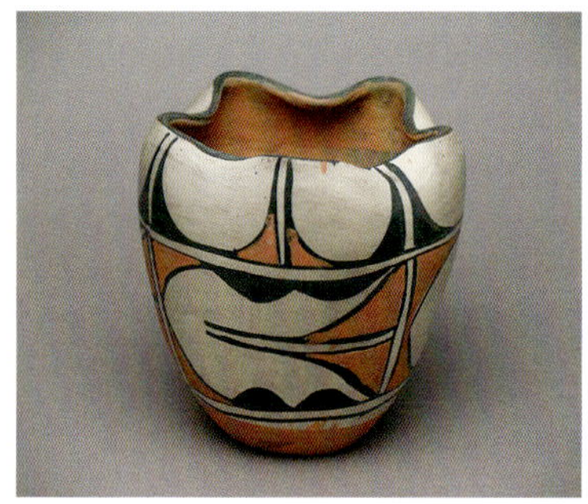

Jar
Lupe Lovato, 1933
14.3 × 13.7
Kenneth M. Chapman Collection
7728

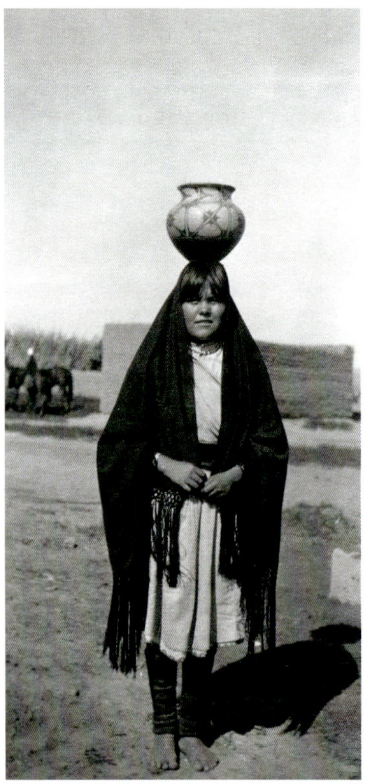

A Santo Domingo woman demonstrates the traditional method of carrying a water jar, 1915. Kenneth Chapman, photographer. Courtesy School for Advanced Research, Kenneth Chapman Files, F41.3.

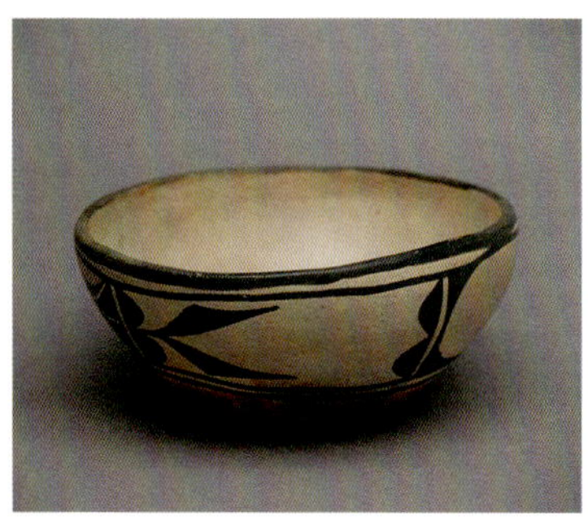

Stew Bowl
Artist Unknown, 1925
7.7 × 16.8
Museum Collection
1160

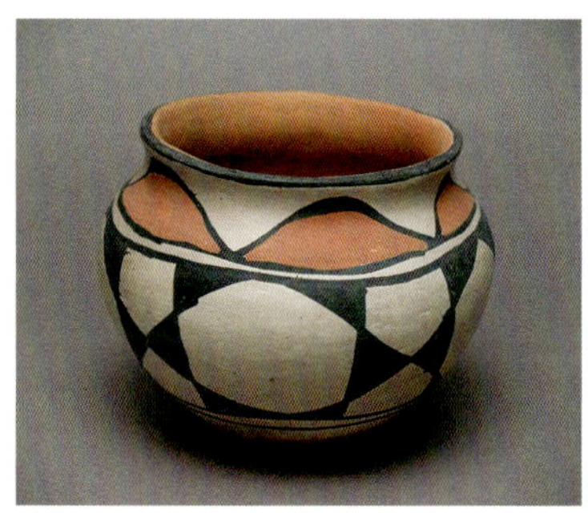

Jar
Lupe Lovato, 1933
14.0 × 11.5
Kenneth M. Chapman Collection
7729

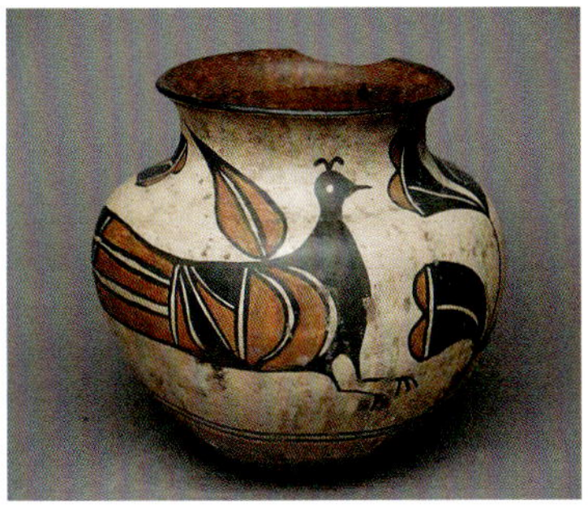

Jar
Artist Unknown, ca. 1900–1910
24.1 × 25.7
Kenneth M. Chapman Collection
7785

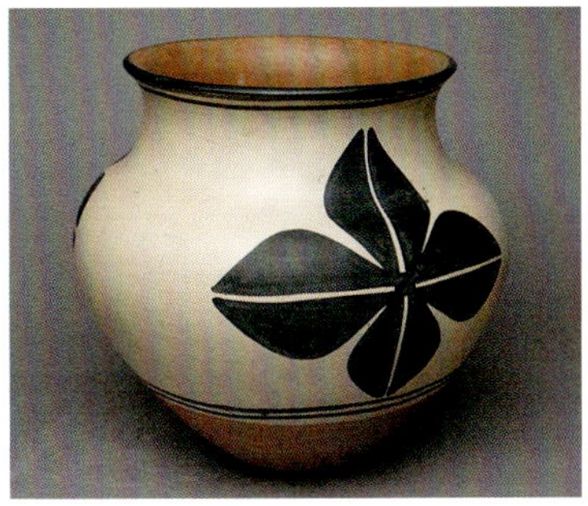

Jar
Artist Unknown, ca. 1945
24.4 × 26.3
Daniel H. McMillan Collection
8113

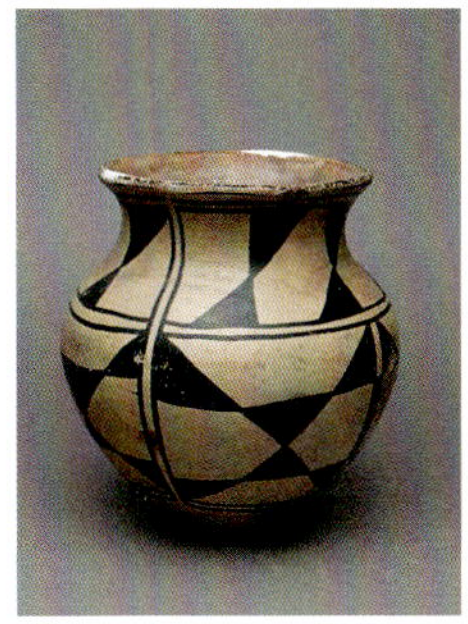

Jar
Artist Unknown, ca. 1910
20.3 × 19.4
Museum Purchase, Rogers and Schafer, Albuquerque
11103

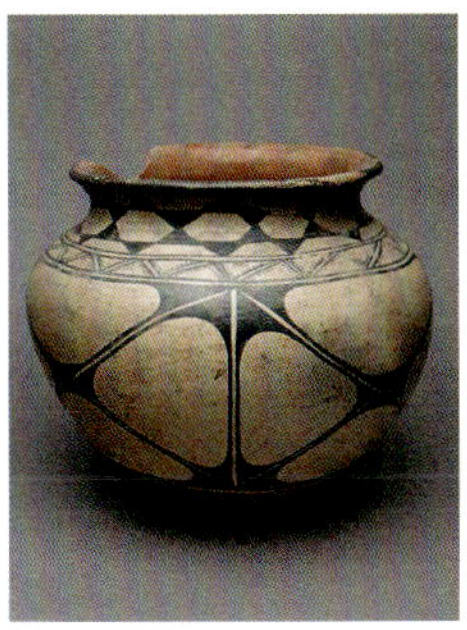

Jar
Artist Unknown, ca. 1890–1910
24.9 × 29.6
Gift of J. E. Fiske
7901

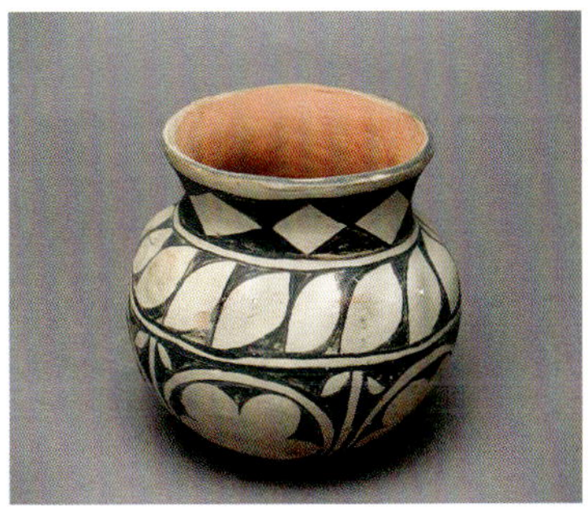

Jar
Artist Unknown, ca. 1930s
12.5 × 12.5
Gift of Alice Myers
8124

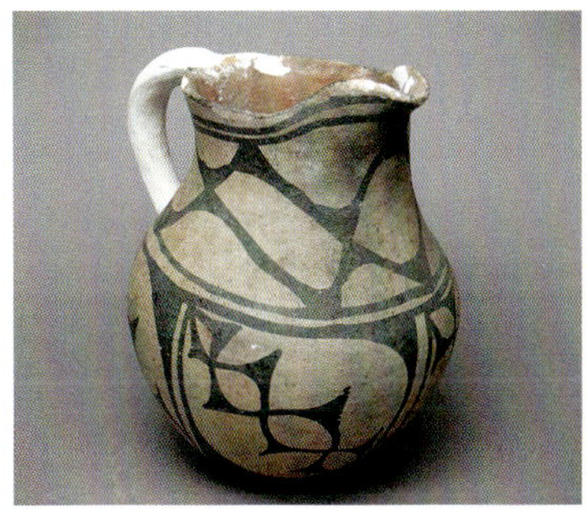

Pitcher
Artist Unknown, ca. 1915
20.8 × 18.5
Museum Purchase, Rogers and Schafer, Albuquerque
11106

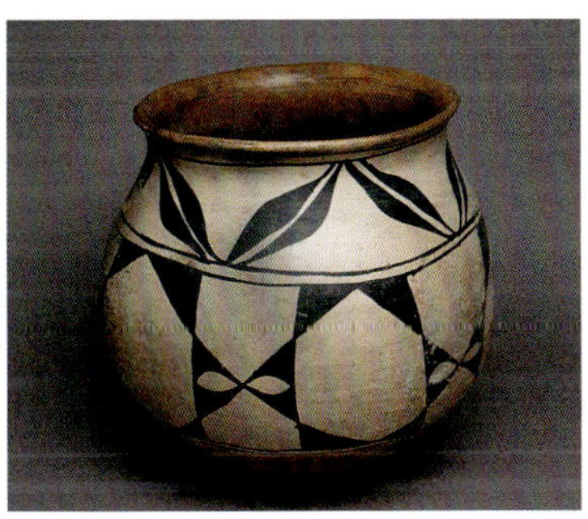

Jar
Artist Unknown, ca. 1900
33.9 × 35.0
Gift of T. B. Williamson
8048

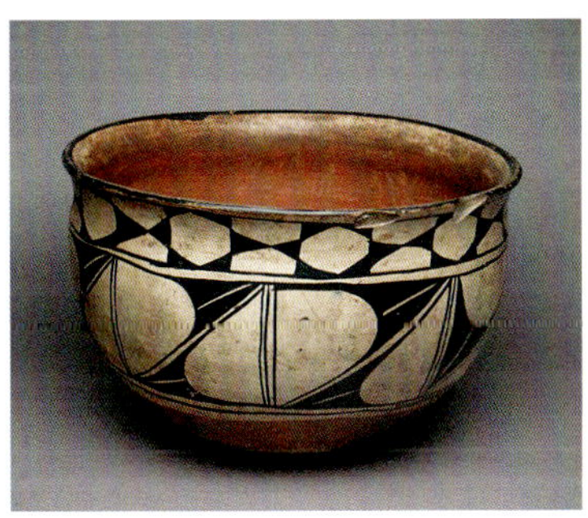

Dough Bowl
Artist Unknown, ca. 1890
23.2 × 37.0
Museum Purchase, Rogers and Schafer, Albuquerque
11102

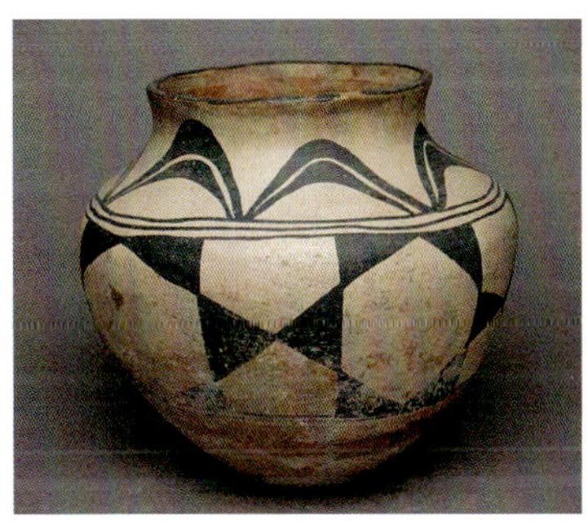

Jar
Artist Unknown, ca. 1920
22.9 × 25.8
Museum Purchase, Rogers and Schafer, Albuquerque
11109

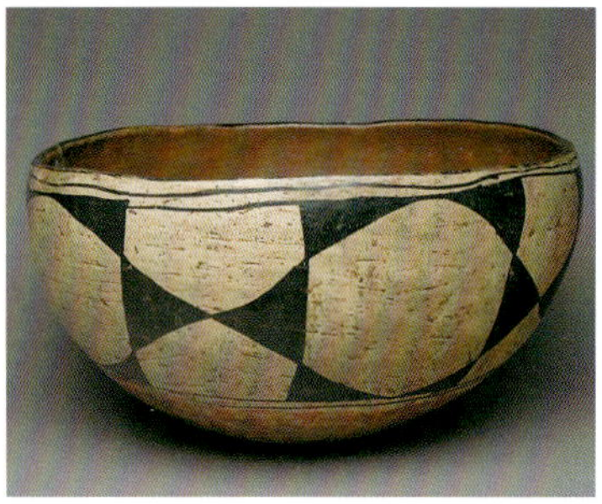

Dough Bowl
Artist Unknown, ca. 1900
18.1 × 36.3
Bequest of the Twichell Estate
11111

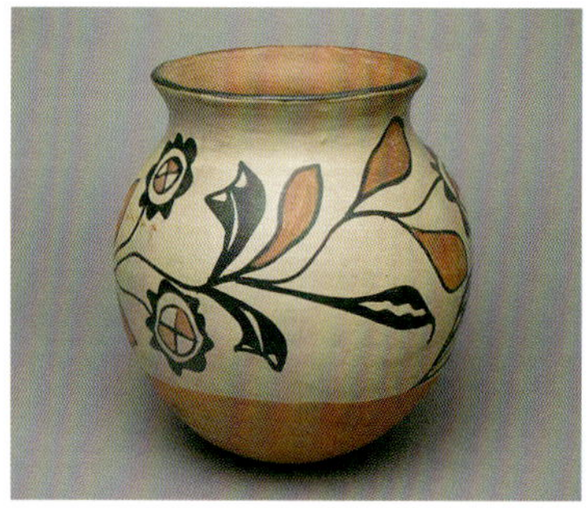

Jar
Artist Unknown, ca. 1910
21.5 × 20.0
Museum Purchase, Twichell Estate
11120

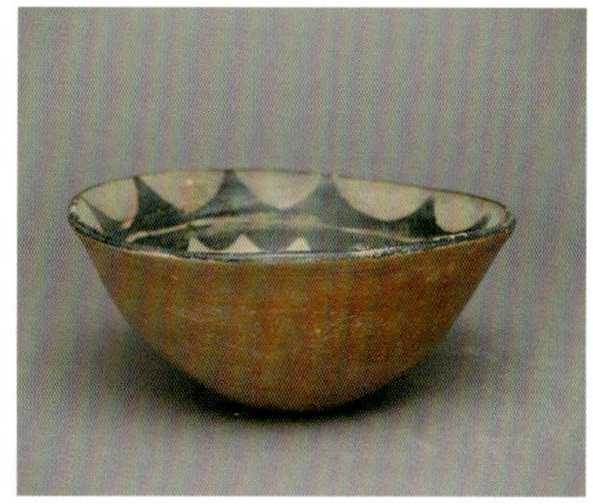

Stew Bowl
Artist Unknown, ca. 1900–1910
8.3 × 19.0
Museum Collection
11239

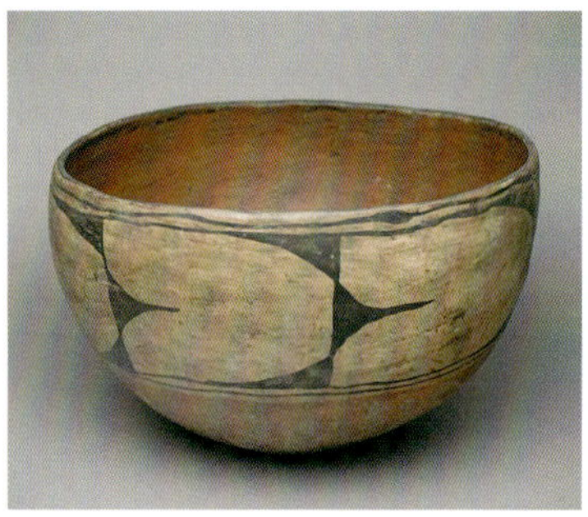

Dough Bowl
Artist Unknown, ca. 1860
21.6 × 36.7
Museum Purchase, Rogers and Schafer, Albuquerque
11115

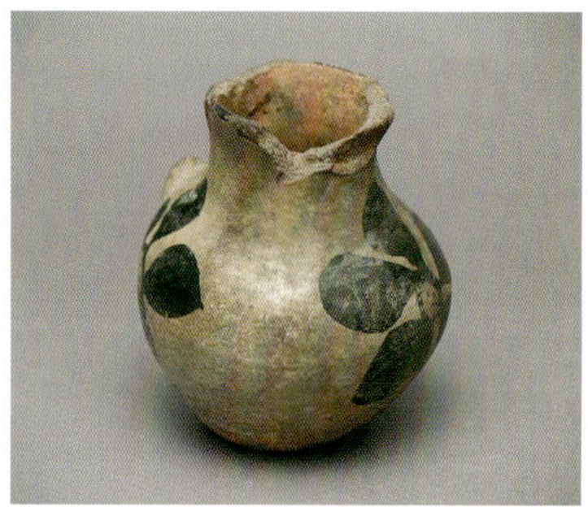

Jar
Artist Unknown, ca. 1915
13.0 × 9.3
Museum Purchase
Twichell Estate
11190

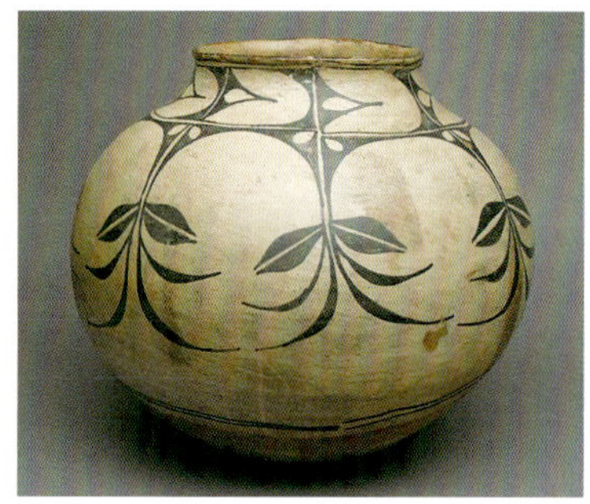

Storage Jar
Artist Unknown, ca. 1880–1890
46.8 × 43.2
Gift of Juan Olivas
12247

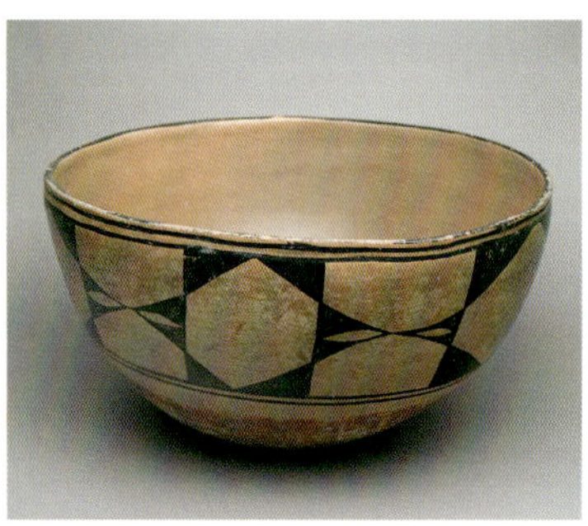

Dough Bowl
Artist Unknown, ca. 1880
23.5 × 45.7
Museum Purchase, Rogers and Schafer, Albuquerque
11117

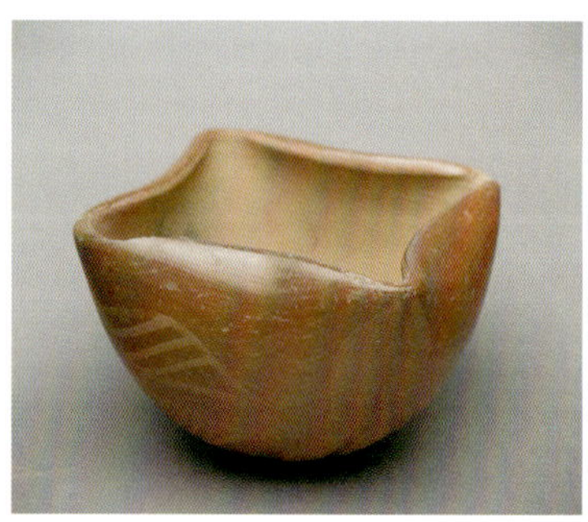

Bowl
Artist Unknown, ca. 1900
7.2 × 12.6 × 10.3
Museum Purchase, Twichell Estate
11192

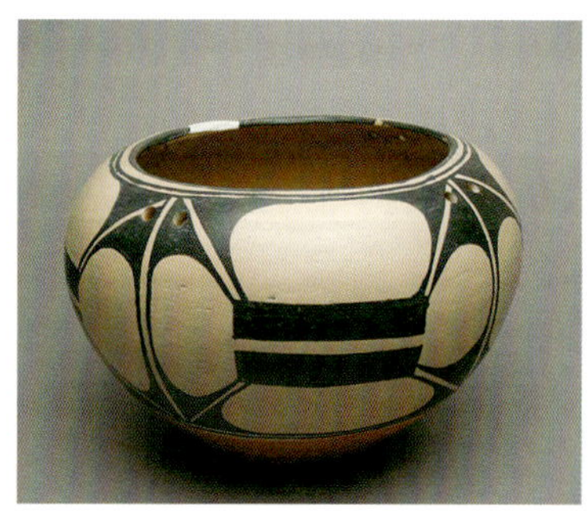

Bowl
Santo Domingo and Santa Clara
Monica Silva, ca. 1930
16.2 × 26.5
Museum Collection
12248

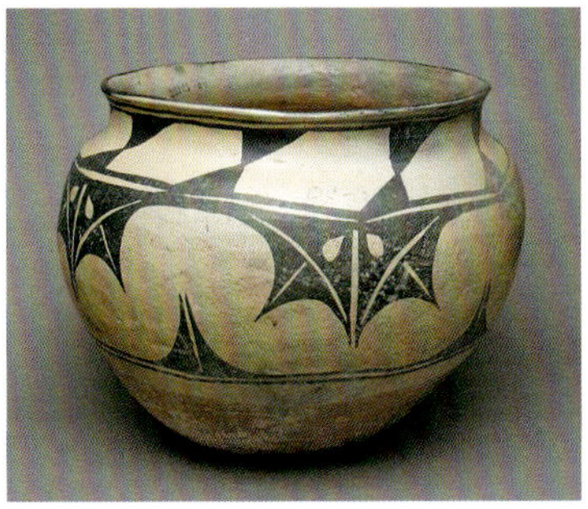

Jar
Artist Unknown, ca. 1910–1920
33.5 × 43.0
Museum Collection
12249

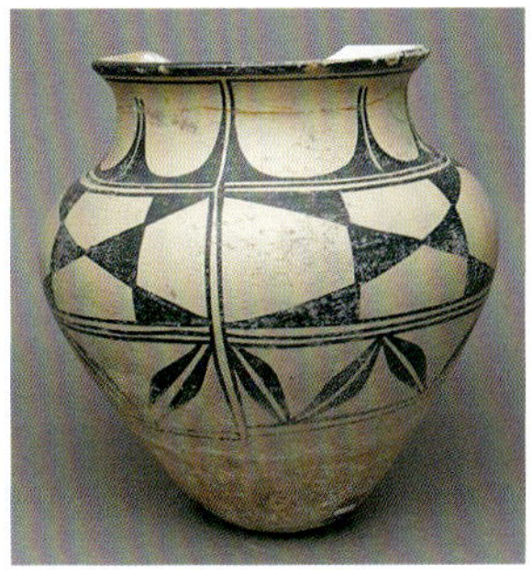

Jar
Artist Unknown, ca. 1920
30.3 × 29.2
Gift of the Historical Society of New Mexico
12256

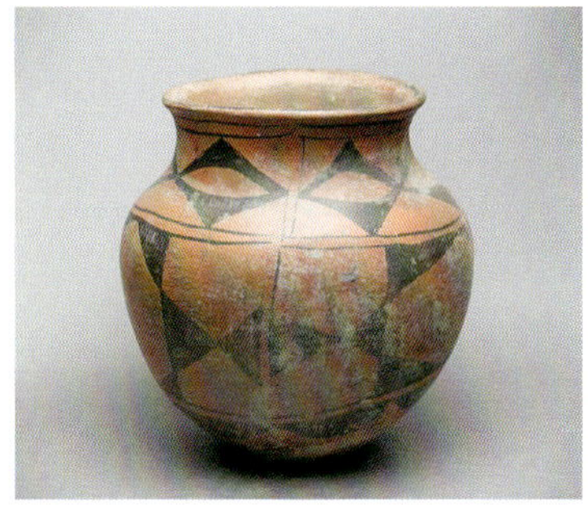

Jar
Artist Unknown, ca. 1915
23.5 × 22.0
Nelson Collection
12262

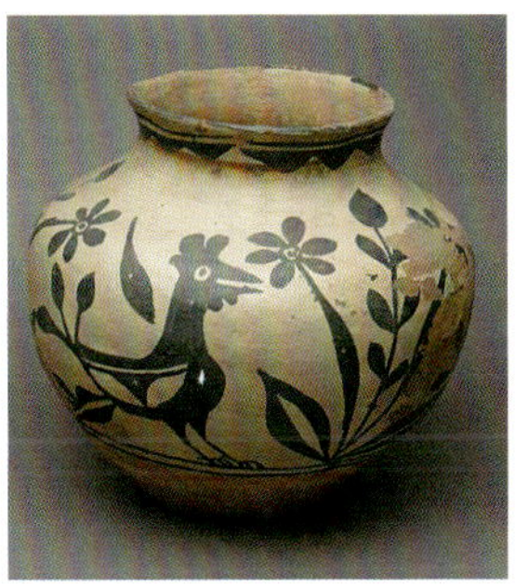

Jar
Artist Unknown, ca. 1920
26.8 × 28.8
Gift of the Historical Society of New Mexico
12252

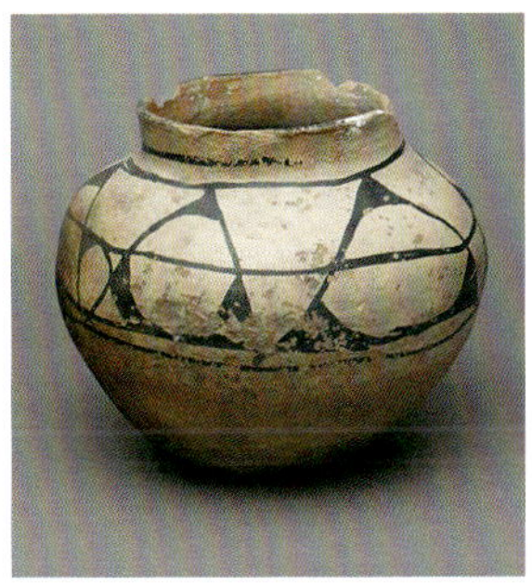

Jar
Attributed to Donaciano Padilla, ca. 1920
17.7 × 21.7
Museum Purchase, Donaciano Padilla
12257

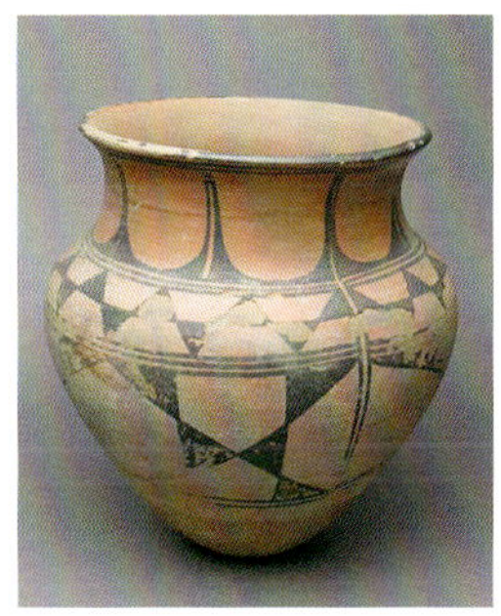

Jar
Artist Unknown, ca. 1920
30.7 × 29.7
Gift of the Historical Society of New Mexico
12263

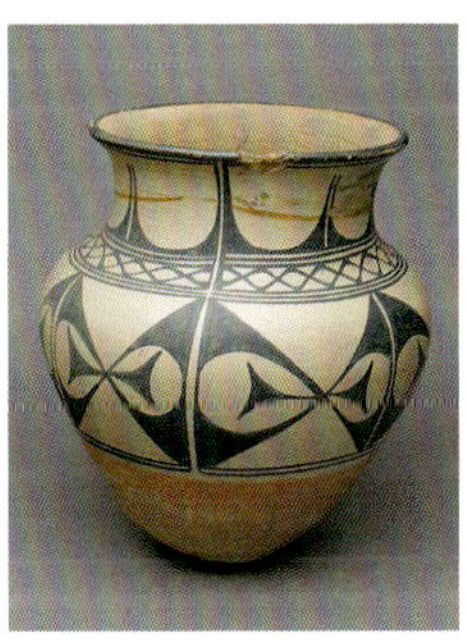

Jar
Artist Unknown, ca. 1920
30.2 × 27.3
Gift of the Historical Society of New Mexico
12255

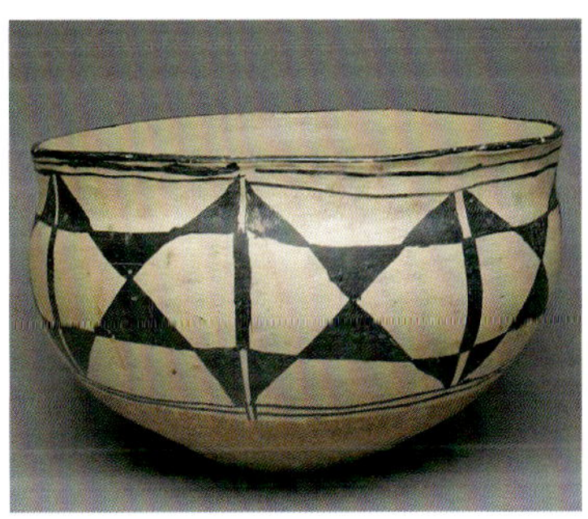

Dough Bowl
Artist Unknown, ca. 1900–1910
22.8 × 37.6
Gift of the Historical Society of New Mexico
12259

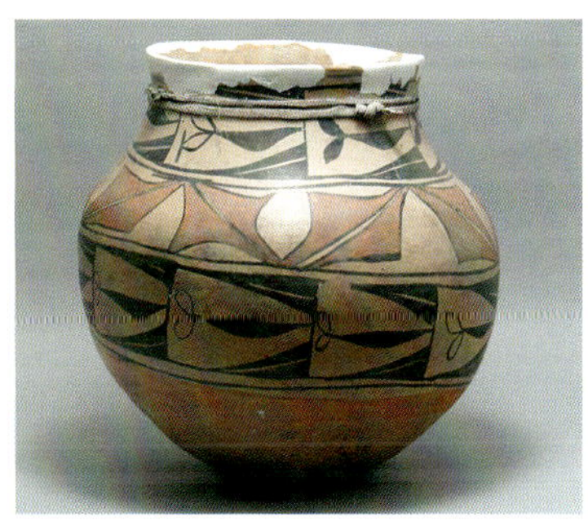

Jar
Artist Unknown, ca. 1910–1920
41.5 × 42.5
Gift of Juan Olivas
12264

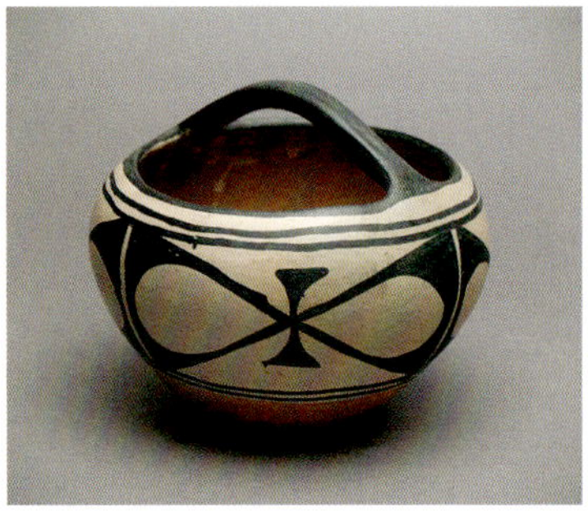

Bowl
Santo Domingo and Santa Clara
Monica Silva, ca. 1925
14.0 × 15.5
Gift of the Historical Society of New Mexico
12398

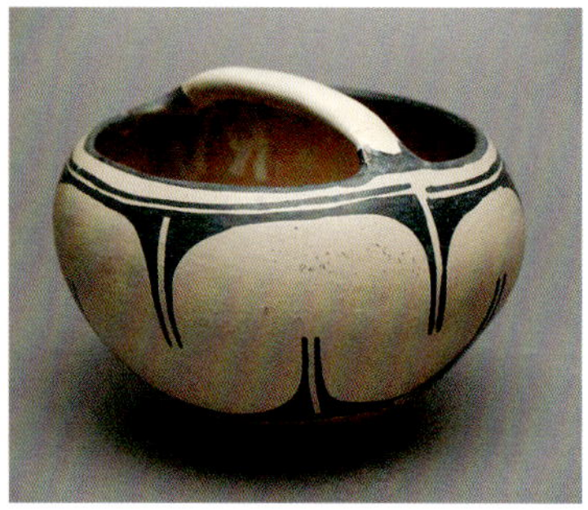

Bowl
Santo Domingo and Santa Clara
Monica Silva, ca. 1925
14.0 × 17.4
Gift of the Historical Society of New Mexico
12403

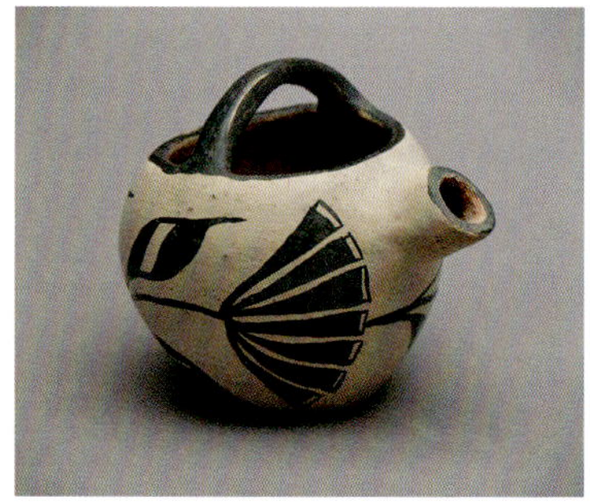

Pitcher
Artist Unknown, ca. 1925
10.7 × 12.6
Gift of the Historical Society of New Mexico
12406

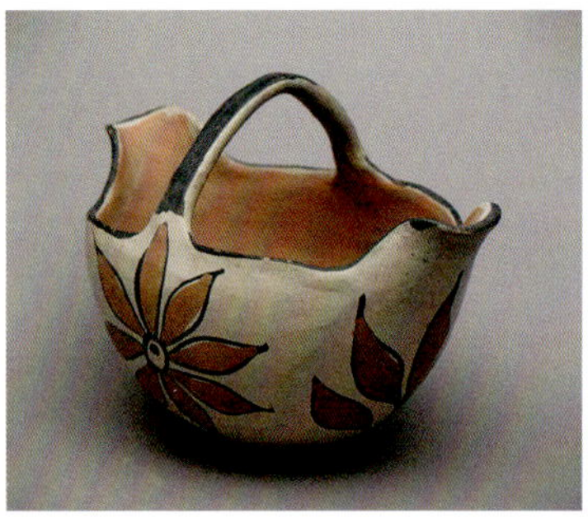

Pitcher
Artist Unknown, ca. 1930
15.7 × 22.4 × 14.3
Gift of the Historical Society of New Mexico
12399

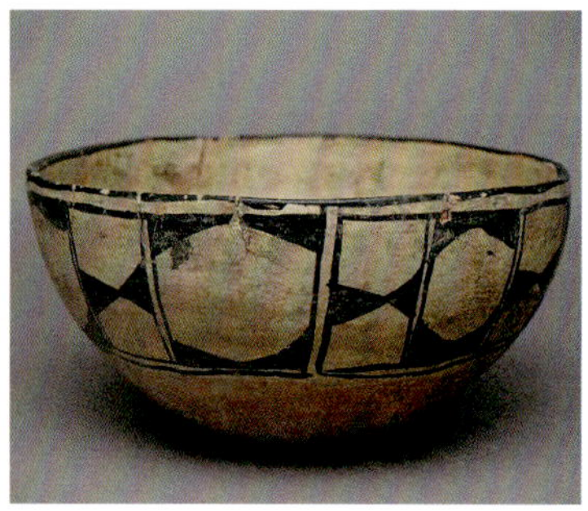

Stew Bowl
Artist Unknown, ca. 1900–1910
11.4 × 23.2
Nelson Collection
12404

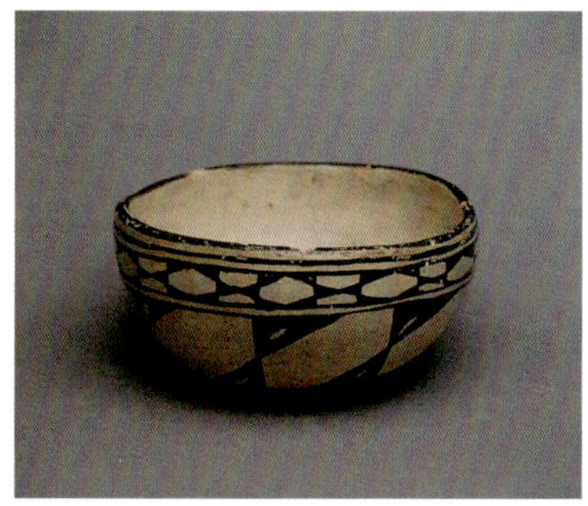

Bowl
Artist Unknown, ca. 1900–1910
7.9 × 16.5
Nelson Collection
12445

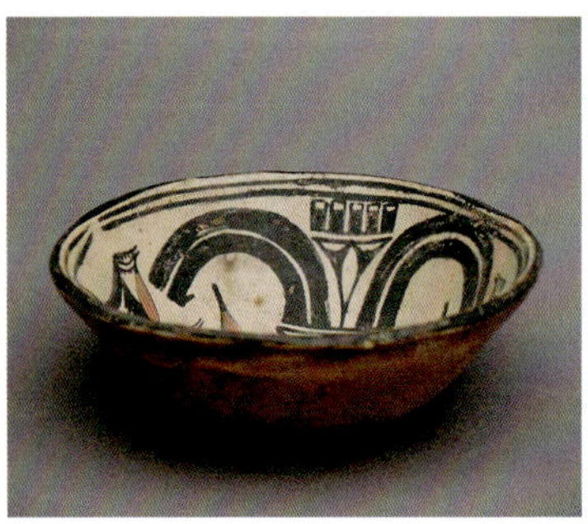

Bowl
Artist Unknown, ca. 1935
6.6 × 18.8
Nelson Collection
12400

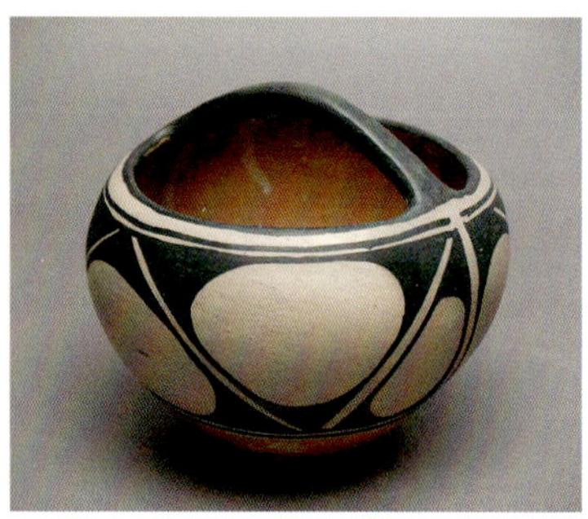

Bowl
Santo Domingo and Santa Clara
Monica Silva, ca. 1925
16.0 × 16.2
Gift of the Historical Society of New Mexico
12405

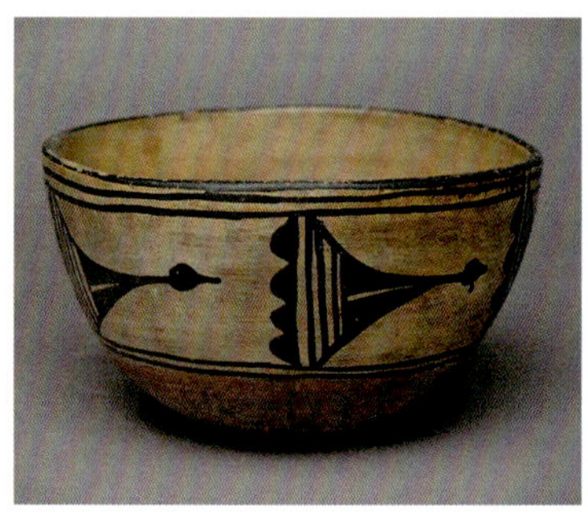

Stew Bowl
Artist Unknown, ca. 1920
11.0 × 20.2
Gift of Arthur Rogers
16174

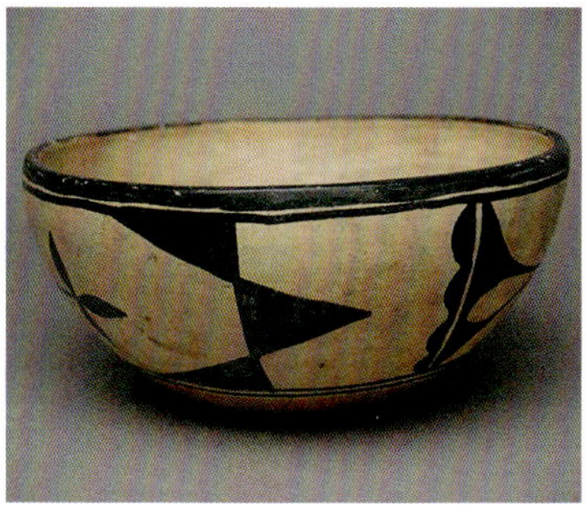

Stew Bowl
Angelita Cata, ca. 1925–1930
10.9 × 23.4
Kenneth M. Chapman Collection
16180

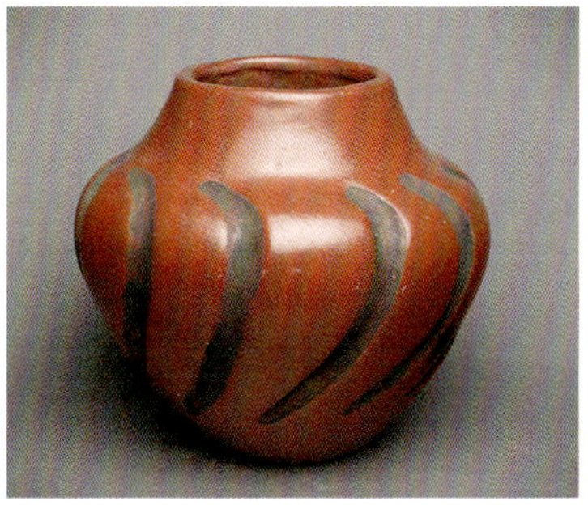

Jar
Santo Domingo and Santa Clara
Monica Silva, ca. 1950
21.3 × 23.4
Gift of Mrs. William J. Lippencott
18669

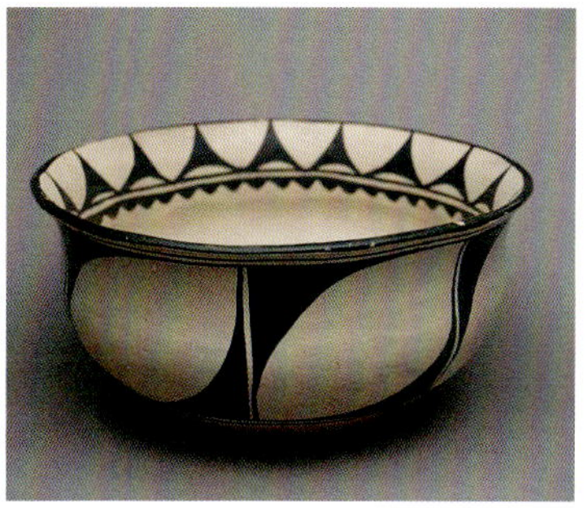

Bowl
Artist Unknown, ca. 1940–1950
11.5 × 24.0
Museum Collection
18772

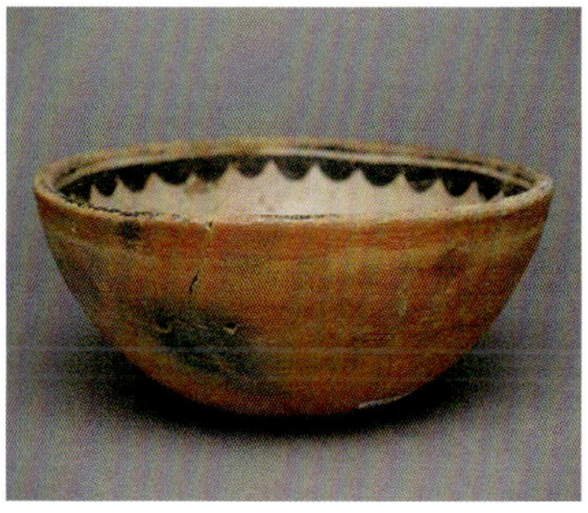

Stew Bowl
Artist Unknown, ca. 1890
9.4 × 21.1
Vivian Gordon Collection
16193

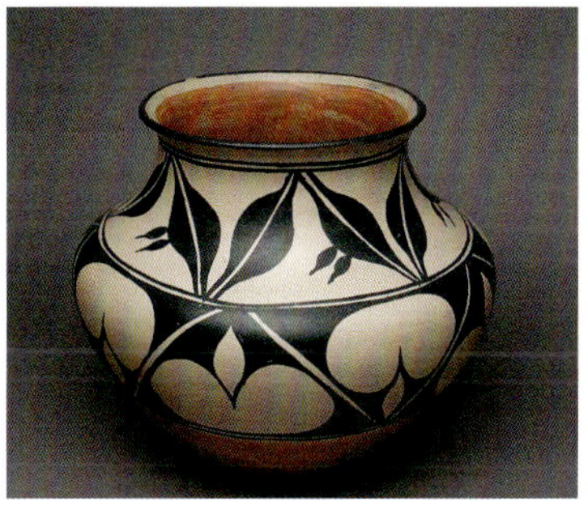

Jar
Felipita Aguilar Garcia, ca. 1915–1925
20.0 × 24.1
Gift of the Historical Society
of New Mexico
18686

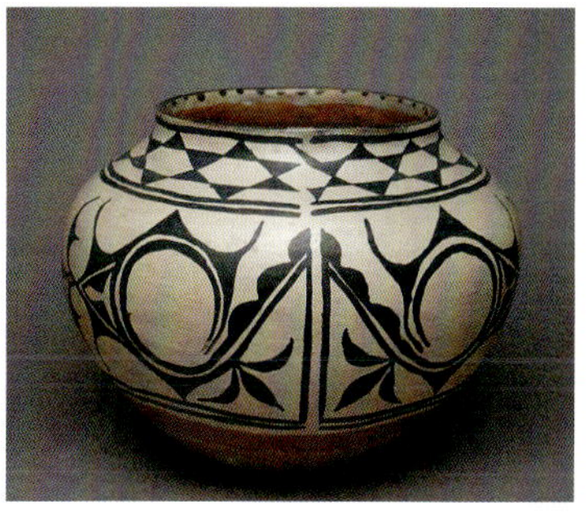

Jar
Artist Unknown, ca. 1910–1920
22.3 × 29.3
Gift of the Historical Society
of New Mexico
18818

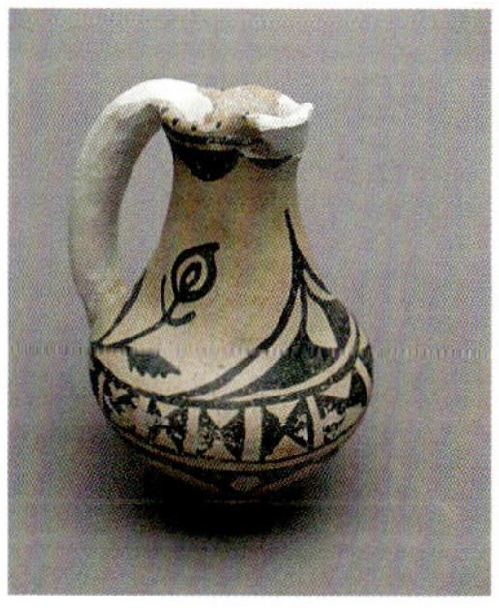

Pitcher
Santo Domingo or San Ildefonso
Artist Unknown, ca. 1890–1900
12.2 × 8.0
Museum Collection
16248

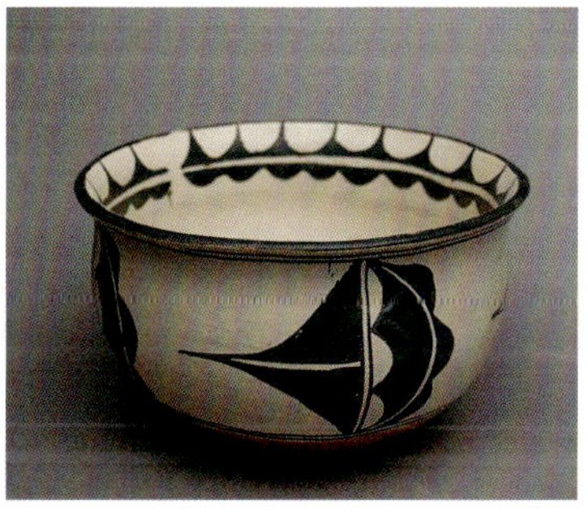

Stew Bowl
Artist Unknown, ca. 1925
11.9 × 19.6
Gift of the Historical Society
of New Mexico
18771

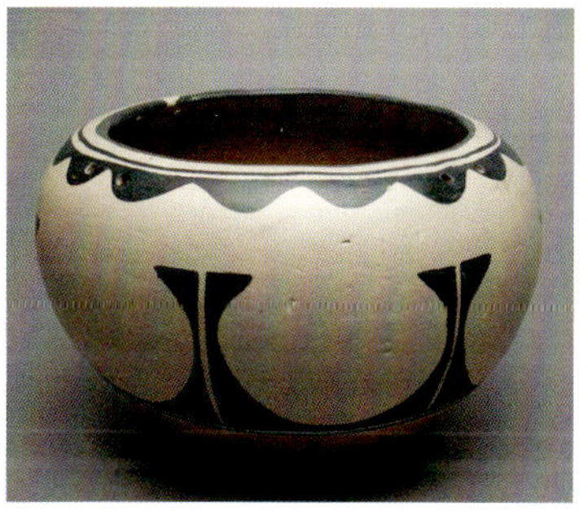

Bowl
Santo Domingo and Santa Clara
Monica Silva, ca. 1920
15.5 × 24.0
Museum Collection
18892

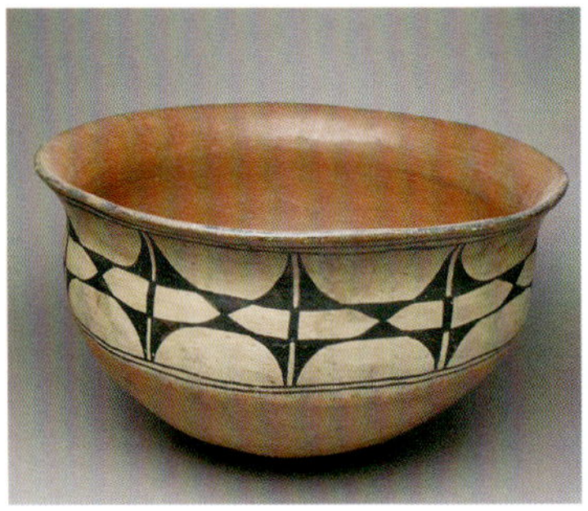

Dough Bowl
Artist Unknown, ca. 1880
28.0 × 49.5
Museum Purchase, Rogers and Schafer, Albuquerque
18895

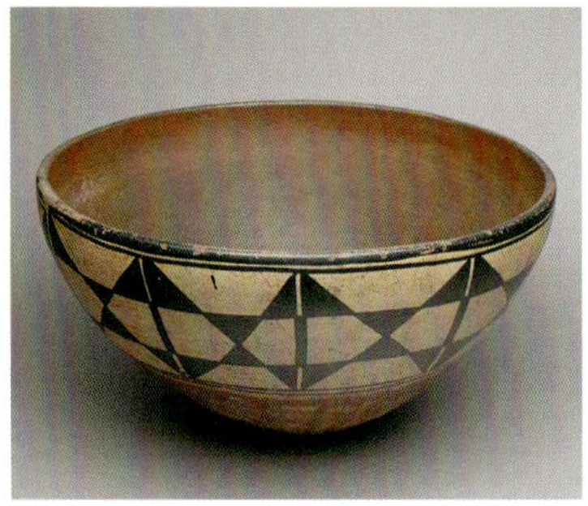

Dough Bowl
Artist Unknown, ca. 1910–1930
33.0 × 16.5
Gift of Hugh Bryden McGill
19064

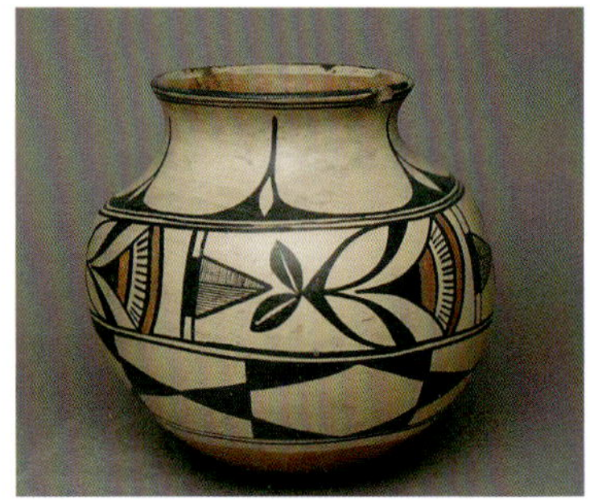

Jar
Artist Unknown, ca. 1910
25.9 × 27.4
Gift of Boaz Long
19137

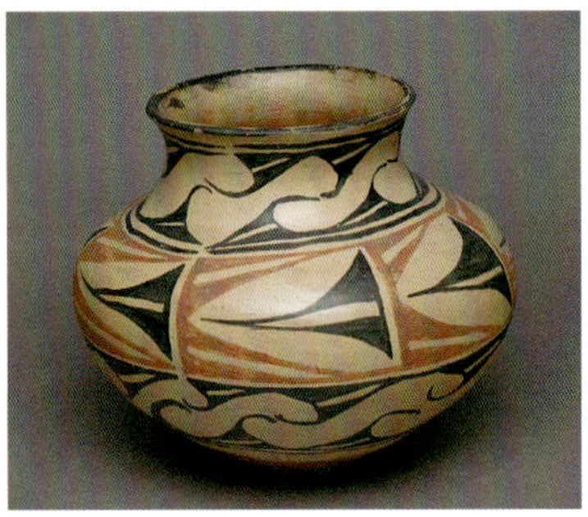

Jar
Artist Unknown, ca. 1920
20.2 × 24.9
Gift of Ina Sizer Cassidy
18897

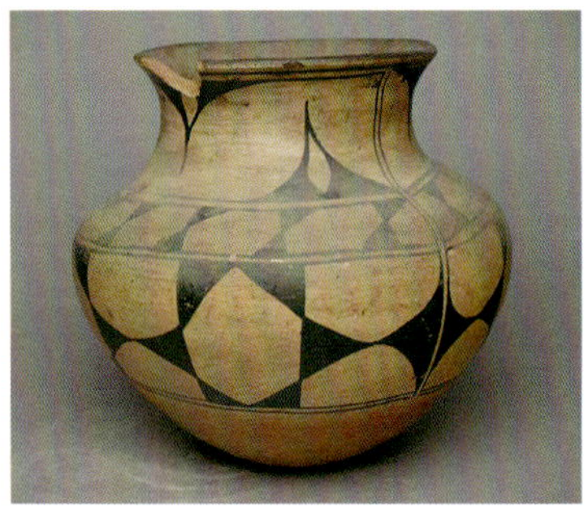

Jar
Artist Unknown, ca. 1910–1920
20.2 × 22.3
Gift of Hugh Bryden McGill
19065

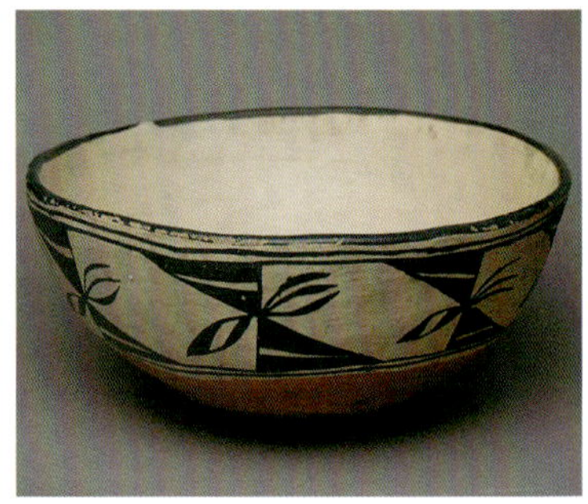

Bowl
Artist Unknown, ca. 1910
15.1 × 33.5
Gift of Boaz Long
19138

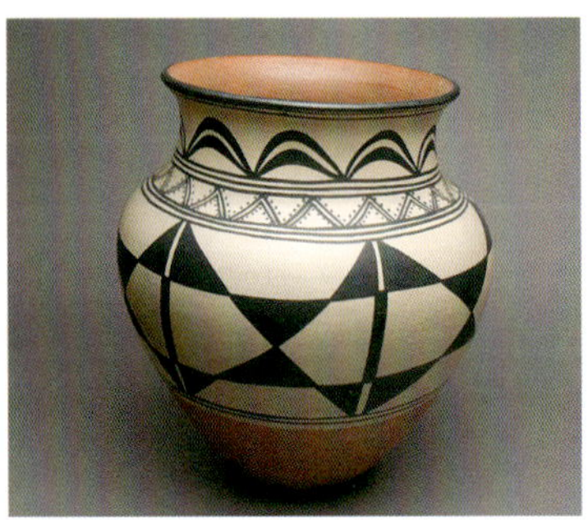

Jar
Felipita Aguilar Garcia, ca. 1920
32.3 × 27.6
Gift of the Alice Fletcher Foundation
18910

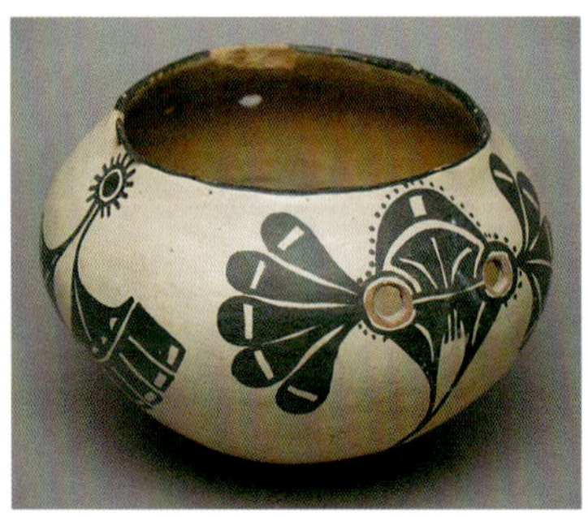

Jar or Flower Pot
Artist Unknown, ca. 1935
14.1 × 21.5
Gift of Henry Dendahl
19132

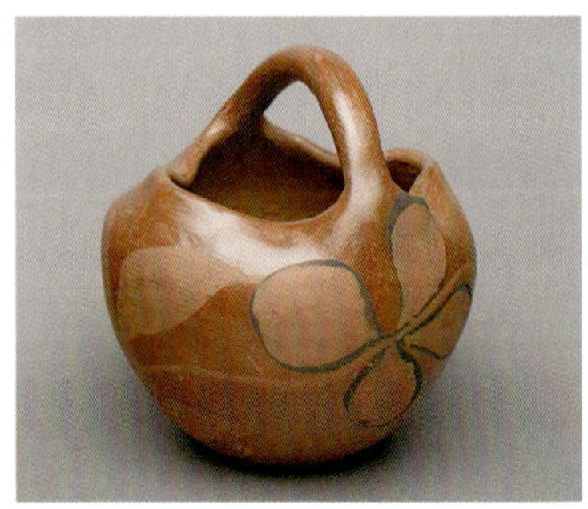

Bowl
Artist Unknown, ca. 1935–1940
12.3 × 11.5
Gift of Henry Dendahl
19202

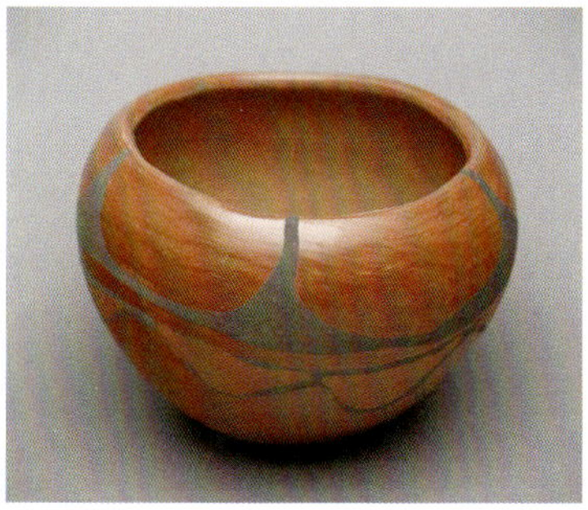

Bowl
Artist Unknown, ca. 1935–1940
8.2 × 11.9
Gift of Henry Dendahl
19203

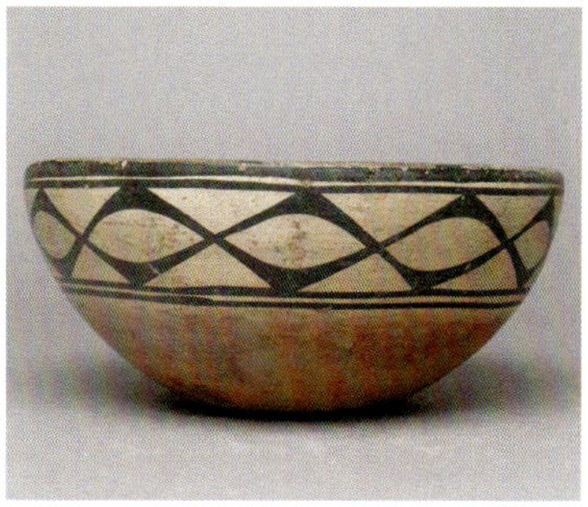

Stew Bowl
Artist Unknown, ca. 1900–1910
8.5 × 19.8
M. M. Lane Collection
19521

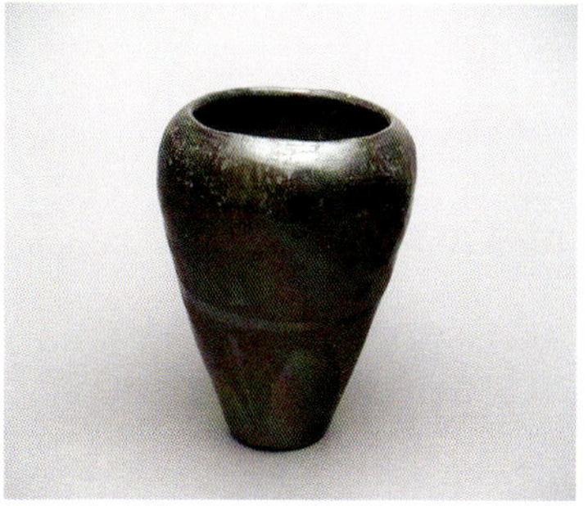

Jar
Artist Unknown, ca. 1930
17.8 × 13.3
Wyland Collection
35695

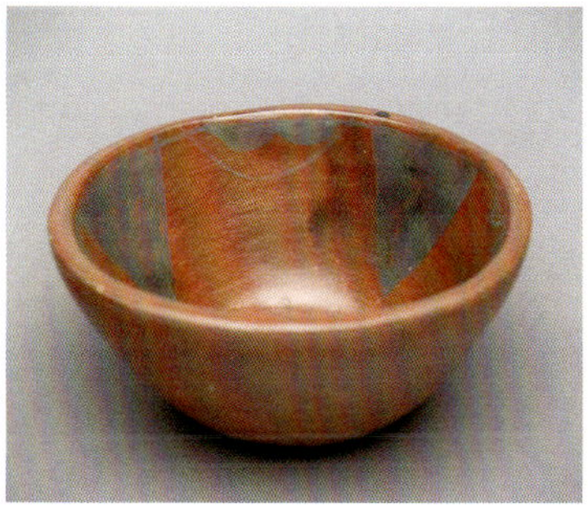

Bowl
Artist Unknown, ca. 1935–1940
5.5 × 12.2
Gift of Henry Dendahl
19204

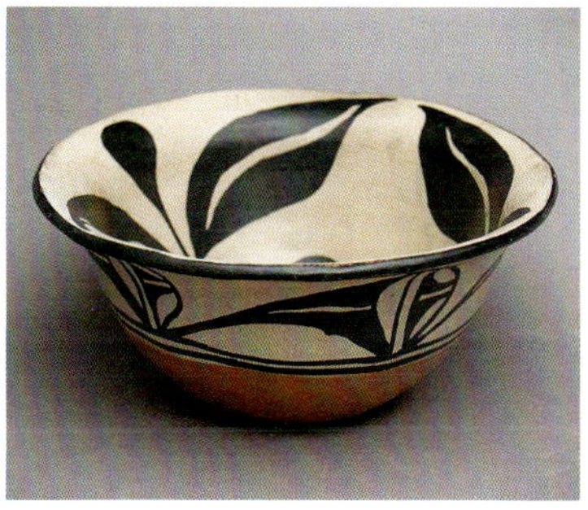

Stew Bowl
Mrs. Juan Cate, ca. 1923
11.3 × 23.4
Gift of Ina Sizer Cassidy
25735

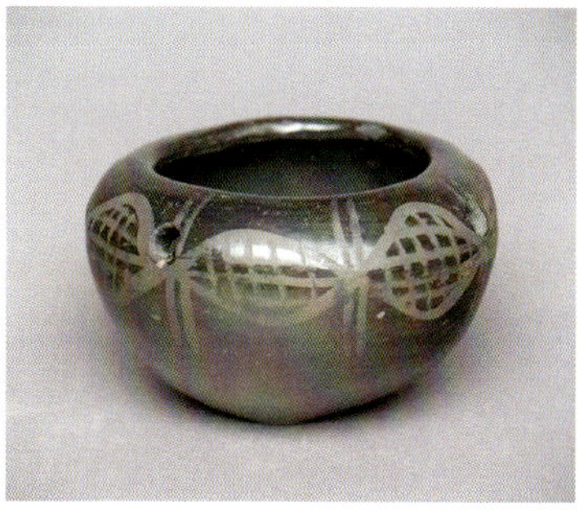

Bowl
Artist Unknown, ca. 1930
7.7 × 13.2
Wyland Collection
35713

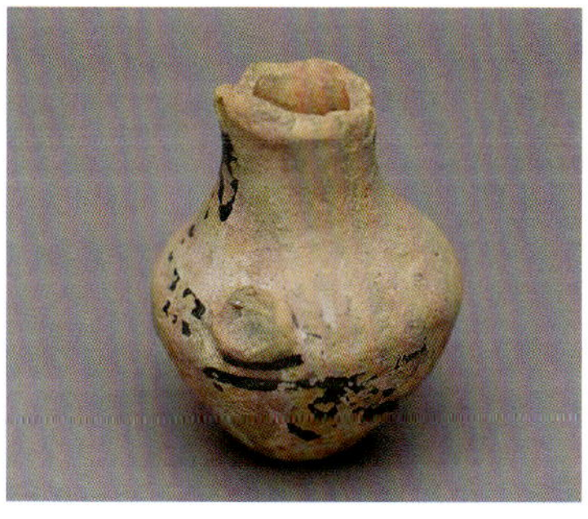

Pitcher
Artist Unknown, ca. 1915
7.0 × 5.7
Museum Collection
19259

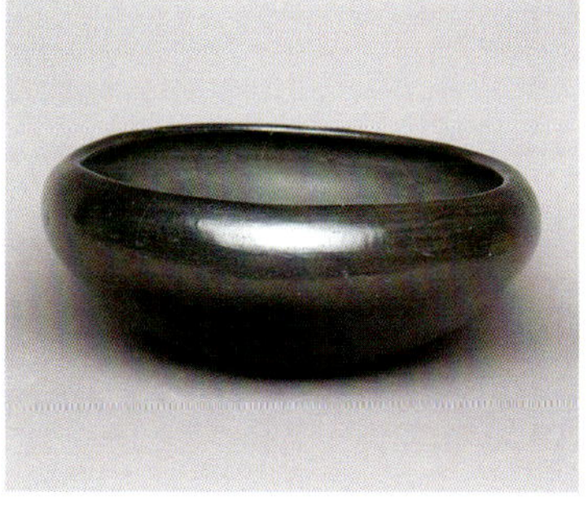

Bowl
Santo Domingo and Santa Clara
Monica Silva, 1935–1960
11.1 × 29.0
Wyland Collection
35691

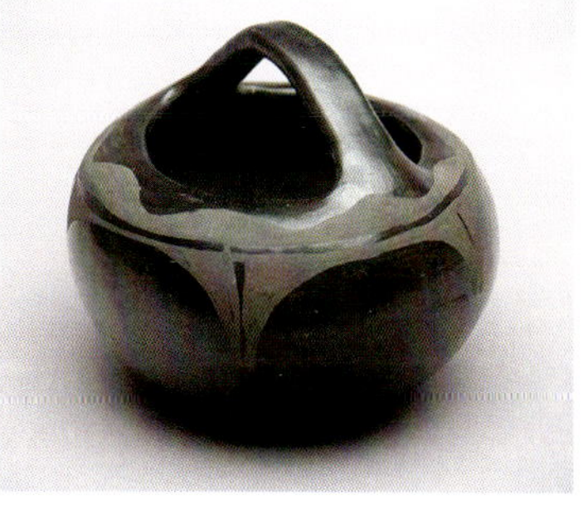

Bowl
Artist Unknown, 1930–1960
14.7 × 18.4
Wyland Collection
35715

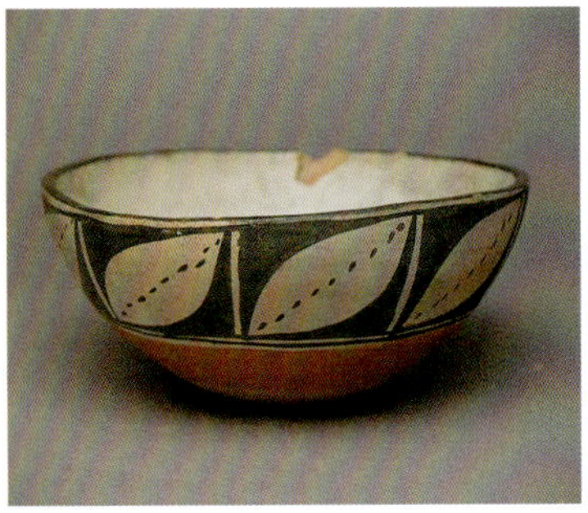

Stew Bowl
Artist Unknown, ca. 1920
8.5 × 19.0
Wyland Collection
35716

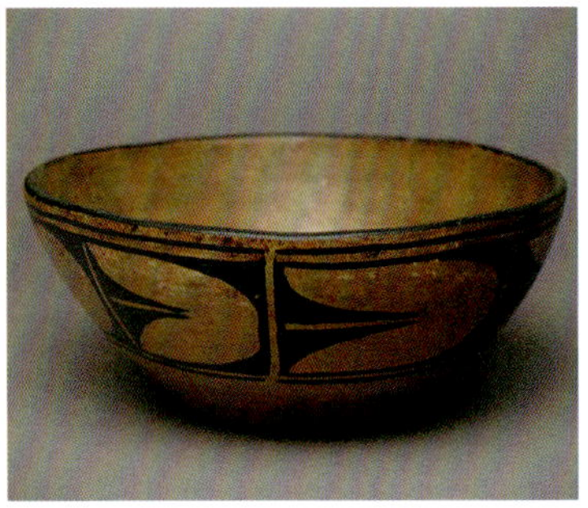

Stew Bowl
Artist Unknown, ca. 1900
9.1 × 18.9
Museum Purchase, Rafael Pacheco
44798

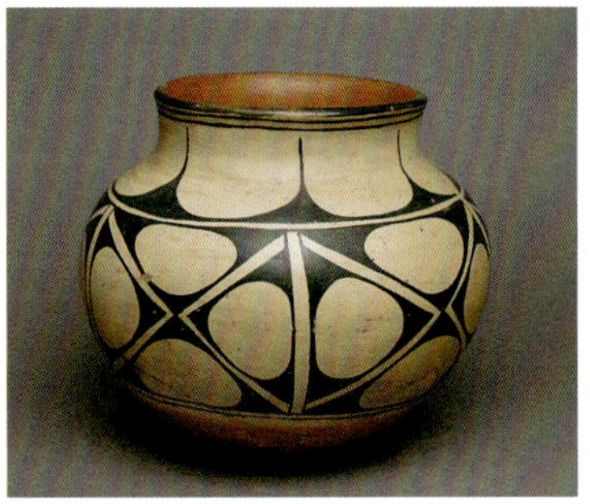

Jar
Artist Unknown, ca. 1910
23.4 × 26.5
Gift of Mrs. Howard G. Gibbs
45484

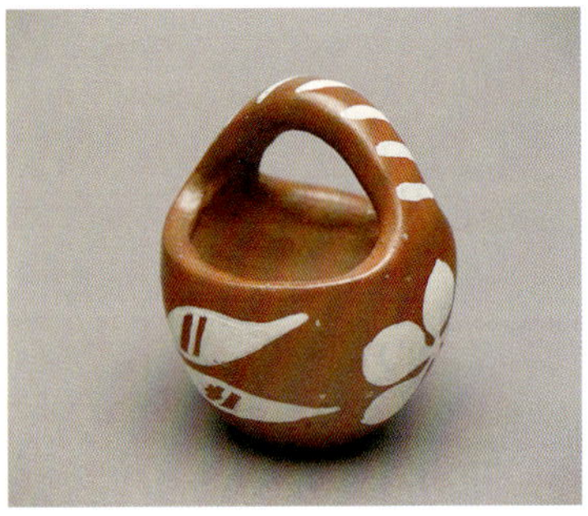

Bowl
Artist Unknown, ca. 1930–1940
6.5 × 5.1
Museum Collection
36544

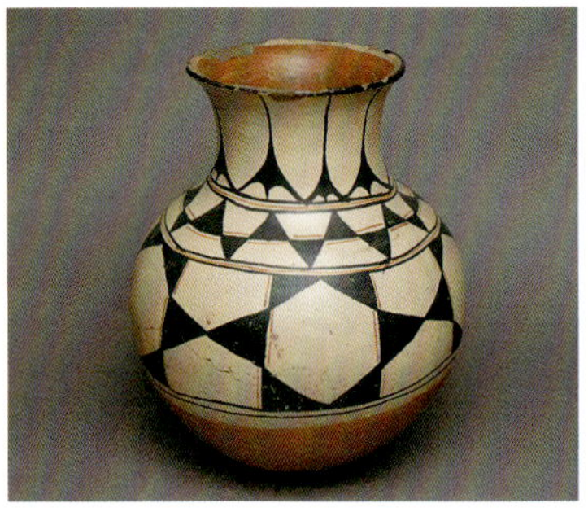

Jar
Artist Unknown, ca. 1900
34.0 × 27.5
Gift of Caskey Settle
44998

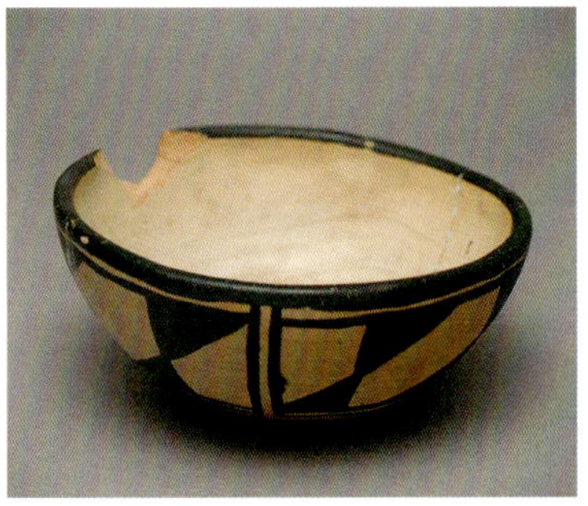

Bowl
Artist Unknown, ca. 1930
5.7 × 11.8
Gift of Mrs. Howard G. Gibbs
45485

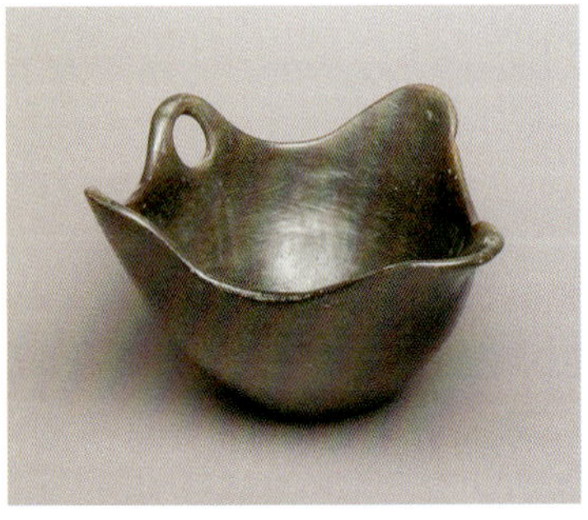

Pitcher
Encarnacion Reano, ca. 1930s–1940s
12.2 × 20.7
Gift of Byron Harvey III
42217

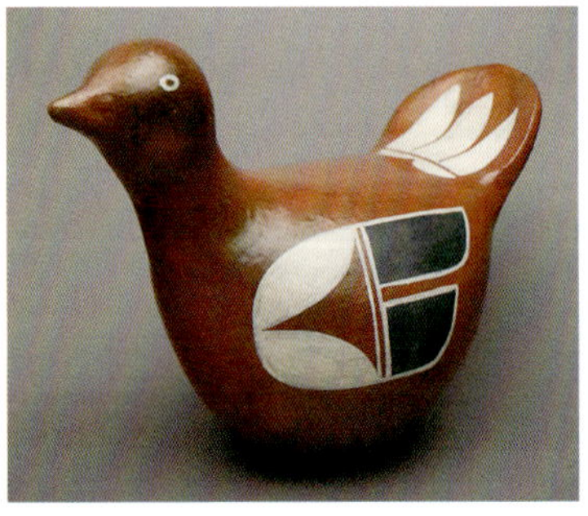

Bird Figurine
Artist Unknown, ca. 1955
16.6 × 11.1 × 21.5
Gift of Fred Bailey
45000

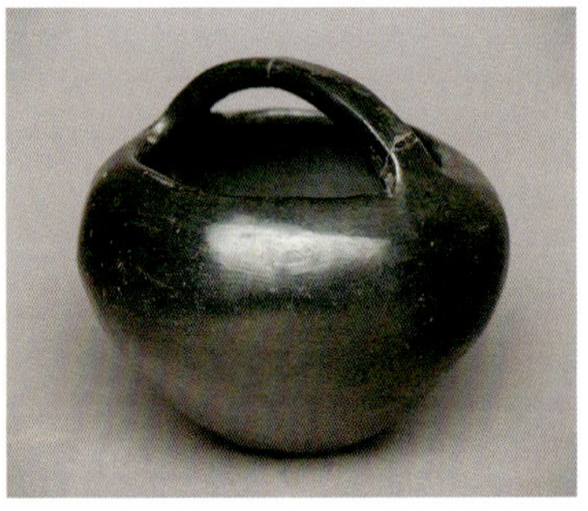

Bowl
Artist Unknown, ca. 1930
11.9 × 13.4
Gift of Mrs. Howard G. Gibbs
45486

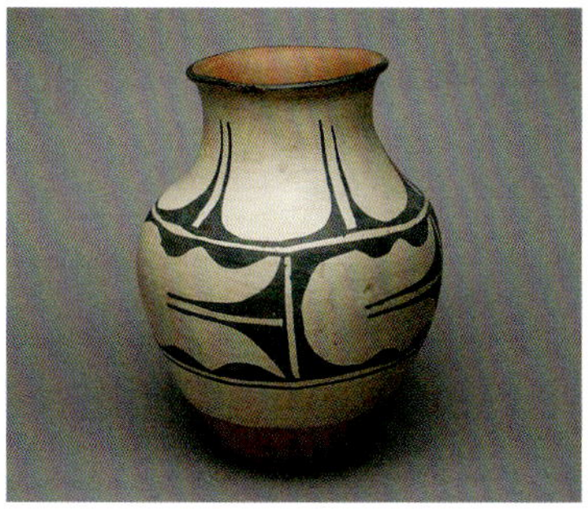

Jar
Artist Unknown, ca. 1935
24.5 × 17.2
Gift of Erik K. Reed
45793

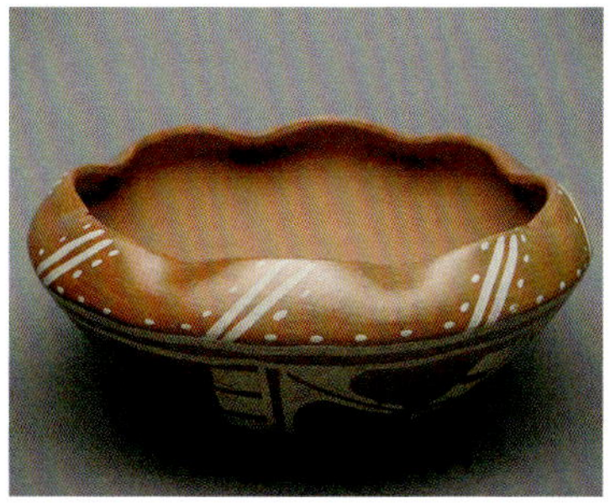

Bowl
Santana Melchor, ca. 1930–1940
9.4 × 21.9
Purchase, A. Kirkpatrick Estate
46050

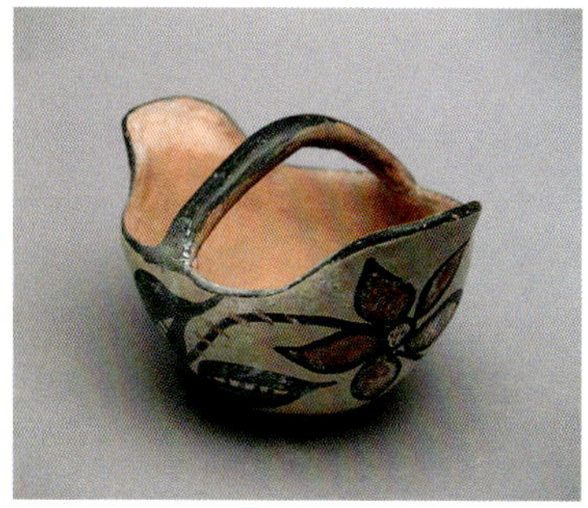

Pitcher
Artist Unknown, ca. 1930
10.2 × 11.5
Pansy Stockton Bequest
46185

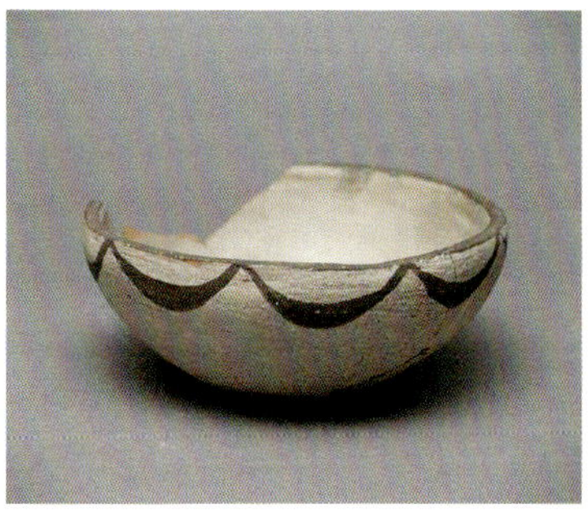

Bowl
Artist Unknown, ca. 1960–1970
5.2 × 13.0
Gift of Stewart L. Peckham
45970

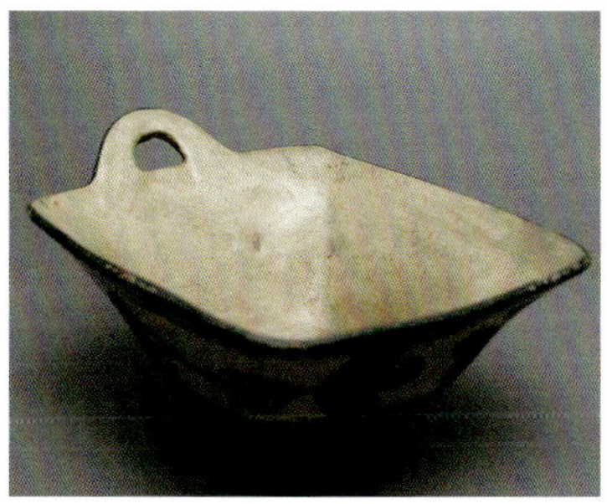

Bowl
Artist Unknown, ca. 1915
8.8 × 6.9
Gift of Marjorie F. Lambert
46086

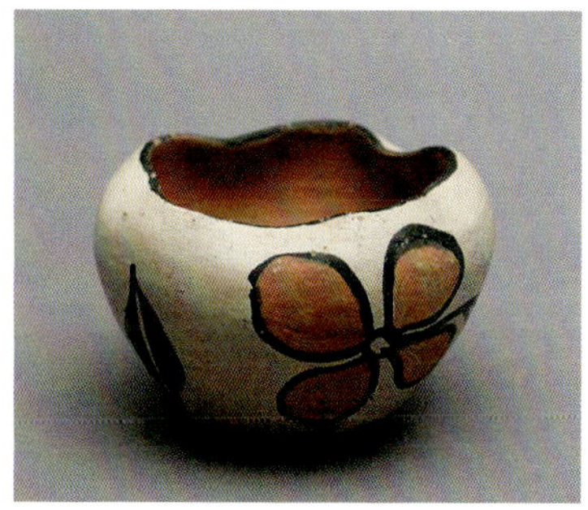

Bowl
Artist Unknown, ca. 1930–1940
6.4 × 10.0
Pansy Stockton Collection
46208

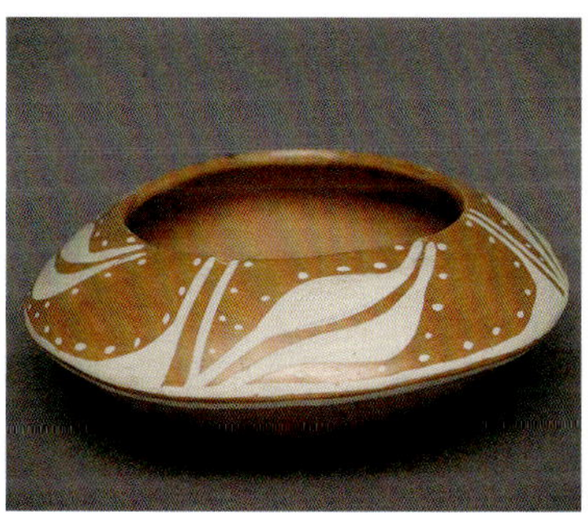

Jar
Santana Melchor, ca. 1930–1940
6.4 × 16.4
Gift of A. Kirkpatrick Estate
46049

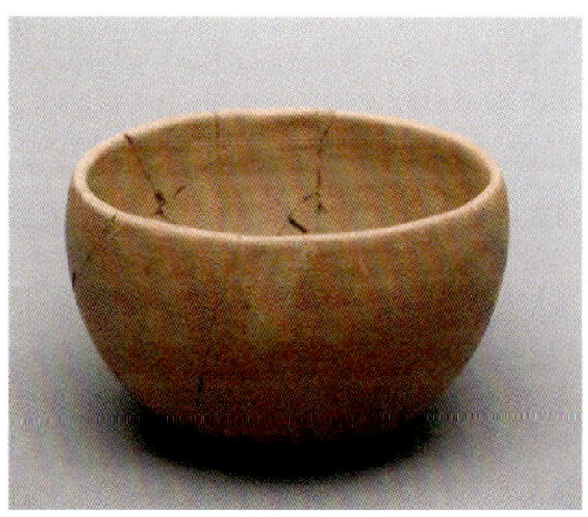

Bowl
Artist Unknown, ca. 1930–1940
10.7 × 17.4
Gift of Louise K. Lauermann
46107

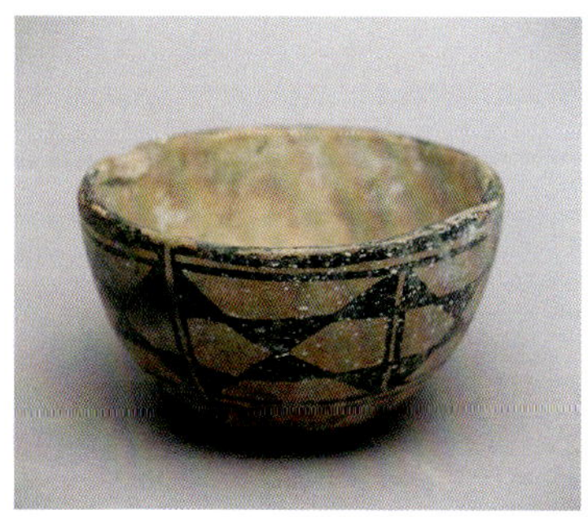

Bowl
Artist Unknown, ca. 1915–1920
6.6 × 11.8
Gift of Dora R. Smythe
46433

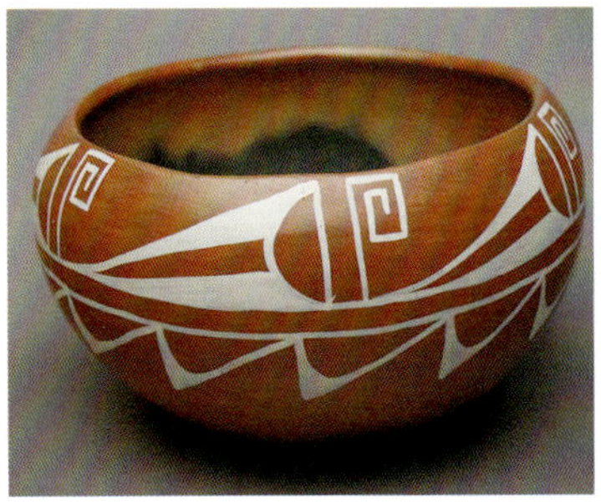

Bowl
Artist Unknown, 1930s
12.8 × 22.8
Gift of Joan Higgins Reed
46559

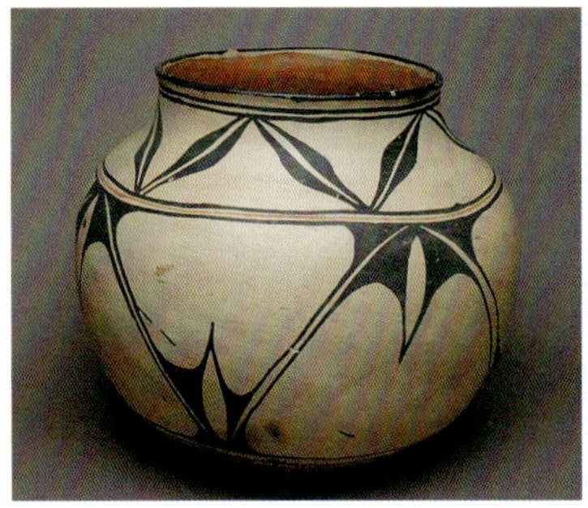

Jar
Artist Unknown, ca. 1900
33.9 × 39.5
Gift of Phyllis Harroun
48146

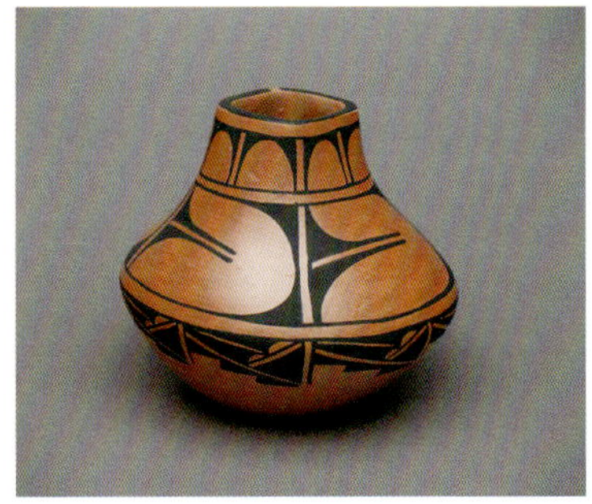

Jar
Marie E. Coriz, ca. 1981
11.2 × 13.3
Museum Purchase, Marie E. Coriz
49764

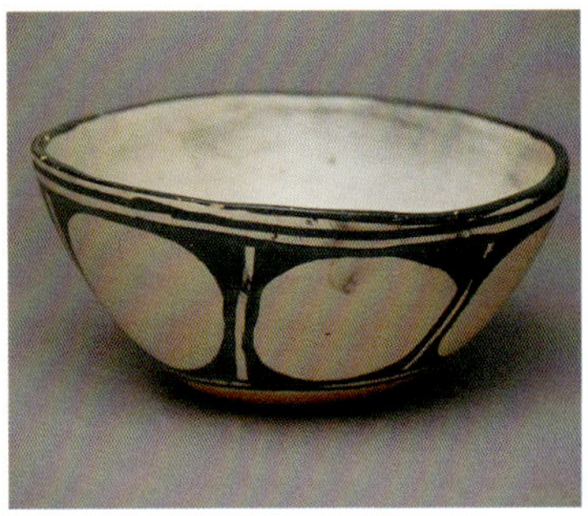

Stew Bowl
Artist Unknown, ca. 1920
9.5 × 20.9
Museum Collection
47355

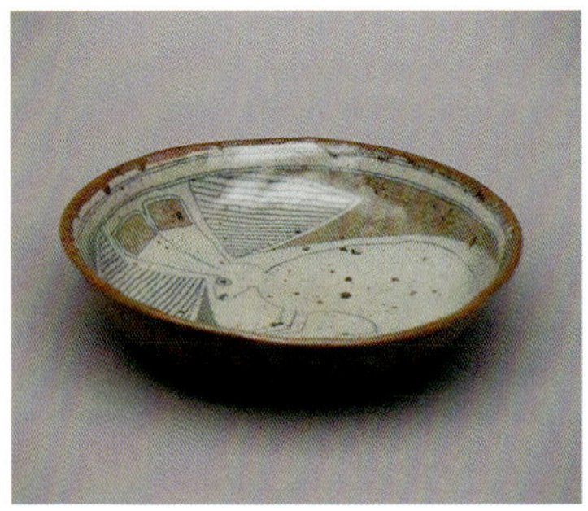

Bowl
Santo Domingo and Laguna
Harold Littlebird, ca. 1977
4.8 × 19.7
Museum Purchase, Harold Littlebird
48666

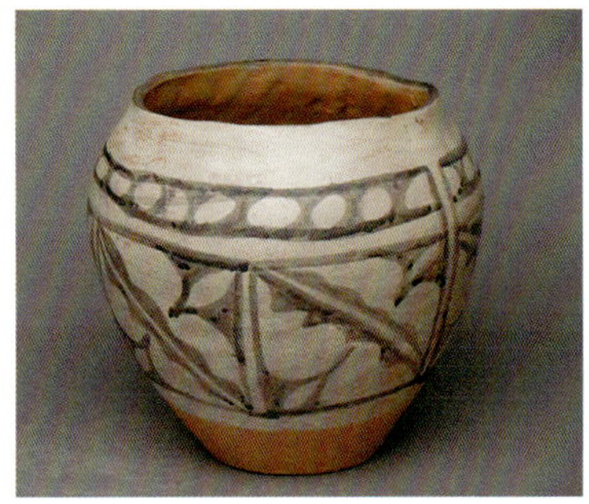

Jar
Attributed to Santana Melchor,
ca. 1971
21.2 × 23.0
Gift of John and Sara Seagrave
49850

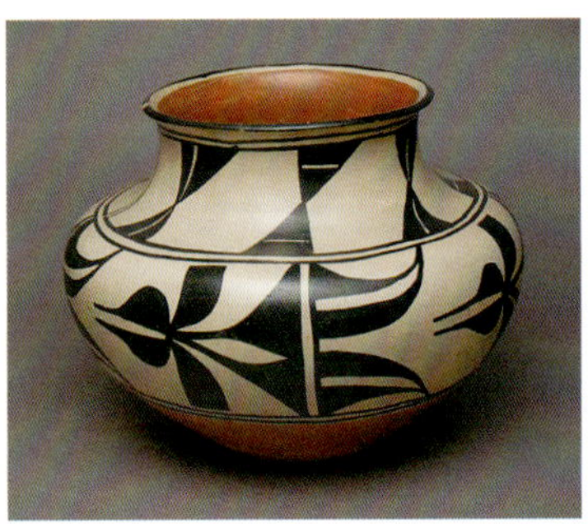

Jar
Artist Unknown, ca. 1910
21.5 × 28.8
Gift of Julia P. Meardon
47724

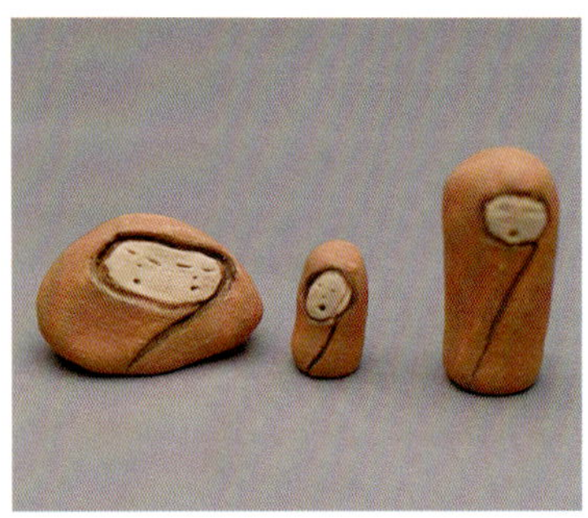

Zingzing Men Figurines
Alissa Chavez, ca. 1981
3.4 × 2.0 × 4.0
Museum Purchase, Alissa Chavez
49760

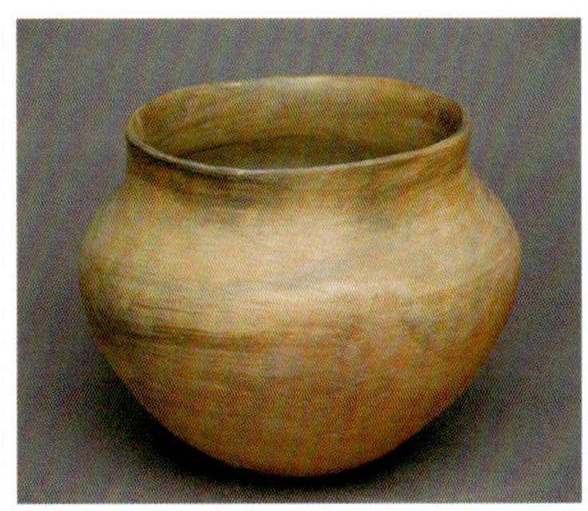

Jar
Santo Domingo?
Artist Unknown, ca. 1960–1970
16.4 × 20.4
Museum Collection
50023

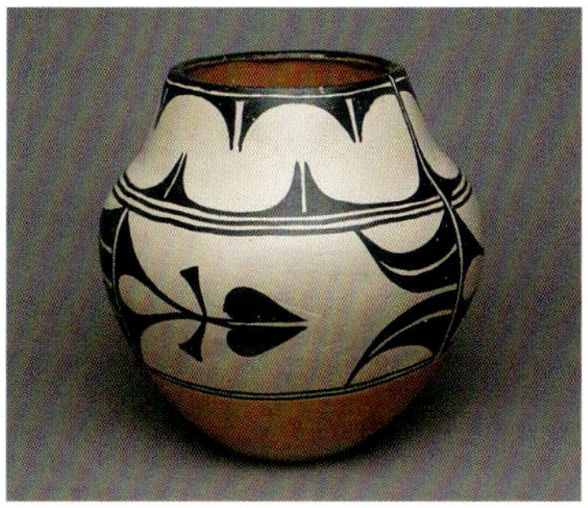

Jar
Artist Unknown, ca. 1930
26.2 × 26.8
Margaret Moses Bequest
50201

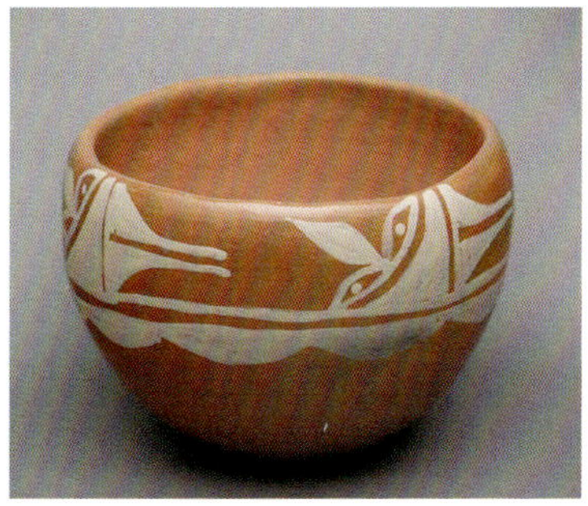

Jar
Manuelita Garcia, ca. 1980
11.3 × 15.6
Gift of Barbara Mauldin
50418

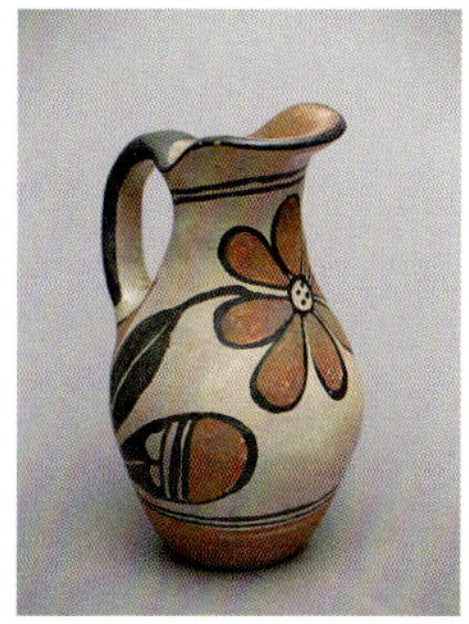

Pitcher
Artist Unknown, ca. 1935
16.3 × 9.5 × 16.3
Gift of LaVerne Hanners
51117

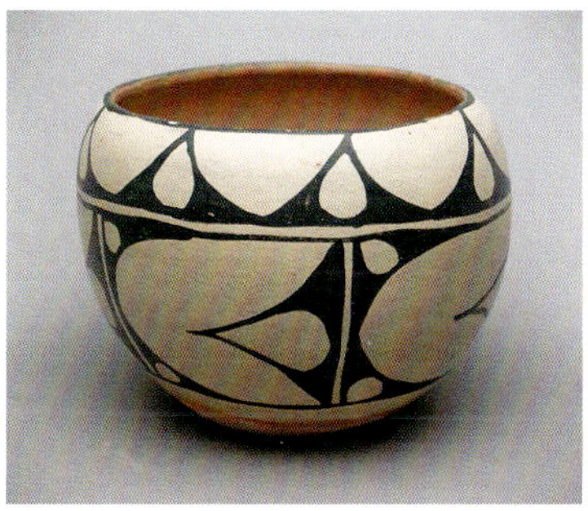

Jar
Artist Unknown, ca. 1940
14.5 × 19.3
Margaret Moses Bequest
50202

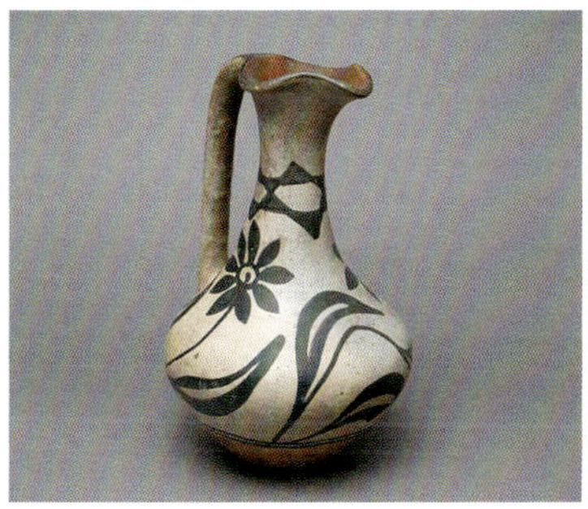

Pitcher
Artist Unknown, ca. 1920
22.5 × 12.4 × 23.1
Gift of Josephine Brokaw
51092

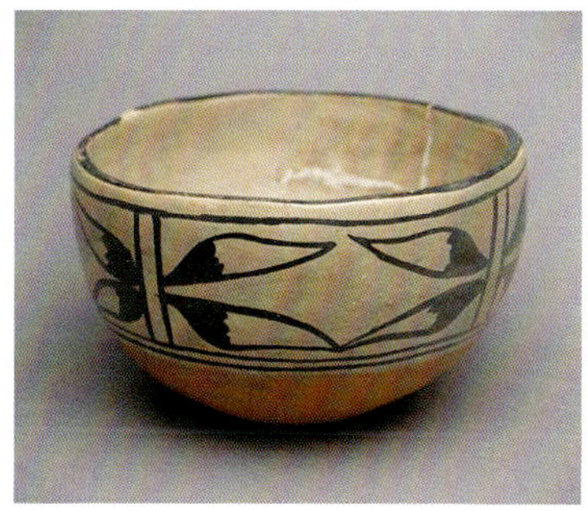

Stew Bowl
Artist Unknown, ca. 1968
10.3 × 17.5
Gift of Regge N. Wiseman
51125

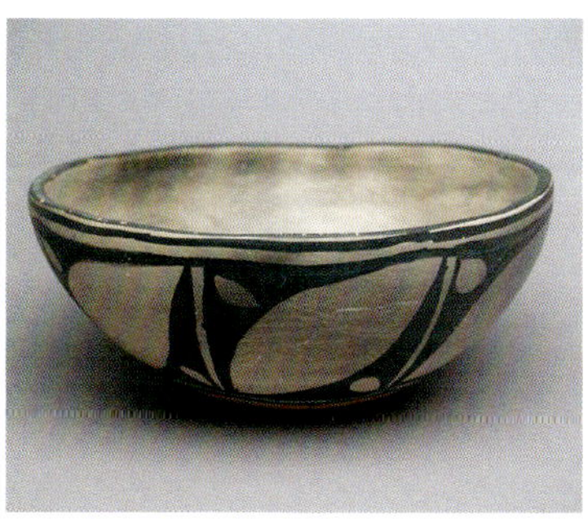

Stew Bowl
Artist Unknown, ca. 1940
9.3 × 22.7
Margaret Moses Bequest
50203

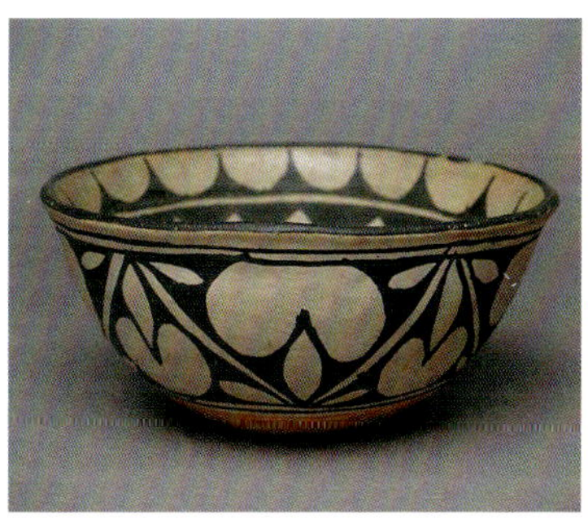

Stew Bowl
Artist Unknown, ca. 1920
9.2 × 20.6
Gift of Josephine Brokaw
51093

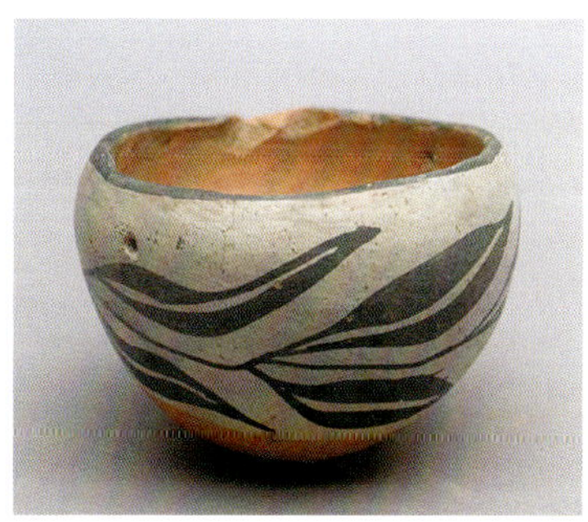

Bowl
Artist Unknown, ca. 1940
7.8 × 11.2
Gift of Laverne Hanners
51180

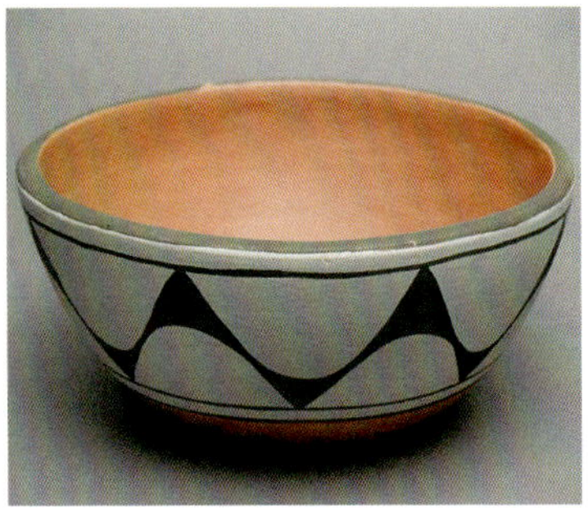

Bowl
Petra G. Garcia, 1989
10.5 × 21.6
Museum Purchase, Petra Garcia
51650

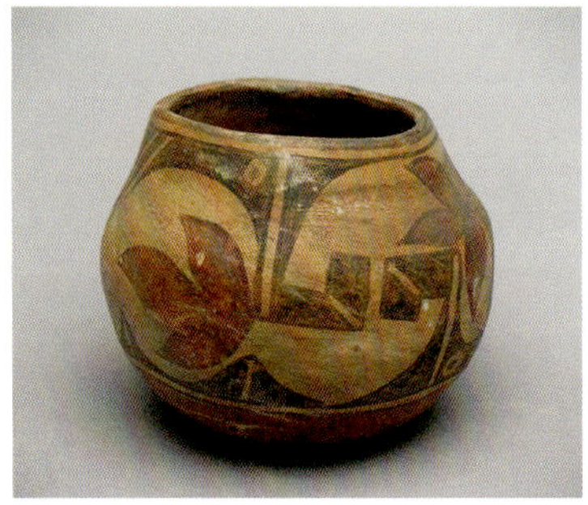

Jar
Artist Unknown, ca. 1880–1900
11.2 × 13.9
Gift of Warren and Lois von Preissig and Sue Bacharach
53087

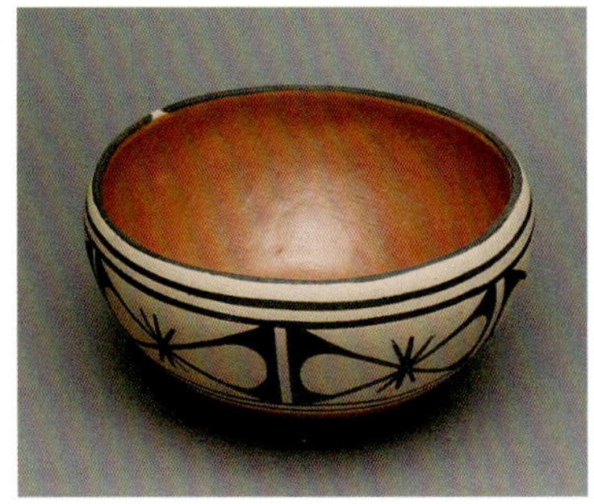

Bowl
Carol and Abel Calabaza, 1992
9.8 × 20.2
Museum Purchase, Carol and Abel Calabaza
53555

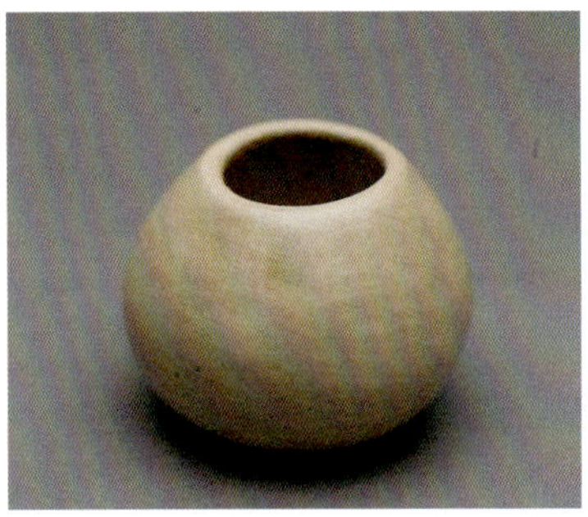

Jar
Terry Reano, 1989
5.0 × 6.3
Gift of Terry and Joe Reano
51755

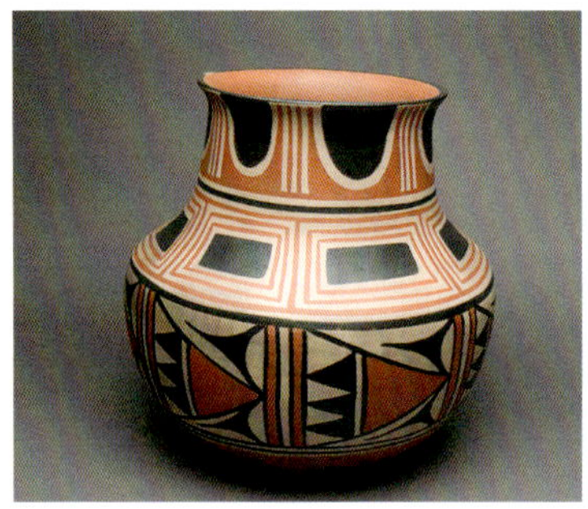

Jar
Robert Tenorio, ca. 1979
34.5 × 35.2
Gift of Richard Spivey
53226

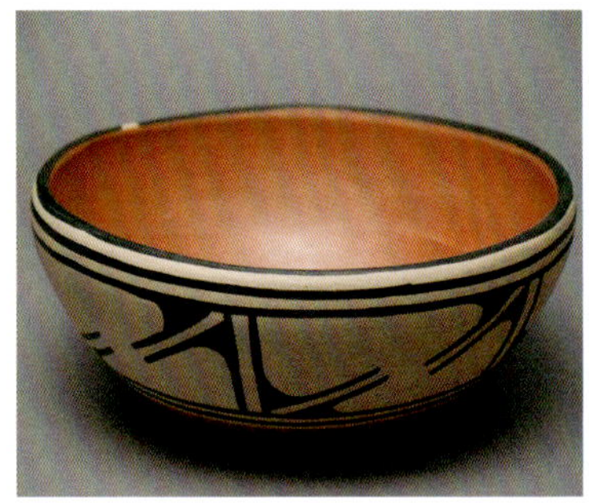

Bowl
Carol and Abel Calabaza, 1992
9.0 × 20.5
Museum Purchase, Carol and Abel Calabaza
53556

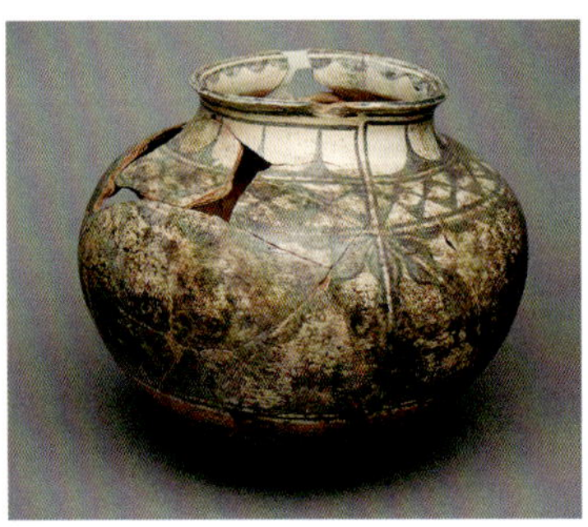

Jar
Artist Unknown, ca. 1880–1900
28.1 × 33.4
Gift of the Fred Harvey Company
52665

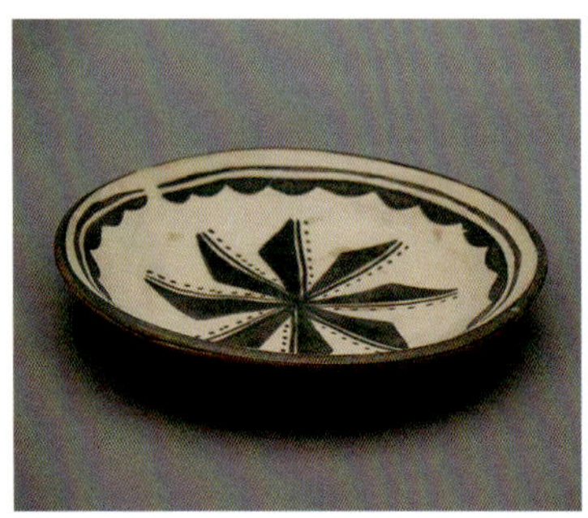

Plate
Paulita Pacheco, ca. 1980
4.1 × 20.8
Rick Dillingham Collection
53394

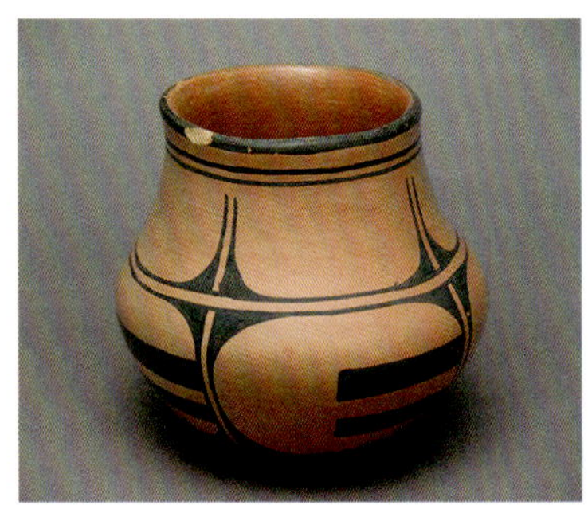

Jar
Santana and Crucita Melchor, 1976
16.0 × 16.2
Rick Dillingham Collection
53670

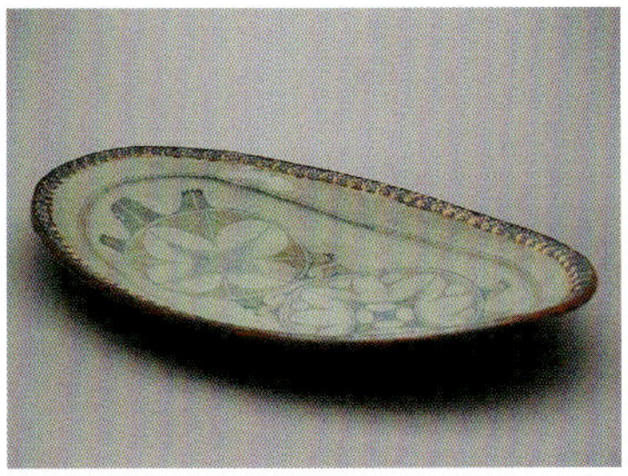

Platter
Santo Domingo and Laguna
Harold Littlebird, 1993
6.7 × 42.9 × 27.6
Gift of the Fred Harvey Company
53873

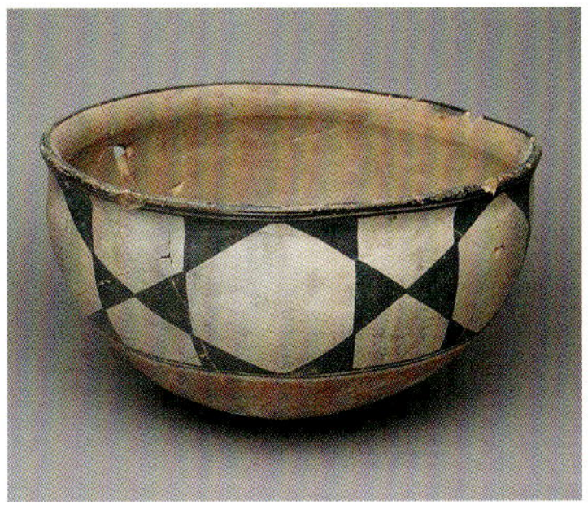

Dough Bowl
Artist Unknown, ca. 1900
21.3 × 38.2
Gift of the Fred Harvey Company
53883

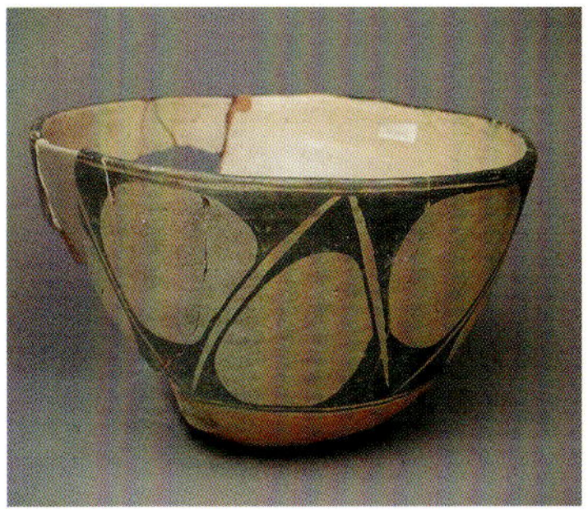

Bowl
Artist Unknown, ca. 1930–1940
15.8 × 27.2
Museum Collection
53890

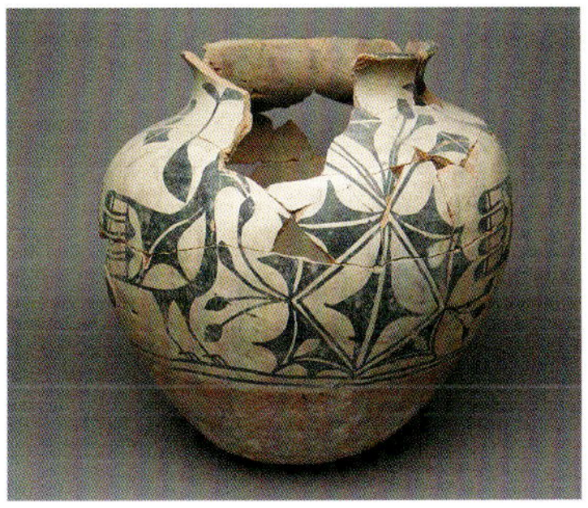

Jar
Artist Unknown, ca. 1900
42.4 × 39.4
Gift of the Fred Harvey Company
53878

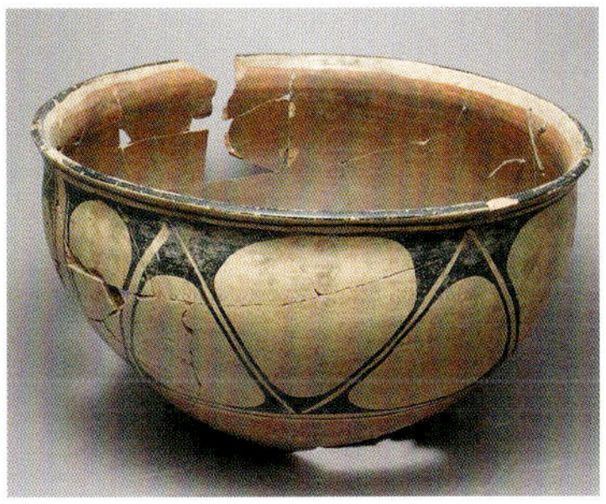

Dough Bowl
Artist Unknown, ca. 1890–1900
36.8 × 39.8
Gift of the Fred Harvey Company
53884

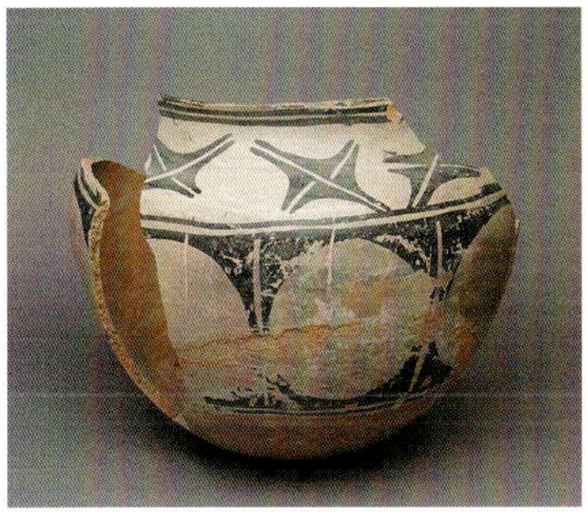

Jar
Artist Unknown, ca. 1920
31.9 × 35.2
Museum Collection
53892

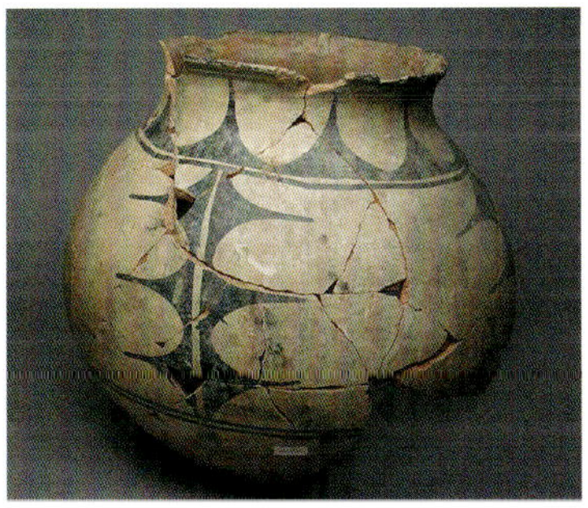

Jar
Artist Unknown, ca. 1870
33.8 × 39.3
Gift of the Fred Harvey Company
53879

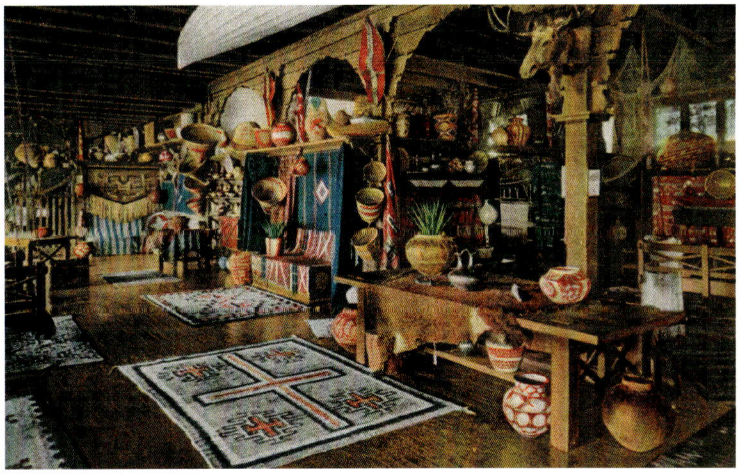

Fred Harvey Indian Room, Alvarado Hotel, Albuquerque, 1905. Courtesy Palace of the Governors (MNM/DCA), 001507. A number of pieces in the museum's collection are from the Fred Harvey Collection. The Fred Harvey Company had a concession agreement with the Santa Fe Railway beginning in the 1890s to serve its stations throughout the Southwest. Herman Schweizer, manager of the Indian Department, purchased most of the pieces that were included in the Fred Harvey Collection, as well as the pieces sold in the stores.

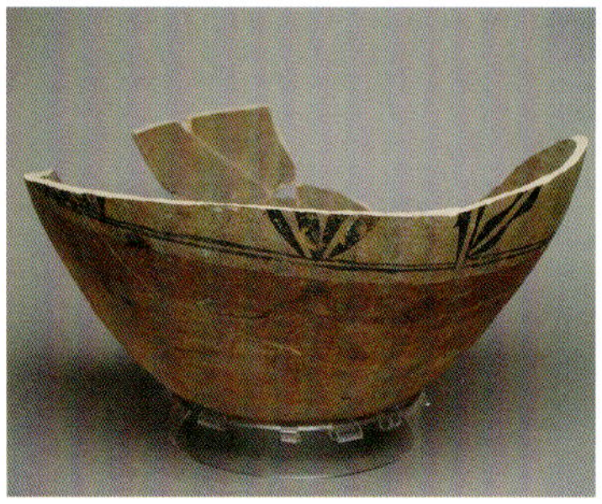

Jar Fragment
Artist Unknown, ca. 1900
31.5 × 41.4
Museum Collection
53901

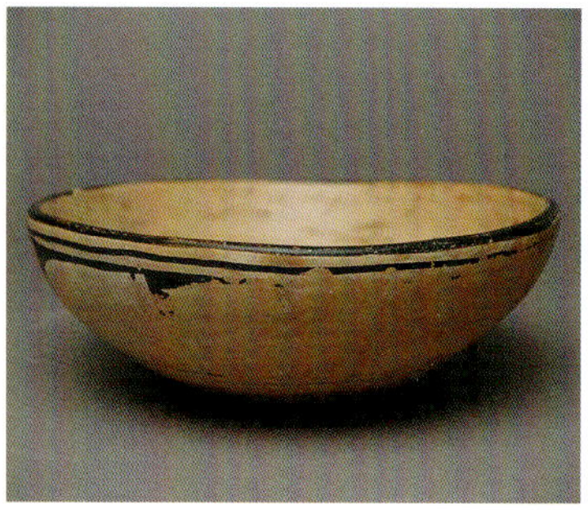

Stew Bowl
Artist Unknown, ca. 1920
7.0 × 19.9
Rick Dillingham Collection
54327

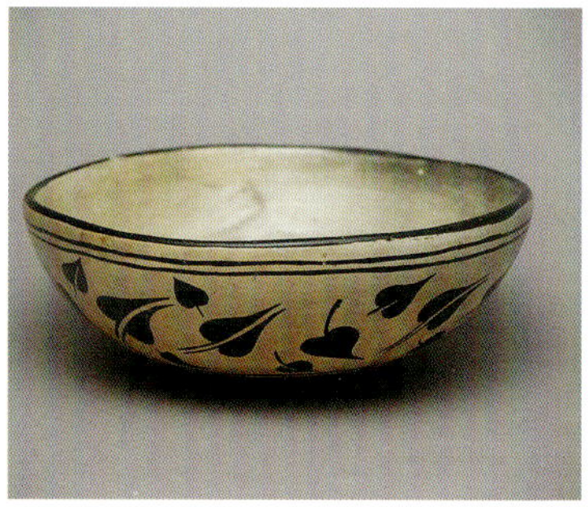

Bowl
Santana and Crucita Melchor, ca. 1975
8.5 × 23.0
Rick Dillingham Collection
54331

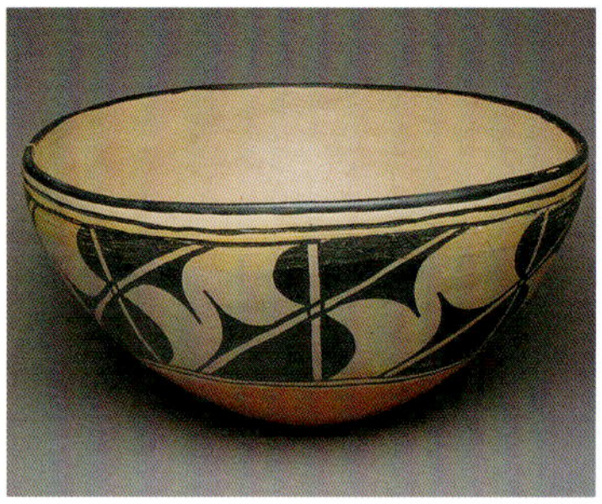

Dough Bowl
Santana and Crucita Melchor, ca. 1950
20.6 × 41.9
Rick Dillingham Collection
54322

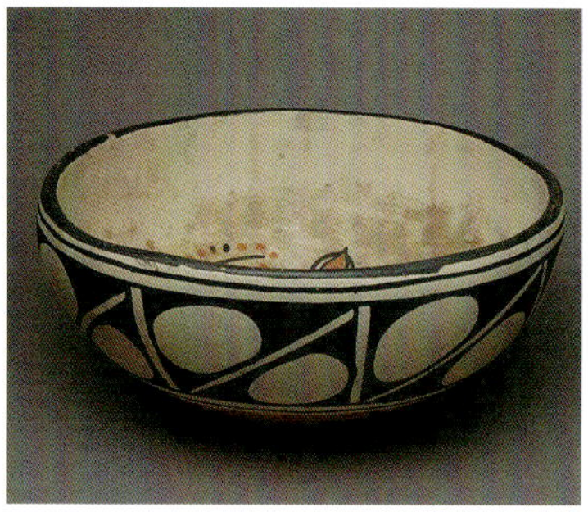

Dough Bowl
Crucita Melchor, ca. 1977
15.0 × 34.5
Rick Dillingham Collection
54328

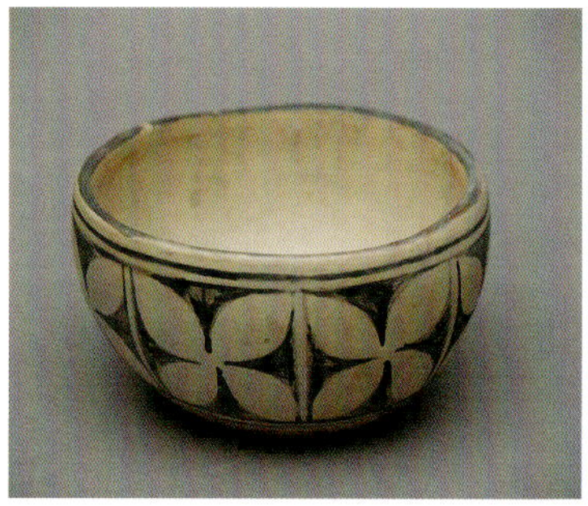

Bowl
Crucita Melchor, ca. 1975
7.0 × 11.9
Rick Dillingham Collection
54333

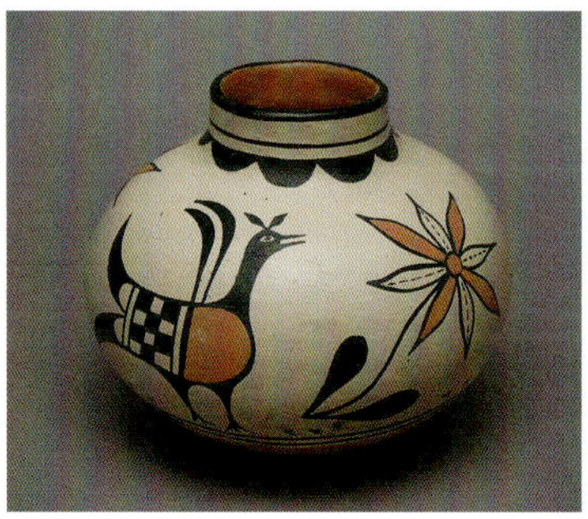

Jar
Santana and Crucita Melchor, 1975
15.6 × 18.2
Rick Dillingham Collection
54326

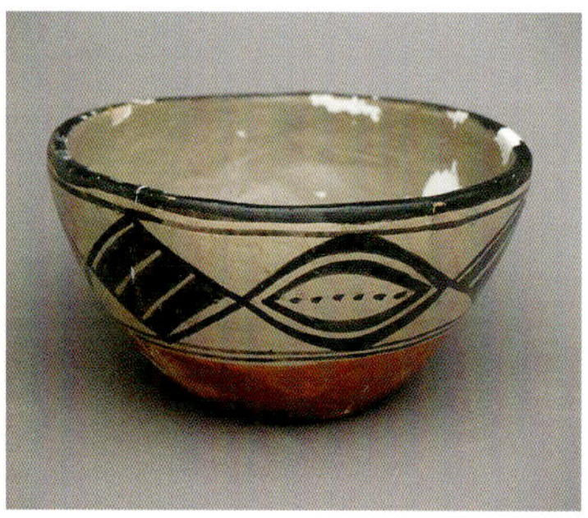

Stew Bowl
Artist Unknown, ca. 1955
10.0 × 19.0
Rick Dillingham Collection
54330

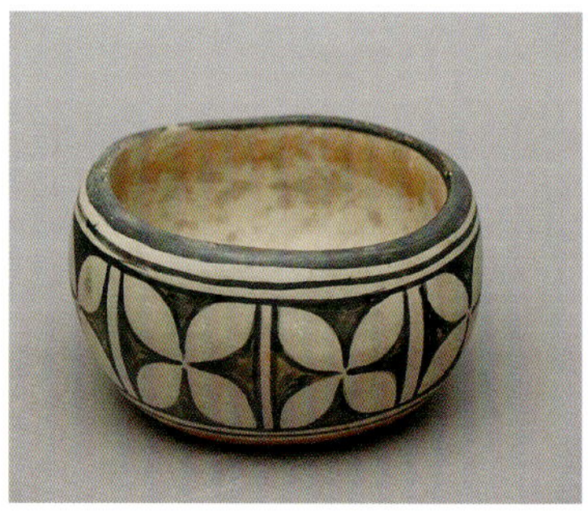

Bowl
Crucita Melchor, ca. 1975
6.0 × 10.9
Rick Dillingham Collection
54334

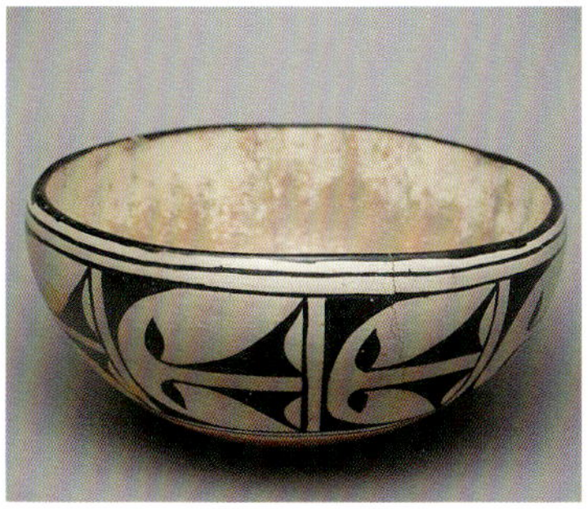

Bowl
Crucita Melchor, ca. 1970
12.5 × 26.0
Rick Dillingham Collection
54335

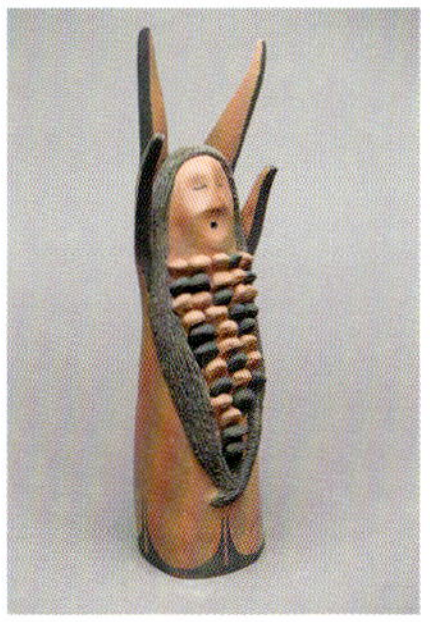

Corn Maiden Figurine
Artist Unknown, ca. 1990
28.5 × 7.0
Gift of Mark and Martha Alexander
54467

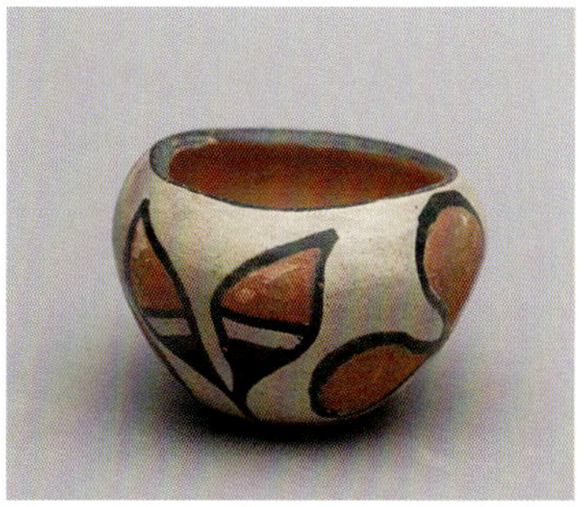

Jar
Artist Unknown, ca. 1930
6.4 × 9.6
Gift of Sanford M. and Diane P. Besser
54728

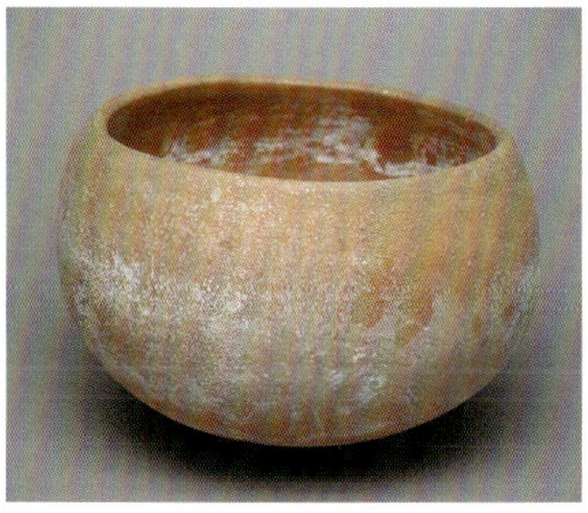

Bowl
Dolorita Melchor, ca. 1980
14.0 × 21.0
Rick Dillingham Collection
54336

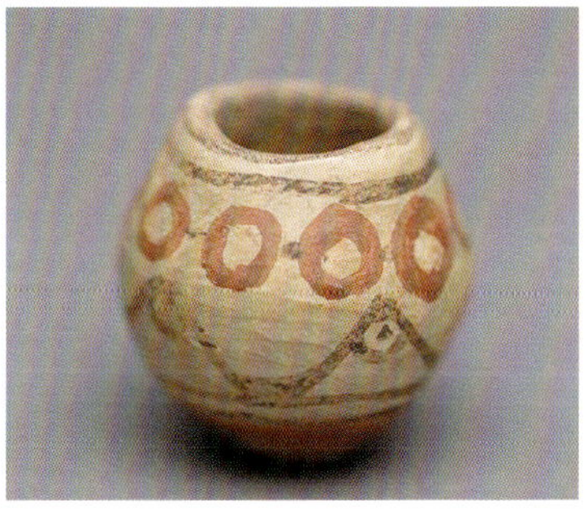

Jar
Santo Domingo?
Artist Unknown, ca. 1920
4.4 × 4.5
Gift of Sallie Wagner
54590

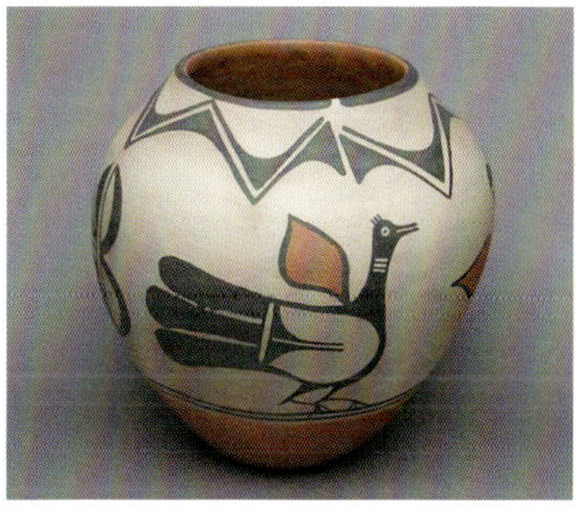

Jar
Robert Tenorio, 1982
20.1 × 21.6
Gift of Sanford M. and Diane P. Besser
54756

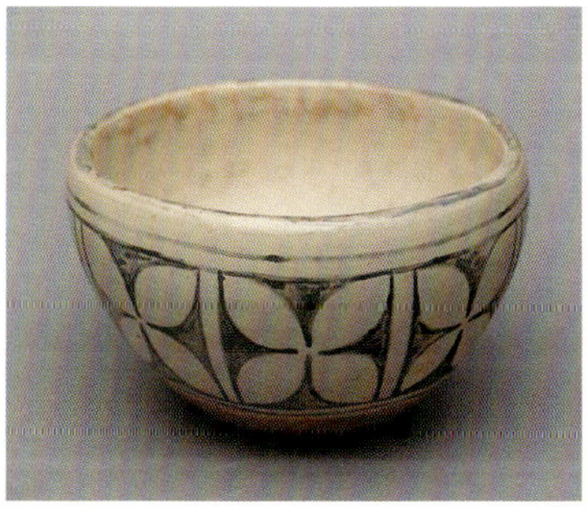

Bowl
Crucita Melchor, ca. 1975
7.2 × 12.2
Rick Dillingham Collection
54337

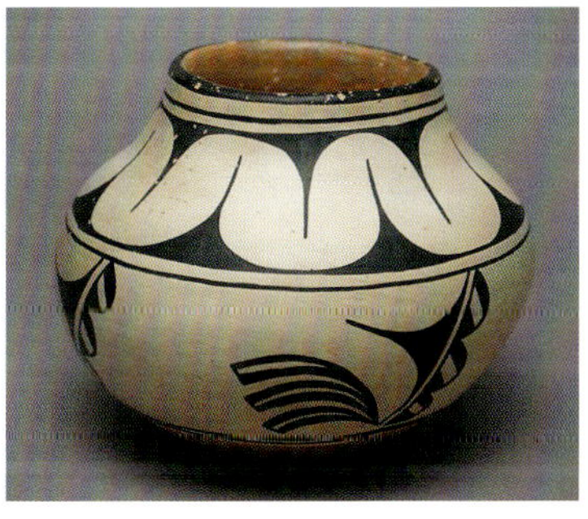

Jar
Santana and Crucita Melchor, ca. 1975
15.0 × 17.6
Gift of Mark and Martha Alexander
54673

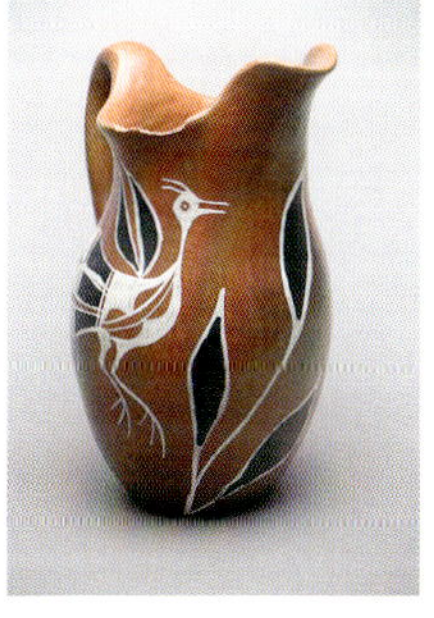

Pitcher
Artist Unknown, ca, 1950–1953
27.3 × 21.0 × 21.9
Gift of Norman and Gilda Greenberg
55352

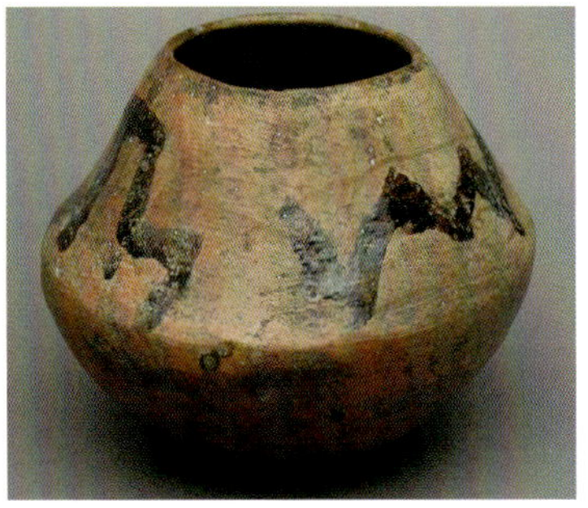

Jar
Santo Domingo?
Artist Unknown, ca. 1600–1650
16.7 × 28.4 × 15.8
Gift of Francis H. and
Patricia N. Harlow
55781

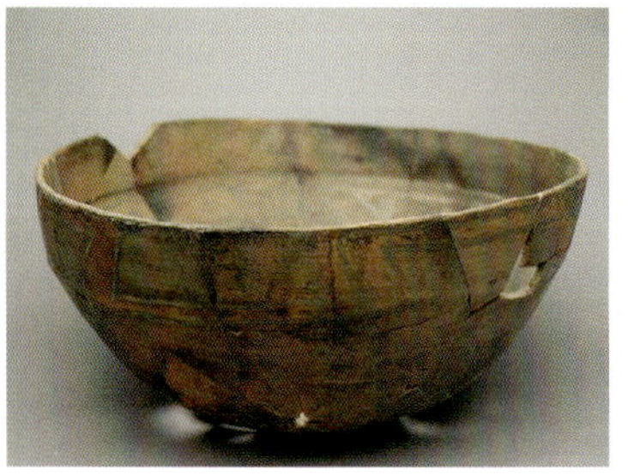

Bowl
Artist Unknown, ca. 1690–1700
16.5 × 33.9 × 15.3
Gift of Francis H. and
Patricia N. Harlow
55824

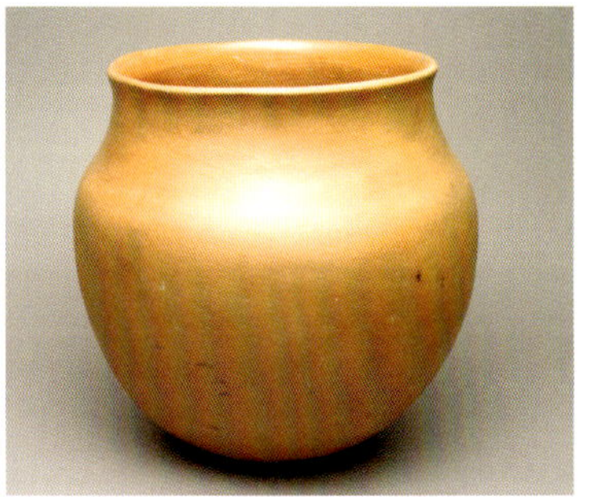

Jar
Santana Melchor, ca. 1961
29.5 × 31.0 × 27.4
Gift of Francis H. and
Patricia N. Harlow
55835

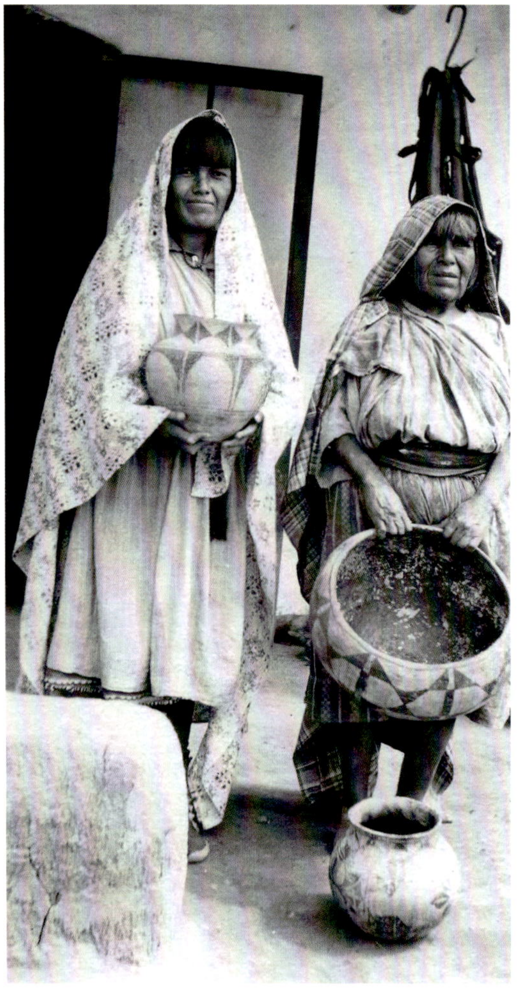

Two Santo Domingo women hold examples of their household pottery, 1929. Kenneth Chapman, photographer. Courtesy School for Advanced Research, Kenneth Chapman Files, F41.3.

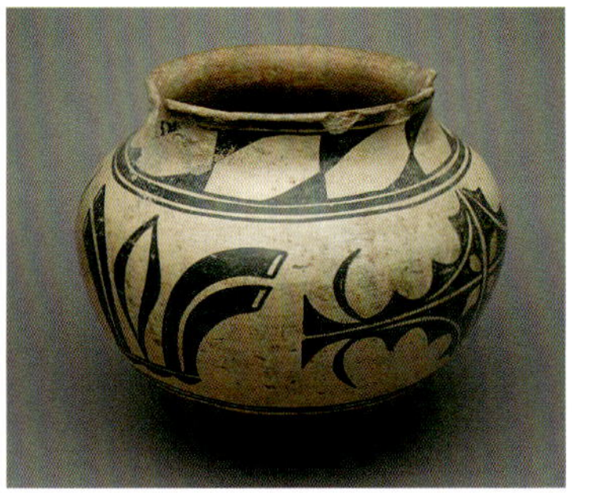

Jar
Crucita Herrera Coriz,
ca. 1915–1920
24.8 × 28.9 × 23.5
Gift of Francis H. and
Patricia N. Harlow
55890

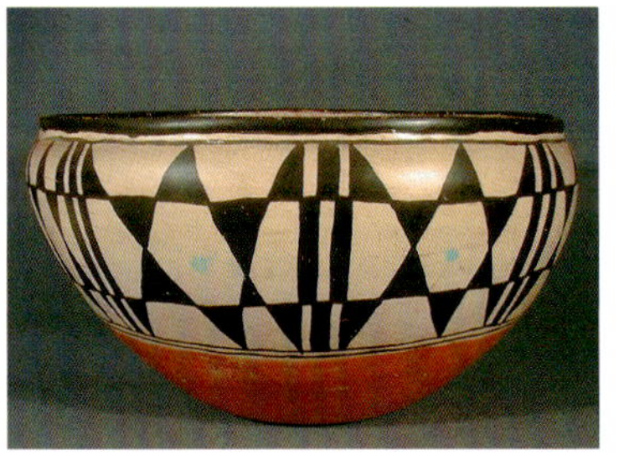

Dough Bowl
Santana Melchor, ca. 1930
25.5 × 47.7
John B. Elliott Collection
55960

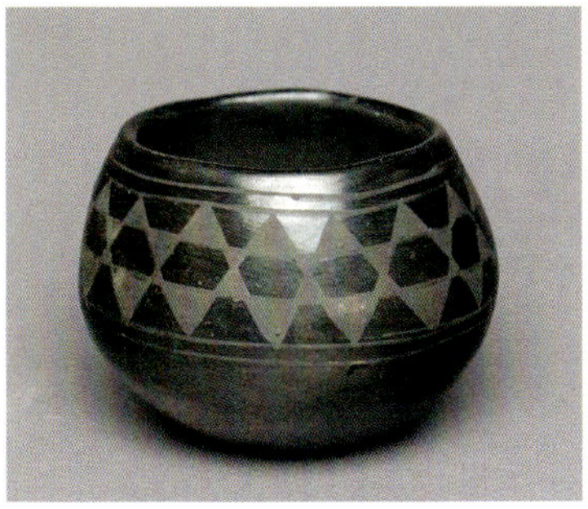

Jar
Josephine Martinez, ca. 1975
6.9 × 9.7
Gift of Judith M. Liersch and Al Jennings
56550

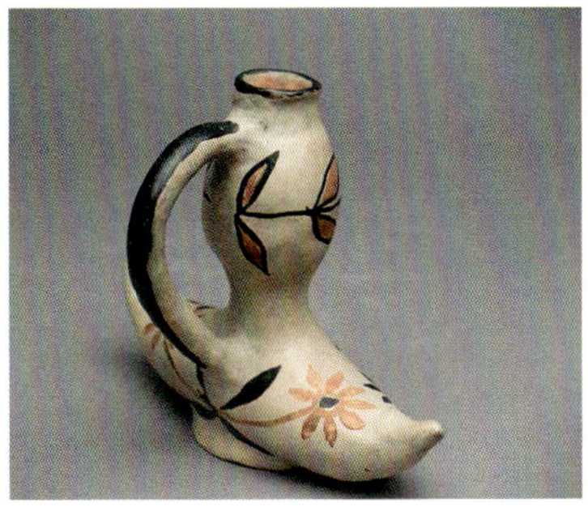

Candlestick
Artist Unknown, ca. 1930
13.0 × 16.0 × 9.0
Gift of Mark J. Sublette
56908

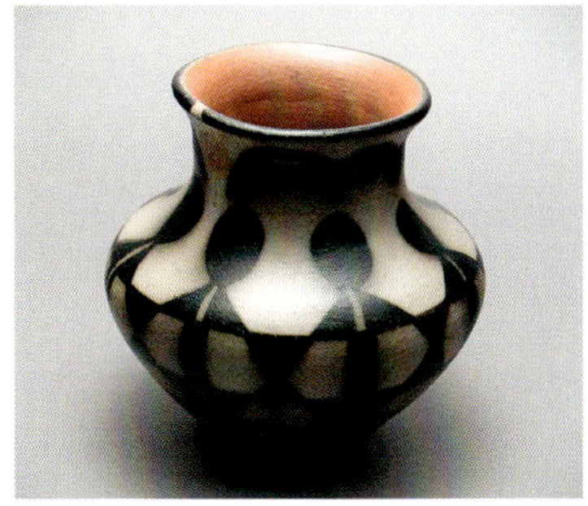

Jar
Robert Tenorio, 2006
13.4 × 13.9
Museum Purchase
57256

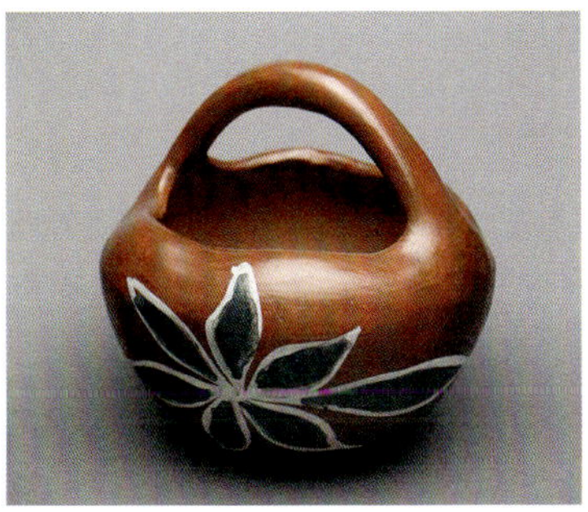

Bowl
Artist Unknown, ca. 1955
13.2 × 13.5
Gift of Norman and Gilda Greenberg
56647

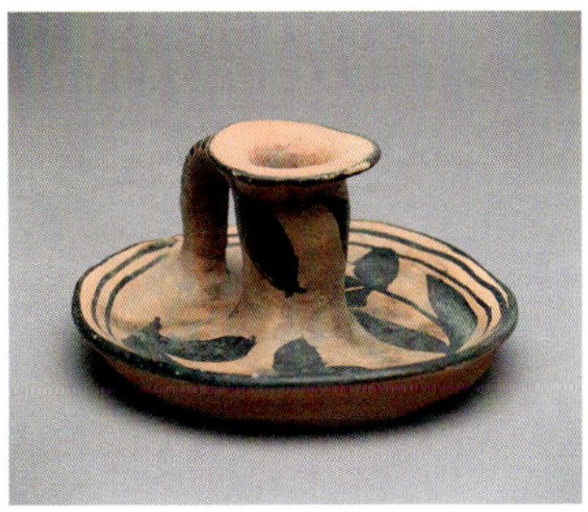

Candlestick
Artist Unknown, ca. 1920
6.2 × 13.7 × 12.8
Gift of Mark J. Sublette
56909

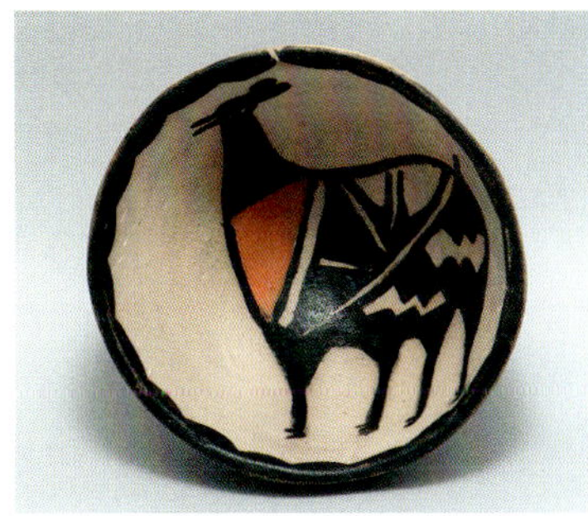

Bowl
Paulita Pacheco, 2007
8.0 × 14.0
Gift of Paulita Pacheco
57333

PART IV

Cochiti or Santo Domingo

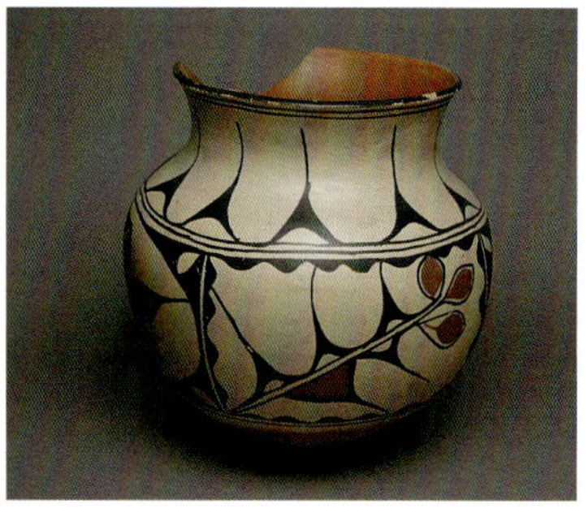

Jar
Artist Unknown, ca. 1925–1935
31.1 × 30.7
Gift of Henry Dendahl
7982

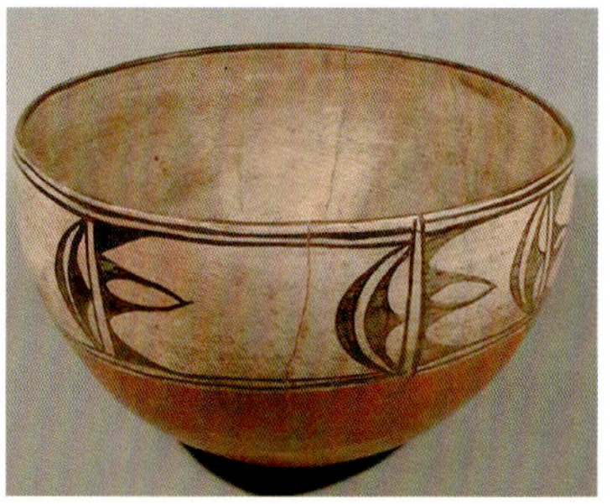

Dough Bowl
Artist Unknown, 1880–1900
29.5 × 49.0
Museum Collection
11114

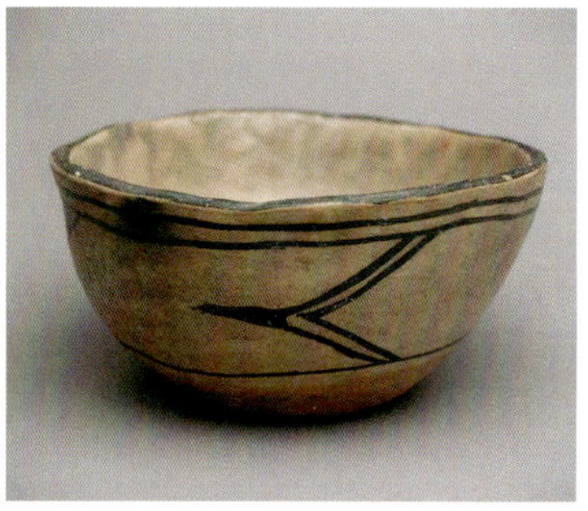

Stew Bowl
Artist Unknown, ca. 1890
8.7 × 17.2
Gift of the Seligman Brothers
8008

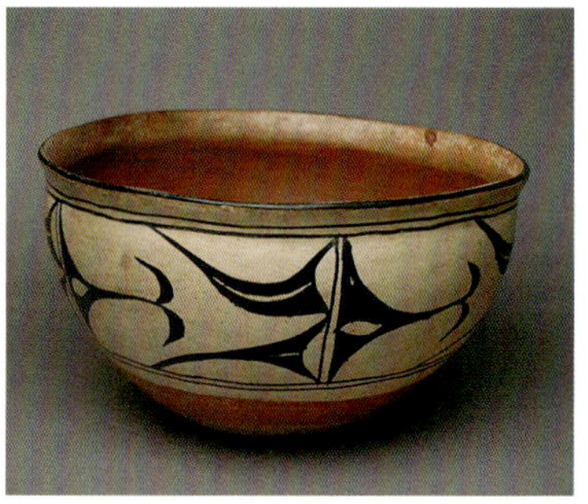

Bowl
Artist Unknown, ca. 1915
19.1 × 33.3
Museum Purchase, Twichell Estate
11116

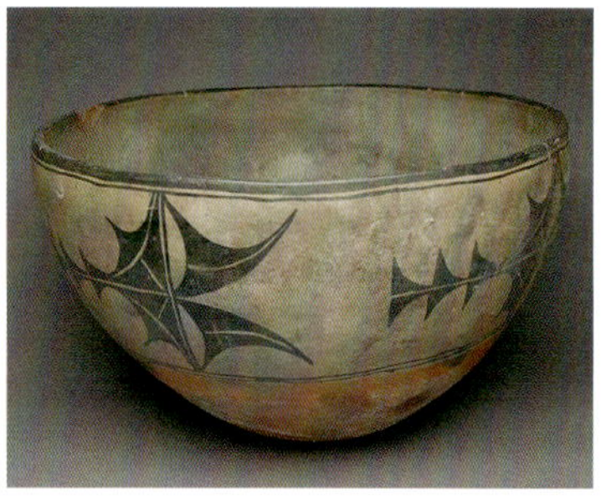

Dough Bowl
Artist Unknown, ca. 1890–1900
28.4 × 48.8
Manderfield Collection
11112

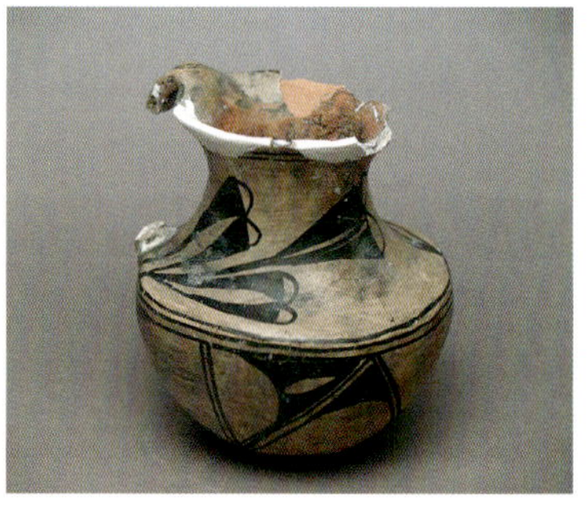

Pitcher
Artist Unknown, ca. 1900
16.8 × 13.5
Museum Purchase, Rogers and Schafer, Albuquerque
11189

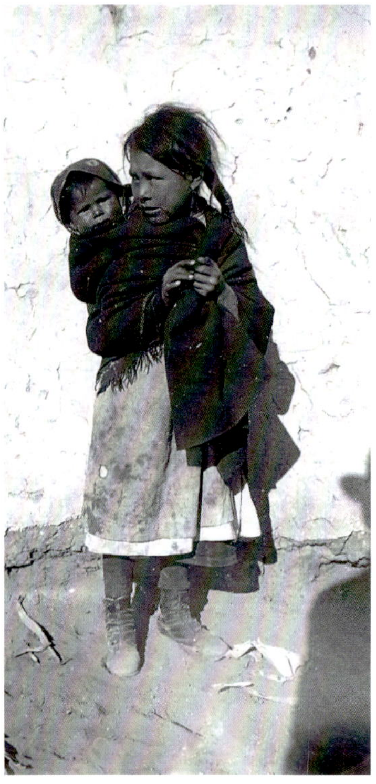

Kenneth Chapman at Cochiti Pueblo. Courtesy School for Advanced Research, Transfile AC02:841. The figure of Kenneth Chapman's shadow (1875–1968) looms large over the historic-period ceramics of both Cochiti and Santo Domingo. With the founding of the Museum of New Mexico in 1909, "Chap" served director Edgar L. Hewett as executive secretary, artist, archaeologist, lecturer, receptionist, and sometime janitor. In 1927, he was a founder of the Laboratory of Anthropology.

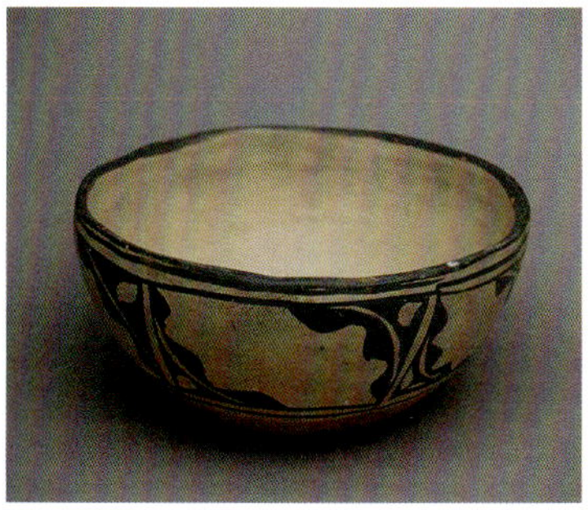

Stew Bowl
Artist Unknown, ca. 1935
9.9 × 20.3
Gift of Henry Dendahl
11193

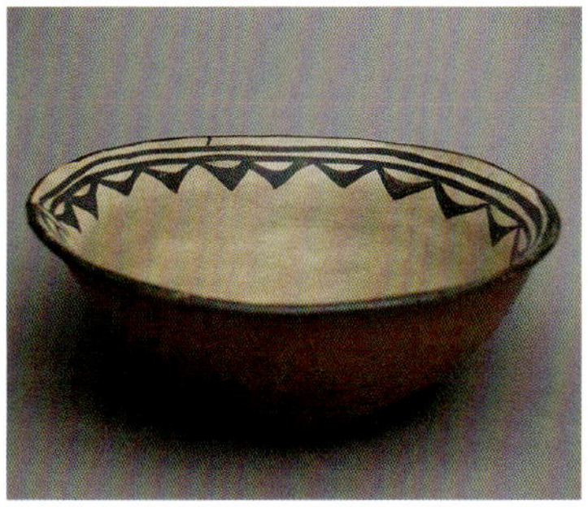

Stew Bowl
Artist Unknown, ca. 1925
9.5 × 23.7
Gift of Frank Patania
19313

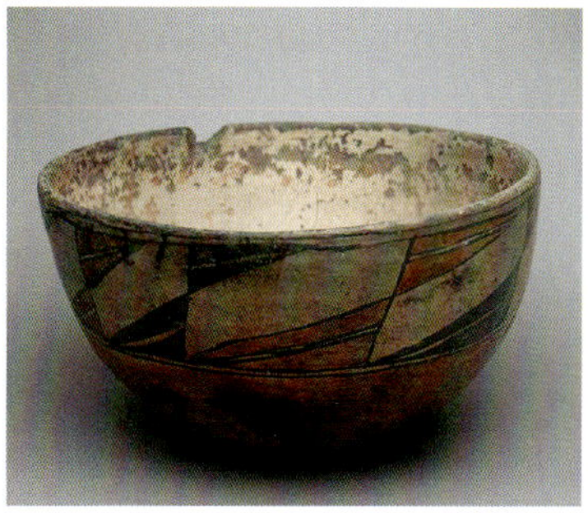

Dough Bowl
Cochiti, Santo Domingo,
or San Ildefonso
Artist Unknown, prior to 1973
17.5 × 33.2
Mr. and Mrs. Harris Masterson
Collection
46430

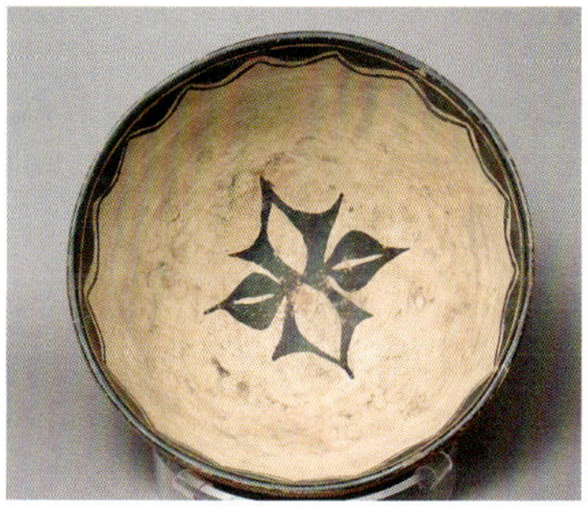

Bowl
Artist Unknown, ca. 1920s
13.7 × 29.2
Nelson Collection
12177

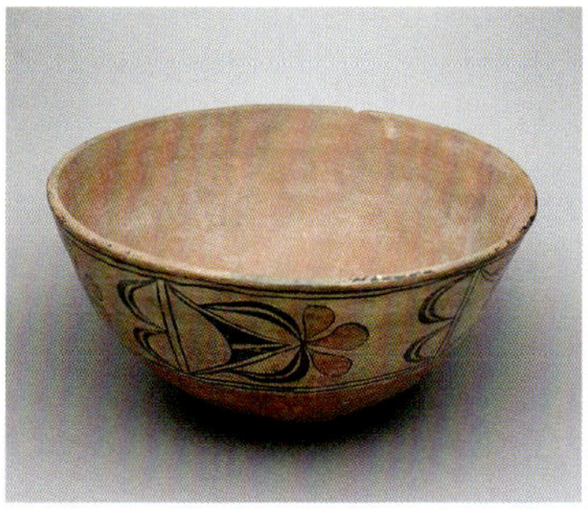

Dough Bowl
Artist Unknown, ca. 1870–1900
19.9 × 40.7
Gift of Elizabeth S. Sargent
30169

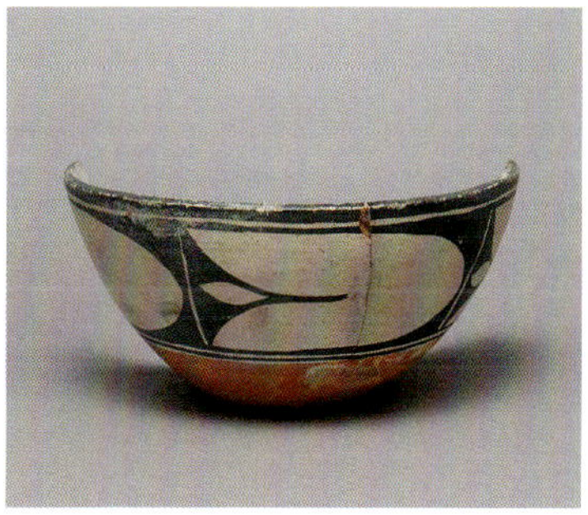

Bowl Fragment
Artist Unknown, ca. 1945
9.1 × 10.3
Museum Collection
50027

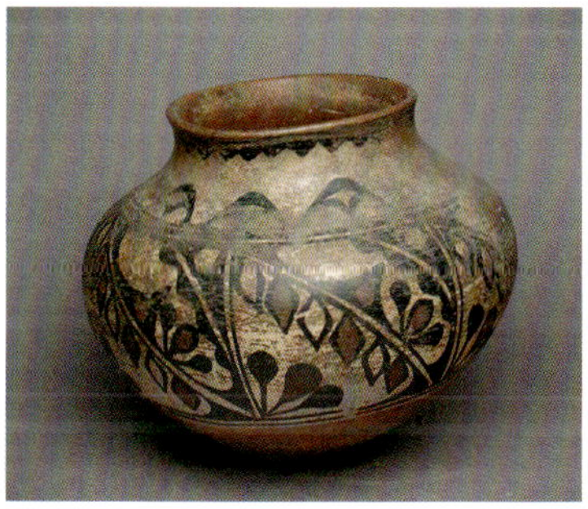

Jar
Artist Unknown, ca. 1890
24.0 × 28.5
Gift of the Historical Society of
New Mexico
12210

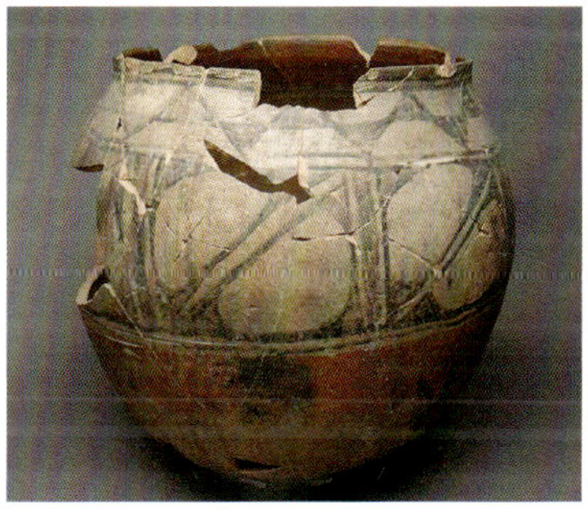

Jar
Artist Unknown, ca. 1900
41.7 × 43.0
Gift of the Fred Harvey Company
44237

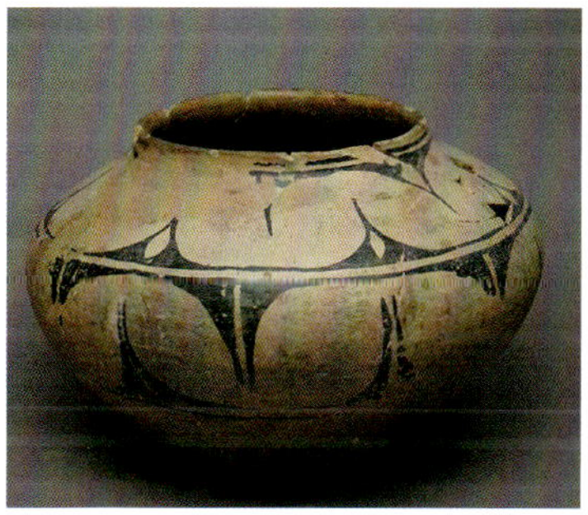

Jar
Artist Unknown, ca. 1880
33.0 × 35.8
Gift of the Fred
Harvey Company
53902

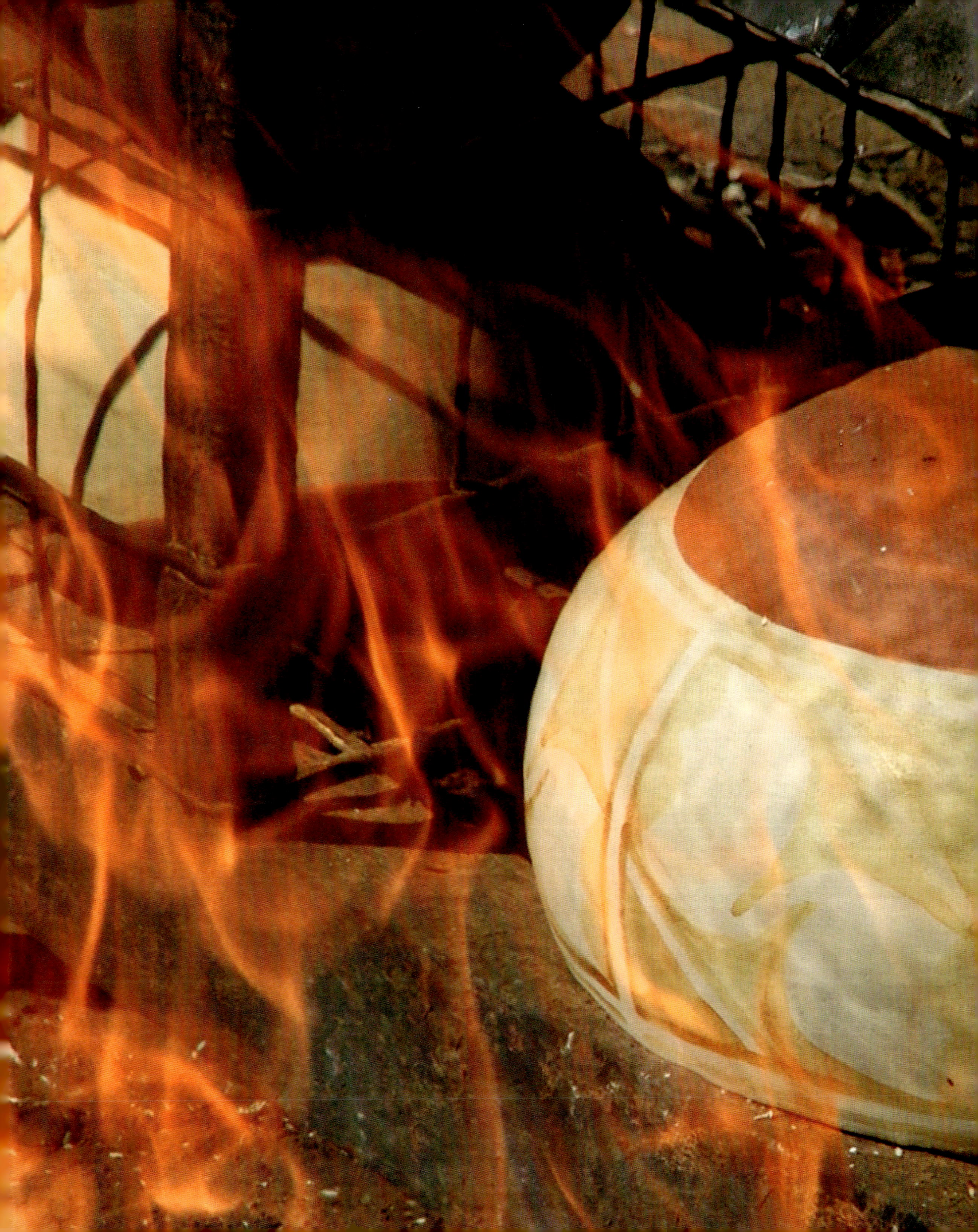

SECTION IV

Appendices

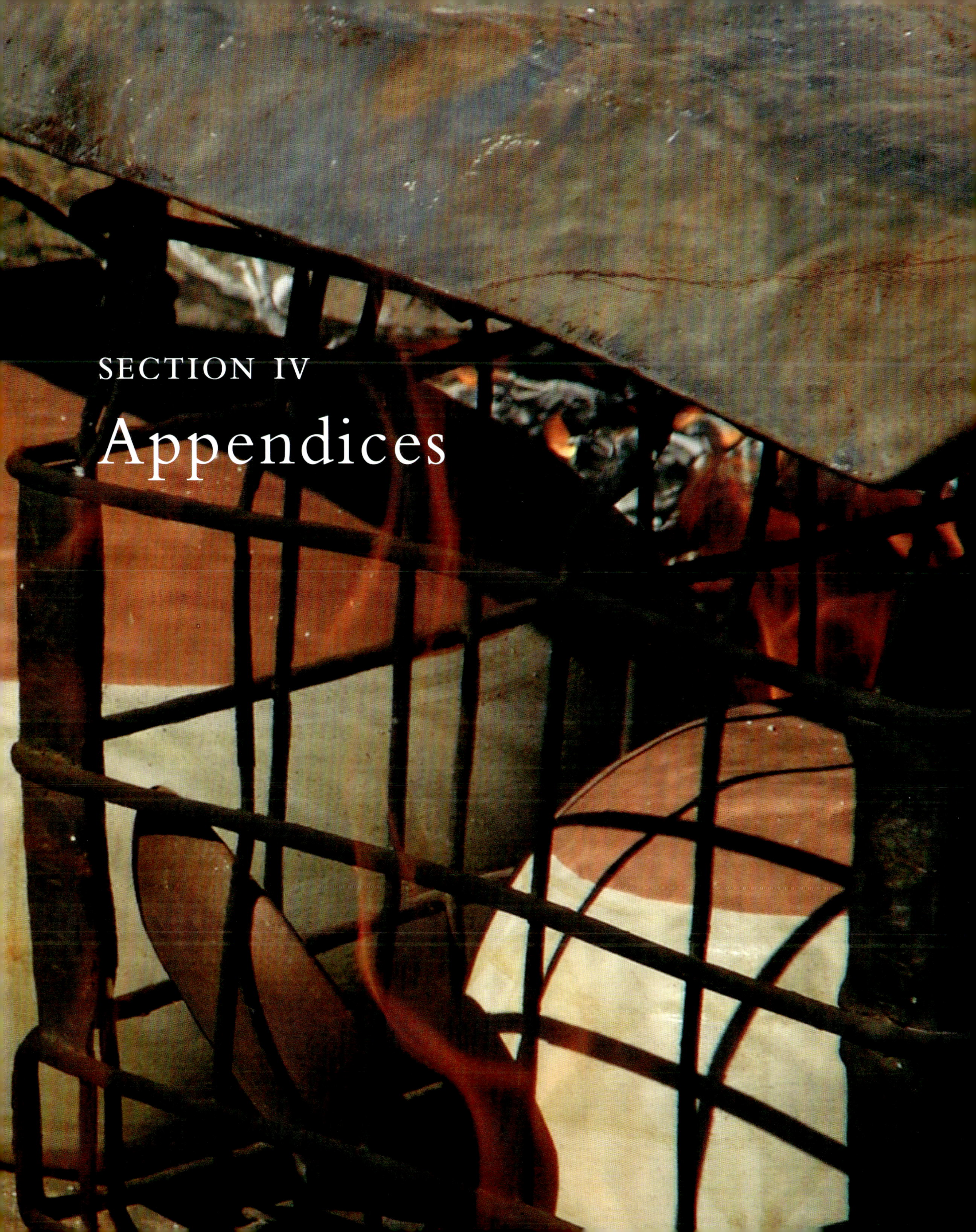

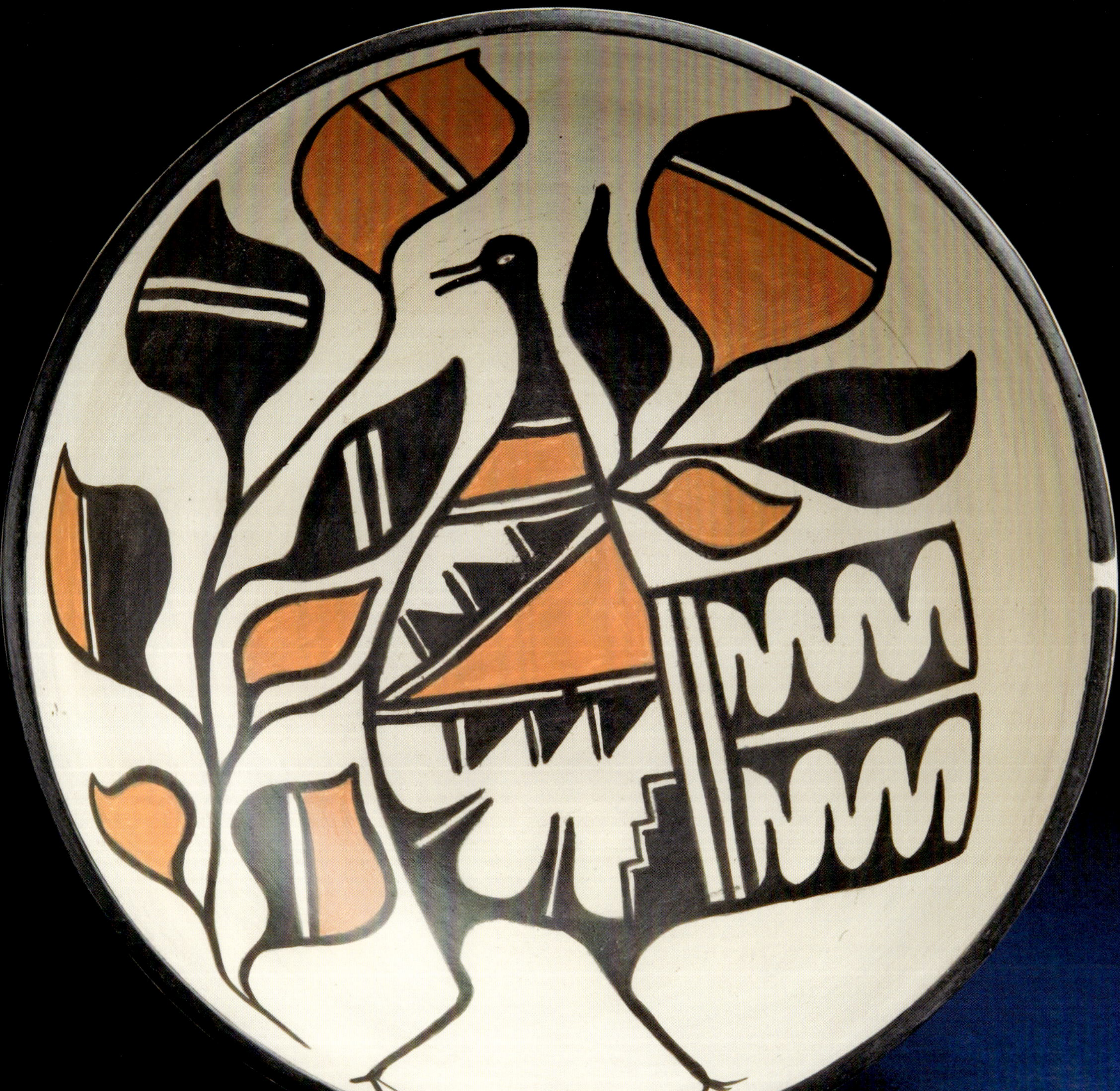

Pueblo Pottery Basics

Materials, Tools, and Techniques

Valerie K. Verzuh

Traditional potters must understand clays, tempers, and pigments, be able to identify their sources, and know how they react when combined and in what proportions. They also must be students of the marks of workmanship left in the molding, shaping, and finishing processes, and of the outcomes of different firing methods. A few anthropological studies at the Rio Grande pueblos document clay, slip, and paint processing; construction methods; and polishing, painting, and firing techniques (Guthe 1925; Shepard 1956); however, strong opinions exist at the pueblos that to survive as an art, making pottery should remain experiential rather than analytic and formulaic. This means that the source, chemistry, and mixture of clay, paste, slip, and paint remain privately held, by individual potters or potting families, so no significant analysis of these raw materials and their combination has been done. In the manner the pueblos are protective of their privacy, pottery artists are protective of their knowledge and materials (see Chavarria in this volume for a more intimate portrait of Pueblo pottery).

Making pottery is a family affair. Individual artists typically learn through observations of family members and through trial and error. Santo Domingo potter Robert Tenorio, who has mentored other potters, says he guides students rather than giving them an exact formula, as "every situation is different and requires a unique approach." Making pottery also is integrated into family life and centered among the daily activities at home. Crucita Melchor, who learned from and worked with her mother Santana Melchor, says that she "always made her pots on the kitchen table."

Clay Preparation

Clay is dug, in dry or moist lumps, out of traditional clay beds. The location of a potter's clay source may be known by pueblo and family, or may be a closely held secret; however, digging clay and transporting it home is hard physical labor, which usually means it is a group outing. At home, the potter allows the raw clay to dry prior to grinding and siev-

figure 122
Jar
Santo Domingo
Paulita Pacheco
1997
12.1 x 27.5 cm

ing it to remove inclusions such as stones and plant materials.

The potter then adds temper to the clay to create what is technically referred to as the paste. Temper is a non-plastic material that lessens the stickiness of the wet clay, reduces shrinkage and the danger of cracking during drying and firing, and coarsens the dense clay body, opening it up to permit the escape of gases which might cause spalling or blistering of the fired pot's surface. At both Cochiti and Santo Domingo, ground volcanic ash and tuff, called sand, is used as temper. The resulting paste is workable, or plastic.

Construction

All prehistoric pottery in the American Southwest was hand built; today, the majority of Pueblo pottery still is made using the coil and scrape method. The base of the pot is formed in and supported by a mold, sometimes the base of an old pot, a basket bottom, or, more recently, a plate. The potter also uses the base mold to rotate the pot as she builds the walls. The walls are formed of ropes, or coils, of clay. The coils are pinched and smoothed together to form a solid bond. Potters use scraping tools—a piece of gourd, stone, or a tin can lid—to smooth the surface, thin the walls, and refine the shape. After the vessel has dried, the surface is sanded to a finer finish with sandstone or commercial sandpaper.

Surface Treatments

The painted designs at Cochiti and Santo Domingo can be Black-on-cream, Black-and-red on cream, Black-on-red, or Polychrome. Prior to painting, the surface of a pot is coated with a watery suspension of very fine clay called slip. Up to ten coats of slip are applied to cover the coarser clay body. The final coat is rag-polished, or smoothed, to create a cream-colored "canvas" which absorbs and binds the paint pigments. (The unique properties of Cochiti/Santo Domingo slip, a bentonite clay, play a crucial role in retention of carbon-based (black) paint during firing, and thus the production of a strong black color. Potters using organic, or carbon-based, paints all prefer Cochiti/Santo Domingo slip.) The pigments, interacting with the slip, adhere to the surface and achieve their color during firing. Paint pigments are still applied with brushes made of narrow yucca leaves; one end of the leaf is scraped or chewed to separate the fibers. Trimming the fibers can create a variety of tip

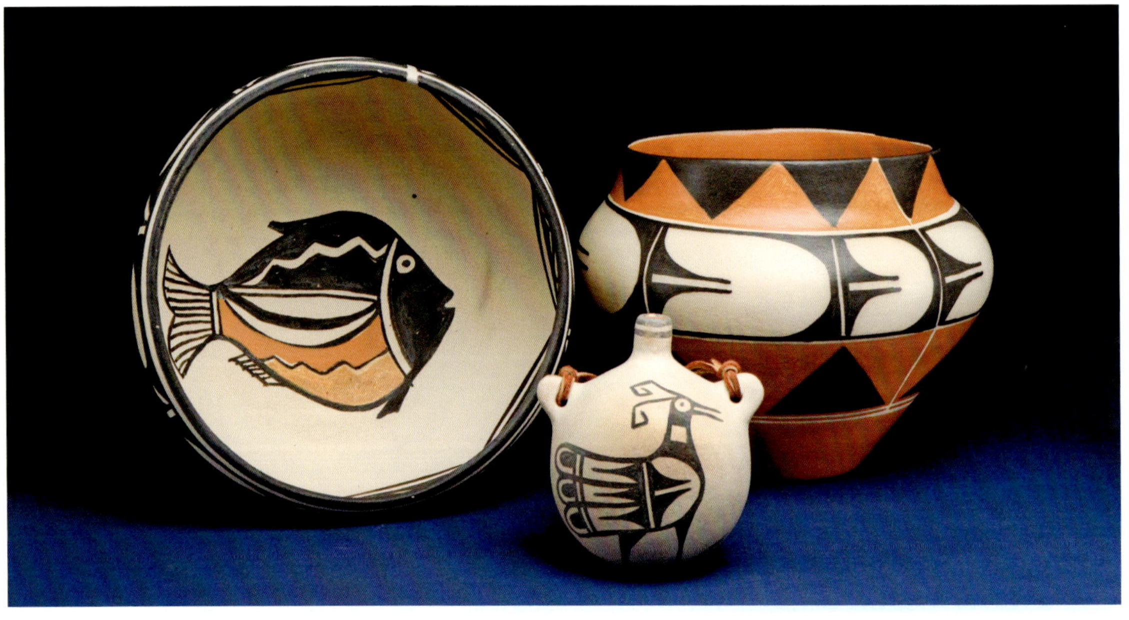

figure 123
Pots from firing at Santo Domingo, June 14, 2007.
Bowl, Robert Tenorio; Canteen, Warren Coriz; Jar, Ione Coriz
14.4 x 29.3 cm; 21.8 x 29 cm; 15.5 x 14 cm

sizes and shapes. Commercial brushes also are used.

Cochiti and Santo Domingo potters make their black paint from Rocky Mountain beeplant, which they call wild spinach. The spinach is boiled down to a gummy mass referred to as *guaco*. The *guaco* can be dried and stored in blocks until needed, at which time it is diluted with water to create the carbon paint. The production of carbon-paint color in an oxidizing atmosphere occurs because of its adsorption into the clay slip. If the paint solution is too thick, the carbon paint won't penetrate and will be burned out; if the solution is too thin, the carbon paint will produce a light gray. The temperature, duration of firing, and firing atmosphere also are crucial to the formation of the desired deep black color. There is some oxygen in all firing to enable fuel combustion, so the absorptive clay slip is essential to retain the carbon paint color through the firing process. Orange to red pigment is obtained from minerals, typically iron, manganese, or a combination of the two. Iron oxide paint is prepared by grinding the minerals to a fine texture, mixing with water, applying the paint to the surface, and polishing before firing .

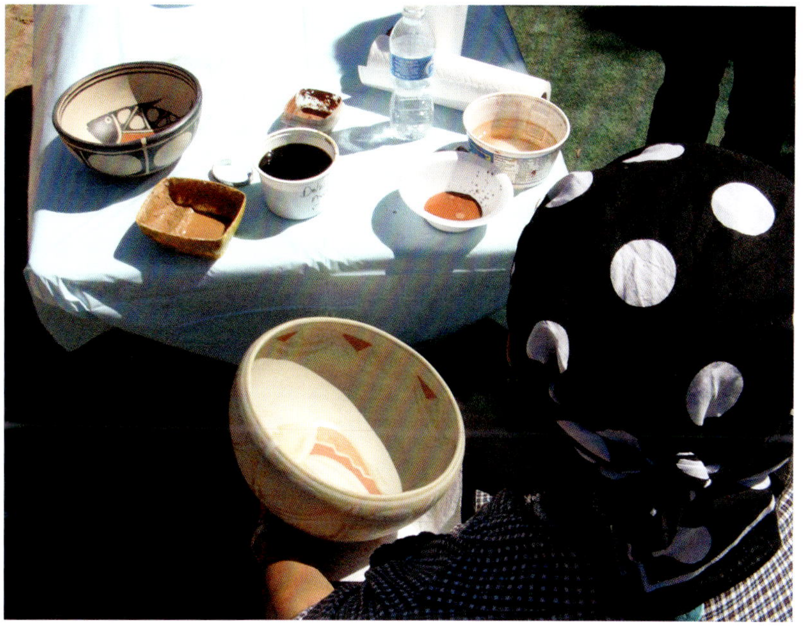

Robert Tenorio and his paints, 2007. An absorbent "canvas" for the painted design is created using a slip of local white bentonite clay. The paints include those made from minerals and vegetal matter. Antonio Chavarria, photographer.

Firing

Pots drying out in the sun still may be seen at the pueblos, although many potters oven dry their pots at a low temperature. Pots must be completely dry before firing, or collected steam in the vessel wall will cause surface blowouts. Dry pots are fired in open air "kilns." Bedsprings, scraps of sheet iron, metal milk cartons, and other recycled metal materials form grates to support, cover, and protect the pots. Fuel is piled around the kiln. Split cedar logs are the preferred fuel, sometimes in combination with cow dung. However, individual potters may go against the norm if something works particularly well for them: Cochiti potter Elizabeth Trujillo says she uses cow dung alone to fire her pots.

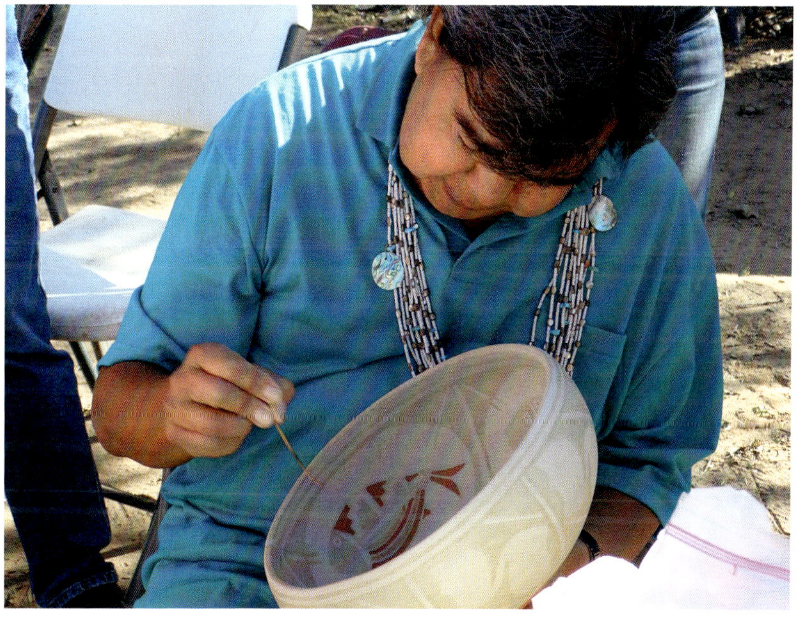

Robert Tenorio painting a pot with a yucca brush, 2007. Although manufactured brushes are part of his tool kit, Tenorio still uses a yucca brush—constructed by chewing or stripping the end of a yucca leaf to free its fibers—to paint aspects of his designs. Antonio Chavarria, photographer.

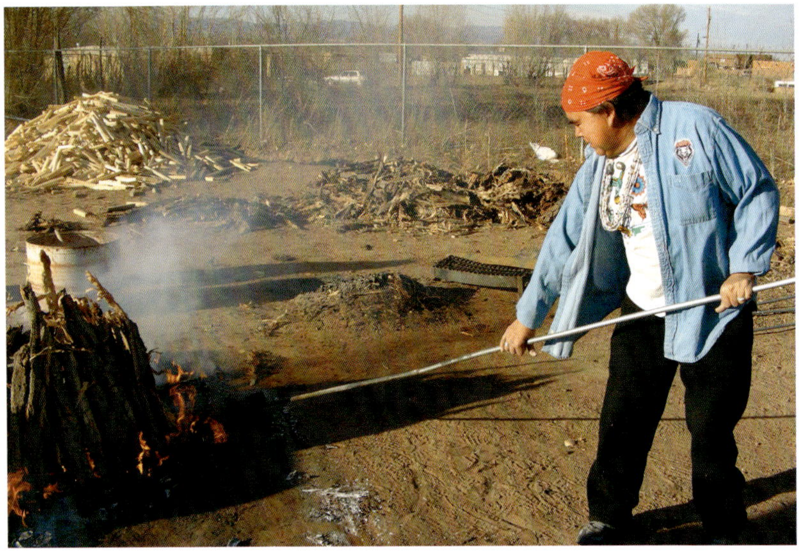

Robert Tenorio tending the kiln, 2007. This is a traditional firing in that it is outside in an open fire, or kiln, created by piling the fuel around and over the pots and igniting it. The metal grills and crates protect the pot surfaces from imperfections caused by direct contact with the fuel. In every firing there is always the chance that imperfections in the clay or air bubbles may cause a pot to explode in the fire, damaging or destroying adjacent pots. Antonio Chavarria, photographer.

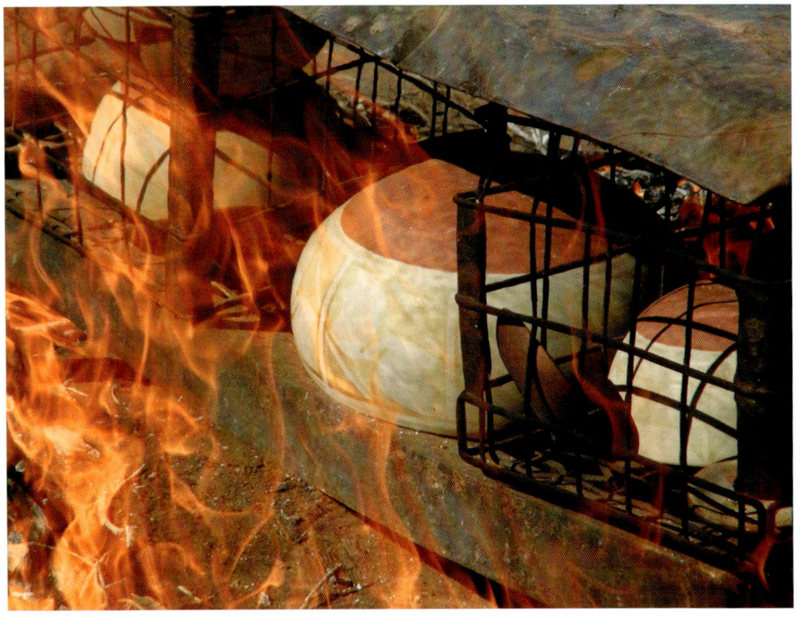

In the fire. Translucent carbon paint chars black in the kiln, 2007. Boiling the leaves and stems of certain plants, usually Rocky Mountain beeplant, produces the black paint. Antonio Chavarria, photographer.

Commercial Materials

As is true with all other contemporary ceramic artists, it is the decision of individual potters alone as to the materials they incorporate into their pottery. Using traditional clays and processes requires a sensuous involvement that culminates in an artistic expression they believe cannot be duplicated with other methods. And, practically, traditional and non-traditional materials and techniques do not mix successfully. Innovations in Pueblo pottery, which extend to the use of commercial materials and techniques, are influenced by three factors: the desire of present-day artists to use modern materials to express contemporary concerns; the desire of collectors and dealers in a competitive pottery market for "perfect" pots; and daily realities of potters who support themselves and their families with their art.

The use of commercial materials exists on a continuum from post-firing touch-ups, through subtle replacement of traditional slips and paints with commercial equivalents, to unabashed use of commercial clays, paints, and glazes. Modern ceramic materials include underglazes that can be painted on greenware (unfired vessels) and burnished, and fired, as well as post-firing ceramic paints, and mica. Recently many potters have begun to use commercial kilns at both pueblos. The irony here is that while a primary impetus for the move to commercial clays, paints, and kiln use is the demand for "perfect" pots, the most valuable and sought after ones are those perfect pots made with traditional materials and techniques. Nevertheless, because most potters still live at the pueblos and remain intimately connected to the seasonal rhythms of the yearly social and religious cycle, to the land that has provided pottery's raw materials for centuries, and to the generations of teachers and students before them, today Pueblo pottery continues to be predominantly hand built of and painted with traditional materials.

Glossary

Appliqué. A decorative method consisting of applying a raised element to the leather-hard clay pot surface.

Bentonite. An absorptive clay formed from airborne volcanic ash. Used as slip at Cochiti and Santo Domingo.

Black-on-Black. A decorative technique in which the designs are described by matte black paint on a polished black background.

Blackware. A surface finish created in an open firing which is smothered with manure and/or sawdust at maximum temperature and then buried in sand, dirt, or ash to trap smoke, causing wares to turn black.

Burnishing, or Stone Polishing. A finishing technique consisting of rubbing a leather-hard clay pot with a tool, typically a smooth stone, to produce a glossy surface. Burnished surfaces can be identified by an irregular luster and visible polishing marks.

Carbon Paint. A black-firing pigment made by boiling the leaves and stems of certain plants to a thick brown juice. The paint soaks into the surface and chars to a black color when the pot is fired. Usually made from Rocky Mountain beeplant at Cochiti and Santo Domingo.

Clay. A mineral substance of very fine texture which becomes plastic when wet, and hard and relatively immune to softening when fired. Clay may be used for the body of a pot, for diluting to cover the surface as slip, or as a decorative paint.

Cochiti Slip. Also called Domingo slip. A fine clay that is applied with a rag or piece of leather and polished by rubbing with a cloth or the palm of the hand. Used at Cochiti and Santo Domingo, and since about 1907 exported to nearby Tewa pueblos. This slip is characterized by the ability to absorb the carbon paint used at both Cochiti and Santo Domingo.

Coil and Scrape. A hand-building technique using long ropes of clay to build up pot walls. The coils are joined by scraping and smoothing the internal and external surfaces. The traditional method of ceramic manufacture at Cochiti and Santo Domingo.

Figure-Ground. The fundamental design relationship between foreground imagery and background or surrounding area. In Cochiti and more significantly Santo Domingo painted-pottery designs, the foreground shapes divide the background, creating additional important shapes.

Fire Cloud. A darkened area on the pot surface. Fire clouds are caused by carbon deposits. They frequently occur in open firings when the smoky part of the flame or an incompletely burned piece of fuel comes into contact with the pot surface.

Firing. A heating process by which clay is converted to ceramic by driving off chemically combined water from the clay molecules in a temperature in excess of 550° C. At Cochiti and Santo Domingo traditional firing is outside in the open, with fuel—either wood or dung—piled around and over the pots and set on fire.

Framing Line. A line tracing the circumference of a pot and delineating a design area.

Glaze. A finely powdered mineral substance painted on the surface of a vessel. Composed of silica, flues, and metallic oxides, glaze melts smooth and bonds to the clay surface when fired at a high temperature. Used by Cochiti and Santo Domingo potters for the design element on Kotyiti Glazeware, 1625–1700.

Guaco. A carbon paint made from the boiled residue of the Rocky Mountain beeplant.

Iron Oxides. The source of the color of most clays, they most commonly contain ferric oxide (hematite), ferrous oxide, or magnetite. If firing is carried out under an oxidizing atmosphere, the pot will be yellow, red, or brown; if fired in a reducing atmosphere, the pot will be dark brown, black, or gray.

Keresan Polychrome. Keresan is used to designate pottery made in the 1760–1900 period by Cochiti and Santo Domingo potters, which, not inconsequentially, is often difficult if not impossible to distinguish from Tewa-made pottery of the same era. This pottery is united by the commonalities created by functional roles in the storage and preparation of wheat and wheat-based foods. There are in addition similarities in design iconography and shape. Frank and Harlow (1974) labeled this style of pottery Kiua; Bruce Bernstein developed the term Keresan Polychrome here to incorporate ground-breaking work while pushing the cultural and contextual considerations further.

Kiln. An oven capable of producing a high, controlled heat for firing pottery. Contemporary Cochiti and Santo Domingo potters may use kilns to produce high-finish wares.

Kotyiti Glazeware. Kotyiti Glazewares are found throughout the northern and middle Rio Grande and date between ca. 1625 and 1700. It is generally accepted that prior to 1700 Kotyiti Glazeware was the traditional pottery of Cochiti and Santo Domingo. The glaze is a mineral paint that solidifies during firing to a shiny, vitreous surface glaze. (In the American Southwest, glaze was not used to waterproof, as is common in other ceramic traditions, but for design lines alone.)

Leather Hard. Clay that has dried to the point that it has lost most of its plasticity and is firm but not dry. Most surface treatments, such as slipping and painting, are applied in the leather-hard stage, as the clay is moist enough for alteration.

Line Break, or Ceremonial Break. A gap in a design or framing line painted around the circumference of a pot.

Mineral Paint. A paint for decorating pottery made of a powdered mineral substance, such as iron oxide, mixed with water. Mineral paint may contain a binder of carbonaceous material.

Negative Design. A secondary design created when a solid color covers all of a space except for selected areas of the lighter background.

Open Firing. A method of firing vessels without a kiln, the most common methods are bonfires or pits. Open-fired pots usually can be recognized by the blotched, multicolored appearance of the surface, or the presence of fire clouds.

Oxidizing Atmosphere, or Oxidized Fire. An oxygen-rich firing atmosphere under which iron oxides present in clay will give a white, buff, orange or red color, depending on the amount and combination of clay impurities, of which iron compounds are the most significant.

Paste. The mixture of clay and temper that forms the structure of the pot.

Plasticity. A quality of clay that allows it to be molded and maintain a shape.

Polishing. The surface finish achieved by stone stroking, or rubbing with fabric or leather, prior to firing while the paste surface is leather hard to produce a uniform and glossy surface.

Polychrome. A surface decorative style that uses three or more colors (usually black, red, and white) to form the two-dimensional design.

Powhoge Polychrome. Powhoge Polychrome was the primary painted-pottery type produced during the late eighteenth, early nineteenth century by Tewa Pueblo potters north of Santa Fe. Although very little material cultural data exists related to pottery production in the middle Rio Grande region between 1700 and 1880, archaeologists do know that at this time both Cochiti and Santo Domingo pueblos discontinued the use of iron-oxide pigments and the production of glazewares and began their carbon-paint tradition—Keresan Polychrome. This style is almost identical to the tradition of their northern Tewa neighbors, Santa Clara, San Ildefonso, and Tesuque—Powhoge Polychrome.

***Puki*.** A container used to form the base of a pot. It is also used to rotate the pot while building up the walls.

Rag Polished, or Rag Wiped. A method of finishing a slipped pot surface with a piece of cloth rather than a polishing stone.

Reducing Atmosphere, or Reduction Fire. An oxygen-poor firing atmosphere. Iron oxides in the clay are not fully oxidized and give a dark color—brown, gray, or black.

Slip. A liquid mixture of clay and water applied to the pot surface when it is in the leather-hard stage to alter color and texture. Slips are only minimally absorbed by the clay body and are distinguishable as a separate layer on the surface. At Cochiti and Santo Domingo the white bentonite slip creates a surface for adherence and carbonization of the carbon paint used in the design elements.

Spinach Paint. Traditional name for the black carbon paint made from boiling the Rocky Mountain beeplant. (See Carbon Paint.)

Stone Polishing. See Burnishing.

Temper. An inert substance mixed with clay to strengthen the wet clay and prevent the walls from collapsing, facilitate drying by allowing water to evaporate more easily, and reduce drying shrinkage. Open-fired pottery temper allows residual water to escape the pot body in the form of steam during the early stages of firing. At Cochiti and Santo Domingo the typical temper is volcanic ash, or pumice.

Type. A classification given to a group of pottery wares based on similar characteristics.

Use Wear. Traces on pots formed as a result of use. Common examples of use wear on Cochiti and Santo Domingo pottery are oil deposits on dough bowls, rim chips on storage and water jars, and salt deposits on water jars.

Volcanic Ash, or Pumice. Fine volcanic particulate expelled from surface vents in a volcanic eruption. Volcanic ash is the temper added to clay by potters at Cochiti and Santo Domingo. Volcanic ash is only suitable for low-fired pots.

Ware. Class of pottery characterized by similar technology, material, and surface treatment.

Time Line of Events in the Southwest

Valerie K. Verzuh

Historic Period 1540–1879

1540 Francisco Vásquez de Coronado arrives at Hawikuh (Zuni), with Spanish soldiers and colonizers. Coronado's expedition is precipitated by the discovery of Hawikuh, a Zuni village, by a Spanish exploratory party in 1539. Friar Marcos de Niza observes the village from a distance and returns to Mexico to declare the discovery of the legendary cities of gold, the "Seven Cities of Cibola." The romantization of the American Southwest begins.

1598 Juan de Oñate takes formal possession of New Mexico for the Spanish Crown. Pueblo leaders meet with the Spanish at Santo Domingo and give Oñate's colonists permission to settle. Pueblo country is divided into *alcaldias*, or districts, and Franciscan missionaries are assigned to each.

1610 La Villa Real de Santa Fe de San Francisco de Assisi (Santa Fe) is established and the Palace of the Governors constructed.

1620 By royal decree of the king of Spain, each pueblo is required to institute a secular governing body, including a governor, lieutenant governor, and other officials. Silver-headed canes are given to each governor as a symbol of his office. The Spanish require the Pueblos to accept the Roman Catholic Church. This marks the beginning of two social systems which oppress the pueblos: *encomiendo,* in which the Spanish collect tribute and taxes in return for maintaining order through an established military and providing instruction in Catholicism; and *repartimiento*, a system of forced labor.

1680 The Pueblo Revolt is successful in driving an estimated 2,500 Spanish colonists in New Mexico back into Mexico. The conquering Pueblos attack Santa Fe and burn most of the buildings, except the Palace of the Governors. Pueblo Indians occupy Santa Fe until 1692.

1692 Diego de Vargas leads the reconquest of New

Mexico. Some pueblos, including the Keresans, resist Spanish resettlement.

1780–1781 An epidemic of smallpox, brought by the Spanish, kills as many as five thousand Puebloans.

1821 Mexico becomes independent of Spain, and New Mexico becomes a province of Mexico. All Indians in the region are declared citizens of Mexico.

1822 Trade is established with the United States, and the Santa Fe Trail is opened.

1824 The United States establishes the Bureau of Indian Affairs as part of the Department of War.

1846 War is declared between the United States and Mexico. The Treaty of Guadalupe Hidalgo ends the war (1848), and New Mexico becomes a territory of the United States.

1849 The Bureau of Indian affairs becomes part of the Department of the Interior. James S. Calhoun is appointed as New Mexico's first Indian agent. Calhoun becomes governor of the Territory in 1851.

1859 The Historical Society of New Mexico is founded.

1879 The Smithsonian Institution's first collecting expedition to the pueblos. Other major museums follow. Tens of thousands of artifacts exported to eastern and European museums.

Modern Period 1880–1950

1880 The railroad comes to New Mexico bypassing Santa Fe, the territorial capital, for Albuquerque. A branch to Santa Fe is completed in February 1880. The railroads link the Southwest and the West to the East, bringing an influx of tourists and transforming the crafts of southwestern Native peoples into a marketable commodity. Original Jake Gold Curio store, later renamed the Original Old Curio Store, opens its doors.

1884 The New Mexico Territorial government approves the use of two rooms in the Palace of the Governors for exhibiting the collections of the New Mexico Historical Society.

1887 The General Allotment Act (also known as the Dawes Act or the Dawes Severalty Act) authorizes the United States to survey tribal lands and divide the areas into allotments for individual Native American families. The intention of the act, with its emphasis on individual land ownership, is to have a negative impact on the unity, self-government, and culture of the tribes. By breaking up reservation lands into privately owned parcels, legislators hope to force Indian assimilation by disrupting the communal lifestyle of Indian societies and impose Western-oriented values.

1890 Santa Fe Indian School is founded.

1907 The Archaeological Institute of America, a private association for the promotion of archaeological studies, establishes its School of American Archaeology in Santa Fe. Edgar Lee Hewett is appointed director. In 1917, it is reorganized as the School of American Research and, in 2007, as the School for Advanced Research.

1909 The Museum of New Mexico is established and housed in the Palace of the Governors. The Territorial Legislature places its administration under the School of American Archaeology.

1912 New Mexico is admitted to the Union as the 47th state.

1919 Edgar Lee Hewett revives Santa Fe Fiesta as an annual event to promote Santa Fe as a tourist destination.

1922 The first recorded meeting of the All Indian

Pueblo Council is held at Santo Domingo. The exact age of the council is unknown, but it is recognized as an ancient political body. Its mission is stated as follows: To foster the social and economic advancement of all the Pueblo Indians, and to preserve and protect our common interest.

1922 Indian Fair is created by Edgar Lee Hewett and the Museum of New Mexico as part of the Santa Fe Fiesta. It continues sponsorship until 1936. From 1923 to 1926, the fair remains part of fiesta.

1922 The New Mexico Association on Indian Affairs (NMAIA) is founded to fight the U.S. Senate's proposed Bursum Bill, which would give Pueblo land to Spanish and American settlers.

1922 The Pueblo Pottery Fund is founded by Wesley Bradfield, Kenneth Chapman, Harry P. Mera, and Elizabeth Sergeant. In 1925, it is reorganized as the Indian Arts Fund, Inc. (IAF).

1924 An Act of Congress declares all Indians citizens of the United States and eligible to vote. Only New Mexico and Arizona fail to approve legislation to grant Indians voting rights.

1927 The Laboratory of Anthropology is organized as a private corporation and Jesse Nusbaum appointed director; Kenneth Chapman and Harry P. Mera are appointed curators. The Indian Arts Fund collections become the base upon which the Lab's collections are built.

1927 An independent Southwest Indian Fair committee takes over the management of the Indian Fair from the Museum of New Mexico. The last Santa Fe Indian Fair is held in 1931. From 1932 to 1935 they are held during Feast Day celebrations at the pueblos.

1934 The Indian Reorganization Act passed by congress reaffirms the right of Indians to govern themselves. Tribal sovereignty—guaranteed by the U.S. Constitution—is the inherent authority of indigenous tribes to self-government. Typically, treaties between tribes and the United States guarantee sovereignty, homeland, and the provision of social services, including health care and education, in exchange for the ceding of traditional lands.

1934 The New Mexico Association on Indian Affairs absorbs the Indian Fair committee, and the fairs return to Santa Fe Fiesta until 1962.

1944 The National Congress of American Indians is formed to mobilize tribes into effective political action.

1947 The Laboratory of Anthropology and the Museum of New Mexico merge.

1948 Indians in New Mexico and Arizona are granted the right to vote.

Contemporary Period 1950–Present

1952 The Relocation Program is established by the Bureau of Indian Affairs. Indians are encouraged to leave their reservations and move to cities. They are offered adult education, vocational training, and city jobs as incentives.

1962 Santa Fe Indian Market is moved to the weekend prior to Santa Fe Fiesta, marking the birth of the modern market.

1962 The Institute of American Indian Arts (IAIA) is established in Santa Fe.

1972 The Indian Arts Fund (IAF) is disbanded and its collections given to the School of American Research.

1973 The first annual Eight Northern Pueblos Annual Arts & Crafts Show is held.

1975 The first annual Santo Domingo Pueblo Crafts Show is held.

1975 The Indian Pueblo Cultural Center of Albuquerque opens. The center is a program of the All Indian Pueblo Council and owned and operated by the Pueblo Indians of New Mexico.

1987 The Museum of Indian Arts & Culture opens as the Laboratory of Anthropology's exhibit venue. The two institutions become the Museum of Indian Arts & Culture/Laboratory of Anthropology (MIAC/LAB).

1990 The Native American Graves Protection and Repatriation Act (NAGPRA) is passed by the U.S. Congress and takes effect the following year. This act establishes a congressional policy for the return to tribes of aboriginal human remains, associated funerary objects, and items of cultural significance.

Credits

(frontis)
Gift of the Fred Harvey Company
55892

(fig. 1)
Museum Purchase, Sallie Lippencott
25005

(fig. 2)
Kenneth M. Chapman Collection
7786

(fig. 3)
Rick Dillingham Collection
54266

(fig. 4)
Gift of Mrs. John Veeder
11087

(fig. 5)
Museum Collection
12251

(fig. 6)
Gift of Jane Baumann
47943

(fig. 7)
Gift of Mrs. Julius Gans
35772

(fig. 8)
Gift of Francis H. and Patricia N. Harlow
56208

(fig. 9)
Museum Purchase, Diego Romero
54131

(fig. 10)
Museum Purchase, Richard Howard
53628

(fig. 11)
Museum Purchase, Richard Howard
53627

(fig. 12)
Gift of Wesley Bradfield
12266

(fig. 13)
Gift of Wesley Bradfield
12401

(fig. 14)
Rick Dillingham Collection
54264

(fig. 15)
Nelson Collection
18812

(fig. 16)
Museum Purchase, Robert Tenorio
47652

(fig. 17)
Rick Dillingham Collection
54323

(fig. 18)
Museum Collection
50060

(fig. 19)
Gift of Daniel H. McMillan
8114

(fig. 20)
Museum Purchase,
Eleanor Bedell
45138

(fig. 21)
Gift of Lydia J. Trowbridge
18928

(fig. 22)
Gift of the Fred Harvey Company
53899

(fig. 23)
Gift of Sallie Lippencott
25004

(fig. 24)
Edgar L. Hewett Collection
11086

(fig. 25)
Gift of Judith M. Liersch and Al Jennings
56545

(fig. 26)
John B. Elliott Collection
55961

(fig. 27)
Gift of Jane Baumann
47934

(fig. 28)
Gift of Mrs. Julius Gans
35771

(fig. 29)
Gift of Mrs. Wesley Bradfield
12254

(fig. 30)
Gift of Juan Olivas
12265

(fig. 31)
Museum Purchase, Mrs. E. L. Hutcheson
19075

(fig. 32)
Museum Purchase, Aurelia Suina and Gift of Gilbert Hitchcock
47653; 54152

(fig. 33)
Gift of Mark and Martha Alexander
54672

(fig. 34)
Rick Dillingham Collection
54269

(fig. 35)
Museum Purchase, Spanish and Indian Trading Company
7873

(fig. 36)
57252

(fig. 37)
Gift of Tony Abeyta
54797

(fig. 38)
Pansy Stockton and Julia K. Shishkin Bequests
46222; 49706
Mary Boyce Collection
25722; 25723; 25724

(fig. 39)
Rick Dillingham Collection
54257

(fig. 40)
Gift of Bernalillo Mercantile Company
7838

(fig. 41)
Rick Dillingham Collection
54325

(fig. 42)
Rick Dillingham Collection
54329

(fig. 43)
Gift of Byron Harvey III
35755

(fig. 44)
Museum Purchase,
Ernest Seligman
7885

(fig. 45)
Gift of the Indian Fair Committee, Courtesy of John and Linda Comstock and the Abigail Van Vleck Charitable Trust
7730

(fig. 46)
Gift of Henry Dendahl
18901

(fig. 47)
Rick Dillingham Collection
54247

(fig. 48)
Rick Dillingham Collection
54254

(fig. 49)
Gift of the Robert Nichols Gallery
55266

(fig. 50)
Rick Dillingham Collection
54268

(fig. 51)
Gift of Henry Dendahl
19139

(fig. 52)
Museum Collection
12250

(fig. 53)
Museum Collection
11101

(fig. 54)
Gift of Mrs. Crawford R. Buell and the Rick Dillingham Collection
47660; 54324

(fig. 55)
Gift of the Historical Society of New Mexico
12179

(fig. 56)
Museum Purchase, Estefanita Herrera
19187

(fig. 57)
Rick Dillingham Collection
54261

(fig. 58)
Rick Dillingham Collection
54265

(fig. 59)
Rick Dillingham Collection
54332

(fig. 60)
Gift of Francis H. and Patricia N. Harlow
55891

(fig. 61)
Gift of Jane Baumann
47941

(fig. 62)
Gift of Pat Lange and Museum Purchase
56613; 670

(fig. 63)
Rick Dillingham Collection
54256

(fig. 64)
Gift of Francis H. and Patricia N. Harlow
55883

(fig. 65)
Field Collection, Edgar L. Hewett
21211

(fig. 66)
Gift of Francis H. and Patricia N. Harlow
55757

(fig. 67)
Field Collection, Stanley A. Stubbs
44731

(fig. 68)
Museum Purchase, Rogers and Schafer, Albuquerque
11119

(fig. 69)
Gift of the Historical Society of New Mexico
12259

(fig. 70)
Peltz Collection
11229

(fig. 71)
Museum Collection
12220

(fig. 72)
Museum Purchase, Native Treasures Art Festival
57254

(fig. 73)
Gift of the Historical Society of New Mexico and Gift of Jane Baumann
12174; 47938

(fig. 74)
Gift of Mrs. Adelheit Keplinger
44857

(fig. 75)
Museum Collection
41805

(fig.76)
Museum Collection
11105

(fig. 77)
Kenneth M. Chapman Collection
7794

(fig. 78)
Gift of the Historical Society of New Mexico
18696

(fig. 79)
Purchase, Spanish and Indian Trading Company
8551

(fig. 80)
Rick Dillingham Collection
54278

(fig. 81)
Gift of Francis H. and Patricia N. Harlow
55767

(fig. 82)
Gift of the Fred Harvey Company
12258

fig. 83)
Gift of the Fred Harvey Company
53852

(fig. 84)
Gift of Francis H. and Patricia N. Harlow
55864

(fig. 85)
Gift of Mrs. John W. Chapman
7931

(fig. 86)
Gift of Alice Patricia Insley
56606

(fig. 87)
Nelson Collection
12397

(fig. 88)
Museum Collection
19178

(fig. 89)
Gift of Jane Baumann
47933

(fig. 90)
Gift of Jane Baumann
47935

(fig. 91)
Gift of Jane Baumann
47936

(fig. 92)
Museum Purchase, Rogers and Schafer, Albuquerque
11100

(fig. 93)
Museum Purchase, Rogers and Schafer
11107

(fig. 94)
Gift of Bruce Cooper
11098

(fig. 95)
Museum Purchase, Marie Sanchez
19322

(fig. 96)
Gift of I. W. Schormoyer
12269

(fig. 97)
Gift of the Robert Nichols Gallery
55264

(fig. 98)
Gift of Ernest N. Stanton
8030

(fig. 99)
Gift of the Historical Society of New Mexico
11238

(fig. 100)
Gift of the Historical Society of New Mexico
18730

(fig. 101)
Gift of the Charleston Museum
54059

(fig. 102)
Bandelier Collection
12267

(fig. 103)
Gift of Byron Harvey III
19332

(fig. 104)
Amelia E. White Collection
51637

(fig. 105)
Gift of the Historical Society of New Mexico
673

(fig. 106)
Gift of the Charleston Museum
54060

(fig. 107)
Gift of Kate Marinoff
45920

(fig. 108)
Pansy Stockton Collection
46178

(fig. 109)
Gift of John Kania
53253

(fig. 110)
Kenneth M. Chapman
Collection
7812

(fig. 111)
Museum Purchase, Joe Moya
19181

(fig. 112)
Museum Purchase
55401

(fig. 113)
Museum Purchase,
Twichell Estate
11118

(fig. 114)
Gift of Ann Higham
49541

(fig. 115)
Gift of A. E. White
36380

(fig. 116)
Gift of Henry Dendahl
19140

(fig. 117)
Museum Purchase, Tony Aguilar
22623

(fig. 118)
Gift of Juan Olivas
12253

(fig. 119)
Museum Purchase,
Petra G. Garcia
51651

(fig. 120)
Gift of Francis H. and Patricia
N. Harlow
55963

(fig. 121)
Museum Purchase, Friends of
Indian Art
57317

(fig. 122)
Gift of the Robert Nichols
Gallery
55281

(fig. 123)
Museum Purchase
57336, 57335, 57334

References

Introduction: A River Apart
Valerie K. Verzuh

Colwell-Chanthaphonh, Chip, and T. J. Ferguson
2006 Memory Pieces and Footprints: Multivocality and the Meanings of Ancient Times and Ancestral Places among the Zuni and Hopi. *American Anthropologist* 108(1): 148–162.

Crapanzano, Vincent
1992 *Hermes' Dilemma and Hamlet's Desire: On the Epistemology of Interpretation*. Cambridge, MA: Harvard University Press.

D'Andrade, Roy
1995 Moral Models in Anthropology. In *Current Anthropology*, 36(3): 399–407.

Foucault, Michel
1970 *The Order of Things: An Archaeology of the Human Sciences*. New York: Pantheon.

Lyotard, Jean-Francois
1984 *The Postmodern Condition: A Report on Knowledge*. Manchester, England: Manchester University Press.
1992 *The Postmodern Explained*. Sydney: Power Publications.

Spiro, Melford E.
1996 Cultural Relativism and the Future of Anthropology. In George E. Marcus, ed., *Rereading Cultural Anthropology*. Durham NC: Duke University Press.

Artist Unknown:
The Significance of Signatures on Pueblo Pottery
Chip Colwell-Chanthaphonh

Basalla, George
1982 Transformed Utilitarian Objects. *Winterthur Portfolio* 17(4):183–201.

Batkin, Jonathan
1998 Some Early Curio Dealers of New Mexico. *American Indian Art Magazine* 23(3):69–81.

Bernstein, Bruce
1993 From Indian Fair to Indian Market. *El Palacio* 98(3):14–18, 47–54.

1994a Potters and Patrons: The Creation of Pueblo Art Pottery. *American Indian Art Magazine* 20(1):70–79.

1994b Pueblo Potters, Museum Curators, and Santa Fe's Indian Market. *Expedition* 36(1):14–23.

Blocker, Gene H.
1994 *The Aesthetics of Primitive Art*. Lanham, MD: University Press of America.

Brody, J. J.
1971 *Indian Painters and White Patrons*. Albuquerque, NM: University of New Mexico Press.

Brovarney, Dot, Susan Billy, and Suzanne Abel-Vidor
1996 *Remember Your Relations: Elsie Allen Baskets, Family, and Friends*. Berkeley, CA: Heyday Books.

Brown, Michael F.
2003 *Who Owns Native Culture?* Cambridge, MA: Harvard University Press.

Bunzel, Ruth L.
1929 *The Pueblo Potter: A Study of Creative Imagination in Primitive Art*. New York: Dover Publications.

Cohen, Beth
1991 The Literate Potter: A Tradition of Incised Signatures on Attic Vases. *Metropolitan Museum Journal* 26: 49–95.

Errington, Shelly
1998 *The Death of Authentic Primitive Art and Other Tales of Progress*. Berkeley, CA: University of California Press.

Fox, Nancy
1976 Poveka, Signature of Maria Martinez. In *Collected Papers in Honor of the Archaeological Society of New Mexico*, ed. Albert H. Schroeder, 259–264. Albuquerque, NM: Albuquerque Archaeological Society Press.

Frisbie, T. R.
1973 The Influence of J. Walter Fewkes on Nampeyo: Fact or Fancy. In *The Changing Ways of Southwestern Indians*, ed. Albert H. Schroeder. Glorieta, NM: Rio Grande Press.

Haus, Mary
2004 Sign Here! *Art News* 103(7):162–166.

Hoerig, Karl A.
2003 *Under the Palace Portal: Native American Artists in Santa Fe*. Albuquerque, NM: University of New Mexico Press.

Matthew, Louisa C.
1998 The Painter's Presence: Signatures in Venetian Renaissance Pictures. *Art Bulletin* 80(4):616–648.

McChesney, Lea S.
1994 Producing "Generations in Clay": Kinship, Markets, and Hopi Pottery. *Expedition* 36(1):5–13.

Naranjo, Tessie
1994 Pottery Making in a Changing World. *Expedition* 36(1):44–50.

Naranjo-Morse, Nora
1992 *Mud Woman: Poems from the Clay*. Tucson: University of Arizona Press.

Nequatewa, Edmund
1943 Nampeyo, Famous Hopi Potter (1859–1942). *Plateau* 15(3):88–90.

Nicholas, George P., and Kelly P. Bannister
2004 Copyrighting the Past? Emerging Intellectual Property Rights Issues in Archaeology. *Current Anthropology* 45(3):327–350.

Peterson, Susan
1977 *The Living Tradition of Maria Martinez*. Tokyo: Kodaansha International.

Price, Sally
1989 *Primitive Art in Civilized Places*. Chicago: University of Chicago Press.

Rubin, Patricia
2006 Signposts of Invention: Artists' Signatures in Italian Renaissance art. *Art History* 29(4):563–599.

Spivey, Richard L.
2003 *The Legacy of Maria Poveka Martinez*. Santa Fe, NM: Museum of New Mexico Press.

Wang, Aileen June
2004 Michelangelo's Signature. *Sixteenth Century Journal* 35(2):447–473.

Wilmerding, John
2003 *Signs of the Artist: Signatures and Self-Expression in American Paintings*. New Haven, CN: Yale University Press.

Zavrel, B. John
2006 Salvador Dalí Signature in Art. *Prometheus* 112(October):
www.meaus.com/112-dali-signatures.htm.

Looking into the Bowl: Part I Artists and Outsiders
Bruce Bernstein

Batkin, Jonathan
1987 *Pottery of the Pueblos of New Mexico, 1700 – 1940*. Colorado Springs, CO: The Taylor Museum of the Colorado Springs Fine Arts Center.

1998 Some Early Curio Dealers of New Mexico. *American Indian Art Magazine* 23(3): 69–81.

Batkin, Jonathan, and Patricia Fogelman Lange
1999 Human Figurines of Cochiti and Tesuque Pueblos, 1870–1920: Inspirations, Markets, and Consumers. In *Clay People: Pueblo Indian Figurative Traditions*, ed. Jonathan Batkin, 41–63. Santa Fe, NM: Wheelwright Museum of the American Indian.

Bernstein, Bruce
1993 Marketing of Culture: Pottery and Santa Fe Indian Market. Ph. D. diss., University of New Mexico.

Chapman, Kenneth
1935 Roadside Shopping. *New Mexico Magazine* 14(6) (June):20-21, 38-39.

1936 The Pottery of Santo Domingo Pueblo: A Detailed Study of Its Decoration. Memoirs of the Laboratory of Anthropology 1.

Eickemeyer, Carl, and Lilian W. Eickemeyer
1895 *Among the Pueblo Indians*. New York: The Merriam Company.

Halseth, Odd S.
1926 The Revival of Pueblo Pottery Making. *El Palacio* 21(6):135 – 154.

Section II epigraph

Babcock, Barbara
1986 *The Pueblo Storyteller: Development of a Figurative Ceramic Tradition*. Tucson: University of Arizona Press.

Benedict, Ruth
1931 Tales of the Cochiti Indians. Washington, DC: Smithsonian Institution Bureau of American Ethnology, Bulletin 98.

Pot Hunters/Pray for Rain
Mateo Romero

Romero, Mateo
2006 *Painting the Underworld Sky: Cultural Expressions and Subversion in Art*. Santa Fe, NM: School of American Research.

The Anomalous Painted Pottery of Santo Domingo and Cochiti Pueblos: A Brief History
J. J. Brody

Batkin, Jonathan
1987 *Pottery of the Pueblos of New Mexico: 1700–1940*. Colorado Springs, CO: The Taylor Museum of the Colorado Springs Fine Arts Center.

Bernstein, Bruce, and J. J. Brody
2001 *Voices in Clay: Pueblo Pottery from the Edna M. Kelly Collection*. Oxford, OH: Miami University Art Museum, Oxford, Ohio.

Crown, Patricia, and Wirt Wills
2003 Modifying Pottery and Kivas at Chaco: Pentimiento, Restoration or Renewal? *American Antiquity* 68:511–532.

Frank, Larry, and Francis H. Harlow
1990 *Historic Pottery of the Pueblo Indians: 1600–1880* (second edition). West Chester, PA: Schiffer Publishing, Ltd.

Harlow, Francis H.
1973 *Matte-Paint Pottery of the Tewa, Keres and Zuni Pueblos*. Santa Fe, NM: Museum of New Mexico Press.

Lange, Charles H.
1959 *Cochiti: A New Mexico Pueblo, Past and Present*. Austin, TX: University of Texas Press.

Powers, Robert P., and Janet D. Orcutt, eds.
1999 The Bandelier Archaeological Survey (vol. II). *Contribution No.9 of the Bandelier Archaeological Survey*, Intermountain Cultural Resources Management, Professional Paper No. 57, National Park Service, Department of the Interior.

Rohn, Arthur H.
1989 *Rock Art of Bandelier National Monument*. Albuquerque: University of New Mexico Press.

Shepard, Anna O.
1956 Ceramics for the Archaeologist. *Carnegie Institution Publication 609*. Washington, D.C.

Stevenson, James
1883 Illustrated Catalogue of the Collections Obtained from the Indians of New Mexico and Arizona in 1879. In *Second Annual Report of the Bureau of American Ethnology to the Secretary of the Smithsonian Institution, 1880–1881*, 307–422.

Washburn, Dorothy Koster
1977 *A Symmetry Analysis of Upper Gila Area Ceramic Design*, 11–22. Cambridge, MA: Harvard University Press.

Zaslow, Bert, and Alfred E. Dittert, Jr.
1977 Pattern Mathematics and Archaeology. *Anthropological Research Papers,* No. 2, Arizona State University, Tempe.

Looking into the Bowl: Part II An Anthropologist's View of Cochiti and Santo Domingo Pottery
Bruce Bernstein

Anonymous
1917 Museum Notes. *El Palacio* 4(1):101.

Bandelier, Adolf F.
1966–1984 *The Southwestern Journals of Adolph F. Bandelier (1880–1892)*. Charles H. Lange, Carroll L. Riley and Elizabeth Lange, eds. Four volumes. Albuquerque: University of New Mexico Press.

Barnett, Franklin
1969 *Tonque Pueblo: A Report of Partial Excavation of an Ancient Pueblo IV Indian Ruin in New Mexico*. Albuquerque, NM: Albuquerque Archaeological Society.

Batkin, Jonathan
1987 *Pottery of the Pueblos of New Mexico, 1700–1940*. Colorado Springs, CO: The Taylor Museum of the Colorado Springs Fine Arts Center.

1991 Introduction in *Style Trends of Pueblo Pottery 1500–1840* by H. P. Mera, 1–4. [1939] Albuquerque, NM: Avanyu Publishing Inc.

1999 Tourism Is Overrated: Pueblo Pottery and the Early Curio Trade, 1880–1910. In *Unpacking Culture: Art and Commodity in Colonial and Postcolonial Worlds*, eds. Ruth Phillips and Christopher Steiner, 282–297. Berkeley: University of California Press.

Batkin, Jonathan, and Patricia Fogelman Lange
1999 Human Figurines of Cochiti and Tesuque Pueblos, 1870–1920: Inspirations, Markets, and Consumers. In *Clay People: Pueblo Indian Figurative Traditions*, ed. Jonathan Batkin, 41–63. Santa Fe, NM: Wheelwright Museum of the American Indian.

Bernstein, Bruce
1994 Potters and Patrons: The Creation of Pueblo Art Pottery. *American Indian Art* 20(1):70–79.

Bourke, John G.
1936–1937 "Bourke on the Southwest," ed. Lansing B. Bloom. *New Mexico Historical Review* vols. 8–13 (1933–1938), *passim.*

Bunzel, Ruth
1929 *The Pueblo Potter: A Study of Creative Imagination in Primitive Art*. New York: Dover Publications.

Capone, Patricia W., and Robert Preucel
2002 Ceramic Semiotics: Women, Pottery, and Social Meanings at Kotyiti Pueblo. In *Archaeologies of the Pueblo Revolt: Identity, Meaning, and Renewal in the Pueblo World*, ed. Robert Preucel, 99–111. Albuquerque: University of New Mexico Press.

Carlson, Roy L.
1965 Eighteenth-Century Navajo Fortresses of the Gobernador District. *University of Colorado Studies, Series in Anthropology No. 10*. Boulder.

1977 Eighteen Century Painted Pottery from the Gobernador District of New Mexico. *American Indian Art* 2(4):38–43.

Carrillo, Charles M.
1997 *Hispanic New Mexican Pottery: Evidence of Craft Specialization 1790–1890*. Albuquerque, NM: LPD Publishing.

Chapman, Kenneth
n.d. Kenneth Chapman Archives. Santa Fe, NM: School for Advanced Research.

1936 The Pottery of Santo Domingo Pueblo: A Detailed Study of Its Decoration. *Memoirs of the Laboratory of Anthropology 1*.

1970 *The Pottery of San Ildefonso Pueblo*: Supplementary Text by Francis H. Harlow. Albuquerque: University of New Mexico Press.

Dauber, Kenneth
1993 Shaping the Clay: Pueblo Pottery, Cultural Sponsorship and Regional Identity in New Mexico. Ph. D. diss., University of Arizona.

Eickemeyer, Carl, and Lilian W. Eickemeyer
1895 *Among the Pueblo Indians*. New York: The Merriam Company.

Ellis, Florence H., and J. J. Brody.
1964 Ceramic Stratigraphy and Tribal History at Taos Pueblo. *American Antiquity* 29(3): 316–327.

Fane, Diana, Ira Jacknis, and Lise M. Breen
1990 *Objects of Myth and Memory: American Indian Art at the Brooklyn Museum*. New York and Seattle: Brooklyn Museum in association with University of Washington Press.

Ferg, Alan
1984 Historic Archaeology on the San Antonio de las Huertas Grant. Sandoval County, New Mexico. CASA Papers 3. Cortez, CO: Complete Archaeological Service Associates.

Frank, Larry, and Francis H. Harlow
1974 *Historic Pottery of the Pueblo Indians, 1600–1880*. Boston, MA: New York Graphic Society.

Frank, Ross
1991 The Changing Pueblo Pottery Tradition: The Underside of Economic Development in Late Colonial New Mexico, 1750–1820. *Journal of the Southwest* 33(3):286–321.

Habicht-Mauche, Judith A., Suzanne L. Eckert, and Deborah L. Huntley, eds.
2006 *The Social Life of Pots: Glaze Wares and Cultural Dynamics in the Southwest, A.D. 1250–1680*. Tucson: University of Arizona Press.

Halseth, Odd S.
1926 The Revival of Pueblo Pottery Making. *El Palacio* 21(6), 135–154.

Hammond, George P., and Agapito Rey, eds.
1966 *The Rediscovery of New Mexico, 1580–1594*. Albuquerque: University of New Mexico Press.

Harlow, Francis H.
1971 *Pueblo Indian Pottery: Painted Jars and Bowls of the Period, 1600–1900*. Santa Fe: Museum of New Mexico Press.

1973 *Matte-Paint Pottery of the Tewa, Keres, and Zuni Pueblos*. Santa Fe: Museum of New Mexico Press.

1990 *Two Hundred Years of Historic Pueblo Pottery: The Gallegos Collection*. Santa Fe, NM: Morning Star Gallery.

Harlow, Francis H., and Jack Silverman
2001 *Pueblo Indian Pottery*. Santa Fe, NM: privately published.

Harlow, Francis H., Duane Anderson, and Dwight P. Lanmon
2005 *The Pottery of Santa Ana Pueblo*. Santa Fe: Museum of New Mexico Press.

Hedges, Ken, and Alfred E. Dittert
1984 Heritage in Clay: The 1912 Pueblo Pottery Collection of Wesley Bradfield and Thomas S. Dozier. San Diego Museum of Man Papers 17. San Diego.

Hill, W. W.
1982 *An Ethnography of Santa Clara Pueblo, New Mexico*. Albuquerque: University of New Mexico Press.

Holmes, W. H.
1889 The Debasement of Pueblo Art. *American Anthropologist* 2(4):320.

Kidder, Alfred Vincent
1931 *The Pottery of Pecos. Volume I: Dull-Paint Wares, with a Section on the Black-on-White Wares by Charles Avery Amsden*. Papers of the Southwestern Expedition 5. New Haven, CN: Published for Phillips Andover Academy by Yale University Press.

Kidder, Alfred Vincent, and Anna O. Shepard
1936 *The Pottery of Pecos. Volume II. 1: The Glaze-Paint, Culinary and Other Wares. 2: The Technology of Pecos Pottery*. Papers of the Southwestern Expedition 7. New Haven, CN: Published for Phillips Andover Academy by Yale University Press.

Lambert, Marjorie
1981 Spanish Influences on the Pottery of San Jose de los Jemez and Giusewa, Jemez State Monument (LA 679), Jemez Springs, New Mexico. In *Collected Papers in Honor of Erik Kellerman Reed*, ed. Albert Schroeder, 215–236. Papers of the Archaeological Society of New Mexico 6. Albuquerque.

Lange, Charles, H.
1959 *Cochiti: A New Mexico Pueblo, Past and Present*. Austin: University of Texas Press.

Lange, Patricia Fogelman
1993 Pueblo Pottery Figurines: Art As Social Criticism. Ph. D. diss., New York University.

1998 Cultural Collecting Fever in New Mexico: Figures and Governor L. Bradford Prince. *Journal of the Southwest* 40(2):217–242.

2002 *Pueblo Pottery Figurines: The Expression of Cultural Perceptions in Clay.* Albuquerque: University of New Mexico Press.

Mera, Harry P.
1932 Wares Ancestral to Tewa Polychrome. *Laboratory of Anthropology Technical Series, Bulletin 4.* Santa Fe, NM.

1933 A Proposed Revision of the Rio Grande Glaze Paint Sequence. *Laboratory of Anthropology Technical Series, Bulletin* 5. Santa Fe, NM.

1939 Style Trends of Pueblo Pottery in the Rio Grande and Little Colorado Cultural Areas from the Sixteenth to the Nineteenth Century. *Memoirs of the Laboratory of Anthropology 3.* Santa Fe, NM.

Mills, Barbara
2002 In *Archaeologies of the Pueblo Revolt: Identity, Meaning, and Renewal in the Pueblo World.* Albuquerque: University of New Mexico Press.

Parezo, Nancy
1985 Cushing As Part of the Team: The Collecting Activities of the Smithsonian Institution. *American Ethnologist* 12(4):763–774.

Preucel, Robert W.
1998 The Kotyiti Research Project: Preliminary Report of the 1996 Field Season. Report Submitted to the U.S. Forest Service, Santa Fe National Forest and the Pueblo de Cochiti.

2000 Living on the Mesa: Hanar Kotyiti: A Post-Revolt Cochiti Community in Northern New Mexico. *Expedition* 42:8–17.

Preucel, Robert W., ed.
2002 *Archaeologies of the Pueblo Revolt: Identity, Meaning, and Renewal in the Pueblo World.* Albuquerque: University of New Mexico Press.

Simmons, Marc
1966 New Mexico's Smallpox Epidemic of 1780–81. *New Mexico Historical Review* 41(4): 319–326.

Smith, Watson, Richard B. Woodbury, and Natalie F. S. Woodbury
1966 The Excavation of Hawikuh by Frederick Webb Hodge: Report of the Hendricks-Hodge Expedition 1917–1923. *Contributions from the Museum of the American Indian Heye Foundation vol. XX.* New York: Museum of the American Indian.

Snow, David
1973 Some Economic Considerations of Historic Rio Grande Pueblo Pottery. In *The Changing Ways of Southwestern Indians: A Historic Perspective*, ed. Albert H. Schroeder, 55–72. Glorieta, NM: Rio Grande Press, Inc.

1983 A Note on Encomienda Economics in Seventeenth-Century New Mexico in Hispanic Arts and Ethnohistory. In *The Southwest: New Papers Inspired by the Work of E. Boyd*, eds. Marta Weigle, Claudia Larcome, and Samuel Larcome, 347–358. Santa Fe, NM: Ancient City Press.

1984 Spanish American Pottery Manufacture in New Mexico: A Critical Review. *Ethnohistory* 31(2):93–113.

Spicer, Edward H.
1962 *Cycles of Conquest: The Impact of Spain, Mexico, and the United States on the Indians of the Southwest, 1533–1960.* Tucson: University of Arizona Press.

Stevenson, James
1883a Illustrated Catalogue of the Collections Obtained from the Indians of New Mexico and Arizona in 1879. In *Second Annual Report of the Bureau of American Ethnology to the Secretary of the Smithsonian Institution, 1880–1881*, 307–422.

1883b Illustrated Catalogue of the Collections Obtained from the Indians of New Mexico in 1880. In *Second Annual Report of the Bureau of American Ethnology to the Secretary of the Smithsonian Institution, 1880–1881*, 432–465.

Toulouse, James
1949 The Mission of San Gregorio De Abo: A Report on the Excavation and Repair of a Seventeenth-Century New Mexico Mission. *Monographs of the School of American Research 13*. Santa Fe, NM: School of American Research.

Wade, Edwin L., and Lea S. McChesney
1981 *Historic Hopi Ceramics: The Thomas V. Keam Collection of the Peabody Museum of Archaeology and Ethnology*. Cambridge, MA: Harvard University Press.

White, Leslie
1935 The Pueblo of Santo Domingo, New Mexico. *Memoirs of the American Anthropological Association 43*. Menasha, WI.

White, Leslie
1962 The Pueblo of Sia, New Mexico. *Bureau of American Ethnology Bulletin 184*. Washington, D.C..

Pueblo Pottery Basics: Materials, Tools, and Techniques
Valerie K. Verzuh

Guthe, Carl E.
1925 Pueblo Pottery Making: A Study at the Village of San Ildefonso. *Papers of the Southwestern Expedition 2*. New Haven, CN: Published for the Department of Archaeology, Phillips Academy, Andover, Massachusetts, by Yale University Press.

Shepard, Anna O.
1956 Ceramics for the Archaeologist. *Carnegie Institution Publication 609*. Washington, D.C.

Index

Project Director: Mary Wachs
Art and Production Director: David Skolkin
Composition: Set in Bembo
Map: Deborah Reade
Manufactured in Singapore
10 9 8 7 6 5 4 3 2 1

Page i, Potter Juanita Trujillo, Cochiti Pueblo, ca. 1940–1945. See page 119.

Frontispiece and front jacket detail from Storage Jar, Keresan Polychrome, artist unknown, ca. 1870, 36.6 x 46.7 cm.

Library of Congress Cataloging-in-Publication Data

A river apart : the pottery of Cochiti & Santo Domingo pueblos / edited by Valerie K. Verzuh. — 1st ed.
p. cm.
Includes bibliographical references and index.
ISBN 978-0-89013-522-8 (clothbound : alk. paper)
1. Pueblo pottery—New Mexico—Cochiti—History.
2. Pueblo pottery—New Mexico—Santo Domingo Pueblo—History. I. Verzuh, Valerie K. II. Title: Pottery of Cochiti & Santo Domingo pueblos. III. Title: Pottery of Cochiti and Santo Domingo pueblos.
E99.P9R536 2008
738.3089'974—dc22
2008013225

Museum of New Mexico Press
Post Office Box 2087
Santa Fe, New Mexico 87504
www.mnmpress.org